York Deeds, Volume 5

You are holding a reproduction of an original work that is in the public domain in the United States of America, and possibly other countries. You may freely copy and distribute this work as no entity (individual or corporate) has a copyright on the body of the work. This book may contain prior copyright references, and library stamps (as most of these works were scanned from library copies). These have been scanned and retained as part of the historical artifact.

This book may have occasional imperfections such as missing or blurred pages, poor pictures, errant marks, etc. that were either part of the original artifact, or were introduced by the scanning process. We believe this work is culturally important, and despite the imperfections, have elected to bring it back into print as part of our continuing commitment to the preservation of printed works worldwide. We appreciate your understanding of the imperfections in the preservation process, and hope you enjoy this valuable book.

YORK DEEDS

BOOK V

EDITED BY
WILLIAM M. SARGENT, A. M.
MEMBER OF THE MAINE HISTORICAL SOCIETY, OF THE MAINE GENEALOGICAL
SOCIETY, AND OF THE GORGES SOCIETY

PORTLAND
BROWN THURSTON & COMPANY
1889

PRINTED BY R. THURSTON & CO.

CONTENTS.

PREFACE . . . . Page 5
REGISTER'S CERTIFICATE . . . . Page 11
ERRATA . . . . . . Page 12

YORK DEEDS,
    Part I . . . . . . Folios 1—121
    Part II . . . . . Folios 1—129

INDEX,
    I. Grantors . . . . . Pages 2— 15
    II. Grantees . . . . Pages 16— 33
    III. Other Persons . . . . Pages 34— 48
    IV. Places . . . . Pages 49— 51
    V. General . . . . . Pages 52— 76

PREFACE.

THE Legislature of the State of Maine for 1889 generously provided, by Resolve, for the publishing of Books five and six of York Deeds under the supervision of the Maine Historical Society. The Maine Historical Society appointed as its Committee to supervise these publications Dr. William B. Lapham, Rev. Dr. Henry S. Burrage, and William M. Sargent, Esq.; and this Committee delegated the labor of editing the books to Mr. Sargent. No longer having the painstaking care and loving labor of our distinguished fellow-member and collaborator, Mr. Hobart W. Richardson, whose conscientious discharge of similar supervision over the four books heretofore printed, and whose compendious but comprehensive Prefaces and Introductions to the preceding books will ever remain a monument to his zeal, industry and erudition, this Committee has felt the necessity of increased watchfulness and care in the proof-reading and comparison of the current work, and confidently believes the diminished list of Errata in this, a work of even greater difficulty, because of its perplexing minutiæ and numberless details, to be the best evidence of their zeal and application to the trust committed to them.

This volume will prove, because of the greater variety of topics embraced in its script, of quite as engrossing historical interest as any of the foregoing volumes. It embraces besides the continuation of the chronological order in the registering of deeds, by filling the gap from 1690 to 1696; the special record of probate business opened by Rishworth, in July, 1680, together with transcripts of earlier records, apparently inserted by him in vacant pages; and finally one hundred and twenty-seven pages of the celebrated Court Records of the District of Maine.

This volume embraces two distinct parts: Part I., the earlier, was opened by Edward Rishworth, April 6, 1680, just after the

PREFACE.

return of President Danforth home to Cambridge from the organization of the new government and installation of officers at York in March, 1680, with a record of a Court of Sessions of the Peace, with Deputy-president Bryan Pendleton, as presiding officer; he continued his entries till July 7, 1686 [fol. 40] : after that date Thomas Scottow as Deputy-register under Edward Randolph took charge of the book and, as Clerk of the Probate Court, made an entry Oct. 8, 1686 [fol. 43ª]. John Wincoll being chosen Clerk of the Court, Dec. 20, 1689,[1] filled in one entry [fol. 43], July 29, 1690, and continued the records till Oct. 5, 1694 [fol. 43ᵇ – fol. 115]. Joseph Hammond, senior, appointed Clerk and Register in Dec., 1694, continued them to the end of Part I., in Jan., 1696, with the exception of Sept., 1695, to Nov., 1695, when John Newmarch acted as Clerk and Register, filling Major Hammond's place during the latter's captivity in Canada.

Part II. pages 1–36 were kept by John Wincoll as clerk of the Inferior Court of Common Pleas and of the Court of Quarter Sessions; and pages 40–127 up to April 10, 1699 by Joseph Hammond as incumbent of the same offices; and one instrument was inserted by him in fol. 128, of an earlier date.

Or, to summarize and further explain the above statements; at the time this book was opened for the probate business, the fourth book was being used for registering of deeds; from 1687 to 1689, the register used the sixth book; from 1690 until 1696, the records were continued in this fifth book; and from 1696 till 1699, the register returned to the fourth book; thus in the confusion of the wars and governmental changes scattering the records of these years through three distinct record-books.

The book itself, in a most dilapidated condition, was very unreliably transcribed in 1872, as the following certificate at the end of the copy shows:—

"The foregoing is a copy of Vol. 5 of York County Record of Deeds, Wills &c., transcribed in the year of our Lord one thousand eight hundred and seventy-two.

By me Samuel Tripp, Register."

[1] Part II., folio 1.

But the work was very carelessly done, no care being taken even to preserve the original pagination.

At the time Mr. Tripp made his copy the first leaf had become detached from the end of the book and Mr. Tripp prefixed the following note to the second part of his copy: —

"The first two pages of Court record are missing, but the date appears to be in 1689."

This leaf containing two pages was fortunately recovered by Mr. Sargent, and although parts have been lost from the bottom of it, it is cause for much gratulation that the heading affords the organization of the first court assembled after the Revolution.

This volume from its double character of a record book and a registry book was long claimed and retained by the Clerk of Courts, but was finally transferred to the Registry of Deeds.[1]

The occurrence herein of so considerable a portion of the famed Court Records of Maine merits more than a passing notice, and were space sufficient and time not too pressing, a learned disquisition might be penned on the gradual evolution of orderly administration of justice from its chaotic confusion, during the triangular controversy between the King's Commissioners, the Gorges claimants and the General Court of Massachusetts, when amidst the contentious factions *inter arma silent leges*. But only a brief outline will be here sketched in of the salient features of the judicial systems in operation during the years 1680-1699, covered by our text, leaving to the coming historian the fuller elaboration, of which the changes disclosed by these pages will supply component parts of situations picturesque and variable as the kaleidoscope.

After Massachusetts had purchased the District of Maine from the Gorges heirs, the question of framing its civil government presented perplexities that were finally resolved by adhering to the forms of Gorges' royal charter, and the election by the Governor and assistants of Thomas Danforth President, and a Council of eight members,— Bryan Pendleton, Charles Frost, Francis Hooke, John Davis, Joshua Scottow, Samuel Wheelwright, John Wincoll and Edward Rishworth, who were to be also the Judges of a Supreme Court, and magistrates throughout the province. As President Danforth's home was in Cambridge,

[1] See p. 15, Preface to Book IV.

he took, as these pages show, no personal share in the public administration of justice, he is mentioned but once in these pages, [Part I., fol. 1,] and his place as presiding officer was filled by a Deputy-president; filled successively by Pendleton, Davis and Hooke.[1] Rishworth was Secretary as well as a Justice,[2] as was Wincoll later, and upon the death of Pendleton Edward Tyng was added to the Council,[3] and other vacancies were filled from time to time.[4]

Under the presidency of Danforth, and with the judiciary thus constituted the government, as well as justice, was satisfactorily administered for six years; but, in 1686, came the decline of the colony charter, the administration of Dudley, and the usurpation, so called, of Andros.

The only mark of the chaotic confusion of the next three years apparent in the pages of this book is the entry of a single inventory by Thomas Scottow, Clerk and Deputy Register under Randolph [Part I., fol. 43*], and this book was no furth erused by him.

After the Revolution the Council of Safety confirmed Frost, Hooke, Davis, Scottow, Wheelwright, Wincoll and Tyng, the former Councilors, and John Wincoll being chosen clerk and recorder, not finding the fourth and sixth books, that had been carried to Boston, and searching for a record book used this fifth book, previously devoted to probate business, for a general record of deeds; and turning the book upside down began at the other end a court record.

Under the restored Presidency of Danforth these magistrates continued their dispensation of justice till 1691, when the Provincial Charter, or Charter of William and Mary, having passed the seal and received the royal sanction, the existing laws were continued in force by Massachusetts from June to November 1692, when she established formal courts of justice, substantially the same as they now exist. These were Justices of the Peace for the trial of small causes; the Quarter Sessions held by Justices of the Peace for the county, corresponding to our Courts

[1] See General Index, under Deputy-president.
[2] Infra, Part I., fol. 4.
[3] This resolves the doubt in which Williamson left it. *History of Maine*, I. 565, 566.
[4] See General Index, under Justices, for their names.

of County Commissioners, the Inferior Court of Common Pleas and the Superior Court.

The Superior Court consisted of William Stoughton, chief justice, Thomas Danforth, Wait Winthrop, John Richards and Samuel Sewall, associate justices. The court held two sessions a year in the principal counties; but the trials of causes arising in Maine were held in Boston, and it was only occassionly that a term was holden in Maine.[1]

A Court of Common Pleas called the Inferior Court was organized for each County, consisting of four judges; their names may be found by the Indices, and their commissions in folios 27, 40 and 100; two terms a year were held in York and two in Wells; trials were held before juries; no very strict forms nor technical rules were employed in the earlier practice, " no special pleadings were admitted, but the general issue was always given and special matters brought in evidence."[2]

The Court of General Sessions of the Peace could be holden by three persons *quorum unus* should always be a regular magistrate; but in practice was usually officered by the same persons as the Court of Common Pleas, and came finally to embrace the functions of the Common Pleas and Sessions. Its jurisdiction extended to all cases, civil and criminal, except divorce, and crimes the punishment for which extended to life, limb or banishment; it had power to summon jurors, appoint clerks and other officers; it also had power to lay out highways, issue licenses to innholders &c., and probate powers in the settlement of estates. It combined the principal jurisdiction and duties of the Superior, Inferior and Probate Courts, as subsequently established, with rights of appeal to, and excepting certain original powers reserved to, the Court of Assistants.

Probate Court powers had been assumed by the General Court and continued by it until the Province was made a part of Massachusetts. After the annuling of the colonial charter the president Dudley and after him Andros from 1686 to 1689 assumed supreme probate jurisdiction, introduced the forms of

[1] Infra. Part II. fol. 52 I am aware that Willis' *Courts and Lawyers of Maine* states that this Court was not held here till 1699; but he must have overlooked the term at Kittery in 1695 here cited.

[2] Dummer, quoted by Willis.

the Spiritual Court in England, and attended personally to all cases of administration where the estate exceeded fifty pounds sterling. He introduced order and system into this branch of the law, but greatly increased the fees, and required all estates to be settled and the records to be kept in Boston.

By the charter of 1691, probate jurisdiction was conferred on the Governor and Council; but they, by virtue of their power of substitution, appointed Judges of Probate in each county. Its officers were, Judges: Joshua Scottow, 1687-1693; Francis Hooke, 1693-1695; Samuel Wheelwright, 1695-1700; Registers, Thomas Scottow, 1687-1693; John Wincoll, 1693-1695; Joseph Hammond, 1695-1700.

The editor acknowledges his obligation to the labors of Williamson and Willis, the fruits of which have become common property, upon which he has largely drawn in the preparation of this Preface. The indices evidence a part of his own labors in the preparation of this volume, in which the contractions and signs employed are the same as in the preceding ones, and which are carefully explained in the preface to the first book.

WM. M. SARGENT.

REGISTER'S CERTIFICATE.

State of Maine.

COUNTY OF YORK, ss:

This may certify that the following printed volume is a true copy of the fifth book of records of the Registry of Deeds for this County; that I have read and compared the same with the original records; and that all accidental variations that have been detected are noted in the table of errata on the following page.

Attest:

Justin M. Leavitt

Register of Deeds for York County.

ERRATA.

☞ The sign — is used to denote a line numbered backward from the end of the folio.

Part I., folio 2, line 16, *for* mps *read* Imps.
    63,   41, " endured " endure.
    84, — 35 *omit* the.

FIRST PART.

[1] At a Court of Pleas houlden by Major Pendleton Deputy Prsident, & severall of the Justs at Wells for the Province of Mayn, June the 30th 1680 : wr severall Administrations were granted, & Inventorys brought in, & Lycences granted, & renewed according to order/

Humfrey Scammon is appoynted, & allowed to keepe a ferry for transportation of horses & men, ouer Sacoe River, at ye Late house wr formerly Hene: Waddocke liued, & for his ferrage of an horse & man hee is to haue nine peence/
Hee is also allowed to keepe a publique house of Intertaymt

Administration granted vnto Mary Oakeman, of the Estate of her late husband Samll Oakemā: deceased/ Capt Josua standing bound & 100£ pound bond yt sd Mary Oakeman shall administer according to Law/

Administration granted to John Graues, of the Estate of Nathell Mitton lately of Cascoe deceased/ Leeft Brackett stands bound with Graues in his administration, in a bond of fourty pounds to ye Treasr yt Jon Graues shall returne in a true Inventory of sd Mittons Estate vnto ye Court of sessions houlden at Kittery for this Prouince

Humfrey Spencer haueing the Select mens approbation for keeping of an ordinary, the Court granteth him a Lycence for the yeare Insewing/ a lycence given him/

PART I, FOL. 1.

William Loue his Lycence, is Continewed to keepe a publique house of Intertaynement for the yeare Insewing/ a Lycence sent him/

Jos: Storys his Lycence Continewd to him for yᵉ yeare Insewing/ his Lycence sent him p Mr Curwine/

ffrancis Littlefeild, his Lycence is Continewd to k[eepe] a publique house of Intertaynement for yᵉ yeare Insewi[ng]

ν At a sessions of pe: houlden at Kittery Aprill: 6: 80:

Wʳas, According to yᵉ Advise of oʳ Honoʳᵈ Pʳsident/ wᵉ yᵉ whoole Estate of Lands houses & Mills being yⁿ brought in & yᵉ apprisall thereof ordered by the Counsell/ Administration was granted to Mary Sayword, Relict or Widdo[w] of Henȩ: Sayword deceased, provided shee give in bond according to Law of all such moueables belonging to yᵉ aforesayd Estate/ Wee Mary Sayword, James Gran[t] & Robert Young, do hereby Ingage our selues in a bond of Two hundred pounds vnto the Treasurer of this Province, that the sd Mary Sayword Administratrix, shall take a true Inventory of the Moueables of the Estate of Hene: Sayword deceased, & shee to make returne yʳof, & of her doeings yʳin, vnto the next Cour[t] of pleas to bee houlden for this Province, & to procure some honest able Indifferent men to make the apprisa[l.] And what other Estate Hene: Sayword was possessed of, in Lands & Mills, are to bee brought in although no[t] apprised/

Wʳas Mary Sayword Relict of Hene: Sayword deceased, had admi[nis]tration granted her of the Moueables of the sd Saywords Estate, at a Court of sessions houlden for this Province Aprill: 6: 80: by [yᵉ] Mary Sayword by her

Part I, Fol. 2.

selfe & suretys were bound in a bond of 200ˡ to returne a true Inventory & apprisall of yᵉ Moueables vnt[o] the next Court of pleas for this Province/ wᶜʰ accordingly she br[ought] not in agreeable to order/ The Pʳmisses Considred/ It is hereby ordered, that Mary Sayword Administratrix to yᵉ E[s]tate of Hene: Sayword abouesd, do & shall forthwith make an . pen Publication in writeing of her Administratrixshipp, & to th . æffectuall Care It bee posted vp at Boston Salem, Ipswich, Stra[w]bury banke & at yorke for this Province, yʳby Pʳfixing a ty . . vpon the last Tuesday of Septembʳ next Insewing from ye date hereof wʳ Crs are to bring or send in yʳ Just Claims of yʳ de . . . due from yᵗ Estate, vnto yᵉ ReCor: at Yorke, wʳby they may haue opertun . . y before the Counsell of this Province to settle the Concernes yʳof, & to make out any Legall rights, due vnto yᵐ from the Pʳmisses/ ✓

[2*] Administration granted vnto Ann Allison of the Estate of Joseph Oliver deceased/

Wee Ann Allison & Nathall Fryer, stands bound vnto the Treasʳ of this Province in an obligation of eighty six pounds that the sd Ann Allison shall bring in a true Inventory of the Estate of sd Oliver deceased, & render a Just Accopᵗ of her doeings yʳin, vnto the next quartʳ sessions houlden for this Province/

Leefteᵗ John Sargeant, allowed to keepe ordinary at Sacoe for the yeare Insewing, who is to haue a lycence granted him/

A lycence sent him by John Harmon/

This is a true Inventory of the Estate of John Phillips

Part I, Fol. 2.

deceased, as they were prised the 9th of March 16⅔ by us vnderwritten

mps his house & Land	10	00	00					
It one Cow 3£ one Heffer 50s	05	10	0	It 3 ould Gouches	0	02	0
It 1 ould feathr bed & bowlster	01	10	0	It one parting gouge	0	02	0
3 blanketts 15s Ciuerlid 8s	01	03	0	It one gouge at	0	02	0
an ould Gun 3s, 1 peyr shoes 3s	0	06	0	It Two turneing Hooks	0	01	4
one peyre briches	0	05	0	A groueing & heading chissell	0	01	6
one peyre Canvis drawers	0	03	0	a Turneing chissell	0	01	0
one peyre of searge briches	0	12	0	It a Joynter at	0	03	0
a 4 Skirted Jacke·t at	0	16	0	It a Jacke playn 2s a frow 8s	0	05	0
It fiue turneing Hookes	0	05	0	It a brest Wimble 18d	0	01	6
one bryar bill 2s and Hatchet 4s	0	06	0	a drawing kniff 3s, a hamer 12d		04	0
two round shaues, & 1 picke axe	0	03	6	an Houldfast	00	01	6
a bottome of a brass pott	0	00	0	one Ryming Iron 12d	0	01	0
one punch 18d ould Iron 2s	0	03	6	A fyle and ould Hooke at	00	01	0
a Twibill & an Hooke shaue	0	4	0	a spoake shaue 12d, a Mare coult 20s	1	01	0
It an ould Kettle	0	02	6		£02	07	10
To punches 4s one Wimble bitt & sisers 1s	0	05	0				
A Chest & ould things yrin	0	10	0				
It foure Copps Irons at	0	02	0				
a hand Saw 2s 6d, a square 2s	0	04	6				
It one square adse at	0	03	6				
It one hollowing adg 2s	0	02	0				
It a handsaw two s 6d a square 2s	0	04	6				
It an ould broad axe	0	02	6				
It a Topping Iron 2s Inch anger 3s	0	05	0				
It an Inch & ½ Auger	00	01	4				
It ½ Inch auger & broad chissell		02	0				
It one hedding Chissell at	00	01	0				
	23	12	4				
	2	07	10				
	£26	00	02				

Enocke Houtchin his marke **E H**

Gowine Willson/

A true Coppy of this Inventory transcribed out of the originall this 16th July: 1680:

p Edw: Rishworth
ReCor:

June 21th 1680:

Capt Francis Hooke, Capt Charles ffrost, & Edw: Rishw[orth] ReCor: Granted Administration vnto John Harmon of ye Estate of John ffoxell deceased/

Wee John Harmon & ffran: Hooke, stand bound vnto authority in a bond of eighty pounds, that ye sd Harmon shall respond all Legall rights apprtayneing to sd John Foxell his Estate, & shall rende[r] a Just Accopt of his Doeings yrin, vnto the next Court of sessions houlden for this Province/

Part I, Fol. 3.

A true Inventory of the Estate of John ffoxell taken by us the 21th of June : 1680 :

	£	s	d
Ims one Cow & Calfe at	4	00	0
It 2 yeareling Heffers & a Calfe	5	00	0
It to a bed & what belongs to it	5	00	0
It 1 Iron pott & 2 small pewter dishes	01	00	0
It To six Acres of Marsh	12	00	0
It one horse at foure pounds	04	00	0
It one hundred acres of Land	10	00	0
	41	00	0

apprised by Peter Bass/
Samll Johnson/

John Harmon doth Attest vpon his oath that this aboue written is a true Inventory of John Foxell his Estate deceased, according to ye best of his knowledg/ If more estate do afterward appeare vpon the same oath hee Ingageth to bring it in/

Taken vpon oath before mee Edw: Rishworth Just: pe: 21: June: 1680:

A true Coppy of this Inventory transcribed out of the original this 16th July: 1680: p Edw: Rishworth ReCor:

A true Inventory of the Estate of Moueables belonging vnto the Estate of Hene: Sayword deceased/ Taken & apprised by us whose names are subscribed this 22th of Aprill 1679:

	£	s	d
Inps 8 sheepe 4£: a Nagg, 2£: a Mare 2£, a Coult 20s	09	00	
It his Weareing apparell given to his Attendants	05	00	0
It a peyr of sheets & one dosen of worne napkines	01	05	
It Towles, a small Gryndstoone, & ye Turneing Mill Towles	01	10	0
It Towles for husbandry 20s: Two cross cutt saws 10s	01	10	
Three Lodgings & bedding belonging therevnto	04	00	0
Ould pewter dishes, a frijng pann, a skellet, & a musket	01	05	0
Twelue wodden dishes, Keelelers, and three Chayres	00	11	
One Chest 9s, 2 Iron potts 2 brass Kettles, 2 ould Tubbs, a Tramell, pot hookes, a spitt, Andirons two water bucketts	3	04	

[3*]

	£	s	d
A peyre of Cards, a spining Wheele, & two table boards	00	10	0
It an ould bible & other Bookes at	00	10	0
It one Meale Troffe, & a Chest at 4s, 2 ould Connows 20s	01	04	0
It 50 or 60 Acres of vpland at 5s p Acker	12	10	0
It one peyre of styleyards at 7s 6d	00	07	6
	42	07	10

This is a true Coppy of ye Inventory vnto wch these apprisers haue set y^r hands vnto

PART I, FOL. 3.

Mary Sayword Came into this Court, & doth Attest vpon her oath, that this is a true Inventory of the moueables, of the Estate of Hene: Sayword her deceased husband, to the best of her knowledg, & If more do appeare hereafter, shee stands bound vpon the same oath to bring y^m in/

      Ric: Banks
      Samll Donell
      Hene: Symson
      Job Allcocke

Taken in Court 2: July: 1680, p, as Attests,
     Edw: Rishworth ReCor:

As for ye Saw Mills & Corne Mills, at yorke, & w^t is else Erected app'taining therevnto, wee leaue to better Judgm^ts, or whom the Hono^rd Court shall see good to appoynt for there apprisall, also the Mills at Cape Porpus river, & ye Mill at Cascoe, with all the appurtenances belonging to them/

      Ric: Bankes
      Samll Donell/
      Hene: Symson/
      Job Allcocke/

Wee whose names are vnderwritten, being requested by Mis Sayword, Administratrix to her deceased Husband Mr Hene: Sayword, to apprise the Mills at Mowsum, & all the app'rtenances y^rvnto belonging/ which accordingly Wee haue valewed at one thousand, two hundred pounds/

witness o^r hands this 20th day of June 1680:

      John Littlefeild

A true Coppy of the Inventory aboue Samll Webber/ written given into ye Court of pleas at Wells June 30th 1680: by Mary Sayword Administratrix to her deceased husbands Estate transcribed out of ye originall this 16: August: 1680: p

More added to this
Inventory in this   Edw: Rishworth ReCor:
booke pa: 31:

Part I, Fol. 3.

At a Court of Sessions houlden at Kittery 29th of Septembr 1680: at the house of Jos: Hamonds/

Administration granted vnto Thomas Pumrey, of the Estate of William Robbines deceased/

In reference to yᵉ Estate of Joseph Pearce deceased/
Pouer of Administration granted vnto Saraih Pearce alias Jones or Mattown of the Estate of sayd Jos: Pearce her deceased brother/
Wee sayd Saraih Pearce, & Nicho: Shapleigh stands bound in a bond of Eighty pounds to yᵉ treasuʳ of yᵉ Prouince that the sd Saraih shall bee Lyable to respond all Legall Claims belonging to yᵉ Estate of sd Jos: Pearce her brother to yᵉ valew of fourty three pounds 13ˢ 10ᵈ/ the one halfe yʳof being her Sister Marys part, according to the Inventory/

Saraih Pearce owneth a Judgmᵗ vnto Majoʳ Nicho: Shapleigh of houses Lands Goods, & wᵗsoeuer other Moueables are belonging to the Estate of her brother Jos: Pearce deceased, according to the Inventory, excepting what Estate was disposed off for payment of her brothers debts/

June
21: 77   New England/
An Inventory of the Goods of Joseph Oliver of blā: Poynt who was slayne at the Garrison yʳof, In the tyme of the late Indean Warr/

Part I, Fol. 4.

They were apprised by John Jordan & Peter Shaw as followeth

	£	s	d
Inprs 5 augers prised at	00	10	00
It foure augers at	00	04	00
It 6 chissells & a Compass at	0	09	00
It 2 drawing kniffs at 3s	00	03	00
It seaven planes at	00	14	00
It a small sale bench Hooke & fiue playne Irons at	00	06	00
It one hould fast ring 2s 6d 2 chissells 3s		05	06
It Hamers 2 syth nibbs & a gymlit	0	08	00
It Two little Adges at	00	05	00
It one square & a falling axe	0	03	00
It one chalke lyne & a houge at		05	00
It 2 chests 16s, one how 3s	00	19	00
It 2 blankett 18s, one Rugg 30s	02	08	00
It one bed & bowlster at	04	00	00
It 2 peyre of shooes & an hatt	1	00	00
It 2 peyre of briches	1	16	00
It 2 ould Coats at	00	04	00
It 3 peyr of drawers & a lining Jackett at 26s	01	06	00
It Tickeing & some other lifig	1	15	00
It Napkines & other lining	00	18	00
	17	14	06

	£	s	d
It 3 peyr of gloues 8s buttons 2s	00	10	0
It one Gymlett & other things 3s, It & books at 16s	00	19	0
It 2 peyre of drawers & a dere skine		12	0
It Remants of Cloath 2s 6d, & amunition a vest & sword 30s	01	12	6
It one Cow 3£ 3 bushls 1 pecke of wheat at 13s	03	13	0
It a pot & bucket 6s, & foure peyre of stockings 7s	00	13	0
It more due to Jos: Oliuer by bill for his wages due from the Countrey	18	00	0
for wch the tickets were	25	19	6
left in the hands of Ann	17	14	6
Allison, who appeard before mee at Bla: Ploynt & oath to ye treuth of ye Inventory, above Totall	43	14	0

2: Septb 1680:

Jos: Scottow
Just pe:

vera Copia transcribed & Compared with ye originall this 27th of Octobr (1680)

p Edw: Rishworth Re . . .

[4*] September 29th 1680: p Major Jon Davess & Edw: Rishworth Justs pe & Rishworth ReCor:

Administration granted to Jesper Pullman of the Estate of John Pullman deceased, wch by the Court of sessions was allowed sd Pullman giveing in bond according to law/

Part I, Fol. 4.

Here followeth the Inventory of John Pullman his goods, being deceased, they being prised by us whose names are vnderwritten this 7th of August: 1680:

	£	s	d
Inprs his weareing Cloaths 9£: 7s: 0d, bed Cloaths & Tickeing of Canvaise 45s	11	12	0
It one Chest 7s, one fowling peece 30s	01	17	0
It for one Muskett at fiueteen shillings	00	15	0
It In money fiue pounds, 6 quintls Cod fish in ye house 3£	08	00	0
It four quintells Refuge fish is 01: 12: 0	01	12	0
It one barrell of Tarr 8s, for Caske in ye house 20s	01	08	0
It one barrell of porke at 2£: 10s: 0d	02	10	0
It Corne in the house 51s, Nett & lynes in the house 30s	04	01	0
It Bread in the house 25s, Lead in the house 14s	01	19	0
It The house at fineteen pounds	15	00	0
It A Boate & all things b longing to her	30	00	0
It Meddow Ground & Ysland is	26	00	0
It a yeareling Heffer & a Calfe at	02	00	0
It Bootes & shooes 10s	00	10	0
	107	04	0

Jesper Pullman Came before Major Davess & my selfe, & tooke oath this 21th of Septembr 1680, vnto the treuth of this Inventory according to ye best of his knowledg, & If any more goods hereafter bee found, vpon the same oath hee stands Ingaged to bring them in as Attests Edw: Rishworth
    ReCor:

Job Allcocke
the marke of
Hen: HD Donell
Edw: Wollcocke

The Testimony of Hene: Donell aged 78 years or there abouts/

Being examined sayth, that hee this Deponent did often heare John Pullman say in his life tyme, that his warehouse that hee ye sd John Pullman built by the water side, was Mary Pullmans house/ this is thy house Mary & the sheepe yt I bought, I bought for thee Mary/ Taken vpon oath before mee this 24th Septembr 80: John Davess Just pe:

Samll Freathy testifys likewise vpon oath yt hee did heare

PART I, FOL. 4.

John Pullman say, that the house was his Cosson Mary Pullmans house/ taken vpon oath the 24th Septemb^r 1680 :
    before mee John Davess Just : pe :
A true Coppy of the depositions aboue written transcribed out of the Originall this 4th of Octob^r 80 :
      p Edw :· Rishworth ReCor :

The Deposition of Richard Carter aged 30 yeares, or there abouts/
Testifyeth, that hee being P^rsent w^n John Pullman bought a Certen Parcell of Marsh of Samson Anger, that hee heard the sd John Pullman say, y^t hee would neuer haue layd out his money, nor bought ye sayd Marsh, If it had not beene for his brother Jesper Pullmans Daughter & sayd y^t hee bought it for her, & shee should haue it/ & further sayth not/ Taken vpon oath this 25th of Septem^br 1680 :
    before mee John Davess Just : pe :

Capt Job Allcocke ownes all the aboue written vpon oath, onely hee doth not remember the words laying out the money/ Taken vpon oath this 25th of Septemb^r 1680 :
    . before mee John Davess Just : pe :
vera Copia of these 2 Testimonys aboue written transcribed & Compared this 5th of October 1680 :
     p Edw : Rishworth ReCor :

    27 : Septemb^r 1680
Jesper Pullman desirs a Confirmation of what his brother John Pullman deceased gaue his Daughter, according to these euidences here P^rsented to this Hono^rd Court/

 Jesper Pullman gives an Accompt of Charges referring to the Estate of his brother John Pullman/

To Charges expended about his funerall, & other necessary occasions all in Generall Comes to.. 04 10 0
To ReCording ye Inventory & Granting letters of Administration............... 0 05 0
vera Copia Allowed in Court/ Edw : Rishworth   04 15 0
      ReCor :

Part I, Fol. 5.

June 16: 1679:

A true Inventory of all the goods & lands of Henery Waddocke of Sacoe River deceased, prised by John Sargeant & Walter Mayre, as followth

	£	s	d
Inprs Two hundred & fiuety Acres of vpland at	31	10	00
It Thyrty Acres of Meddow apprisd at	30	00	00
It one Cow & Calfe 4 pounds, 2 sheets 5s, one pillow 5s	04	10	00
It two sheets one Pillow 10s one Rugg 50s, 2 yds of broad Cloath 20s	04	00	00
It one yd & halfe of kersey, & 1 yd & an halfe of sheard	00	10	00
It one pott one kettle one skellet 20s	01	00	00
It one bed Tickine at 15s	00	15	00
Totall	72	05	00

Jane Waddocke the abouesd Hene: Waddocks Widdow maketh oath that the Inventory aboue expressed, is the whoole Estate of what shee at P^rsent knoweth off, this 9th of Octob^r 1679 before mee ffran: Hooke Comisso^r

vera Copia of this Inventory as aboue Attested transcribed & Compared with ye originall this 27th of October 1680:

p Edw: Rishworth ReCor:

[5*] The Inventory of the Estate of the late Samell Oakemā: deceased made by the subscribers/

	£	s	d
Inprs to 2 Cows eight pounds, two stears & one Heffer 7: 10: 0	15	10	00
It one horse Three pounds, 120 Acres of Land 6: 10: 0	09	10	00
It tenn Acres of Inland 50s, Tenn Acres of Marsh 10£	12	10	00
It to bed & bedding 5: 10: 0, to Andirons Iron kettles Crocks & other Irons one pound tenn shillings	07	00	00
It To two panns 20s, & 3 pewter dishes & house hould goods	03	02	00
It to one share & Cowlter & other workes at	02	00	00
It to an house at Tenn shillings	00	10	0
	£50	02	0

June 28: 1676:   John Tynny/
Mary Oakeman appeared before mee &   Edw: Bennett/
made oath to ye Treuth of this Inventory above, & wⁿ shee knows of more shee will reueale It

Jos: Scottow Just: pe:

Mary Oakeman prayeth the worship^{ll} Court now sitting to grant her Administration to the Estate of her late deceased husband/ Blā: Poynt 28 June 1680:

Mary Oakemā:

Part I, Fol. 5.

A true Coppy of this Inventory as Attested with w^t was vnderwritten, transcribed & Compared this 2^d of Novb^r 1680 :
p Edw : Rishworth ReCor

Portsmouth 9th of August (1677)

I Bryan Pendleton sometyme of Sacoe In ye County of Yorke, Now rescident in Portsmouth, on Pischataq River in N : E : do make & ordajne this to be my last Will & testament, hereby reuoakeing all former Wills by mee made/

1 : I giue vnto my beloued Wife Ellner Pendleton (besid^e what I here reserved for her in a Deed of Gyft to my Grandchild Pendleton Fletcher) all my househould goods, togeather with all that peece of Land belonging to mee lijng between my son James & Mr Dereings, vpon ye great Ysland which I haue excepted, & reserved out of my deed of Gyft of all to my son James/ Furthermore, I give vnto my wife, all my houseing & land at Cape Porpus, which Richd Palmers wife hath the vse of dureing her life, togeather with my six hundred & fourty Acres of Land more or less lijng on the East side of Wests brooke, neare Saco ffalls, which I bought of John West, & Majo^r William Phillips as by Deed will appeare, & also Tymber Ysland at the little River, all which I giue to my wife absolutely to bee at her disposall/

2ly vnto my grandchild James Pendleton Junjo^r, I giue my hundred acres of vpland, & Tenn Acres of Meddow which I bought of Jo^n Bush & lyeth with in the Towneshipp of Cape Porpus adioyneing to princes Rocke/

3ly all my houseing & Land at Wells with all the priuiledges & appurtenances I giue vnto my two grandchildren Mary, & Hannah Pendleton wch my son had by his former wife to be æqually diuided between them/

4 : I giue to my wife all my weareing Cloaths to bee disposed off as shee shall see meete, desireing her to remember some poore/

5 : Finally I make my wife my executrix & Joyne my

Part I, Fol. 5.

beloued son James Pendleton executo[r] togeather with his Mother, willing my executrix to disburse what is meete for my funerall Charges, & my executo[r] to pay all my debts/ And I request Mr Josua Moodey, & Mr Ric: Martyne, to bee ouerseers to this my last Will & testament/

In witness to all & singular the P[r]misses, I haue set to my hand & seale, this 9th day of August 1677:
Witness   Bryan Pendleton (his Seale)
   Josua Moodey/
   Ann Moodey/

As a Sedule to this my last will & testament, I giue vnto my beloued son James Pendleton, all my land on the East of Wests brooke butting on the great River of Saco, six hundred Acres more or less, my farme & all my land at Cape Porpus, in all three hundred acres in the occupation of Ric: Palmer, all my seuerall yslands in or neare Cape Porpus, y[e] one halfe of my stocke of Cattle of w[t] sort so euer vpon my farme at Winter Harbour, found after mine & my wiues decease, with all my weareing apparrell & one third of my househould goods (except my vtilensills of husbandry)

And to Mary & Hannah Pendleton daughters to my sayd son James all y[e] My lands In Wells, being those Plantations or Lotts bought of Mr ffletcher, Hamond, & West Improued by Joseph Cross, & to each of them one third part of my househould goods, after mine & my wiues decease/ Ite[m]: to Bryan Pendleton my Grandson, y[e] remajnd[r] of my land on Great Ysland/ w[t] is Contayned there in is addition to my will, any thing in the sd will notwithstanding/

This Sedule signed & sealed   Bryan Pendleton (his Seale)
   In y[e] Presence of vs/
   Joseph Dudley/

Josua Moodey made oath that y[e] writeing on the other side, was signed & sealed by Majo[r] Bryan Pendleton &

PART I, FOL. 6.

declared by him to bee his last Will & testament, & that Mr Joseph Dudley did write & was a witness to ye Sedule, annexed in ye foote of ye aforesd page

Taken this 5th day of Aprill 1681 : before us/

A true Coppy of this Will the Sedule & the Attest, within & aboue written, transcribed out of ye originall & y^r with Compard this 23 : of Aprill 1681 :

John Wincoll
ffran : Hooke } Jus^ts pe :
Charles ffrost

p Edw : Rishworth ReCor :

[6] :23 : of May 1681 :

Administration of the Estate of Samell Biss deceased, granted to John Twisden Clar : of writts, more fully Entred into the New booke of ReCords for the Prouince at y^t Court 6th of Aprill 1680 :

An Inventory of the Estate of Samell Biss, deceased taken & apprised by vs whose names are vnderwritten to ye best of o^r Judgm^ts, this 23 : of May 1681 :

Inprs his weareing Cloaths & hatt	01 05 00	
It in siluer one pound 13s, 2d.....	01 13 02	It one hundred & six skines of
It 9 yds ½ New cotton Cloath.....	01 03 09	silke & an Inke horne........ 00 09 06
It Tow yards of Cotton Cloath...	00 04 00	in lining foure shirts & one
It 8 yards of Osenbridg at........	00 06 00	peyre of drawers............. 01 06 00
It Two yards of Cotton Cloath at	00 05 00	It 1 neckcloath 2 Hankerchers... 0 08 06
It foure yards of Cotten Cloath..	00 08 00	It 3 peyre of stockings & one
It 6 yds ½ of Cotten Cloath......	00 13 00	peyre Cotten gloues......... 00 07 00
It 4 yards ¼ of Cotton Cloath at..	00 08 06	It one Chest 5s................. 00 05 00
It one yard of Canting at........	00 03 03	It 1 kniff 1 Come case 2 thybles.. 06 00
It two peyre of worsted stock-ings at............	00 08 00	6 19 08 03 02 00
	£06 19 08	3 02 00
		10 01 08

witness o^r hands the day & yeare aboue sayd/
vera Copia of this Inventory transcribed & Compared with the originall this first day of June 1681 :

Richd Bankes/
Abra : Preble/
John Harmon/

p Edw : Rishworth ReCor :

Part I, Fol. 6.

June: 23: 1681:
An Inventory of the Estate of Major Bryan Pendleton deceased, taken & apprised by us vnderwritten/

	£	s	d
Inprs Too feather bedds, two ruggs, too feather pillows	08	00	00
eight blanketts, 2: 8: 00, foure Carpetts & too Coverlids 3: 2: 0	5	10	00
It 3 feather bowlters fiue feather pillows	02	10	00
It seaventeen peyre of sheetes	07	13	00
It 2 Towells 2s 7 table cloaths, 28s fourty one Napkines 3: 61: 6	4	11	06
It 3 ould blanketts, & two New blankents at	01	18	00
It one small Remnant of Cloath	00	10	00
It 1 wollen rugg 20s 3 Cussions 6s, 3 leather Chaires 9s	01	15	00
It one pann 8s, one drippine pan 4s, one Iron skellet 3s	00	15	00
It one silver Tankard & three silver Cupps	06	01	00
It Two peyre of Hangers 6s one peyre of tonges & a fyre shovell 5s		11	00
It 2 Iron spitts 7s, a Copper Kettle 18s, 1 brass skimmer & candle sticke 5s	01	08	00
It 4 brass Kettles 35s, 3 brass skelletts 9s	02	04	0
It one brass Morter & Pestell 5s, two brass Candlesticks 3s 6d	00	08	6
It a warmeingpan 4s, foure Iron potts 20s	01	04	00
It 5 small pewter basons, & one pewter bason at Twenty shillings	01	00	00
It 3 pewter dishes & one pint pot all goes into the some aboue vidz 20s			
It 3 chares, milke tubbs & wodden ware, 20s	01	00	0
It one Coate, one Raper & belt, & one peyr of shooes at	02	00	0
It to vntinsells for husbandry	07	00	0
It to Cattle of seuerall sorts one hundred pounds	100	00	0
	155	14	00
	4	18	00
	£159	12	00
It one smothing Iron one lanthorne & a grater at 5s	00	05	
It 11 pewter plates 6 pint sawcers 8s 6d 1 quart pot one pewter flaggon 8s	00	16	0
It 10 pewter dishes 01: 10: 00, some ould broaken pewter 6s	01	16	0
It a Collender 3s, 1 ould Cross Cutt saw & a small chayne 4s	00	07	00
It 2 ould musketts, 2 peyre of ould bandaleres	01	00	00
It ould Iron 2s 6d, yarne 2s, 2 Iron Kettles 9s	00	13	06
	04	18	00

apprisers Israell Harding   John Elldridg/

An Inventory of Lands belonging to the Estate of Major Bryan Pendleton deceased, by Deed of gyft & will disposed of/

That Necke of Land at Winter Harbour & Marsh at wth other vpland belonging to sd Necke	500	00	00
It to seuerall yslands & Marsh land at Cape porpus	050	00	00
It 600 Acres of Land neare Sacoe ffalls at	050	00	00
It to the land on the great Ysland	007	00	00
It to one hundred acres of vpland & tenn Acres of Marsh	020	00	00
	627	00	00

Part I, Fol. 6.

A true Coppy of this Inventory transcribed & Compared with ye originall this 24th of June 1681: p Edw: Rishworth ReCor/

Capt Pendleton was not free in giveing his Attest to this Inventory because hee Conceived severall goods were disposed of, before hee could haue oportunity to come to looke after y^m/

29th June: 1681:

This day Tho: Turner Came & Entred Caution, to Prevent the granting of Administration to any P^{r}son vnder any Pretence, In referrence to that Land now possessed by Tho: Turner, w^{r}of hee houlds his possession by a Judgm^t of Court/ y^{r}fore Partys agreiued must make vse of ye Coman Law for y^r releife

July
6: 69

At a Court of sessions houlden at wells 27th Septem^{br} 1681: Administration granted unto Ann Bedford the relict or widdow of Nathan Bedford deceased, joyntly with Mr Robert Elliett of the great Ysland in Pischataqu. M'chant of the Estate of Nathan Bedford aforesd/ with whome Capt ffran, Hooke stands Ingaged with administrators in a bond of one thousand pounds, unto the authority of this prouince, that ye Partys aboue mentioned shall administer according to law, & to respond all Legall rights any way belonging to sd Bedfords Estate, w^n Called y^{r}vnto by the authority of this prouince/

Richmans Ysland 28th of August: 1681:

An Inuentory of Nathan Bedford his Estate taken by Mr John & Robert Jordan/

Inprs 38 Hodgeads of sault at 11s p Hodgsd....................	20	18	0
It Too boates & theire furniture................................	44	00	00
It one barrell of flower 3: 10: 00: six bushells of Mault 24s.............	04	14	00
It 7 barrells of oyle 8: 10: 00| seuerall ould Caske 1l's.............	09	05	00
It too Ankers at 40s| 120 quitlls of fish at 10s p qutl 60£: 00: 0............	62	00	00
It 2 halfe C at 7s p...	02	17	00
It one grindstoone one ould saddle & one skellett....................	00	04	00

Part I, Fol. 7.

It one gunn one barrell of porke 3: 7: 0: 500 of bread 4: 0: 0: It 2 Mayres his sonns 00: 0: 0:.	07	07	00
It one peece of ould Junke, & one new standing part.	02	00	00
It one Grapper at 12s, & fiue Netts at 8 pounds.	08	12	00
It 3 peyre of playne shooes 15s & too peyre of boys shooes 8s.	01	03	00

[7]

It 7 hatts at 5s p hatt 1£: 15s: 0d.	01	15	0
It one hundred fiuety one yd of best Nowells at 21d p yd.	15	02	0
It good bookes at 12s.	00	12	0
It 50 yds of Kersey at 5s p yd is 13: 10 00.	13	10	0
It 91 yds of Breames, at 2s p yd 9£: 250 yds of Leanells 5: 10: 0.	14	12	0
It ½ doz: lines & 3ld of Twine at 2s p ld 12s, 7 yds of heyre Cloath 14s.	01	06	0
It 10 yds of searge at 1: 16: 6d| 5 yds ½ of Kersey at 5s p yd, 27s 6d.	03	04	0
It 32 yds of sougers lineing at 2s p yd, is.	03	04	0
It 3 Inke hornes & 2ld of thread 7s 6d, 1¼ld of thread & fiue Capps all 7s 6d.	00	15	0
It one dozen of worsted stockeings at 2: 8: 0.	02	08	0
It 9 yds ¼ of searge at 3s p yd 01: 8: 6: 33 yds of ball Cloath at 2s p yd 3: 6: 0.	04	14	6
It 6 peyre of Cloath stockeings 9s: one bed & bowlster, rugg & blankett 3: 10: 0	03	19	0
It fiue peyre of stockings & one peyre of drawers at.	00	12	0
It one Chest 5s, 2 small peeces of leather 2s, 50ld spikes 25s.	01	12	0
It tape & thread 6s, one Moreing & Anker 10£.	10	06	0
It all the ould dishes & platters 4s one peyre of still yards 6s.	00	10	0
It to a Neager Man 30£, an ould Chayne fiueteen shillings.	30	15	0
It Tenn Cod lines at 2s 6d p line twenty fiue shillings.	01	5	0
It ½ hodged Molosses one pound 10s, 2 Peces Paragon 18d.	02	8	0
	275	06	9

Spurwinke riuer the 28th August 1681:
The Accompt & Apprisall of Nathan Bedford his Estate there/

His house & land at 36£: 00: 00| foure pewter dishes 8d.	36	08	0
It 2 porrengers two shillgs, one pint pott 18d.	00	04	0
It 3 Iron potts & a Kettle Too pounds too shillings.	02	02	0
It 2 Andirons 7s, 114ld of woll at 8d p ld, 8: 16: 00.	04	03	0
It too Coates & one peyre of briches 20s one Camlett Coate 45s.	03	05	0
It too small bedds too ruggs & too shirts, 2: 15: 00.	02	15	0
It one bed & furniture 3: 15: 00, 2 peyre of sheetes & blanketts 30s.	5	05	0
It 3 shirts & three payre of drawers 50s, 3 Neckecloaths 2 Hankerchers 10s.	03	00	0
It three wastcoats 24s It one greate Coate 01: 10: 00.	02	14	0
It Sowes & piggs, 3: 10: 0, one great Chayre 2s.	03	12	0
It a frijinpane & one ould Chayre, 3s, 2 Cows & Calfes at ye Cape 6: 0: 0.	06	03	0
It too yeareling fourty shillings.	02	00	0
	£71	11	0

Apprizers, John Jordan/
     Robert Jordan/

	275	06	09	
Spurwinke	071	11	00	The 3ds of the fish & oyle to be Deducted, the 3d £ s d
blew Poyt	156	00	00	of 120 qutlls of refuge fish for the men...... 20 00 0
3ds of	502	17	09	It the 3d of seauen barrells of oyle........... 02 16 8
fish &	22	16	08	£22 16 8
oyle De-	480	01	01	
ducted				

Part I, Fol. 7.

An Apprisement of Nathan Bedfords Plantation house & Marsh at blew Poynt, by John Jackeson & James Wiggens August the 29th 1681:

	£	s	d
Inprs one house, & one hundred & twenty acres of Land with Twenty Acres of Marsh at prisd at 90£	90	00	00
It Thirty six Ackers of Marsh more at	48	00	00
It too oxen at 10£ & too steares at 8£	18	00	00
	156	00	00

vera Copia of this Inuentory as aboue & with in written of the Estate of Nathan Bedford as delivered in Court, 27: Septem^br: 81: transcribed & with originall Compared this 8th day of Octob^r 1681:

   p Edw: Rishworth Re: Cor:

The Marke of John Jackeson

The Marke of James Wiggens

Kittery in New England Aprill 11th 1682:
An Inventory of the Estate of Mr Francis Tricky deceased/

	£	s	d
vizt to his house & Land Adjoyneing to it at	35	00	0
It to too Heffers & too yearelings at 10£	10	00	0
It one Mare at thirty shillings, & 3 swine at fourty 5s	03	15	0
It to a skiffe & a Conow at 5£: 15s: 0d, to his weareing Cloaths yt now remaines 25s	07	00	0
It to Pewter brass & Tynn: 3: 10: 00, 2 spitts 2 Tramells one peyre of tonges 12s	4	02	0
It to three small ould Iron potts at eighteen shillings	00	18	0
It to one Diaper table Cloath, & one dozen of Diaper Napkines at	02	10	0
It one Table Cloath & one dozen of Napkines at	01	12	0
It one peyre of Cotton sheetes, & 4 Napkines at 22s	01	02	0
It one ould peyre of sheetes 8s, one peyre of sheetes 16s	01	04	0
It Too small Course table Cloaths and three pillow drawers	00	06	0
It 3 ould feather bedds, & feather pillows, & too feather bowlsters	07	00	0
It Too ould Ruggs 20s, too peyre of ould blankett 18s	01	18	0
It to a Hamake & a feather Bowlster at Twenty shillings	01	00	0
It More the aboused Widdow Tricky ownes yt is due to ye Estate from ye Prouince	12	00	0
It to so much due to the Estate from Ric: Downs of Ysles of shoals in fish	09	00	0
It to some other things wch were forgotten at this apprisall	01	00	0
	£99	07	00

Wee whose names are underwritten being desired by Mis Tricky & her sonn John to apprise the abouesd Estate, wch wee haue done according

Part I, Fol. 8.

to o' best skill, & Judgm^ts, as witness o' hands
the 11th day of Aprill 1682 :

William ffurnald/ Saraih ye wife of ffran^s : Tricky
Elihew Gunnison/ Came before ye Councill of this
prouince Aprill 12th 1682 : at yorke,
& doth Attest vpon her oath that to ye best of her knowledg
this aboue written is a true Inventory of sd ffran : Tricky
her husband his Estate deceased, & if more y^rof afterwards
do appeare, shee stands ingagd by uertue of ye same oath to
bring it in to Authority/

Taken vpon oath in Court the 12th of Aprill 1682 :
p Edw : Rishworth Re : Cor :

vera Copia of this Inventory aboue written as Attested,
transcribed & with originall Compared ye 17th of Aprill
1682 : p Edw : Rishworth Re : Cor :

[8*] An Inuentory of Nicholas Edgscome deceased
apprised by us underwritten/

	£	s	d
Inprs 20 Acres of Marsh land, at....	020	00	00
It Thirty Acres of upland at.....	15	00	00
It one Cow & Calfe at foure pounds	04	00	00
It one Iron pott at eight shillings	00	08	00
It one Musket 15s, his weareing Cloaths 5£	05	15	00
	45	03	00

Willmot Edgscome wife to Humphrey Scamon
the late Nicolas Edgscome ap- George Page his marke O
peared before mee the 28th day of March 1681 : & made
oath y^t this writeing aboue is a true & full Inventory of the
Estate of the late Nicholas Edgscome deceased, her hus-
band/ Josua Scottow Just^s

vera Copia transcribed & Compared this 12th May 1682 :
p Edw : Rishworth Re : Cor :

Judeth Gibbines aged fiuety fiue years or there abouts,
sworne sayth that this deponent was desired by the late
Nicho : Edgscome of Sacoe to understand from him what his

will should bee relateing to what hee had after his decease, & then hee tould her hee would Settle It so as none of the rest of his children should wrong his sonn Robert, & y'fore his intent was, to leaue all to his sonn Robert, to Mantaine his mother, & this was spoaken about three weekes or a Moenth before his death, & further sayth not/ Taken vpon oath the 18th of March 1681: before mee Jos: Scottow
Just^e

John Bonighton aged thirty 4 yeares, sworne testifyeth, to ye trueth of the substance of w^t is aboue testifyd/

Josua Scottow Just^e taken vpon oath before mee 29th of March 1681:

A true Coppy of these testimonys transcribed & Compared this 12th May 1682: p Edw: Rishworth Re:Cor:

24th day of July: 1680:
A true Inuentory of the Estate of William Robbins deceased/

	£	s	d
to one peyre of new shooes 7s, one hatt at 5s	00	12	0
one peyre of New briches 3s, one peyre of Kersy briches 8s	00	11	0
to foure ould Musketts 6s, to too peeces of ould drusline 8s	00	09	0
It to too ould peeces of briches, one wollen ye other lining at	00	03	0
It one ould Kersy Coate & Capp 3s, 5 peyre of ould stookings 5s	00	08	0
It to a New wastcoate Cloath 19s too peyre of Cannice drawers 7s	01	06	0
It to 3 ould shifts	0	08	0
It to 4 ould Necke Cloaths & one ould swash at	00	05	0
It to too ould pillows with feathers in them, 3s 6d	00	03	6
It one peyre of ould bootes 4s one Chest 8s	00	12	0
	£05	04	6

Apprised by Robert Heines/ :13th Septem^{br} 1680:

Jeffory Currier his marke *IC* his marke *RH*

Thomas Pomrey Came & made oath to ye treuth of ye aboue Inuentory hee being to ye Charge of the Doctor, & also to his funerall before mee the day & yeare aboue written/ Roger Kelly Commiso^r/

vera Copia of this Inuentory transcribed out of the originall & Compared this 12th day of May 1682:
p Edw: Rishworth Re:Cor:

Part I, Fol. 8.

In the name of god Amen/ the twenty seauenth of August 1675 : I Ellner Pearce the unprofitable seruant of god, though weake in body yet of good & Perfect remembrance, praysed bee almighty god, knowing y^t I am naturally borne to dy, & to pass from this transcitory life, minding to putt in order mine Estate, to the Intent y^t should bee no striffe for the same after my decease, & to auoyd all Occasions of trouble & Charge I do hereby make this to bee my true last & onely will & testament in manner following/

Ip^m I Commend my soule to almighty god, & his sonn Jesus Christ my saujo^r & redeemer, in whose prætious blood I set ye whoole & onely hope of my saluation, my body in hope of a Joyfull resurrection, I Committ to ye earth to bee decently buried, & touching the distribution of my mortall goods, I dispose of ye same as followeth/

1. first I will y^t all my debts I ow should bee truely payd/

It I giue to my sonn Jos: Pearce my house & Land, only hee is to lett his two sisters, Saraih & Mary, each of them an house lott, If they come into the Countrey & demand It : or otherwise allow the ualew of It, If they should bee in want/ also I giue vnto my sd sonn all my Cattle, as also too feather beds, & the furniture belonging to them, as bedsteads & else, as too fine Holland^s pillows, one new Holland sheete (& w^t y^r is not underneath excepted) & one Diaper board Cloath, foure pewter platters of the biggest sort, on ye vpper shelfe with the earthen dishes, on each side of them as also too of the smallest platters, too plates, foure porringers, too small basons, halfe a pint pott, a beare bowle, a Candlesticke & sault seller, also the biggest brass Kettle, & ye smallest with one Copper Kettle, two skelletts, too Iron potts, one Iron Kettle, one dripinpane, one grediron one spitt, with Andirons & pott hangers, one warmeing pann & brass morter, as also all ye furniture in ye Hall as It stands (excepting 3 leather Chajres, which are Saraihs) also I giue

Part I, Fol. 9.

unto my sonn 4 Napkines & the other eight to bee diuided between his sisters/ also I gaue unto my sd sonn one Siluer Cupp a silke Twilt, & foure siluer spoones, with a Gould ring, one Chest, one deske, one Case of bottles, with 4 round bottles with a drippinpan, one great knott bowle, & too small knott dishes, 6 round trenchers, & 6 square, one fowling peece too Meale Ciues, 19 platters & bowles & trayes, but 2 3ds of them for his too sisters, as also w^t earthen ware y^r is to bee diuided, with ye glasses between my sonn & daughter Saraih/ as also I giue unto my sonn Joseph my scarffe, with the too wodden porringers, & a Cann, with three pounds in siluer, from my daughter Saraih, or else to keepe her siluer bowle/

[9] It I giue unto my daghter Saraih too brass Kettles, one brass candlesticke, one brass morter, one spitt on ye other side/ Moreouer I giue unto my daughter Saraih, one gould ring, one new feather bed provided shee return y^t to her brother, which shee carried away with her, also one holland pillow beare, one hollane sheete, one great knott bowle, one Indean knott dish, 6 new trenchers one Iron Posnett, one sleightstoon, a Chaffine dish one table board, too boxes one baskitt/ furthermore, It is my desire y^t all my weareing Cloaths togeather with three pewter basons, fiue platters six porringers should bee diuided between my too daughters/ further I giue vnto Saraih a Cotten Ciuersid

It I giue vnto my daughter Mary, one Copper Kettle, one brass Candlesticke, one hollane pillow beare, one ould holland sheete, one Iron Posnitte, one box/ further It is my will, that if either of my Children should die before the receipt of the afore mentioned lagaceys, then his or her part to bee deuided between the Partys, or else to ye Party suruiueing: forthermore, I do by these Presents, make & ordajne my deare & well beloued sonn Jos: Pearce before mentioned, to bee my full whoole & onely executor, of this my last will & testament, hereby giueing & bequeathing,

Part I, Fol. 9.

vnto him all ye remayender of my Estate, wch is not in this my last will & testament disposed off/

Lastly I do appoynt my loueing frejnd M^r ffran^s Hooke to bee ouer seer of this my last will & testament, desireing of him not onely to keepe my sd will in safe costody but also after It shall please god to take mee out of this world to open it & to take care y^t each Perticular may bee Performed as neare as may bee, as alsoe to take æffectuall & speedy Care, that all my obligations be fully satisfyd, by my executor or through his defect to make saile of the portion giuen unto him to satisfy the same, whither It bee debts y^t now I am Ingag'd, or funerall expences/ also it is my desire y^t my friend & ouer seer Mr Hooke do take Care y^t my sonn do not waste or Imbessell the sd Estate, but upon such considerations as sd Hooke shall see to his aduantage/ In witness w^rof I sd Ellner Pearce haue subscribed this my last will & testament, with my own hand, & y^runto putt my seale the day & yeare aboue written/

```
                               The marke of
Signed Sealed & deliuered,   Ellner Pearce  𝐸𝑃  (her seale)
   in the Presence of us whose
   names are here underwritten/
   Benjamen Johnson/  Hannah
                her    Langleigh/
   Joane Bray  B
            Marke
   ffrancis Hooke
```

Mr Fran^s Hooke, Joane Bray the Ellder were both Present & see Ellner Pearce set to her marke or hand & seale, & owned this her last will to bee her Act & Deede, before y^m/

Taken upon oath this 24th of Janu : 1675 : before mee
        Edw : Rishworth Asōte/

This will allowed off & Confirmed p this Court Aprill 4th/ 1676: & a true Coppy w^rof is transcribed this 6th day of Aprill 1676 : as Attests Edw : Rishworth Re : Cor :

Part I, Fol. 9.

January 5th 1675:

Wee whose names are underwritten did by ye request of Joseph Pearce take an Inuentory of the Estate left by his mother deceased/ which wee did accordingly, & is as followeth/

	£	s	d
Inprs A dwelling house & land apprtaineing to it	0110	00	00
It too oxen too Cows one yeareling steare & too Calfes	024	00	00
It Too Chaines a Dogg & a Copspine, an Iron Hooke & ring	001	02	00
It 3 feather bedds & the furniture belonging to them	014	00	00
It 2 bedsteads one Chest, one deske one Case of bottles	002	17	00
It one great brass Kettle, 2 Copper Kettles, too skellets	003	10	00
It 2 brass Kettles 25s one brass morter & a warmeing pan at	001	15	00
It one Chaffine dish 4s, too Iron potts 40s	002	04	00
It 1 Iron kettle a dripinpan, one Gredirone & too spitts	000	14	00
It 2 Andirons 3 pott Hangers & Curten rodds at 20s	001	00	00
It one Iron p snitt one Iron skellet 10s, table boards, Joynt stoules & 3 leather Chares 4: 0: 0	004	10	00
It one slpris board, one Cubbard & three leather Cussions at 2: 05: 0	002	05	00
It 9 picturs too Chargers painted 8s, 3 chaires, 4 basketts, 3 boxes a lookeing glass 10s	00	18	00
It one peyre of wiminse shooes, one bible & a practice of piety	000	16	00
It too raysors, one smouthing Iron three heaters, at	000	11	00
It a prospect glass too runletts & too round glass bottles	00	06	00
It 2 small hammers 18d one fowling peece 30s	01	11	6
It 1 Iron plate 1 peyre tonges, earthen ware stoone buttles & one gredIron all at	00	12	00
It 3 Tubbs 5s, 2 Clues 2s, one water buckett 3s	00	10	00
It 2 platters trays dishes 6 trenchers, & three Cheesefaits	01	00	00
It one Table board, one glass case, one Lamp & one ould Chaire at	00	13	00
It Debts due on Accopt from seuerall Persons	05	00	00
It 1 2 yeareling Heffer 50s, 1 chamberpot 3s, 3 pewter potts 5s. 5 basons 15s: 23s	03	13	00
It 11 pewter dishes 2: 15: 0, 3 Cupps & one Candlesticke at 6s	03	01	00
	186	08	6
It 9 porringers at 9s, 2 platters 4 sawcers, one sault seller 4s a brass morter & a Candlesticke 10s	001	03	0
It 6 lysborne dishes 5s 6d, platters a puddinpan & trenchers 2s	00	07	6
It too knott dishes & a funnill, 12d, 2 otter Muffs 8s, 2 brushes 18d	00	10	6
It one peyre of scales & stillyards 5s, 8 sheets 40s, 1 doz: Napkines & 2 Towells 32s	03	17	00
It 4 pillows 12s, 3 table Cloaths 12s, 4 Cubbard Cloaths 10s	01	14	00
It 2 Chests a blanket & a swath 5s, & 5 handkerchers 2s 6d	00	07	6
It 5 dressings 5 Coiues, 3 necke handkerchers, & three head bands	01	13	0
It one whiske one silke howd 20s, 10 earthen dishes & potts 5s, 3 Cocer Nutts 5s	01	10	0
It three wastcoats, three petticoates & a Caster hatt at	07	00	0
It 2 peyre of stockings & glasses all 8s, some peeces of lace at 3s	00	11	0
It 3 gould rings 24s, one peece of gould 20s	02	04	0
It too siluer dram Cupps a siluer thymble & a Claspe 10s: 2 purses 5s a kniffe & 1 peyre of sisers	00	15	00
It 4 Course Napkines two headbands 6 Capps & an ould NeckeCloath	00	10	0
It two turky Cussions 10s, one petticoate, one peyre of bodys & a Chest 25s	01	15	00
It fine wedges too beetle rings & a searge hood money at	00	17	00
	211	03	00

Part I, Fol. 10.

The P'ticulars herein expressed apprised by us this 5th of Janv: (1675)   Fran' Hooke Joⁿ Bray/

Joseph Pearce doth Attest vpon his oath y' this Inuentory aboue written is a true Inuentory of the Estate of his father John Pearce & of his Mother Ellner Pearce lately deceased to ye best of his knowledge, & if remember any more vpon same oath hee promisseth to bring it in/ taken vpon oath this 24th Janva : 75 : before mee Edw : Rishworth Assote/ A true Coppy of this Inuentory transcribed & Compared this 8th day of March: 76: p Edw: R... worth . . . . .

In the name of god Amen/

[10] I Edw: Hayes of Kittery in the County of yorke In New England being at Present uery sicke, & weake of body, but of Perfect mind & memory, & without fraude or deceipt not knowing how It may please ye Lord to dispose of mee as to things of this life, to whose gratious dispensations I humbly submitt, w'fore I do Committ my soule unto god that gaue It & my body to the earth, to bee Inter'd in a decent & orderly manner, ordering & appoynting this to bee my last will & testament, in manner & forme following/

1 : Imp': I giue & bequeath unto my Elldest sonn Joseph the some of seauen shillings & 6d in Currant pay of New England to bee payd by my executrix imediately so soone as my sonn shall Attayne unto, & accomplish the age of Twenty one yeares If demanded/

2 : It I giue & bequeath unto my yonger sonn William the some of seauen shillings 6d of Current pay aforesd, to bee payd. by my executrix imediatly & as soone as my sd sonn shall Attajne unto & accomplish ye age of 21 years if demanded/

I giue unto my 3 daughters, Elizabeth, Saraih & Ann, the sume of seauen 6d a peece, of Current pay aforemen-

Part I, Fol. 10.

tioned, to bee payd unto them by my sd executrix, as soone & Immediately as they Attayne to y⁶ age of 18 yeares, is demanded as aforesd/

3 : I giue & bequeath unto my most deare & affectionate & intirely beloued wife Phylodelphia Hayes, my iust & due debts being first payd, & satisfyd all the rest of my goods, wares M'chandise Cattle househould stuffe Implemeᵗˢ debts goods whither in my owne Costody, or possession or others, of wᵗ nature kind quality or Condition w'soeuer (nothing excepted or reserued) whither mouables or unmoueables whom I do hereby & my will is, do make my whoole & soole executrix, to execute & see Prformed this my last will & testameᵗ according to the purport, true & Intent & meaneing thereof/ In witness wʳof I haue here unto sett my hand & seale in Kittery aforesd, this secund day of July one thousand six hundred seauenty fiue Anno Dom̃ : 1675 :

Signed sealed & deliuered,   The signe of
  in the Presence of us,   Edw : ╪ Hayes (ʰⁱˢ Seale)
Jabes Jenken his
    signe H
Joseph Ham̃onds/
Richd Allexandʳ/

Richd Allexander & Jabez Jenkens, do Attest upon their oaths, yᵗ this Instrument or will aboue written to which Leefᵗ Hayes his hand or marke, & seale is afixed, was the Act, & Deed of sd Edw : Hayes now decessed

Taken vpon yʳ oaths this 9ᵗʰ day of March 167⅘ before us
A true Coppy of this will tran-   Edw : Rishworth
  scribed & Compared with   John Wincoll Assots
the origi nall the 20ᵗʰ day of
Aprill 1676 :   p Edw : Rishworth Re : Cor :

Part I, Fol. 10.

Kittery in Pischataqua Riuer in New England March 28 : 76 :
An Inuentory of the Estate of Mr Edw : Hayes deceased/

	£	s	d
Inprs 4 pewter platters 30s one bason 5s: & six porringers 6s	02	01	00
It one pewter plate & too ould pewter Cupps at	00	04	00
It one frijinpan 6s, one Tynn pann 4s one skellet 6s	00	16	00
It 2 peyre of Cards 3s, one Gread Iron 3s, 6 dishes earthen 5s	00	11	00
It 2 earthen potts, one earthen Jugg 2s, wodden dishes & trays 5s	00	07	00
It 3 Chayers 10s, one Chest & too boxes thirteen shillings	01	03	00
It Two bedds, one bowlster, & foure pillows at	04	10	00
It one rugg 18s foure ould blanketts 30s	02	08	00
It one peyre of sheetes one peyre of Cotton pillow beares	01	00	00
It one table Cloath 4s, one uallance & ould Curtanes at 16s	01	00	00
It 1 Trundle bed stead 8s, one Coate one peyre of briches 55s	03	03	00
It one peyre of sheres, one pressing Iron & one smothing iron	00	14	00
It one Iron pot & an Iron Kettle at 20s	01	00	00
It one Table & foure Joynt stooles at sixteen shillings	00	16	00
It one barrell of beife & seauen buslls of Indean Corne at	03	00	00
It 2 Cows 6£ too Heffers flue pounds, 2 yearlings 40s, 1 horse 3£	16	00	00
It fluety Acres of Land at Newgewanake at	05	00	00
	£43	13	00

This is a true apprisall of the Estate aboue mentioned to yᵉ best of our Judgments, as witness our hands the day & yeare first aboue written/ John Shapleigh/ Jos : Ham̄ond/
vera Copia of this Inventory aboue written transcribed out of originall & yʳwith Compared this 20ᵗʰ of Aprill : 76 :

p Edw : Rishworth Re : Cor :

Philadelphia Hayes doth Attest vpon her oath yᵗ this Inuentory aboue written is a true Inuentory of the Estate of her husband Edw : Hayes his Estate to the best of her knowledg, & if afterwards any more of her sd husbands Estate do or shall appeare, shee will bee ready to giue it in vpon the same oath shee hath now taken/

Taken upon oath this 29th of March 1676 : before us

Edw : Rishworth
John Wincoll Assōtˢ

Part I, Fol. 11.

An Inuentory of the Estate of John Cross senior Deceased, apprised by us whose names are underwritten 18th Decembr 1676

	£	s	d
Inprs to House & Land & Marsh at home, Marsh at Ogunquent & Marsh & vpland at Drakes ysland all in Wells, at..................................	140	00	0
It to 7 Cotten sheetes at seauen shillings p sheete.............................	002	09	0
It 15: Cheeses 15s: one table cloath 4 Napkines & a pillow beare 12s.........	01	07	0
It wanescott Chest 10s, a rugg, 2 blanketts a Ciuering & a pillow 3£.........	03	10	00
It one bed one bowlster too pillows & three blanketts at......................	05	00	0
It butter dishes, 2 Candlesticks & spoones at...................................	01	01	0
It 2 potts & pot hookes, 2 small Kettles & a frijinpan at.....................	01	10	00
It one brass Kettle at 10s 1 Chest bed 2 Clues 2 cabbines at 30s...............	02	00	00
It one Cart 3 Cleueeses 3£: 4 yoaks, 1 peyre of hookes & a staple at 20s,.....	04	00	00
It foure axes, one shayre & Cowlter & a plow at 28s...........................	01	08	00
one peyre of betell rings, 5 wedges & foure forkes at......................	00	13	0
It 2 spades a shed sh uell & a roape all at 20s................................	01	00	0
[11] It one horse Coller syth tackeling & three Hammers at.......	01	00	0
It too Adges, 2 Augers, one Chissell & a small Gouge all at.................	00	06	0
It 1 Chayre & Carpet 10s, 4 baggs 11s, 1 peyre tongus 1 spitt & pot hangers 12s 6d...	01	13	6
It Conows at 20s, a Wheele, Cards & a sleade at 15s..........................	01	15	0
It 3 fat Hoggs nine pounds, old hows 5s, a skellet 3s........................	09	08	0
It 16 harrow teeth & one Haulter 8s, Meate Hides & Caske 4: 15:.............	5	03	0
It eight Hoggs & 1¼ piggs 17£: a Proell of Woll 20s.........................	18	00	0
It Too horses, too Mayres & too Cowlts at....................................	16	00	0
It Caske & a Churne & seuerall other small things at........................	00	11	0
It 4 busls of Rie, 19 bushlls & an halfe of peas at 4s p bushll	04	14	0
It seauenty seauen bushlls of Indean Corne at 4s p busll is 15: 08: 0	15	08	0
It 25 busls ½ of good Wheate at 5s p busll...................................	06	07	6
It More 4 oxen at 30£ 6 Cows at 4£ 10s p Cow..................................	27	00	0
More to foure oxen at 30£..	30	00	0
It Two steares & a bull at three pounds p beast..............................	09	00	0
It Two yearelings & one yeareling is fiue pounds.............................	05	00	0
It 19 sheepe at ten shillings p sheepe is 9£: 10s: 0.........................	09	10	0
It one pillion a Proell of trays & Pales	00	10	0
	325	06	8
Debts due p balls:....	07	04	00
Totall	332	10	08

Sammuell Wheelewright
ffrancis Littlefeild/

John Cross his Estate
to seuerall Prsons is Dr/   Estate p Contra is Cr/

					£	s	d
to Mr Fryer for a debt............	2	10	0	Inprs p a Cow Impressed for ye Countrey......................	4	00	0
to Jos: Cross for threshing Corne		19	0	p dyet for souldgers on ye accopt.	4	15	0
	03	09	00	p dyet for fiue weeks dyet from Mr Buss....	1	05	0
Cr 11 03 00				p a debt due from Richd Palmer...	0	15	0
Dr 03 09 0				p a small debt from Natll Cloyce..	0		
p balle 07 04 0				p a debt due from Frans Backeus..	0	8	0
					11	03	0

Part I, Fol. 11.

January 2 : 1676 :

Joseph Cross doth Attest vpon his oath y^t this is a true Inuentory of the Estate of his father John Cross Senior deceased, to the best of his knowledg & If anything more do appeare which is at Present forgotten hee is ingaged by the same oath to bring it into ye Court/ Taken before us
      Edw : Rishworth
      Samell Wheelewright
       Assotiates/

An Inventory of the Estate of John Cross Junior deceased, taken by Sam^{ll} Wheelewright Decemb^r 18 : 1676 :

	£	s	d
Inprs to a Tract of land lijng in the Countrey all at	10	00	0
It one Cow & yeareling, one spade & betle rings at	05	01	0
	£15	01	0

vpon the same oath taken by Joseph Cross to ye Estate of his father John Cross deceased, hee doth Attest to the treuth of this his brothers Inuentory, before us aboue written as Attests
    Edw : Rishworth Re : Cor :

A true Coppy of these two Inuentorys aboue written transcribed out of the originall & there with Compared this 5th day of January 1676 :   p Edw : Rishworth Re : Cor :

An Inventory of the Estate of James Gouch lately deceased the 24th of Septemb^r 1676 :

	£	s	d
Inprs one dwelling house & barne, Land & Meddow belonging to It lyjng in Wells where hee liued, & the ysland	180	00	00
It a Parcell of vpland & Meddow at Epiford	20	00	00
It 2 oxen at sixteen pounds & eight Cows at thirty 6 pounds	52	00	00
It 2 steares & eight pounds too yearelings at three pounds	11	00	00
It 3 Calfes 40s, too Mayres & one Cowlt tenn pounds	12	00	00
It six swine foure pounds, weareing Cloaths & Table lining 16 : 19 : 0	20	19	00
It In new stuffe searge & Canuince	03	06	00
It too feather bedds & bedding 14£ 00s 0d, househould stuffe 06 : 16 : 00	20	16	00
It yoakes Cheynes & husbandry tackeing	02	15	00
It a sword & belt 13s, one bible & another booke 7s	01	00	00
It single board nayles 23s Twoles & Iron things 30s	02	13	00
It to wheate in the straw. Judgd 18 bushells	01	10	00
It fourty five busils of Indean Corne at	07	00	00
	£337	19	00

PART I, FOL. 12.

Apprised by us John Wells/
Jonathan Hammonds/
Jonathan Hammonds giues in vpon his oath before this Court that this is a true Inuentory of James Gouch his Estate, & what more doth afterwards appeare, upon the same oath stands Ingaged to bring it in/ taken upon oath in Court y⁰ 13ᵗʰ Decembʳ 1676 : as Attests

Edw : Rishworth Re : Cor :

An Inuentory of the Estate of Mis Ruth Gouch, Deceased/

Inprs too steares, too Cows with part of one Calfe	18	8	00
It one horse too pounds	02	00	00
	20	08	00

Apprised by us this 6th day of Decembʳ 1676 :

Samll Wheelewright
A true Coppy of these Inuen-   John Wells/
torys transcribed out of yᵉ originall & yʳwith Compared this 11ᵗʰ day of January 1676 :   p Edw : Rishworth ReCor :

A true Inuentory of the Estate of George ffarrow deceased taken the 28ᵗʰ of September 1676 :

Inprs an house & land, with all ye vpland Meddow & March belonging to it.	230	00	0
It one Parcell of vpland lijng at the little riuer	010	00	0
It one Prcell of Meddow & land at Coxwell	015	00	00
It too steares 10£: too Heffers 4 pounds, 2 yearelings 3£ one Calfe 15.	017	15	00
It too Mayres & Too Cowltes nine pounds, fiue swine £5: 10: 00	14	10	00
It bedding Cloathing 8s, househould stuffe 6: 18: 0	07	06	00
It a bible & another booke 7s a weauers lowme slays & harness 3£	3	7	0
	£297	18	0

[12]   In the name of God amen/
I Thomas Spencer of Newgewanacke in the Townshipp of Kittery being sicke of body, but through the mercys of god, sound of Mind & memory, and not knowing how soone my Change may come, desire to dispose of that Estate which god hath giuen unto mee as followith, uidzᵗ :

Part I, Fol. 12.

Inp^{rs} I giue unto my Elldest sonn William Spencer after my decease, & the decease of Patience my loueing wife, my now dwelling house & all out houseing by It, or belonging to it, & all the Land adioyneing to it, being now in my possession & lijng on the North side of the high way, by my sd dwelling house, whither It bee Gardens oarchards, pasture Meddows Corne Land to him the sd William Spencer my sonn, & to his heyres for euer; prouided hee pay or Cause to bee payd unto my Too daughters, namely Susanna & Elizabeth, with in six weekes, after my decease & of my loueing wife Patience, the full & iust sume of Tenn pounds, a peece in money or pay æquiuolent ther unto: The houses & sd land lijng responsable, untill ye Legacys abouesd bee fully payd/

2ly I giue to patience my louing wife all the rest of my Estate, whither It bee in lands Chattles, Cattle, goods debts house hould stuffs Meddows &c: not mentioned as abouesd, for her to distribute & dispose of amongst my Children at her own discretion, except what I haue already giuen to my Elldest son as abouesd/

Lastly I do nominate & appoynt patience my sd loueing wife to bee my soole executrix of this my last will & testament/ In Confirmation where of I haue here unto set my hand & seale, the secund day of June in the yeare of our Lord one thousand six hundred seauenty nine/ 1679:

Signed sealed & Deliuered   Thomas Spencer
  in Presence of
  Gillbard warrine his   his marke   (his Seale)
  marke **G**
  George Pearson/

Thomas Spencer appeared before mee, & acknowledged this Instrument to bee his act, & Deede, this 18th of June
(1679)   Samuell Wheelewright Assotiate

Part I, Fol. 12.

An Appendix to my last will & testament as on the other side of this paper, appeareth my further will in that, where as formerly I gaue unto my sonn in law John Gattinsby who married my daughter Susanna a Certen Tract of land being part of that too hundred acres that the Town of Kittery granted to mee, ioyneing to my house lott, & the sd Gattensby sould his sd right or tract of land unto my sonn in law Thomas Euerington who married my daughter Mary, & the sd Gattingsby was fully Contented, & payd by the sd Euerington my sonn in law, for his sd land & the sayd Euerington my sonn in law possessed the sd Land his life tyme, & left it to his heyres; And w^r as I also gaue unto my sonn Etherington a Certen Tract of Land ioyneing to the land hee bought of the sd John Gattensby, on which the dwelling house of the sayd Etherington now standeth, & both Tracts of land Contajneing about Twenty foure Acres by Estimation, bee It more or less, as they are now bounded with Richard Nason & the high way on the South, William Spencers land on the West, Daniell Goodins land & Humphrey Spencers land on the North, & that part of my land Called Parkers Marsh on the East: And although some writeings haue been Prused about the Premisses, yet nothing y^t I know upon record about It, & that the sd Land according to my true intent discend unto the right heyres of it, both by the sayd Etheringtons purchase of the sayd Gattensby in part, & my gift unto the sayd Etherington of the rest of the sd land: Now my will is that the sayd Land with the dwelling house vpon it, & all the appurtenances & priuiledges y^r unto belonging, should bee & remajne the proper right & Inheritance of John Wincoll Junjor, sonn of John Wincoll of Kittery & of Mary his wife deceased, who was the daughter of my sd sonn in law Thomas Etherton & Mary his wife deceased, to haue & to hould the sd tract of Land, dwelling house with all the appurtenances, & priuiledges there unto belonging to him the sd John Wincoll Junjo^r &

PART I, FOL. 13.

his heyres lawfully begotton of his body for euer: & If hee dy with out such lawfull heyres, my will is that the sd Tract of Land houseing & all appurtenances & priuiledges y^r unto belonging shall bee & remajne the proper right & Inheritance of patience Atherton daughter unto sd Thomas Etherington & Mary his wife deceased, to haue and to hould to her & her heyres for euer/ In witness where unto I haue afixed my hand & seale, this fifth day of June one thousand six hundred seauenty nine 1679:

Signed sealed & deliuerd in   Thomas Spencer
 the Presence of,
 Gillbard Warrine   his marke (his seale)
 his Marke G
 George Pearson/

  Thomas Spencer appeared before mee, and acknowledged this Instrument to bee his Act & Deed this 18th June 1679:
     Samuell Wheelewright Assōte

A true Coppy of Thomas Spencers will with in written, & of an appendix, or deed of gyft aboue written transcribed out of ye originall & there with Compared this, 15th day of June 1682:   p Edw: Rishworth ReCor:

[13] An Inventory of the Lands, Cattle Chattles, goods & moueables of Thomas Spencer, late of Barwicke in the Town of Kittery deceased, 15th Decemb^r 1681:

	£	s	d
Inprs His weareing Cloaths 5£: in the vpper Chamber, one feather bed Couerlid blankett, 1 peyre of sheetes 2 pillows & a bowlster 3: 10: 00	08	10	0
It one peyr of sheetes 10s, 3 yds of Cayrsey 12s, a Carpet 3 ould Chests & forme 1s	01	18	0
It In the lower Chamber, one feather bed, 3 blanketts a rugg 2 pillows It a bowlster 5£: A little Table Carpet ould Chest a forme earthen dishes 10s	05	10	0
It In ye leantow, a rugg a blankett ould bedding wodden dishes trays 12s trenchers 3s	00	15	0
It in the Hall 2 Copper kettles a brass skellett one warmeing pann It one little kettle & a skimmer too pounds	02	00	0
It 8 pewter dishes, 8 porringers, 5 pewter potts & a bason 40s & a bason & Vre 10s	02	10	0
It 6 earthen dishes 5s, 2 Tynn panns 2s, a siluer Cupp & spoone 12s	00	17	0
It one Iron pott fyre pann pott hookes & tramell 10s Chayrs & Table 10s	01	00	0
It Two small Gunnes at 30s, in seller leantow a little Molosses & barrells 5s	01	15	0
	24	15	0
It 5 swine at three pounds 9 Harrow teeth at Tho: Holms his 19s 3 19 00			
24 15 00			
28 14 00			

Part I, Fol. 13.

The home stall of house barne Oarchard & about tenn Acres of Land	100	00	0
The rest of the Land neare the home stall supposed about 100 Acres	50	00	0
It 100 Acres of Land by the Marsh at lower end of Willcocks pond.	25	00	0
It the Meddow about 14 Acres & 30 Acres of vpland by it at	20	00	0
It Thee Cows & three foure years ould stears at	18	00	0
It 2 3 years ould stears 4£ too stears 3 years ould 3£	07ˢ	00	0
It A Mare 30s horses in the Woods at fiue pounds	06	10	0
It 3 Chanes hooks & staples a ring for a Copp yoake beetle & 2 Wedgs } It one peyre of Cart Wheel hoopes all at }	02	10	0
	229	00	0
	28	14	0
	257	14	0

Apprised this first day of May 1682 : Richard Nason
A true Coppy of this Inventory transcribed & Compared with originall this 15th June : 82 :   Moses Spencer *M*
   John Wincoll/
p Edw : Rishworth Re : Cor :

In the name of god Amen/

I John Bready of the Town of Kittery in the Prouince of Mayne, being at this Instant on my bed being sore sicke yet through the goodness of Almighty god, as Prfect in my understanding & memory as at any other tyme heretofore : & haueing by the goodness of god through his blessing vpon my lawfull Endeauoʳˢ, attajned to some outward Estate, I do by this my last will & testament signify to the world my soole purpose & intention in the disposeing of it as followeth/

1 — first I do hœrtily & really bequeath & freely render my spirit & soule to god, that gaue It, hopeing that in the meritts & mediation of yᵉ Lord Jesus Christ, I shall Inheritt euerlasting life/ secundly I do will that all my Acts of dealeing bee paid, & all my lawfull debts discharg'd/

3ly I will that all my necessary Charges, whither in sickness or buriall of my Corp . . bee fully discharged/ 4ly & lastly I do hereby will & bequeath to Saraih my wife, all & singular my Estate remajneing after the defraijng the Premisses aforesd : as well wᵗsoeuer is at Present in reuersion out of my hands as wᵗ is in possession in hand, in maner & kind wᵗsoeuer, bee It houses lands Chattles, Cloathing, debts by

Part I, Fol. 13.

Accompts, or w^tsoeuer is found to Pertajne to my Estate, I do as aforesd fully & freely bequeath to my trusty & loueing wife/ to all which I subscribe this 30th of August in the yeare of o^r Lord 1681: as witness my hand/

witnesses/   The signe of

    Job Cleamons Senjo^r   John ╫ Bready/
    The signe of Thomas
    Roberts **T R**

Prouince of New Hampshire/ At a quarter Court of pleas held in Hampshire the 6th day of Decemb^r 1681: Job Clements Esqr & Thomas Roberts made oath that this is the last will & testament of John Bready who signed the same by his marke In y^r Presence, & that ye same tyme hee was of a disposed mind/   Elyas Styleman ReCor:

Job Clements Esqr & Thomas Roberts, did attest vpon the oath they had taken as aboue written, the aboue will of Joⁿ Bready with his hand to it, was the last will & testament of sd Bready signed wⁿ hee was of a disposeing mind/

        owned before us May 8th 1682:

vera Copia of this will aboue   John Wincoll ⎫ Just^s
written as Attested tran-   Fran^s Hooke ⎬ pe:
scribed & with originall   Charles Frost ⎭
Compared this 16th day of
June 1682: p Edw: Rishworth ReCor:

An Inuentory of the Lands Cattle, Chattles & moueables of John Bready late of Kittery deceased/ October 9th: 1681:

	£	s	d
His wearing Cloaths apprised at six pounds	06	00	00
It his Muskett Carbine & all his amunition at	03	10	00
It the home stall of Twenty Acres of land, vidzt a dwelling outhouses oarchard Corne Land, Meddow wood land tane yard Barke Mill &c all at	70	00	00
It Lands about Seauenty Acres	05	00	00
It English & Indian graine about fluety busils	06	10	00
It Hay about three loade & some other ffodder	03	00	00
It too stears 2 Cows too yearelings & an horse	15	00	00
It 8 sheepe & eleauen swine at	09	00	00
It 2 axes plow Irones, a beetle & wedg, an ould saddle & bridle & a yoake	01	10	00
It one feather bed a bowlster, 2 pillows too blanketts, one Rugg Curtains & bedstead all at fiue pounds	05	00	00
It one little bed 2 blanketts & one bowlter at	02	00	00

Part I, Fol. 14.

[14]

It 2 peyre of sheetes, 12 napkines, 1 table Cloath & foure pillow beares.......	02	00	0
It prouissions vidzt Mollosses meale & Meate at........................	05	00	0
It too Iron Potts one kettle, 2 Tramells & pott hookes at	01	00	0
It pales trays Earthen ware dishes trenchers & spoones......................	00	10	0
It Chests Chares stooles, 2 spinning wheeles Cards one box 1 fryinpan peyre of bellows & other trumpery at	01	10	0
It about Twenty Hides in the Tann ffatts at.	10	00	0
It due from James Stagpoole 22s..	01	02	0
It Twenty yards of home made Wollen Cloath.	04	00	0
It Twenty shillings payd towards seateing the meeteing house................	01	00	0
	£152	12	0

Apprized this 21th day of Nouemb^r 1681 : by us
                        John Wincoll
                        Charles Frost/

A true Coppy of this Inventory transcribed & Compared this 16th day of June 1682 : p Edw : Rishworth-Re : Cor :

The last will & testament of Robert Mendum of Kittery taken this first of May 1682 :

I Robert Mendum being weake in body, but of Perfect mind & Memory, do ordaine this as my last will & testament, hereby reuoakeing all wills by mee formerly made/

My house w^{r}in I now dwell, with all the houseing, & land belonging y^{r}unto, & all the priuiledges app^{r}tajneing, I giue to my sonn Jonathan Mendum for his use, dureing his life, & after his deccase, to his two younger sons, Jonathan & Dauid Mendum, to be æqually deuided between them, & If either of them dy before they Come to age the Suruiuer shall haue ye whoole, & If both of them die, then my Grandsonn Robertt Mendum shall haue It/

All my land in Spruse Cricke I giue to my Grandson Robert Mendum with all the priuiledges belonging there unto/ Further unto my sonn & daughter Mendum I giue tenn of my Cattle, & to my three Grandchildren aforesd, fiue Cattle a peece, to bee diuided amongst them as æqually as they may, my sonn & daughter to haue ye Improuement of all both land & stocke, till my grandchildren Come to

Part I, Fol. 14.

age, & as each of y^m Come to ye age of Twenty one years, then y^r portion of moueables to Come into y^r hands All the rest of my Moueables & house hould goods I leaue in hands of my sonn & daughter, oblieiging them to giue each of my Grandchildren a share of it, as they Come to age/

Moreouer, I will that my grandsonn Robert Michamore shall haue an Heffer which my sonn Jonathan shall deliuer to him, when he comes to age/ & Robert Mendum shall haue his land at Spruse Chicke, w^n hee Comes to the age of Twenty one yeares, or to bee married/

Finally I make my sonn Jonathan my soole executor of this my last will & testament, giueing to him w^tsoeuer Estate I haue not expressly mentioned aboue, whither in debts, or moueables or otherwise, willing him my sd executor to pay all my iust debts, & funerall Charges, & to burry mee in my fejld by my last wife/ I also require my Hono^rd frejnd Richd Martyn Esqr to bee my ouerseer, to see the Prformance of this my last will & Testament/ In witness to all & singular the Premisses, I set tow my hand & seale the day & yeare aboue written/

Robert Mendum of Kittery,
 did signe & seale the
 aboue written Instrument
 & declare It to bee his last
will & testament this 1 : May 1682 :
In Presence of us/ Josua Moodey/
Christeian Ramach/

the marke of (his Seal)
Robert R M Mendum

Mr Josua Moodey affirmeth on oath to the uerity abouesd, this 18th day of May 1682 before mee ffran : Hooke Just : pe :

Christian Ramach testifyed vpon oath y^t hee saw Robert Mendum signe seale & deliver this Instrument, as his last

Part I, Fol. 15.

will & testament, & that Mr Josua Moodey, & hee sd Ramach set y^r hands as witnesses/ May 22 : 1682 : before us/

vera Copia of this will transcribed & Compared this 17th June 1682 : p Edw : Rishworth ReCor :

John Wincoll
ffran : Hooke
Charles ffrost
} Just^s pe :

An Inventory of the Estate of Robert Mendum of Kittery deceased as It was taken & apprized by us whose names are here underwritten/ May 16th : 1682 :

	£	s	d
Inprs the dwelling house, & all the out houses with all the Land adjoyneing yrunto being about seauenty acres	100	00	00
It to the land in Spruse Cricke by report 100 Acres, be ye same more or less	050	00	00
It 4 oxen at six pounds p oxe & Ditto 6 pounds	030	00	00
It too stears 3 years ould 7£ It 9 Cows 4£ p Cow, 36£	43	00	00
It one Heffer of three years ould with her Calfe at	03	10	00
It one Heffer of two years ould with her Calfe at	03	00	00
It too Heffers of two years ould at flue pounds	05	00	00
It 1 3 yeare ould bull three pounds, 5 yearelings at 30s a peece 7£: 10s: 0d	10	10	00
It 7 hoggs of one yeare ould 7£: It 8 shotts at 3: 4: 0	10	04	00
It In the bed Chamber one bed & furniture at 6: 10: 0	06	10	00
It one great Chaire 5s, one Chest 10s, one ould Cloake 00: 00: 00	00	15	00
It 1 stuff Coate lyned 25s, one Cloath Coate ditto lyned 25s	02	10	00
It one Cloath Ditto 25s. & one Cloath Coate 15s 1 Torne Coate 5s	02	05	00
It too peyre of Cloath briches one peyr 12s, other 8s	01	00	00
It one peyre of leather briches 10s. one new searge wastCoate 15s	1	05	00
It a Red broad Cloath wastcoate 20s, 1 peyre of ould drawers 5s	01	t5	00
3 ould wastcoats at 3s	00	03	00
It 6 peyre of wollen stockeings 18s: 2 peyr of Mittons 18d	00	19	06
It 2 kiues 12d, 1 peyre sizers 6d, 2 rubstones 18d & 1 peyr leather pockets 12d.	00	04	00

[15]

	£	s	d
It 2 yds of penistone 7s, 2 Hatts 5s one yd of Scotch cloth 2s: one sash 2s	00	16	00
It 3 yds ; of locerum 4s 1d, 4 yards Scotch Cloath at 12s	00	16	01
It 3 new shirts at 01: 10: 00, 4 ould shirts at 20s	02	10	0
It 4 peyre of Cotton drawers 12s, 1 Daper Table Cloath 10s	01	02	0
It one ould sheete 5s, one peyre of lining sheetes 16s	01	01	0
It one peyre of new Cotton sheetes 20s	01	00	0
It 6 Cotton Napkins 15s, too Cotton table Cloaths 5s	01	00	0
It 1 table Chayre & 5 ould Chayres eight shillings	00	08	0
It a fyrelocke Muskett 14s, a long fowling peece 20s	01	14	0
It foure siluer spoones 40s & one silu-r wine Cupp 14s	02	14	0
It 6 six pewter dishes seaventeen & 6d	00	17	6
It one brass Pestle & Morter 10s, one brass skellett 8s	00	18	0
It one pewter Candlesticke sault 3 pewter potts one beaker	00	08	0
It too brass skimmers & a flesh hooke at	00	04	0
It one great ould brass Kettle at Twenty shillings	01	00	0

Part I, Fol. 15.

It one small kettle Twelue shillings...	00	12	
It one ould Iron skellett 2s, 3 Iron potts & one Kettle 40s...................	02	02	0
It too Trammells, 2 peyre of pot hookes & one peyr of tongs................	00	14	0
It one Iron skellett 3s, & one warmingpan 5s.................................	00	08	0
It one peyre of bellows 2s, & foure pailes at 5s...............................	00	07	0
It one barrell of porke 3£, & ½ of barrell of beife at 7s.....................	03	07	0
It 12 Trays 12s, one Churne 4s, 3 Tubbs 7s	01	03	0
It 3 pewter potts 3s too butter firkines 4s....................................	00	07	0
It 1 pressing Irone, glass bottle 4s a packe of small towls 10s.	00	10	0
It 2 beare barrells 6s, one peyre of Scales & Weights 10s...................	00	16	0
4 axes & a spitt at 16s..	00	16	0
It one broad axe flue shillings, one hand saw 12d...........................	00	06	0
It one Crow of Iron 8s, one plow Chayne & Copps 12s at..................	01	00	0
It 2 Mattockes 7s, & one plow shayre & Cowlter at 10s	00	17	0
It flue hows 12s, & one spade foure shillings................................	00	16	0
It 3 pitchforks 4s, one whipp saw 12s, & one griad stoone 6s..............	01	02	0
It one syth 4s It too yoak s with Iron works 10s...........................	00	14	0
It one Cross cutt saw 10s, too plaine stocks & Irons 6s....................	00	16	0
It 3 Augers 4s 6d foure ould Agses at seauen shillings.....................	00	11	6
It a parcell of small Towles 12s foure syth 6s..............................	00	18	0
It a bed bowlster & pillows in the Chamber.................................	05	00	0
It a Hammocke Twenty shillings a whitt Couerlidd 12s....................	01	12	0
It a flocke bed a feather bowlster & too Couerlidds........................	03	00	0
It 3 siues a Meale trough 4s, & too busils of wheate 10...................	00	14	0
It Twenty busils of Corne at...	04	00	0
It one Tenant saw 7s, too Nibbs for a syth 18d.............................	00	08	6
It one Cannow 5s, one drawing kniff 2s.....................................	00	07	0
It to Money omitted to be sett down as aboue..............................	16	00	0
	336	02	01

Debts due to this Estate, Dr/

Thomas Ryce by bill............	2	12	6d
John Hoole by bill..............	7	12	0
	10	4	06

Christian Ramaich/
William ffernald/

Mary Mendum Came & made oath this is a true Inventory of all the Estate of Robert Mendum deceased wch at Present shee knows off, & y^t shee will render an Accomp^t if any more should hereafter Present/ taken this 18th day of May 1682 : before mee ffran : Hooke Just pe :

vera Copia of this Inventory transcribed & with the originall Compard this 20th day of June : 1682 :

p Edw : Rishworth ReCor :

A true Inuentory of the Moneys goods Cattle & Chattles belonging & app'rtaineing to the Estate of Major Nicho : Shapleigh, of Kittery in the Prouince of Mayn In New England deceased, taken and apprised by us whose names

Part I, Fol. 16.

are here subscribed, this 9th day of May 1682 : which are as followeth/

	£	s	d
Inprs to so much In Cash or ready money	065	17	00
It to 70 ounches of plate at 6s p oz	021	00	00
It to his weareing apparell thirteen pounds 13s	013	13	00
It to a Prcell of worne Pewter, at 6 pounds 7s	006	07	00
It to a Parcell of New Pewter apprised at	009	03	00
It 68lb of beauer at 5s p lb at Otter skine 5s, a Mowse skins 8s	017	13	00
It two hatts & a Case 20s, his rideing horse & furniture 5: 10: 00	006	10	0
It The home stall, dwelling house out houses oarchards grandings pastures feilds with all appurtenances yrunto belonging with all other out-lands yrto adjoyneing, the Tymber of ye saw Mills onely, excepted	500	00	00
It the saw Mill & Grist Mill, and their accommodations at Kittery unlewe l...	300	00	00
It William Ellinghams Interest purchased by Major Shapleigh in his life tyme lijng on the North side of the Cricke	050	00	00
It about thirty Acres of Marsh lijng at Sturgeon Cricke	090	00	00
It Tenn thousand foote of boards or yrabouts at ye Saw Mills	010	00	00
It Three horses apprised at 50s p horse	007	00	00
It eleuen oxen 38£: eleuen Cows: 27: 10: 00, 3 3 yeare ould Cattle: 7: 10: 00, foure two years ould at six pounds	079	00	00
It foure yearelings 4: 00: 00: 11 sheepe & flue lambs 4 pounds	008	00	00
It a Prcell of swine at 10£: 4 Neagers 3 men one woman & one little Neager all at ninetie pounds	100	00	00
	1273	10	0
[16] It Two Irish boys, one to serue about two yeares. & one 3 yeares	010	00	0
It Great Gunnes & Carages seauen pounds, a great fowling peece that samson Whitte borrowed 30s, foure New Musketts foure pounds 4 small gunns 40s: a blunderbuss 15s	015	05	0
Two Tymber Cheynes 40s six draught Cheynes 48s, 6 yoakes ready fitted with rings & staples 24s, too plows 16s, too Cleuesses 5s			
It a Cart & wheeles 35s one peyre logging Wheeles & draughts 4: 10: 0	012	18	0
It Too peyer of Mast Wheeles decayed with Iron worke 3 pounds } It Two Mast Cheynes & ⅓ of another Cheyne at 5£ }	008	00	0
It 12 ould axes, two spades, 1 peyre of hand screws, too syths two drawing kniffs, Carpenters twoles & Turneing towles flue pounds	005	00	0
It one peyre of large styleyards at Mr Richd Waldens	003	00	0
It In ye smyths shopp one peyre of bellows, small Towles & ould Iron	002	10	0
It one ould liter, one shallop with ould Riggine & furniture at	010	00	0
It 3 great hay Conows & a Coasting Canow	005	00	0
It one ould Cloake at 35s	001	15	0
	73	08	0

wt was apprised in the Inner rowme/

	£	s	d
One feather bed too bowlsters, 3 blanketts, too pillows one peyre of sheetes, one Rugg & bedstead Curtaines & uallance all at 10£	010	00	0
A ovell Table, & Carpett 40s one Chest of drawers & Cubbard Cloath foure pounds, 6 Turky chayres 3£ 4 leather Chares 15s, a Trunke 10s	10	05	0
It one peyre of Andirons & tongues 1 pound	001	00	0
It In the Hall 3 Tables & a Carpet 3 pounds, 12 Chares 2s 6d a peece 30s	004	10	0
It 2 peyre of still yards 40s, one peyre of ould scales at 12d	002	01	0
It one peyre of Doggs 12s, 2 smoothing irons 5s	000	17	0
	28	13	0

Part I, Fol. 16.

In the Majors Lodging Rowme/

One standing bed, & a tumble bed with furniture belonging..................	010	00	0
It a little table & a Carpet 5s, a Court Cubbard 40s.............................	002	05	0
It 1 peyre of Andirons 6s, a iron bound Case 5s, 2 Chares 1 settle 15s.........	001	06	0
It one spanish Chest 25s, another Chest & trunke 8s...........................	001	13	0
It a Tubb 4s, a Candle case Candle-ticke & syllibub pott 5s...................	000	09	0
It one hat & hatt Case 4s, 5 peyre of Course sheetes & one ould sheete 50s....	002	14	0
It 6¼ Napkines 32s It 15 hand Towells seauen shillings 6d.....................	001	19	6
It six Course table Cloaths, & one fine one 40s, a chamberpot 2s 6d	02	02	6
It one ould table Cloath 2s, an ould Turky Carpet 3s........................	000	05	0
	22	14	0

In the Hall Chamber/

One feather bed, one bowlster & one pillow one peyre sheets & other bed Cloaths belonging thereunto	004	10	0
A table & an ould Carpet 10s an ould Trunke 10s ould sheets 5s..............	001	05	0
It 1 peyre ould sheetes 6s, one peyre of sheetes 6s........................	0 10	12	0
	006	07	0
It lineing in ye great Trunke, sheetes, pillow drawers, pillowes Napkins & the whoole yrin yt Trunke at nineteen pounds 2s 6d	019	2	6

In the Parlor Chamber/

Too feather bedds, one bed steade, one peyre of sheets, 2 pillow beares, one bowlster one rugg & too blanketts all at nine pounds....................	009	00	00
It one small table Cloath & a table at thirty shillings, 30s	001	10	00
It one pewter Chamberpott 2s 6d, one looking Glasse 4s....................	000	6	6

In ye little Canopy Rowme ouer ye Hall/

Bedding Ruggs, blanketts with other things belonging yrunto................	005	10	0

In another little Rowme/

One bed, bowlster, blanketts at Curtaines all at three pounds................	003	00	00

In ye darie/

Too stills at 40s earthen Potts Milke panns tubbs trays barrells, & other Lumber with a Churne & other things 40s.....................................	004	00	00
In the Citchen leantow, severall things at................................	002	10	00

In the Chitchine/

Too tables & forme, 10s 6 Iron Potts & too Iron Kettles 4 pounds............	004	10	0
It one Corper Kettle 35s 4 skellets 3 ould brass Kettles 25s................	003	00	00
It one Iron Kettle three brass Candlesticks...............................	000	12	00
It Too frijng pannes flue spitts & a Jacke at 40s..........................	002	00	00
It one peyre of Iron Doggs, 3 peyre of Tramells one peyre of pott hookes 1 peyre of tonges, & two peeles 40s.....................................	002	00	00
It too Iron Drippinpans, one skimmer, one small skellet one flesh-forke at twelve shillings...	000	12	00
Bowls trenchers wodden dishes, tables, pales & Canns at..................	000	10	00

In the New house/

One peyre of Iron Rackes, one Cheese press, too spinning Wheeles tubbs & Kettles & other Lumber 41s...	002	01	00

PART I, FOL. 17.

In the Brew house/

one Copper at foure pounds tenn shillings, too Kettles at three pounds, & Tubbs & brewing uessells at 10s...	008	00	00

In the Garrett/

Too ould Ruggs one blankett & too Mowse skines at........................	002	10	00
It to eighteen yards of Courase Canuice at 24s...............................	001	04	00
It to 18 yards of Red Cotton at one pound 16s...............................	001	16	00
It to Three yards & an halfe of Kayrsey at...................................	000	17	00
It Three yards more of Kayrsey at 12s..	000	12	0
It To three quarters of a barrell of powder at 3 pounds.....................	003	00	00
It to three Coursae hatts at flue shillings p hatt 15s........................	000	15	00
It to one Parcell of nayles at flueteen shillings.............................	000	15	00
It 2 peyre of shooes 8s, to a Prcell of Dagger kniues brass Rings sizers, horne rings, and some ould fishing Hookes at 5 pounds...................	005	08	0
	065	18	6

[17]   In the ware house/

Too barrells of powder at eight pounds.....................................	008	00	00
It a Prcell of Leade 10s, 2 quarters of Spanish Iron 3: 10: 0..................	(04	00	00
It one ould scale one beame & Weights at	002	00	00
It 3 Hodgseds of Tardodous sault..	001	01	00
It A Parcell of Daggers & kniues at 1: 10: 0.................................	001	10	00
It to ould boxes & Caske & other Lumber at................................	002	00	00
It to one peyre ould Still yards at Twenty shillings........................	001	00	00
It an ould Winch for a Grin-lstonel & too ould Grindstoons at............	000	10	00
It thirty six yards of home made Cloath at..................................	003	12	00
It nine yards of Coursae Holland at 1: 2: 6d.................................	001	02	6
It 19 yds of bleue lining at 15s, 16 yds of breams...........................			
It 7 yds of Scotch cloath, & 52 yds ½ of Locerum at......................	(03	16	4
It 100 yds ½ of Coursae broad cloath at......................................	001	02	0
It too blanketts 2s, 5 yds of red searge at 30s..............................	002	10	00
It 14 striped sashes 28s, 29 peyre of small stockings 29s.................	002	17	00
It 7 peyre of sockes, & one soyle skine & a Trunke........................	000	12	4
It one large bible at 20s...	001	00	00
	036	12	2

The Widdows bed & furniture to bee Deducted out of ye Inventory/ Lands at ye Poynt not apprisd/

Mis Aylce Shapleigh Came before the Generall Assembly at yorke June 28 : 82 : & did affirme as in the Presence of

Apprized by
Edw: Rishworth/
Charles ffrost/
Joseph Hammonds/
James Johnson/
Richard Otis his marke r o/

god, that this was a true Inuentory of Major Shapleigh her husband his Estate, to the best of her knowledge, & if more

Part I, Fol. 17.

Estate did appeare afterwards, vpon the same Attest or affirmation shee will bee Carefull to bring it in/ taken in Court as Attests Edw: Rishworth Secre^{ty}/

vera Copia of this Inuentory transcribed & Compared this 7th of July 1682, p Edw: Rishworth R$_c$Cor:

At a Councill houlden at yorke, 12th August 1682: for the Prouince of Mayn In order to make way for the better & more æffectual settleing of the Estate of Major Nicho: Shapleigh deceased/ It is hereby ordered & declared y^t all Crs shall bring in there Claimes & demands, relateing to the sd Estate, before the Committee hereby substituted for the settleing y^{r}of, at such tyme or tyms as they shall Judg meete to appoynt, which is to bee done by such as liue in the Countrey within the tyme of six Moenths from ye date hereof, & all such who dwell in forraine parts, & all such as do liue out of the Countrey haue one twelue Moenths lyberty from this tyme, with in the lymitts whereof, all P^{r}sons Concern'd there in are to bring in their Claimes & Challenges, at tymes & places appoynted by the sd Committee, in order to ye Legall Settleing of the Estate/ & payment of due debts/ to which end, this Court hath ap-

order a—
Major
Shapley his
Estate|
& Comittee

poynted, Major John Dauess, Mr Richd Walden Junior, & Mr John Hinkes (who if they accept) are Impoured to approue of what debts are legally due, & not any debts to bee payd, or Estate dis-

posd of out of the sd Estate, without Consent & approbation of sd Comittee/ who in order to the execution of the Premisses, unanimously haue appoynted, the first Thursday in Octob^r next Insewing, at ye house of Mis Aylce Shapleigh at Kittery, the tyme & place before y^{m}selues w^r all Prsons Concern'd, haue free lyberty to make out their just Legall demands, as law requires/

Part I, Fol. 18.

An Inuentory of the Estate of Thomas Cleuerly & his wife deceased, taken at blã: Poynt the 27th of June: 1682: & then apprised as is here underwritten, by Anthony Roe, & Hene: Ellkines, sworne thereto by Walter Gyndall Commissio^r/

	£	s	d
Inprs by all her weareing Cloaths, 47s, 3 yd of Lining 3s.......	02	10	0
It 2 white aprons one peyr bodys with head & Necke Lining........	02	07	0
It one peyre of shooes, 1 peyre of stockings 1 silke hudd, & a peyre of wollen sleeues all at.......	00	08	0
It 2 thread knitting needles, 2 peyr of sizers one Grater, pinns ould Riggs....	00	05	6
It to Earthern Ware 2s, a wodden dish 1 peyre of Cards & one slue........	00	04	3
It to a Chest & a box 8s to 6 trenchers & a little Iron pott 7s 6d.......	00	15	6
It an Iron pot & pott hookes 7s, to an ould frijngpane 2s 6d........	00	09	6
It To a Trammell, one fyre pann & one peyre of Tongs........	00	07	0
It one peyre of blanketts, one Rugg worne........	01	14	0
It to one bed & bowlster of Canvice worne........	00	14	0
It to an ould axe 12d, a small Prcell of Woll 5s, a small gould Ring 5s.......	0	11	0
It to an how & one peyre of post Hooes 3s, a padlocke 3d........	00	03	3
It To the dwelling house 55s a shift & 2 ould petticoa:s 5s........	03	00	0
It to one sow, & three small piggs at 25s........	01	05	0
It to Cattine ware & flue spoones at 4s 6d........	00	04	6
Totall	14	18	6

John Pickerin in behalfe of John Palmer & by his order tooke administration of y^e Estate at y^e last Generall Assembly, & hath now returned an Inuentory y^r of/

{ apprized by Anthony Roe/ & Hen = ᕼᕼ ery Ellkins his marke

vera Copia of this Inuenory transcribed out of y^e originall, & Compared this 10th of Octob^r 1682: p Edw: Rishworth ReCor

ffebru: 27: 1682: Winter Harbour/ the goods of Joseph Penwell apprised by us, John Leighton & John Dauess as followeth/

Inps 2 Heffers 2: 7: 6 p Heffer.......	04	15	00
It 1 suite of Cloathes & a wastcoate 2: 15: 00, one hatt 5s.......	03	00	00
	07	15	00
[18] on the other side.......	7	15	00
More one horse 20s, 2 quitils of scale fish 20s.....	2	00	00
	09	15	00

Part I, Fol. 18.

March 6 : 1682 : Walter Penwell testifyeth y^t this Inventory is all the Estate y^t at Present hee knoweth of belonging to Joseph deceased, & if more do Appeare hee will giue Accop^t y^rof/ Sworne in Court

Fran^s Hooke Jus𝔱 pe :

A true Coppy of this Inventory transcribed out of the originall this 9th day of March 1682 :

p Edw : Rishworth ReCor :

March secund 168$\frac{2}{3}$

An Inventory of Edmund Cocks his Estate deceased, taken by us whose names are vnderwritten/

	£	s	d
Inprs his lands	25	00	00
It one Table & a forme 20s.	01	00	00
It one house standing vpon John Cards Land as hee sayth	12	00	00
	£38	00	00

A true Coppy of this Inventory tran- Apprised by us/
 scribed, & with y^e originall Com- Abraham Preble/
 pared this 23^d day of March 168$\frac{2}{3}$ Phillip Addams/
 p Edw : Rishworth ReCor : John Twisden/

Nouember 29 : 1682 :

An Inventory of John Hills Estate taken & apprised, by us whose names are here underwritten/

Some other Cattle John Hill hath at y^e Eastward but at Present they know what they are E: R: more added to y^e Inventory on pa: 40:

	£	s	d
Inprs eight acres of Land & houseing	25	00	0
To too thousand seaven hundred of boards at 30s p thousd & one hundred of pine slabbs at 15s.	04	18	0
It Too Cows & 2 Calfes at 7£: 10: 0	07	10	0
It Too steares at foure pounds	04	00	0
It To three yearlings at 3: 15: 00	03	15	0
It to nine Swine at seaven pound fineteene shillings	7	15	0
It About one hundred Cocks of Hay	5	00	0
It bedding & a little other househould stuff	2	10	0
It about 12 busils of Indean Corne at 3s p bushell	1	16	0
	£62	04	0

vera Copia of this Inventory tran- p us
 scribed out of the originall, & y^r William Scriuine
 with Compared this 5th day of John Graues/
 Aprill 1683 : p Edw : Rishworth
 ReCor :

Part I, Fol. 18.

Capt Fran^s Champernown refused to take his oath to this Inuentory because hee did not so certenly know was goods y^r was, but was willing & stands ingaged to this authority in a bond of one hundred pounds, to respond any Estate which may hereafter appeare, app^{r}taineing y^{r}unto, as Attests Edw: Rishworth Jus: pe: 5th March: 83:

The last will & testament of John Hill/
Inp^s: I bequeath my soule into the hands of my mercifull God/
2ly my body I desire should haue a decent buriall/ & as for my worldly Concernes I giue as followeth, vidz^t: to Mis Champernoown all my Cattle, & swine (except one three years ould Heffer, to Mary Gullisson to haue in the spring follow the date here of, one of my best hoggs also, & Corne to fatt him, Conueniently, as also to ye sd Mary Gunisson I giue my househould Moueables & Wheele) as I haue given to Mis Champernown all my Cattle, I also bequeath all my hay & Corne, except what is aboue mentioned/ & in reference to my houseing & Lands I giue to Capt: Champernoown, as also the boards & slabbs y^t lie vpon my sd Land/
Witness, John Graues/   John Hill/
 Allexsand^r Dennett/

John Graues doth Attest vpon his oath y^t hee was Present & see John Hill signe this Instrument aboue written as his last Will & testament/ Taken before mee this 3d day of Aprill 1683: p order of Court Edw: Rishworth ReCor:

Allexand^r Dennett doth Attest vpon his oath that John Hill did sign this his last Will & testament as his Act & deed in his Presence, as a witness/ Taken vpon oath this 12th of Aprill 1683: before mee Edw: Rishworth Jus: pe:
uera Copia of this Will aboue written, with ye Attests y^{r}unto annexed, transcribed & Compared with ye originall this 13th day of Aprill 1683:   p Edw: Rishworth ReCor:

Part I, Fol. 19.

An Inventory of the Estate of James Jackeson deceased, taken by the Towns men of Yorke, this 25th of Octobr 1676: & apprised by Richard Bray & John Mayne/

	£	s	d
Inprs one Cow 8: 10: 00, one steare one pound 15s & 3 yearlings 3£	8	05	0
It one Cow & Calfe fiue pounds, one Cow foure pounds, 1 Heffer 3 pounds	12	00	0
It One Heffer thirty shillings one Heffer 10s	02	00	0
It one Cow & Calfe eight pounds, & Tenn sheepe foure pounds	12	00	0
It vpland & Marsh Thirty pounds	30	00	0
It The swine apprised by Richd Bankes & Ric: Bray	11	05	0
It Goods & some prouisions appri*ed by Edw: Rishworth & Siluester Stouer about ye 16th of Octobr 76: with a Proell of butter 10 Cheeses & a Parcell of ould Cloaths, all Comeing to 3: 01: 00	3	01	0
	78	11	0

John Smyth Senior attesteth vpon his oath, that this a true Inventory of the Estate of James Jackson deceased, & wt more shall afterwards appeare belonging yrunto (if not forgotten) vpon ye same oath hee stands bound to bring it in/ Taken vpon oath in Court ys 13 : of Decembr : 76 :

p Edw : Rishworth ReCor

An accopt of wt Charges John Smyth Senior hath been out about securcing of James Jackesons Estate, & wt Charges hath been expended in payment of seuerall debts [19] & for Schooleing & Cloaths for Elizabeth Jackeson, given in to ye Court of Assotiats at Wells, the 12th day Decembr 1676 :

To John Twisden & 12 men Impressed by Mr. Rishworths order one day for fenceing in James Jackesons Corne & hay to Prserue it	01	06	0
To fiue men one day for fetching his Cattle & Sheepe to yorke	00	10	0
To 5 men another day for fetching more of his Cattle to yorke	00	10	0
To expences layd out vpon ye men yt brought those Cattle seuerall tyms	00	10	0
To Ric: Carter for diging a graue for 2 children 2s & Goody shears Tendance of the sicke Child 2s	00	04	0
	03	00	0

ffor Cloathing layd out by John Smyth Senior for Elizabh Jackeson/

Inprs 4 yds lining Cloath, at 2s p yd, eight shillings, 3 yds of Red Cotton at 4s p yd 12s	01	00	0
It one peyr of gloues 4s, 1 peyre of stockings 1s: 10:	00	05	10
It to makeing her a suite of Cloaths & a shift at 3s 6:	00	03	6
It to a peyr of bodys bought of Mr Smyth for her	00	07	0
It 32lb of porke made Mr Wollcott for hir scooleing	00	10	8
It to a Town rate more payed Capt Dauess 9s, & tenn shillings payd sd Dauess for too bushills of sault	0	19	0
	03	06	0

Part I, Fol. 19.

Seuerall Debts payd by John Smyth Senior due to seuerall Prsons out of James Jacksons Estate/   Estate Dr.

	£	s	d
To George Snell as hee Charges p Accopt	02	18	0
To the Ministers rate due to Mr Shuball Dumer	01	02	9
To the Countrey rate 40s, To ye Town rate 21s	03	01	0
To Capt Dauess, for hay owing him by James Jackeson	01	00	0
To Mr Rishworth for letters of Administration ReCording the Inuentory & other Accopts all at	0	6	6
	£08	8	03

A true Coppy of the Inventory within written & of the Accopts aboue written transcribed & Compared this 10th day of ffebru: 1676: p Edw: Rishworth ReCor:

More payd out: 27: Novbr 79: of James Jackesons Estate for debts due as p ye Administrators Accopt appeareth   ffebru: 10: 79:

To Micum Mackeyntire	04 00 00	Capt Dauess Certifyd to mee by a Note under his hand yt John Smyth Senior had as much Cloathing of him for Elizabeth Jackeson as Comes to 00 17 6
To Robert Junkines	03 09 00	
	07 09 00	
To Edw: Rishworth due from James Jackesons Estate, & for seuerall ReCords about it, pd him by the Administrator	00 11 7	
	08 00 7	
To Capt Dauess as on ye other side	0 17 6	Edw: Rishworth ReCor:
Totall	08 18 01	

vera Copia transcribed out yº Accopts given in by John Smith Senior ye Administrator, as Attests Edw: Rishworth ReCor:

In the name of God Amen/

I John Heard of Kittery in the County of Yorke, In New England yeamon, being by the prouidence of god by reason of age weake of body, but of Prfect mind & memory, & with out frawd & deceate, & not knowing how it may please ye Lord to deale with mee, as to matters of this life, Now to take mee out of this troublesome & transitory world, to whose Most gratious dispensations, I do humbly submitt, w^r for I Commit & Comend my soule into the hands of god y^t gaue it, & my body to Christean buriall, ordering & appoynting this Present Instrum^t to bee my last will & testament, in manner & forme following/

Inp^r: I giue & bequeath my grandaughters Mary & Elizabeth, daughters to my well beloued sonn James Heard late whilst hee liued of Kittery in New England, aforesd deceased, all my Land Improued & mot Improued, being by Computation sixty Acres, or y^r abouts bee It more or lesse, lijng or scituate in Kittery aforesd, at a place Comanly Called & known by the name of Tomsons Poynt, imediately from & after the decease of Jo^n Ross, which sd land or part y^r of, is now in the houlding possession & Occupation of the sd John Ross, togeather also with an house Erected, & built y^{r}on for ye tearme of his Naturall life; with all & singular ye profitts, & Comoditys belonging & app^{r}tajneing y^{r}unto, to bee aequally diuided amongst them & y^r heyres, or to the suruiuer of them, & y^r heyrs for euer, ye Ellder always to bee Preferred before ye younger, & ye Males before ye females/

Item I giue & bequeath unto my 3 younger Grandaughters, Katterine, Abigale & Ann, ye daughters of my Intirely beloued sonn James Heard, late whilst hee liued of Kittery aforesd, deceased, the full some of Twenty pounds, a peece to each & euery of them, either in money or other good payment, which I shall leaue to ye discretion of my ouerseers, in trust, whom I shall here in & here after Nominate, & appoynt to bee made Immediatly after: And as soone as they or either of them, shall accomplish to Attajne ye age of eighteen years, or bee maried by my executor/

Item my will is y^t in case one of the three last mentioned, Katterine, Abigaile & Ann, should Come to decease before they accomplish & Attaine to ye age of eighteen years, or bee married as abouesd, then my Will is, y^t ye legacy herein & hereby given, & bequeathed unto such shall redown unto my executor, but If ye two of the before ye aforementioned y^r in, should happen to decease befor the Attajne to ye aforesd age, or bee married, then my will is, that ye legacys herein & hereby given & bequeathed, unto y^m shall desend unto ye Too Elldest girles, Mary & Elizabeth, as an augmentation to w^t is giuen unto y^m, as aboue to bee æqually diuided, betwixt them & y^r heyrs lawfully begotten/

[20] Ite: I giue & bequeath unto my grandaughter Elizabeth, aboue mentioned, two Cows to bee deliuered unto her or her Assignes, two or 3 yeares after my decease, if they bee then liueing, otherwise this gyft to cease, & bee voyd, by my executors or ouerseers, in trust whom I shall in these nominate/

Ite: I giue & bequeath vnto my grandsonn John Heard, all the rest of my goods & Estate, to witt my farme, & all w^tsoeuer doth belong, & apprtajne y^runto, lijng & scituate at Sturgeon Cricke, in Kittery aforesd, togeather also with all & singular my whoole stocke of Cattle, of w^t nature, kind quality or Condition soeuer, & also all my debts wares, M^rchandizes, dues, or demands, w^tsoeuer, my iust & due debts being first payd, & discharged: Either in my own Costody or possession, or in the hands keepeing Costody or possession of any other Prson, or Prsons rescident in New England aforesd or else where, whom I do hereby make my soole heyre, & executor, & to the heyres of his body lawfully to bee begotten for euermore/

Always prouided that ye sd John Heard should happen Mary, but decease with out lawfull Issew, then my will is in such a Case, that his widdow possess & inioy such a Competency of his sd Estate dureing ye tearme of her naturall life, as ye law directs & appoynts, but ye remajnder of ye Estate to witt ye farme aforementioned, being Composed of vpland Meddow, Marsh^s Orchards, houseing, & all other & singular the app^rtenances, y^runto belonging, or any wise app^rtajneing, with ye Estate of Cattle, as aboue bequeathed, & intended to bee bequeathed unto him y⁰ sd John Heard, shall discend unto y⁰ aforementioned Mary, & Elizabeth Heard Jointly, & unto there heyres for euer, lawfully to bee begotten on yʳ bodys, & in default of such Issew, to the next sister & her heyres for euermore, prouided the sd Marry & Elizabeth relinquish yʳ Clajme & right to & in the Land at Tomsons Poynt, afore mentioned, the which in such a Case shall descend vnto y⁰ three youngest daughters before named, or unto y⁰ suruiuer or suruiuers of them, or either of them, & her or yʳ heyres, lawfully to bee begotten on her, or yʳ bodys, for euer more, the Elldest always to bee Preferred before y⁰ younger, & y⁰ Males before y⁰ femals of yʳ Issew/

My will is also yᵗ in Case it should please god yᵗ I decease before my indeared Wife, Isbell Heard, then my Will is, that my ouerseers in trust take spetiall Care, yᵗ shee bee Carefully & duely prouided for, for a Comfortable subsistance out of the aforesd Estate at Sturgeon Cricke, dureing the tearme of her naturall life, & do hereby Impoure my sayd ouerseers hereafter mentioned, & nominate so to do/

My will is also, yᵗ in Case my daughter in law Susanna Heard see meete to abide at Sturgeon Cricke with her Children, that shee & they bee carefully prouided for, & mantayned out of y⁰ pduce of the farme, & stocke prouided shee use her utmost Care & diligence, in the Managemᵗ & Improuemᵗ there of, & this to Continew dureing the tyme of her Widdowhoodship, & till such tyme as the Children be Capable of being disposed of by her, with the aduise & approbation of the ouerseers, & this to Preuent unnessary Charge, & expence to my executor; my Intent & meaneing in the first Article is, that John Ross with in named may haue free lyberty, quietly & peaceably to possess & inioy, the dwelling house & Tomsons Poynt, & likewise y⁰ Land yʳ fenced in & Improued by him dureing the tyme of his naturall life, as aforesd, but not to debarr, or prohibite y⁰ aforesd

Part I, Fol. 20.

Mary & Elizabeth or y^r Assigns for Improueing at y^r will, & pleasure, the remajnder of the sd Lands, & to ye Intent y^t this my will & testament, being the last I euer intend to make, & irreuocable, may bee duly & truely executed & Prformed, according to ye tenour purport, true Intent & meaning y^rof, I do hereby nominate make Choyce of, & appoynt my trusty & beloued frejnds Majo^r Nic : Shapleigh, John Shapleigh, Jos : Hāmonds William Spencer, & James Chadborne all of Kittery, & New England aforesd, & ye suruiuer & suruiuers of them, any or either of them, vpon trust & Confidence in them reposed, to bee my ouerseers in trust, requesting them to bee Assisting in the execution of the same ; In testimony y^t this is my last will & testament, irreuocable as aforesd, I do here unto put my hand & seale/ Dated in Kittery in Pischataqua Riuer, in New England aforesd this third day of March, in the yeare of o^r Ld god, according to y^e Computation of y^e Church of England one thousand six hundred seauenty & fiue & six/ Anno Dom̃ : 167$\frac{5}{6}$

Signed sealed & Deliuered,   John Heard ($_{Seale}^{his}$)
  in the Presence of us/
  Fran^s Smale/
  Elizabeth Leighton/
  Ric : Allexander/

Richd Allexander, & ffrancis Smale do Attest vpon y^r oaths that this Instrument, the will of John Heard within written, was y^e Act & Deed of the sd Heard, & they were Present, & see him sign & seale the same, & was of a Composed mind wⁿ hee did it/
  Taken vpon oath this one & Twenteth of ffebru : 1676 : before us/   Edw : Rishworth/
A true Coppy of this Instrument,   Samell Wheelewright
  or will within written tran-   Assōtes/
  scribed this 16th day of March
  167$\frac{5}{6}$ p Edw : Rishworth Re : Cor :

Part I, Fol. 21.

An Inventory of the Estate of William Roanes deceased, taken In Aprill 1677: by us whose names are underwritten/

Inprs Too Cows nine pounds, too yearelings 3 pounds	12	00	0
It one steare of 2 years ould, 45s, 3 swine 50s	·04	15	0
It one Vrine pott, one peece of a pot & a Tramell & 1 peyr of pott hookes	0	8	
It for halfe of one Conow 8s, one Cow at foure pounds	4	8	0
It one yeareling 30s, a Conow, a Coate & peyre of britches	2	08	0
	£23	19	0

A true Coppy of this Inventory tran-   Abra: Preble/
scribed & Compard with the originall   Samll Twisden
this 27th Septembr 1677:   Hene: Symson/
    p Edw: Rishworth Re:Cor:

[21]   George Parker Junior deceased/

An Inuentory of his Estate taken by us, whose names are subscribed & Compared with the originall, ys 27th Septembr: 1677: Edw: Rishworth Re: Cor:

Inprs to his weareing Cloaths	01	10	00	It one 3 years ould Heffer	03	00	0
It to a Capp 8s, 1 peyre shooes 5s.	00	13	0	It one 2 yearling Heffer at	02	00	0
It 2 yds ½ peunistone at	00	07	10	It one yeareling Cowlt	01	05	0
It 3 yds ¼ of searge	00	14	8	It 1½ of a saw & fyle	00	06	0
It buttons & silke 4s 6d, a saddle 28s	01	12	6	It ½ a Conow at	09	06	0
It a horse 5li, a broad axe 7s	02	17	0	It Two sheepe at	00	16	0
It an how 2s 6d, a Cow 4 pounds	04	02	6	It 28 oars Containeing foure hun-			
It a Cutless & belt at	00	11	0	dred sixty 4 foote	01	18	8
	£12	08	6		£9	11	8

   12   8   6   John: Twisden/ Abra: Preble/ Hen: Symson
    9 11   8   vera Copia transcribed & Compared this 27th of
   £22 00   2   Septembr 1677: p Edw: Rishworth ReCor:

John Palmer deceased, Aprill 27: 1677:

An Inventory of his Estate taken by us whose names are underwritten/

Inprs too Cows & two Calfes at	09	10	00
It one Heffer of three years ould & a Calfe	04	00	00
It one yeareling bull 30s, six swine fiue pounds	06	10	00
It Meate 18d, one Iron pott & Two Hookes 7s	00	08	06
It one young horse at foure pounds	04	00	00
It one Mayre at foure pounds	04	00	00
	28	08	06

Part I, Fol. 21.

vera Copia transcribed & Com-   John Dauess/ Ric: Banks/
pared, this 27th of Septebr   John Twisden/
1677: p Edw: Rishworth
ReCor:

June 23: 1677:

A true Inuentory of the Estate of John Cirmihill, taken & appriz'd by us whose names are here underwritten/

Inprs 12 Acres of Land wron he liued, with a little house upon it	20	00	0
It one Cow foure pounds, one 2 yeareling Heffer 40s	06	00	0
It 1 yeareling 20s, 3 swine 3 pounds, Two piggs 2s	05	00	0
It one Iron pott 12s, Tow ould hows at 2s	00	14	0
It Two bettle Rings 2s Two blanketts 10s	00	12	0
It 3 busils & three peckes of Indean Corne at 4s p buall	00	15	0
It 700 C of Whitte Oake pipe staues at 7s p C, 2: 9: 0 an ould Chest 12d	02	10	0
	£35	11	0

Apprised by us Tho: Bragdon his marke, **T B**
A true Coppy transcribed &   Jere: Mowlton
Compar'd this 29th of Sep-   his marke *ʃ*
tembr 1677:

p Edw: Rishworth ReCor:

:26: June 1677:

An Inventory of the Estate of Lewis Beane deceased, taken & apprised by us whose names are here underwritten/

Inprs 45 Acres of Land 21 £: foure Cows 12£	32	00	00
It 3 Heffers of three years ould at 50s a peece	07	10	00
It too yeareling Heffers 30s, one yeareling steare 15s	02	05	00
It Too Calfes 10s, one horse 40s, one ould sow 20s	03	10	00
It 5 shoats 25s, 2 yarne potts 12s, 2 pewter dishes 3s	2	00	00
It one Tramell 2s, 50 lb of Cotton woll at 30s	01	12	00
It 7 Gallons of Rumme 15s, one barrell of Molosses 20s	01	15	00
It 2 axes & a pitch forke 6s, a Proell of ould yarne 12s	00	18	00
It one broad Cloath Coate 30s	01	10	00
It 7 yds of searge too peyre of stockings, 1 peyr of shooes	01	11	00
It one hat 6s, one Ladle & Skimmer 6s, a smoothing Iron 12d	00	10	00
It Table lining 26s, 2 peyre of sheetes & 2 peyre pillow bears 20s	2	06	00
It Necke Cloaths foure shillings, a gould Ring 8s	0	12	00
It one Chest & too hows at 7s	0	07	00
seuerall debts due to ye Estate if recouerable	04	00	00
	62	06	00

Part I, Fol. 22.

A true Coppy of this Inventory transcribed & Compared with originall this 29th of September 1677:

p Edw: Rishworth ReCor:

An Inventory of the Estate of Trustrum Harris, late of Kittery deceased, brought into ye County Court June 1677: & afterwards into ye same Court 6 Noveb': 77: apprised 15th of Octob' 1677:

Inprs an home stall & dwelling house between 30 or 40 Acres of Land.........	40	00 00
It 50 Acres of Land lying in ye woods 8:00: 00 hay & Corne 4£...............	12	00 00
It Too Cows fiue pounds, 2 Calfes 18s..	05	18 00
It one steare of 4 years ould 3£ one of 3 years ould 2£: 10....................	05	10 00
one It one 2 yeareling Heffer 35s, one Heffer of one yeare ½ ould 30s...	3	05 00
Calfe It one yeareling 20s, tenn swine nine pounds...................	10	00 00
dyed It Indean Corne & beife at Capt Frosts house.....................	00	13 00
within It 1 bushl; smutty Wheate at 4s 6d, ould Cutless 5s....	00	09 06
few days It an Iron pot a Trauell, an ould peyre of shooes & stockings....	0	15 00
It a small plow & Irons, at ould spade 8s, more added a frin pan & a skellett 5s	0	13 00
	£79	03 06

Will Gowine alias Smyth, Apprisers/ Tho: Holms
Administrator made oath   his marke ⊤
to ye treuth of ys Inven-   Willi: Spencer/
tory, as aboue written 6:   the remaindr of this Inventory Entered in the
9: 77:   24th pa: Libris
        Jos: Dudley Assistant

A true Coppy of this Inuentory transcribed & Compared with ye originall this 23: of Janu: 77:

p Edw: Rishworth ReCor:

[22] Winter harbour, this 4th day of Novemb' 1682:

Wee whose names are underwritten, being Chosen by authority, to prise & ualew the Estate of Walter Penwill Senior deceased/

Inprs to one yeareling, one Cow, & one Calfe..................................	07	10 00
It to hay and wintering thyrty shillings..	01	10 00
It to tow nets for a boate at three pounds.....................................	03	00 00
It to one Table & two Chayres at thirteen shillings............................	00	13 00
It to one peyre of Tongus 4s, to two Chests at 25s..............................	01	09 00
It to one Wheele 8s, to two tramells 12s 6d....................................	00	15 06
It to Two pewter dishes & one Cliffe at a 7s...................................	00	07 00
It to pales & a payre of bellows fiue shillings................................	00	05 00
It to 3 dishes toe spoones & a funnell at.....................................	00	08 00
It to two quills of fish Twenty shillings.....................................	01	00 00
It To Land & Marsh at the little Riuer.......................................	20	00 00
	£36	12 06

PART I, FOL. 22.

Phinæas Hull
Richd Tarr apprisers of the Estate/
Mary Penwill relict & widdow of Walter Penwill her late husband deceasd came before mee this 21th day of May 1683 : & did Attest vpon her oath, that this is a true Inventory of her husbands Estate, & if any more belonging do afterwards appeare, vpon ye same oath shee Ingageth to bring it in/ Edw: Rishworth Jus: pe :

A true Coppy of this Inuentory transcribed out of ye originall, this 24th day of May 1683 :

p Edw: Rishworth ReCor/

An Inventory of the Estate of Judeth Tozier, administratrix to ye Estate of her husband Richd Tozier deceased/

	£	s	d
Inprs to ye houses, & 75 Acres of Land being the homestall	50	00	00
It Twenty Acres of Meadow land at Bally hocke	02	10	00
It To 100 Acres of Land granted by ye Town of Kittery	05	00	0
It one Cow, one Heffer, 3 yearelings	07	00	0
It 5 swine three pounds, Three sheepe 15s	03	15	0
It one feather bed, one bolwster, too pillows one b'anket one peyre of sheetes a bed blankett, all at	04	00	0
It to one flocke bedd & three blanketts	01	00	0
It 1 Iron pott, 1 tramill, 2 peyre of pot hooks, one fringpan	00	14	0
It Too wodden dishes, spoones, trenchers, pale aiue & other tymber	01	00	0
It 2 axes, one Adge, & a drawing kniffe at	00	05	0
It one plow, one broad how a Hammer	00	12	0
It to one Copps yoake, & a peyre of Hookes	00	05	0
	76	01	0

Apprised this 30th day of March : 1683 : by us
John Wincoll
Geo: Broughton/

Richard Tozier Came before this Court this 30th day of May 1683 : & doth Attest vpon his oath, y^t this is a true Inuentory of the Estate of his deceased Mother, Judeth Tozier senior, according to his best knowledg, & vpon ye same oath, pmisseth to bring in w'soeuer more doth, or shall hereafter appeare, belonging y^{r}unto/ hee will bring in vpon ye same oath, as Attests Edw: Rishworth ReCor :

Part I, Fol. 22.

A true Coppy of this Inventory transcribed, & with originall Compared this 18th June 1683:

p Edw: Rishworth ReCor:

An aprisall of yᵉ Estate of Gabrigall Bonighton deceased/

	£	s	d
Inprs one horse at two pounds tenn shillings	02	10	00
It one horse at two pounds 10s	02	10	00
It for a Prcell of fish at Twenty foure shillings	01	04	00
It one blankett halfe worne	00	03	00
It Too yds ½ of Tickeing at 6s	00	06	00
	06	13	00

James Gibbines/
John Sharpe/

Mr John Bonighton doth Attest vpon his oath, that this is a true Inventory of what at Present hee remembreth of his brothers Gabrigale Bonightons Estate, & vpon yᵉ same oath, If hee remembres more afterwards hee will bring it in/ Taken vpon oath this first of June 1683: in Court

p Edw: Rishworth ReCor:

vera Copia transcribed into the booke of Inventorys for yᵉ prouince of Mayn this 18th June: 1683:

p Edw: Rishworth ReCor/ pa: 22:

In the name of God Amen/ Bee It known unto all, unto whom this shall Come, that I John Lybby Senjoʳ, do giue unto my children fiue shillings a peece to euery one of them, & to my too younger sonns Namely, Mathew & Daniell shall haue fiuety shillings out of yᵉ Estate when they Come to age/ & my wife shall haue It all to her disposeing to mantayn the Children/

Witnesses
John/
Anthony Roe/
the marke of

Leefᵗ: Ingersall

Part I, Fol. 23.

9th February 1682:

An Inuentory of the Estate of John Lybby Senior deceased, taken by us whose names are underwritten/

Inprs to 4 Cows at.............	12	00	00
It Two Heffers, at	04	00	00
It to foure steares at...........	12	00	00
It to fiue yearelings at.........	08	00	00
It to one Calfe at tenn shillgs..	0	10	00
It Two sheepe at................	00	16	00
It eleuen swine at 40...........	02	00	00
It one horse at 20 shillings.....	01	00	00
It to weareing apparell & to househould Goods all at...	8	00	00
It to house & Lands at.........	70	00	0
	£118	06	0

William Burren & Andrew Brown appeared before mee this 5th day of May 1683: & made oath to this aboue writeing before mee
Josua Scottow Just^s pe:

Testes William Burrine/
Andrew Brown/
apprisers/

vera Copia transcribed, & with originall Compared this 2cund of July 1683: p Edw: Rishworth Sere^{ty}

[23] An Inventory of the Estate of Mr Joseph Boolls late of Wells deceased, September 25th 1683: and apprized the 8th day of Octob^r next following/

Inprs his weareing Cloaths with other Wollen & Lining......................	15	05	00
It Too bedds & bowlsters, & bedding belonging to them......................	06	00	00
It To fourty pounds of Yarne at 4d	04	00	00
It To foure Chests, one box, & one Trunke at.......................	01	10	00
It to too Tables & fiue Chayres at...........................	01	04	00
It to Iron potts, too skellets, pewter, brass, & dishes...............	04	00	00
It a peyre of Andirons, & one peyre of Tonges at..................	01	00	00
It Iron & Towles fiue pounds...................................	05	00	00
It one saddle pistolls Howlsters, one pillion & Cloath................	02	05	00
It Bookes 20s, one Gunn 25s...................................	02	15	00
It Indean Corne Wheate & Rie at...............................	12	00	00
It Butter & Cheese 3: 5: 0......................................	03	05	00
It Too barrells of Cider 18s....................................	00	18	00
It Three bedsteds at 18s.......................................	00	18	00
It three yoakes, one plow shayre, bettle & Wedges at...........	02	00	00
It three Coults at foure pounds................................	04	00	00
It Twenty one swine at.......................................	21	00	00
It eight steeres at fourty pounds...............................	40	00	00
It seauen Cows at 4: 10: 0 p Cow............................	31	10	00
It four yearelings at six pounds...............................	06	00	00
It fiue Calfes at 3: 15: 00.....................................	03	15	00
It Twenty sheepe at tenn shillings p sheepe	10	00	00
It 2 Acres of Marsh at eight pounds...........................	08	00	00
It 30 loade of Hay at 10s p loade.............................	15	00	00
	200	15	00

Part I, Fol. 23.

Apprised by us/ Joseph Storer/
Nat͞l Cloyce/

Mary Bolls came before mee this 21th day of Novemb^r 1683 : & did Attest vpon her oath, y^t this aboue written is a true Inventory of ye Estate of her husband Mr Jos : Bolls deceased, to ye best of her knowledg, & if afterwards anything more should Come into her mind belonging y^runto, by uertue of ye same oath shee will bring it in to added to the Inventory/ Taken before mee Edw : Rishworth

Jus : pe : & ReCor :

A true Coppy of this Inventory as Attested transcribed out of ye originall & y^rwith Compared this 21 : Novemb^r 1683 : p Edw : Rishworth ReCor :

An Inventory of the Estate of Patience Spencer deceased Noveb̄^r 1683 :

	£	s	d
Ipr͞s weareing Cloaths, & a greene Coate & wastcoate	01	10	00
It a Coate & wastCoate 20s, her head lining 10s	01	10	00
It 2 workeing steeres 8£, one Cow & 3d part of corne & hay in ye barne, 3: 10: 00	11	10	00
It one bed at 50s, one Mare 1 sow & piggs, 2: 15: 00	05	05	00
It one Cow & one ¼ part of her hay & Corne in ye barne	03	10	0
It one Calfe a two sows at three pounds fiue shillings	03	05	0
It one Tapistrey Covering one pound fiue	01	05	00
It one Cow & ¼ part of her hay & Corne in the barne	03	10	00
It one bowlster, one Hammacher. & a small blankett	02	02	0
It 2 barrows & one small pigg 2: 05: 0	02	05	0
It Two steeres 6: 05: 0, one fowling Mault & a Chest, 27s	07	12	0
It 1 Table Cloath & Napkines 20s, 1 pillowbeare & sheet 7s 6d	1	07	6
It 1 peyr gloues & 1000 M of pinns 2s 6d, 2 pewter platters & one spoune 7s 9d, one porringer & salt seller 2s 9d	0	13	0
It lysborne dishes & a Cann, silke & thread	09	03	6
It one sheete 10s, one Chest foure shillings, ¼ small things 3s	0	17	00
to 1 peyre of stileyards, an Iron pott & pot hookes one spitt one Tramill & thread	01	10	0
It Too pewter dishes 7s 6d, a porringer 15d	00	8	9
	40	08	9
It Two drinking Cupps, 18d, 2 lysborne dishes, 1 spoone & one butter pott 3s, 9d, one blankett 10s, one Chest 4s	00	19	03
It to seuerall things 3s, 2 chaines 1 peyr of Hookes & staple It one Neb ring & staple an ould axe & 2 pillows & tramell 1: 16: 0 }	01	19	00
It one whitt aprone, one blew aprone, one whitte wastcoate, & one blacke Hansltt Chayre, 18s	00	18	00
It 2 pewter dishes, 1 small bason, & a drame Cupp	00	07	06

Part I, Fol. 24.

It one porringer, one Cadale Cupp 2s 9d, lisborne dishes 1 spoone, 2s 3d.......	0	05	00
It 2 Earthe Juggs, & silke & thread 18d, one Rugg 10s.	00	11	06
It 1 Chayre Table 4s, pewter dishes & one porringer 8s 9d.....................	00	12	09
It 1 pewter Cupp one brass skellett 18d, to lysborne dishes			
It one spoone, one earthen Jugg, 2 baskets & 1 earthen pann 3s 9d	00	05	03
It 1 peece of Cayrsey & ffianill, & 5lb of Cotton Woll.........................	00	10	00
It 1 Chest 4s, 3s in small things, 2 pewter dishes & 1 porringer 8s 9d..........	00	15	09
It 2 small porringers, 2 earthen Cupps 18d, to Lysborne dishes one spoone, one Chamberpott, one earthen pann 3s 9d..	00	05	3
It 1 blanket one Chest, one barrell, & in a nall things 3s all....	00	17	00
	£08	06	08
[24] It one brass Candlesticke, one Iron Candlesticke, 1 brass scimer...	00	08	00
It one Iron Morter 3s, one warmeinpan 2 pillows 17s 6d	01	00	06
It In Cash 2: 8: 9..	02	8	9
It To 100 C Acres of vpland Neare Willcoxs his b nd.........................	25	00	0
It halfe ye further Meddow 3£ one dripinpann 18d............................	03	01	6
It one hide at Daniel Sto ns ye shoemakers	00	08	0
Cloath at ye weauers the quantity unknown				
	32	06	9

```
48 03 9
08 06 3
32 06 9
─────────
88 16 9
```

Wee whose names are hereunder written, being made Choyce of by William, Humphrey & Moses Spencer, Ephraim Joy & Thomas Chicke, to take a list of all their Mothers Patience Spencers Estate deceased, the 7th of Nouember 1683 : & also to diuide ye same æqually amongst them, as may appeare under yr own hands/ wrof Wee haue æqually diuided It moueables & unmoueables, onely the Land & Meddow to ly responsible Six Moenths If any debts should appeare, wrunto wee sett or names this 15th of Nouember 1683 :

vera Copia transcribed out of the originall & yrwith Compared this 28th of November 1683 by Edw: Rishworth ReCor:

Richard Nason his ◯ marke/
James Emery/

Moore to bee Added to ye Estate of Trustrum Harrss/ pa : 21 :

Received of John Bready/

Inprs draught Cheane one Cleuice & pinn 8s...	00	08	0
It one Coate 1 peyre of britches & a doublett.................................	01	04	0
It one ould sheete & one ould bagg at...................	00	04	0
	01	16	0

Part I, Fol. 24.

Apprised 28 : Novemb^r 1677 by us   John Wincoll
Attested by John Bready &   William Spencer/
his wife to bee all the goods they know off belonging to ye Trustrum Harriss his Estate vpon oath before Capt Wincoll, June 30 : 79 :

more to bee added to ye Estate a lame oxe found in the Costody of James Chadborne apprisd at foure pounds fiue shillings by Christ : Banefeild & Will Spencer

Decemb^r 4th 1677 :

Administration granted unto Mathew Raynkine, relict of Andrew Raynkins Deceased, of sd Raynkine her husbands Estate, with whome as Administratrix Arther Bragdon Senr stands bound with sd Mathew in a bond of one hundred & eighty pounds, to the Treas^r of this County that shee shall be lyable to respond all Legall rights belonging to the Estate wⁿ y^runto Called by lawfull authority/

An Inventory of the Estate of Andrew Raynkine deceased taken & apprised by us, whose names are vnderwritten, December 18th 1677 :

	£	s	d
Inprs Sixty Acres of Land & houseing at.....	60	00	0
It Two Cows 10£ Too 2 yeareling Heffers fiue pounds.........	15	00	0
It one yeareling 20s one horse fiue pounds 3 swine 52s..........	08	12	0
It to a beetle foure Wedges & a frow 12s, 1 Reaphooke 18d...........	00	13	6
It one Chamberpott 5s, 1 axe & an how fiue shillings...........	00	10	0
It one Chayne one pott & a fryinpane 20s........................	01	00	0
It one brass Kettle 5s, an Iron Trammell fiue shillings..............	0	10	0
It A Joynting plane 3s, Two bibles 8s..........................	0	11	0
It 1 peyre of fyre Tongs 18d, 4 yds ½ of penniston 13s 6d...........	0	15	0
It 2 Hodgeds & 1 powdering Tubb 12s, 35lb of sheeps Woll 85s......	02	07	0
It one beauer hatt fiueteen shillings...........................	00	15	0
	90	13	06

Arther Bragdon/

The Inventory of the Estate of Annas Littlefield deceased apprizd by Samell Austine & Joseph Boolls this 7th day of March 167¾

PART I, FOL. 25.

Inprs one Cow fiue pounds, one steare fiue pounds.............................	10	00	0
It 2 stears 6£, one Calfe 20s, 1 bed & bowlster 4: 10: 0.	11	10	0
It 1 Rugg 20s, 5 yds of penistone 25s, 4 yds of blew linning & foure yards & an halfe of Dowlass at 16s..	03	01	0
It 4 yds of Cotten 12s, 3 yds of ffannill 9s 1 searge Coat 20s....................	2	01	0
It one wastecoate & petticoate 30s 2 pillow bears 1 wastcoate & ould lining 30s	03	00	00
It a grein aprone 5s, 1 skellet a bason 1 ould pewter pott 4s...............	00	09	00
It one aprone 4s, 19 buslls of Indean Corne 3: 16: 0...........	04	00	00
It 3 buslls & one peake of wheate at Merribah's.............................	00	16	00
It foure buslls of wheate due from the Corne Mill.	01	00	00
It foure buslls of Indean Corne Due from ffrans Littlefield for his Ysland.....	00	16	00
It for his Ysland................................	00	02	00
	£36	15	00

Apprised by us Samull Austine
Jos: Bolls/

Thomas Littlefield tooke oath the aboue written is a true Inventory of the Estate of his Mother Annas Littlefeld Deceased, & If any more yrof appeare hee will add It yrunto vpon ye same oath/ Taken in Court Aprill 2: 78:
as Attests Edw: Rishworth ReCor:

[25]   12th December: 1677:
In the name of God Amen/
The last Will & testament of Annis Littlefejld/

1: first I bequeath my soule into the hands of Almighty god, my maker, my body to bee buried in Christcan buriall, at ye discretion of my executor hereafter mentioned/

1: I do giue unto my daughter Hannah Cloyce my bed & bowlster, & Katterine Wakefejld to deliuer It to her/

2: I giue unto my three daughters, Elizabeth Wakefejld Mary Barrett, & Hannah Cloyce, all my lining & Wollen New & ould to bee æqually diuided amongst them/

I giue unto my sonn John Littlefejld my Cow Gentle & fiue buslls of Corne/

I giue to my daughter Merribah foure buslls of Wheate due from ye Mills

I giue to my Grandchild Katterine Wakefejld my Rugg & eight buslls of Corne/

I giue to my sonn Peter Cloyce too Acres of Marsh bee

Part I, Fol. 25.

it more or less, y^t lyeth on the South West side of Mr Whelewrights Necke of Land/

I giue vnto my sonn Thomas Littlefejld, who hath taken a great deale of care of mee, all the rest of my househould goods Corne & Chattles, & I do make my sd sonn Thomas Littlefejld, my whoole & soole executor, & to receiue all debts comeing to mee, & to pay all If any thing there bee that I do ow, & to take all the remajnd^r to him selfe, & to see my will fullfilled/

Signed, & Deliuered,   Annis Littlefejld
  In ye Presence of us,
  Joseph Bolls/   her marke   X
  William Symonds/

Mr William Symonds, & Mr Joseph Bolls, tooke oath y^t they saw Annis Littlefeild, signe & deliuer the aboue written, as her last Will & testament, w^n shee was of a disposed mind/ Sworne in Court Aprill 2 : 78 : p Edw : Rishworth/
vera Copia transcribed out of ye originall as Attests
                         Edw : Rishworth Re : Cor :

A true & Prfect Inventory of the goods Cattle & Chattles Moueables, & unmoueables of Abraham Conley lately deceased, & made & taken by Thomas Abbett, & Jonathan Nason, which Prsons liue in the Town of Kittery 18th day of March Anno Dom Regi Caroly secundo 30th & in the yeare of o^r Lord 167$\frac{7}{8}$

	£	s	d
Inprs his weareing apparell apprised	05	00	00
It his bed & bedding ualewe t at three pounds	03	00	00
It one Cow one yearelling 4£ too potts one saddle 16s	04	16	00
It one peyre of stillyards, 1 peyre of Hookes & staples & a peyre of pincers 20s	01	00	00
It one Chissill, one Hatchett 2s, one Cross Cutt saw } It 2 Wodden dishes or bowles & one pitcher 14s }	00	16	00
It His farme at Sturgeon Cricke, namely vpland It & swampe, being 80 Acres more or less with It the house & appurtenances belonging to it on the North side of Sturgion Cricke	55	10	00
more follows	£70	02	00

Part I, Fol. 25.

It His Marsh at Stergeon Cricke with the fenceing ⎫ It & all the Marsh within fence, heretofore it & now ⎬ known by ye name of Abra: Conleys great Marsh ⎭	55	00	00
It one Chest & one powdering Tubb at	00	10	00
It more due on bills for goods, & other Desperate debts	30	06	04
It more fourty acres of Land granted him by the Town of Kittery Lijng on the South side of Sturgeon Cricke, adjoyneing to Abra: Conleys great Marsh aforesd nalewed at	05	00	00
	£160	18	04

       Thomas Abbett
      Jonathan ℱ Nason apprisers

Nathan Lawd Senior tooke oath unto the treuth of this Inventory aboue written, & by uertue of the same oath stands Ingaged to bring in wᵗ else hereafter shall appeare to belong unto this Estate/ Taken In Court this 3ᵈ of Aprill 1678 :   p Edw: Rishworth Re: Cor:

vera Copia of this Inventory aboue written transcribed & ReCorded this 22th Aprill 1678 :
       p Edw: Rishworth Re: Cor:

An Inventory of the Estate of Joseph Allcocke deceased the 30ᵗʰ of July 1678 :

Inprs one small house as siluer 6: 10: 0 other pay	09	10	0

as attests oʳ hands & apprised by us/
      John Tomson Richd King
      his marke ℭ ℛ

More of Joseph Allcocks Estate prised the same day/

one Rugg 20s, 1 peyre of sheetes 10s ould blanketts 4s.	01	14	0
It one bed & bowlster 25s, 3 small pewter dishes 1 quart & pint 16s	01	11	00
It one small Iron pott 4s	0	04	00
	£03	09	0

 apprised by us, Richd King his marke Peter Dixon his
       ℛ   marke ℘

Part I, Fol. 26.

[26] More apprised of the Estate of Jos: Allcocke the same day/

on ye other side....	12	19	0
Inprs one suite of Cloaths at 3 pounds..........................	03	00	00
It a Wastconte 6s, one Cutless & a belt 10s........................	00	16	00
It to a broad axe 4s too drawing kniffes 4s.........................	00	08	00
It 1 narrow axe & an edge 5s 6d, bettle Rings & Wedges 5s............	00	10	06
It one playne & a locke shaue at 2s..................................	00	02	00
	17	15	6

Apprised by us William ffurnald   Geo: Letten/

More to bee Added to this Inventory belonging to the Estate of Jos: Allcocke lijng in the Town of yorke/

Inprs one Parcell of vpland apprised at 20£	20	00	00
It foure Acres of Marsh at	10	00	00
	30	00	00

More 3 Acres of Marsh not prised but left to pay ye Widdow Allcocke sd Jos: Allcocks mother, being seauen pounds & 10s, If the Honord Court allow of it, otherwise It is apprised at the same rate, y^t the other foure Acres are apprised at/

This 28th of Septemb^r 1678: by vs vnderwritten this three Acres of Marsh was ordered by the approbation of this last Court, y^t shee the sd Widdow Allcocke should haue w^t was most sutable for her in Land to bee payd or Marsh for y^t seauen pounds tenn shillings, which her Joseph should haue payd her yearely at fiuety shillings p Ann:

A true Coppy of this Inventory   Apprisers
transcribed & with originall   John Dauess/
Compared this 7th of Decem^{br}   Nathe^{ll} Preble/
1678: p Edw: Rishworth Re: Cor:

Know all men whome It may Concerne that I Arther Bragdon Senior do giue my whoole Estate, house, & Land & marsh, & Cattle unto my sonn Thomas Bragdon, so long as I & my wife do liue, vpon this Condition that my sonn Thos Bragdon do prouide for mee & my wife, all Necessary things y{t} either of us shall stand in neede of, so long as Wee do liue/ Dated this fiue & Twenteth day May 1678 :

 Nathāll Maysterson/   Arther Bragdon his
 Jere : Mowlton his
           marke
    Marke/
          Thomas Bragdon his
          Marke

A true Coppy of this writing transcribed & Compared with the originall, this 18th of Decembr 1678 p Edw : Rishworth Re : Cor :

An Inventory of Arther Bragdon Senior his Estate/

Inps 30 Acres of vpland, & fiue Acres of Marsh & house & barne apprised as money at.........	40	05	0
It Two Cows as money at seaven pounds.....	07	00	0
It One Cripled Heff-r at Thirty shillings......	01	10	0
It one Too yeareling Heffer 30s, one yeareling Heffer 15s.....	02	05	0
It one young Calfe at 8s, Three Swine at Three pounds........	03	08	0
It Three swine 40s one ould horse 50s............	04	10	0
It 5 wedges & a beetle ring 7s, 3 ould axes & an how 8s.....	00	15	0
It one hatt 5s, too ould Coats & one peyre of briches 30s.....	01	15	0
It 1 pott 12s, one skellett 5s, ould pewter 3s 6d............	01	00	6
It more Added since by the Administrator........	1	17	6
	64	06	0

         Nathall Maisterson/
         Arther Caime his
          Marke/

Thomas Bragdon doth Attest upon his oath unto the treuth of this Inuentory to ye best of his knowledg, & If more of ye Estate do appeare afterwards by uertue of the same oath hee stands Ingagd to bring it in/ Taken in Court this secund of October 1678 :

       p Edw : Rishworth ReCor :

The last will & testament of Allexandr Cooper of Barwicke in the Town of Kittery in the prouince of Mayne, though weake in body, yet of Prfect memory & of a disposed mind

Part I, Fol. 26.

(do Committt my soule unto god) and my body to the dust from whence It came, & do dispose of my outward Estate as followeth/

I do in the Presence of these Prsons now with mee too of whome I haue desired to subscribe it as witnesses hereto, Namely John Taylo^r & George Gray, giue & bequeath my whoole Estate of Land, Cattle Chattles, & all moueables & all other appurtenances belonging thereunto, vnto my onely sonn John Cooper, as the true & proper heyre of the sd Estate, & for the better Improueing Preserueing & secureing y^r of till ye sayd John Cooper come to age of Twenty one yeares, being now about sixteen years of age; It is my will & desire to Commit under god, both my sonn, & my estate left him vntill hee come to age, unto my Loueing freinds vidz^t Richard Nason Senjor, James Warrine Senior, & Peter Grant whome I leaue as feofees in trust, faithfully to take Care both of my sonn & Estate, & for the Improuement & security there of, for my sonns best aduantage; before these witnesses John Taylour & George Gray Inhabitants of the aforesd place & James Warrine Junjo^r there, Pattericke Bryce traueller, being desired to bee scribe, by the aforesd Allexand^r Cooper, of the aforesd will/ Dated at Barwicke this ninth day of February one thousand six hundred Eighty three/

Testes/ John Taylor   George Gray his marke

    his marke   Pattericke Bryce

PART I, FOL. 27.

[27] John Taylour & George Gray came before mee this Twenty eight day of February 168¾ & do Attest vpon there oaths that yt ys Instrument aboue written, was the last will & testament of Allexandr Cooper deceased/ Edw: Rishworth

Jus: pe:

Mr Pattericke Price being ye subscriber of this Instrument doth euidence to the same thing which these Witnesses haue done/ Taken vpon oath before mee Edw: Rishworth Jus: pe

At a Court of sessions at Wells, this Will allowed in Court this 25th day of March 168¾ as Attests Edw: Rishworth ReCor

vera Copia of this will aboue written transcribed & Compared with ye originall this first day of Aprill 1684: p Edw: Rishworth ReCor

An Inventory of the Lands, Cattle, Chattles, & Goods of Allexandr Cooper late of Barwicke deceased ffebru: 11th 1683: 84:

May: 2 :84 Moore brought in to bee added, by Peter Grant unto wt formerly was given in, to Allexandr Coopers Estate | In Corne flesh & some Cloathing, & other Lumber as barrells ould Hodges belonging to ye Estate.............................. 10 00 00

	£	s	d
Inprs his weareing Cloaths at Three pounds....................	03	00	0
It his homestall with 24 Acres of Land with houseing.........	030	00	0
It A peece of Medd ow lijng at WhittesMarsh at 15£	015	00	0
It An house & eighty acres of Land by Will: Spencers Marsh..............	30	00	0
It Two oxen, 2 three yeareling steres & three Cows.................	20	00	0
It a Too y. are ould Heffer too Calfes, & one Mare & horse..........	07	00	0
It A sow too barrows, & six young swine at............................	06	00	0
It One feather bed & bowlster. 7 blanketts Two ruggs & 5 sheetes	11	00	0
It lining Cloath 2£: Wollen Cloath 4: 10: 0.....	06	10	0
It Three pewter dishes, one bason, & one quart pott....................	01	00	0
It one brass Kettle, one Iron kettle, one Iron pott at......................	01	13	0
It Thee small gunns, a sword, a peyre of bandaleres..................	02	05	0
It a betle fiue wedges, foure axes, & an handsaw............................	01	00	0
It A New plow, a small Cheyne, & a Cleuice at............................	01	05	0
It Too Hows, too yoakes & a spade, & a Tramell all.........................	00	13	0
It Hay & Corne & a barrell of porke at.................	07	00	0
143-6-00	143	6	00

Peter Grant came into the Court of sessions March the 25th 1684: & did Attest this Inventory aboue written to bee a true Inventory (to the best of his knowledge) of the Estate of Allexand[r] Cooper deceased, & If any thing more appeare hereafter, hee will add it y[r]unto by uertue of the same oath/ Taken vpon oath In Court, as Attests Edw: Rishworth ReCor:

A true Coppy of this Inventory, transcribed out of the originall & there with Compared this first of Aprill 1684:

p Edw: Rishworth ReCor:

I James Grant of Kittery In the County of yorke shyre, In New England, being weake In body, yet through gods mercy of a disposed mind, & Memory, Comitting my soule to god that gaue it, & my body to the earth to bee decently buried, do declare this to bee my last will & testament as followeth/

1: I bequeath vnto Elizabeth Grant daughter of Joane, the wife of Peter Grant of Kittery aforesd, Twenty Acres of Land at the head of my house lott, being at the North East end of it, reseruing a Convenient highway through it into the rest of my Land beyond it & y[e] way to lie on that side next Goodman Keys Land, It being the South East side: And also I giue unto the sd Elizabeth Grant Tenn Acres of Land, It being part of that Lott of Land, which I haue at y[e] place Called nine Noches/

2: I bequeath unto the aforesd Peter Grant Senjo[r] of Kittery my best cloath sujte, & Cloake, & my searge sujte, & my great broad axe & a narrow axe, & my square axe, & Compasses my ads, & an Inch & an halfe Auger, & an Inch Auger/

3: I giue unto James Grant the sonn of Peter Grant aforesd, my fyrelocke Muskett, & my sword, & belt/

4: I giue unto Peter Grant the sonn of the aforesd Peter Grant, one Heffer of one yeare ould/

5: I bequeath unto John Wincoll Junjo[r], one steare of one years ould and vpwards/

Part I, Fol. 27.

6 : I bequeath unto Elizabeth my Loueing wife, all the rest of my Estate, of dwelling house, out houseing Oarchard, with all my Lands whither ye home stall, or out lands, with all my Cattle of all sorts, & all my houshould Goods, tooles, vtensills, with in doores, or with out, or w'soeuer is not bequeathed as abouesd/

7 : I do nominate & appoynt my loueing wife Elizabeth Grant, to bee the soole Executrix of this my last Will & testament, & do desire & Impoure my Loueing father in law, James Euerell of Boston, to bee ouerseere of this my last Will, & for Confirmation hereof haue sett too my hand & seale, this twelfth day of November : 1679 :

Witness Niuen Aignew   James Grant (his seale)

 his marke)

James Grant acknowledged this aboue written Instrume^t to bee his last will & Testament, this 12th day of Novemb^r 1679 :   before mee John Wincoll Assotiate/

John Wincolls testimony taken in Court the 25 : of March 1684 : p Edw : Rishworth ReCor & doth attest to this will/

Niniue Aignew tooke oath y^t James Grant being of a disposed frame hee saw him signe & seale this Instrument as his last will & testament, & set too his hand as a witness/ Sworne March 19 : 168¾ before mee Jo^n Wincoll Jus : pe :

At a Court of sessions at Wells 25th March 1648 : this will allowed In Court as Attests Edw : Rishworth ReCor :

A true Coppy of this will as Attested & proued transcribed out of the originall & y^r with Compard this 2cund of Aprill : 1684 :   p Edw : Rishworth ReCor :

Part I, Fol. 28.

[28] An Inventory of the Estate of James Grant late of Barwicke deceased, Nouember the 6th 1683:

	£	s	d
Inprs his wearing Cloaths at Tenn pounds.	10	00	0
It a home stall of houseing Orchard & one hundred & 20 Acres of Land	80	00	0
It Twenty Acres of Land in the woods 20 Acres of swamp land remote	02	00	0
It Thee 3 yeares ould steeres, & a bull tenn pounds	10	00	0
It Three Cows, one Two yeare ould & three yearelings	09	00	0
It six swine at foure pouud, New Cloath in seurell peeces 4£	08	00	0
It Two bedds bedsteads, 7 sheetes 5 blanketts ruggs bowlsters & pillow curtains	12	00	0
It six pewter dishes, 12 porringers, potts & other small peeces at	02	00	0
It brass Tinn, earthen & Wodden Ware 20s, 1 Iron pott 2 kettle 1 skellet 30s	02	10	0
It 3 bibles & some other bookes 20s, Carpenters fowles at 40s	03	00	0
It Towels & Tackelline for husbandry foure pounds	04	00	0
It Wheat Barley Indean Corne peas & porke 5:10:0	05	10	0
It an ould Cubbard Wheeles Chests, chares, with some other Lumber	2	00	0
It Andirons a fyre shouell, tonges, spitt, & a tramell	01	00	0
It Too Muskets a sword & belt & a saddle	02	00	0
It more Aded at ye Court Two siluer Cupps 10s	00	10	0
It one round table & three Joynt stooles at 20s	01	00	0
	£154	10	0

Apprised this 19th day of March 168¾
    p us   John Wincoll
           John Key his
           Marke B

Elizabeth Grant came before the Court this 25th day of March 1684, & doth attest vpon her oath that this is a true Inventory of her deceased husbands Estate, so fare as shee knowes, & on ye same oath shee will bring what euer after may appeare further to bee added y^{r}to belonging to y^t Estate/ Taken in Court by Edw: Rishworth ReCor:

A true Coppy of this Inventory transcribed out of the originall & y^{r}with Compared this 2cund of Aprill 1684:
                      p Edw: Rishworth Re:Cor:

The last will & Testament of Joseph Cross of Wells In ye prouince of Mayn yeoman, being of Perfect Memory & understanding though weake In body/

1: I Committ my soule into the hands of god, who is ye father of spirits/

2: I Committ my body into the hands of my executrix,

Part I, Fol. 28.

to bee decently buried, & after funerall expences are discharged, & all due debts payd, I do dispose of my Estate as followeth/

3: I do giue & bequeath unto my Cosson Samell Hill of the Land that was my fathers, Twenty rodds In breadth, with the Meddow the same breadth, & so to runne vp into the Countrey, as other lotts runne togeather with all my vpland, & Meddow at Drakes Ysland, to him the sayd Hill, & his heyrs for euer/ I do further giue to my aforesd Cozen, two Heffers, & two Steares of Two years ould a peece, & one feather bed with bedding belonging to it/

4ly I giue vnto my Cossons John & Joseph Hill, Thirty fiue rodds of Land in breadth, from the Town Lands towards my house, with the Meddow between the Town Land, & the remajnder of my land; a streight line being drawn between the Two Parcells of Land; And I do further giue unto my aforesd Cossons, all my vpland & Meddow at Epiford, to them & y^r heyres for euer, & my will is that Cossons Jo^n & Joseph Hill, do fence in a quarter of an Acre of Land neare ye Clumpe of pines, & keepe it well fenced for a burijng place, for mee & my relations/

5: I do giue unto my Cosson Elizabeth Backehouse tenn pounds in pay with two suites of apparell, In Case shee liue with my wife vntil shee bee seaventeene years of age or Marry/

6: I giue & bequeath unto my Loueing wife, my dwelling house with all other out houses, vplands, & Meddows stocke & househould stuffe, with all other of my Estate, In debts or other wise with out doores, & with in, not disposed of, In this my will dureing her naturall life, & at her death, my will is, y^t my Cossen Samll Hill, shall haue an Addition to his land as fare as the brooke, on the Easterly side of my house, which vpland is to bee bounded by the brooke, so fare as the highway, & then to runne into the Countrey as other lots runne/ & the Meddow to bee bounded by ye Cricke that cometh vp to my house, all which Land, I giue unto my Cosson Samuell & his herys for euer/ & further my will is, that the remajnder of my land both vpland & Meddow between Samll Hills, & John & Joseph Hills land, & all the other Meddow, or Land vndisposed of in this my Will I giue unto my wifes sonn Willi: Breeden, with halfe my stocke & househould Goods, not disposed In this my Will, always prouided that ye sayd Breeden liue to Attaine to the age of twenty one yeares, to him the sd Breeden & his heyrs for euer/ but my will is that my wife shall haue the vse & Improuem^t of the sd Land, stocke & househould stuff dureing her life, & the other halfe of the Stocke, & househould stuffe then In being, at my wifes decease, to be æqually diuided, between John Samuell & Joseph Hill/

[29] Further my will is that In Case William Breeden should dy before hee come to age, then my will is that all the Land, Stoke Househould Stuffe, willed to Willia: Breaden, at my wifes decease, bee æqually diuided, between John Samell & Joseph Hill, to them & thejr heyres for euer/

7: I do Constitute ordajne & appoynt, my loueing wife Mary Cross, to bee my soole executrix of this my last Will & testament, by whome all iust debts are to be payd, & all legacys to bee discharged/

8: I do appoynt my loueing frejnds Mr Parciuall Greene, & Samell Wheelewright, to bee ouerseers of my will/ In witness & testimony whereof, I haue here unto sett my hand, & seale, this 2nd: of March/ 1683: 1684:

Signed, sealed, &   Joseph Crosse (his Seale)
Deliuered, in Pre-
sence of us/
Samuell Wheelewright/
John Wheelewright/

This Gyft & bequest made by mee Joseph Cross unto Samell Hill, togeather with all my vpland & Meddow, at

Part I, Fol. 29.

Drakes Ysland, in the eleaueth lyne of this my last Will vpon good after Considerations, I do totally reuoake, & make null, haueing legally past away the sd lands by a bill of saile, beareing date the 29th: May: 1684: to Samuell Austine of Wells, as witness my hand June 11th 1684: Testes/ Samell Wheelewright/   Joseph Cross his

Marke ⚘

Mr Samell Wheelewright, & John Wheelewright his sonn who as witnesses, haue subscribed theire names, came before mee this secund day of August 1684: & did Attest vpon oath, that they see Joseph Cross, signe & seale this his within written will, as his act & deede/

Edw: Rishworth Jus: pe:

A true Coppy of this will aboue written transcribed out of the originall & there with Compared this 24th day of August (1684)   p Edw: Rishworth Re: Cor:

An Inventory of the Estate of Joseph Cross Deceased, the 18th of June 1684:

Six oxen at fourty six pounds	46	00	00
It 14 Cows, & one bull at 5£ p beast	75	00	00
It Tenn Calfe at 8s p Calfe	04	00	00
It foure beasts of two years ould at 50s a peece	10	00	0
It 9 beasts of one yeare ould at 25s a peece	11	05	0
It one horse at flue pounds	05	00	0
It 17 swine at Twenty shillings p swine	17	00	0
It one dwelling house, barne out housen & land & Meddow	250	00	0
It yorke Chaines Cart sleads, axes, bettle Rings wedges	06	00	0
It 3 Connows, fyre shouell tonges & other Towles	02	05	0
It 4 Ceader Pales, shouell Table & Towles	01	10	0
It Pewter & 1 siluer Cupp 5 bottles & one Tankard	01	16	0
It Barrells & other Tubbs 10s	00	10	0
It one saddle one pillion & pillion Cloath 30s	01	10	0
It Chests, & a Trunke & boxes & a saw	02	01	0
It baggs & houses 5s, gunnes & swords & bandelers	03	05	0
It Powder & shott at three shillings	00	03	0
It Money six pounds eleuen & three p ence	06	11	3
It 17 Napkins, 7 peyre of sheetes, one Couerlidd, six Table Cloaths	04	10	0

Part I, Fol. 30.

It Two bedsteads, 2 feather bedds one bowlster & bedding to them And Two other bedds with bedding to them	15	00	0
It one peyre of stillyards........	00	15	0
It three brass kettles, 2 Iron potts, & one warmeingpann....	05	10	0
It some more lining at eighteen shilling........	00	18	0
It to one barrell of Molosses at one pound 12s......	01	12	0
It Corne & meale........	07	00	0
It Two Chirnes & a frijngpan at........	00	15	0
It Butter & Cheese Twenty shillings........	01	00	0
It Two small peeces of lining Cloath at........	00	10	0
It 5 bookes, one Morter, one Chaffindish, one Gridiron & one Dripinpane It one spitt one peyre of bellows, one houre glass, one lookeing glass	01	05	0
It some housebould stuffe, Twenty shillings........	01	00	0
It One Wheele & Cart........	00	06	0
It one Carpett & fiue yds of penistone at........	01	06	0
It 5 cheesefatts, one Chesfatt, one siue, 4 pickeforkes........	00	14	0
It one Gryndstoone........	00	04	0
It one peyre of bootes, too peyre of shooes........	01	09	0
It Weareing Cloaths........	13	09	0
	500	05	3

These aboue Prticulars was prised p us this 23th day of June 1684: Joseph Storer
John **B** Barrett
his marke

Mary Cross came before us this secund day of August 1684: & doth Attest In the Presence of god, that this Inventory aboue written, is a true Inventory of her husbands Jos: Crosses Estate deceased, to ye best of her knowledg, & if any thing more do afterwards appeare, shee will bring it in/ vpon the some oath/ Edw: Rishworth Jus: pe: & ReCor: Samll Wheelewright Jus: pe:

A true Coppy of this Inventory transcribed, & with originall Compared this 25th day of August 1684:

p Edw: Rishworth ReCor:

[30] A true Accomp^t of Nathan Lawd, Administrator to the Estate of Abraham Conley deceased, of w^t debts the s^d Administrator hath payd, & secured to bee payd, in bills M^rchants bookes or otherwise, also w^t trauell & expences hee hath expended & other disbursements, for & Concerne-

Part I, Fol. 30.

ing the sd Conleys Estate, the Inventory w'of being apprised did amount to the sume of 160 : 18 : 04 : as appeareth vpon oath unto y^t Court y^t granted Administrat

Inprs for his Dyett & tendance vidzt Abra: Couleys one whoole yeare & seuerall Moenths..	20	00	00
It to br:nging of his goods from Sturg:on Cricke...	01	00	00
It payd unto Capt Doneill due by bo ke,..	29	01	06
It payd unto Mr Wi:l: Vahan on booke: 8: 16: 3: by bill........................	08	19	05
It pd Mr Ellner Cutt due by booke flue pounds..	05	00	00
It payd unto Mr Nathaniell Fryer on booke..	08	16	03
It more pd him for 2 syths & other things...			
It payd to Mr John Cutt on booke Accopt...	01	14	04
It payd to Mr Thomas Ha:vy...	03	05	00
It pd to John Morrall on bill..	03	07	06
It more for my selfe & 2 men for expenses at Court 3 days......................	00	18	00
It for my owne Trauell down the R ver, with an Accoptant }			
It three days to search the Mrchants booke 20s }	01	00	00
It more for 3 men six days, & one man t.o dayes to lay out }			
It & diuide yt Land yt was between Abra: Conley & John Heard & yr dyett }	04	00	00
It Too days to get ye men together & procure a Compass	00	08	00
It payd Mary Forgisson Wid low 01: 01: 00...	01	01	00
It payd Ri:: Greene 24s, to Mr Ric: Styleman, 2: 15: 00............................	03	19	00
It by seauen days to get John Wentworths money......................................	01	01	00
It pay i vpon an execution being sewed by Nichos Frost Concerneing the Land yt father Couley sould him...	03	15	00
It mor · to Capt Frost. John Hearle, & will: Hookely...................................	02	00	00
It to too rat :s payd due in his life tyme 11s...	00	11	00
It payd more for fencing of his Marsh...	05	00	00
It more payd for too shirts for him..	01	00	00
It on- peyre of drawers for him 10s: 1 peyre of stockeings & a Necke Cloath 6d	0	16	06
It for his windeing sheete wrin hee was buried...	00	15	00
It more for Trau ll 4 days t) get Jinkens money...	00	12	00
It for his funerall Charges 5 pounds..	05	00	00
It more on bills Desperate Debts hard to bee recouered.............................	44	00	00
It to makeing of the Accopt & for charges of seuerall Courts to answere Ni·hols Frost, & at diuerse meeteings Concerneing that Land............	04	00	00
	161	00	02

A true accomp^t as given in apperttaineing to the Estate of Abra : Conley deceased by Nathan

Lawde seno^r his marke ✗

Testes Edward Rishworth / Sep^b^{r} ; 12 : 1684 :

    Peter Grant /   A true Coppy transcribed out of ye originall by Edw : Rishworth Re Cor : 23 : of Octob^r 1684 :

Part I, Fol. 30.

Kittery In New England July 16:th 1684:
An Inventory of the Estate of John Tompson deceased/

Inprs to sundrey Towles one pound 5s 6d.....................................	01	05	6
It to one sword 5s to one syth at 3s..	00	08	00
It to sundrey Towles, one Iron pott & Tonges at............................	01	07	00
It to Oyle Caske & Wodden Ware at 7s..	00	07	00
It to fiuety Acres of Land which will appeare vpon reCord in the Prticular grants, with ye buildings yron included...................................	50	00	00
It one Iron Pott, ketle rings Wedges & other small Towles................	01	12	06
It to sundrey Towles, one Tramell & fiue Wedges..........................	01	00	06
It to a Parcell of Wodden Trays 4s 6d...	00	04	06
It to pewter brass & earthen ware at...	01	09	11
It Two tables 10s, 3 ould Chayres 18d, 2 boxes 3s 6d.....................	00	15	00
It one bible & 3 other small bookes..	00	04	00
It Sundreys of bedding at 3: 05: 00...	03	05	00
It fiue Cows at 20£ & one 3 yearleing at 3£..................................	23	00	00
It Two of Two yeare ould beasts at...	04	00	00
It 2 yearelings at 40s, & three Calfes at 15s.................................	02	15	00
It to fiue swine at fiue pounds..	05	00	0
It One Conow & two bucketts at foureteen shillings........................	00	14	00
	97	07	11

These aboue written Goods were apprised as for Current speties at ye prise Current by us/

William ffernald

Christian Ramacke tooke oath in   Jacob Ramich/
Court the aboue written is a true Inventory of ye Estate of John Tompson deceased to the best of his knowledg, & if any thing more appeare afterwards hee will add it/ at a Court of sessions taken the 29th of Octob 1684:

                p Edw: Rishworth ReCor:

vera Copia transcribed & with originall Compared this 17th Decembr   p Edw: Rishworth ReCor:

More of Estate in ye possession of Hen: Sayword/ The one Cascoe Mill is here namely apprised vnder, & Mowsume Mill & appurtenances, left to Wells men to apprise it/ this

PART I, FOL. 31.

is a true Coppy of the Originall Inventory vnto·wch these apprisers haue set y^r hands vnto/

For y^t new Mill at Cascoe In y^t Capacity, as wee left it which were workemen vpon it, besid^s the grants of Land & Tymber is apprised fiue hundred pounds by us whose names are subscribed

      Ric: Bankes Samll
      Donell/ Hen: Symson
      Job Allcocke
      The marke of J John Freathy
      Samll Webber/

[31] A true Inventory of the Mansion or dwelling house y^t Henery Sayword late deceased dwelt in, & the Saw Mills & Grist Mills at yorke, & other things left vnapprised at the last apprisall Aprill 22 : 1679 : are hereby apprised by us whose names are here vnderwritten, June 28 : 1680 :

	£	s	d
Inpr^s one dwelling house valued worth	040	00	0
It one little Houell or sheepe house	001	00	0
It one barne & Cow house fiueteen pounds	015	00	0
It an ould shopp 10s, a Turneing Mill apprisd 15£	015	10	0
It the Saw Mill vtilences & Dame	150	00	0
It Too Corne Mills & an ould shopp	060	00	0
	281	10	00

Also more Lands are apprised by us of Hene: Saywords whose names are subscribed/

	£	s	d
Twelue Acres of Land on the South side of ye New Mill Cricke 5s p acre	03	00	00
300 Three hundred acres of Land on the West side of yorke Riuer & Twenty Acres of swampe & 15 Acres of Land the whoole being 347 Acres	30	00	00
	314	10	00

vera Copia transcribed this 3 :
ffebru : 84 :
p Edw: Rishworth ReCor :

  Tymothy Yeales/
  Samell Sayword
  John Freathy his
    marke

Part I, Fol. 31.

September 24th : 1684 :
The Inventory of the Estate of Charles Martyne latly deceased/

	£	s	d
Inprs one Chamlett Coate Twenty shillings..................................	01	00	00
It one hatt one peyre of briches at at 17s.....................................	00	17	00
It one peyre of briches & a wast Coate at.....................................	00	06	00
It one Coate one peyre of drawers 4s...	00	04	00
It one Coate & doublett at Twenty shillings..................................	01	00	00
It p more in linning shott & nayles at 12s.....................................	00	12	00
It one Chest & a Gunn at Twenty shilling.....................................	01	00	00
It p Twenty nine pounds of feathers at 29s...................................	01	09	00
It 1 yd of Tickeine 2s, one 3 yeareling Heffer 30s...........................	01	12	00
It one Mare at Two pounds...	02	00	00
It by flueteen Acres of Land Three pounds...................................	03	00	00
It one flue shillings peece of siluer at 5s......................................	00	05	00
It 700 C foote of boards due from Jeremiah Mowlton...................	00	14	00
It Due from Samll Bragdon tenn shillings.....................................	00	10	00
	£14	09	00

An Inventory of the Estate of Joseph Pearce latly deceased, taken by us by whose names are here subscribed, this 8th day of ffebru : 1678 :

	£	s	d
Inprs an home stall, a dwelling house & an orchard, with too Acres of Land besides yt Necke of land wron the house is built, and now standeth vpon out of which by his Mothers will one acre of Land was given to her too daughters Saraih & Mary Pearce, wn by them demanded................	60	00	0
It one peyre of streight garters 2s..	00	02	0
It three Cubbard Cloaths 4s, one linine Cubbard Cloath 3s 6d......	00	07	6
It one small blankett & a wrought Table Cloath at.........................	00	12	0
It 1 lining awath 2s, 1 pillowbeare a bagg & 2 ould Table Cloaths 3s..	00	05	0
It a fine Hollane pillowbeare 5s, one fine hollane sheete at 11s.......	00	16	0
It flue Dowlass Napkines & one Towell at.....................................	00	13	0
It one Dyaper Table Cloath 7s, foure ould Napkines at 2s 6d.........	00	09	6
It one peyre of Thread stockeings 4s, 1 womans Caster 14s..........	00	18	0
It 4 glases 3s, Two turky worke Cussions 8s.................................	00	11	0
It Plate of di pleasure or Jackeanaps plate at................................	00	10	0
It 2 Callibashes 2s, flue purs s & baggs at 3s................................	00	05	0
It Basketts & boxes 2s, one peece of gould Twenty shillings...........	01	02	0
It one gould Ring & one gould pine at...	00	18	0
It one plue Cussion & a veluett purse at.......................................	00	03	0
It 2 siluer Cupps, & one siluer Timeble with other plate at..............	00	18	0
It one Ceader Chest, locke & key 20s, one Ciuerlid & 2 blanketts 20s..	02	00	0
It Twenty eight pound of pewter at 2s p lb....................................	02	16	0
It Two paynted Cussions & a Cubbard Cloath..............................	00	06	0
It one peyre of Curtens & valence Twenty flue shillings.................	01	05	0
It one peyre of scales at foure shillings 6d....................................	00	04	6
It Platters, bowles, Trays, 2 bottles, 6 Trenchers & a small Cann....	00	05	6
It 2 brushes & a Minitt glass 2s, 6d, 3 Indean Trays at 3s.............	00	05	6

Part I, Fol. 32.

It an ould warmeinepann a little Iron Kettle, one small brass kettle, a little brass skellett & a pestell at 17s.	00	17	0
It 1 Copper kettle 33s, a Cattiue Drippinpan & 1 pewter Chamberpot 2s	1	15	0
It 2 ould Chayres & Cussions 6s, a Court Cubbard Cloath 20s.	01	06	0
It a spanish dish at Two shillings, a Case with 6 3pint bottles 12s	0	14	0
It 2 small Andirons 7s, a Table board with turnd leggs 18s.	01	05	0
It a small Table board 5s a Parcell of ould pictures 12d.	00	06	0
It a bedstead at 14s 1 peyre of ould stillyards 2s.	00	16	0
It an ould Chest without a locke 4s 3 Leather Chayres at 27s.	01	11	0
It 7 Joynt stooles at 10s 6d, one brass pistoll & 2 other gunns 3: 02: 0.	03	12	6
It one Neate basket 4s, & a Morter & pestell at 9s.	00	13	0
It 1 feather bed & Two pillows poyse 60lb at 15d p lb	03	15	0
It another feather bed & 2 bowlsters poyse 82lb at 15d p lb	05	02	0
It The ould brass Kettle about halfe worne at	01	10	0
It One Iron pott at Tenn shillings	00	10	0
	99	05	0

Seuerall Goods of Joseph Pearces at the house of Mr Francis Hooke/ as on the other side/

[32] The Lands & Goods on ye other side come to..	99	05	0
It more at Mr Hookes Two Cows at eight pounds	08	00	0
It one 3 yeares ould Heffer at 2: 15: 00	02	15	0
It one small Calfe 5s, one Gryndstoone at 9s.	00	14	0
It one broaken Iron pott & a Tramell at 8s.	00	08	0
It An Iron spitt & Two Curten Rodds poyse 13 lb at	00	06	8
It a small Rapeyre 9s, 1 silke Twilt much worne 3: 10: 0.	03	19	0
It one blac silke Gowne at Thirty shillings.	01	10	0
It one siluer Wine Cupp & foure siluer spoones at	02	05	0
	119	02	08

Apprised by us this eleuenth day of Febru : 1678 :
vera Copia of this Inventory tran-　Edw: Rishworth
scribed & Compared with the　Roger Deareing/
originall this 22th day of Febru :　Ephraim Crockett
1678 : p Edw: Rishworth ReCor :　his marke/ 𐅁

March 5th 167⅞
An Inventory of the Estate belonging to John Præsbury/

Inprs 27 yds at 4s p yard 5: 8: 0, 1 bed bowlster & new tickine 4: 10: 00	9	18	0
It one checkard blankett 20s, & three blanketts at 12s	01	12	0
It one Couerlid 7s, 6 yds ½ redd Cotton 14s 6d	01	01	6
It 1 Coate 10s, on hatt 7s, one brass Kettle 30s.	02	07	0
It 3 Augers & a gouge 4s, ould Tickeing 4s, one Charye & ciue 3s	00	11	0
It one Iron pott with Crooks & Tramell 1 frijinpan & hatchett	00	17	6
It 2 squid lynes 2s, one lookeing glass 18d, 1 hoode 1 scarff & 1 whiske 6s	0	09	6
It one bowle & 139 peeces of linning, 40s, 2 peyre of gloues & one shift 7s	2	7	0
It one aprone 5s, 1 sheete 1 aprone 2 Towells & one Table cloath 8s	00	13	0

Part I, Fol. 32.

It one peyre of french fall shooes 5s, 4 yards of blew lining 6s.................	00	11	0
It 3 yds 3-4 quarters of whitte lining at 7s 6d, a New Coate 30s................	01	17	6
It 1 wastCoate 12s, a pillow & drawers 6s, one searge semare 30s....	02	08	0
It a Wollen Wastcoate & 3 petticoats 15s, a rideing hoode 3s, 10 peeces small lining 3s 4d.............................	01	01	4
It one Childs Coate 2s 6d, 32 peeces of lining & Childs Cloaths 8s..............	00	10	6
It one pillow beare 18d 1 greine say aprone 4s, 1 peyr sleeus 15d..............	00	06	9
It one Childs blankett & strip't Cloath 2s 6d, 4 pewter pla'ters 12s............	00	14	6
It 4 porringers 3 spoones foure shillings, 1 aprone & pewter pot 2s............	0	06	0
It 6 trenches one pewter Candlesticke 8s 4d, 2 peyre of Cards 2 dishes & spoones 5s 4d......	0	13	8
It to an Iron box & too frows 3s 6d, one brass skellet 2s......................	00	05	6
It To Lands & Meddows 26 pounds...	26	00	0
It Thee quintlls ½ of Codd fish Deliured to Major Clarke.....................	01	11	6
It three quintlls ½ of stocke fish more sent to Major Clarke....................	01	06	0
It More In fish sent to Major Clarke..	00	11	0
It to a Parcell of Meddow bought of Major Phillips..........................	10	00	0
more one peyre of blew britches & a Crooper at 3s d.......	00	03	6
It 1 peyre of whitte hose 4s, 2 Cod lynes 6s, an hand ulce 2s 6d.................	00	12	6
It to 1 peyre of red hose 3s, a Rayser 18d, 15 Cod hookes 3s 6d.................	00	08	0
It to a Chest 5s...	00	05	0

To bee Abated out of the Estate/

It one great Kettle & 3 Augers wch were walter Mares.............	1	14	0
more to be abated out of ye bed & bowlster.......................	00	10	0
	02	04	0
Rest due to the Estate as apprised............................	67	06	00

p Bryan Pendleton & John Sargeant/

Majo^r Bryan Pendleton doth Attest vpon his oath to the best of his knowledg, this is a true Inventory of John Presbury his Estate, & if more afterwards do appeare hee will bring it in/ Taken In Court this j day of Aprill 1679: as Attests   Edw: Rishworth ReCor:

A true Inventory transcribed, & with originall Compared this 2: of Aprill 79:   p Edw: Rishworth ReCor:

In the name of God Amen, I John Leds husbandman, In the County of yorke being very sicke & weake, & drawing neare to my last end, make this my last will & testament, being of a naturall good vnderstanding & of a disposed mind; I bequeath my soule unto god, In ye strength & merritts of my Lord & Saujo^r Jesus Christ, in hope of a Joyfull resurrection, & my body to the earth to descent buriall; As for y^t little Estate the Lord hath giuen mee I do dispose as followeth/

First that all my debts lawfull shall bee payd, & my funerall charges out of y^t little I haue; I do giue vnto my sonn John Leads my house & Land now In yorke, with ye writeings deeds, & Assurances, as also my too guñs my sett of Wedges, my mortissing axe & my sword/

I will also giue to my wife, my weareing Cloaths with my Chest, & what is in it, & all my debts that are due to mee/ I also give to Samell Sayword my broad axe/ & that this my last will & testament bee truly Performed, I do make & Constitute Mr Hene: Sayword, & his wife Mis Mary Sayword executors, as Witness my hand this 15th day of Novemb^r 1678:

Attests John Jefferys/
 & Tymothy Yeales/   John Leads his marke ✗

Tymothy Yeales doth Attest vpon his oath that this will of John Leads, was his last Act & Deede, which both himselfe & John Jefferys see him signe & are witnesses vnto/ Taken vpon oath in Court the 10th of Nov$\tilde{b}$ 1678:

                        Edw: Rishworth ReCor:

John Jefferys doth attest vpon his oath y^t this will aboue writen was the Act & Deede of John Leads taken vpon oath the first of Aprill 1679: p mee Samll Wheelewright

                        Assotiate/

This will Confirmed & allowed in Court as Attest

                      Edw: Rishworth ReCor:

A true Coppy of this Will, transcribed out of ye originall & y^{r}with Compared this 4th of Aprill 1679:

                   p Edw: Rishworth ReCor

Part I, Fol. 33.

[**33**] 20th of November 1678 :

An Inuentory of the Estate & Goods of John Leads deceased/

	£	s	d
Inprs to a peece of Land, & a frame vpon it at..	15	00	0
It Cash in his Chest 1: 19: 6d..	01	19	6
It 2 remnants of new lining 01: 01: 0, a remnant of siluer lace 7s	01	08	0
It to buttons silke & thread 3s a Come & Parcell of flints 12d	00	04	0
It a peece of red silke Ribbine 3s 3yds of searge 18s	01	01	0
It 1 yd ¼ of Red broad Clotth 22s one searge Coate & 1 peyr lining trowsers 30s.	02	12	0
It 1 Cloath Coate & briches, & a searge Wascoate at 3£	03	00	0
It foure peyre of gloues & 3 shirts 22s one bible & 4 peyre of stockings 16s. ...	1	18	0
It Two Parcells of nayles 40s, fowleing shott & bulletts 15s	02	15	0
It a Parcell of powder & a powder horne at 10s	00	10	0
It 4 ould Wastcoats, an ould Coate 3 peyre of briches with an ould Closs body'd Coate & one peyr of Worsted Stockings at 30s	01	10	0
It one hatt & one peyre of new shooes 18s, 6d 17 Gousewings & a glass bottle 23d	01	00	6
It 3 Necke Cloaths & a quantity of Cheeses 10s 6d	00	10	6
It 3 small Hatchetts, one sett of Wedges & a beetle Ring, 8s 2 Rowls of Toba: 14	1	02	0
It to a small quantity of flints one Grater 1 powdr horne & a fishing leade.....	0	02	0
It 2 ould Chests & a broad axe 12s 1 fowleing peece 1 Musket & a Cuttless 70s..	4	02	0
It one Cow & halfe a steere 5£ one peyre of ould shoos & a walking staffe 2s 6d	5	02	6
It one Runlett an ould kniff & one peyre of Toba: tongues	00	02	6
	43	19	05

A true Coppy of this Inventory transcribed out of the Originall & yr with Compared Aprill 4th 1679 :

p Edw : Rishworth Re : Cot :

These are to order Mary Sayword, executrix to John Leads his Estate to deliuer all those things which were in John Leads his Chest, wn hee deceased which by will hee bequeathed to his wife, to Mr Dummer in the behalfe of John Leads his wife, & shee to take a receipt of him for what shee deliuereth vnto him in ye behalfe of John Leads his wife, & it shall bee in Mary Saywords behalfe her full discharge/ Signed this 6th of Octobr 1681 : p John. Dauess Depty Presidt. Edw : Rishworth Jus : pe :

Part I, Fol. 33.

ffebru: 26: 1678:

Here followeth the true Inventory of Benjā: Donells Estate now Deceased/

Inprs The boate with all her appurtenances yrto belonging Ankers, Cables, Sails, Compass, barrell of Tarr & glass.............	40	10	0
It one Conow 20s a fyre locke Muskett at 1: 16: 0..............	02	16	0
It six worne shirts 4 peyre of lining drawyers & 2 Necke Cloaths............		15	0
It 1 peyre of silke Camlett briches 30s 1 searge Coate & briches 25s.............	02	15	0
It an ould Searge Wastcoate 5s, 1 peyre of new searge drawers 7s 6d...........	00	12	6
one Keyrsy suite at 20s, 8 peyre of ould Stockings 6s.....................	01	06	0
It an ould stuffe Coate 5s, 1 ould wastcoate 1 peyr of briches 2 peyr of drawers 7s..............	0	12	0
It one Trunke & too Chests 17s, a bible & 2 sea books 8s.	01	05	0
It flue other small books 9s a Gunters Scale Compass & Staff 6s............	0	15	0
It Tenn yards & a halfe of searge at 3s 6d p yd..........................	01	16	8
It 2 Splitters, one Gutter 16 Cod hookes at 7s 6d..........................	00	7	6
It 47 lb of lead 11s 9d, one lb powder 2s 1 barrell & strade 5s...................	00	18	9
It Too new lynes, & one ould line 9s, a Sea Compass 5s........................	00	14	00
It 15lb of Tobā: 5s 7d 14 gallons of Rume 2s 6d p gallon 15.0................	02	00	07
It one Jarr of Oyle 6s too Raysors at 3s............................	00	09	00
It one large lynd Coate 10s, one shirt & a peyre of drawers 14s.....	01	04	00
It one Caster hatt 12s, one Hamacke 20s, 1 Canvis bagg 18d.............	01	13	06
It 1 peyre of shoe buckells, & 3 siluer bottones for a shirt....................	00	05	06
It one Redd Couerlid 18s an ould blankett 3s a yarne Couerlid 4s.............	01	15	00
It a small greine Carpet & a Rugg 4s.	00	04	00
It one feather pillow bowlsters & pillows Containeing 84lb................	04	04	00
It 2 Netts at Two pounds 15s, In money to Samll Donell 14: 07: 8	17	02	08
It In Boston due by bill from Mr Powle...........	16	00	00
	100	01	08

These goods were ualewed by us
    Edw: Woolcocke/
    Job Allcocke

More to bee Added to this Inventory/

Inprs one Parcell of Cod & Hake dry fish supposed to bee 20 quintls less or more, the Cod at 10s, the Hake at 8s, p quintll...............	£ 09	s 00	d 00
It more in money 03: 10: 8d a gould Ring 20s...................	04	10	8
It 1 barrell of oyle 22s, one Cann & Tinn funill 2s 3d..........................	01	04	03
It A brass Kettle 22s an Iron pott 6s a Necke Cloath & drawers 5s.............	01	13	00
It 1 peyr of red drawers a wastcoate, 1 peyr of searge drawers & a searge Coate	1	06	00
It one Stuffe Coate at Twenty eight shillings...	01	08	00
It 1 peyr of searge briches a wastcoate, 1 peyre of lining drawers & a shirt....	1	00	06
It 4 Handkerchers 3 Necke Cloaths 8s 9d 1 peyr of shoos & stockings 5s.......		13	09
	£ 20	16	08

A true Coppy of this Inventory transcribed & Compared with the originall this 4th day of Aprill 1679:

        p Edw: Rishworth Re:Cor:

Part I, Fol. 34.

In the name of god Amen/ the 18th of September 1678: deceased I Joseph Boolls of Wells in the County of yorke shyre Gentlē being in Perfect memory & remembrance praysed bee God, do make & ordajne this my last Will & testament In manner & forme as followeth/

1 : I do bequeath my soule into the hands of almighty god & maker, hopeing that the meretorious death, & passion of Jesus Christ my onely Saujo^r & redeemèr, to receiue free pardon & forgiueness of all my sins, & as for my body to bee buried in Christian buriall, at the discretion of my execcutrix hereafter mentioned/

1 : I giue & bequeath unto my Elldest sonn Thomas Bolls Tenn pounds/

[34] I bequeath unto my sonn Samell Tenn pounds/

I do bequeath unto my daughter ffrost tenn pounds/

I bequeath unto my daughter Becke Thirty pounds/

I bequeath vnto my daughter Locke Tenn pounds/

I bequeath unto my daughter Mercy Thirty pounds, & as much searge as will make her a Gowne, & Tickeine for a bedd & a bowlster, which is in the house & my will is that Twenty pounds bee payd to my sd daughter by my executrix, w^n shee shall Antajne the age of Twenty yeares, or marry, which shall first happen, & the other tenn pounds to bee paid by my sonn Joseph/

I bequeath unto my sonn Joseph all my houseing, vpland Meddows & Marsh belonging to my home place, to him & his heyres for euer, after the death of my wife, not doubting of his Dutifullness & care to his Mother, hee paijng fiuety pounds to my Children hereafter mentioned to my sonn Thos tenn pounds, to my sonn Samell Tenn pounds, to my daughter Frost tenn pounds, to my daughter Chadborne tenn pounds, & to my daughter mercy tenn pounds/

Further, my will is, that my wife shall haue my whoole Estate both with in doors & with out, in this Town or else w^r to dispose of to w^t children shee sees good, excepting the

Part I, Fol. 34.

houseing & Lands that I haue given unto my sonn Joseph after her decease, shee to haue the use of it dureing her life, & my wife to pay all debts & legacys, but onely w^t Joseph is to pay; And I do hereby nominate & appoynt my deare & loueing wife Mary my soole executrix of this my last will & testament, & do hereby nominate & appoynt my loueing frejnds, Mr William Symonds & William Symonds to bee the ouerseers of this my last Will & testament, all other Wills & testaments being made uoyd/ In witness where unto I haue sett my hand sett my hand & seale, the day & yeare aboue written/

Witness Sam̃ell   Joseph Boolls (locus Sigilli)
  Wheelewright/
  William Symonds/

An Inventory of the Estate of Jos: Bolls Gentlemā: who deceased lately/

	£	s	d
Inprs houses lands & Meddows belonging to the home lotts apprised by us vnderwritten at foure hundred & eighty pounds....................	480	00	00
It for oxen thirty pounds, 3 Cows 3 Heffers & 3 three yeare oulds 27£........	057	00	00
It 1 yeare ould Heffer 3£, 4 yearelings 6£, 4 Calfes 4£ 2 Horses 8£..........	021	00	00
It 19 swine at 20£: 10s: 0d, Three Acers of Marsh at ye Necke of land 15£....	035	10	00
It Two Acers of Land at Ogunquett 30£, 50 Acers of land at Cape Porpus 20£	050	00	00
It Wollen & liuing Cloathing 30£, 18 yds of Dowless at 3s p yd 54s	032	14	00
It lining Cloath 15s, 2 yds of broad searge at 16s.............................	001	11	00
It 9 yds of Cayrsey at 6s p yd 2: 14: 0, 8 yds of searge at 48s................	005	02	00
It 11 yds of broad Cloath at 22s p yd 12: 02: 00, silke thread buttons gallone Trimg 6£...	18	02	00
It 8 yds ½ Cotton Cloath, 25s 6d, 7 yds ½ of Tickeing 30s.......................	002	15	6
It 3 feather bedds 3 bowlsters, 3 pillows belonging to ym.....................	014	00	0
It 6 ruggs apprisd at 5£: 10: 00, 5 blanketts 3: 15: 00, 8 sheetes nine pounds....	018	05	00
It 3 flocke bedds & some other bedding 7£ Curtains & Carpents 4£...........	11	00	00
It 12 pillow bears & Napkins 35s, 18 Napkins 2 Table Cloaths 45s.............	04	00	00
It 2 Tables & 2 formes 32s, 7 Chests 42s, 5 Chares 15s........................	004	09	00
It Indean & Inglish Corne of of all sorts 28£.................................	028	00	00
It porke & beife 11£, 20 Loade of Hay at 15s p loade 15£	026	00	00
It Butter Cheese & suett 4£ & Bookes foure pounds..........................	008	00	00
It 3 Iron potts & 3 peyr pott hookes 45s 1 Iron kettle & skellett 15s...........	003	00	00
It one frijngpan & 2 Tramells at 13s...	000	13	00
It to an Iron Morter 4s to brass Kettle a stew pann & other brass 35s pewter dishes & other pewter 40s.....	03	19	00

Part I, Fol. 35.

It Earthen Ware & glass bottles 20s Hodgs barlls & Tubbs 35s	02	15	00
It Molesses 15s, one peyre of bellows two peyre of shooes 7s	01	02	00
It one peyr of shott Moulds 18d, Toba: tenn shillings	00	11	06
It a Churne & Milke vessell 15s Garden stuffe & pipkins 30s	02	05	00
It one Grindstoon 6s, Axes Rings, Wedges a marking Iron Hookes 40s	02	06	00
It Wheeles & Cart 30s, Clues pitchforkes racks saws & takelin 12s	02	02	00
Sleads shares plows & Cowlters 1: 14: 00, yoaks Cheains & Tackeing belonging to the yoakes 24	02	18	00
It 4 Cussions 4s, one Muskett 4lb of powdr & bull-tt 36s	02	00	00
It nayls 10s a smoothing Iron 2s, 6 baggs 6s	00	18	00
It one warmeing pann at three shillings 6d	00	03	06
	842	01	06

An Inventory made & apprised by us the 29th of Nouembr 1678: William Symonds/
Joseph Storer/

Mis Mary Bolls taketh oath that this is a true Inventory of the Estate of her husband Mr Joseph Bolls Deceased, according to the best of her knowledg, & wt more shall afterwards appeare vpon ye same oath shee is bond to bring it in/ taken in Court ye 7th of Aprill 1679:

p Edw: Rishworth Re: Cor:

vera Copia of this Inventory transcribed & Compared with the originall Aprill 7: 1679 p Edw: Rishworth Re: Cor:

[35] An answere to an Administration granted mee the last Generall Court of Thomas Turners Estate, that were small Moueables in the house apprised at 3 pounds 9s, or tenn shillings & 6d/

Wrof I haue pd to the funerall Charges & Peter Staple	01	06	0
It to Richd Greene for digging the Graue 5s & to Gemmer Greene for weeding the Garden foure shillings	00	09	00
It to Goody Rogers for cureing of his Legg	00	04	00
It Two men yt made ye apprisall too days	00	04	00
It for my own Charges & money layd by Christian Ramacke	1	04	00
	£03	09	00

Octobr 28: 84:

This Accopt given in by Christean Ramacke, & by ye Court ordered to bee Re:Corded, as Attests Edw: Rishworth ReCor: & is here done/

Part I, Fol. 35.

A true Inventory of the Estate of John Præbury deceased which left at the house of Pendleton Fletcher, as followeth/

	£	s	d
Inprs 3 peyre of petticotes 15s, one snymarr 20s.	01	15	00
It Three wast Conts 15s, & one rideing Hood 5s	01	00	00
It 3 wimmines sleeues 5s 6d, It 3 aprones 6s 8d	00	12	02
It 3 blanketts for a Child & one pillow beare 4s 6d	00	04	6
It one Childs Coate 5s, 32 Clowts 18 d, 1 peyre of gloues & 2 Coyffs 18d	00	08	00
It one Capp & a swath 4s 6d, 1 peyre of stockings & shooes 1s 10d	00	06	4
It one pillow beare 6d, 3 Iron staples 15s	00	15	6
It 3 Chests, 4 platters 3 porringers, one pint pott 20s 6 trenchers 6d	01	00	6
It one Candlesticke, one Couerlid 20s, 1 peyre of Tongus & fire shouell 3s 6d	1	03	6
It Could Chissell 5s, 6 wodden dishes 3s one hatt 2s 6d	00	10	6
It one frijnp n & one steile box 4s, 6d, a Tramell 2s	00	06	6

This Inventory taken & Goods apprised by Pendleton Fletcher & Phineas Hull, according to ye best of y^r knowledg on the 3d of November 1684 :   Pendleton Fletcher/
                                           Phineas Hull/
further to bee Added/

It a box of 30s, p a debt due from Pendleton F'etcher 16s 8d.	04	06	8
It To a debt from Capt Frans Hooke due	04	14	0
It Land & Meddow Twenty pounds	20	00	0
	29	00	8

John Dauess
Phineas Hull
apprisers/

William Præsbury made oath to the uerity of this Inventory, & this all hee knows of at Present, & doth Ingage that If hee find any more hee will giue an Accop^t of it/ taken this 27th of March 1685
                    before mee ffrancis Hooke Jus : pe :

A true Coppy of this Inventory so fare as I Could read & understand it transcribed out of ye originall this 5th of Aprill 1685   p Edw : Rishworth Re : Cor :

In the name of god Amen, this Twenty sixt day of September one thousand six hundred seaventy nine, I Thomas Withers the vnprofitable servant of god, though weake in body, yet of good & Perfect remembrance blessed be god, &

Part I, Fol. 35.

knowing y^t I am naturally borne to dy, & to pass from this transitory life, minding to put in order my Estate, to the Intent there should bee no striff for the same after my decease: I do here by make this to bee my true last & onely will, & testament in manner followeth/

Imp^{rs}: I commend my soule to almighty god, & his sonn Jesus Christ my sauio^r, in whose prætious blood I set ye whoole & onely hope of my saluation, my body in hope of a Joyfull resurrection, I comitt to ye earth to bee decently buried, & touching the distribution of my mortall goods, I dispose of as followeth/

I will all my debts should bee satisfyd/

I giue vnto my beloued wife Jane Withers, the one halfe of all y^t I haue, both of Land & Cattle, for ye tearme of her life, vidz^t: too oxen, too Cows by name, starr & Jentle, & also my land next to Goodman Mendums, which I giue her dureing her life, & after wards to my daughter Mary/ also I giue vnto my sayd wife the vse of Eagle poynt, dureing her life, after wards to bee for euer my daughter Elizabeths; Also I giue vnto my wife all that Land on the Eastward side ouer against John Shapleighs, between John Hoole, & Lewis, dureing her life, & afterwards to bee my daughter Elizabeths/

I giue vnto my daughter Mary Ryce one Red Heffer/

I giue unto my two Grandchildren, Allexand^r & Aeilce Shapleigh one Red heffer/

I giue unto my sonn In law John Shapleigh a Necke of land Called Oake Poynt, with ye Marsh next to his house/

I do by these Presents make & ordaine, by well beloued wife aboue mentioned, to bee my soole executrix of this my last will & testament, here by giueing & bequeathing unto her all the remajnd^r of my Estate, as househould stuff & else which is not mentioned in this my last will & testament In testimony of Which, I haue here vnto set my hand & seale this Twenty sixt day of Septem^{br}: 1679:

Thomas Withers (his seale)

Part I, Fol. 36.

Francis Hooke testifys that y⁰ will on the other side was writt by him, & wᵗ was there written, was nothing but what Mr Thomas withers desired

<small>The aboue written compared with the originall will hath divers fundament mistakes in it Augst 30th 1690 as attests   John Wincoll Recordr</small>

[36] mee to write, to the uerity of which, I do here unto set my hand this 30ᵗʰ day of March 1685/

                                   ffrancis Hooke

Capᵗ ffranˢ Hooke testifys vpon his oath in Court to the treuth of this Euidence, aboue written relateing to Mr Withers his will, as Attests Edw : Rishworth ReCor :

I William Heynes beareing often Company with the Cheefe author of this Instrument, Mr Thoˢ Withers by name, when I Preceiued him grow feeble & weakely, Aduised him to putt his worldly Estate in order, If hee had not, but hee tould mee at sometyms hee had, & I haue heard him Confess it to his wife & daughter/ but who had it I understood not/ but gathering often by his answers that Capᵗ Hooke was the man hee depended vpon as his trustee & ouerseer/ witness my hand this 13ᵗʰ day of Febru : 84 :

Mr William Heynes came & made oath to the uerity aboue sayd this 13ᵗʰ of Febru : 168⅘ Francis Hooke Jus : pe :

Mary Ryce aged 25 yeares or there abouts, sayth that about three Moenths before her father Mr Thomˢ Withers Dyed, shee heard him say that hee had made his Will/ & further sayth not, taken vpon oath this 30ᵗʰ of March 1685 :

                     before mee ffrancis Hooke Jus : pe :

This euidence ownd in Court 1 : Aprill 1685 :

                           Edw : Rishworth Re : Cor

A true Coppy of Mr Thomas Withers his will as on the other side, & of the euidences here aboue written transcribed out of the originall & yʳwith Compared this 8ᵗʰ day of Aprill 1685 : p Edw : Rishworth ReCor :

At a Councill held at yorke for yᵉ Prouince of Mayn Aprill 27ᵗʰ 1685/

Part I, Fol. 36.

An Inventory brought in by Samuell Donell Aministrator to his sister her Estate Margerett Donell deceased/

Wee whose names are vnderwitten being desired by the relations of Margerett Donell, haue apprised a Percell of Goods that was Margerett Donells Deceased/

To fine weareing suites of apparell, with one Trunke & a box valewed at 10: 15: 00	10	15	00

Besides some other goods left in the hands of Goody Pullman, by sd Margerett Donell, by Information, vapprised/

        Job Allcocke
        John Morris
        his marke **2**

A true Coppy of this Inventory as brought into the Councill transcribed this 5th day of May 1685:

      p Edw: Rishworth ReCor:

An Inventory of the Lands & Chattles of John Batson deceas'd taken May 6: 1685:

Inprs foure oxen 15£: 00s: 0d & flue Cows 12£: 10s: 0d	27	10	00
It three two yeare oulds 5: 05: 00 | one foure yeare ould 50s	7	15	0
It Too Calfes 20s, To twelue sheepe at 3: 12: 00	04	12	0
It Chaynes Clenice hookes & Rings at 25s	1	05	0
It one Mayre & Cowlt at 3: 00: 00 | 7 swine 3: 10: 00	6	10	0
It To halfe a Saw Mill at 28£	28	00	0
It To houseing Lands & Meddows at 40£	40	00	0
It to a feather bed & furniture 10£ to a pott Kettles & tramell	12	00	0
It to a spitt & a fryinpane 5s, househould goods 10s	00	15	0
It In weareing Cloaths 20s, 4 Wedges & 1 peyre of Rings 10s	01	10	00
It Three axes & one peyre of Tonggs 10s	00	10	00
	129	07	00

    Apprised by us/ John Barett his
        marke
        John Purrington/

Apprised by us about that tyme aboue written

Elizabeth Batson relict to John Batson Deceased did Attest vpon her Oath, yt this is a true Inventory of her husbands Estate, & if more appeare afterwards, vpon the same oath shee will bring it in/ Taken In Court this 26th May 1685:

    as Attests Edw: Rishworth ReCor:

Part I, Fol. 37.

June 12th 1685:
An Accompt of the Perticulars of the Estate of Jonathan Fletcher deceased, the 9th day of June 1685:

	£	s	d
Inprs one new Cloath Coate at 1: 10: 00	01	10	00
It 1 ould broad Cloath Coate 10s, one ould Coate 6s	00	16	00
It other ould Cloath 6s, a Caster Hatt 20s	01	06	00
It one Whitte Jackett & a peyre of drawers & some necke cloaths		16	00
It one ould hatt 12d, one bible 3s, one siluer Clasp 2s	00	06	00
It One Gunn one powdr horne, & one ould belt all at	01	00	00
It 1 ould peyre of gloues 6d, too axes, too or 3 other small towls at 8s, one peyre of plow Irons halfe worne 6s	00	14	6

[37]

his home stall of house & three Acres of Land Inclosed one acre & halfe yr of broaken vp with Corne yron, with 43 Acres of vacant Land Joyneing to the sd Homestall, the whool house & Land Esteemed at	30	00	0
It bedding at 3: 06: 00, a small quantity of beife 3s: 4d	03	09	4
It one bedstead at 6s, 1 Chest 6s, a few wodden Implmts for housekeepg	0	17	0
It a spineing Wheele with a little yarne 9s, a Meale bagg 2s	00	11	00
an horse bridle & saddle 4: 10: 0, 3 fowles at 18d	4	11	6
suma totalis:	45	17	4

Apprised by us Will: Gowen/
& James Emrey/

vera Copia of this Inventory transcribed & Compared this 2: of July 1685: p Edw: Rishworth Re:Cor:

Katterne Fletcher came before mee this 14th of August 1685: & did Attest vpon oath yt this is a true Inventory within written of all her deceased husbands Estate, to ye best of her knowledg/ If afterwards any thing more come to her mind, vpon the same oath already taken shee will bring it in/ taken vpon oath at ye Present date/

Edw: Rishworth Jus: pe:

vera Copia transcribed this 14: Augst 85:

p Edw: Rishworth ReCor:

Saco the 14th of August 1685:
Inventory of the Estate of Tobias Cawly deceased apprised by us Henery Smith, & Richard Peard/

Inprs 2 redd wast Coates, 6s, too blew shirts 5s	00	11	00
It 4 silke Hankerchers 6s, 2 Whitte Necke Cloath 18d	00	07	6
It a Parcell of ould Cast of Cloathes at 5s	00	05	0
It ½ a blew Rugg 3s, a gray hatt & a red hatband 6s	0	09	0
It Too EllElay shirts 10s, too peyre of whitte drawers 8ss	0	18	00

Part I, Fol. 37.

It Too whitte wast coates 10s one peyre searge Trowsers Coate 8s	0	18	00
It one searge Coate & briches 10s, 1 peyre of gloues 1 peyre Mittons 12d		11	00
It one peyre of britches 8s, 1 peyre of stockings 5s	0	13	00
It Toba: 18s 6d bookes & shirts & Come 5s	01	08	6
It one peyre of bootes & one peyre of shooes 10s	0	10	0
It one peyre of shooes at 2s 6d	0	02	6
	05	11	6

The whose appraisem^t is fiue pounds seaven^s & six peence as testifys Hene: Smith/ Richard Peard/

vera Copia transcribed out of ye originall this seound of Septeb^r 1685 :   p mee Edw: Rishworth ReCor:

An Inventory of the Estate of Mr George Munjoy, senior deceased, being In the Townshipp of Falmouth in Casco Bay, or Elsewhere as was apprised by us underwritten the 24th of Septem^{br} 1685 :

		s	d
Inprs a Tract of Land at Tewissicke	030	00	00
It one Tract of Land bought of Thoms Brackett at	020	00	0
It a Tract of Land lijng at long Cricke, with Marsh to it	110	00	0
It an Ysland called house ysland at	030	00	0
It a Tract of Land at Pischataqua at	040	00	0
It An ysland Called Bastines ysland	020	00	0
It a Tract of Land on ye other side Ammongungon Riuer	020	00	0
	£270	00	0

Debts due to Geo: Munjoys Estate deceased/

Inprs Geo: Ingersall senior by bill	25	00	00
It Arther Hews	04	00	00
It Jo: Meane	02	12	00
It Jo: Mosier	01	08	00
It Elias Redding	12	00	00
It John Atwell	03	00	00
It Thomas Skilline	10	00	00
It Aron ffelt	02	12	00
It James Wiggins	00	13	03
It Anthony Brackett	01	05	00
It Thomas Brackett	02	04	00
It Jo: Whittefoote	03	08	6
It Robert Corbene	0	15	6
It Geo: Barnard	2	10	00
	71	08	10

A true Coppy of this Inventory, with ye Accot y^{r}unto Annexed, transcribed out ye Originall & y^{r}with Compared this 6th day of Septeb^r 1685 : p Edw: Rishworth ReCor:

This Land aboue was by us apprised
    Anthony Brackett   William Rogers/

Part I, Fol. 38.

In the name of god Amen/
Rowland young Senjo^r of yorke in the Prouince of Mayne, declareth this to bee his last will & testament; I Rowland young aforesayd, being at this Present of a sound mind, & of a memory substantiall, though very sicke in body, & willing to dispose prudently of what god in his pleasure hath possest mee with all, declare as followeth/

first ⁋ bequeath my soule to god, that gaue it in & through ye meritts of my deare Ld & saujo^r, Jesus Christ, in hopes of a Joyfull resurrection, at the great Tribunall : & my body to the earth y^r to bee Inter'd, in order & Decent buriall/

2ly I will that all my funerall Charges shall bee fully & duely payd, with all my other iust & due debts, which may appeare/

3 : I will that my dearly, & beloued wife, Johanna young shall inioy all my Estate y^t I haue in this world, the same to possess & improue, & to take the full produce of from tyme to tyme, & at all tyms dureing the tyme of her naturall life, & If in case the produce of ye same shall not bee a Competent measure for her Comfortable subsistance [38] I do hereby Impoure my well beloued to sell, aliene or dispose of all or any of my Estate. not yet disposed off, for y^t end, & shall desire any Court or seale or Judicature, in such case of extremity, to ayd & Assist my beloued wife y^rin, & also so to order that shee may haue a comfortable liuelyhood according to her Ranke, & quality out of ye same/ And further I order my well beloued wife to will bequeath & dispose off what part of my Estate, shee shall leaue at her decease, to whom shee pleaseth ; I also will the possession Present of all my Estate, houses Lands Marshes, or any or any thing y^r unto belonging to my dearely beloued wife, to whom I Committ soole execution, & Administration,

PART I, FOL. 38.

desireing this my wellbeloued wife to act as soole executrix, in all respects to see my last will & testament Performed/ Signed & deliuered in the   Rowland young
    Presence of,
    Jeremiah Mowlton/   his marke
      his $\mathcal{L}$ marke/
    Timothy Yealls/

Jeremiah Mowlton, & Tymothy yealls came before mee this 6th of Noveb^r 1685 : & made oath that they see Rowland young signe the abouesd Instrum^t as his last will & testament/ Taken vpon oath before mee John Dauess
                                      Dep^{ty} President/

A true Coppy of this will aboue written, transcribed & with ye originall Compared this 24th day of Novemb^r 1685 :
                    p Edw : Rishworth Re : Cor :

An Inventory of the Estate of Rowland young of yorke deceased, taken by us whose names are vnderwritten, this 25th of Sepb^{er} 1685 :

Inprs his weareing Cloaths	008	19	00
It for houses Lands & Marsh	140	00	00
It one small boate with what doth belong to her	010	00	00
It for a stage fishing house & flake rowme	003	05	00
It Cattle 2 stears, 4 Cows one Two yeareling Heffer	026	00	00
It three yearlings and Too Calfes at	005	00	00
It one horse three swine & foure piggs	006	10	00
It two Iron potts & one Irone Chissell at	001	10	00
It for pewter & a warmeingpan	000	15	00
It a frijngpan & one brass morter at	000	05	00
It Tenn sheepe 4£ for bedding six pounds 15s	010	15	00
It for a saw betle Rings & two axes at 20s	001	00	00
It one fowling peece at	002	00	0
It 2 Cheeses 6 Milke pans two butter potts	000	18	00
It one Churne Tubbs, pales, with other small things	005	05	0
It Cloath at the Weauers fourty shillings	002	00	00
	224	06	00

    witness our hands Abra : Preble Arther
                            Bragdon/
Joane young came before us this 26th day of Septemb^r 1685 & doth Attest vpon her oath y^t this is a true Inventory

Part I, Fol. 38.

of ye Estate of her husband lately deceased Rowland young senior to ye best of her knowledg, & if any more of sd Estate shall afterwards appeare, by vertue of the same oath shee will bring it in/ John Dauess Dep^ty Presid^t

Edw: Rishworth Jus: pe:

A true Coppy of this Inventory within written transcribed & with the originall Compared this 24: Novemb^r 1685:

p Edw: Rishworth ReCor:

yorke 19th of December: 1685: Wee whose names are here vnder written being Chosen by Mr Robert Eliett to prise the Estate of Samuell Frethy deceased, haueing prised as followeth vidz^t:

	£	s	d
22th Inprirs to one 35s to one horse 4: 5: 00 |	06	00	00
It 1 Chest & one peyre of shooes halfe worne at	00	09	00
It one Hatt & Ribbine 6s, 1 peyr of stockings 2s	00	08	00
It one peyre of Hoses 12d, 2 ould shirts & one yd of lining all	00	04	00
It locke 9d, a ball of Tyine 9d, 1 p yre Trusers 5s	00	06	06
It a new bridle 2s 6d, a searge Coate 30s	01	12	06
It a Cloath Coate Twenty fiue shillings a Rugg 20s	02	05	00
It a pill w 5s, Too hornes & ½ lb of powder 3s 6d	00	08	06
It Canvice bed sacke 16s a Lyne 2s 6d	00	18	6
It 18 lb of Leade 6s, 20 Cod Hookes 2s 6d one horne 3d	00	03	9
It one pillow beare 3s a silke Necke Cloath 18d	00	04	6
It in a syth 2s 6d, a glass bottle 6 d	00	03	00
It 3 yds & ½ of searge 24s 6d, 3 yds of Callico 7s 6d	01	12	00
It one Come Case & saile Needles 5d, 7 doz buttons 4s 8d more buttons 15d	0	06	4
It one Chest locke & key the Goods are in	00	08	00
It 1 Raysor Inkehorne and too peyre of small Cisers	0	02	00
It 2 Kintalls & 76 lb of Cod fish at 26s 9d	01	06	9
It 3 quinlls & one hundred & 4 lb of Refuge fish 33s, 5d	01	13	5
It one Cow pray ed at foure pounds	04	00	0
March 17 One Rugg fiue shillings 5s, 2 peyr of stockings 2s 6d£	00	07	6
It a peyr of 2s, one barrell 9d one lyne at 2s	00	04	9
It 7 Hooke 14 d, 3 lynes, & one peece of a lyne 3s 8d	00	04	00
It one peyre of Canvice briches, & one ould Coate at	00	02	06
In the boate, & yrunto thin,s belonging, that is say part of A Roade, 18 fathome 2: 10: 00, one Iron pott 6s 6d — In the boate 3 oars, 2 Mast bucketts & yds & Tackelling yrunto belonging, & foure blockes 12d, one Mainesale 2£: 05s: 00d, foresale 9s, 1 Compass & buckett 6s	17	16	06
	41	12	10

Part I, Fol. 39.

[39]

March 23 At Goodman Frethys Goods prised as followeth

It 16 sprice oares 410 C ft at three halfe peece p foote & qr	02	11	3
It 4 ash Oares 83 foote & an halfe at 2d p ffoote	00	13	11
It one Grindstoone wch as Jon sayd promised p his bror to him	00	07	0
It one ax 2s, one ½ part of a Grindstone 1s 6d	00	03	6
It 300 C of barrell staues & 3 Oares 7s 6d	00	07	6
	45	16	00

This is a true Inventory of the Estate of Samūll Freathy deceased, taken by us, whose names are here und^r written/ yorke 23 : March 168¾

for ye apprisemet of the sd Estate £ s d
01 10 00

John Penwill/
William Wormewood

vera Copia of this Inventory aboue written transcribed & Compared with Originall this 14th of Aprill : 1686 :

p Edw : Rishworth ReCor :

May : 17th 1686 :

Then by us whose names are here underwritten, was an Inventory taken of the Estate of Mis Saraih Tricky, & of her sonn Tricky deceased/

	£	s	d
To the houseing & Land being Twenty Acres at	90	00	0
It too Cows & yr Calfes 9£ Too Heffers 4 : 10 : 0	13	10	0
It to one Mayre three pounds, one sow & one Hogg 40s	05	00	0
It John Trickys Chest & Cloaths 4 : 7 : 0 & 2 gunns 40s	06	07	0
It Two hand saws & a whipp saw 30s, a hand & a cross cutt saw 7s	01	17	0
It to his workeing towles 37s to Iron 10s, to a saddle 10s	02	17	0
It 3 table Cloaths, Too dozen of Napkines	03	10	0
It 2 peyre of ould sheetes 01 : 8 : 0, ould Lining 3s	01	11	0
It one bed greine rugg & bowlster 3 : 10 : 0, 1 bedstead Curtains & uallence 40s	5	10	0
It one ould peyre of blanketts & pillows 10s, six Chares 10s	01	00	0
It 1 small table & table Cloath 15s, an ould bed bowlster blanketts & ould Rugg 40s	02	15	0
It 2 Trammells & ould Iron 8s an ould brass Kettle & warming pan 30s	01	18	0
It an ould pott and brass Kettle 12s, ould pewter & Lattine ware 20s	01	12	0
It ould bed & beding, 37s Due from ye Countrey 12£	13	17	0
It to Eleuen days worke from Roger Dereing at 3s 6d p day	1	18	6
	£153	02	6

John Diament/
Ephraim Crocket/   John Diament & Ephraim Crocket
his marke E   gaue in their oaths as apprisers to this Inventory this 18th of May 1686 :

before mee Francis Hooke Jus : pe :

Part I, Fol. 39.

Saraih Tricky came before this Court vidz‍ᵗ Capᵗ Wincoll, Capᵗ Frost & Edw: Rishworth ReCor & his Majestys Justˢ at yᵉ Present date, & did Attest vpon her oath this to bee a true Inverity of her sonn John Trickys Estate, & afterwards any more appeare shee will bring it in vpon the same oath Edw: Rishworth Jus: pe:

vera Copia transcribed out of originall this 5ᵗʰ of June 1686 p Edw: Rishwort ReCor:

An Inventory of the Lands, Chattles & goods of William Gowen alias Smith late of Barwicke deceased, Aprill secund 1686:

	£	s	d
Inprs his weareing Cloaths & apparell	05	00	0
It one dwelling house barne oarchard with 60 acres of Land more or less with ye Addition	100	00	0
It one hundred Acres of Land lijng neare Yorke lyne	010	00	0
It thirty eight acres of Land by the third hill	005	00	0
It Sixty Acres of Land on ye South side of Sturgeon Cricke	025	00	0
It 5 oxen 15£, tenn Cows 22£ seaven three years ould 11£	049	00	0
It 5 cattle of Too years ould, and fiue yearlings at 10£	010	00	0
It Too horses fiue pounds & Thirtene swine 8£: 10s: 0	08	10	0
It In the fyre roume foure 4 gunnes and a backe sword	003	10	0
It 3 Iron potts & Hookes, 3 skelletts, Too friinpanes	002	04	0
It 14 earthen dishes & wood, a Wodden Morter and sume ould Twine	000	4	6
It 12 spoones, one spining wheele & Cards a Cettle too Chayrs & Lumber	000	11	0
It 3 Tramells, Tonges, a smothing Iron & an hour glass at	00	10	0
It in the vpper chamber Wheate peas, & Indean Corne 20s, bed & bedding 40s	3	00	0
It Empty Caskes, bedsteads, 3 ould slues, & other Lumber 20s	01	00	0
It 2 sackes, 1 winnowing sheete 2 bare skines fiue sawes	01	05	0
It a broad axe & Adgs 6s, 4 Augurs 4 Chissells 6s, 1 square Compass & frow all 2s	0	14	0
It in ye yard 9 howes 10s, 5 axes 8s, 4 pitchforks 3s, 6 wedgs and a rule 6s	1	07	0
It 5 beetle Rings 2s, a sledg 12d, An Iron for horse tackleing 2s	0	05	0
It plow Irons 10s, wheels Cart & sleade 25s, 4 yoakes 4 Chaines & staples 1 peyre of Hooks 30s	3	05	0
It ould syths, sickles, tackling & an ould drawing kniffe	00	05	00
It 1 ould saddle & bridle six shillings, & 2 Hamers 12d	00	07	00
In ye lower chamber a feather bed, bedstead bowlster 2 pillows Two peyre of sheets & one blankett, & one Rugg all at	04	00	00
A trundle bed 2 blanketts & a Rugg, and too feather pillows	01	00	00
It 3 Chests 10s one peyr of stillyards & a warmeing pan 4 glass bottles	00	16	0
It 1 bible & diuinity bookes 20s, new Cloath 40s, Cradle gally potts & salve 2s	03	02	0
It 6 pewter dishes 15s, 10 small peecs of pewter porringers & a Chamberpott	01	00	0
It earthen potts, panns, palles trays cheese press 1 Churne barrell & lumber	01	00	0
It flax tow & yarne 20s, one small Case of bottles & too Cheeses 4s	01	04	0

PART I, FOL. 40.

It beife & porke 15s, tallow & Lard 10s, Wool & Cotton 40s.................	08	05	0
It boards loggs at seuerall places 20£. debts due to ye Estate six pounds......	26	00	0
Moore in the Chamber 2 peyre of shirts & an ould hamaker, & a Table Cloath at..	01	5	00
	265	09	00

Apprised this 21th of May 1686 : John Wincoll
            Nicholas frost/
            his marke ⋏⊢

Elizabeth Smith alias Gowen doth Attest vpon her oath that this Inventory aboue written, of William Smiths alias Gowein deceased is a true inventory to yᵉ best of her knowledg, & yᵗ If more do appeare afterwards vpon the same oath shee will bring it in/ Taken vpon oath in Court this 21ᵗʰ of May 1686 :   p Edw : Rishworth Re : Cor :
  vera Copia transcribed & Compared, this 6th of June 1686 :
         p Edw : Rishworth ReCor :

[40] An Inventory of the visible Estate of James Chadborne, of the Town of Kittery, In the prouince of Mayne, lately deceased, apprised by us, whose names are vnderwritten/ Dated 26 : March 1686/

	£		
Inprs his weareing apparell 6£ ould books 5s.................................	06	05	00
It one feather bed & furniture Curtaines & bedsteade........................	10	00	00
It Too bedds with ould furniture in one Lodging.............................	04	00	00
It a small Lodging for a boy 40s, one barrell of beife 30s...	03	10	00
It 3 busils of Indean Corne 7s 6d, one Table Cloath 1 doz: Napkins 30s.........	01	17	06
It ½ dozen of ould Napkins 6s, 1 ould painted Callico Carpitt 6s................	00	12	00
It one peyre of stocke Cards, 1 peyre of small Cards & a wheele at............	00	09	00
It one Table 3 Cheyres 16s, & one Trundle bed stead 5s.......................	01	01	00
It Two Iron potts 01: 16: 0, 1 brass Kettle 1 ould brass skellett 6s.............	02	02	00
It 3 water payles 3s, 1 peyre of Tramells, 1 peyre of tonges 1 spitt 9s...........	0	12	00
It one ould frijngpane & some other Implmts about ye house..................	00	11	00
It A Parcell of ould Iron Towles about ye house..............................	02	15	06
It Too grindstoons 16s, ould sleads 20s, an ould axe 18 6d.....................	01	17	06
It Logg Wheeles 50s, yoakes and Chaines & a Cleuis 14s......................	03	04	00
It 17 Cattle at 31: 13: 00, but Abigaile Heards portion taken out, yn remains..	11	13	00
	£50	09	06
It 8 swine 5£: 10: 00, 1 Chest 2 sackes 13s 6d, his house & land bought of Nathell Lord, & joynes to John Heards farme at Sturgeon Cricke, Twenty too pounds, 1 tenant Saw 5s...	28	08	06
	78	18	00

PART I, FOL. 40.

More to bee Added/

a grant for 50 Acres of Land in the woods six pounds, an Addition to his mothers farme unknown to us 20s.	07	00	00
To Thomas Roads his bill for Thirty pounds	30	00	00
James Smith, bill 20s.	01	00	00
	38	00	00
Capt Geo: Broughtons & Richd Otis yr bill for 120000 foo'e of Mrchanble pine boards, onely flueteene thousand foote payd	120	00	0
of the bill, which are to bee deducted 15£.	015	00	00
Due	105	00	00
It to one Mare to be Added one pound 10s.	01	10	00
	£106	10	00

James Emery Senior/

Elizabeth Chadborne doth at attest vpon her oath that this is a true Inventory of the Estate of James Chadborne her husband deceased, according to best of her knowledg, & if afterwards more do appeare shee will bring it in vpon the same oath/ Taken vpon oath this 27ᵗʰ May 1686: In Court as Attests Edw: Rishworth Recor:

78	18	0
38	00	0
120	00	0
01	10	0
07	00	0
245	08	0

A true Coppy of this Inventory transcribed & with yᵉ Originall Compared this 6ᵗʰ June 1686:

p Edw: Rishworth ReCor:

more given in by Mis Champnown in Cattle to bee added to John Hills Inventory recorded pa: 18: as followeth July 7:86/

Inprs 2 Heffers of three years ould, 2 small Cattle of Two years ould,
It too small yearelings |

as Attests Edw: Rishworth/

Kittery in New England ffebru: 19ᵗʰ 167$\frac{5}{8}$/
An Inventory of the Estate of William Dyamont, deceased/

Inprs Twenty Acres of Land, lijng between Mr Cutts his Land, & Thomas Wills his Land, neare Cooked lane, wrof tenn acres by Town Grant, wrby it comes to bee nalewed at	40	00	00
It 4 Cows 10£ & 2 young Cattle vnder one years ould 30s.	11	10	00
It flue swine flue pounds, two sheepe 20s.	06	00	00
It 2 small feather bedds, & one bowlster at seauen pounds	07	00	00
It ould Ruggs 20s: 3 feather pillows 1 peyre of Cotton sheetes one bowlster drawer & one pillow drawer Too pounds tenn shillings	3	10	00

Part I, Fol. 40.

It 2 peyre of blanketts 20s, a downe bed & two pillows 20s.....................	02	00	0
2 Chests & 3 Chares 18s Pewter & Clome 15s.................................	03	03	0
It one suite of Curtains 10s, to his own weareing Cloaths 50s..................	3	00	0
It Three small Iron potts & a kettle thirty shillings.........	01	10	0
It 2 brass Kettles, 1 Grediron too skelletts 40s, & a fowling gunn at thirty shillings..	03	10	0
40lb of Cotton woll 30s & wodden wares at 12s.............................	02	02	0
It too Tramells, one peyre of Tonges & a spitt all at..........................	00	10	0
It one two handed saw, & an hand saw 10s, 2 ould axes 2 Hamers 6s...........	0	16	0
It one bettle Ring & Wedges foure shillings...................................	0	04	0
	£85	05	0

Joane Dyament giues in vpon her oath that this is a true Inventory of her husbands Estate, according to the best of her knowledg, & If more come to her remembrance afterwards vpon the 'same oath shee will bring it in/ Taken in Court 1: of Aprill 1679: as Attests Edw: Rishworth
             ReCor:

vera Copia transcribed p Edw: Rishworth ReCor:

An Invenory of the Estate formerly Thom^s Crocketts, now deceased as it was shewd unto vs whose names are vnderwritten, this 20th day of March 167$\frac{8}{9}$

	£	s	d
Inprs one Necke of Land, neare unto Spruse Cricke, bounded at the head with a little Ysland, & doth Containe as we do judg one hundred eighty eight Acres, or yr abouts at 50s p Acre...................................	141	00	0
It one horse 50s, one Heffer at three pounds....	005	10	0
It To six acres of Marsh or yr abouts at tenn pounds........................	10	00	0
It to Iron potts, a pott hooke, & Crookes at................................	01	00	0
It 3 Chests & things in them 12s, Earthen & wodden ware 13s................	01	05	0
It a spitt, two ould axes betle rings and other Iron...........................	00	10	0
It a frijnpann 4s, & other seuerall ould Calkes 6s....	00	10	0
It 4 pewter dishes, one Cupp, bason & Candlesticke at.......................	00	11	00
It one Gryndstone & too baskette 3s 6d, a Cubbard 2s 6d	01	06	00
It too Wedges 2s 6d, Cloathing lining and Wollen 40s.......................	02	2	6
It a debt due from Ephraim Crockett...	07	00	0
It an ould Connow at 16s...	00	16	0
	170	10	06

apprised by us the day & yeare aboue written/
    Francis Hooke/ William Scriuine/

Ann Crocket giues in vpon her oath in Court, that this is a true Inuentory of her husbands Estate, & if more appeare

Part I, Fol. 41.

afterwards shee vpon the same oath will giue it in/ taken in Court 1: of Aprill 1679: as Attests Edw: Rishworth
ReCor:

[41] An Inventory of the Estate of Nathaniell Trustrum deceased, taken this 4th of March 167$\frac{8}{9}$

	£	s	d
The house land & Marsh apprized at	12	00	00
It one Gale & halfe of one Gale	06	00	00
It 2 shirts 5s, one brass Kettle 25s, 3 50s, 1 Iron square 2s	04	02	0
It barrells of Indean Corne 14s, 1 busll of meale 2s 6d one bridle 5s	01	01	6
It one Hatt 8s, 2 yds ½ of scarge 15s, 4 yds Dimitty 8s	01	11	0
It 1 peyre of Dimitty breeches, 1 shirt 2 Necke Cloaths, 2 handkerchiefs	0	14	0
It bla: Coate 30s, one peyre of french fall shoes fiue & 6d	01	15	6
It 2 pistolls & one peyre of Howlsters at 18s	00	18	0
	28	02	0
It more 1 yd of Curle 18d, one Hamers & 2 Raysors 4s			
It one peyre of shott moulds 5s, one fyle 6d Molesses 11s	01	02	0
It 1 booke 18d, buttons & Silke 2s	00	03	6
It 1 Cow one Calfe & yeareling 6£: 5: 00, one horse at 3£, 10s, 0d	09	15	0
It An halfe boate & furniture 7£ an ould Raper at 3s	07	03	0
It an ould Chest at 2s	00	02	0
	46	07	6

A true Coppy transcribed & Compared with y^e originall this 11th of Aprill 1679: p Edw: Rishworth ReCor:

March 4th 167$\frac{8}{9}$

An Inventory taken of the Estate of Ralph Trustrum late of Winter harbour deceased/

Inprs Too feather bedds one bowlster 5£ 6 blanketts one Rugg 30s			
It 2 shirts 6s one p·tt & Crookes 12s, one Iron Kettle 2s 6d	07	10	6
It one brass Kettle 7s, 1 frijupane 7s, 1 pewter flaggon bason & plate 8s	01	02	0
It 1 peyre of Andirons 1 fyre shouell 6s, 2 Hatts 8s, 1 Chamberpott 3s	00	17	0
It 1 brass skellett 8s Iron Crookes & hangers 3s, ould spikes & nayls 2s	00	08	0
It Cross cutt saws & 1 peyre of shoes 9s 6d	00	09	6
It 3 Towells 18d 1 plow share a Copps yoaks staples & rings 8s	00	09	6
It 1 skirt 1 s, the house goods & Meddow 60£	60	10	0
It the house stage & moreing 16£ to halfe an yeareling at 15s	16	15	0
It to one halfe of a boate and furniture 7£ one Grindstoone & a Rugg 36s	08	16	0
It 2 Whitte blanketts 20s, 8 yds sleasy holland 24s. 3s p yd	02	04	0
It 2 ould sheets 5s, 6 napkines 20s, 3 pillow bears 1 table Cloath 8s	01	13	0
It 7 pewter platters & one bason 21s, 3 porrengers 3s, 1 pewter pott & 6 platts 7s	01	13	0
It 3 panted dishes 2s, an ould chest 4s, to 1 whit shifft & a blew scarfe 7s	0	13	0
It an ould silke Necke Cloath 2s, 3 Cod lynes 9s 1 dozen of Cod hookes 5s	00	16	0
It 1 bible & 4 small bookes 12s, to one new hatt 10s	01	02	0
It 2 peyre of drawers 1 peyre of briches, one Coate & wast Coate all at	02	00	0
It one bed & bowlster 3£, 5s, 0, one Iron pott & Kettle 25s, 1 barell of oyle 22s	05	12	0
It 2 Chests 2s, to a quantity of Molosses 11s too Iron Wedges 2s	00	15	0
	113	03	0⁶

Part I, Fol. 41.

Dominicus Jordan giveth in vpon his oath y⁺ this is true Inventory of Ralph Trustrum his Estate deceased, & if hee find any more belonging thereunto vpon the same oath hee will bring it in/

Taken in Court 1: Aprill 1679: as Attests

Edw: Rishworth ReCor:

vera Copia transcribed & Compared this 12ᵗʰ of Aprill 1679: p Edw: Rishworth Re:Cor:

Winter Harbour Janv: 25ᵗʰ 167$\frac{8}{9}$ An Inventory taken of the Estate of Benjã: Trustrum/

one ye other side	45	9	6
Inprs 114 yds of Canvice at 20d p yd 9: 10: 00 13 new Cod lynes new 3s p Line 01: 19: 00	11	09	00
It 7 doz: of Hookes at 2s p doz 14s 6 fishing lines apprised 8s	01	02	00
It 6 yds of Colord Callico 6s, a Compass 2s, 1 Razer 3s	00	11	00
It powder 18d about 80lb of shott at 3d p lb 20s, 3 ould lynes 3s a Nett 30s	02	14	6
It Ditto 15s, 2 n w lynes 5s, 6 barells of Micharell at 16s p barrell 4: 16: 0	05	16	00
It Three barrels of porke at nine pounds	09	00	0
It 4 barells ¼ of Tarr 27s, 72lb of Cordidge 6d p lb, 8: 6: 0	04	13	0
It Three new Empty barrells 6s, 5 9 Inch blockes 3s, 9d, 5 6 Inch blocks 2s 6d	00	12	3
It 4 7 Inch Blockes 2s 4d, Judgd about 11 Hogsheads of sault 8£: 5:	08	07	4
It foure pounds of Twine 6s, 2 squid lyns 3s	00	09	00
It 13 doz: ¼ of pewter buttones 9s 11 glasses at 6d p glass 5s 6d	00	14	6
It 12 rings 2s, 3 doz: of Hooks 8s, 9d, 10), 3 qrs 18d nales, 2s 7d	00	13	04
It 2C: 3qr: 6lbs of bread at 16s p C, 45s, 2 Cows & 2 yearling Calfs 9: 10: 0 in Jon Sargents hands	11	15	00
ffish to bee Weighd at Present Judgd to bee 25 qntills			
It one New Anker 25s, one ould Grapnell at 1d ¼ p lb 7s 6d	01	12	6
	59	09	11
It A Deck'd boate, Roade 2 Ankers fore sale & apprtenances			
It & one shallope, 1 Roade 2 Ankers Mayne sale & Riggine nalewd	45	00	0
	104	09	11

These to whome these may Concerne do testify y⁺ I Syluanus Dauis did take yᵉ Inventory aboue expressed, for yᵉ behalfe of Majoʳ Thoˢ Clarke of Boston, the sd Clarke to Administer on sd Estate, & to giue an Accomᵗ to yᵉ Court & yʳ to giue a Just Accomᵗ to the whoole disposeing of the sd Estate, as aboue expressed, & wᵗ else shall appeare, that yᵉ

Part I, Fol. 42.

sd Clarke shall receiue vpon y⁰ Accōt of sd Estate, as witness my hand this 25th of Janva: 1678 : p mee Siluanus Dauis
agent for Majo^r Thos Clarke/

This is a True Coppy as Attests/   Siluanus Dauis/

More one Gunn 20s one gunne 10s | 01 10 00
One halfe of the house & Stage Rowme, belonging to Ralph Trustrum, hee gaue ye halfe to Benja: Trustrum | 08: 00: 0 |

Bryan Pendleton
John Sargeant his
marke ◠

as Attests John Sargeant his marke ◠

The 2 new Lines In the Inventory is Geo: Joanes/

George Joanes his marke ✚

           s d
more 50lb of Lead at 3d plb   12 6
19 gallons of wine at 20d p
Gallon.................... 01 11 8
         02 4 2

01 10 00
08 00 00
&underline;2 04 2&underline;
11 14 02

besids the fish not as yett apprised/

104 9 11
&underline;11 14 2&underline;
116 04 01

Totall some is

A true Coppy of this Inventory transcribed & with the originall Compared, the 21th of Aprill 1679 :

p Edw: Rishworth ReCor:

[42]   Aprill third 1679 :

An Inventory of the Lands of Mr Henery Norton formerly deceased/

The Land & Pasture lijng at ye home Lott about 9 or tenn Acres more or less.
Tenn Acres of vpland on ye North side of Scituate high way granted by Mr. Will: Hooke, part yrof planted & Improued............................
Tenn Acres granted by the Town on the sam ; side of Scituate high way......
Twenty acres of vpland granted by the Town of york lijng behind Scituate feild part wrof was planted and improued............................
Six acres more of vpland was granted by Mr. Vines being on the North side of Scituate high way............................
One Parcell of Marsh lijng on the North West branch of the East side of yorke Riuer............................
About the quantity of flue or six Acres of Meddow more or less, lijng from or by the Mouth of th ould Mill Cricke on the South side of Yorke Riuer, so fare vp the sd Riuer as Mr. Rishworths Marsh ouer against Allexandr Maxells............................
ffourty Acres of vpland upon the South west branch of the Easterne side of Yorke Riuer granted by Mr. Godfrey, Adjoyneing to ye side of Phillip Addams his Land............................
It Sixty Acres of Land lijng upon the South West side of of Cape Nuttacke Riuer, between Siluester Stouers Land & the Land of Nichols Greene & part thereof lijng at ye head of Nicholas Greens his lot of vpland.......

Part I, Fol. 43.

A true Coppy transcribed & Compared with the originall, this 15th of August 1679 : p Edw : Rishworth Re :Cor :
[The second page of this folio is blank]

[43] Kittery in the county of yorke
1675 July 22

Know all men by these presents that I Thomas Wither of the same towne and Countrey aforesaid haue and doe by these presents giue vnto my Daughter Mary and Thomas Rice her husband in consideration of their Marriage after my Decease a tract of land lieing and being on the northeast side of pascatque river where the said Withers now dwells begining at the Water side at the corner of Robert Mendums orchard and so to Goe on a northeast line 276 rod to a bound marke tree which is the bound-marke betweene the said Withers & Mendum and from y^t corner tree to a marke tree y^t is the wester bounds of Eagle point lott and so far as the said Withers his land goes, to the southermost extent of his breadth that way and then the breadth being Measured over the neck Justly I doe hereby these presents giue vnto my sone in law Thomas Rice & Mary his wife in Consideration of their Marriage after my Decease, the one halfe of the foresd tract of land vnto the said Thomas & Mary his wife vnto them their heires executors Administrators ore assignes for ever from me my heires executors administrators & assignes ore any from by ore vnder mee whatsoever with all the priveledges therevnto belonging ore any way appertayning with all the houseing Gardens orchards, feilds, meadowes, pastures timber woods vnder woods, and whatsoever therevnto belongeth vnto the only vse and behoofe of the sd Thomas Rice and Mary his wife for their heires and Assignes forever from me my heires executors or assigns whatsoever and furthermore the

Part I, Fol. 43ᵃ.

said Withers doth Ingadge myselfe for the said premises be free and Clearer from all bargaines Gifts Grants mortgadges sales whatsover from all manner of psons for ever in Witness my hand and seale the Day and yeare aboue written

    Witnes   Tho Withers
    John Deament   (seale)
    Samll Knight

                    february the 25 16$\frac{8}{8}$

Jnº Diamond and Samuell Knight personally appeared before me and made oath that they saw Thomas Withers signe seale and deliver the aboue Instrument as his act & deed and that Mrs Jane Withers his Wife and their Daughter Elizabeth was present and heard the same read and shewed no dislike therat but seemed verry well satisfied therewith:

                               Francis Hooke Just. pe

The aboue writen is a true Coppie of the originall Deed of Tho Withers to his sone and daughter Rice with the wittnesses oathes thereto as attests

    July 29·1690//   John Wincoll Recordr

[43ᵃ]   page (1)
               [The first page of this folio is blank]

                   An Inventory of the Estate of John Moor
July 27th
  1686   deceased as it was taken & apprized by us undr-written

	£	s	d
To a Catch & furniture now riding in ye Road	55	00	00
To 85 Qt of Summer at 10s p Quintall	45	00	00
To one Canoa, & Gundeloa	03	00	00
To one Iron Beame for gt Skailes	01	00	00
To one dwelling house & Land with othr small buildings	80	00	00
To 50 Acres of Land in Spruce Crick	60	00	00
To 11 Peuter Platters & a Bason	02	08	00
To 6 plates 5 porringers, one Candlestick & other peutr	00	18	00

Part I, Fol. 43ᵇ.

To a Iron pot, a Kettle, & frying pan...	01	08	00
To 3 Iron Wedges, 2 beetle Rings, & ould Ax...................................	00	07	00
To a table board, 6 chayrs, & other old wooden ware..........................	01	00	00
To 3 feather beds, with their furniture much worne...........................	18	00	00
To 2 Chests, one Cupboard...	02	00	00
To one Warmping pan...	00	07	00
To his wearing Cloaths...	08	00	00
To 12 yds of Serge..	02	00	00
To a silver Tanker, a Beaker, 2 dram cups, four silver spoones...............	09	00	00
To a Qradrant scale & other sea Instruments....................................	01	00	00
To peices of Kentin & bream..	02	10	00
To Cows 8£, 2 yearlings 45s, a Mare 2£, 15s, 0 4 swine at 3£, 15s, 0d......	18	10	00
	£321	08	00

      William Screven.
      Roger Dearing.
 A true Copy of the Originall Inventory transcribed, & compared by me this 8ᵗʰ of October 1686
           Tho: Scottow Clericˢ
One line left out in the Inventory as above

To Service of one Servtman being one year..	00	10	00

  which sd sum makes up the Totall, 321£ 8s
      as above p me Tho Scottow Clericum.

 [**43ᵇ**] [The first page of this folio is blank.]
 An Inventory of the lands and Chattells of Samuell Lord late of Barwick Deceased November 20ᵗʰ 1689//

	£	s	d
His wearing Cloathes...	05	00	00
a Dwelling house barne & fortie acres of land adjoining to it.................	36	00	00
Two oxen at...	06	10	00
Two Heifers...	03	00	00
One Cow	02	05	00
Two Calues..	01	10	00
The halfe of a grindlestone..	00	02	00
	54	07	00

 Apprised this first Day of march 16⁸⁹⁄₉₀
    By vs   John Wincoll
           Benjamin Barnard
 Abraham Lord presented the aboue Inventory to the Court of sessions and tooke oath to the truth of it and If any more estate appeare that he will ad it therevnto: March 4ᵗʰ 16⁸⁹⁄₉₀ as Attests
          John Wincoll Cleric͠:

Part I, Fol. 44.

The aboue written is a true Coppy of the originall Inventory & therewith Compared this 18th Day of of February 16 89/90   p me John Wincoll Record{r}

[44] An Inventory of the Estate of John Endell late of y{e} town of Kittery in the province of mayne Deceased Taken and apprized the 7th Day of July 1690//

Inprs one new sarge coate & one old Coate & jaquet	01	14	06
Two old Hats	00	02	06
one pair of shoes	00	02	06
four yards of Linen cloath at 20d p yard	00	06	08
A small remnant of fustian	00	01	03
a sword belt & bandeliers	00	08	00
Three powder horues a qur of a pound of pouder Shot puch bullets & other small trifles	00	02	00
one paire of Sarge britches	00	02	00
one red Wascoate	00	04	00
one old Stuff coate	00	02	06
one old Carsey coate 5s & one old Jaquett	00	05	06
two shirts and two air of Drawers	00	08	00
one old p of stockens	00	00	06
Two heifers and two calues	03	10	00
Seaven old ewes & 4 Lambs	01	13	00
Two horses	05	00	00
one old axe	00	01	00
Two old Neckcloathes	00	00	04
a parcell of sheeps wooll vnwashed	00	07	00
one syth	00	03	00
a parcell of Timber	01	00	00
Seaven pigs	03	10	00
one White Wastcoate	00	07	00
Suma totalls	19	16	09

p the marke of: Nic{s} Weekes } Apri
William Hooke } zers

Province
of mayn

A true Coppie of the originall Inventory Transcribed & compared July. 30th 1690//
          p me John Wincoll Record{r}

Know all men by these p{r}sents that I Walter Boaden fisherman of the Iles of Showles viz{t}: of Smuttinose in the countie of portsmouth being by Gods providence at the house of George Litten of the towne of Kittery in the Countie of yorke & of firme memory & Vnderstanding Doe make this my last will and testam^t vizt:

Inprimis I Dispose of my outward Estate in maner as followeth vizt: my will is that all my debts be duely and truely paid by my Executor

2. I giue & bequeath all my estate whatsoevor vnto my verry Loving frends George Litten and Sarah his Wife & my Will is that all those that haue any estate of mine in their custodie or that Doe owe any Debt vnto me Doe deliver & pay the same vnto the sd Litten or his Wife after my Decease vppon their demand or either of them their heires Executors Admis^{trs} or Assignes in species as the same is to be delivered or paid vnto me

3^d I doe Nomi^{te} and appoint the abouesd George Litton of the town of Kittery in the Countie of yorke to be the Executor to this min Last will & testament and doe here by Injoine him faithfully to performe all and every of the premises aboue mentioned in Wittnes Whereof I haue here vnto set my hand and seale the eighteenth Day of Sebt^{br} in the yeare of o^r lord god one thousand six hundr^d seventy six

The Marke of 𝒽 John Shepard

The Marke of 𝒻 John Morgradge

John Morgradg & John Shepard appeared before vs & tooke oath that they saw Walter Boaden signe and deliver the aboue written as his last Will & tes^t he being then in a disposeing capacitie this 7th day of May 1690

    Francis Hooke John Wincoll: Jus^{tes} of peac
   As attest Jno Wincoll Cleric:

The aboue written is a true coppie of the original will and witnesses oathes transcribed & compared this 30th Day of July 1690//

    John Wincoll Record^r

PART I, FOL. 45.

The Chest & goods of Walter Boaden apprized by John Shepard & John Alcock vppon their oath May 7th 1690 amounts to 14£. 1s. 2d as attests Jn° Wincoll: Cleric:

[45] Province An Inventory of the Estate of Joseph
of main Whinick late of Scarburough deceased

Imprs 2 Iron pots and pot hookes....	00	15	00
a water bucket and a ladle.	00	01	00
2 Woodden Dishes and a crooke.	00	02	00
a heifer of two yeares old.	01	10	00
a young cow.	02	00	00
	04	08	06

Apprized July 15 1690 p vs Elihu Crocket
Joseph Crocket

Sarah Whinick relict of the aboue Joseph Whinick appeared before Francis Hooke & John Wincoll Justces of the peace & gaue oath that the aboue written is a true Inventory of the estate of her husband Joseph Whinick deceased & If any more shall appeare shee will ad it hervnto
July 15 1690 : as attests John Wincoll Cleric:

Sarah Whinicke & Elihu Crocket bind themselues to our soueraigne lord the King in the penall sum of eight pound seaventeene shillings sterling that the said Sarah Whinick shall administer on sd estate according to law/ July 15 1690/ as Attests Jn° Wincoll Cleric:

The aboue written are true Coppies of yr originalls Transcribed & compared July 30 1690//
p me John Wincoll Recordr

To all Christian people to whom these presents shall Come Wee James Gibbons of the towne of Kittery in the province of maine And Thomas Gibbons sone and heire to the said

PART I, FOL. 45.

James Gibbons send Greetting &c : Know ye that wee the said Thomas and James for and in Consideration of the Naturall loue & affection wee haue and doe beare vnto Elizabeth Sharpe Daughter to the said James Gibbons, sister to the said Thomas Gibbons and Grandchild to Mr Thomas Lewes deceasd Haue Giuen & Granted and by these presents doe Giue grant Enfeoffe and confirme vnto the said Elizabeth Sharpe and her heires for ever All that tract or parcell of Land Containing about one Hundred acres lyeing and being in the town of Sacoe in the foresaid province bounded with Sacoe river on the Southwest, land of Hubertus Mattoon on the northwest, and land late in the possession of Edmond Andrewes on the South part thereof, together with a parcell of Marsh adjoining to ye sd land lyeing between the sd land and the sd river of an equall breadth with the sd land, And also one other parcell of marsh lieing in the said town of Sacoe bounded with a run of water comonly called fresh water Crick on the Southwest and Marsh of John Bonigtons on the Northwest part therof together with all wayes, waters water courses woods vnderwoods comons profits priviledges and advantages whatsoever to the same belonging or in any wise apertayning And the reversion and revertions Remainder and Remainders therof and all the Estate right title and Interest of vs the said James Gibbons and Thomas Gibbons or either of vs of in or to the said parcells of land and marsh or any part therof, To Haue and To Hold all and singular the said parcells of land and marsh vnto the said Elizabeth Sharp for and during her Naturall life and after her Decease the one moyety or halfe part thereof to be equally devided amongst so many of the Children of the sd Elizabeth Sharp as shall be then liveing, to them and their heires and assignes for ever and the other moyetie to the proper heires of the said Elizabeth Sharp for ever and to and for none other vses intents

Part I, Fol. 46.

or purposes whatsoever And further wee the said Thomas Gibbons and James Gibbons and our heires all and singular the abouesaid hereby giuen and granted parcells of land and Marsh to the said Elizabeth and her heires to the vses aforesaid against all people shall and will-warrant and forever defend by these presents: And further Know ye that wee the said James and Thomas haue put the said Elizabeth Sharp in possession of the sd premises In Witness wherof wee haue herevnto set our hands and seales [**46**] the seaventeenth Day of July in the yeare of our lord God one thousand Six hundred and ninety/

          The marke of
      James   Gibbons
       (a seale)

   Sealed and delivered by the within named
    James Gibbons in the presence of vs
          John Wincoll

Memorandum that this day being the eighteenth Day of July Año dom one thousand six hundred ninety the within named Thomas Gibbons gaue his free consent to the within writeing and relinquished all his right and title to the within land and Marsh and did then Engadge for himselfe and his Heires not to molest or trouble the said Elizabeth Sharp or her heires in the possession or enjoyment of the said premises/ Before mee & in the presence of Francis Hooke Just pea John Wincoll William Hooke	Elihu Gunnison William Hooke July 18th 1690 James Gibbons personally appeared before me and owned the within Instrument to be his act and Deed Francis Hooke Just pea

Part I, Fol. 46.

Province of main: This is a true Coppie of the originall Deed as it is written in parchment and now transcribed and therewith compared this first Day of August 1690   p me John Wincoll Record^r

The last Will and testament of John Bray of Kittery in the province of maine in New England
January 22. 1688.89
In the name of god Amen

I John Bray being sensible of my frailty of mortallitie & yet retaining my perfect reason & vnderstanding for the preventing of all trouble about the worldly estate that god hath blessed me with I doe constitute and appoint this following as my last will and testament

Imp: I doe giue vnto my loueing Wife Joan Bray the house in Plimouth in England & the rent of it to be hers & at her Dispose only with y^t limitation that it goe to some of my Children at her Decease/ Also I giue vnto my loueing Wife Joan Bray the new end of my now Dwelling house in Kittery Dureing the terme of her naturall life and at her Decease I giue it to my son John

It. I giue vnto my sone John Bray my fiftie acres of land or thereabout giuen to me by the towne adioining to Cap$\bar{t}$ Hookes land lieing spruce creeke Also I giue vnto my sone John the Midle part of my now Dwelling house adjoining to the new end and my building yard & the bed and Chest & Court Cubbard that stands in the Esterly end of my house & this in reference to wages Due to him Also I doe freely to my sone John al my tooles Instruments and tackling y^t belongs to building of vessells

3 I giue to my wife Joan Bray & to my sone John Bray Jointly and equally in partnership my farme at braueboat harbour vpland & marsh except so much marsh as hereafter

excepted & otherwise Disposed/ also I giue to my wife and sone the land belonging to my house being about 24 acres in Joint & equall partnership excepting the building yard before expressed & what shall be afterwards excepted Also I giue to my wife and son Jointly my 2 barnes & all my stock & all my household goods excepting what is before giuen to my son Distinctly & what shall be afterward Excepted

4 I giue to my daughter Joan Dearing ye one halfe of y^t piece of marsh y^t lies betweene 2 points at braueboat harbour Also I giue her a piece of land lieing in the southeast corner of my land ouer against my house runing from the said corner to the barrs & backe to the old fence be it two acres more or less with this proviso that after her Decease both these parcells of land revert & returne to her Eldest sone John Dearing

5. I doe giue to my Daughter Margery Pepperill besides the land already giuen the other halfe of that peece of marsh lieing between 2 points at braue boat harbour aboue mentioned which after her decease is to revert & returne to her sone Andrew Pepperill

6 I doe giue to my Daughter Mary Bray a peice of marsh lyeing at brauboat harbour bought of John Andrews and his mother only reserving a highway for the carrieing of timber and hay, also I giue her the Grassie feild at the northeast corner of my land lieing over against my house from the back Creeke [47] to the land giuen my Daughter Deering and westward to the old fence Also I giue her part of my Dwelling house vizt: the leantoo & Chamber over it & the east roome & as much of the chamber as is over that yet it is to be vnderstood that If the said Mary Dye without heires of her body y^t what is giuen to her shall at her decease revert & returne to my son John Bray and his heires. Also it is my Will that when she comes to be Married shee shall

haue one of my cowes, And further that shee shall haue the one halfe of the Garden that we now Emproue

And lastly it is my Will that all my debts should be paid and al y^t is that is owing to me should be receiued by my wife Joan Bray and by my sone John Bray whom I doe desire & appoint to Execute this my last will & testament And it is my desire that Capt: Francis Hooke and Mr Benj: Woodbridge may be overseers

Witnesses Benj: Woodbridge   John Bray (seale)
Francis Hooke

Memorand: that this Day being the 15th Day of July 1690 m^r Benjamin Woodbridge personally appeared before me and made oath that the within written Will was written by this deponent and dictated by the testator and y^t he saw the sd testator m^r John Bray deceased signe and seale ye same as his act and Deed and that he was at that time Compos Mentis and not any wayes disturbed in his mind but as full in his sences as at any other time of his

Mr Benjamin Woodbridge   Francis Hooke Just: pea:
owned his aboue oath   John Wincoll Jus: pea
before mee

Capt Francis Hooke Gaue oath in Court July: 15: 1690 that he was present and saw the within named testator John Bray signe seale and deliver the within Instrument as his last Will and testament when he was in a Disposeing Capacitie

                as attests John Wincoll Record^r

Province of
maine   This is a true Coppie of the originall Will and of the probat therof transcribed and therewith Compared this first Day of August 1690:

             p me John Wincoll Record^r

Part I, Fol. 47.

An Inventory of the lands tenements & Chattells of Mr John Bray Deceased : New England January 31 16⁸⁹⁄₉₀

	£		
Imprimis The home lott of land qty 24 acres apprised at 20s p acre.............	24	00	00
The lot of land lying at bradford harbour qty 116 acres of vpland and Marsh at 5s p acre vpland marsh 40s p acre..	60	00	00
The lot of land at spruse creeke qty 50 acres at 5s an acre....................	07	10	00
All they housing and Tenements........ :	100	00	00
Foure oxen 3 cowes & 1 heifer 2 horses 1 mare 2 steares of 2 yeares old 1 of a year old 14 yewes............	030	10	00

Household goods

In the Haull some Goods and furniture.......................................	030	00	05
In the Linto Chamber...	005	03	00
In the Kitching brass puter Iron pots & other nesesarys........	020	09	00
In the bed Chamber...	005	17	00
In the Haull Chamber...	006	00	07
In the porch Chamber...	002	10	00
Plate 9 peeces..	009	00	00
foure hogs 2 yeares old, 3 ditto of a yeare old..............................	005	10	00
	306	10	00

A true appraisment made by William Fernald
        Roger Dering
        John Bly/

July : 15th 1690

Mrs Joan Bray appeared before vs and gaue oath that the within writen Inventory is a true Inventory of the estate of her Husband John Bray late of Kittery deceased and If any more Estate shall hereafter appeare that shee will ad it herevnto

Province of maine   Francis Hooke ⎱ Justices
        John Wincoll ⎰ of ye peace
    as attests John Wincoll Cleric⁓

This is a true coppie of the originall Inventory & oath transcribed and therwith compared August 2^d 1690/
       p me John Wincoll Record^r

Part I, Fol. 48.

[48] To all Christian people to whom this Deed of morgage shall Come Nathaniell ffryer of piscataway river in New England Merch' sendeth Greeting Know ye that I the said Nathaniell ffryer for and in Consideration of the sume of four hundred pounds in Curant money of New England to him in hand well and truely paid by Robert Bronsdone of Boston in New England aforesaid Merch^{t} the receite wherof he doth hereby acknowledge and himselfe therewith to be fully satisfied and contented and therof and of & from every part and parcell thereof for himselfe his heires Executors and Administrators doth Exofiate acquit and discharge the said Robert Bronsdon his heires Executors Administrators and assignes firmly and forever by these presents hath Giuen Granted bargained sould Aliened Infeoffeed & Confirmed And by these presents doth fully freely Clearely and absolutely Giue grant bargaine sell Alien Infeoffee Convey & Confirme vnto the sd Robert Bronsdon his Heires Executors and Assigns all that his Island scittuate lieing and being on the Eastern side and at the mouth of the said river Comonly Called and Known by the name of Champeroons Iland which he the said which hee the said ffryer bought of Capt ffrancis Champeroone of piscataway river aforsd Gent: containing one thousand acres of land be it more or less Excepting Eightie acres of land lieing vppon the said Iland which the said ffryer hath giuen vnto his sone in law John Hinckes together with all houseing and buildings vpon ye sd Iland & all the land as well vpland as marsh or meadow sault and fresh to sd Iland belonging and all the wood vnderwood timber and timber trees mines mineralls liberties priviledges Immunities and appertenances w'soever to the said Iland belonging or in any wise appertaining and also all the stock of cattle both great and small being vppon the sd Iland to say twentie cowes three breeding mares foure oxen

This is a coppie of a Deed Brought to me by Major Davese Dept president and Entred into the records this 17th Day of August 1680 p me John Wincoll Recordr

foure and twentie sheepe foure hogges and all other Catle now being vppon the said said Iland of what Kind soever all which Iland Excepting as before excepted and all other the afore bargained premises and Appurtenances he the said Robert Bronsdon his to haue and to hold and peacably to possess and to him his heires Executors Administrators and assignes forever to his and their sole and proper vse benefit and behoofe from henceforth for ever and the said Nathaniell ffryer for himselfe his heires Executors and Administrators doth covenant promise and grant to and with the said Robert Bronsdon his heires his heires Executors Administrators and assignes that he the said Nathaniell ffryer is the true right sole and proper owner of the aforesd Iland and of all and singular other the bargaind premises and appurtenances and hath in himselfe full power good right and lawfull authoritie the same to giue grant bargane sell alien and confirme vnto the sd Robert Bronsdon his heires Executors and assignes in manner as aforesd and that the sd Iland and all other the bargained premises and appertenances, Excepting as before Excepted are at the sealing and Delivering of these presents free and Cleare and Clearely acquitted and Discharged off and from all former and other Gifts grants bargains sales leases morgadges Inventories Dowryes Wills Entailes Judgments Executions titles troubles acts alienations and Incombrances whatsoever and that y⁶ sd Robert Bronsdon his heires Executors and Administrators shall and may from henceforth for ever hereafter peaceably and quietly haue hold vse Emproue posess and Enjoy the aforsd Iland and other the aboue bargained premises and appertenances without the lett trouble hindrance Molestation or Disturbance of him the said Nathaniell ffryer his heires Executor Administrators or assignes or of any other parson lawfully Claiminge any right thereto or Interest therein from by or vnder them or any or either of them and that hee the said Nathaniell ffryer shall and will warrant the said Iland

and other the barganed premises to him the said Robert Bronsdon his heires Executors and assignes for ever by these presents, Provided allwayes and it is the true intent of these presents that If the sd ffryer his heires Executors administrators or assigns doe doe or shall well and truely pay or cause to be paid vnto the aboue named Robert Bronsdon or to his atturney his heires Executors Administrators and assignes the full and whole summ of four hundred Eighty and fiue pounds in Currant Mony of New England at or before the fiue and twentieth Day of october which will be in the yeare of our lord one thousand six hundred and ninety one with the Interest that shall be due vppon all to be paid in bosto aforesaid and the Interest after the rate of six p cent at the end of every twelue month during the sd terme then this Deed of Morgage is to be vtterly void and of none Effect to all intents and purposes But in default therof to stand remaine and abide in full pouer force strength and vertue in witness whereof the sd Nathaniell ffryer hath herevnto set his hand and seale this six and twenty Day of october Anno Domine 1688/ Anoque Regis Jacobi Secundi Angle & quarto

Signed sealed & deliv^r d
  in ye p^r sence of vs
    Jonathan Evans
    Joseph Bronsdon
    Thomas Kemble

Acknowledged ye 26 of october 1688 the instrument aboue written
    Edw Randolph :

Memorandum y^t wheras there is mentioned aboue all other Catle of what Kind soever it is to be vnderstood y^t ye s^d Fryer make over only twenty Cowes three breeding mares four oxen four and twenty sheepe and foure hogs
    Nathaniell Fryer (seale)

Part I, Fol. 49.

Jonathan Evans apeared before m3 the 9th of octob' 1690 & made oath y' he saw m' Nathaniell Fryer seal & signe this aboue Instrum' as his act & deed and likewise saw Jos : Brondon & Tho Kemble sign with my self taken vpon oath the Day aboue writen   John Daves Dep' p'sdent

[49] To all Xtian people to whom these p'sents shall come Greeting, Know ye That I Walter pennywell of Winter harbour in the towne of Sacoe in the Province of Maine in New England weaver for and in Consideration of the summe of Thirteen pounds Currant money of New England to me in hand paid before thensealing & delivery of these p'sents by Edward Sergeant of Winter harbour in the towne and province aforesaid Planter the receipt whereof I doe hereby acknowledge and of every part and parcell thereof Doe Clearly acquitt and Discharge the said Edward Sergeant his heires and Assignes and every of them for ever, by these p'sents Haue giuen Granted Bargained sold Aliened Infeofed and Confirmed and by these presents Doth fully Cleerly and absolutely Giue grant bargaine sell alien Infeoffe and confirme vnto the said Edward Sergeant his Heires and assignes for ever All that fiftie acres of vpland lieing and being at litle Riuer formerly called Scadlocks river which said River boundeth the towne of Sacoe aforesd on the Westward side and is adjoining to the litle falls on a branch of the said river and also seaven acres of Marshland lieing and being neer the said litle river abbutting on the sea wall to the East ward and on the said litle river to the Westward and bounded with a parcell of Marsh in the possession of John Abbot to the Southward and with a litle Creeke from the said river to the Northward All which fifty acres of land and Marsh was purchased by my father Walter Pennywell

Part I, Fol. 49.

deceased of Major William Phillips as by his Deed reference therevnto being had may more plainly appeare And also all the Estate right title or Interest vse possession Claime and Demand whatsoever which I the said Walter Pennywell now haue may might should or in any wise ought to haue of in and to all and singular the said bargained p'mises or any part thereof together with all and singular Evidences Deeds Scripts Writeings and Muniments whatsoever concerning the same To Haue and To Hold all and singular the said fifty acres of vpland and seaven acres of Marsh land and all other the aforesaid p'mises and all and singular their appurtnances before in and by these p'sents Bargained and sold and every part and parcell therof to the said Edward Sergeant his heires and assignes for ever And the said Walter Pennywell for himselfe his heires Executors and administrators doth Covenant and grant to and with the said Edward Sergeant his heires & assignes by these p'sents in maner and and forme following that is to say that he the said Walter pennywell at the time of thensealing Hereof is and vntill the first Execution of an Estate to the said Edward Sergeant his heires and assignes by force of these presents shall stand and be lawfully seized to him his heires and Assignes of and in the before bargained p'mises and of and in every part and parcell thereof of a good sure lawfull and Indefeazible Estate of Inheritance And also that the said Walter Pennywell now hath full power good right and lawfull authoritie and true title to grant Alien Bargane sell and confirme the before bargained premises and every part & parcell thereof vnto the said Edward Sergeant his heires and assignes in manner and forme aforesaid and according to the true intent purport and meaning of these p'sents And further that the said granted and bargained premises and every part and parcell thereof on the Day of the Date hereof and from time to time and at all times hereafter for ever shall remaine and continew to the said Edward Sergeant his heires and assignes free and

Part I, Fol. 49.

Cleare and freely and Cleerly acquitted Exonerated and Discharged or otherwise by the said Walter Pennywell his heires and Assignes sufficiently saued and kept harmlesse or and from all and all manner of former bargaines sales Joynturs Dowers leases Annuities rent charge arrerages of rent Mortgadges Recognizances Judgments and Executions and of and from all other Charges titles troubles and Incumbrances whatsoever had made and Comitted suffered or done by the said Walter Pennywell his Heires or assignes And Lastly I the said walter Pennywell for my selfe my heires and assignes and all and every person or persons now haveing or lawfully Claiming or which shall hereafter rightfully any mañer of Estate right title or interest of in & to the said Bargained p'mises or any part thereof by from or vnder the said Walter pennywell his heires & assigns shall and will at all times hereafter for and during the terme of one yeare next ensueing the Date of these p'sents doe make acknowledge execute and suffer or cause to be made Done acknowledged executed and suffered all and every such further lawfull act or thing Device or devices Conveyance and assurances in the law as shall be by the said Edward Sergeant or his assignes or Councell learned in the law reasonably devised or required for the makeing of the said Bargained p'mises with the appurtenances sure vnto the said Edward Sergeant his heires and assignes for ever In Witness whereof I the said Walter Pennywell haue herevnto put my hand & seale This thirteenth Day of July Anno Domini 1687/ Annoq, RR^s Jacobi Secdi &c tertio :

Signed Sealed & deliv'd in the   the Marke of
Presence of vs George Turfrey   Walter P Pennywel (seale)
the marke of Roger H hill   a true coppy of the originall
          John Hill   Deed transcribed this 26 :
          Wm Milborne   Day of August 1690/
                       p me John Wincoll Record.

Part I, Fol. 50.

[**50**] The following words are wanting between the 24th & 25 lines on the other page vizt
for my selfe my heires Executors & administrators Doe Covnant and grant to and with the said Edward Sergeant his heires and assignes that I the said Walter pennywell

This following is on the back side of the Deed
vizt Possession was giuen to Edward Sergeant as it is within mentioned by turfe and twig by Walter Pennywell the fourteenth Day of July 1688

In the p^rsence of vs   Walter pennywell
 Samuell 2 Scadlock his ◯ marke
 John ⊗ Churchwell
  their marke

In the Name of god amen This twentie six Day of September one thousand six hundred & seaventy nine

I Thomas Withers the vnprofitable servant of god though weake in Body yet of good and perfect remembrance blessed be god, and knowing that I am naturally born to Dye & to pass from this Transitory life, Minding to put in order my estate to the intent there should be no striue for the same after my Decease I doe hereby make this to be my true last & only Will & testament in manner follō :

Imp^{rs} I comend my soule to almighty god & to his sone Jesus Christ my Saviour in whose precious bloud I set the whole and only hope of my salvation, my body in hope of a Joyfull resurection I comīt to the earth to be decently buried and touching the Distrebution of my mortall Goods I Dispose of as follō :

I will that all my debts should be satisfied

I giue vnto my beloved Wife Jane Withers the one halfe of all that I haue both of land & catle for the terme of her life vidz^t two oxen & two Cowes by name Star & Gentle & also my land next to goodman Diam^s which I giue her Dureing her life and afterwards to my Daughter Elizabeth: also I giue vnto my said Wife the Vse of Eagle point Dureing her life, afterwards to be forever my Daughter Elizabeths, also I giue vnto my Wife all that land on the Eastward side over against John Shapleighs between John Hole & Lewes During her life & afterwards to be my Daughter Elizebeths/ I give vnto my Daughter Mary Rice one one Red heifer/ I giue vnto my two Grand Children Alexander & Alice Shapleigh one red heifer

I giue vnto my sone in law John Shapleigh a neck of land Called Oake point with the marsh next his house

I Doe by these presents make & ordaine my welbeloved Wife aboue mentioned to be my sole Executrix of this my last will & testament herby giueing and bequeath vnto her all the remainder of my estate as household stuffe land & else which is not mentioned in this my will & testament

In testimony of which I haue here vnto set my hand & seale this twenty sixt Day of Septr 1679

Tho Withers (Seale)

The aboue written is a true coppie of the originall will of Mr Thomas Withers Transcribed and therewith compared This 30th Day of August 1690 p me John Wincoll Record^r

[51] Francis Hooke testifieth that the Will on the other side was writ by him and what was there written was nothing but what Mr Thomas Withers desired me to write to the verity of which I Doe herevnto set my hand this 30 of March 1685

Francis Hooke

Capt Francis Hooke testifies vppon his oath in Court to the truth of this Evidence aboue written relateing to Mr Withers his Will   As Attests Edw: Risworth Recor:

I William Heines Scoole Master, Bearing often Company with the Cheife author of this Instrument Mr Tho Withers

Part I, Fol. 51.

by name when I perceiving him Grow feeble & weakly Advised him to put his Worldly Estate in order If he had not, but he told me at sometimes he had & I had heard him confess to his Wife and Daughter but who had it I vnderstood not but gathering often by his Answers that Capt Hooke was the man he depended vpon as his trustee or overseer Witness my hand this 13th Day of ffeb: 84

Mr William Heines Came & Made oath to the veritie abouesd this 13th of ffebr: 168 4/5

Before me Francis Hooke Just pea:

a true Coppie of the probat of mr Thomas Withers his taken out of the originall & there with Compared this 30th Day of August 1690/ p me John Wincoll Recordr

the Inventory

The Inventory of all the goods lands and Chattells of Thomas Bragdon in yorke in the province of Main planter late Deceased had seen and praised by Arthur Cane and John Houie of the same parrish and province aforesd plantors the fourteenth of october 1690 as followeth

	£	s	d
To his wearing apparrell a coate a pair of breeches 1£ 11s a hatt 1s 6d........	01	12	06
Item a womans hat 2s. two oxen 5£ 10. three cowes 7£ three young catle 4£...	16	12	00
Item a kaff 5s a pot 10s a speet tongs and shovell 3s two poots a ketell 1£....	02	03	00
Item a freaying pan 4s 2 tylers goas two pair of pot hooks tramell...........	00	14	00
Item a skillit 1s 6d pruter and spoons 1£ all earthen ware & wooden ware...	01	06	06
Item two earthen butter poots 1s three hoos brood axe Narrow axe spoods 1£	01	01	00
Item houling axes 5s two plaines hamber gamlet two inch ager 7s 6d.	00	12	06
Item a knif a Chisel 2s 6d a old yron 5s two betle rings fiue augers 12s..... ..	00	19	06
Item Cheare and coulter 12s two pichforks forks 3s one gun Cutlash 1£......	01	15	00
Item a sadle 6s a croscut sea 10s two pound powder 4s......................	01	00	00
Item lead and bullets 6 pounds 2s. three hundred shoo nailes 1s.............	00	03	00
Item a file 6d a Chist 1£ 5s two old Chists one boxe boxe 5s	01	10	06
Item two old Chests some old Caske 3s a ring slue and reddell 2s............	00	19	00
Item ten sheepe 7£ 10s foure sheepe 1£................	08	10	00
Item a booll a meel slue and bellos two peals 6s............................	00	06	00
Item a bedsted 6s a feather bed and boulster 3£ curtaines & valans..........	04	02	00
Item two pillos three pillo kases 1£ two blankets Coverlet 15s...............	01	15	00
Item a old fether bed bolster 1£ 10s foure ould blankets Coverlet 1£	02	10	00
Item a bolster 8s two shirts 4s a pair of wodden skells 6s	00	12	06
Item a tabell 6s old Roope 2s 6d a greedayron 1s 6d..........................	00	10	00
Item Housen lands Marshes	110	00	00
Tota suma Est........	156	06	00

Part I, Fol. 52.

Witness the aboue Inventory had seen and apraysed by vs
   The marke of Arthur *A C* Came
   The marke of John *I H* Houie

Arthur Bragdon sone of the abouesd Thomas Bragdon tooke oath to the truth of ye abous^d Inventory & If any more estate appeare to ad it hereto:
  Sworne in Court Dec : 3^d 1690
    John Wincoll Cleric̃ :
A true Coppie of the originall Inventory
  Jan : 15 16¾   p me John Wincoll Cleric̃ :

[52]   An Inventory

The Inventory of all the lands goods Chattells of James Freathie of yorke in the province of Mayne plantor late Deceased had seen praysed by Arthur Came John Hovie of the same parrish and province aforesaid plantors the fourteenth of october 1690 as followeth

Inprimis Three kous 6£ four stears two years old a heifer of two years old one yearling 8£ 10	14	10	00
Item six swine a fraying pan thre pots 17s 6d	00	17	06
Item a broad axe narrow axe two Hoos trambell betle ring sayd	00	10	00
Item two hand saas 5s a sweething box 1s 6d a saath 4s	00	10	06
Item three traas on vater paall two kellers 5s	00	05	00
Item a tabell Craddell great Cheir 10s a Mel sive 1s	00	11	10
Item Eight pound of sheeps Wooll 8s a spining wheele 3s	00	11	00
Item a gun bandoliers 1£ a cutlash 5s a canon 10s	01	15	00
Item a bel two blankets a roug 1£ an axe 4s	01	04	00
Item a horse 4£ twentie four acres land house & barren 45£	49	00	00
Suma tota est	66	14	00

The aboue said Inventory had seen and Apraysed by vs
   The marke of Arthur *A C* Came
   The marke of John *I H* Hovie

Mary ffrethy relict of the deceased tooke oath to the truth of the abouesd Inventory & if any more appeare to ad it Sworn in Court dec : 3 1690 Jn° Wincoll Cleric :

The aboue written is a true coppie of the originall Inventory January 20 16¾ p me John Wincoll Cler̃

Part I, Fol. 52.

An Inventory

An Inventory of all the Goods and Chattels of Daniell Bragden of yorke in the province of Maine plantor late Deceased had seen praised by Arthur Came & John Houie of the same pish and pvince aforsd plantors the fourteenth october 1690 as followeth

	£	s	d
Inpr: his weareing Cloathes a coate 16s a Jacket 10s Coat breeches 5s.........	01	13	00
Item two oxen 6£ on Cow one Calfe 2£ 10 one meare & Colt 2£ 10............	10	00	00
Item one ewe & lamb 7s two yards home spun Cloath 6s.....................	00	13	00
Item one Gun Bandalers and sword 1£ 3s	01	03	00
Tota suma est	18	09	00

Witness that the abouesd Inventory to be had seen and apraised by vs

The marke of Arthur A C Came

The marke of John | H Hovie

Arthur Bragden took oath to the truth of this Inventory and If any more appeare to ad it: Sworn in Court dec: 3. 1690 Jn° Wincoll Cleric:

A true Coppie of the originall Inventory Janᵣʸ 21 : 16⁹⁰⁄₉₁

p me John Wincoll Cleric

An Inventory

The Inventory of all the Goods lands Chattells of Arthur Bragdon of yorke in the province of Maine plantor late deceased had seen and praysed by Arthur Came and John Houie of the same pish & Countie aforesd plantors the fourteenth of october 1690 as followeth

	£	s	d
Imprs his wering Cloathes a Coate 12s old Coate breeches Hand Cursher 9d...	01	06	00
Item Neckcloth 9d a p of shoos 5s a p of stockens 2s a shirt 5s................	00	12	09
Item two guns a pair of of bandaliers 1£ 10s, a Cutlash 10s two pound powder	02	04	00
Item two pound bullets 3d a meer 1£ a hat 1s 6d a pair of stockens one hand saa	01	01	02
Item Two oxen 6£ on steer 2£ 10s two kous 4£ on kaff 10s six swin 3£: 15s.....	16	15	00
Item six sheep 1£ 10s on slea two pair of harnesses 1£ a loome 15s............	03	05	00
Item two porengers a quart pot wooden vear Chamber pot 9s..................	00	09	00
Item a syron pot 5s a fraying pan butter tobe 1s sheeps vool 1£ 2.............	01	08	00
Item three agors a Chisel two sikcls 8s old ayron 4s three Hoos 3s..........	00	15	00
Item two yoakes two huks two rings & Chain 10s a pitch forke 1s............	00	11	00
Item saath vag ring nobes 4s a broad axe 5 a Chist 3s........................	00	12	00
Item a narrow axe 3s bed bolster 3£ bed Clothen 1£...........................	04	03	00
Item house barren Lands Maush 90£ two barrells 2s 6d two glas botles 1s.....	90	03	00
Tota Suma Est........	121	08	05

one oxe If not found 3£ to be abated for him

Part I, Fol. 53.

ve Witness the abouesd Inventory to be had seen and appraysed by vs the of Arthur A C Came
the marke of John I H Hovie

Arthur Bragden sone of the deceased tooke oath to the truth of the abousd Inventory and If any more appeare to ad it and Arthur bragden and John Twisden doe Ingadge themselues to o^r sov'aine lord & lady the king and Queen in the sum of two hundred fortie two pound that the said Arthur Bradgden shall administer according to law

Sworne in Court dec: 3 1690   John Wincoll Cleric̄

The aboue is a true Coppie of the originall Inventory Jan^{ry} 21 16⁹⁰⁄₉₁   p John Wincoll Cleric:

[53]   An Inventory

The Inventory of all the goods lands Chattells of William Wormwood of yorke in the province of Maine plantor late deceased had seen praised by Arthur Came and John Hovie of same provence and parrish aforesd plantors the fourteenth of october 1690 as followeth

	£	s	d
Impr his vering Cloathes a Coate 4s one two year old heifer one yearling	02	00	00
Item three swine 1£ 10s two poots 10s a fraying pan 2s trambell 3s	02	05	00
Item vooden veare 1s 6d two plaine Irons hand saw Agor drawing knife gug three chissells brood axe narow axe	01	10	00
Item a meale slue twentie pound sheeps wooll	01	01	00
Item three barrells a toobe 3s old chest 1s a trunnel bed 2s 6d	00	06	06
Item a bed sted a Chist 8s a bed bolster pillo two blankets a sheet Coverlet 1£ 10s a horse 4£ on pound half pouder	06	01	00
Item six pound lead 8s a two foot Rull 1s 6d	00	04	00
Item house and land 12£	12	00	00
Tota Suma Est	25	07	06

Ve Vittnes the abousd Inventory to be had seen & praysed by vs

The mark of Arthur A C Came
The mark of John I H Houie

Sworne in Court by Mary Wormwood & If any more appeare shee will ad it Sworne in Court dec: 3 1690

John Wincoll Cleric̄

PART I, FOL. 53.

A true Coppie of the originall Inventory taken this 22th Day of Jany 16$\frac{90}{91}$

p John Wincoll Record^r

An Inventory of the estate of John Billing Deceased taken and appraised by vs whose names are vnderwritten this third day of December 1690.

	£	s	
To 5 pecks of meale	00	04	00
To one gun at	00	15	00
To one axe at 3s 8d 2 old pots 2 hangers & frying pan	00	13	00
To 2 bushels of wheat & barley vnthreshed	00	06	00
To seurl small trifles 3s 6d woole & two old ruggs 2s 6d	00	06	00
To old bed-sack and bolter and pillow	00	02	06
To one Grindstone & an old speenning wheele & some other small trifles all at	00	06	00
To 10 bushells of Indian corne vnsheiled	01	00	00
To other small trifles	00	04	00
To a parcell of hay neare the house	02	00	00
To 2 stacks of hay at	03	00	00
To one mare and Coult at	03	00	00
To 2 heifers at	03	00	00
To one Cowe & calfe at	02	04	00
To 2 thoeowe Cowes at	04	04	00
To one small thorowe Cowe at	01	16	00
To a sow and 5 pigs	00	15	00
To a sword 5s			
	23	15	00

Apprysed by vs
Nicholas Weekes
Joseph Weekes

Some swine in the woods praysed by vs
Land & Marsh vnknowne what it is
More 4 piggs cont 455 lb at 2d p lb is 03 15 10

Capt Francis Hooke came and made oath to the verity of this Inventory & is oblidged if he can find any more estate of the sd Billings deceased to bring it into the Court
Taken vppon oath this 8^t Day of December 1690
Before me John Daues Dep^ty p^rsident

Francis Hooke & Lf^t Abraham Preble Ingadgeth themselues in the sum of forty six pounds sterling that the sd Hooke shall Administer and act in the p^rmises abouesaid according to law

Part I, Fol. 54.

Francis Hooke and Leftnt Abraham Preble own'd this bond   Before me John Daves Dep pre^dt

The aboue written is a true coppy of the originall Inventory : oath & bond as it was p^rsented to me p Capt Francis Hooke : Entred on record this 17th of Febr^y 16$\frac{90}{91}$

p me John Wincoll Record^r

[54] Province of Maine An Inventory of the Estate of Mr Andrew Searle late of Barwick Deceased November 25. 1690//

	£	s	d
His wearing cloathes	03	00	00
His loome for weaveing the warping pins box & wheele	03	00	00
Two reeds and harness	00	10	00
an Iron pot 7s Chamber pot 2s 6d a frying pan thre woodden Dishes & a Jarr.	00	14	00
a bed and bedding	01	00	00
provision Beefe &c	02	10	00
3 old Caske	00	03	00
a cow & calfe in Ben: Hodsdens hand	03	00	00
an oxe in the hands of John Neale	03	00	00
13 lb of cotten wooll and yarne	00	13	00
an axe and hatchet	00	04	00
a Dore lock 2 bottles three pecks of pease and a meale trongh	00	04	00
Two stooles	00	03	00
	18	01	00

a Chest of writings & bookes left with Benoni Hodsden

The rest as aboue apprized this 8^t Day of December 1690
By vs   Thomas Abbott
Bennony Hodsden

Dec 10: His printed bookes apprized at	01	05	00
Due to him by bills	09	03	08
The whole is	28	09	08
More found since 1 lb of twine & 3s money	00	05	00
an old paile and some Cane	00	03	06
his shop built in the garrison	00	15	00
Debts due by his booke from severall	09	04	01
december 10: 1690	38	17	03

december 10 : 1690

Andrew Neale Gardion to James Neale gaue oath to the truth of this Inventory and If any more of sd Searles estate shall appeare that hee will ad it heret and William Wittam

Part I, Fol. 54.

and Nicholas Gowen are bound to our soveraigne lord & lady the King & queen in the sum of eighty pound that said neale shall administer according to law : John Wincoll Cleric͞:

The aboue written is a true Coppy of the originall Inventory Compared this 18th Day of February 16⅜⅞

p me John Wincoll Record^r

To all Christian people to whom these p^rsents shall Come Greeting &c Know ye that I Richard White of the towne of Kittery in the province of Mayne for and In Consideration of the sum of twelue pounds ten shillings to me in hand paid or secured to be paid at or before thensealing & delivery of these p^rsents by John Moore of the towne and province aforesaid haue bargaind and sold and by these p^rsents Doe Bargaine Sell Infeofe and Confirme vnto the said John Moore all that my parcell of Marsh lieing on the Northeast side of broad boat harbour Crick from Rails there belonging to Captⁿ Raines to the vpper end of the said Crick lyeing in the towne of yorke and in the province aforesaid together with all profits priviledges and advantages therevnto belonging and all my right title and Interest in the same or any part thereof To haue and to hold the said parcell of marsh vnto the said John Moore his heires and Assigns for ever And the said Richard White Doth hereby Couenant promise and Grant that I the said Richard White haue good right and lawfull authority to sell and convay the said land vnto the said vnto the said John Moore his heires and Assigns for ever And that I will Warrantize and Defend the same vnto him his heires and Assigns for ever in witness hereof I haue herevnto set my hand and seale this fourth Day of January Ano Dñi one thousand six hundred and eightie nine.

Sealed and delivered   The marke of
   in the p'sence of   Richard White (seale)
Francis Hooke
William Hooke   This Deed or Instrument was acknowl-
Mary Hooke   edged by the aboue said Richard White this fourth Day of January 1689 as his act and Deed
                         Francis Hooke Just pea

Memorandum that this Day being the fifth Day of august the yeare of our lord 1690 ye aboue named Richard White Delivered vnto the abouesaid John More possession of the aboue p'mises by delivery of a twig & turfe in the p'sence of
vs   Dominicus Jordan   & Coram me
      William Hooke   Francis Hooke
                                Just pea :

The aboue is a true Coppie of the originall Deed of Richard White to John Moore Entred this 25^t day of february 16$\frac{90}{91}$ p me John Wincoll Record^r

[55]   In the name of god Amen

I John Taylor of Barwicke in the province of Maine being weake of body and yet Through the Mercies of god sound in mind and Memory and humbly Comitting my soule to god that gaue it and my body to the earth by Decent burieall not knowing how soone my Change may come Doe declare this Instrument to be my last Will and Testament/

Imp^r I bequeath vnto my Daughter Katherne Cahan thirtie acres of land to be taken out of my land at the rockie hills to run the whole length of it & to be to her & her

Part I, Fol. 55.

heires for ever and also a cow and a calfe & an Ewe & a lambe

It : 2dly I bequeath vnto my Daughter Mary Taylor thirtie acres of land to be taken out of my land at the rockie hills to run the whole length of it & to be to her and her heires for ever and also a cow and a calfe & an Ewe & a lambe

3dly I bequeath vnto my Daughter Sarah Taylor thirtie acres of land to be taken out of my land at the rockie hills & to run the whole length of it, to be to her and her heires for ever also I giue her a cow and a calfe and an Ewe and a lambe

4^{thly} I Bequeath vnto my daughter Deliverance Taylor thirtie acres of land to be taken out of my land at the rockie hills & to run the whole length of it to be to her and her heires for ever also I giue her a Cow and a calfe and an Ewe and a lambe

5^{tly} I bequeath vnto my Daughter Abigaile Taylor thirtie acres of land to be taken out of my land at the rockie hills and to run the whole length of it to be to her and to her heires for ever also I giue her a cow and a calfe and an Ewe and a lambe

6^{tly} The rest of my Estate of Dwelling house out houses orchards Gardens lands Cattell Chattells household goods Vtencills whatsoever at home or abroad within Dores or without I bequeath vnto Martha my loveing Wife to be and remaine to her for her Maintenance and comfort and Dayly vse dureing the whole terme of her Naturall life and what shall remaine at her decease she shall haue power to Dispose of at her Discretion amongst her fiue Daughters aboue named and to haue liberty to cut & take off ten cords of Wood per annem for her firewood During her life out of those lands aboue giuen to our aboue written fiue daughters, and the lands giuen by Nyvan Agnew to me & my Children I leaue to my sd wife

The cattell aboue giuen to my Daughters not to be taken away from their mother till their respective marriage

Part I, Fol. 55.

to Dispose of it amongst our Children at her Discretion/ I Doe also Nominate & appoint the sd Martha to be the sole Executrix of this my last will & testament & to take Especiall care for payment of my Just debts as Witness my hand & seale this 7th Day of May 1687

Signed sealed and delivrd in presence of vs
Stephen Hardison
John Wincoll

John Taylor
his ✝ mark ($_{Seale}^{a}$)

A true Coppy of the originall Will Entred March 4th 168⅞

p me John Wincoll record^r

Province of Main At a meeting of Major Frost Esqr Justice of the peace and John Wincoll Justice of the peace & recorder of this pvince the 23th Day of February 168⅞

The two witnesses to the will on the other side vizt Stephen Hardison & John Wincoll Tooke oath that they saw the within named John Taylor signe seale & Deliver this Instrument as his last Will & testament while he was of a Disposeing mind,   as attests John Wincoll Record^r

A true coppy of the probat on record

p me John Wincoll Recor^r

An Inventory of the lands Goods Chattels and Cattell of John Taylor late of Barwick in the pvince of Maine in New England Deceased

	£	s	d
Impr all his weareing Cloathes at	05	00	00
a fether bed bolster seven blankets and a rug	12	00	00
a fether bed bolster 2 pillows 2 blankets 2 pair of sheets and a rug at	12	00	00
a Brass ketle a scillet 3 Iron pots an Iron ketle & a tramell	04	00	00
7 pewter Dishes, 4 basons quart pot 1 porenger & a puter dish	02	10	00
6 spoones and six Wooden Dishes	00	03	00
3 buckets 3 keelers 10s a Musket at 16s	01	06	00
3 old augers, 2 Chisels, 7 wedges, 2 betles 2 narrow axes, an Ads, 4 old hacthets & 3 old howes	00	10	00
one Draft Chaine & a peece & a p of hookes	00	12	00

Part I, Fol. 56.

	£	s	d
8 cowes. 2, 3 year old 5, 2 yeare old at	15	00	00
5 swine 4£ and 18 sheepe 4£ 10	08	10	00
2 old bedsteds & a Chest	00	10	00
3 pitchforkes & a hay knife	00	03	00
ten bushells Indian Corne: 1 bushell barley	01	00	00
beefe and porke at	03	00	00
his homestall of house barne orchard and land adjoining	60	00	00
his lands giuen by Nyvan Agnew	20	00	00
the remainder of his land at rockie hills	10	00	00
	156	04	08

Apprized this 28th Day of January 16 8/9

p vs Richard Nason
his O marke
Thomas Abbott

Martha Taylor Executrix to her Deceased husbands Will tooke oath that the aboue written is a true Inventory of her said husbands Estate and the said Martha and Stephen Hardison and John Turner acknowledge themselues bound to our sovraign lord & lady the King & Queen in the sum of three hundred and twelue pound that the said Martha shall perform according to the said Will of her sd husband

March 4 : 169 8/9

prouince of Maine   Before me John Wincoll Jus^tce of peace

the aboue are true coppyes of the originall Inventory; oath and bond March 4th 169 8/9 p me John Wincoll Record^r

[56] Feb: the 18 1689

An Inventory of the Estate of Mr Edward Rishworth Deceased

	£	s	d
His waring Cloaths	05	00	00
one bed and furniture	08	00	00
1 old Cubard and Cloath	01	05	00
1 Chist and 1 box and 3 old Cheares	00	18	00
3 pare of And Irons and thre Iron pots & 1 small kitle	02	00	00
3 tramells 1 old brass kitle	01	00	00
2 old Cases and botles and 6 round bottles	00	07	06
1 brass Chafindish 1 candlestick 1 small skelet	00	06	00
1 warmenpan 1 small morter and pesell	00	05	00
1 pare of old steyards and 1 pare of old Scales	00	07	00

Part I, Fol. 56.

2 spits 1 sadel and bridel...............	00	14	00
1 horse 1 bull 1 Cow and Calfe...............	07	10	00
by silver...............	12	10	00
1 great Chist pear of Cob Irons...............	00	18	00
	39	00	06

Taken by vs
Abra: Preble
Matthew Austin

M⁽ʳˢ⁾ Mary Hull took oath in Court that the aboue written is a true Inventory of the Estate of her deceased father Edward Rishworth and if any more Estate appeare she will ad it

February 25 16 88/89   John Wincoll Record⁽ʳ⁾

The aboue written is a true Coppy of the Inventory & oath giuen in Court as aboue

p me John Wincoll Record⁽ʳ⁾

The Inventory of the Estate of M⁽ʳ⁾ Phillip Foxwell deceased the 20 of october last as followeth

	£	s	d
Three beds and Furnitare 9 pound...............	09	00	00
To brass Citils...............	01	10	00
Thre pots and on Iron Citil...............	01	05	00
puter...............	00	12	00
The warmingpan and Morter and skilit...............	00	15	00
The flinpan and Gridiron...............	00	06	00
The old Iron...............	00	18	00
The ax and spade...............	00	07	00
The linen...............	02	10	00
The to boxes and on Chest...............	00	10	00
To oxen...............	07	00	00
and foure Cowes...............	09	00	00
fower swin...............	01	04	00
all which sum amounts to...............	34	17	00

The aboue Riten is a true Inventory of all the Estate besids land and Marsh at the Eastward taken by vs as witness our hands this. 19. of febr: 1690

witnes Richard Brian
        Thomas Litchfield

M⁽ʳˢ⁾ Elinor Foxwell tooke oath in Court that the aboue written is a true Inventory of the Estate of her husband deceased and If any more Estate can be found shee will ad it hervnto and the said Elinor Foxwell and Joseph Curtis acknowledge themselues bound vnto our soveraigne Lord and Lady the King and Queene in the sum of seventie pound sterling that the sd Elinor shall administer according to law

Feb 24 16$\frac{8}{9}$ John Wincoll Record^r

1691

[57] In the name of god Amen march y^e thirtie first one thousand six hundred ninty & one to all psons to whom this shall or may come Know y^e: that I william more of yorke in the province of Maine being sick of body but of Good and perfect Memory thankes be to god for it, Doe make this my last Will and testament in maner & forme as followeth

Imp^r: I giue & bequeath my poore imortall soule to god that gaue it to me hopeing through the only merits of our lord & sauior Jesus Christ to Inherit everlasting happiness/ And I giue & bequeath my body to the earth whereof it was made therin to be decently interred

I giue & bequeath to my loueing wife Dorathy More all my house, lands, goods Chattells & Moueables as also all Debts due to me.

I giue to my sone John More one Cow to be Delivered within a twelue month after my Decease.

I giue to my Daughter Elizabeth Trafton fiue shillings in good pay within a twelue month

I giue to my sone Robert More one shilling in good pay

I giue to my Daughter Sarah Welcom fiue shillings in good pay

I giue to my sone William More fiue shillings in good pay

I giue to my Daughter Elianor More fiue shillings in good pay

I giue to my Daughter Ann More fiue shillings in good pay

Part I, Fol. 57.

I giue to my Daughter Mary More fiue shillings in good pay

I giue to my sone Thomas More five shillings in good pay and If he proues a good loueing & Dutifull sone to his mother and liue with her Dureing her Naturall life then I giue & vnto my sone Thomas More my house that I now liue in and the land that I haue to him and his heires for ever after the Decease of his Mother

And I leaue my wife Dorathy More my sole Executrix Witness my hand & seale the Day and yeare aboue written

Witness   Willm :   More (Seal)

Francis Tucker   his marke

Rort   Souden his marke

Sarah   Anger her marke

Province   The within named Francis Tucker Robert of maine   Souden and Sarah Anger Tooke oath that they saw William More signe seale & deliver the within Instrument as his last Will & testament & that he did it when he was in a Disposeing Capacitie

Taken vppon oath this 2^d Day of June 1691 before two Justices of the peace & the Recorder of this province as attests John Wincoll Record^r

The aboue written is a true Coppie of the originall Will and probat: this 3^d day of June 1691 p me John Wincoll Record^r

The Inventory of the Estate & goods of William More Deceased in the province of in yorke fisherman had seene & appraised by Jesper Pulman fisherman and Arthur Came in the aforesd town & province this 12th of May 1691 as Followeth

	£	s	d
In Primis two oxen 7£ two Cowes 4£ 10s two 3 yeares old 3£	14	10	00
Item two kous 5£, 3, 2 years old 3£ 10s three yearlings 2£ 5s	10	15	00
Item ten sheepe 2£ 10s, one horse 1£ 10s one Mear 1£ 15s, hogs	07	05	00

Part I, Fol. 58.

Item House & barren a Houndred acres of land four acres three quarters of Marsh 84£ His wearin Cloathes 3£ 16s..	87	15	00
Item one Hat 4s one rug & blanket 17s 6d..	01	07	06
Item two pair of shooes 6s, bed boulster 2£ two blankets roug...............	04	06	00
Item boulster two pillows 15s a bed two blankets boulster 12s.................	01	07	00
Item a bed furniture 1£5 six hoos 8s two forkes 3s..................................	01	16	00
Item three axes 10s a speed 4s flue wages a bettell 8s............................	01	02	00
Item one krow of ayron 2s two Chaines 8s twelue pound of wooll............	01	02	00
Item six pound wooll 6s one whell 2s one gunn 15s pewter 12s................	01	15	00
Item one Morter 1s six pots a kettell 1£ 10 two agers a Cross cut saa a Drawing knife 12s two trambells speet pair tongs......................................	01	04	00
Item foure pair of pot houks 4s one fraying pan 1s.................................	00	05	00
Item a poot poot hookes 10s Clevis hoo 2s..	00	12	00
Item yoake stepell & ring two whels 4s the boate furniture 7£ 10s flue Cleues 5s old skellit 1s 6d two milking peals..	08	02	00
Item Wooden Dishes spoones a warming pane 3s...................................	00	05	00
Item nine Treas 7s Milk boules 2s two Earthen pans 1s 6d.....................	00	10	00
Item four butter poots 4s foure glass bottells 1s 6d...............................	00	05	06
Item old twobs barrells 3s one Churne 1s two seiues 2s....,....................	00	06	00
Item a flasket & hougset 2s a meale troffe old Chists.............................	00	05	00
Item Money 11s old panell two bags 12	01	03	00
Item three konowes 30s a gundillo 30s two axes froo Drawing knife.......	03	06	00
Item three shirts a pair of Drawers 18s two pair sheets 1£ 1s.................	02	13	00
Item two Hamoker 2£ tabell cloaths Napkins 12s..................................	01	12	00
Item two bibells 3s three Earthen porrengers, a gallipot 8s....................	00	06	00
Item a pair of britches 12s three Earthen sasars 1s................................	00	13	00
Item flue pewter Dishes 1£ 5s three porrengers 1s 6d.............................	01	06	06
Item two old saiethes a reap hooke 4s four Chists 16s...........................	01	00	00
Item old Caske 7s Stage and house 2£..	02	07	00
Tota suma est........	159	07	00

This Estate apraysed by vs

    the marke of **I P** Jesper Pulman

    the marke of **A 6** Arthur Came

Dorathy More tooke oath to the truth of this Inventory to her best Knowledge And If any more Estate appeare she will ad it herevnto June 3^d 1691 before me John Wincoll

                                  Just^{ce} of peac

The aboue written is a true coppy of the originall Inventory and oath June 3^d 1691. p me John Wincoll Recorder

[58]   pvince of Mayne

Thes Deed Made the twenty Day of March 1644 between Richard Vines Steward Generall for Sir Fardinando Gorges in the pvince of Main on the one party and Thomas Withers of puscat : on the other party Witnesseth. Know ye therefore that I Richard Vines Steward generall aforesaid haue bargained and sold vnto Tho : Withers for and in Consideration of tenn pounds sterling already paid vnto me Richard Vines by the said Tho Withers and other good Considerations me herevnto Especially mouing a Certaine tract of vpland and Medo conteining Six hundred ackers lieing and being at ye head of Spruce Crick at the marsh where the said Tho : Withers haue formerly bin possest of : by Mr Tho : Gorge and made vse of, bounded with two other Creekes one on the Easter side and ye other on the West side vntill the said six hundred acres be accomplished with all the timber and preveledges whatsoever which belongeth therevnto for the only vse of the said Tho : Withers his heires Executors administrators and assignes for ever yealding and paying yearly vnto Sr Ferdinando Gorges or his assignes fiue gratts a yeare If Demanded on the twenty ninth Day of September, and furthermore I the said Richard Vines Steward Generall for Sr Ferdinando Gorges Doe ratific and Conferme all the said premises vnto the only vse and behalfe of hee the said Thomas Withers his heires and assignes for ever in Witness whereof I haue herevnto set my hand and seale the Day and yeare aboue written

Sealed Signed and Delivred   Rich Vines
  in the presence of vs   (seale)
William Waldron
  the marke of
Alexander A Jones
    Vera Copia of this Instrument aboue written
      Entred in the records of the pvince of
    Maine this 7 : June 1666
        p Edw : Rishworth Re : Cor :

Wheras some scruple amongst some to arise about the validitie of this within grant written made by m^r Richard

Part I, Fol. 58.

Vines vnto Tho: Withers, vpon what former Experience wee haue had of M`r` Vines his hand and his vsuall manner of makeing Grants Do Conceiue and adjudge this Instrument within writen to be a good suficient grant signed and giuen by M`r` Richard Vines vnto Thomas Withers

      Witnessed by our hands June 1667:

This Deed I Doe approue of to be y`e` act and Deed of M`r` Richard Vines Witness my hand

      July 13`th` 1667
      Henry Jocely
      Edward Johnson

    The Deposition of Alexander Jones

Saith that this Deed of M`r` Richard Vines that hee made to M`r` Thomas Withers for his land in the Spruce Creeke: that William Waldren and this Deponenant were wittnesses vnto was made at M`rs` Linns where she now Dwells and that his bounds on the Easter side of the Creek did begin at the Easter Crick at neck of land called pine point and so on the Wester side of the Crick it begineth at the Wester Creeke that goeth in West at Eagle point Marsh and so vp along the Creeke as the Deed doth express, and sworne by the said Jones

    Before vs Henry Jocely Justice peace
At a Court held at yorke: Edward Johnson Comision`r`
8. f`r` y`e` 4`th` 1667:

The aboue written with the deed in the foregoing page are true Coppyes of the originall Deed and the testimonyes to it transcribed and Entred this 4`th` Day of June 1691:

    p me John Wincoll, Record`r`

Part I, Fol. 59.

[59] An Inventory of the Estate of Thomas Holmes late of Kittery Deceased

	£	s	d
Impr His Wearing Cloathes			
Six Cowes 12£: 3 yearlings 2£,	14	00	00
3 2 yeare old and one bull	05	00	00
4 Calues 2£ 2 horses 2£	04	00	00
a young oxe sold 4£ & two oxen 6£	10	00	00
The home lot of land 20£. 50 acres Vacant land 10£	30	00	00
Six catle kild at 11£; 5s	11	05	00
one sow	00	19	00
one feather bed two bolsters 1 rug & three blankets	06	00	00
3 Iron pots a brass ketle, 1 frying pan 1 Warming pan	02	10	00
5 pewter peeces 3s: 1 keeler 1s: 2 seiues 2s, a flesh forke	00	07	00
a short gun, 2 axes: fire shovell. tongs: bridle & sadle	01	10	06
a Chissell: Candlestick pot hooke spining wheele	00	05	00
an old Chest & trunke a great Jug two pailes	00	06	06

Apprized Jan^{ry} 16. 16$\frac{89}{90}$ p vs   Daniell Goodin Senr
                                       William Spencer

His land at yorke 30 or 40 acres	20	00	00
	85	12	06

Mrs Joana Holmes tooke oath to the truth of this Inventory and what more Estate of her deceased Husband shall appeare shee will ad it herevnto Jan^{ry} 16$\frac{89}{90}$ Before Me John Wincoll: Jus^{tce} of peace

Adition to the Inventory of her Husband Tho Holmes, June: 9: 1691:

a parcell of household Goods at portsmouth	17	18	06
Mony receiued at Boston	32	19	08
Mony receiued of Mr Horell	14	05	00
	65	02	02
	85	12	06
the Whole Sum	150	14	08

Walter Allin and Gilbert Warren stand bound to o^r Soveraigne lord & Lady the King & Queene in the sum of three hundred & one pound eight shillings & eight pence that the said Joana Holmes shall Adminester on sd Estate according to law June 9th 1691: Ownd Before me John Wincoll Just^{ce} of peace

The aboue written is a true Coppy of the Inventory of Tho: Holmes deceased with the oath and suretys as Attests June 9th 1691:   John Wincoll Record^r

Part I, Fol. 59.

Let all men know by these presents that wheras I Thomas Newberry of Newgewannke by my bill vnder my hand Doe stand Justly Indebted vnto Thomas Homes of Dover in the Just sum of Eight pounds lawfull mony of New England which bill beareth Date with these presents for the secureing of which Debt I the said Thomas Newberry haueing a house and fiftie akers of land which I the said Newberry am now legally possest of by vertue of town grant and other towne order of the towne of Kittery Doe not only make the said Thomas Homes my true and lawfull atturney for me and in my steed and place to Improue sett and lett the said house and land for my best advantage in my absence and whereas that I the said Newberry am bound for England and so to returne againe If god permitt: but Doe further heerby Giue and grant vnto the said Thomas Homes all that my house and land for the payment of the foresaid Debt with such adventure and Interest as they the said Newberry and Homes are agreed on (viz) that is for the Eight pounds adventure to pay on pound seven shillings and six pence for the forbearance adventure and Interest of the foresd sum of Eight pounds Debt to be paid by the said Newberry vnto the said Homes for every yeare that the said Newberry shall be wanting or before hee come for New England or send his assigne or legall atturney to pay the said Debt with the Interest and Demand the house & land aforesaid, and If that I the said Newberry Do Die on the sea or before I Doe returne or send for New England againe without eire then the said house & land shall be wholely and solely the said Homes his owne pper right and Interest so firmely to all Constructions as it is now mine owne and If I the said Newberry Doe not returne or send some lawfull attorney within seven yeares next after the Date hereof that then the land and house aforesaid is pperly and legally the said Homes his to him and his heires & assignes for ever in as large a mañer to all Constructions as I the said Newberry can or may Giue,

Grant or estate the same, Notwithstanding If that I the said Thomas Newberry my Executors Administrators or assignes Doe returne from England to NewEngland at any time within seven yeares and pay or cause to be paid vnto the said Homes the full and Just sum̄ of Eight pounds lawfull mony with on pound seven shillings and six pence for every yeares Interest from the Date hereof for the Interest of the said sum of Eight pounds, that then the said Newberry his Executors Administrators or assignes shall haue repossesse and haue againe the said Estate house and land as his first and former Estate butt in the meane time the said Homes to vse it, lett it or sett to his will and pleasure for the said Newberry and If any profitt Doe accrue to render account, Witness my hand and seale even the twenty fourth Day of July one thousand six hundred seventy & fiue

Sealed signed & deliv- Thomas Newberry(seale)
ered in the pᵣsence of vs
The marke
of Henry H Child : Andrew Searle witnesses

[60] Let all men Know by these presents that I Thomas Newberry of Newgewanick Cordwiner doe hereby acknowledg and Confess myselfe to owe and to be Indebted vnto Thomas Homes of Dover in the full and Just sum of Eight pounds lawfull Mony in NewEngland to be paid vnto the said Homes his heires Executors Administrators or assignes or to one of them at one Entire payment at in and vppon the twenty fourth Day of June next Ensueing the Date hereof with one pound and fiue shillings for the Interest and other Considerations for the foureance and Curtesies received of the said Homes and for the true payment hereof with the Interest I doe bind mee my Estate heire Executors and Administrators firmly by these presents wit-

ness my hand and seale even the twenty fourth Day of July in the yeare one thousand six hundred seventy and fiue
Sealed and Delivered in   Thomas Newberry (seale)
    the presence of vs
    The mark
    of Henry **H** Child ⎫
    & Andrew Searle ⎭ witnesses

The aboue written Thomas Newberry appeared before mee & did acknowled the aboue written Instrument to be his act and Deed the 26ᵗ Day of July : 1675 :
                    John Wincoll Asotiate
The aboue written with the Deed in the foregoing page are true Copies of the originall Instruments transcribed and here Entred on record this 9ᵗʰ Day of June 1691 :
                    p me John Wincoll Recordʳ

To all Christian people to whome these presents shall Come Henry Child of Barwick in the township of Kittery in ye province of Maine in New England planter and Sarah his wife sends Greetting, Know ye that I the aboue named Henry Child and Sarah my wife for Divers good Causes and Considerations vs hervnto moueing, but more Especially for and in Consideration of the sum of fiue pounds in Currant money in New England and thirty one Thousand foot of Mᵇˡᵉ pine boards already in hand received before the signing and sealeing hereof of Samuell Lord of Barwicke aforesaid in the province of Maine in New England where with wee acknowledge ourselues ffully satisfied contented and paid and thereof and of every part and parcell thereof Doe hereby acquitt and for ever Discharge the said Samuell Lord his heires and assignes by these presents haue absolutely giuen Granted Barained bargained sold Aliened Infeoffed and Confirmed and Doe by these presents absolutely Giue Grant bargain sell Alien Infeoffe and Confirme vnto the aboue named Samuell Lord a peece or parcell of land being by Measure fouerty acres and lyeing in a certaine place Comonly called & Knowne by the name of post wiggwam being one hundred and twenty poles in length from Newichawanick river north west and by north and in breadth fiftie & three poles & a halfe Northeast & by east, and South West and by west bounded on the South west by the land of phineas Hull and on the South east with the river on the North east with the land of John Cutts and on the north west with the Comons with foure pole in breadth at the north west end of the said land in leiw of the highway passing through it with a Dwelling house and all ye fences vppon the Land with all the wood and timber that is either standing or lyeing vppon the land aforesaid, Excepting the pine trees belonging to Mr Leaders Grant of timber, To Haue to Hold the aboue mentioned land & house & fences with all the wood and timber standing or lyeing vpon the said land not excepted to him the said Samuell Lord his heires and Assignes for ever and to his and their only proper vse benefit behoofe for ever and the sd Henry Child & Sarah his wife for them selues their heires and assignes Doe Covenant promise and Grant to & with the sd Samuell Lord his heires & assignes that they the said Henry Child and Sarah his wife haue in themselues good right full power and lawfull authoritie the aboue giuen and Granted premises to sell & Dispose of & that the same and every part and parcell thereof are free & Cleare and freely & Clearely acquitted Exhonorate and Disharged of [61] and from all and all maner of former Gifts, Grants, leases, Mortgadges wills, Entailes, Judgments, Executions, pouer of thirds and all other Incumbrances of of what Nature and kind soever had made Done acknowledged Comitted or suffered to be Done or Comitted where-

Part I, Fol. 61.

by the sd Samuell Lord or his assignes shall or may any wayes be molested, in, Evicted or Ejected out of the aboue Granted p'rmises or any part or parcell thereof by any person or persons haueing Claiming or pretending to haue or Claime any legall right title Interest Claime or Demand of in or to ye aboue Granted premises and the said Henry Child and Sarah his Wife Doe for themselues their heires Executors, administrators and assignes Covenant and promise & grant to & with the said Samuell Lord his heires & assignes the aboue giuen and Granted peece or parcell of land house and fences with all the priviledges & appurtenances therevnto belonging to Warrant & for ever defend from all persons whatsoever, Excepting the lord proprietor In Witness whereof the said Henry Child and Sarah his Wife haue herevnto sett their hands and seales this Eighteenth Day of March 168$ and in the third yeare of the raigne of Soveraigne lord James the Second of England Scotland France and Ireland king Defender of the faith &c.

Signed sealed & deliv'd   Henry Child (seal)
  in presence of ous   Sarah S Child (seal)
  George Broughton
  Joseph Barnard
  Pern Broughton

The aboue written Henry Child and Sara his wife acknowledged the aboue Deed of Sale to be their free act and Deed June 13th 1691:

  province   Before mee
  of maine   John Wincoll Just^{ce} of peace

The aboue written with the rest of this Deed on the other side is a true coppy of the originall Deed and ye acknowledgment transcribed and here recorded this 13th Day of June 1691: p me

                       John Wincoll Record^r

Part I, Fol. 61.

In the name of god Amen

The last Will & testament of John Amerideth Coop late of Dartmouth in England & Now of Kittery in the province of Maine in New England, being Weake of body but of perfect Memory & of a disposeing mind Doe ordaine this as my last Will revoake all former Wills & bequests whatsoever thinke meett to sett my house in order & Dispose of that Estate as god has giuen me as followeth

Imp^r: I bequeath my soule to god that gaue it me in hopes of a Glorious resurection & my body to be Decently buried

It: That estate I haue in Dartmouth abouesaid of housen & Gardens I giue and bequeath the Moietie or one halfe to my beloved wife Joane Amerideth Dureing her Naturall life & the other halfe vnto my sone & Daughter John & Joanna Alcock and their heires for ever: & after my said viues decease the whole to be and remaine to sd sone and Daughter for ever;

It: I giue & bequeath to my sd Wife the oue halfe of the house and land I now liue vppon Dureing her Naturall life and after her Decease the whole Vnto my Sone & Daughter John and Joaña Alcock Dureing their Naturall liues & the longest liver of them and after their Decease to be and remaine to Joseph & Joanna the Children of the sd Jno And Joanna aforesd: & twelue acres of land in broad Coue vnto Joanna last aboue named

It: I giue & bequeath vnto vnto my two Grand Children Abigail & Mary Alcock a bill of six pound in Mony Due from Cozen John Shapleigh to be equally Devided between them.

It: I giue & bequeath the rest of my Estate in Chattells & Cattell within Dores and without Dores vnto my beloued wife Joane hopeing shee Will be provident so of it that shee may leaue to my Children what remaines at her decease appointing & makeing my sd Wife my sole Executrix and

Part I, Fol. 62.

Elias Stileman & John Shapleigh my ouer seers in Wittness whereof I haue here vnto set my hand & seale the 26 January 1690:

The marke of John Amerideth

(Seale)

Richard King and William Tetherly tooke oath that they saw John Amerideth sign & seale this Instrument as his last Will and testament while he was of a Disposing Capacitie & that they with Elias Stileman set to their hands as witnesses to it this 16 Day of June 1691 before two Justices & the recorder of this province: as attests: John Wincoll

ReCord^r

A true Coppy June 24: 1691 p Jn° Wincoll Record^r

[62] A true inventory of all and singular the Goods & Chattells of John Ameredeth of the town of Kittery in the province of Maine who deceased the 26th of Jan^r 16$^{90}_{91}$ praysed by vs whose names are vnderwritten June 16th 1691://

	£	s	d
Impr^s To 6 Neate Cattle one with another	08	00	00
To the bedding & Furniture	23	10	00
To the Table linen	03	00	00
To plate 10 oz ½	02	13	00
To peuter new and old	02	19	00
To brass	01	07	00
To Iron Ware about the house	01	05	00
To Armes & armer	02	00	00
To Chests Trunks and Join Stooles Chaires and tables	03	00	00
To 6 swine	03	00	00
To his tooles belonging to his trade	01	18	00
To housing and land 32 acres	100	00	00
Totall sum Errour Excepted	152	12	00

This is a true account taken by vs as it was shewed vnto vs by m^{rs} Joan Ameradeth relict & executrix of the Deceased abouesaid

  Peter Dixon
  Wm Godsoe

PART I, FOL. 62.

Province   Mrs Joan Ameradeth tooke oath to the truth
of Main   of the aboue Inventory and If any More of
the Estate of her deceased husband shall appeare she will
ad it herevnto and the said Joan and John Alcock stand
bound to our Soveraigne ld and ladie the King and Queen
in the sum of 305 pound that the said Joana shall Execute
according to the Will before two Justices & recorder June
16: 1691   as Attests John Wincoll Recorr
  The aboue is a true Coppie of the originall Inventory the
oath and bond giuen June 16: 1691//
                    as Attests John Wincoll Recordr

  This Indenture made the Ninteenth Day of aprill in the
yeare of our lord god according to the computation of the
Church of England one thousand six hundred and Eighty
nine Betweene Benjamin Woodbridge of the towne of
Kittery in the province of Mayne in New England Minister
on the one parte And William Peprell of the towne of
Kittery aforsaid in the sd province Marriner on the other
parte Witnesseth that the said Benjamin Woodbridge for
and in Consideration of the sume of twelue pounds of currant money of New England vnto him in hand paid by the
said William Peprell at and before the sealeing and Delivery
of these presents the receipt he doth hereby acknowledge
and therof and of every part and parcell thereof Doth
remise release and Discharge the said William Peprell his
heires Executors and Administrators and Every of them by
these prsents and for Divers other Good causes and considerations Him therevnto moveing Hath Giuen Granted bargained sold Enfeoffed and confirmed And by these presents
Doth Giue Grant Bargayne sell Enfeoffe and confirme vnto
the said William Peprell his heires and assignes for ever

PART I, FOL. 62.

All that tract or parcell of land containing by Estimation twelue acres (be it more or lesse) lyeing in the said towne of Kittery between a crick comonly called Crockets Crick and the salt water comeing in at Piscataqua harbour mouth from a pine tree lyeing on the banke of the said Crick vnto a stake Driven in South two Degrees Easterly eleven Chaines and a halfe or forty two rodd and from a stumpe lyeing likewise on the banke of the said Crick to a fence belonging to m{r} John Bray South Westerly Eleven Chaines fifty eight links and the breadth to hold out to amount to twelue acres and a halfe as it was laid out and measured the twenty sixth of March one thousand six hundred and Eighty nine by Richard Clemens Dep{ty} Survayor (He the said William Peprell leaveing a Convenient Highway according to law) which sd land is part of a certaine tract of land sold by John Ameredith and Joane his wife John Gilman and Elizabeth his wife and Lucy Wells vnto the said Benjamin Woodbridge his heires and assignes for ever by Deed bearing Date the 24{th} of July 1688 And was formerly land belonging to M{r} Alexander Shapleigh and after to Major Nicholas Shapleigh as in and by the said Deed may more at large appeare, and all wayes waters water courses woods vnderwoods comons profits priviledges and advantages whatsoever to the same or any part there of belonging or appertayning and the revercon and revertions remainder and remainders thereof and of every part thereof and all the estate right title and Interest Claime and Demand whatsoever both in law and Equity power and Equity of redemtion of him the said Benjamin Woodbridge of in or to the same or any part thereof, And Coppies of all such Deeds Evidences and writeings which concerne the same, To Haue and to Hold the said twelue acres and a halfe of land with the appurtenances vnto the said William Peprell his heires and assignes for ever to the sole only and proper vse and behoofe of the said William Peprell his heires and assignes for ever and the said Benjamin Woodbridge Doth for himselfe and his heires Covenant promise and grant to and with the said William Peprell and his heires and assignes by these p'sents in maner & forme following That is to say That he the said Benjamin Woodbridge [63] Doth stand lawfully seized of and in the said parcell of land of a good perfect and absolute and Indefeazible estate of Inheritance in fee simple and that he hath full power good right and lawfull authority to grant and Convay the said land vnto the said William Peprell and his heires and assignes for ever And also that he the said William Peprell and his heires shall and lawfully may from time to time and at all tymes hereafter peaceably and quietly haue hold vse ocupy possesesse and enjoy the hereby granted and sold premises wth the appurtenances without the lawfull let suite trouble Deniall Ejection Eviction or Disturbance of him the said Benjamin Woodbridg or his heires or any other person or persons whatsoever Clayming to haue any Estate title or Interest therein And also that the said hereby bargained and sold p'mises with the appurtenances now are and be and soe from time to time and at all times hereafter shall be remaine and continew vnto the said William Peprell and his heires free and cleare and freely and clearly acquitted Exonorated and Discharged of and from all and all manner of former and other guifts grants bargains sales Dowers Judgm^{ts} Execucons Extents and of and from all titles troubles charges and Incumbrances whatsoever had made comitted suffered or executed by him the said Benjamin Woodbridg or any other person or persons whatsoever And also that he the said Benjamin Woodbridge & his heires from tyme to tyme and at all tymes hereafter for and Dureing the space of seaven yeares next Ensueing shall vppon the reasonable request and at the cost and charges of the said William Peprell his

This Deed of Sale Copied and Entred on record this first Day of december 1691 it being a true Coppy of the originall Deed p me John Wincoll Recordr

Part I, Fol. 63.

heires or assignes make perform acknowledge leavy and Execute or cause to be performed acknowledged leavied and Executed all and every such further & other lawfull and reasonable assurances acts and conveyances in the law whatsoever for the better and more perfect & absolute assureing of the said land with the Appur̃tences vnto and to the vse of the said William Peprell and his heires and assignes for ever as shall be required be it by fine feofm^t or confirmation or any other way Act Deed or meanes whatsoever All which said acts so hereafter to be Done shall be and endured to the only and proper vse and behoofe of the said William Peprell his heire and assignes for ever.

In Witness whereof the said Benjamin Woodbridge hath herevnto set his hand and seale the Day and yeare first aboue written

Sealed and delivered Benj: (seale) Woodbridge/ and livery and seizen giuen and deliverd according to law of the p'mises within mentioned the word hereby betwene the twenty six and twenty seventh lines and the words as shall be required, between thirty third & thirty fourth lines being first Interlined in the presence of vs as likewise the words by Deed bearing Date the twenty fourth of July 1688: between the fourteenth and fifteenth lines and the word lawfull between the twenty fourth and twenty fifth lines was Interlined before the sealeing hereof

Aprill the ninteenth 1689
Mr Benjamin Woodbridge personally before me & acknowledged the wthin Instrument to be his act & Deed and Deborah Woodbridge wife of the sd Benj: Woodbridge being secretly examined acknowledged her free consent to the wthin Deed
Coram Francis Hooke
Just peace & Quor:
{ John Bray
  William Hooke
  Robert Mitchell

PART I, FOL. 63.

Know all men by these pʳsents that I Benjamin Woodbridge of the Towne of Kittery in the province of Mayne in New England Minister haue now had and receiued of William Peprell of the towne of Kittery aforesaid in the said Province Marriner the sume of twelue pounds of currant Money of New England being the full consideration money mentioned in one Indenture of bargaine and sale bearing equall Date with these pʳsents made betweene me the said Benjamin Woodbridge on the one parte and the sd William Peprell on the other parte And therefore I the said Benjamin Woodbridge Doe hereby remise release and for ever Discharge the said William Peprell his heires Execʳˢ and Admʳˢ of and from the said sume of twelue pounds and of every parte thereof in Witness wherof I haue herevnto set my hand and seale this nineteenth Day of Aprill Año Dⁿⁱ 1689

Sealed and Delivered   Benj: Woodbridge (a seale)
  in the pʳsence of John Bray
             William Hooke

The aboue written is a true coppy of the originall Discharge transcribed compared and here Entred this 2ᵈ Day of December 1691.   p me John Wincoll Recordʳ

Know all men by these pʳsents that I Benjamin Woodbridge of the towne of Kittery in the Province of Mayne Minister Doe ow and stand Indebted vnto William Peprell of the towne of Kittery aforesaid in the said Province marriner in the full and Just sume of twenty foure pounds of currant mony of New England To be paid to the said William Peprell or to his certain atturney his Executors Admʳˢ or Assignes to the which payment well and truly to be made I bind me my heires Executors and Admʳˢ firmely by these pʳsents Sealed wᵗʰ my seale Dated this Nineteenth

Day of Aprill in the yeare of our lord God one thousand six hundred and Eighty Nine

The condition of this obligation is such that if the aboue bound Benjamin Woodbridge his heire Exec^{rs} and Adm^{rs} Doe and shall well and truly obserue performe accomplish fullfill and keepe all and singular the Covenants grants Articles Clauses and agreements which are and ought to be observed performed accomplished fulfilled and kept mentioned and Comprized in one Indenture of Bargaine and sale bearing equall Date wth these p^{r}sents made betweene the said Benjamin Woodbridge on the one parte and the aboue named William Peprell on the other parte in all things according to the true Intent and meaneing of the same Indenture of bargaine and sale: That then this obligation to be void and of none Effect or elce to be and remaine in full fforce effect and vertue   Benj: Woodbridge ($_{seale}^{a}$)
Sealed and Delivered in
  the p^{r}sence of John Bray
          William Hooke
         Robert Mitchell

This is a true Coppy of the originall obligation transcribed Compared and Entred this 2^d Day of December 1691:
                   p me John Wincoll Record^r

[64] This Instrument Declareth that I George Foxwell Mar^{nt} resident at Boston in New England haue Bargained sold and Emptied myself of all my right title and Interest of Eighteene head of Cattell And the halfe of all my Vncle Mr Richard Foxwells plantation which I the said George formerly bought of my said Vncle at black point in the towne of Scarburough alias Black point vnto James Robinson Cooper resident at the said Black point, For and   Consideration of

PART I, FOL. 64.

two hundred pounds to be paid according to the tenure of foure bills by the said Robinson signed and sealed and Delivered vnto me and for my vse that is to be fifty pounds p annem and to Confirme the truth hereof I Doe herevnto set my hand and seale this 26th Day of August Anno: one thousand six hundred seaventy one

Signed Sealed and Delivered   George Foxwell (seal)
  in the p'sence of vs   William Pitman made oath this
  Henry Jocelyn   22th of August 1685 that he
  William Pitman   did see George Foxwell sign
  Ambrose Bouden   seale and Deliver the aboue
    written Deed
        Robert Mason Just Pe

Ambrose Bouden Sen' made oath this 16th of June 1686 that he Did see Mr George Foxwell sine seale and Deliver the aboue written Deed

      Before me John Hinckes of the Counc̄ll

The aboue written is a true Coppy of the originall Deed Transcribed and here Entred this 2d Day of December 1691
         p me John Wincoll Recorder

To all Christian people to whom this p'sent Deed of sale shall Come. Joshua Scottow of Boston in the County of Suffolke in the Collony of the Massachusets bay in New England Merchant and Lidia his wife send greeting Know yee that the said Joshua Scottow and Lydia his said wife for and in Consideration of ffourteene pounds fifteene shillings of currant money of New England to them in hand paid at and before thensealing and Delivery of these presents by Samuell Sewall of Boston aforesaid Esq' the receipt whereof they Doe hereby acknowledge and themselues therewith to be fully satisfied and contented and thereof and of every

Part I, Fol. 64.

part thereof doe acquitt Exonorate and discharge the sd Samuell Sewall his heires Executors and Adm[rs] and every of them for ever by these presents Haue Giuen Granted bargained sold aliened Enfeoffed Conveyed and Confirmed And by these presents Doe fully freely Clearely and absolutely giue grant bargaine sell aliene Infeoffe convay and Confirme vnto the said Samuell Sewall his heires and assignes for ever A Certaine tract or parcell of Land scittuate lyeing and being on a Neck of land Commonly called and knowne by name of Maricaneeg Neck neere vnto North Yarmouth in Cascoa bay in the province of Maine in New England aforesd Containeing by Estimation fiue hundred acres be the same more or less granted vnto the said Joshua Scottow by the Hon[ble] Generall Court of the sd Massachusets bay in the yeare 1684 and confirmed vnto him the said Joshua Scottow his heires and assignes for ever by the said hon[ble] generall Court held at Boston by the Govern[r] and Company of said Massachusets Bay 27th May 1685 who then appointed Capt Edward Ting and Dominicus Jordan to lay out y[e] aforesd grant And the said Edward Tyng and Silvanus Davis Deputed therevnto by and in behalfe of sd Jordan in obedience to authority accordingly laid out the same vnto the sd Scottow as by their returne vnder their hands at falmouth Dated the sixt Aprill 1686: more plainely appeares: Which sd tract is bounded as followeth viz[t] Begining at a red oake tree Marked on the foure sides beareing Northeast Northerly from pulpit Island Comeing in at New Damaris Coue Sound and also to runn from the abouesaid Marked tree northwest and by north to run over the first Creeke vnto a litle river comonly called litle or Crooked lane Also to run from the first said red oake Marked tree northeast vp by the water side vp the bayward to Come vp to Sandy point takeing in all that small point of Marsh or meadow further to run vp from the head of the aforesaid litle river or Crooked lane northeast into the woods and so

PART I, FOL. 65.

far vp along fronting to the bay at Sandy poynt to run on a parralell line vntill two hundred acres be Expired being aded to aboue parcell to make vp the aforesd sum or quantyty Together with all and singular the lands Grounds Meadows marshes timber trees woods lyeing Growing [**65**] vppon and Contained within the said tract and all waters fishings commodytyes profitts priviledges hereditaments rights and appur^{ces} whatsoev^r to the same belonging or in any kind appertaineing – and the revertion and revertions remaind^r and remainders thereof and all their Estate right title Interest Inheritance Claime property and demand whatsoev^r of in and to the said bargained premises with all writeings & Evidences relating thereto To Have and to hold all the aboue granted and bargained premises with the appurtenances and every part and parcell thereof vnto the said Samuell Sewall his heires and assignes for ever to his and theire only sole and proper vse benefit and behoofe for ever And the said Joshua Scottow and Lydia his said wife for themselues their heires Executors and Adm^{rs} Doe hereby covenant promise and Grant to and with the said Samuell Sewall his his heires and assignes in manner and forme following that is to say – That at the time of this present grant bargaine and sale and vntill the Executeing of these presents they are the true sole and lawfull owners and stand lawfully seized in their own proper right of all the aforebargained premises in a good perfect and absolute estate of Inheritance in fee simple without any manner of condition revertion or limitation of vse or vses whatsoev^r so as to alter Change defeate or make void the same, Haueing in themselues full power good righ and lawfull authority to grant sell convey and assure the same in manner as aforesaid And that the said Samuell Sewall his heires and assignes shall and may by vertue of these presents from henceforth and for ever hereafter lawfull peaceably and Quietly haue hold vse occupie possess and enjoy the aboue granted premises Free and Cleere and Clearely acquitted and Discharged of and from all and all Manner of former and other gifts grants bargaines sales leases Mortgadges Jointures Judgments Executions Entailes forfeitures and of and from all other titles Charges & Incumbrances whatsoever had made Comitted Done or suffered to be done by them or either of y^m at any time or times before the Ensealeing hereof And shall and will at all times henceforth and for euer hereafter warrant and Defend all the aboue granted premises with the appurtenances thereof vnto the said Samuell Sewall his heires and assignes forever against the the lawfull Claimes and Demands of of all person & persons whomsoev^r by from or vnder them or either of them their or either of their heires or assignes —

In Witness whereof the said Joshua Scottow & Lidia his wife haue herevnto sett their hands and seales the twenty ninth Day March Anno Dom^i 1690 Annoq. RR^s et Regine Gulielmi et Marie nunc Anglie &c secundo

· Josh (seal) Scottow/   Lidia (seal) Scottow

Signed Sealed & deliv^rd in p^rsence
of vs William Paine
Samuell Mears
Eliezer Moody Scr :
Boston Aprill 10th 1690/
Recorded with the records of the county of
Suffolke for Deeds
att^r Is^a Addington Cl̃re

Joshua Scottow and Lydia his wife psonall appeareing in Boston this third Day of aprill 1690 Acknowledged the within Insrument to be their free act and Deed
Before Is^a Addington Assist^t

This is a true coppy of the originall Deed of Sale and here Entred this 3^d Day of December 1691

p me John Wincoll Record^r

Part I, Fol. 65.

Inventory of the Estate of Major John Davies Deceased Taken and appraised by me Ric[d] Bankes and me Abraham Prebell Aprill y[e] 3[d] 1691

	£	s	d
Impr His weareing Apparell	12	03	00
Two oxen 7£: 3 cowes 6. 15.	13	15	00
One heifer of 3 yeares old, two of 2 yeares 2£ 10	04	10	00
Two steares of 3 yeares old 4£ one of 2 years 25s	05	05	00
Twenty sheepe and six lambs 7£: 12s halfe a caffe 5s	07	17	00
To four hoggs and flue piggs	04	00	00
One horse a two year old Coult and a year old Coult	06	00	00
To one pair of Dowlas sheetes 20s 5 pair Cotton sheets	05	10	00
one pair of holland sheets 22s 2 diaper board Cloaths 30s	02	12	00
fiue table cloaths 25s sixteen Napkins 30s	02	15	00
Two towels 4s flue pilobers 15s, 8 napkins 10s	01	09	00
Three yards new Canvis 7s one long & two short Carpets 30s	01	17	00
In the new roome one featherbed and furniture	04	05	00
One tabell two formes 25s a bedsted 10	01	15	00
A tabell and forme in the Chamber 25s a bedstead 20s	02	15	00
In the chamber over the kitchen two beds and ruggs or	03	00	00
A table board 16s old tubs & Caske 2is	02	01	00
Three Iron and one brass pott two pair pot hookes Iron skilet	02	00	00
Two old brass kettles Chafing dish Candlestick Drip pan	02	06	00
Three flagons three quarts three platters pint Cups &c	02	10	00
Earthen Ware 1s one saddell 15s two ould tabell 10s	01	06	00
One Musquett 18s Double barrell Carbine 20s one Carbine 12s	02	10	00
Three paire of Andirons two tramells fire shouell } Two paire of tongs two spitt Chafing dish	03	10	00
one hide 12s a warming pan and lanthorne &c	01	04	00
Fiue Chests and a box 30s, a cubboard 15s, flue Chaires 20s	03	05	00
An ould Chest and box 6s, Cart wheeles and slid 32s	01	18	00
A plow plou Irons & Chaine 16s an Ax 4s bookes 22s	02	02	00
A grinding stone 4s paire stilers 5s	00	09	00
Plate and the Warehouse Wharfe & land 8£	18	12	00
The Dwelling house: barne: out houses and two acres of land adjoining	200	00	00
Soma	331	11	00

The marke of

Richard ℞ Bancks

Abra: Preble

A true Coppy of the originall Inventory recorded December 14th 1691 p me John Wincoll record[r]

Part I, Fol. 66.

[66] An Inventory of parte of the Estate of Maj^r John Daves taken by vs whose names are here vnderwritten Septemb^r 21th 1691 :/

	£	s	d
In primo One small mill to grind malt	02	00	00
It 15 putr Dishes and one bason	02	00	00
It 6 Cushings	00	12	00
It Two feather beds & furniture belonging to them	08	00	00
It 4 Chambr potts	00	06	00
It 1 putr plattr	00	10	00
	13	08	00

March ye 11th 1690 Disbursments on the funerall of Maj^r Daves

	£	s	d
In primo: For expences for the funerall	10	00	00
It being for funerall Charges			

Abra͠: Preble
John Twisden

Yorke March the 19th 169½

Wee whose names are vnder written ware desired by Mrs Mary Davis to aprise a sloope which was Major John Davies late Deceased of yorke which accordingly wee haue Vallued at twenty & three pounds currant money of New England In Wittness hereof wee haue herevnto set our hands

Samuell Donnell
Samuell Banks

The aboue written are true Coppys of the originalls this 14th Day of december 1691   p me John Wincoll Record^r

An Inventory of William Milberrys Estate lately deceased taken and aprised by vs whose names are here vnder written this 2^d Day of october 1691

	£	s	d
His wearing Cloathes	05	00	00
Two Cowes 5£ halfe a stere & a calfe 3£ 10s, 8 sheepe 2£	10	10	00
4 pigs 1£ 5s, a bed and bed Cloath 5£ 10s, 2 peuter dishes an axe 5s	07	00	00
Land and Marsh at bass Coue	16	00	00
A gun	01	00	00
	39	10	00

The marke of
John **H** harman
John Twisden

Part I, Fol. 67.

This is a true Coppy of the originall Inventory Entred this 14th Day of december 1691/ p me John Wincoll
Record^r

An Inventory of Steven Preble Estate lately Deceased taken and aprised by vs whose names are vnder subscribed this 3^d Day of October 1691/

	£	s	d
His wearing cloathes	04	10	00
A bed and bed Cloathes belonging to it	06	00	00
In Cash	02	02	00
23 yards of new Cloath	03	00	00
one hatt	00	04	00
2 Iron pots pot hookes one tramell	01	00	00
plow Joyring Chaine axes and other Joyrn	01	10	00
A gun and Cutlas	01	10	00
A horse bridle and sadle	03	00	00
A mayre and two Colts	05	00	00
14 sheep 3£ 10s 9 swine 8£	11	10	00
4 Cowes 10£ one oxe 4£	14	00	00
2 hafer and 2 steares	07	00	00
2 yearlings and 3 Calfes	03	00	00
old syths and rings	00	00	00
his Dwelling house & barne and aboue 40 acres of land and Mowing land adjoining to his house	100	00	00
20 acres of wood land	005	00	00
1 acres of marsh vp the north west branch of yorke river	003	00	00
	171	12	00

And more 36 shiling
mony: 01: 16: 00

The marke of
John | H Harman
John Twisden

A true coppy of the originall Inventory Entred on record this sixteenth Day of Decemb^r 1691/ p me John Wincoll
Record^r

[67] Inventory of Joseph Prebles Estate lately Deceased Taken and Aprised by vs whose names are vnder subscribed this 3th Day of october 1691/

	£	s	d
His Wearing Cloathes	04	00	00
In Cash	03	00	00
5 yards of sarge	01	00	00
5 yards of lining Cloath	00	10	00

Part I, Fol. 67.

26 yards of Cotten Cloath	02	10	00
2 beds & bed cloaths to them	10	00	00
8 pounds of yarne and Wooll	00	16	00
6 yards of Cotten Cloath	00	18	00
In puter	01	00	00
and axe and other tulls	00	10	00
1 gun and a Cutlash	01	10	00
3 Joyron pots a ketle and skillet	01	10	00
2 Cowes 5£ 4 hafers 7£	12	00	00
2 oxen one steare a Calfe at	10	00	00
8 swine	01	10	00
13 sheepe	02	05	00
a Multle	00	10	00
1 Mayre and Colt and sadle	03	00	00
House and barne and about 100 acres of land adjoining to it	40	00	00
1 acres of marsh vp the north west branch of yorke river	03	00	00
	99	19	00

2 wedges 18d

John Harman

his | H marke

John Twisden

A true Coppy of the originall Inventory Entred on record This 16th Day of december 1691 p me John Wincoll Record^r

Know all men by these presents that I Joane Cartter now of the great Island in piscataqua Widdow Doe for Divers good Causes me moueing therevnto but more Especially that naturall affection which I beare vnto my beloued sone John Dimand doe by these p^rsents freely and volentarily giue and bestowe vnto my said sone Jn° Dimand a tract of land of ten acres in Crooked lane with the house vpon it which land I formerly purchased of Joshua Downing and was the land on which my husband William Dymand deceased & my selfe Did formerly build and liue vpon, as also a tract of land of about Eight acres giuen vnto my sd husband Dymand by the town of Kittery as may apeure by their grant which tract of land lieth at the head of the abouesd tenn acres of land together with tenn acres of land be it more or less lying between my brothering laws lotts, to say John Dymand And

Part I, Fol. 67.

Andrew Dymand formerly giueinge by my father in law Jn° Dymand deceased vnto my late husband William Dymand Deceased with all the priviledges & appurtenances thereunto apertayning or belonginge vnto each & every parcell of land aboue specified to be the proper Estate of John Dymand my aboue said sone his heire Executors and Administrators for evermore To haue & to hould and improue as his and their Estate for ever without any lett or molestation by me my heires Executors Administrators or assignes, alwayes prouided that he the sd John Dymand shall well and truly pay vnto his two sisters now liueing fiue pounds to each of them and that he shall not Alienate or sell the abouesd land or any part of it but shall receiue it for his posterity : but in case he should alter his condition and Marry and Dye without Issue then the sayd house and land abouesd to be Improued by his Widdow Dureing her naturall life and then to returne into my hands again as my proper estate or elce If I am deceased, into the hands of his two sisters equally to be devided or otherwise If them or either of them shold be Depated out of this world then to be dvided amongst their children that are surviueing and in the meane time If penury or want should overtake me that then I may haue an abideing place in the abouesd house & land Dureing my liue, all which being Duely performed I doe then giue & grant the abousd house & lands as aboue for ever vnto the performance of all which I doe herevnto sett my hand & seale this twenty second Day of Decemb^r 1691

Signed sealed & delivered
  in the presence of vs
  Francis Hooke
  Jeremy ✝ Walford

The marke of
Joan ✝ Carter ($_{scale}^{a}$)
A true Coppy of y^e originall
Entred Jan^{ry} 12 169½
    p Jn° Wincoll Reco^{rdr}

Part I, Fol. 68.

[68] This Indenture made the ninteenth Day of January Anno Dom̃ one thousand six hundred and Ninety Annoq̨ RRˢ et Regine Gulielmi et Marie nunc Anglie &cᵃ secundo between John Alden Senʳ of boston in the County of Suffolke within their Majᵗⁱᵉˢ Collony of the Massachusets bay in New England Marrinʳ and Elizabeth his wife one of the Daughters of mʳ William Phillipps late of boston aforesd Gent̃ Decd, on the oue part and Simeon Stoddard of boston aforesd Shopkeeper on the other part Witnesseth that Whereas the sd John Alden Senʳ by an obigatory bill vnder his hand and seale It heareing Date the ninth Day of September A D 1689 stands Indebted vnto the sd Simeon Stoddard in the full and Just sum̃e of two hundred seventy Foure pounds seven shillings and six pence currant Mony of New England made payable vnto the sd Simeon Stoddard his heires &cᵃ on or befor the first Day of October next Ensuing the Date of sd bill And wheras the time of payment therof is elapsed and the said Alden Desires twelue monthes time more from the Date hereof for the Discharge of sd bill with Interest vpon sd mony as is hereafter Expressed wᶜʰ sd Stoddard hath consented vnto Now Further Witnesseth this Indenture that the sd John Alden and Elizabeth his wife as part security for payment of the aforesd summe of Two hundred seventy foure pounds seven shillings and six pence with Interest for yᵉ same as is herevnder mentioned and Expressed to the sd Simeon Stoddard his heires &c Haue giuen granted bargained & sold Aliened Enfeoffed conveyed and Confirmed and by thes presents Doe fully freely Clearely and absolutely giue grant bargaine sell alien Enfeoffe convey and Confirme vnto the sd Simeon Stoddard his heires and assignes for ever One hundred acres of land in a place called Decaied Neck alias pechague together with one Eight part of all the meadow ground belonging to the sd neck And one hundred acres of

John Alden & Elizabeth his wife & daugr of Wm Phillips to Sim. Stoddard

land at a place called Rooty brooke together with a sixteen shilling purchase being the fifteenth lot in that devision all which parcels are within the limits and precincts of the town of Midleborough within the Jurisdiction of New Plimouth in New England aforesd also one hundred acres more being the first in a Devision of a thousand acres within bridgwater bounds in sd Jurisdiction all which was granted to the sd John Alden by Deed of gift vnder ye hand and seale of his father John Alden dec^d of Duxbury bearing Date ye thirteenth Day of January 1686 reference wherto or the record thereof being had more fully may appeare Also one Eighth part of a tract of land scittuate lyeing and being between Kinibunk riuer and Batsons river (so called or Known) within the Province of maine (al^s yorkshiere) contaning by Estimation foure miles and more by the sea side that is to say from river to river and is to extend reach and run vp Eight miles into the land being butted and bounded by the sea on the Southeast (the Islands lyeing betweene the mouths of the two rivers of Kinibunke and Batsons to be alwayse reckoned and accounted to be belonging to the said aboue menĉoned and Included therein) and is also bounded by the two rivers one to the north East and the other to the South west or pointing thereabout and so to extend or run vp Eight miles within the land there to Cross with a head line at the end of the sd Eight miles right vp from the sea side from one river to the other which prescribed bounds are to be the limitts and Extent of the aforesd tract or parcell of land which was purchased by the sd William Phillipps of an Indian Sagamore Comonly Knowne to the English people about that part of the Countrey by the name of Moghiggin with other lands therevnto Adjoining he being formerly the true Indian proprietor and posessor thereof as by the Deeds thereof vnder his hand and sealle vppon record in the publick office of the Province of Maine aforesd relation whereto being had more fully may appeare and wch said tract hath since been Confirmed to ye sd Wm Phillips and his heires in the Kingdome of England by Fardinando Gorges Esqr the true & right heire and successor of Sr Fardinando Gorges Kn^t the lord proprietor of the sd province of Maine al^s yorkshiere as by the pattent vnder the great Seale of England granted by the Kings Maj^{tie} to the sd Sr Ferdinando Gorges his heires and successors or by the true transcript or Coppys therof may more at large appeare and which sd Eighth part by Deed of Sale vnder the hand and seale of the said William Phillipps beareing date the twelfth Day of June Anno Dom: 1676: was granted vnto the sd John Alden as by the sd Deed or record thereof in the 3^d booke of records page 4th for the province of Maine reference whereto being had more fully may appeare Also one thousand acres more of land Giuen and granted vnto the sd Elizabeth Alden by sd William Phillips her father by Deed vnder his hand and seale vppon record in the aforsd third booke of records beareing Date the fifteenth Day of June Anno Dom: 1676 being a part and parcell of a tract or parcell of land scittuate lyeing and being in the foresd Province of Maine and on the Westerne side of Kennibeck river containing by Estimation Eight Miles square to extend Eight Miles from the sea and adjoining to the Inland head line of the township of Wells and so to be as aforesd Eight Miles square all which was formerly purchased by the said William Phillips of an Indian Saggamore comonly known by the English people in and about that part of the Country by the name of Fluellin formerly the true Indian proprietor owner and possessor thereof and since Confirmed to him the sd William Phillipps by sd Fardinando Gorges esq^r the heire and successor of Sr Ferdinando Gorges Kn^t the lord proprietor of the whole Province of Maine al^s yorkshiere as by the aforsd pattent relation whereto being had more fully may appeare As also one quarter or fourth part of a Saw mill with sawes Dogs Crowes and all maner of vtensells goeing geare and tooles therevnto belonging scittuate vnder Sacoe falls with the benefitt of the place (which said Saw mill was built by the sd Alden) and also with sufficient Meadow land pasture land and timber for the sd quarter part porportionaby to the other three quarter parts which sd quarter part was granted [69] and Giuen to the sd John & Elizabeth Alden by Deed vnder the hand & seale of the sd William Phillipps bearing Date the twenty Eighth Day of November Anno Domī 1662 as by the sd Deed or record thereof on the 35 & 36 pages of the new booke of records for the aforesd Province of Maine reference wherevnto being had more fully and at large Doth and may appeare Together with all and singular the lands grounds meadowes marshes woods vnderwoods timber trees swamps beach flats mines quarries rivers strĕames Dams̄ ponds water courses wayes Easments waters watercourses fishing fowleing hauking hunting within the limītts of the aboue granted premises with all other rights profitts priviledges advantages Imunityes Com̄oditates hereditaments town rights Com̄odityes and appurtenances whatsoever to the same or any part or parcell thereof belonging or in any Kind appertaining or therewith now vsed occupyed or enjoyed or accepted reputed or taken as part parcell or memb^r thereof And Also all the Estate right title Interest Dower Claime Inheritance propriety and demand whatsoever of the sd John and Elizabeth Alden and either of them of in and to the same & every part thereof with the revertion and reverc̄ons remainder and remainders thereof and of every part thereof To Haue and to Hold all the aboue granted and bargained Premises with their and and Every of their rights, members hereditaments and appurtenances and every part and parcell thereof (in as large and ample mañer & forme as the same were granted to the sd John and Elizabeth Alden & their heires and assignes by vertue of the aforementioned Deeds) vnto the sd Simeon Stoddard his heires and Assignes for ever, to the only

Part I, Fol. 69.

proper vse benefitt and behoof of him the sd Simeon Stoddard his heires and Assignes from henceforth and for evermore And the said John Alden and Elizabeth his wife for themselues their heires Executors and Administrators Doe hereby Covenant promise grant & agree to and with the said Simeon Stoddard his heires E^{rs} Administo^{rs} and assignes in manner and forme following that is to say that at the time of this present grant bargaine and sale and vntill thensealing and Delivery of these presents the sd John and Elizabeth Alden are the true sole and lawfull owners of all the aforebargained premises and stand lawfully seized thereof in their own proper right of a good perfect and Absolute Estate of Inheritance in Fee simple without any mañer of Condicon revercon or limitation whatsoever so as to alter Change defeat or make void the same Haueing in themselues full power good right and lawfull authority to grant sell Convey and assure the same in mañer and forme aforsd And that the sd Simeon Stoddard his heires and assignes shall and may by force and virtue of these presents from henceforth and for ever hereafter lawfully peaceably and Quietly haue Hold use ocupy possess and Injoy the aboue granted p'misses with the appurtenances thereof Free and Cleare and freely and Clearely acquitted exonorated and Discharged off and from all and all mañer of former and other Gifts grants bargaines sales leases Mortgadges Jointures Dowers Judgments Executions Extents Intaile forfeiturs seizures fines Amerciaments rents and of and from all and all maner of other titles troubles Charges and Incombrances whatsoever And Further the said John Alden and Elizabeth his wife Doe hereby Covenant promise bind and oblidg themselues their heires Executors and Administrators from henceforth and forever hereafter to Warrant and Defend all the aboue granted premises with their and every of their appurtenances vnto the sd Simeon Stoddard his heires and assignes for ever against the

PART I, FOL. 69.

lawfull Claimes and demands of all and every person & persons whomsoev' Provided allwayes and these presents are vppon this Condition any thing herein to the contrary thereof Notwithstanding That if the aboue named John Alden Sen' his heires Ex'ⁿ Administrators or assignes or either of them shall and Doe well and truely pay or Cause to be paid vnto the within named Simeon Stoddard or to his Certaine atturney heires Ex'ⁿ Administoⁿ or assignes in Boston aforesd the full and Just summe of three hundred and twelue pounds Currant money of New England on or before the nineteenth Day of January which will be in the yeare of our lord one thousand six hundred Ninety and one/₉₂ without fraud or farther delay That then this p'sent Indenture Sale and grant and every Clause and Article therof together with the aboue recited bill obligatory to be null void and of none Effect or elce to abide & remaine in full force and virtue to all Intents and purposes in the law whatsoever In Witnesse whereof the sd John Alden and Elizabeth his wife haue herevnto set their hands and seales the Day & yeare first aboue written/

Signed sealed & Deliv'ᵈ   John Alden Sen' (seal)
in p'sence of vs   Elizabeth Alden (seal)
Delivernce Torner   Cap' John Alden and Elizabeth his
Eliezer Moody Scr :/   wife acknowledged this Instrument to be their act and Deed, before Elisha Hutchinson Assist:
Boston March. 2. 169½

This aboue written Instrument or deed of Mortgadge is Recorded in Plimouth Counties new booke of records for deeds and Evidences of lands—begining at page 117 and Ending in page
    120 Aprill 24. 1691   p Sam¹ Sprague Recorder
This aboue written is a true Coppy of the originall Deed of Mortgadge and here Entred on Record January 30. 169½
                p John Wincoll Record'

Part I, Fol. 70.

[70] The deposision of Henry Brookin, aged about forty foure years and Sarah Brookin, aged about nineteene years sworn saith that about october last past wee these Deponents was Desired by Mr Thomas Withers to goe over with him to his Island lieing betweene his house and Strawberry banke where wee did see ye sd Mr Withers giue his Daughter Elizabeth Withers posession of the one halfe part of the said Island, next to Strabery banke by Deliver-

together with ye house so that it was not Intended yt side ovr against Strawbery bank but ye vpper end & ye halfe of ye same Island

ing her a turfe and twigg of the sd Island and Did put his Daughter Elizabeth in posession of the house that is now on the Island, and further Mr Withers at the same time Did say that he Did give the litle Island that lies northeast from ye abouesd Island y^t Elizabeth Withers hath posession of: vnto his sd Daughter the said Mr Withers pointing with his finger towards it and said, Betty I will giue thee that litle Island and further saith not

Henry Brookin & Sarah Brookin Came and made oath to the verity abouesaid this 6 of Ap^r 1685

Before me Francis Hooke Jus^t pe

William Heynes aged about 49 yeares being with ye abouesaid Mr Withers Deceased, and More over wheras it was at one and the same time when the deponents aboue Mentioned & the said Withers gaue his Daught^r Elizabeth free possession both of the house and also of the vpper end, to wit the vpper halfe of the same Island aforsd scittuated over against Strawberry banke and the manner of the sd possession giuen was by turfe & twig & more over by the same token shee his Daught^r put presently ye said Deponent that am here subscribed in possession for her friend or tenant Dureing her pleasure   William Heynes

Mr William Haynes came and made oath to ye verity

Part I, Fol. 70.

aboue sd this 7 of Ap^r: 1685 Before me Francis Hooke Jus: pea

The aboue written are tru Coppies of the originall deposisions of Henry Brookin Sarah Brookin and William Heynes and here Entred on record this 16th Day of February 169½   p me John Wincoll Record^r

An Inventory of the Estate of Henry Child late of Barwick deceased Sept 25 1691/

His wearing Cloathes	01	06	00
A peece of searge at 5s p yd 13yds	03	05	00
Two feather beds, 2 bolster, 2 pillows one p of sheets 1 p blanckets, 2 rugs, an old Coverlet & 2 old blankets	10	00	00
Seven Earthen milkpans and some Dishes	00	04	00
two Iron pots a kettle and 3 pailes	01	08	00
three Chests 20s sixteene yds linen Cloath	02	12	00
Hoopes, boxes, axle trees pins for 2 p wheeles	02	00	00
two log Chaines two Draft Chaines	03	00	00
two paire of plow Irons	01	00	00
four old axes and a croscut saw	00	12	00
A homestall of forty acres of land and thirty acres bought of phineas Hull & 50 or 60 acres of land a town grant			
four oxen and two 4 year old steres at	21	00	00
foure Cowes 8£, 1: 2 year old 1: 3 year old and three calues and one horse	14	10	00
seven swine	03	00	00
	63	17	00

Apprized this 10th Day of february 169½ p vs

                         Richard ◯ Nason
                                his marke

Province   John ⁊ Nason
of Maine Feb^ry: 10: 169½   his marke

Sarah Child tooke oath that the aboue written is a true Inventory of her deceased Husband Henry Child his Estate and If any more estate appeare shee will ad it thereto and the said Sarah Child and Richard Nason her father acknowledg themselues bound to o^r sov^rn lord and lady the King & Queene in the sum of a hundred twenty and seven pounds

PART I, FOL. 71.

fourteene shillings that the said Sarah Child shall administer on said Estate according to law
                    Before me John Wincoll Just^{ce} of peace

The aboue written is a true coppy of the originall Inventory wth the oath & bond acknowledged & is here entred on record this 16th Day of February 169¼
                    p me John Wincoll Record^r

[71] The Inventory of the Estate and Goods of Joseph Hodsden lately Deceased had seene and apraised by Richard White and John More this 15th Day of June 1691/

	£	s	d
T·) foure Cowes	08	00	00
To two Steares	06	00	00
To two heifers three yeares old	03	10	00
To two heifers two years old	02	10	00
To one yearling	00	16	00
To one Mare and Colt	03	00	00
To foure Ewes	01	04	00
To flue swine	03	00	00
To one Dwelling house & one barne	20	00	00
To two plow Chaines	00	12	00
To one yoake	00	02	06
To two small Gunes	01	10	00
To peuter	00	12	00
To one pot scelet, Cetle one frienpan	00	14	00
To Edg toole and Iron worke	01	00	00
To two Chests and one Box	00	09	00
To woodden ware	00	10	00
To two beds and furniture	08	00	00
To one sadle and one pillion	00	14	00
To one Cannoe	01	00	00
	63	02	06

The aboue Inventory had seen and appraised by us
        John More   Richard White
            ✝   ⊖
        his mark   his marke

John Hodsden made oath to this Inventory This 9 day June 1691 and If any more apeare to ad it
            Before me Francis Hooke Jus peace :

A true Coppy of the originall Inventory here Entred on record this 19th Day of february 169¼
                    p me John Wincoll Record^r

Part I, Fol. 71.

June 15 91 Samuell Sawords Cloathes apprised by John Fost and Walter Allin which is in the hands of William Spencer

	£	s					
It one new Coate...............	03	13	00	Samuell Saword Debter To Wil-			
It on pair of woosted stockens.	00	04	00	liam Spencer...	1	18	00
It two old shirts................	00	02	00	To arthur Bragden	1	03	00
It one homespun Coate........	00	12	00	To Nicholas Turbet..............	0	05	06
It one pair briches	00	07	00	To Mary f..st.....................	0	02	06
	03	18	00	To Ephm Joy for a razor....			
one pair of shoos paid to Nicholas Turbett for Diging his Graue					3	09	00

Jan'y 26 169½ William Spencer tooke oath to the truth of this Inventory and If any more appeare he will ad it hereto

     Before me John Wincoll Just^{ce} of peace

A true Coppy of the originall Inventory here Entred Feb: 19 169½   p me John Wincoll Record^r

Be it knowne vnto all men by these presents that I Christian Ramick of the town of Kittery in the province of mayn Doe for Divers good considerations me moueing therevnto but more Especially the fatherly affection and tender care and loue that I beare vnto my beloved sone Isaak Ramick Doe by these presents freely grant and giue vnto him my beloved sone aforesaid and to his lawfull heires begotten of his own body for ever a sertayn tract and parcell of land with a Dwelling house vppon it scittuate and lying in the aforsaid province of Mayn in Kittery in the great Cove behind Thomas Spineyes Contayning thirty acres of vpland to say twenty poale breadth by the water side north and south and Eight score pole into the woods vppon an East and west line, and also forty pole square East and West, north and south Joyning to the aforesaid tract of land on the north side all which maketh vp thirty acres of

Part I, Fol. 71.

land as abouesaid all joining to Richard King and John fernalds land To haue and to hold the abouesaid land to him and his heires for ever as aboue said without any lett or molestation by mee or any vnder me alwayes provided that my sone Isaack abouesaid shall without any lett or hindrance giue way to me or any by my appointment to Cutt and carry of the abouesaid land two hundred cord of wood provided that I or mine shall cut the said wood within twenty yeares from the Date hereof, If not then to be freely my sone Isaack for ever vnto which Dayly Gift I doe hereby freely & voluntaryly giue and Grant as abouesaid vnto my sone Isaack as abouesd for ever but If in case the said Isaac shall Dy without Isue his wife If he haue any shall Injoy the said land Dureing her life together with the said house vnto which Deed of gift I doe herevnto freely set my hand and seale this sixteenth Day of Octob^r Añ Dom̃ 1686/

Signed Sealed & deliurd Christian Remick (a seal)
  in the presence of vs   Christian Remick came before me
  Francis Hooke   this 9th of March 1686 and ac-
  The marke of   knowledged this Deed or
  Nicholas /M weekes   writing to be his act and
                                  before
                    John Hinckes of the Councill

I vnderwritten doe freely & voluntary giue my Consent and aprobation to the act and Deed of my father Christian Remich of the other side mentioned vnto my brother Isaak Remich & doe hereby Promise and ingadge never to Disturbe him or any of his on the said land which is within mentioned

PART I, FOL. 72.

vnto which I doe herevnto set my hand this sixteenth Day of october 1686/

 Witness   Jacob Remich
 Francis Hooke   Jacob Remich Came before me this
 The marke of   9th of March 1686 and acknowl-
 Jonathan Ⅎᴧ Nason edged this aboue wrighting to be
          his ackt and ded before
         John Hinckes of the Councill

The aboue written are true Coppyes of the originall Deed of gift and of the writing on the back side of it transcribed & here entred on record this 25 Day of February 169¼
        p me John Wincoll Recorder

[72] Inventory of Mr Shubaell Dumers Estate left in yorke when he was Killd and substance destroyed Jan^{ry} 25. 169½ p vs whose names are vnderwritten

	£	s	d
Impr 4 Cowes and one young bull	10	00	00
To one horse and one mare	05	00	00
To 4 pigs of last Spring	04	00	00
To fifteene sheepe	04	10	00
To three Acres of marsh	07	00	00
To one small Iron pott and Ketle	00	17	00
To 150 pound Gross of old peuter	01	12	04
	32	19	04

Inventory of Mr Shubaell Dumers   Thomas Clarke
Estate in pascataqua   the marke of
February 26 169½ p vs vnderwritten   Henry H Milbery

Imprimis one barrell of porke at fifty shillings	02	10	00
To three barrells of beefe at thirty shillings each	04	10	00
	07	00	00
To two Chests locked contents not yet Knowne | totall:	39	19	04

   Mr George Snell made oath to this Inventory & that it is all at p^rsent he knoweth of and as more Doe or may p^rsent

Part I, Fol. 72.

he will giue it in to the Court or such as ought to haue Cognisance hereof

 Sworne in Kittery this 19th March 1691-2 before vs
    Francis Hooke Dept pre͞:
    John Wincoll Justce of peace

A true Coppy of the originall here Entred this 23th Day of March 169½   p me John Wincoll Recordr

An Inventory of some goods found in two Chests belonging to the Estate of Mr Shubaell Du͞mer late of yorke deceased mentioned in the Inventory

	£	s	d		£	s	d
Impr 28 yds of blanket cloath new out of ye loome at 2s 9d p yd	03	17	00	A Sheet of fine brins	00	10	00
one p of Curtaines & Valance	01	04	00	3 hand towels 2 shirts & 1 p drawers	00	15	00
one p home spun Curtaines being 3 with Valence	01	00	00	3 pair of stockens	00	07	00
one small Carpett	00	06	00	a bolster 2 pillows & two Cushions	00	18	00
3 petty Coats & a mantle of her wearing Cloaths	02	00	00	a slick stone 1s 10 peeces earthen ware dutch	00	09	00
an old turkie Coverlate	00	10	00	33 pound of pewter	02	04	00
3 homespun blankets	01	10	00	4 peeces latin ware	00	04	00
2 old narrow green Curtaines one broad & valance	00	05	00	a brass bason of 4 lb waight	00	10	00
another small Carpet	00	06	00	2 skirts Kenting 5 caps & 7 bands 2 neck cloathes, half sleeues, 4 Kenting handkercheefs, 2 p cotton gloues & a cubbard cloath	01	15	00
6 napkins & a table cloath brins 5 yds ¼	00	15	00	two trunkes & 2 chests	01	00	00
6 napkins & a table cloath Dowlas 5 yds	00	10	00	a silver tankerd, a wine cup & a spoon 19½ ounces	05	10	00
6 napkins & a table cloath Diaper 5 yds	00	13	00		30	16	00
6 pillowbers cotton	00	10	00				
4 pillowbers Dowlas	00	08	00				
10 sheetes of cotton Cloath	03	10	00				

   Apprized by vs this 16th Day
    of May 1692
      Francis Hooke
      John Wincoll

This is a true coppy of the additionall Inventory here Entred this 16th Day of may 1692 :
    p me John Wincoll Recordr

An Inventory of the estate of Jonathan Nason Deceased taken and prised this nintenth Day of march one thousand

Part I, Fol. 72.

six hundred Nintti one two by left^t John Tuttle and Petter grant Senr

ffurst To ye waring apparrell	05	00	00
pr Armes and Amenishon	04	00	00
pr mony noat	000	00	00
pr The houses and housen with all the land adjoining to it Containing one hundred accores prised at	170	00	00
pr Land and Marsh lyeing at Sturgeon Creek in partnership abot	25	00	00
pr one hundred Accores off land lieing near ye rocky hills	015	00	00
pr Two oxen foure Cowes two 3 yerere olds	021	10	00
pr one yearling 4 sheepe one horse	001	10	00
pr fifteen swine at the prices of	006	09	00
pr one fether bed and furniture to it	004	00	00
pr a flock bed and bedding	002	00	00
pr eleven pewter platters 4 plates & pr 8 porringer & other peuter	004	00	00
pr a small p of scales & waites	000	06	00
pr a Cubbrd	003	00	00
pr two tables & Chaires & Jonte stooles	002	01	00
pr two Chests and two bedsteds	000	18	00
pr flax and Cotton yarne & woollen yarne & flax yarne	006	10	00
pr two payre of lomes and Gares	005	10	00
pr oyeren puts & tramells Dodges & tonges	002	12	00
pr botles locken glasses & other small th!ngs	000	09	00
pr Two woollen wheales two lenen wheales one pair Cords	000	10	00
pr Enden Corne & English Corne & proveshen	007	08	00
pr sadle & bridle & sadle Cloath	000	12	00
pr old kaske & tubs and one sefe	000	16	00
pr one Hackell one warmenpan & more short flacx	000	13	06
pr boockes and table linen	000	07	00
pr pales Dishes spones and trenshers	000	10	00
pr three Chanes 2 Clefeses one pair of bettell rings 4 wedges	001	16	00
pr one Cart & Wheeles plowe & slede one yocke	002	06	00
pr a Cyder press	000	06	00
pr three axes 2 howes one Ades 2 pich forckes	001	01	00
pr one Crosscut saw one sieth	000	11	00
pr one saw 2 Hacke 3 beles & other small toules	000	13	00
pr one Cannue one friing pan	001	05	00
as to a parcell of staues in partnership vndevided	000	05	00

      John Tuttle, Peter O Grant
         his marke

Sara Nason relict and Administratrix to the Estate of her late husband Jonathan Nason tooke oath to the truth of this Inventory and If any more shall hereafter appeare shee will ad it herevnto

 Sworne this 24th day of march 169½ Before me
      John Wincoll Just^ce of peace

Part I, Fol. 73.

The aboue written is a true Coppy of the originall Inventory & the widdows oath to it here recorded March 28th 1692

p me John Wincoll Record^r

[73] To all Cristen People to whom this pressent Rightting shall Come and Appeare, I Steven Jenkenes of oshter rever in the tounshepe of Dover in the provence of Nue Hampsheare in New England sendeath Greatting know ye that I the sad Steven Jenkenes ffor Good Cases and Considdrationes him mouenig thearevnto and More Espeshally ffor and in Consideration of the sum of AEleven pounds in money in hand paid before the Insealing and delivering of thes presents by ye hands of my brother Jonathan Nasson of the toune of Barweck in the provence of Main the receipt whareoff I Doe acknowledg myselfe Satisfied and paid and of every pence theareof Doth for ever acquet and Discharge my Brother Jonathan Nasson his Hires Executores Admenestratores and Assines by these presents hath obsolutly giuen Giuen Grantted barganed sold Infefed asshured and Confermed and by these presents Doth giue Grant bargan and sell vnto my brother Jonathan Nasson two peases of Marsh liing in Sturgen Creeke in the provencs of Main one peas liing neare to Capt ffrosts marsh and the other peacs liing at ye south west end of ye aforesd marsh which two peases of Marsh containing two Acores more or less that was formerly my father Jenkenes with all preveledges and Appertanses theareto belonging and Appertaining vnto the sd Steven Jenkenes shall be for the sole vse benefit and behoufe of the sd Jonathan Nasson his hires Executores Admenestratores and assines for ever To Haue and To Hold the premeses aforesd and the sd Steven Jenkenes Doth for himselfe hires Executores Admenestratores Covenant &

Part I, Fol. 73.

promes a varant to maintaine that he hath In himselfe good right full poure and lawfull athoretti to sell & Dispoes of the premeses abouesd that he hath in himselfe good right full poure and lawfull athoretti from all poure of thirds and that it is freely acquetted and Discharged from all other gifts barganes sales wills Judgments Intales or any other Incombrances of what Nattur or Kind soever without any Molestation frome me my Hires Excutores Admenestratores or by my meanes consent permet Consent or procurement In Witns heareof I the sd Steven Jenkenes haue hearevnto set my hand and scale this third Day of Aprall in the yeare of oure Lord one thousand six hundred and nintti one and in the third yeare of oure soverin lord William by the grace of god King of England Scotland and France and oyrland Defender

Sealed Signed and Delivered   The sine of
   In the presents of vs   Steven O Jenkenes (a seal)
Benjamin Nason Edward Allen
Joseph Abbott

   A true coppy of the originall Deed here recorded This 28th Day of March 1692   p me John Wincoll Record^r

   An Inventory of the Estate of phill Adams in the pvince

	£	s	d
His Home place	40	00	00
to 3 acres of meadow	12	00	00
to 40 acres of land behind the towne	20	00	0c
to 40 acres of land vp the river	10	00	00
to 29 acres of swamp land	30	00	00
3 cowes	09	00	00
3 3year old	04	10	00
3 Cafe	01	10	00
to 10 swine	10	00	00
	102	00	00
more 2 chines	000	10	00
2 guns	001	10	00

Prised by Job Alcock

the marke of John I H Harman

   A true coppy of the originall Inventory here Entred may 17th 1692   p me John Wincoll Record^r

PART I, FOL. 74.

An Inventory of the Estate of Jonathan Masterson late of yorke Deceased

His weareing Cloathes, brass, penter, Iron two feather beds 2 rugs, 1 bolster two pillow bers, 2 Chests, 3 sheets 4 Napkins............................ 036 00 00
His Dwelling house barne 16 acres of land and other lands Adjoining........ 100 00 00
136 00 00

March 3ᵈ 169½ Apprized by phillip bab & John Linscott
A true coppy of the originall Inventory here Entred on record May 17ᵗʰ 1692   p me John Wincoll Recordʳ

[74]
In the name of god Amen I Abraham Conley of the town of Kittery in the County of yorke in New England being weake and sickly of body but perfect of memory thanks be to god Doe make and ordayne this my last will & testament in maner & forme as here followeth/ And first I Doe giue & bequeath vnto Nathan Lord and Abraham Lord the two sones of Nathan Lord the Elder my sone in law all that lot or tract of land with the appurtenances called or Comonly known by the name of Coole harbour which I lately purchased of James Emery of Kitry and all that pte of my land that lieth at Sturgeon Creeke which is now lett & Disposed of to one Francis Small with this pviso that If the sd Small Doe hold his bargaine made with me for the said land then the sd Nathan Lord & Abraham to receiue & haue all such pay either Money or other Engadgments as he oweth to and hath bound himselfe to pay for it but If hee the said Small Doe relinquish or otherwise make void his bargaine that he made with me for the said land then my will is that they shall haue the land as aforesaid to the only vse benefit and behoofe of them the said Nathan and Abraham Even all that land that was barganed granted or In-

This is a true Coppy of the originall written will of Abraham Conley June 8th 1692 & entred on Record p me John Wincoll Recordʳ

Adrian Fry & Sarah his wife attested on oath to the truth aboues'd June 8th 1692 Before vs Charles Frost } Justices John Wincoll } of the peace

tended to be granted vnto the said ffrancis Small/ And my Will is that this shall be the devission betwixt them the said Nathan and Abraham the one to haue the aforesd land at Sturgeon Creeke or the rents and profits therof and the other the land Called Coole harbour lately purchased of James Emery as aforesd with this pviso & pvisoes that Nathan Lord the Eldest brother to take his Choice which of they two he will haue And to haue it as they shall Come to the age of twenty one yeares each of them, the Eldest first as he Comes to the age aforesd and the other sucsessiuely and in the mean time to be in their fathers Disposall after my Decease Also I Doe giue & bequeath vnto Nathan Lord thelder my sone in law all that land that Nicholas Frost now holdeth of me and all the other land either marsh meadow or vpland that I now haue or ought to haue at Sturgeon Creeke, (besides that I haue lett or granted vnto the aforesd Francis Small) by vertue of any town grant or grants or other wise to his own pper vse benefit & behoofe for ever/ Also I doe giue and bequeath vnto Adrian Fry with whom I doe now liue nine pounds or there abouts which is due vnto me on two bills and Doe acquitt him thereof for ever also I doe giue vnto John White my Neighbour all such debts as he oweth me and Doe thereof acquitt him Also I doe giue vnto Robert Allen all such Debts as he oweth me either by bill or otherwise and thereof Doe acquitt him : All which Debts aforesd If I doe happen to Dye before they are Due to me or before they are paid my meaning and will is that I Doe acquitt them against my Executor for ever/ All the rest of my Goods & Chattells or lands Moueable or Vn-moueable bills bonds or other Debts what soever not here-tofore in or by this my last Will and testament not giuen or bequeathed I doe giue and bequeath vnto Nathan Lord thelder my sone in law whome I doe make my whole and sole Executor to see my Debts paid and my legacies per-formed in Witness hereof I haue Caused this my Will to be

Part I, Fol. 74.

made and haue here vnto sett my hand and seale Even the first Day of March in the twenty seventh yeare of the raigne of our Soveraign Lord Charles the Second by the grace of god of England Scotland France & Ireland King Defender of the faith : And in y⁰ yeare of oʳ Lord 1674/
Sealed & Acknowledged in the
   pʳsence of vs here vnderwritten The marke of
   Andrew Searle
   The marke of **A F** Adrian Fry Abraham Conley (Seal)

Province   Adrian Fry & Sarah his wife tooke oath that
of main   they saw the aboue Abraham Conley set to his
          hand & seale to the aboue written will when he was of a disposeing Capasity & that Andrew Searle and Adrian Fry set to their hands as wittnesses then
   Sworn this 5ᵗ Day of March 16⅞?
    Before me John Wincoll Justᶜᵉ of pease

To all Christian people to whome this prisent Deed of Sale shall Come Greetting whereas the select men of Kittery within yᵉ Province of Mayne in New England vpon the 24ᵗʰ Day of March 1678 granted twenty acres of Land to Robert Allin Senʳ of Could harbour to him his heires or assignes for ever Know ye that I Robert Allin of yᵉ Town of Kittery in the province of Mayne on the one party & Adrian Fry of yᵉ said town & province Witnesseth that said Robert Allin for & in Consideration of the sum of six pounds in hand received before the Ensealing & Delivering of these presents well & truly paid of Adrian Fry & for every part & parcell thereof Doth acquit and Discharge the said Fry Eaires Execettʳˢ Administratʳˢ & Assignes and every of them for ever & also for Divers other good cases and Considerations him the sd Allin therevnto of speciall moueing

PART I, FOL. 74.

hath Giuen Granted bargaind & sold Aliened and Confirmed and by these presents Doth Giue Grant bargaine & sell Alenat Infeofe releas Deliver and Confirme vnto said Adrian Fry his heires & Assignes for ever all the right title Claime & Interest that the said Robert Allin hath Ever had: May Might or ought to haue whether by Improuement or possession or any other lawfull wayes or meanes whatsoever six acres of said Allen Town grant aboue said To Haue And To Hold standing & lieing with the liberties previledges Comodities benefits Appurtenances therevnto belonging whereof the six acres of land is now in the possession of Adrian Fry and alredy laid out by ye Survaer of this town of Kittery baring Date the 16th of December 1679 to be vnto the only proper vse benefit and behoofe of the said Adrian Fry his Ares & assignes for ever Farthermore I Robert Allin for and in Consideration of the wintering of a mare well and truly paid whereof the sd Allin Acknowledgeth him selfe to be fully satisfied I the abouesd Robert Allin haue Giuen Granted bargaind sold and by these presents Doe fully and Absolutely giue grant bargain sell release infeoffe and confirme vnto the sd Adrian Fry for the abouesd wintering of a mare which sd Allin acknowledgeth himselfe to be fully satisfied & content & paid whereof he Doth Acquitt and Discharge the said Fry his heires Excetitor Administrat^{rs} and Assignes and every of them for ever and by these presents I also alinate one acre of land Deliver and Confirme vnto the said Adrian Fry his hears & assignes for ever all the right title Cleame & Intres that the said that the said Robert Allen hath ever had may might or ought to haue whether by possession or Improuement town grant or any other lawfull ways whatsoever To Haue & to Hold standing & lieing with the liberties previledges Comodities benefits and appurtenances there vnto belonging which land is to be laid out and is adjoining to Adrian Fry lot north from his house foure powl wide & so to run West till one

Part I, Fol. 75.

acre be accomplished And the said Adrian Fry for himselfe his heires Executors Admis^rs and Assignes shall or may at all time or times for ever hereafter lawfully peaceably quietly haue hold vse ocupy possess by & Injoy all the said parcell of land with the previledges therof without the least lett hindrance Claime Challenge by or vnder the said Robert Allen In Wittness whereof I haue herevnto sett my hand and seale this 13 Day of February one thousand six hundred ninety and one

Signed Sealed and deliv^rd   Robat Allen (a seale)
   in p^rsence of Christo : Bampfield   The aboue named Robert
           William Stacie   Allen appeared before me
                                    in Kittery this 24th Day
                                    of March Anno Dom̃ 169½
A true coppy of the orignal   and did acknowledg the
   deed here recorded June   aboue written Deed of
          8 : 1692   Sale to be his free act &
   p John Wincoll Record^r   Deed
                           pvince of maine : Before me :
                                John Wincoll Just^ce of peace

[75] Wheras there hath beene a controversy betweene us Kathern Lidden and Sarah Trickie widdowes both of Kittery in the Province of Maine in New England concerning the deviding line betweene our house lotts in Crooked lane in the lower part of Kittery aforesaid, it is now by our voluntary consent agreed and determined that the deviding line shall be from a certaine beech stump standing on the South side of the highway South west so much southerly as will goe Cleare of the sd Kathern Liddens Dwelling house and so to run on the same line to the water side (the sd beech stump being proued by Evidence to be the antient bound marke betweene the two foresaid lotts) and from the fore-

said beech stump Northeast or nearest northeast to the roote of a certaine Hemlock tree lieing vppon the ground which Hemlock tree appeared by Evidence to be another bound marke betweene the two foresd lotts, and from the roote of the said hemlock tree to run Due northeast to Spruce Creeke & these to be and remaine the standing bounds between vs and our heires for ever for Confirmation whereof Wee the aforesd Kathern Lidden and Sarah Trickie Doe bind our- selues our heires Executors and Administrators each to other in the penall sum of one hundred pounds sterling not to Molest Interupt or hinder one the other in the quiet and peaceable Enjoyment or Improuement by setting vp fence and standing in the said line from time to time or at any time from henceforth for ever, and for the further Confirma- tion of the premises Wee the aforesaid Kathern Lidden and Sarah Trickie haue herevnto sett our hands and seales this Eighteenth Day of Aprill Anno Dom̄: one thousand six hundred ninty two and in the third yeare of the reigne of our soveraigne lord and Ladie William and Mary by the grace of god of England Scotland France and Ireland King and Queene defenders of the faith &c :

Signed Sealed and Delivered   Katherin Letten (seale)
  in the presence of vs   Sarah Trickey (seale)
Witnesses: William Screven
        Elihu Gunnison

Province of maine

Katherin Letten and Sarah Trickey acknowledged the aboue written Instrument to be their free act and Deed this 18th Day of Aprill 1692/
               Before me John Wincoll Just^{ce} of peace

The aboue written is a true Coppy of the originall agree- ment here Entred this 9th Day of May 1692/
            p me John Wincoll Record^r

Part I, Fol. 75.

1692 Sept 26 County of yorke
in the Province of the Massachusetts bay
A Inventory of John Pears Astate Deceased at yorke

	£	s	d
on Iron pot: 7s shillings	00	07	00
on Frying pan 4 shillings	00	04	00
on Ax on shilling	00	01	00
one old roug 2 shillings	00	02	00
to mete at ten shillings	00	10	00
to one ketle at 3 shillings	00	03	00
to one booke at on: 1:	00	01	00
to a house and barne and land	30	00	00
to on Cow and Calfe three pound	03	00	00
to halfe a Calfe at 8 shillings	00	08	00
to one sheepe at 7 shillings	00	07	00
	85	03	06

the aboue is a true Coppy of the
originall Inventory Sept 26 : 1692   James Plaisted
p me Jn° Wincoll Cleric̃:   Matthew Austin

Articles of agreement made and Concludes betweene William Godsoe of Kittery in the County of yorke and province of the Mathatusets bay in New England of the one party and John ball of the same town and County as followeth Viz^t

That Whereas there hath beene a long controversy between ye p^{r}decessor of the abouesd William Godsoe in his life time and the said John Ball as also betweene the now Wife of the sd Godsoe in her Widdowhood and since betweene the sd Godsoe and the said Ball concerning a devideing line betweene the land of William Godsoe and the homestall of the said John Ball in Spruce Creeke in the town of Kittery aforesaid as also a like controversy Concerning the fulfilling of a deed of sale from the late Thomas Withers to the sd Ball his homestall as abouesd

Therefore for a finall Issue of all Controversies between the sd Godsoe & Ball in the premises abouesd it is agreed and Concluded between the sd William Godsoe and John Ball that the deviding line between the lands of the sd Godsoe and Ball shall be from between certain two rocks lieing about a foote asunder neare the salt Marsh and from between the sd two rocks west south west vnto a certain white rock about three or four foot broad neare the midle of the length of sd balls land and from the Midle of sd rocks west south west vnto a certain Hemlock tree growing at the southermost and westermost end of sd Balls land marked on the foure sides neare the ground and from sd Corner tree twenty six pole north north west vnto John Shepards fence [76] and from thence bounded by sd Shepards land till it come to the western Creeke and then bounded by said western Creeke till it come to the marsh and then bounded by said marsh till it come to the Midle betweene the two rocks where the deviding lines began, and these lines to stand as the deviding lines betweene the said Godsoe and ball and their heires for ever and the present fence is to stand as it is so long as it shall be serviceable and when it shall be decayed it is then to be new made at the Equall Charge of both partyes and sett in the true devideing lines betweene the sd William Godsoes and John Balls lands and the timber that makes the said new fence is to be taken off the sd William Godsoes land

And for the true performance of all the articles premised the said William Godsoe and John Ball Doe hereby Bind themselues their heires Executors and Administrators Each to other in the penall sum of forty pounds sterling to be forfeited and payed by the party that shall breake the abouesd articles or either of them to the party that shall obserue and performe the same, For confirmation whereof the said William Godsoe and said John Ball haue herevnto

Part I, Fol. 76.

sett their hands & seales this sixt Day of October Anno Doṁ : one thousand six hundred ninety two :

Signed Sealed & delivered Wm Godsoe (a seale)
 in the presence of vs John Ball
The marke of
Enoch *E H* Huchin ᴗᴗ (a seale)
John Wincoll his marke
John Alcock A true Coppy of the originall articles taken and here Entred this 13th Day of October 1692
 p me John Wincoll Cleric :

To all Christian people to whom this present writing shall com Know ye That I Ephraim Crocket of Kittery in the province of Maine in New England and An my wife Doe for Divers good Causes & valuable considerations me herevnto moueing, and for and in Consideration of the sume of forty six pounds sterling in hand receiued of Richard White of Kittery aforesaid Doe acknowledg and Confess myselfe to be fully satisfied and paid for a pcell of land and accordingly Doe hereby Giue Grant bargaine and sell vnto the aforesd Richard White his heires Executors Administrators and assignes ninty acres of vpland begining at the bridge at the head of broad bote harbor and runing from thence north west along by yorke line one hundred & sixty poles into the woods and ninty poles in breadth southwest being bounded on the southeast with a small pees of salt marsh which said Crockets father did vsially mow leaveing out the places where John billinge and James Wigins built their houses, And further Know ye that I the said Ephr : Crockett and An my wife Doe by thes presents Giue Grant Alienat sell Infeof and confirme vnto the abouesd White all the marsh :

Part I, Fol. 76.

begining at the bridge and so runing in the breadth of fifty acres of the abouesaid vpland on the southeast of it, which marsh is bounded with ye sd vpland on one side and brod berd harbor Crick on the other side, as also a small strip of Marsh lieing on the north east side of the neck aboue the bridge To Haue and to Hold all the aboue bargained premises both vpland and marsh with all the singular appurtenances and privilidges thereto belonging or in any wise appertaining to him the said Richard White his heires & assigns for ever, he the said White his heires or assigns paying twelue pence in silver to the said Crocket his heires or assignes on the twenty fift of March yearely acknowledgment, further I the said Ephri: Crockett and An my wife Doe for our selfs our heyrs Exequt^{rs} Administrat^{rs} promise and Ingadge for ever to warrent and Defend the abouesd title both of vpland & marsh against all manner of person or persons whatsoever makeing any lawfull Claime or demand therevnto or to any part or parcell thereof by from or vnder vs or either of vs our heires Exequtors or Administ^{rs} And more over I the said Crockett Doe couenant to & with the said White his heires Executors and Administrat^{rs} and to Every of them by these presents that all the aforesd vpland and marsh at the sealeing hereof shall remaine Clearly acquitted Exonorated and Discharged or otherwise saued and kept harmless from all former gifts barganes and sales whatsoever, and that forevermore vnto the confirmation of the truth hereof I the said Ephraim and An my wife haue hervnto set our hands and seales this twenty seventh Day of Aprill 1686

Signed sealed & delivered   The marke of
in the presence of vs
Francis Hooke   Ephraim E Crocket (seale)
John Daues   by the abouenamed The marke of
William Hooke   Ephraim Crocket   An A Crocket (seale)
               vnderwriten

Part I, Fol. 77.

Wheras there was formerly a Deed of Sale giuen by the abouesaid Ephraim Crockett to the aboue named Richard White of [77] fifty acres of land part of the land mentioned in the aboue written Deed, which sd Deed of Sale now remaines recorded in the records of the province of Mayne, these presents testjfy that the said deed is from henceforth to be void and of none Effect and that the said Richard White is to take no advantage by reason of the same in witness w^rof the partyes to these presents haue herevnto sett their hands and seales this twenty fourth Day of May one thousand six hundred and Eighty Eight

Sealed in the presence of   The marke of
   John Daves
   William Hooke   Richard *D* White (seale)
                                    The Marke of
                                   Ephram *E* Crocket (seal)

Ephraim Crocket and An his wife cam and Did acknowledge this Instrument to be their act and Deed this twenty sixt Day of Sept 1688/

                Before me Francis Hooke Jus^t Quor :

I Richard White of Kittery doe hereby for myselfe my Heires &c Assigne and set over vnto Henry Dering of Boston & his heires &c all my right title and Interest of the within written bill of sale as witness my hand Sept : 28. 1692

   Witness   Richard White
   Saml Wentworth   his marke
   Jno Wentworth
                Boston Sep^t 28th 1692 Richard
                  white Came & acknowledged the
                  aboue assignm^t to be his act &
                  Deed
                  Before me Sam̃ Sewall J. P.

Part I, Fol. 77.

These three last afore written are true Coppys of three Instruements written in one sheete of paper and here Entred this 13th Day of October 1692
p me John Wincoll Cleric:

To all Christian People to whom this present wrighting shall come Know ye that I Richard White of Kittery in the province of maine in New England Do for Divers good Causes and valluable Considerations me herevnto moueing and for and in Consideracon of the summ of forty two pounds Mony in hand Recd: of Henry Dering of Boston Do acknowledg and confess myselfe to be fully sattisfied and paid for a pcell of land houseing and marsh and Do giue grant bargaine & sell vnto the aforesd Henry Dering his heires Execrs Admrs & assignes, Ninty acres of vpland begining at the bridge at the head of broad boat harbour and runing from thence along by yorke line one hundred and sixty poles into the woods and ninty poles in breadth south west being bounded on the southeast with a small peece of salt marsh (which Ephraim Crockets father did vsually mowe) leaveing out the places where Jnº Billing & Ja: Wiggin built their houses And Further Know ye that I the said Richard White Do by these presents Giue Grant alien sell Infeoff and Confirme vnto the abouesd Henry Dering all the Marsh begining at the bridge aforesaid and runing in the breadth of ffifty acres of the abouesaid vpland on the southeast of it which Marsh is bounded with the said vpland on the one side and broad berd Harbour Creeke on the other side As also a small strip of Marsh lyeing on the North East side of the neck aboue the bridge aforesaid To Haue & To Hold all the aboue bargained premises both vpland and Marsh and houseing now standing vpon sd land

Part I, Fol. 78.

and all vnderwood, trees, timber, & fences with all and singular appurtenances and previlidges thereto belonging or in any wise apertaining To him the said Henry Dering his heires and Assignes for ever. Further I the said Richard White Do for myselfe my heires Execⁿ Admʳ promise and Ingadge for ever To warrant and defend the abouesaid title of vpland & Marsh &c vnto 'sd Henry Dering his heires and assignes for ever Against the lawfull Claimes and Demands of all and every person and persons whatsoever And the said Richard white for himselfe, his heires Execⁿ & Admʳ Doe hereby Covenant promise Grant and agree to and with the said Henry Dering his heires and Assignes that at the time of this present grant and sale and to th'ensealing and delivery of these presents he the sd Richard White is the true sole and lawfull owner and stand lawfully seized of and in all the aboue bargained and Granted premises in his own proper right of a good perfect and absolute estate of inheritance in Fee simple without any manner of condition revertion or limetation whatsoever so as to alter change defeate or make voyd yᵉ same Haueing in my selfe full power good right and lawfull authority to grant sell Convey and assure the same in Manner as aforesaid And that the said Henry Dering his heires and assignes shall and may by force and vertue of these pʳsents from henceforth and forever hereafter lawfully peaceably and quietly haue hold vse occupy posses and Enjoy the aboue granted premises with the appurtenances thereof free and Cleare and Clearly acquitted and Discharged of and from all and all manner of former and other Gifts Grants Bargains sales leases Mortgadges Joyntures Dowers [78] Judgments, Executions, Entailes, Forfeitures, and of and from all other titles, troubles, charges, and Incumbrances whatsoever, In Witness whereof the said Richard White haue herevnto sett his hand and seale the twenty seventh Day of September Anno Domⁱ one thousand

PART I, FOL. 78.

six hundred ninty two Annoq R Rˢ et Reginæ Gulielmi et Mariæ nunc Angliæ &c Quarto./

Signed Sealed & delivered   Richard ⊗ white (seale)
  in presents. of vs   his marke
  Samˡˡ Wentworth   Boston in New England Sept : 28 :
  Jnº Wentworth   1692 Richard White Came &
                             acknowledged the aboue Deed
                             of Sale to be his act and Deed
                     Before me Sam̃ Sewall Justice of peace
The above is a true coppy of the originall Deed of Sale transcribed and here Entred this 14ᵗʰ Day of october 1692

            p me John Wincoll Cleric̃ :

By vertue of a letter of atturney from the within mentioned Richard White vnto myself beareing Date the 27ᵗʰ Day of September last past I haue giuen by turfe and twigg posession of the within mentioned pʳmses vnto the within mentioned Henry Dering as witness my hand this 5ᵗʰ Day of october 1692

  The marke of   Francis Hooke
  John ✕ More   This is also a true coppy of the write-
  Eliz Parsons   ing on the back side of the aboue
                     Deed of Sale oct : 14 1692 p me
                     Jnº Wincoll Cleric̃ :

To all Xtian People to whom this present Writeing shall Come Know ye that I Richard White Late of Kittery town on piscaqua river Do for Divers good Causes and valluable considerations me herevnto moueing and for and in Consideration of the summ of tenn pounds secured to be paid by Henry Dering of boston shopkeeper Do Giue, Grant, bargaine, and sell vnto sd Henry Dering his heires Execⁿ Admⁿ and assignes Sixty acres of vpland lyeing and being in Kittery township bounded by the land of the township of yorke Easterly and by my land of ninety acres I sould sd Dering South Eastwardly and by James Wiggins land Southwardly : and Kittery Comons North Westerly or however otherwise bounded To Haue & to Hold to haue and to hold all the aboue bargained premises be it more or less as it is laid out with all the trees timber and vnderwood with all and singular the appurtenances and priviledges thereto belonging or in any wise apertaineing to him the sd Dering his heires & assignes for ever Haueing in myselfe full power thus to Do And Do for myselfe my heires &c warrant the same vnto sd Dering his heires & assignes against any person and persons whatsoever lawfully Claiming the same In Witness whereof The said Richard White haue herevnto sett his hand & seale this twenty seventh Day of September one thousand six hundred ninty two Annoq̄ R Rˢ et Reginæ Gulielmi et Mariæ nunc Angliæ &c : Quarto

Signed sealed & delivered
  in presents of vs
  Samˡˡ Wentworth
  Jnº Wentworth

Richard white (seal)
his marke
Boston in New England Sepᵗ 28ᵗʰ 1692 Richard White Came & acknowledged the aboue Instrumᵗ to be his act & Deed Before me
  Sam̄ Sewall J. peace

A true coppy of the originall Deed of Sale transcribed & here Entred this 14ᵗʰ Day of October 1692
    p me John Wincoll Cleric͠:

october 5ᵗʰ 1692 possession by turfe and twigg giuen vnto the within mentioned Henry Dering by Capᵗ Francis Hooke

Part I, Fol. 78.

as Attorney to the within Mentioned Richard White which letter of Attorney bears Date the 27th Day of Septembr last past as witness our hands this 5th Day october 1692

 The marke of   Francis Hooke
 John ✝ More   a true coppy of the originall as it is
 Eliza Parsons   written on the back side of the
          Deed of Sale
    October 14th 1692 p me John Wincoll Cleric:

Boston in New England

 Know all men by these prsents that I Richard White late of Kittery town on Piscataqua river haue made ordained, Constituted & appointed and by these prsents Do make ordaine & appoynt Capt ffr: Hooke and Mr Samll Kease or either of them my true and lawfull Attorney for me and In my stead & name to Enter and Come Into and vpon my farme and lands lyeing and being at the head of braue-boate harbour which is between piscataqua and yorke rivers, or vpon any part thereof and there to Deliver vnto Henry Dering or any by his order by turff and twig full posession of all my houseing, vpland & meadow that I haue and posessed there, And their or his so Doeing shall be as my verry act & Deed to all Intents and purposes in the law whatsoever, Rattifieing and holding for firme and stable whatsoever my said atorneys or either of them shall Do herein In Witness whereof I haue herevnto sett my hand and seale this 27th Day of September on thousand six hundred ninty and two: Annoq RRs et Reginæ Gulielmi et Mariæ nunc Angliæ &c Quarto/ Nota. This is More fully in complyance with my Deed of Sale for the same vnto the

Part I, Fol. 79.

said Henry Dering beareing Date with these presents

Signed sealed & dd   Richard ⓢ white (seal)
in p^rsents of vs   his marke
Saml Wentworth
Jno Wentworth   Boston Sep^t 28th 1692. Richard
White acknowledged this Instrument to be his act and Deed
Before me Sam Sewall J. peace

The aboue written is a true coppy of the originall letter of attorney transcribed and here Entred octob^r 14th 1692

p me John Wincoll Cleric:

---

[79] An Inventory of the estate of John Preble lately Deceased taken by vs whose names are hervnder written October ye 26th 1692

	£	s	d
Imprimo 2 cowes 5£, 2 hafers 4£, 2 yearlings & 2 calues	12	00	00
7 swine 6£ one pott 7s one gun 20s	07	07	00
on Carsie coate and a pair of breaches	01	00	00
3 sheets 1£: 10s:, 28 pounds of sheepes wooll 1£: 1s and yarne 1£: 3s:	03	14	00
Land and Marsh	50	00	00
on sheepe	00	05	00
	74	06	00
Some old Iron	00	08	00
	74	14	00

Abraham Preble
John Harman

Octob^r 1st 1692 Sworne to In court p Hanna Preble that this is a true Invent^ry of the Estate of her deceased husband and If any more Estate shall hereafter appeare that shee will ad it herevnto

as Attests John Wincoll Cleric:

The aboue is a true coppy of the originall Inventory & the oath to it transcribed & here entred this 14th Day of Feburary 169¾   p me John Wincoll Cleric

Part I, Fol. 79.

An Inventory of the Estate of Henry Simson lately deceased taken by vs whose names here vnder written this 7th Day of may 1692/

	£	s	d
Inpr: 2 cowes and 2 Calfs	05	00	00
2 heifers 3 yeare old	04	00	00
1 bull of 3 year old	02	00	00
1 stere on hafer of 2 year old	03	00	00
1 yearling Hafer	01	00	00
6 sheepe	02	02	00
9 swine	07	00	00
1 mare & colt	03	00	00
on Coate	01	10	00
12 napkins & a table Cloath	01	02	00
2 pilo Drayer	00	06	00
2 neck cloaths	00	02	00
books	00	04	00
on payr of White Curtain	01	04	00
on Wascoate	00	03	00
3 puter platter and Dishes	01	03	00
1 sheet	00	15	00
working tulls	00	14	00
Three Joyrn pots	02	08	00
14 acres of salt marsh	42	00	00
His planting land and paster ground & a barn & vacant land adjoining to it	40	00	00
	218	13	00

April 4 1693 more Estate found & aprized since at 15s................. 000 15 00

Daniell Simson took oath in Court   Abraham Preble
to the truth of this Inventory   Joseph Banks
and If any more Estate appear
to ad it hereto : Nov : 1st 1692/
         as Attests John Wincoll Cleric:

These are true Coppyes of the originall Inventory and the oath to it transcribed & here Entred this 14th Day of February 169¾   p me John Wincoll Cleric:

An Inventory of the Estate of Phillip Coper lately Deceased taken and aprised by vs whose names are here vnder written october 31th 1692/

	£	s	d
Impr 2 cows 5£ 2 calfs 20s	06	00	00
2 Joron pots 12s : 4 sheep 1£ Trame pot hookes	02	00	00
1 axe	00	02	00
his Dwelling house and barne and ten acres of land In fence one swine found since: 00£: 14: 00	30	00	00
	38	02	00

PART I, FOL. 80.

Benjamin Preble took oath in Court to   Abrã Preble
the truth of this Inventory & If any   John Harman
more estate shall appear he will ad it
_{Nov: 1st} as attests John Wincoll Cleric:
₁₆₉₂
     A true coppy of the originall Inventory p me
     feb^{ry} 14 169¾   John Wincoll Cleric

         yorke Aprill 18th 1692
An Inventory of the estate of Mr Peter weare lately deceased taken by vs whose names are here vnderwritten

	£	s	d
Inpro About 200 acres of land at Cape nedok and housing	170	00	00
and thre acres and halfe of salt marsh	015	00	00
3 brass ketles	002	10	00
1 Joyron pot & pot hookes & tramell	000	16	00
a frying pan & Iron skile beame	000	17	00
2 axes & a Iron skillet	000	10	00
2 spits a brass morter an passell watch bill	000	10	00
Chaines & Churn augers & other things	001	16	00
[80] A bedsted a spining wheele and other things	01	16	00
on table a paile a cup	00	10	00
on Mayre and six sheep	03	00	00
for puter 43s and two brass candlesticks 13s	02	09	00
on paire of streaked Curtings	01	04	00
on paire of Black curtings	00	07	00
on raper	00	12	00
one booke called the key of the bible	01	00	00
and other bookes	00	18	00
2 silver spons and a silver Cup	01	00	00
2 Cushens and some linnen	00	17	00
on Coate	00	10	00
2 great trunkes and a small one	01	05	00
on bed and bolster and the bed cloathes to it	02	05	00
on old bed and bed cloathes belonging to it	01	10	00
on warming pan & a paire of stilards	01	00	00
on bible	00	07	00
six swine	03	10	00
in Cash	00	04	00
4 Cows 10£ on hefer & 2 steres 4£ 10s	14	10	00
3 yearlings 3£ a saw & other things	04	00	00
	231	18	00

        Abrã Preble
        John parker
Mrs Mary Weare tooke oath in Court that the aboue written is a true Inventory of the Estate of her deceased hus-

Part I, Fol. 80.

band Peter Weare to the best of her knowledge and If any more shall appeare she will ad it herevnto: Nov: 1st 1692
as attests John Wincoll Cleric͞:

The aboue written is a true coppy of the originall Inventory & the oath to it here entred this 14th Day of February 169¾   p me John Wincoll Cleric͞:

An Inventory of the Estate of Nathaniell Preble lately Deceased, taken by vs whose names are here vnder written October ye 16th 1692

	£	s	d
Inprimo his Wearing Cloaths	01	10	00
in mony	03	11	00
3 Cowes 7£ 10: 2 yearlings & one Calfe 2£ 15s.	10	05	00
4 sheep 1£ 4 pogs 2£ one horse	04	10	00
beds and bed Cloaths	04	10	00
2 Iron pots & one Iron ketle	01	00	00
for puter 2s Dishes spoons & tubs & a Chest	00	16	00
his Dwelling house & barn & about 100 acres of land and 3 acres of salt marsh	70	00	00
2 paires of old Cards & a wheel & wooll	00	11	00
Cotten wooll	00	10	00
A broad axe and other tuls	01	00	00
plow share & Colters, Chaines & other Iron things	01	05	00
1 Gun and a Cutlass	01	05	00
a bible 4s & a tramell	00	08	00
	101	03	00

Abr͞a Preble
John Harman

Sworn in Court p Abraham Preble Junr the first Day of November 1692. that this is a true Inventory of the estate of Nathaniell Preble Deceased & If any more Estate shall appeare he will ad it hervnto as attests
John Wincoll Cleric͞:

These are tru Coppys of the originall Inventory & ye oath giuen to it here Entred this 15th Day of February 169¾
p me John Wincoll Cleric͞:

Part I, Fol. 81.

[81] A true Inventory of the Estate of Jn° Parsons who Deceased January 25. 169½.

	£	s	d
To three Cowes	06	00	00
To a yeareling bull	01	00	00
To a Horse & a mare	04	00	00
To nine swine	04	10	00
To a grind-stone	00	05	00
To three Iron p. ts	01	10	00
To four barking knifes	00	04	00
To a barke shaue	00	03	00
To a last knife	00	03	00
To an old sadle 8s and one sheepe 5s	00	13	00
To a Keeler a tub & a beer barrill	00	07	00
To an oyle Jar and two Gun barralls	00	11	00
To 10 lb Rosin & Curring knife	00	10	00
To a pair stiliards 2 Chests and a box	00	18	00
To three pitch forkes and plow Irons	00	09	00
To an Iron tramell & two Chaires	00	10	00
To an old Cart & slead	00	13	00
To a spining Wheele & Cards	00	06	00
To three Hoos & woodden ware	00	10	00
To two hogsh of lime	00	14	00
To a paire fetters & a thousand of nailes	00	08	06
To a Dwelling house orchard & other land	35	00	00
To a Barne	00	08	00
To a barrill of beefe	02	05	00
To two Oagers & a hollowing Ads	00	07	00
To an Iron spit and two shop hainers	00	09	00
To two pair pinsers & one pair of nipers	00	04	00
	62	17	00

John Harman
Thomas Dunnell

Sworne in Court Nov^br 1st 1692 p Elizabeth parsons that this is a true Inventor of the Estate of her Deceased husband John Parsons & If any more Estate shall appeare she will ad it hereto as attests John Wincoll Cleric:

The aboue written are true coppys of the originall Inventory and the oath to it, & here entred Feb^ry 15th 169⅔

p me John Wincoll Cleric:

PART I, FOL. 81.

Know all men by these presents that I Abraham Parker of yorke Doe for and in Consideration of the sum of sixteen pounds sterl: to me already payd in hand by Capt Francis Hooke of piscataqua Doe sell Bargayne Infeoffe and alianat vnto the sayd Hooke his heyrs Exequtors Administrat[rs] and assignes one dwelling house with fifty acr̃s of vpland or there abouts lying one the western side of yorke river it being part of a tract of land containing about one hundred Acrs which I formerly purchased of Capt Job Allcock of yorke butted & bounded as followeth to say of the vper side it is bounded by Thomas Adams his land & runs from the water side South west into the Woods vnto piscataqua bounds & so to run at the head of sayd piscatqua bounds halfe the breadth of the one hundred acres of land purchased as abouesayd from Capt Alcock & there to run north east vnto the river side, To Haue and to hould the abouesaid land and house with all the priviliges and apurtenances thereof to the proper vse and behoof of the sayd Hooke his heyres Exequtors administrators and Asignes for ever without any lett or any molestation by me my heirs Exequt[rs] & Administrat[rs] for ever or any person or persons by or vnder me & moreover I doe by these Presents empty myselfe my heyers Exeq[rs] & administrat[rs] of all my rite title and Intrest which formerly I had vnto the abouesayd hous and land granting & giueing vnto the abouesd Hooke all my right & titell thereine with warrenty from all persons whatsoeuer and moreover I Doe by thes presents Declare at the signinge & sealing hereof the sayd house and land is prperly my own Estate & is free from all sales and Mortgades whatsoever and shall from this time & hens forward Disowne any propriety therein giuing and grantinge my sole & proper right which formerly I Did enjoy vnto the abouesayd Hooke his Eyers Exeqt[rs] Administ[rs] and asignes for

Part I, Fol. 82.

evermore as witnes my hand & seale this tenth Day of June one thousand six hundred ninty and two

Signed Sealed & Deliu^d in the presents of vs
Hanno Jordan
the marke of
Elizabeth ─┼─ Crusey
Robert Mitchell

the marke of
Abraham ⟫ parker (Seale)

Legall posesion giuen by Abraham Parker vnto Capt Francis Hooke of the house abouesd as also of the land by twigg & turff in leiw of the whole land abouesd this thirteenth Day Augst 1692 in presents of vs

the marke of
𝓘 H
John Herman
the marke of
Thomas 𝓘𝓓 Daniell

Abraham Parker came & owned every particular of this instrument to be his act & deed vnto Capt Francis Hooke this 8th Day of decemb^r 1692
Before me Charles Frost J : pe. qu^r

a true coppy of ye originall Deed here Entred Febry 17 169¾
p Jno Wincoll Clerke:

[82]
In the name of god Amen one thousand six hundred ninty & one I John Card of yorke in the province of Maine Cooper being sick of body but perfect Remembrance all laud & praise be giuen to allmighty god for it, Doth Revoakeing all former Wills make and ordaine this my present testament Contayning herein my last will in manner & forme following, that is to say first I bequeath my soule to Al-

mighty god My Maker & redeemer, and my body to be buried in Christian buriall

Item I bequeath to my Eldest sone William Carde the tract of Land being bounded from the lower end of the Coue nigh to Edmond Cooks lott soe running vppon a north east line Joyning to my owne loot and so Joining in Breadth vpon the line of Edmond Coks Loote so running backward so farr as my loot Doth/ Item I doe bequeath Annas Carde my Daughter twelfe pence in silver to be paid by my Executor after my buryall/ Item I bequeath to Mary Card my Daughter twellf pence in silver to be payed by my Executor after my buriall/ Item I doe bequeath vnto my now wife Elesabth Card I doe bequeath the one halfe of my Goods and Chattells of what kind or nature soever and also the one halfe of my home loot and half of all my marsh hom and a brood during hir life not giuen nor bequeathed before, my funerall Expences and Debts discharged/ Item I doe bequeath to my Grandson John Card twenty shillings to be paid by my Executor after my buriall/ Item I do bequeath to my Grand Daughter Mary Card twenty shillings by my Executor after my buriall/ Item I doe bequeath to my younger sone Thomas Card whom I make my sole Executor, all the goods and Chattells & land of what kind or nature soever the one halfe not giuen nor bequeathed before my funerall expences & Debts and demands discharged olny after the desase of my now wife Elesabeth the land & Marsh of what kind or Nature so ever not now bequeathed to my younger sone Thomas my soll Exequetor

Signed Sealed published
  in the presence of vs
  William young
  Samuell Bragdon

The marke of
John ✗ ✚ Card
(seale)

William young personally appeared this 21ᵗʰ februᵧ 169¾ and made oath that he was present & saw John Card signe & seale & heard him declare and publish the within written

Part I, Fol. 82.

Instrument to be his last Will & testament & y^t ye sd John Card was at the same time of right sound & Disposeing mind & that Samuell Bragden was present at the same time & set to his hand together wth himself

Dated in Salem. 21. 12mo 169¾ Before me Jonathan Corwin : of ye Councill & Just^e peace

Samuell Bragdon tooke oath in Court at yorke, the same william young as aboue: Aprill 5. 1693 as attests John Wincoll Cleric

The aboue written are true Coppys of the originall Will & probat Compared & here entred April 7th 1693

p me John Wincoll Cleric

An Inventory of the Estate of John Card lately Deceased taken & aprised by vs whose whose names are here vnder written october 28th 1692

	£	s	d
Inpr: His Wearing Cloaths	02	00	00
one table cloath 9s 8 sheets 3£ 4s 2 pillow Drayers 10s	04	03	00
28 pound of wooll & 2 pound of yarne 1£ 11s	01	11	00
puter 6s, 3 Iron pots & pot hookes & little Iron Ketle	02	00	00
old brass and a warming pan 1s 2d 8 Iron Wedges 8s	01	10	00
2 paire of betle rings and other Iron thing	00	13	00
a Crascut saw and his tuls	01	02	00
one skiff	03	00	00
3 hogsheds and barrells and tubs and other woodden things	01	00	00
Catle: 2 oxen 7£: 5 cowes 12£: 1½s: 2 hafers 3 year old 3£ 10s	23	00	00
one horse 2£: 12 sheepe 3£ 5 swine 4£	09	00	00
3 Chests	01	00	00
2 fether be ls 2 bolsters 3 pillows 3 rugs & a blanket	11	10	00
one gun	01	00	00
In Cash twenty pounds	20	00	00
	82	09	00
his Dwelling house and barne & houslott land and Marsh at home & one acres an halfe of Marsh vp the river	80	00	00
and 60 acres of wood land vp the old mill Crick	10	00	00
one old sword	00	10	00
	172	19	00

Abra: Preble
John Harman

April 5^t 1693

Thomas Card tooke oath in Court to the truth of this Inventory & If any more Estate appeare hereafter hee will ad it

p Curiam John Wincoll Cleric

PART I, FOL. 82.

The aboue written is a true coppy of the originall Inventory & here Entred this 19th Day of Aprill 1693
     p me John Wincoll Cleric⁓

 Samuell Donell aged 45 yeares maketh oath that about 7 or 8 yeares since hee was in Company with Major John Davis then of yorke and Humphrey Chadburne and I heard the said Davis verry much vrge & Importune the said Chadburne to chang a horse with him : the said Chadburns horse being a gray horse and a verry sollid horse : and as said Davis said fit for his riding the said Chadburne Denied the sd Davis request at present and told him sd Davis that the horse was his wiues horse and for her riding : the said Major Davis said hee must haue the horse of said Chadburne in Exchange for his young horse : the said Chadburne still manifested himselfe very loath and vnwilling to part with his horse : but at length said Davis promising said Chadburne that If hee would let him haue said horse hee would not only giue him his young horse but further promised that hee would never Dispose of said horse while he liued, and at the Day of said Davis his Death if the horse were aliue : hee said Chadbourne should freely haue him to his own proper vse : and also promised said Chadbourne to giue him freely his case of pistols : on which condition said said Chadbourne lett said Major Davis haue his horse
  Taken vpon oath the 10. of November 1691
     Before me Job Alcock Comeēre

   nath{ll} Raines took   Ric{d} King toke oath
   oath the truth abosd   to the truth abouesd
   except the pistols   Aprill 11th 1693 before
Jan{ry} 19 : 169½   Francis hǒoke Jus. pe
 before Francis Hooke
 John Wincoll Justices of pe

Part I, Fol. 83.

This is a true coppy of the originall oath and here Entred Aprill: 19th 1693   p me John Wincoll Cleric:

[83] An Inventory of some part of the goods of Mr Joseph Moulton who was taken by the Indians in January ye 25th 1691 and left in a Chest at Lieut Prebles Garrison Taken this 12th of Octor 1692:

	£	s	d
Impr It one Cotten Cover-led	00	10	00
It 1 Vallin	00	02	00
It 1 shash	00	01	06
It old Peuter	00	02	08

More some Cattell belonging to sd Moulton apprised October 31: 1692

	£	s	d
Impr Two steres of 4 yeares & vantage	06	10	00
Two Cowes & a calfe at	04	15	00

         Apprised by Charles Frost
                   Samuell Small

An Inventory of part of the Estate of Joseph Moulton lately Deceased Taken by vs whose names are heare vnderwritten

	£	s	d
For Iron	01	16	00
one bull	01	08	00
one Grining stone	00	06	00
one Chaine	00	07	00
on Tammie pettecoate 16s and a black manto	01	06	00

August 29: 1693   Abra Preble
                       Lues Bane

The aboue written are true coppyes of the originall Inventorys here Entred Septbr 12 1693
                 p me John Wincoll Cleric:

A list of wt swine of Joseph Moltons hath bin prised at this 5th of December 1692

	£	s	d
To 1 Breeding Sow at 12s	00	12	00
To 10 swine at 11s p swine	05	10	00
To 4 young swine at 7s p swine	01	08	00

Part I, Fol. 83.

This part of the Inventory found & Entred this 9th Day of novbr 1693   p me John Wincoll Cleric̃

Wheras there hath been a Controversy between Joshua Downing and John Leighton, both of Kittery in the County of yorke in the Province of the Massathusets bay in New England concerning a devideing line betweene them in the lower parts of their house lots in Kittery neare the river and Arbtrators chosen by both parties and an award given accordingly

Know all men by these presents that wee the said Joshua Downing and John Leighton are freely and Mutually agreed that the Deviding line betweene our foresaid lots of land in the lower parts of it neare the river as aforesd shall begin at a certaine crooked white oake tree standing and growing by or neare a certaine corner of an old fence belonging to the sd Downing, and is a bound tree mentioned in the Deed of sale from Mrs Alice Shapleigh to sd Downing and also mentioned in the foresd award and is to stand as a fixed bound tree, and from the said Crooked white oake tree to run on a straite line which runs nine foote Distance from a certaine great walnut tree on the northwest side of said line and hath a hole in the Southward side of sd walnut tree and from thence said line runs the same course to the river side vnto a certain great stone appointed to stand for a bound marke between our said lands for ever and for confirmation of the truth hereof wee the said Joshua Downing and John Leighton herevnto sett our hands and seales this nineteenth Day of September in the fifth yeare of the reigne of our soveraign lord and Lady William and Mary of England

Part I, Fol. 84.

Scotland France and Ireland King and Queen Defenders of the faith &c:

Signed Sealed & Delivrd Joshua Downing (seal)
  in the p^{r}sence of vs   John Leighton (seal)
  Peter Wittum
  Alexander Dennett
  John Wincoll

The aboue Written is a true coppy of the originall agreement transcribed and here Entred This 26th Day of Septemb^r 1693

[84] To all Christian people to whom this present wrighting shall Come greetting: Know ye that I Harlackenden Symonds Gentleman, of Ipswich in the County of Essex in New England: haue for and In Consideration of a valluable sum̄ of good pay to me in hand payd and other waise to me secured to be paid by the persons vnder mentioned as purchesers before the confirmation hereof in full satisfaction and for Divers other good and lawfull causes and considerations me therevnto moueing; Haue giuen Granted bargaind sold Enfeoffeed and Confirmed and by these presents Doe fully Clearely and absolutely Giue Grant bargain sell alienate and Infeoff and confirme vnto Roger Haskens Edward Bishop William Baker George Herrick Thomas Edwards Samuell Ingalls Jn^{er} John Low Jn^{er} William Dixey Thomas Shepherd William Goodhew Samuell Gittings Barnett Thorne Michell farlo Mesheck farlo, Moses Bradstreete Mathew Perkens John Gitting Senr Paull Thorndick Isack Fellows Richard Walker John Browne farmer Nathaniell Browne Zachary Herrick Thomas Higginson John Stannford Thomas low Sen^{er} Samuell Ingalls Sen^{er} Robert Lord Junr Robert Bradford Nicholas Wooberry Marke Haskell William Haskell

PART I, FOL. 84.

William Cleeues John Harrise John Burnam Nathaniell Rust Sen{r} and Andrew Elliot Jun{r} To them and their heires and Assignes for ever a Certaine Tract of land six miles in length and foure Miles in breadth Known by the name of Cokshall in the County of yorkshiere in the Province of Maine and Is bounded as followeth viz : at the Southeast end partly vpon the line of the township of Wells and partly vppon the line of the Township of Cape porpus and on the north east side partly bounded by the line of the land formerly Maj{r} William Phillips his land and partly vppon the Coman . land and on tthe northwest end the said land is bounded on the Comon land and bounded on the southwest side with the land of the sd Symonds, and I the said Harlakenden Symonds for myselfe my heires Executors and Administrators Doe Covenant and promise to and with the said Roger Haskins and the rest of the Joint purchasers according to their severall proportions as they are entred in a list of their names beareing even Date herewith, their heires Executors Administrators and Assignes that the said bargained premises and every part and parcell thereof is free and Cleare and freely and Clearly Exonorated Discharged and acquitted of and from all former gifts grants bargains sales Alienations Changes Mortgadges dowers Jointures Extents Judgments Executions and all other Incumbrances whatsoever and I the said Harlakenden Symonds for myselfe my heires Executors and Administrators Doe and shall from time and at all times Warantize and Maintaine the said bargained premises with all and singular the appurtenances and priviledges and Comodityes as namly the the trees woods vnderwoods standing or lyeing vppon the said land with all meadows swamps waters water courses mines or Mineralls in or vppon the said land whatsoever or wheresoever it be, against all maner of persons whatsoever haueing Claiming or pretending to haue any Just and lawfull right and title or Interest into the said bargained premises or any part or parcell thereof To Haue And to Hold the said bargaind premises and every part thereof to them the said Roger Hoskins and the rest their heires Executors Administrators and assignes for ever, In Wittness and confirmation of all the aboue written I the said Harlakenden Symonds haue hereunto sett my hand and seale Dated this twelfth Day of June in the yeare of our lord god one thousand six hundred Eighty and Eight And in the fourth yeare of the reigne of Soveraigne Lord King James the Second

The words according to their severall proportions as they are Entred in a list of their names bearing even Date herewith in the twentieth line were Enterlined before signing   Harlakinden Symonds (Seale)

Signed Sealed and Delivered in
   the presence of vs, as witnesses
   Walter ffayerfeild
   Daniell Davison Juner
   Joshua Browne   Boston 22^d June 1688
     Harlakinden Symonds personall appeareing before me one of the Councell of this his Maties territory and Dominion of New England acknowledged the aboue written Instrument to be his act & Deed

         Jno Usher

A true coppy of the originall Deed Deed of Sale transcribed and here Entred on Record this 12th Day of Octob^r 1693

      p me John Wincoll Cleric:

Part I, Fol. 85.

[85] A list of the names of those persons that haue bought land of Mr Symonds and the Quantity of land

Roger Haskins	200 acres	John Browne Farmer	300
Edward Bishop	200	Nathaniell Browne	300
William Baker	200	Zachariah Herrick	100
George Herrick	100	Thomas Higginson	100
Thomas Edwards	100	John Stanford	200
Samuell Ingalls Junr	200	Thomas Low Senr	200
John Low Junr	200	Samuell Ingalls Senr	100
William Dixee	200	Robert Lord Junr	100
Thomas Sheperd	200	Robert Bradford	100
Nathll Fuller William Goodhue	500	Nicholas Woodbury	100
		Marke Hascall	100
Samuell Gittins	200	William Hascall	100
Barnard Thorne	100	William Cleaues	100
Michaell Farlo	200	John Harris	600
Messeck Farlo	200	John Burnam	600
Moses Bradstreete	200	Nathaniell Rust Senr	200
Mathew Perkins	200	Andrew Elliot Junr	100
John Gittins Senr	200	For publick vses	500
Paull Thorndick	200		
Isaac Feellows	300		
Richard Walker	300		

June the 12th 1688

October ye 12th 1693

We whose names are herevnto subscribed being desired by Richard Walker & Thomas Edwards both of Ipswich to acompany them to Coxhall to see the Delivery of a pcell of land sold by Mr Harlackenden Symonds of Ipswich to sd persons together with severall more Wee Doe testify that sd Mr Symonds Did make Delivery by Turff and twigg to sd Walker and Edwards in behalfe of the rest of the Company Joint purchasers wee being with sd persons at Mousum falls within a few rods of sd falls

Captaine John Hill and Anthony Combes Made oath that they were personally present and saw Delivery of sd land as is above Exprest before me

John Hill
the marke of
Anthony ⋏ Combes

Sam^{ll} Wheelwright
Octobr 12 1693
Jus: peace

PART I, FOL. 86.

The above written are true coppys of the originall list & Delivery of land & here Entred Oct[obr] 13th 1693
p me John Wincoll Ceric:

Septemb[r] 15th 1693 At a meeting of the Majo[r] part of the within named Company it was voted that Jacob perkins and Nath: ffuller is admitted in the roome of Samuell Giddins and John Giddins
 As attests Geo. Herrick by order of sd Company

Sep[t] 15 it also voted by sd company that M[r] Christopher Pottle is admitted in the roome of M[r] Nathaniell Rust Sen[r]
Geo: Herrick as aboue

October y[e] 13th
 M[r] Joseph Gerrish Minister of Wenham is Admitted in the roome of Thomas Low Sen[r] by the Company
Attests Richard Walker
Thomas Edwards
The aboue written are true Coppyes of the originalls written on the back side of the foresd list of the names of the purchasers and here recorded this 13th Day of octo[br] 1693/   p me John Wincoll Cleric:

[86] Know all men by these presents that I Nacodumiah my Indian name, called by the English by the name of Dony with the consent of Robert my Eldest sone haue Bargaind & sold & by these presents Doe bargaine sell & Deliver vnto Harlackenden Symons formerly of Wells: now of Ipswich my land about the pond now called Coxhorne within and about the land which was formerly in the possession of Sagamore Sawsewen and confirmed by his son Fruellion his only

PART I, FOL. 86.

son: whith Indian witnesses as by Deed by record Doth appeare and further I the said Dony doe allow the sd Simons to advance for length and breadth Northward by soe farr as Sawsewen and his only son Fruellion had any thing to doe with the land ponds meadows or any appurtenances in reference to wood timber or anything therevnto belonging or any way appertaining to Harlacinton Simons his heire and assigns for ever, it is to be vnderstood it is for a Considerable sume in hand receiued before the delivery of all aboue Expressed, I Doe ratifie and confirme from any by or vnder me in Witness wherevnto wee haue sett our hands and seales, Signed Sealed in the presence of vs 11th of august 1686

Test Sam`ll` Whelewright   Robert alias Dony his Ɉ mark
   Sam`ll` Whelewright Jun`r`   Robert his

marke
(seal)
(seal)

The aboue written is a true coppy of the originall Deed of Sale here Entred on record This 10th Day of Novemb`r` 1693
       p me John Wincoll Cleric:

Know all men by these presents that I Sarah Goodin of Barwick in the pvince of Maine formerly the wife of Peter Turbet Sen`r` late of Cape porpus and with the consent of Nicholas Turbet my Eldest sone liueing of the sd Peter Turbett Sen`r` with the consent of Elizabeth his wife Doe make Deed and full Conveyance of their third part of the land, both meadow and vpland aboue the township of Wells and Capeporpus that John bush & John Sanders Sen`r` &

Part I, Fol. 86.

Peter Turbett Senr bought of Sosowen Saggamore of the tract of land comonly called Coxshall and confirmed by his onely sone Fluellen vnto Harlackenden Simonds of Ipswich and to his heires & assignes for ever, this is to be vnderstood that the land abouesd was purchased of Sosowen before the people here Inhabiting being English submitted themselues vnder the government of the Massachusets and confirmed since by his only sone Fluellen, the land, the said tract of land lieth adjoining to the river called Cape porpus river alias Mowsum and so runs along as the trees are Marked within foure Miles of Sawco river with an Equall proportion both in length and breadth, it is to be vnderstood that Sawco river lieth Northeasterly foure miles from the marked tree being a great pine tree the lower crocth of the said tree being wide beareth from the body Southerly the vpper forke or graine of the said tree being straite vp: this Confirmation & Deed wee whose names are within written Doe hereby ratifie & confirme all our right and title to or in all the said tract of land both meadow and vpland with all the priviledges and appurtenances belonging therevnto or any way apperteining vnto the sole & pp vse and behooffe of the said Harlackenden Symonds his heirs & assignes for ever In Witness wherof wee whose names are within Expressed haue setto our hands and seales.

Know also wee haue receiued satisfaction from the said Symonds before the sealeing and delivery hereof

Dated in barwick June 29 : 1687   Sarah **3** Goodin (seal)
Signed sealed and Delivered   her marke
  in the presence of vs
witnesss Nathaniell Harris   Nicholas X Turbett (seal)
    Jon fellows   his marke
    John Wincoll   Elizabeth ⌒ Turbett (seal)
                                       her marke

Part I, Fol. 87.

A true Coppy of the originall Deed here Entred on record this 10th Day of November 1693/
    p me John Wincoll Cleric͞:

[87] March 29 : 1679

Measured and laid out vnto Peter Staple fiue acres of land by town grant to his wife in her widdowhood bearing Date in december 13. 1669 and ten acres by a town grant to himselfe bearing Date december 5. 1671 : at the head of his house lot in the long reach begining at a litle brooke and runs north east and by east twenty and three pole in breadth as p the marked trees
    John Wincoll Surv'

    December 24. 1679

Measured and laid out vnto Peter Staple his town grant of thirty acres of land beareing Date July 28. 1679 Eight acres of it at the Northeast End of Christopher Bidles tenn acres and runs north east and by east into the woods twenty and three pole in breadth and the other twenty and two acres at the north east end of Richard Rogers his land and runs north east into the woods Eighty pole and is forty and two pole in breadth as p marked trees
    John Wincoll Surv'
Entred in the tow booke p Jos : Hamond Cleric͞:

At a Court of sessions of yͤ peace held at yorke aprill 4. 1693 Ordered that the surveigher of Kittery shall lay out the land within Mentioned according to the grants & to be Done forthwith
    as Attests John Wincoll Cleric͞:

Part I, Fol. 87.

September 6th 1693

By vertue of the aboue written order of court I haue measured and laid out vnto Peter Staple the within Mentioned fifteene acres at the head of his house lot twenty pole wide northwest and by north till it run seventy pole into the woods northeast and by East In length and then is twenty three pole wide till it run a hundred and twelue pole in the whole length to William Tetherlys bounds on the north east and bounded on the northwest with Christopher Bidles and his own land p me John Wincoll Surv^r

Septemb^r 7th 1693

Measured and laid out to sd Peter Staple the within mentioned thirty acres of land : Eight acres of it at the head of Christopher bidles land nineteene pole in breadth northwest and by north and seventy pole in length north east and by East : and the other twenty two acres acres at the head of Richard Rogers land on the north east and runs in length Eighty pole north east & by east and fourty pole in breadth north west and by north

p me John Wincoll Surv^r

The aboue written are true coppys of their originalls here Entred on record this 9th Day of November 1693

p me John Wincoll Cleric :

Know all men by these P^{r}sents that I Elizabeth Plaisted of Portsmouth in the province of New hampshier the relict and Executrix of Elisha Plaisted deceased for and in Consideration of the sume of forty pounds of lawfull mony of New England in hand before ye ensealing & Delivery of these P^{r}sents well and truely paid the receipt whereof said Elizabeth Plaisted acknowledgeth, and herselfe to be fully satisfied content and paid and thereof and of every part and penny thereof doth acquit exonorate and discharge John Plaisted Senr of said Portsmouth & Province Merchant his heires Executors Administrators and assignes and Every of them for Ev^r by these p^{r}sents as also for Divers other good Causes and Considerations her the said Elizabeth Plaisted therevnto Especially moueing hath Giuen Granted Bargained & sold aliened Enfeoffed released Delivered and by turfe and twigg confirmed and by these p^{r}sents doe giue grant bargaine and sell alien Enfeoffe release deliver and by turfe and twigg confirme vnto said John Plaisted his heires and assignes for ever a certain parcel of land scittuate & being in the town of Kittery in the pvince of Maine bounded on the South with a brooke y^t runs along by Nicholas Hodsdens land into birch point coue and so Down ye Coue till it comes to Elder Nutters salt marsh which is the westernd board and ye north with the great river in part and the rest of that side with James Emerys house lot and y^o East with towns land it being the length of the rest of ye lots it being by Estimation near Eighty acres more or less as it was formerly granted by ye towne of Kittery vnto Capt: John Wincoll, as also the marsh Commonly called the new marsh or Meadow lieing in the line between Nechewonnook and yorke, neare to Agamenticus hills together with all profits priviledges and advantages therevnto belonging — To Haue and to Hold the before giuen granted and Bargained premises and every part & parcell thereof vnto the said John Plaisted his heires & assignes for ever And the said Elizabeth Plaisted for herselfe her [88] heires Executors Administrat: and Assignes Doth Covenant promise & grant to & with the said John Plaisted his heires Execut: Administrat and assignes & to & with Every of them by these p^{r}sents that all and singular the said premises with all the profits priuilidges & advantages in and by these p^{r}sents before giuen granted bargaind and sold and every part & parcell thereof at ye time of the Ensealeing and Delivery of these p^{r}sents are & be and at all times hereafter shall be remaine and continew Clearely acquitted Exonorated Discharged and kept Harmless of and from all and all Manner of former and other Bargaines sales guifts grants leases Charges Dowers titles troubles or incumbrances whatsoever had made suffered or Done or to be had made Committed suffered or done by said Elizabeth Plaisted her heires Executors Administrat͞ or assignes or by any of them or any other person or persons whatsoever by her or their meanes acts titles consents and procurement, As Witness my hand and seale this sixth of July one thousand six hundred and ninety three

Memorandum Interlined before the Ensealeing delivery of these pʳsents between the first and second line these words [& Executrix

Signed sealed & Delivered   Elizabeth Plaisted
   in presence of vs   her *e e* Marke (ᵃSeale)
     Thomas Goodin   Elizabeth Plaisted acknowledged the
     James Allin   aboue Instrument or Deed of sale
     John Barsham   to bee her act & Deed: Portsmᵒ
                           July 17ᵗʰ 1693
                  Before Me Richd Martin Justˢ pˢ

A true Coppy of the originall Deed of Sale taken & here Entred on record this 20ᵗʰ Day of Novembʳ 1693
               p me John Wincoll Cleric͞:

An Inventory of the Estate of Jonathan Sayword lately Deceased taken by vs whose names are here vnder written this 25ᵗʰ of November 1689

	£	s	d
His wearing Cloathes...	03	00	00
one bed and bolster and other bed Cloathes belonging to it.................	02	00	00
two loomes slayes and haruess to them.	05	00	00
housall stuff 3 Iron pots and peuter platters and other things................	03	00	00
30 pound of sheeps wooll...	01	10	00

two guns	01	16	00
3 yards of woollen Cloath and 20 pound of yarn	02	10	00
one paire of sheets	01	00	00
20 sheepe	05	00	00
6 swine	05	10	00
one Mare and Colt	01	15	00
one Dwelling house and Cow house twenty acres of land	30	00	00
and 20 acre of land aboue the fal mils	03	00	00
foure oxen, 4 Cowes, 2 yearlings 4 Calfs	20	00	00
	83	01	00

Witness our hands
the Day & yeare aboue
written

Abra: Preble
The [mark] marke of
Henry Simson

Mrs Mary Sayword appeared before vs and tooke oath that the aboue written is a true Inventory of her deceased husbands Estate as far as shee knowes and If any more appeare she will ad it hereto dec: 25 1689 Jn° davess Jn° Wincoll Jus: peac

Administration is granted vnto Mrs Mary Sayword of the Estate of her Deceased husband Jonathan Sayword and the said Mary Sayword and Matthew Austin Doe acknowledg themselues bound vnto our sovereigne lord the King in the sum of a hundred sixty six pounds sterling that the said Mary Sayword shall Administer on sd Estate according to law

a true Coppy of the originall Inventory and the oath to it and the grant of Administration this 9^t Day of december 1693   p me John Wincoll Cleric:

[89] To all Christian people to whom these presents shall Come Know ye that James Littlefield Senior of wells yeoman in the province of maine & in the County of yorke in New England in america sendeth greetting Know ye that I the sd James Litlefeild Senr for the sum of sixty pounds in Currant pay of New England to me in hand payd by my

father Francis Litlefeild Senr of wells as abouesd yeoman before the Ensealing and delivery of these presents which I doe acknowledge to haue received & therewith my selfe fully satisfied contented and paid haue Bargained and sould and Doe by these presents absolutely & Clearely Bargaine, sell, alien, assigne and set over & confirme vnto my said father Francis Litlefeild Senr his Heires Ex^{rs} Administro^{rs} & assignes all that house and land which I bought of Abraham Tilton Lieing and being in the township of wells vizt one hundred & fifty acres of vpland on the north side Augunkitt river begining Eight poles from the said river & so to run vp into the Country bounded on the northeast side by Francis Backhouse his lot vntill one hundred and fifty acres be Compleated : also a grant of tenne acres of Meadow in the woodds where it may be found fre from any Claime by any person : also one hundred and fifty acres of vpland bounded on the north East side by the lott of Joseph Crosse and on the South west side by Nagunkit river vntill it come to be forty poole wide at which wideness it is to run vppon a west norwes line vntil it be fully accomplished and compleated ; also two acres of Salt Marsh meadow bounded by Mr Sam^{ll} Wheelwrights on the east side and Joseph Cross on the west and foure acres of marsh that my father Francis Litlefeild Senr gaue formerly to me ; with all my right title & Interest that I haue or ought to haue at the time of the sealeing of these presents in all the aforesaid houseings or land vpland or Meadowes with all mines Mineralls Comonages profits priviledges & appurtenances thereto belonging To Haue and To Hold all & singular the aboue granted & bargained premises with every part and parcell thereof with all the timber timber trees woods vnderwoods profits prevelidges and appurtenances to every part and parcell thereof vnto me belonging with all my right title and Interest therein vnto the said Francis Litlefeild Senr my father his heires Ex^{rs} Administrators to his and their ow proper vse

Part I, Fol. 89.

benefit and behoofe for ever, And I the sd James Litlefeild doe by these covenant and promise for myselfe my heire Ex^m & Administrators to and wt the said Francis Litlefeild Senr my father his heires Ex^rs Administrators and assignes, that at and Imediately before the Ensealeing of these presents was the true and lawfull owner of all & singular the afore bargained premises and that I haue good right and lawfull authority in my own name to Grant bargaine sell and Convay the same as aforesaid and that the said Francis Litlefeild Senr my father, his heires Ex^m and assignes shall and may by vertue and force of these presents from time to time and at all times for ever hereafter lawfully peaceably and quietly haue hold vse occupy and Enjoy the aboue granted premises with their appurtenances free and Cleare & freely and Clearely acquitted and Discharged of from all Mañer of former Gifts grants bargaines sales leases Mort gadges Jointures Dowers Judgments Executions forfeitures troubles and Incumbrances whatsoever, had made Done or suffered to be Done by me the said James Litlefeild or my heires or Ex^m assignes at any time or times before the sealing & delivery of these presents and I the James Litlefeild Senr my heires Executors and Administrators shall and will from time to time and at all times for ever hereafter warrant and defend the aboue granted premises with their appurtenances and every part and parcell thereof vnto the abouenamed Francis Litlefeild Senr my father his heires Ex^m and Assignes against all and Every person or persons laying Claime thereto or any part thereof from by or vnder me my heires Ex^m Administrators In Wittnes whereof I haue herevnto sett my hand and seale this twentieth Day March one thousand six hundred Eighty & two: three Annoq, Regni regis Caroli Secundi: xxxv. 168$\frac{2}{3}$/ (acres) in the eight row & (giuen) in the fifteenth row and (me) in the nineteenth rowe was Interlined before signeing & sealeing hereof (by Mr Samuell Wheelewrights on the east and Joseph Crosses on the west) in the fourteenth row and that a litle rased before signing and sealing hereof.

Signed Sealed & Delivered   James Litlefeld sa (his seale)
   in presence of   James Littelfeild acknowledged
     Rob: Hilton   this aboue writen Instrument
     George Pearson   to be his act and Deede this
                                3^d Day of May 1683
                Before me Sam^{ll} Wheelewright : Jus : peace
These two sides are a true coppy of the originall Deed of Sale of James Litlefeild Senior to his father Francis Litlefeild Senr here entred on record this 15th Day of decem^{br} 1693
                    p me John Wincoll Cleric:

[90] To all Christian people to whom these presents shall Come Know ye That Francis Litlefoild Senr of wells in the Province of Mayne & in the County of york in New England in america sendeth greeting Know ye that the said Francis Litlefeild Senr out of that naturall loue and affection that I beare to my sone Daniell Litlefeild and Divers & other good Causes me therevnto moueing Haue Giuen Granted & doe by these presents freely Clearely and Absolutely Giue Grant aliene assigne and sett over & confirme vnto my said sone Daniell Litlefeild his heires Ex^{rs} administrat^{rs} & assignes all y^t tract of land with houseing therevnto belonging which formerly belonged to Abraham Tilton of this place, one hundred & fifty acres of vpland on the north side of Augunkitt river beging Eight pooles from the said riuer & so to runne vp into the Country bounded on the northeast side by Francis Backhouse his lot vntill one hundred and fifty acres be accomplished & tenne acres of meadowes in the woods w^r it may found free from any Claime by any person, Also one hundred & fifty acres more of vpland bounded on the northeast side by the lot of Joseph Crosses, and on the Southwest

side by Nagunkitt river vntill it come to be forty poles wide at which wideness it is to run vppon a west nor west line vntill it be fully Compleated & accomplished & two acres of salt marsh meadow bounded by Mr Sam^{ll} Wheelwrights Sen^{rs} marsh on the East side & Joseph Crosses on the West : and foure acres of Marsh that I formerly gaue to my sone James Litlefeild Senior and tenn acres of salt marsh meadow more or less lyeing at the lower end of my own Marsh from the Island so called, Downward bounded with webhanicke river on one side & end & on the Southeast side by Joseph Crosse and two young heifers and two young steares all being one yeare old a peece, all the particulars abouesaid is in lew of his portion with all my right title & Interest, I haue or ought to haue at the time of the sealeing of these presents in all the aforesd houseings arable land fenceing vpland and meadowes with all mines mineralls Comonages timbers timber trees profits previledges & appurtenances therevnto belonging To Haue and to Hold all & singular the aboue granted and bargained premises & every part and parcell thereof with all woods vnderwoods profits &c and to every part and parcell ther of vnto me belonging w^t all my right title and Interest therof vnto the said Daniell Litlefeild my sone his heires Ex^{rs} Administrat^{rs} to his & their owne proper vse benefit & behoofe forever And the said Francis Litlefeild Senr doe by these presents Covenant & promise for my selfe my heire Ex^{rs} Administrat^{rs} or assignes to & wth the sd Daniell Litlefeild my sone his heires Ex^{rs} Administrators & assignes that at and Imediately before the Ensealeing of these presents was the true and lawfull owner of all and singular the afore bargained premises and that I haue good right and lawfull authority in my owne name to grant giue bargaine Conuay the same as aforesaid and that the said Daniell Litlefeild my sone his heires Ex^{rs} Administrat^{rs} & assignes shall & may by vertue & force of these presents from time to time & at all times for ever hereafter lawfully & peaceably & quietly Haue hold vse occupy & Inioy the aboue granted premises w{t} theire appurtenances free and Cleare & freely Discharged & Clearely acquitted of & from all manner of former gifts grants bargaines sailes leases Mortgages Jointures Dowers Judgments Executions forfeitures troubles & Incumbrances whatsoever had made Done or suffered to be Done by me the said Francis Litlefeild senior or my heires Ex{rs} or assignes at any time or times before the Ensealing and Delivery of these presents, and I the said Francis Litlefeild Sen{r} my heires Ex{rs} & administrators shall & will from time to time & at all times for ever hereafter warrant & defend the aboue giuen and Granted premises with their appurtenances and every part & parcell thereof vnto the aboue named Daniell Litlefeild my sonne his heire Ex{rs} administrat{rs} or assignes against all & every parson or parsons laying Claime thereto or any part thereof from by or vnder me my heires Ex{rs} administrat{rs} In Witness whereof I haue herevnto sett my hand and seale this twenty eight Day of March one thousand six hundred Eighty and three Annoq, Regis Regis Caroli Secundi xxxv-1683 : It is to be further vnderstood that my sone Daniell Litlefeild is now to haue imediate posession of the aboue giuen & granted premises only his father Francis Litlefeild Sen{r} is to lett it out for said Daniell Litlefeild his sone as to Improue it as he shall see most convenient vntill his said sone Daniell Litlefeild shall come to the full age of twenty one yeares : the said Daniell is to haue the Improuem{t} and benefitt of the farme whatever is made of it vntill he come of age Excepting fiue acres marsh that I Francis Litlefeild Sen{r} reserue in my own hands and to my own vse vntill my sd sone Daniell Litlefeild come to be twenty one yeares of age, then to be his, his heires Ex{rs} & administrators for ever

PART I, FOL. 91.

In the forty eight row (is haue) was Interlined before signing sealing and Delivery hereof

Signed Sealed & delivered   ffr: Litlefeild Sen[r] (his seale)
in presence of   Francis Litlefeild Senior acknowledged
Robert Hilton   this aboue Instrument to be his act
George Pearson   and Deed this 3[d] of May 1683/
         Before me Sam[ll] Wheelewright
                          Jus peace

These two sides are a tru coppy of the originall Deed of Francis Litlefeild Sen[r] to his sone Daniell Litlefeild: here Entred on record this this 15th Day of Decemb[r] 1693
                p me John Wincoll Cleric:

[91] To all Christian people to whom these presents shall come Know ye that Francis Litlefeild Sen[r] of wells yeoman in the province of Maine & in the County of yorke in New England in America sendeth Greeting Know ye that the said Francis Litlefeild Sen[r] out of that naturall loue & affection that I beare to my sonne Dependance Litlefeild and for Divers & other good causes me therevnto moueing Haue giuen granted & by these presents frely Clearely & absolutely giue grant alien assigne & set over and Confirme vnto my said sonne Dependance Litlefeild his heire Ex[rs] Administrators & assignes all my farme of land y[t] I now liue in or vppon w[t] all my houseings barnes: out houseings arable land pasture land oarchards meadowes fresh & salt that is now in my Imediate possession Excepting what I haue Giuen vnto my sonne James Litlefeild Sen[r] as by his Deed on the twentieth this Instant March Eighty two Eighty three more at large appeareth & ten acres salt marsh which I haue giuen vnto my sone Daniell Litlefeild as by his Deed beareing Date the twenty Eight Day of march Eighty three

PART I, FOL. 91.

may & Doth appeare all which land & houseing as abouesd is bounded by my sonne James Litlefeilds sen^r his land on the north side & by William Ashleys land and Mr Samuell Wheelwrights land on the South : and all the marsh that lieth neare m^r Sam^{ll} Wheelewrights sen^r neck of land and all other marsh now in my Imediate possession after my Death and the Death of my now wife Rebecka Litlefeild with all my right title and Interest I now haue or ought to haue at the time of the sealeing of these presents in all the aforesd houseings arreable land fences Marsh or Meadowes lands out houses mines Minerals Comoditye s timber timber trees woods vnderwoods profitts priviledges and appurtenances therevnto belonging To Haue and To Hold all & singular the aboue granted & bargained premises to every part & parcell thereof with all & singular other preveledges & to every part & parcell thereof vnto me belonging with all my right title & Interest thereof vnto the said Dependance Litlefeild my sonne after the decease of myselfe and Rebecka my now wife and to his heires Ex^{rs} administrators to his and their own proper vse benefitt & behoofe for ever : and the said Francis Litlefeild Senr Doe by these presents Covenant & promise for my selfe my heires Ex^{rs} administrators & assignes that at & Imediately before the Ensealeing of these presents was the true and lawfull owner of all & singular the afore bargained premises and that I haue good right & lawfull authority in my owne name to grant giue Bargaine & convay the same as aforesaid and that the said Dependance Litlefeild my sone after myselfe and Rebeckah my now wifes decease his heires Ex^{rs} administrators and assignes shall & may by vertue & force of these presents from time to time and at all times forever hereafter lawfully & peaceably & quietly Haue hold vse occupy possess & injoy the aboue granted premises with their appurtenances fre & Cleare & freely Discharged & Clearely accquitted of and from all maner of former gifts grants bargaines sailes leases mortgadges Jointures Dowres Judgments Executions forfeitures troubls and Incumbrances whatsoever had made done or suffered to be done by me the said Francis Litlefeild Sen[r] or my heires Ex[m] or assignes at any time or times before the sealeing & Delivery of these presents And I the said Francis Litlefeild Senior my heires Ex[m] and administrators shall & will from time to time & at all times for ever hereafter warrant & defend the aboue giuen & granted premises with their appurtenances & every part & parcell thereof vnto the aboue named Dependance Litlefeild my sonne his heires Ex[rs] administrators or assignes against all & every parson or parsons laying Claime thereto, or any part thereof from by or vnder my heires Ex[m] administrators In Wittnes whereof I haue herevnto sett my hand and seale this twenty ninth Day of March one thousand six hundred Eighty and three Annoq, Regni Regis Caroli Secundi xxxv.

It is to be vnderstood that If my said sone Dependance Litlefeild should Dye before he come to age of twenty one yeares or Dye w'out Issue of his body lawfully begotten in Wedlock then the houseings lands as is aboue Expressed shall returne to my sonne James and Daniell Litlefeild to be equally Devided between them : & if either of my sonnes as abouesd should Dye then to returne to the Surviver his heires Executors & assignes for ever the Day and yeare aboue Expressed

Signed Sealed & delivered   ffr Litlefeild Sener (his Seale)
  in presence of   Francis Litlefeild Sen[r] acknowledged
  Robert Hilton   this aboue Instrument to be his act
  George Pearson   and Deed this 3[d] day of may 1683
            Before me Sam[ll] Wheelwright. Jus. peac

These two sides are a true coppy of the originall deed of francis Litlefeild to his sone Dependence here Entred on record this 16th Day of decemb[r] 1693
             p me John Wincoll Cleric:

[92] Be it knowne vnto all men by these presents that I John Butland of wells in the County of yorke in the province of ye Maschusets bay in New England: Divers good Causes and Considerations me therevnto Moueing and More Especially for and in Consideration of a valluable sume of full satisfaction to me already payed, by Daniell Litlefeild of the aboue sayd towne and County Doe bargaine Covenant sell Infeofe and Conferme and by these presents haue from my selfe my heires Executors and administrators bargind Covenanted sold Infeofed and Confermed vnto the aboue saide Daniell Litlefeild his heires Executors administrators and assignes for ever, a Certaine tract or persell of Meadow contaings two Acres scittuate and being in the towne of wells and bounded as followeth lieing neare or Joyning to a certaine psell of land comonly called the neck of land which belongs to Mr Samuell Wheelwright and from thence running towards a small pond the sea wall or beach on the one side Southestward and a psell of Marsh called Coles Marsh lying on the other side North Westward to him the said Daniell Litlefeild his heires Executors and Assigns To Haue and to hold and peacably Injoy for Ever without any Matter of Chalenge Claime or demand of me the sd John Butland my heires Executors Administrators or assigns or any other person or persons either from by or vnd^r me and I doe farther covenant and promise to and with the said Daniell Litlefeild that before the Insealing hereof I am the right owner and true posessor of the sd meadow and haue full power and right to make lawfull sale thereof and y^t ye said meadow is free and Cleare from all former gifts grants Leases legacies Judgments Dowryes Executions and all other Incombrances whatsoever and that I will maintaine and defend the right and title of the premises sold to the said Daniell Litlefeild his heires Executors administrators and assigns for ever from any psons or pson whatsoever laying any Just Claime therevnto In testimony whereof I haue

set my hand and seale this 15th Day of may in the yeare of our lord Anno Dom : 1693 and in the 4th yeare of the reigne of our lord and lady william and Mary King and Queene of England Defenders of the faith &c :

Signed Sealed and Deliverd
in prence of
Jonathan Hamond
Jeffrey Massey

John ⨍ Butland (his Seale)
his marke
John Buckland appered before me this 17th of may 1693 and did acknowledg this Instrument to be his act and Deed as attests Sam[ll] Wheelwright : Jus peac

A true coppy of y[e] originall deed here entred decemb[r] 19 : 1693   p me John Wincoll Cleric :

Be it Known vnto all men by these presents that I James Litlefeild of the towne of wells in the province of Mayne in New England yeoman severall good Causes and considerations me therevnto moueing and more Especially for and in Consideration of certaine tract of land and meadow containing six hundred acres to me in hand delivered and sesion and posession giuen by John Buckland of the abouesaid town and province wherewith I Doe acknowledge to be fully satisfied and contented Haue bargained sold granted and Exchanged and Doe by these presents grant bargaine Make over Infeoffee and confirme freely fully and absolutely vnto the abouesaid John buckland from mee my heires Executors Administrators and assignes my now Dwelling house and out houseing with my vpland and meadow containing one hundred and seventy foure acres scittuate and being in the town of wells bounded as followeth, the lower end next the sea begining at the river and so bounded by a small brooke next to my father Litlefeilds on the South west side and

Part I, Fol. 93.

Joseph Litlefeilds on the North east side till it come vnto the cart bridge and then to be one and thirty poles in breadth and so to continew that breadth vp into the Country till one hundred and fifty acres be Compleated fiue acres of Marsh lieing be it more or less at the lower end of the said land and seven acres of marsh be it more or less lieing betweene the greate river and the ridge and foure acres more Joining to Ezekiell Knights marsh and so by an Island next the sea on the other side together with the said Island containing by Estimation about twenty acres be it more or less and also three acres of marsh lieing on the Southwest side of Mr Samuell Wheelewrights neck of land, also one hundred acres of vpland at a place called meryland and ten acres of meadow the vpland lyeing on the Southwest side of the meadow at sd Meryland next the greate swampe and so to run from the meadow Southwestward forty poles in breadth till one hundred acres be Compleated the ten acres of Meadow begining next to Thomas Litlefeilds meadow and so to run vp the river till ten acres be compleated with all the singular appurtenances and previledges in any wise appertaining or belonging to the premises granted and sold, woods and vnderwoods comons and comonage together with all other conveniencys whatsoever in any wise appertaining or belonging [93] Freely and quietly To Haue and To Hold without any Matter of Challenge Claime or Demand of Me the said James Litlefeild or any person or persons either from by or vnder mee my heires Executors Administrators and assignes for ever hee the said John Buckland his heires Executors Administrators and assignes I doe hereby Declare to bee truly and rightly possesed of each and every part and parcell of the premises aboue mentioned and hee the said John Buckland his heires Executors administrators and assignes shall haue hold and Enjoy all and every part and parcell of the premises granted and sold to them for ever and I doe hereby promise and Covenant to and with the said

PART I, FOL. 93.

John Buckland that I am before the Ensealeing hereof the true lawfull and right owner and possessor of all the aboue mentioned premises and that I haue full power of myselfe to make lawfull Exchange and seall of the said premises and I doe further Covenant and promise to and with the said John Buckland that all and every part & parcell of the premises granted and free and Cleare from all former gifts grants bargaines leases Dowryes legacies Jointures Judgments morgages Executions and all other Incombrances whatsoever and Doe promise to warrant and Defend the title and Interest of the premises from mee my heires Executors Administrators and assignes and from all other person or persons whatsoever vnder me or by my means or procurements In testimony whereof I haue herevnto sett my hand and seall the fourteenth Day of Aprill in the yeare of our L^d anno Dom one thousand six hundred and Eighty seven and in the 3^d yeare of the reigne of our soveraigne Ld James the 2^d of England Scotland France and Ireland King Defender of the faith

I Katherne Litlefeild the wife of James Litlefeild doe freely consent to this aboue bill of seall wherevnto I haue set my hand and seale   James Litlefeild (Seal)
Signed sealed & delivered   Katherine Litlefeild (Seal)
  in p'sence of
  Jona: Hamond   her ◯ marke
  James Gooch

Know all men by these presents that I Harlakinden Symonds of Ipswich in the County of Essex in their Maties provence of Masachusets bay in New England Gent: For and in Consideration of a valuable some of mony or other Goods paid to my satisfaction in hand already received of Leiut Thomas Baker of Topsfield in the County abouesd Haue Given

PART I, FOL. 94.

Granted bargened and sold Alienated Infeofed and Confirmed and by these presents doe give Grant bargin sell Alienate Infeoffe and Confirme vnto said Baker his Heires Executors Administrators and Assignes for ever a sartaine parsell of land in a place called Coxhall now called Swansfeild containing by Estimation fiftene hundred Akers which is part of that tract of land of six miles square which I formerly purchased of Leiut John Saunders Senr John Bush and Peter Turbet who purchased the said land of ye Indian Sagamore called Sosowan and was Confirmed as by writeing will appeare by ye said Sagamores only sone called Fluellin and by ye testimony of severall Indians as well as English which Land by this wrighting Granted is bounded as followeth to wit: by the land sold to to the six and thirty men towards the South which is but foure miles brode and it is bounded by Caporpus river alias Mousum river towards the West and ye East End is bounded towards Sacoe riuer and from the sutherly side to the northerly side is six score and fifteene rods in breadth all along from End to End lyeing six miles in length: all the abouesaid fifteene hundred Acres as it is bounded: I the said Symonds doe acknowledge I haue bargained and sould and made over to the said Baker with all the woods rocks mines swamps vpland and meadow and ponds and water corses and whatsoever Doth properly belong vnto the said land with all the previledges and appurtenances therevnto belonging contained in the length and Breadth aboue Mentioned To Haue and To Hold and peaceably to Enjoy without any lett hindrance Molestation Deniall or or Disturbance and I the abouesd Symonds doe Ingadge to defend it from any lawfully laying Claime to all or any part of the abouesaid premises from by or vnder me or any or any other person whatsoever and to the true performance hereof I doe bind bind myselfe my heires Executors Administrators and Assignes to said Baker him his heires Executors Administrators and assignes for ever [**94**]

PART I, FOL. 94.

In Witness whereof I haue herevnto set my hand and Seale this Eleventh of aprill one thousand six hundred and Ninty three

Signed Sealed and Delivrd   Harlackinden Symonds ($_{Seale}^{a}$)
in the presence

Deed
H. Symonds
to Baker
169¾

of vs witnesses   Mr Harlackenden Symonds personally appeared & owned this aboue written Instrument to be his act & Deed Janry ye 18th 1693 (4)
Ephraim Dorman
Thomas Waite
Timothy Dorman
Ebenezer roxxell

Before me Thos Wade Justice of peace

A true coppy of the originall Deed of Sale taken and here Entred this 22th of february 169¾

p me John Wincoll Cleric:

Know all men by these presents that I Harlackinden Symonds of Ipswich Gent: in the County of Essix in their Majesties Province of the Massachusets bay in New England for and in Consideration of a valuable some of money or other good pay to my satisfaction in hand alredy receiued of Tymothy Dorman of Boxford Husbandman in the County aboue sd Haue Giuen Granted Bargained & sold Alienated Infeoffed and Confirmed and by these presents Doe Giue Grant Bargaine sell Alienat Infeoffe and Confirme vnto said Dorman his heires Executors Administrators and Assignes for ever a certaine parcell or Quantity of land scittuate lyeing and being beyond Wells in ye province of Maine in New England at a place called Coxhall now called Swansfeild containing by Estimation fiue hundred acres be it more or lesse which is parte of that tract of land of six miles square which I formerly purchased of Leiut Sanders Senr John Bush Peter Turbett who purchased ye said land of the Indian Sagamore called Sosowan and was confirmed as by wrighting will appeare by sd Sagamores only sone called Fluellin and by the testimonys of severall Indians as Well as Inglish which land by this Wrighting granted is bounded as followeth, to wit, bounded by leiut Bakers land towards the South and bounded by Caporpus river alias Mousum river towards the West: and the East end bounded towards Sacoe river and from the Southerly sid to the Northerly side forty fiue rods in breadth all along from End to End lyeing six Miles in length: All the abouesaid fiue hundred acres as it is bounded: I the said Symonds doe acknowledge I haue bargaind and sold and made over to the said Dorman with all the trees rocks Mines swamps vpland and meadow and ponds and water coursis and whatever Doth properly belong to the said Land with all the previledges and appurtenances belonging therevnto contained in the length and breadth aboue mentioned To Haue and To Hold peaceably to Injoy without any lett hindrance Molestation denieall or desturbance and I the abouesd Symonds doe Ingadge to Defend it from any lawfully laying Claime to all or any part of the abouesaid premises from by or vnder me or any other person whatsoever and to the true performance hereof I Doe bind myselfe my heires Executors Administrators and Assignes to the sd Dorman him his heires Executors and Assignes for ever in Wittness whereof I haue herevnto sett my hand and seale this Eleventh of aprill one thousand six hundred and ninety three.

Signed Sealed and Delivered   Har. Symonds (ᵃSeale)
  in the presence of vs
    Witnesses   Mr Harlackenden Symonds personally
    Thomas Baker   appeared & owned this aboue written
    Ephraim Dorman   Instrument to be his act & Deed
    Thomas Waite   June ye 18th 1693 (4)
    Ebenezer rocwell
                     before me Thoˢ Wade Justice of peace

PART I, FOL. 95.

A true coppy of the originall Deed of Sale taken and here Entred on record this 22th of february 169¾

p me John Wincoll Cleric:

[95] Know all men by these presents that I David Trustrum of Sacoe in the province of Maine in New England for and in Consideration of thirteen pound starling to me in hand paid by Edward Sergent of the same town and pvince before the Ensealeing & delivery of these presents to full content and satisfaction and of every part and parcell thereof Doe clearely acquitt and Exonorate & Discharge the said Edward Sergent his heires Executors and Administrators for ever Doe by these Giue Grant Bargin sell Alienate Infeoffe and Confirme vnto the said Edward Sergent a certaine tract of vpland scittuate and being in the towne of Sacoe aforsd it being part of that tract of land that my father Ralph Trustrum formerly Inhabited ocupied and Improued and now lawfully desended vnto me the aforesd David Trustrum sone of the aforesd Ralph Trustrum deceased and it lies in Winter harbour adjoyning to the aforesd Edward Sergents Dwelling house containing about thirty acres be it more or less bounded on thenortheard side with John Sergents Land & to a lot of Land which was formerly Richard Randelles and now in the posession of the aforesd Edward Sergent and bounded on the Southwest side with a brouk and adjoining to a orchard of David Trustrums abouesd with a peas that is now fenced in vpon the Sudeard side of the brouk/ that is to say all the Land betweene the brouk on the Southwest of the said Sergents house : and on the northeard side bounded as is aboue Expressed/ and now by the aforesaid David Trustram sold vnto the aforesaid Edward Sergent To Haue and to hold the

<small>a true coppy of yo originall here
Entered february 23 169¾
p me John Wincoll Cleric:</small>

Part I, Fol. 95.

said trackt of vpland with all and singular the apurtenances and previledges therevnto belonging or in any wise appertaining to him the said Edward Sergent his heires Executors Administrators or assignes for ever fully and Clearely exonorated from all former other gifts grants sales mortgadges or other Incumbrances whatsoeuer made suffered to be done by me David Trustram or any other person or persons by from or vnder me and for confirmation the premises I y² sd David Trustram haue herevnto put my hand this sixth Day of January in one thousand six hundred and ninty :
Signed Sealed & deliv?? in y?   the marke of
  p?sence of vs
  Benjamin Sergent   David ╪ Trustram (Seale)

The marke of Edward ╞ Randuell

Benjamin Sergent & Edward Randell made oath that they saw david Trustram sign seal & Deliv? the aboue Instrum? as his act & Deed vnto which they sett y? hands as witnesses: Portsm? July 14 : 1693 :
                      Before me Richard Martin
                                   Justis pe :

To all Christian People to whom this publick Instrument of deed of sale shall come or may concerne Arthur Hughes Senior Inhabitant of the towne of portsmouth in the province of New Hampshiere within their Majes?? territory and Dominion of New England planter and Sarah his wife the late widdow and relict of Samson Ainger of yorke in the province of Maine Deceased sendeth greetting — Know ye that wee the sd Arthur Hughes and Sarah my wife Administrators to y? Estate of the late Samson Ainger are become lawfull owners of and good right vnto the said Estate and thereby for and in Consideration of a valluable

Part I, Fol. 96.

sume of money to vs in hand paid for our future subsistance being both of vs antient, by Mʳ John Partridge of portsmouth aforesaid Vintner the receipt whereof and of every part and parcell thereof Doe hereby acknowledg ourselues to be therewith fully satisfied and contented for which doe Exonerate Discharge and forever acquit &c : Haue Giuen Granted Bargained sold Aliened set over and confirmed and by these presents Doe Giue Grant bargain sell set over Alienate and Confirme all that our right and title to and Interest in and vnto all that our predecessor Samson Ainger had at the Day of his Death in the towne of yorke in the province of maine and that wee now haue and ought to haue since the Decease of the sd Samson Ainger Together with the house and land he last liued in and vppon and therevnto belonging sittuate lyeing and being in the Towne of yorke fronting to the maine river on the South and to a highway on the East next vnto the land that was formerly Mʳ Edward Rishworth and on the west adjoining vnto the land of Mʳ John Penwills and on the north the bounds as yet unknowne togather all other gifts and town grants highwayes waterwayes woods vnderwoods meadows mowing ground Arrable or pasturage comons Comonages & priveledges whatsoever to the said Samson Ainger belonging or to vs the sd Arthur and Sarah Hughes haue therevnto or ought to haue therein by vertue of the sd Ainger right vnto any of the forementioned bargained premises &cᵉ : To Haue and To Hold to him the said John Partridge Senior his heires Executors Administrators and assignes For ever and to his and their owne proper vse benefit and behoofe without any lett or molestation of vs the sd Arthur and Sarah Hughes our heires Executors and Administrators or assignes or any other person or persons from by or vnder vs them or any of them [96] And wee doe heareby further Covenant promise and grant to saue harmeless and Defend the said John Partridge his heires Execu-

Part I, Fol. 96.

tors Administrators and assignes from all or any former Gifts grants bargaines sales Mortgadges Dowrie or right of Dowries Widdows thirds Joynters and all other Incumbrances heretofore whatsoever, In Testamony whereof wee the said Arthur Huges and Sarah my wife to this our Deed put our hands and Seales this twentieth Day of January anno Domini one thousand six hundred ninety and three, foure and in the fifth yeare of the reigne of our sovereigne Lord and Lady William and Mary King and Queen by the grace of god over England Scotland france and Ireland Defenders of the faith &c :

Signed Sealed and Delivered in the presence of vs
William Bedford
James Levitt
Henry Crown Nata͞: publick for the province of New hampshiere

Arthur **H** Hughes (Seal)
his marke

Sarah **W** Hughes (Seal)
her marke

and whereas the land and premises is aboue and seems to be bounded and mentioned yet notwithstanding the bound are not perfectly Knowne vntill a survay

January the 22^d 169$\frac{3}{4}$
- Arthur Hughes and his wife Sarah Hughes acknowledged the aboue Instrument to be their act and Deed

Before me Thomas Parker Just : p^s :

A true coppy of the originall Deed of Sale taken and here Entred on record February 23^d 169$\frac{3}{4}$

p me John Wincoll Cleric͞ :

PART I, FOL. 96.

May 16th 1692

Capt Job Alcock of yorke appeared before vs this 16th Day of may 1692 and Did testifie that the three acres of salt marsh giuen by the Court at yorke to his mother Elizabeth Allcock widdow and relict to his father John Alcock late of yorke Deceased was by the will of his said Mother Elizabeth Alcock vnder her hand in a written will left in her own Chest in Mr Dumers house and there lost in the fire as wee conceiue in which will his sd mother gaue the said three acres of marsh to her said sone Job Allcock Dureing his life and after his Decease she gaue the said three acres of marsh to her two Grand Children Samuell Snell and John Snell

Capt Job Alcock came and made oath to ye verity of all that is aboue writen this third Day of June 1692

    Before me Francis hooke Just pea

A true coppy of the originall oath here Entred march 17 1693/4   p John Wincoll Cleric:

Know all men by these Prsents that I Thomas Fernald of the towne of Kittery in the province of Main shipwright & Temperance my wife for and in Consideration of the sume of thirteene pounds in goods and Merchandize already in hand paid mee by my Brother William Fernald of the towne and province aforesaid shipwright with which sume of goods and Merchandize I doe acknowledge myselfe to be fully satisfied and paid and Doe hereby Exonerate acquitt and Discharge the said William Fernald his heires Executors & Administrators from the same, and every part & parcell thereof for ever: Haue granted bargaind and sold And Doe by these presents Grant bargaine sell alien Enfeofe confirme and make over vnto the said William Fernald his heire Executors & Assignes a certain parcell or tract of land containing

Part I, Fol. 96.

thirty acres laying and being on the head of Spruce Creeke in yᵉ towne and province aforesd which said land is in length one hundred and sixty poles West and be South & East & bee North, and thirty two poles in breadth North & be West & South & be East bounded with the land of Margrett Adams (now sold to William Fernald aforesd) on the South with the Comons, on the North with a slipe of Comons on the East and Joynes with the land of John Morrill on the West To Haue and to Hold to him the said William Fernald his heires Executors Administrators & Assignes, all the aboue mentioned thirty acres of land being butted & bounded as aforesaid with all the previledges & appurtenances therevnto belonging for ever, And I the said Thomas Fernald and Temperance my wife Doe by these presents bind our selues our heires Executors & administrators to warrant & Defend vnto the said William Fernald his heires Executors Administ^rs & assignes all the aboue mentioned premises with all the previledges & appurtenances therevnto belonging for ever from any person or persons whatsoever that shall pretend any legall title or claime therevnto from by or vnder vs. in Witnesse whereof wee haue herevnto sett our hands & seales the fourth Day of March in the yeare of our lord one thousand six hundred Eighty & nine

Signed Sealed & Delivered in the presence of vs	Thomas Fernald (Seale) Temperance Fernald (Seale)
Abraham Spiller William Waye	Thomas Fernald & Temperance his wife acknowledged the aboue Instrument to be their act & Deed & shee freely renders vp her thirds of of Dowry in the aboue mentioned premises vnto the abouesd William Fernald & his heires &c for ever this fifth Day of may 1693 :
A true coppy of yᵉ originall Deed compared therewith and here Entred this 17ᵗʰ Day of March 169¾ p me John Wincoll Cleric:	
	Before me Richd Martin Jus^tᵉ p^e

Part I, Fol. 97.

[97] Know all men by these presents that I Margret Adams of the towne of Kittery in the province of Maine Widdow and relict of Christopher Adams Deceased for and in Consideration of the sum of thirteene pounds in goods and Marchandize already in hand paid me by william Fernald of the towne and province aforesaid shipwright with which sume of goods and Merchandize I doe acknowledge myselfe to be fully sattisfied & paid and Doe hereby Exonerate acquit and Discharge the said William Fernald his heires Executors and Administrators from the same and every part and parcell thereof for ever Haue Granted bargained & sold and Doe by these presents Grant bargaine sell Aliene Infeofe confirme & Make over vnto the said William Fernald his heires Executors Administrators & Assignes a certaine parcell or tract of land Containing Thirty acres laying & being on the head of Spruce Creeke in the towne & province aforesaid which said land is in length one hundred and sixty poles west and be south & East & East & be north and thirty two poles in breadth north & be west and South & be East bounded with the land of said William on the South & with the land of Thomas Fernald on the north with a slipe of Comons on the East and Joines to the land of John Morrill on the West: To Haue and To Hold to him the said William Fernald his heire Executors Administrators and Assignes all the aboue mentioned thirty acres of land being butted and bounded as aforesaid with all the priviledges therevnto belonging for ever And I the said Margerit Adams Doe by these presents bind myselfe mine heires Executors and Administrators to warrant and defend vnto the said William Fernald his heires Executors and Administrators and Assignes all the aboue mentioned premises with all the priviledges and appurtenances therevnto belonging for ever from any person or persons whatsoever that shall pretend any legall Title or Claime therevnto from by or vnder mee

In Wittnesse whereof I haue herevnto sett my hand and seale the 4th Day of march in the yeare of our lord one thousand six hundred Eighty and nine

Signed sealed & delivered   Margret Adams (seale)
  in the presence of vs   Margret Adams acknowledged
  Nicholas Bennett   the aboue written Instru-
  Richard Seward   ment to be her act and Deed
                            Portsm° December the 27th 1692
                     Before me Richd Martyn Juste pe

A true coppy of the originall Deed compared therwith and here Entred this 17th Day of March 169¾
                     p me John Wincoll Cleric :

Be it Knowne vnto all men by these presents that I John More Doe assigne over this present Deed together with the land within mentioned together with all previledges and appurtenances therevnto belonging vnto John Seward of portsm° his heires Executors or assignes for ever being fully satisfied to Content for the same in Witness whereof I haue herevnto set my hand and seale ye 13th June 1674

      Witness   signe of
      Gregory Williams   John ⟼ Moore (Seale)
      Elias Stileman

Great Iland 13th June 1674 John Moore Came & acknowledged this Assignemt to be his free act and Deed
                     Before me Elias Stileman Comiss :

The aboue written is a true Coppy of the assignment of a deed of sale from John More to John Seaward the fourth Day of June in the twentieth yeare of the reigne of our sovereigne lord Charles the second and therewith Compared this 24th Day of March 169¾ & here Entred on record
                     p me John Wincoll Cleric :

PART I, FOL. 98.

Agnis More Widdow and Relict of John More Junr deceased Came and acknowledged the assignement on the other side to be Done with her consent and Doth freely surrender her thirds of Dowry in the land therein Mentioned to John Seward and his heires for ever Aprill 27th 1678
     Before me Richard Martin Comis^r
The aboue written is a true Coppy of the acknowledgment of Agnis More therewith Compared & here Entred with the records of the County of yorke this 24th Day of March 169¾
     as attest John Wincoll Cleric⁑

[98] Know all men by these presents that I James Emery Junr of Kittery in the County of yorke and in the province of the Massatusets bay in New England with the Consent of Marget my wife and for many Good Causes and Considerations me moueing herevnto Especially for and In Consideration of a certaine tract of land sold and delivered vnto me in Exchange from John Searle of the same towne and County aforesaid as by Deed vnder his hand and seale beareing Date herewith more fully appeareth wherewith I ye said James Emery Junr acknowledge myselfe fully Satisfied & paid Doe by these presents for myselfe my heires Executors and Administrators Giue Grant bargaine sell Infeoffee and in Exchange Confirme vnto the aforesaid John Searle a certaine tract of land containing fifty acres scittuate and being in the towne of Kittery aforesaid in that part of the towne called the long reach on the East side of ye place called Simmons Marsh forty two acres of the aforesd fifty acres being vpland Is bounded with John Greenes land on the north and William Tetherlyes land on the South and the other Eight acres being Meadow and swampe is bounded on the West

with Christian Remichs land: Stephen Paulds land on the North and on the East is bounded in part with sd Tetherlys land and in and in part Comes vp to said forty two acres all which fifty acres of land was Giuen to me by my father James Emery Senr as by Deed of Gift vnder his hand and seale Dated September 3^d 1693 more fully appeares and now by me the aforesd James Emery Junr sold in Exchange vnto the aforesd John Searle To Haue and To Hold the aforesaid fifty acres of land with all and singular the appurtenances and previledges thereto belonging to him the said John Searle his heires Executors Administrators and Assignes for ever. For Confirmation of the premises I the aforesaid James Emery and Marget my Wife haue herevnto set our hands and seales this 20th Day of March 169¾

Signed sealed & Delivrd in   James Emery Junr (his Seal)
  presence of vs   Maraet Emery (her Seal)
  John Linscot   James Emery and Margret his wife
  John Belcher   acknowledged the aboue written
  Charles Frost Junr Instrument to be their act & Deed
                            this 20 of march 169¾ Before me
                            Charles Frost Jus^t of peace

The aboue written is a true coppy of the originall Deed of Sale from James Emery Junr to John Searle & therewith Compared march 26 : 1694
                     p me John Wincoll Cleric

To all Christian People to whom these presents shall Come Moses Spencer of Kittery in the Coutty of yorkeshiere now in the Massachusets Jurisdiction in NewEngland yeoman send Greeting Know ye that I the aboue mentioned Moses Spencer for Divers good Causes and Considerations me moueing therevnto More Espeially for and In Consideration of y{e} sume of twelue pounds in hand receiued before the signing and sealeing hereof of Daniell Goodden Senior wherewith I acknowledge myselfe fully satisfied Contented & paid and thereof & of euery part & parcell thereof Doe acquit & for ever Discharge the said Daniell Goodden Senior his heires and Assignes by these presents Haue absolutely Giuen granted bargained sold Aliened Infeoffeed and Confirmed and by these presents Doe absolutely giue Grant Bargaine sell aliene Infeoffe and Confirme vnto the aboue named Daniell Goodden Senior a peece or parcell of land being twenty fiue acres more or lesse being by Nequichawanick litle river and bounded as followeth Viz one the South west with the land of Moses Spencer on the north west with Isaack Botts land on the southeast with the aforesd river and on the north east with the Comon land and it being in length from Newichawanick litle river one hundred and twenty poles north west and in breadth thirty foure poles To Haue & To Hold y{e} aboue mentioned peece or parcell of land to him the said Daniell Goodden Senior his heires and assignes for ever and to his only proper vse benefitt and behoofe for ever & the said Moses Spencer for himselfe his heires & assignes Doe Covenant promise & Grant to and with the said Daniell Goodden Sen{r} his heires and Assignes that hee the said Moses Spencer hath in himselfe good right full power and lawfull authoryty the aboue Giuen and Granted Premises to sell and Dispose of & that the same & every part and parcell therof are free & Cleare and freely & Clearely acquitted Exonerated & Discharged of & from all and all maner of former Gifts Grants leases Mortgadges Wills Entailes Judgments Executions power of third and all other Incombrances of what nature and kind soever had made Done acknowledged Comitted or suffered & to be done or Comitted whereby the said Daniell Goodden Senior his heires or assignes shall or may any wayes be molested

Evicted or ejected out of the aboue granted premises or any part or parcell thereof by any person or persons whatsoever, haueing Claiming or pretending to haue or Claime any legall right title Interest Claim or Demand [**99**] of in or to yᵉ aboue granted premises and the said Moses Spencer Doth for himselfe his heires Executors Administrator & Assignes Covenant promise and Grant to and with the said Daniell Goodden Senʳ his heires and Assignes yᵉ aboue granted peece or parcell of land with all the appurtenances and priviledges thereto belonging to Warrant and forever Defend by these presents in Witness Whereof yᵉ said Moses Spencer hath herevnto put his hand and seale this Eighteenth Day of December in the yeare of our lord one thousand six hundred and seventy foure and in the twenty sixth yeare of the reigne of our Sovereigne Lord Charles yᵉ ($\frac{d}{n}$) Secund of England Scotland France and Ireland King Defender of the faith

Signed Sealed & delivered   his marke
   in the presence of vs   Moses ⋀ Spencer (Seale)
George Broughton
Humphry Chadbourne

The aboue written Deed of Sale was acknowledged by the within named Moses Spencer to be his act and Deed this 18ᵗʰ Day of december 1674/./

                 Before me John Wincoll Assotiate

The aboue written is a true Coppy of the originall Deed of Sale from Moses Spencer to Daniell Goodden Senʳ Compared & here Entred on record this 27ᵗʰ Day of March 1694:   p me John Wincoll Cleric:

Barbados

To all People to whom this present Writing shall Come I John Hole late of the towne of Kittery in New England Planter now resident in the said Island send Greeting Know yee that I the said John Hole for Divers good Causes & considerations me therevnto Moueing Haue Made Assigned Constituted Authorized & appointed, and by these presents Doe make Assigne Constitute authorize and appoint and in my stead and place put & depute my loueing wife Elizabeth Hole of the towne of Kittery aforesaid to be my true and lawfull Attorney & procurator for me in my name and to my vse by all lawfull wayes & meanes whatsoever to enter into & vppon and take possession of all and singular such lands and plantations as are or shall be belonging or apperteining vnto me the said Constituent in the towne of Kittery aforesaid or elce where in New England together with all and every the houses Eddifices buildings Catle stock and other Appurtenances therevnto belonging or appertaining And more Especially to Comence sue and prosecute any actcon or actcons of Ejectm^t or other accons whatsoever (as the case shall require) against William Furnall of piscataqua in New England shipwright (or any other person or persons whom it Doth shall or may concerne) of and for all that my plantation conteining by Estimacon ninety acres of land scittuate lieing and being in the towne of Kittery aforesaid; together with all and every the houses, Edefices & buildings Cattle & stock goods & Chattells rights Members profits priviledges & appurtenances therevnto belonging or in any wise apperteining; And being posessed thereof the same plantacon and p^{r}mises with ye Appurtenances and Every part thereof for me & in my name to sell and Dispose of, Grant, Alien & convey to such person or persons and for and vppon such tearmes and Conditions, sum & sums of money as to my sd Attorney

PART I, FOL. 100.

shall be thought most for the benefitt & advantage of me the said Constituent; And to that End to make, pass, & Execute such Acts, Contracts or Agreement and to signe seale & Deliver such, Deed or Deeds of Sale and conveyances as shall be requisite in that behalfe; And the moneys goods or Effects ariseing vppon sale of the said planta: & premises with the appurtennces to Demand, procure & receiue to the vse of me the said Constituent, And according to my order to Consigne or otherwise Dispose of ye same, And vppon receipt thereof to make and giue sufficient acquittances or Discharges in the law; And in Case my sd Attorney can not or Doe not sell & dispose of my said plantation with the buildings stock and appurtenances thereof, then I Doe hereby authorize and Impower my sd Attorney to manuage imploy and improue the same from time to time to & for my best profit benefit and advantage as she shall see meet with all other my Estate whatsoever in New England aforsd [100] As also for me and in my name, and to my vse to aske demand sue for Levie recover & receiue all and singular such debt and Debts sum & sums of money Goods and Chattells wares Merchandizes & Comodities, effects and things whatsoever as now are or hereafter shall be Due, Oweing & payable, belonging or appertaining vnto me the said Constituant by or from any person or persons whatsoever in New England or elswhere, be the same arriseing by Judgment Bond bill bookedebt $acco^t$ Couenant Contract, promise, Will, bequest $Consignem^t$ of goods or otherwise howsoever (nothing Excepted nor reserved) together with all Costs Charges Damages and Interests for nonpayment already suffered and yet to susteine vntill full satisfaction be made, Giueing and by these presents granting vnto my sd attorney & procurator all my whole power strength and authority in & about the p^rmises And vppon the rec^t of the said Debt and Debts sum & sums of money Goods and Chattells wares merchandizes and Comodities

Effects and things whatsoever & wheresoever as aforesaid or any part thereof sufficient acquittances or other lawfull Discharges for me and in my name to make seale giue & deliver, And vppon refusall or nonpaym^t the sd person or persons every or any of them to sue impleade and prosecute pursue arrest attach Imprison & condemne and out of prison to deliver And if need be to recon and accompt Compound and make Composision Covenant Contract and agree with any person or persons for and Concerning the premises also to refer any difference to Arbitration and to End finish and Determine the same Moreouer One Attorney or more with like full power and authority vnder her my sd attorney to sett & substitute and at her pleasure the same againe to revoake and all & every other act & acts thing & things needfull or nessesary to be Done in & about the premises and ye dependences thereof for me and in my name to Doe Execute & p^{r}forme as fully amply and Efectually in every respect to all intents and purposes as I the said Constituent myselfe might or could doe being personally present, Ratifieing allowing & Confirming all and whatsoever my said Attorney or her substitute or substitutes shall lawfully Doe or Cause to be Done in & about the premises by vertue of these presents In Witness whereof I the said John Hole haue herevnto set my hand & seale th twelfth Day of August Annoq, Dom̄ one thousand six hundred & Ninty

Signed Sealed & Delivered in   John Hole (Seale)
   in the p^{r}sence of witnesses   Portsm^o In the Province of
   Elisha Plaisted   New Hampshire 8 ber 28th
   Roberd Rously   1690. then Robert Rousley &
                                  Jno Patee mad oath that they
     his R R marke   saw Jno Hole signe sele & deliver ye aboue Instrument as
   John Patee   his act & Deed & they set to
                                  there hands as witneses before
                                  me
                                  William Vaughan Jus^{ts} Ps :

PART I, FOL. 100.

This is a true coppy of the originall letter of Atorney of John Hole to his wife therewith Compared & here Entred March 27th 1694/

p me John Wincoll Cleric͞:

To all Christian People I Richard Cutt send Greeting in our lord god everlasting, Know ye that I the said Richard Cutt of the towne of Kittery in the province of Maine yeoman for the Consideration of the loue I beare vnto my brother leiuetenant Richard Bryer of the same place Haue Giuen and Granted and by these presents doe Giue Grant and Confirme vnto the said Richard Bryer all that Creek of water lyeing betweene the land of him the said Richard Briar and John Muggridg generally Knowne by the name of long Creeke goeing in att the mouth of broad Coue with all and singular the rights titles and prehemenences therevnto belonging as all priuiledges runs of water small Creekes or riuelets or any waters that pass therein out of any brooke or swampe into the aforesaid Creeke as also liberty to Dam over the said Creek in any part thereof for the Erecting of a Corne mill or sawmill or fulingmill for the sole vse of him the said Richard Bryer his heires or Assignes for ever and that it shall not be lawfull for mee the said Richard Cutts or any vnder me to stop any waters or Divert them out of their Naturall Course or streame that pass into the said Creek and that the said Richard Bryer his heires or assignes shall haue their free Egres and Regress to open or scoure any run of water that may be brought into the said Creek for the vses aforesaid To Haue and to Hold all and singular the Creek of water and all the priviledges aforementioned and all the members thereof vnto the said Richard Briar his heires or Assignes for ever 'to their owne proper vse and behoofe for

PART I, FOL. 101–102.

ever, And further that the said Richard Briar shall peaceably and Quietly Enjoy the same without any Claime Challenge or Demand of me the said Richard Cut or any vnder mee or my heires or assignes for ever and the peaceable posession therof to warrant maintaine and defend against al persons laiying Claime therevnto our soveraign lord and their lawfull heires Excepted Witness my hand and seale this sixteenth Day of December 1693

in presence of vs   Richard Cutt (Seale)
    Robt Eliot   M{r} Richard Cutt cam and owned this
    William Peperell   Instrument to be his act and Deed
                      to M{r} Richard Briar this 29{th} o
                      March : 1694 :
                  Before me Francis Hooke Just. pea :

The aboue written is a true coppy of the originall Deed from M{r} M{r} Richard Cutt to M{r} Richard Briar and here Entred this 2{d} Day of Aprill 1694
                p me John Wincoll Cleric :

[101] (This folio is blank)

[102] Memorandum that I John Vgraue of Kittery vpō the Riuer of Pascataquah haue sold vnto Abraham Conley of the same one house or tenement with six acres of ground or land whereof pte is impaled and the rest of the ground he the said Abraham is to pale in Eastward which house the said Abraham Conley now posseseth and for the performance of the sale I haue herevnto sett my hand the first Day of January 1638//

Memorandum that the said Abraham Conley is to haue a way twelue foote wide along by his pales vp into the woods
Witnesses Hñsrd Knollys   John Vgroufe
    Mary Crae Vgroufe
    her marke

Part I, Fol. 102.

A true coppy of the originall here Entred Aprill 13th 1694// p me John Wincoll Cleric:

This Indenture made the 24th of June in the yeare of our lord one thousand six hundred forty Eight witnesseth that I Abraham Conley by and with free consent of my wife Doth grant sell assigne and set over vnto Thomas Jones my house & feild inclosed with all the appurtenances therevnto belonging Cittuate lyeing and being in the bounds of Kittery next adjacent vnto the house and feild of William Everett Know all men therefore that I Abraham Conley for Divers Causes and Considerations me therevnto moueing as also for vallueable consideration to him in hand payed as Doth and may appeare by three bills giuen vnder my hand the Day and yeare aboue written Know all men therefore that I Abraham Conley Doe by these presents Giue Grant sell assigne and sett over the aforesaid premises wth the appurtenances vnto the foresayd Thomas Jones and his heires for ever To Haue and to Hold Quietly to posess and injoy wth-out any Molestation from this time and for ever In Witnes whereof both the partyes haue setto their hands and seales Interchangeably the Day and yeare aboue written

Signed sealed and Delivered
   in the p'sence of
   Basill Parker
     the marke of
Joseph ┼ Austen

The marke of
Abraham ⨍ Conley (his Seale)

The aboue written is a true coppy of the originall Deed of Abraham Conley to Thomas Jones here Entred on Record Aprill 13th 1694//

p me John Wincoll Cleric:

PART I, FOL. 102.

To all People before whom these presents shall Come Know yᵉ that I Thomas Jones of Kittery in the province of maine in New England for Dyvers good Causes me therevnto more Especially for and in consideration of a valluable sum̄ to mee in hand payd by John Leighton of the town and province aforesd the receipt whereof I accknowledge, and of Every part and pcell thereof and therewith fully Satisfied contented and paid haue giuen granted bargaind sold Aliened made over and Confirmed and by these presents Doe for me my heires Executʳˢ Administrators and assignes freely Clearly and absolutely giue grant bargaine sell Alien Make over and confirme, vnto him the said John Leighton his heire Executʳˢ Administrators and assignes for ever all that piece or parcell of land which I bought of Abraham Conley scituate lyeing and being in the towne of Kittery aforesd on the river of piscataqua butting vpon the said river on the south west and so running back betweene two lotts of sd Leightons that is to say his lott Joining to his Dwelling house on the North west & his lot comonly called the six acres on the South east till six acres be Compleated To Haue & to Hold the said six acres of land together with all my meadow at the heathy Marsh so called, with forty acres of vpland which was granted me by the towne of Kittery lyeing and being on the south west side of sd marsh with all the priviledges and appurtenances therevnto belonging or in any wise appertaining to him the said John Leighton his heires Executʳˢ Administrators and Assignes for ever from me the said Thomas Jones my heires Executors Administrators & Assignes and that the said Leighton shall and may from time to time and at all times hereafter make vse of and Improue the aforesd premises without any Molestation lett or hindrance from me the said Jones or any other person or persons Claimeing any right title or Interest therevnto from by or vnder mee In Witnesse whereof I

Part I, Fol. 103.

haue herevnto sett my hand and seale this Thirtieth Day of November one thousand six hundred Eighty and six 1686
Signed sealed and Delivered   Thomas Jones
   in presence of vs   his mark I (Seale)
   Richard Paine   Mr Richard Paine and Elicha Briard
   Elisha Bryard   made oath to the truth of Thomas Jones being verry sencible when he signed and sealed the aboue Deed as his act and Dede this 17th June 1687 before
            John Hinckes, of the Councill

The aboue written is a true coppy of the origniall Deed of Sale from Thomas Jones to John Leighton and here Entred on record this 13th Day of Aprill 1694
            p me John Wincoll Cleric

[103] Know all men by these presents that I Thomas Rice of Kittery in the province of Maine in New England with the consent of Mary my wife for and in consideration of fiueteene pounds currant pay of New England to me in hand paid to full Content & satisfaction haue Giuen Granted bargained sold Infeofeed & Confirmed and Doe by these p^{r}sents for my selfe my heires Exec^{rs} Administrators or assignes Giue Grant bargaine sell Infeoffe and Confirme vnto Samuell Spiney of the town & province aforesaid a Certaine pcell of land scittuate and lyeing neare Spruce Creeke in the towne of Kittery aforsd Containing twenty acres it being a town grant Granted vnto the said Rice at a generall town meeting June 24th 1682 and Measured & laid out by Captn Jno Wincoll Surveyor october 9th 1682 it being 123 pole in length west & by south and 32 pole in breadth bounded with the land of Mr John Shapleigh on the South Mr Withers land on the East Jno Shepheards land on the north &

PART I, FOL. 103.

Thomas Spineys land on the west and now sold by me Tho. Rice vnto the sd Sam^ll Spinney To Haue & to Hold the aboue bargained 20 acres of land be it more or less as it Is laid out with all and singular the the appurtenances & priveledges therevnto belonging to him the sd Sam^ll Spinney his heires Ex^rs Admin^rs ore Assignes for ever Clearely acquitted from all former Mortgadges sales Gifts Dowryes or titles of Dowries Done by me ore by any other person ore psons by from ore vnder me ore my Assignes in Confirmation of the truth hereof I the sd Thomas Rice & Mary my Wife haue sett to our hands & seales this fowerth Day of January in the yeare of o^r lord 1689 90/

Sealed & Delivered in the presence   Tho Rice (a seale)
    of vs witnes   Mary *M* Rice (a seal)
    Sam^ll Knight   her marke
         his
   John *FS* Shepbard   Thomas Rice gaue possesion by
       marke   turfe and twig according to law vnto Samuell Spinney the 13th of December 1690 of this twenty acres of land within written before vs witnesses

    John *JS* Sheapard his marke :   John Spinney

Thomas Rice & Mary his wife Cam and Acknowledged the Deed of Sale within written to be their act & Deed vnto Sam^ll Spinney of Kittery the seventeenth Day of feb^r one thousand six hundred ninty on & two 169½
                     Before me Francis Hooke Just pea
A true Coppy of the originall Deed here Entred on record this 26^t Day of May 1694 p me John Wincoll Cleric:

To all Christian People to whom these presents may Come Know ye that I Richard Carell of Kittery in the province of maine in New England for many Good Causes and Considerations me herevnto moueing Especially for and in Consideration of nine pound starling in hand receiued of Samuell Spinney of the same towne to full content and satisfaction haue Giuen Granted Bargaind sold Infeoffed and Confirmed and Doe by these presents for my selfe and my heires Giue Grant Bargaine sell Infeoffee and Confirme vnto the said Samuell Spinney a certaine tract of land scittuate & lieing in the lower part of Kittery aforsaid in the great Coue containing six acres as it is bounded on the West with the said great Coue and bounded on the East with John Greens Jun : land and bounded on the north and south with the said Samuell Spinneys own land which six acres of land is part of a town grant and now by me sold as abouesd vnto Samuell Spinney To Haue and To Hold the aboue bargained six acres of land with all and singular the appurtenances previledges and Comodities whatsoever thereto belonging or in any wise appertaining to him the sd Samuell Spinney his heires and Assignes for ever freely Dischargeing from all former sales mortgadges or any other Incumbrance by me made or Done whereby the said Samuell Spinney his heires or assignes may be Evicted or Disturbed out of the premises or any part or parcell thereof and for Confirmation of the premises I the aforesd Richard Carell haue herevnto sett my hand and seale this third Day of May Anno Doñi one thousand six hundred ninety and three and in the fift yeare of the reign of our soveraigne lord and Lady William and Mary by the grace of god King and Queene of England Scotland france and Ireland Defenders of the faith

Signed sealed and Delivered   Richard
   in the p^rsence of vs witnesses   Carell (his Seale)
     John Spinny   November ye 4. 1693 Richard Carell
     John Furneld   gaue posession of the within written
     his F marke   six acres of land vnto Samuell Spinney this 4th Day of november before vs witnesses
                                       John Spinney
                John Fernald   J F his marke

Part I, Fol. 104.

Richard Carell Cam and Acknowledged this Instrument to be his act and deed to Samuell Spinney this 18th Day of Aprill 1694 Before me Francis Hooke, of ye Councill & Just. pea

The aboue written is a true coppy of the originall Deed here Entred on record this 26^t Day of may 1694

p me John Wincoll Cleric ̃

[104] Know all men by these present that I Thomas Spinney Senr of the towne of Kittery in the County of yorke in New England yeoman for the naturall loue I beare vnto my beloued sone John Spinney of the same place, Haue Giuen Granted Infeoffed and Confirmed, and Doe by these presents freely Giue Grant Alienat and Confirme vnto my said sone John Spinney all this my Messuage house houseing and land wherein I now Dwell and posess, as orchards gardens feilds and pastures and whatsoever therevnto apertain, as fences trees wood or vnderwood being bounded on the South with the Maine Riuer of piscataqua and on the East with Samuell Fernalds land and the Greate Coue, and on the North with the lands of Peter Dixon, and on the West with the land of John ffernald my said sone, to haue all the abouesaid Giuen and Granted premises Imediately after the Decease of me the said Thomas Spinney and my now wife Margrey Spinney and not vntill our decease, and that Dureing our naturall liues the abouesaid premises are to remaine in our own hands to vse and ocupy as our proper Estate and after our Decease the aboue Giuen and Granted premises are to come into the hands of my said son John Spinney and his heires for ever, To Haue and to Hold all the abouesd house and houseing and outhouseing, lands feilds pastures orchards Gardens whatsoever therevnto belong with all apurtenances and previledges high wayes and landing fishing and fouleing with

Part I, Fol. 104.

all Comodities therevnto belonging vnto the said John Spinney, To him and his heires lawfully begotten of his body, To him and to them to their owne proper vse and behoofe for Ever and further I the said Thomas Spinney Doe by these presents Covenant and Engage the premises to be free from all Incumbrances whatsoever as Gifts sales Jointures or Dowries whatsoever and that I am the proper owner therof at the sealeing hereof, and the same to warrant and defend and the peaceable posession thereof to Maintaine against all Manner of persons laying lawfull Clayme therevnto our soveraigne lord and lady the king and Queens Majesties excepted, In Confirmation I haue herevnto sett my hand and seal this twenty third Day of March one thousand six hundred ninety and foure in the fifth yeare of their Majesties raiyne King William and Queene Mary alwayes to be taken and vnderstood that If my said sone John Spinney shall Decease without Issue or heires of his body as is aboue Expressed, the aboue Giuen and Granted premises shall Desend to my sone James Spinney, to him and his heires for ever.

Memorandum that on word is blotted out in line the twenteth six and one word Interlined between line the twenty sixth and twentieth fifth viz the word third

Signed Sealed and Delivered in   Thomas Spinney (Seale)
  ye p^{r}sence of vs who haue subscribed
  James Spinney   Mr Thomas Spinney Came ac-
  Wm Godsoe   knowledged this Instrument to
                              bee his act and Deed vnto his
                              sone John Spinney this twenty
                              ninth Day of March 1694//
            Before me Francis Hooke Just : pe :

A true coppy of the originall Deed of Thomas Spinney to his sone James Spinney here Entred this 19th Day of June 1694
                      p me John Wincoll Cleric :

PART I, FOL. 105.

Know all men by these presents that I Thomas Spiney Senr of Kittery in the County of yorke in New England yeoman with the free consent of Margrey my wife for Divers Good Causes & Considerations vs moueing therevnto, and for the naturall loue we beare vnto our loueing sone James Spinney of the same place, Haue freely Giuen granted and alienated Infeofet and Confirmed, and doe by these presents freely Giue Grant Allien and Conferm vnto our said loveing sone James Spinney a Certaine tract of land lieing in the towne of Kittery and is part of our homestall, and is bounded on the South side by the Maine river of piscataqua and on the Westward sid with John fernald land three pole in length and on the northermost sid with my owne land fourteen pole in length, and on the Eastermost sid with my owne land fifteene pole in length to the river aforesaid To Haue and To Hold the aforesaid tract of land with all the appurtenances and priveledges thereto belonging or apertaining to him the said James Spinney and his heires for ever and for Defect of heires lawfully Desending from him the said James Spinney, then the abouesd tract of land to desend to our yonges Sone John Spinney to him and his heires for Ever as his and their proper Inheritance, And further I the sd [105] Thomas Spinney doe Ingage Couenant and Warrant the premises to be free from all Incombrances and sales, Gifts Grants and Mortgadges and that I am the proper owner thereof at the Signeing and Sealeing hereof, and for Confermation of the premises I the said Thomas Spinney and Margrey my wife herevnto sett our hand and sealls this twenty second Day of March, on thousand six hundred Ninety and four and in the fifth yeare of their Majestyes Reign, William and Mary by the grace of god King and

PART I, FOL. 105.

Queen of England Scotland France and Ireland Defenders of the faith &c:

Signed Sealed & Delivered   Thomas Spinney (Seal)
   in the presence of vs   the sign +++ of
   John Spinney   /   Margrey Spinney (Seal)
   Wm Godsoe

Mr Thomas Spinney cam and acknouledged this Instrument to be his act & deed to his sone James Spinney this 24th of March 1694 Before me Francis Hooke Just. pea :

A true coppy of the originall Deed of Thomas Spinney to his sone James Spinney here Entred this 19th Day of June 1694 :   p me John Wincoll Cleric

To all Christian People, To whom this bill of sale shall Come or May Concerne Know ye that I Arthur Hughes late of Sawcoe in the County of yorke in the province of Maine at president in portsmouth in New hamshiere in New England and Sarah my now wife for and in Consideration of the sume of six pounds Currant Money of New England to me in hand paid by my sone Arthur Hughes of the same place the receipt whereof and of euery part & parcell thereof I doe acknowledg ourselues to be therew^th fully satisfied contented and paid Doe by these p^rsents Giue Grant bargaine Alien Assigne set over and Confirme vnto my sd sone Arthur Hughes his heires Executors Administrators and Assignes for ever from me my heires Executors Administrators or Assignes for ever a parcell or necke of land licing on ye Eastward side of Sacoe river and butted and bounded as followeth To say the river on one side and bounded on the northward side by a swampe Comonly called the great swampe on the Eastward side by a creeke Called Padges Creeke and the westw^rd End to a hill called the flying hill

PART I, FOL. 105.

To Haue and to Hold the abouesd land with all the priviledges and profits, wayes high wayes water wayes, woods vnderwoods with all other the Appurtenances to y⁶ sd land belonging or any wayes Apertaining &cᵃ to him yᵉ sd Arthur Hughes my sone his heires Execut^rs Administrat^rs & assignes and to his & their prop^r vse benefit and behoofe for ever, and I the said Arthur Hughes and Sarah my wife for vs our heires Execut^rs & Administrat^rs doe avouch the sale hereof by these presents by vs Giuen, and that wee haue good right of lawfull authoritie to sell and Dispose of the sd land as by our deed from John Bonighton of Sacoe bearcing Date the 24th Day of May last past vizt 1694 : and that the sd land and premises is free and Cleare from all Titles Claimes troubles Mortgages leases rents Dowries Rights of Dowries widdows thirds Jointers or any other Incumbrances whatsoever, and further we bind ourselues our heires Execut^rs and Administrators to warrant and defend the sd land title with all the priviledges aboue mentioned from all persons w^tsoever Claimeing or pretending any right title or Interest in any of the abouesd p^rmises vnto him the sd Arthur Hughes my sd sone his heires Execut^rs Administrat^rs and assignes for ever : In Testimony whereof I the sd Arthur Huges Senr and Sarah my wife haue to this our Deed put our hands and seales this fifteenth Day of June one thousand six hundred Ninety foure in the sixth yeare of the reign of our soveraigne lord and lady William and Mary King and Queen over England Scotland France and Ireland defenders of the faith &c :

Signed Sealed and Deliv^rd
 in ye p^rsence of vs
 William Partridge Junr
 Henry Crown Sec^r

      his
Arthur **H** Hughes (ₛₑₐₗₑ)
    marke
    her
Sarah *ll* Hughes (ₛₑₐₗₑ)
    marke

Part I, Fol. 106.

Arthur Hughes and Sarah his wife came & acknowledged this Instrument to be their voluntary act and Deed wherevnto they haue put their hands and seales vnto their sone Arthur Hughes this 15th day of June 1694
     Before me Roger Kelly Jus : peace
A true coppy of the originall deed from Arthur Hughes to his sone Arthur Hughes here Entred on record June 19th 1694
     p me John Wincoll Cleric :

[106] Know all men by these presents that I John Bonighton late of the towne of Sacoe in the County of yorke in New England Doe for and in consideration of ye sum of thre pounds ten shillings sterl to me already paid in hand by Arthur Hughes late of the same towne abouesayd Doe sell bargaine Infeoffee and Alienat vnto the said Hughes his heyers Executors Administrators and Assignes a percell or necke of land lying one the Easterne side of Sacoe river and butted and bounded as followeth to say the river on one side and bounded on the Northerne side by a swampe commonly Called the great swampe and the Easterne side by a Cricke formerly called Padges his Cricke and the Westerne end to a hill formerly and vsually called the flying hill To Haue and to hould the abouesaid land with all the priviliges and appurtenances thereof to the proper vse of the sayd Arthur Hughes his heires Executors Administrators and Assignes for ever without any lett or any Molestation by me my heires Executors and Administrators for ever, or any person or persons by or vnder me, and Moreover I doe by these presents from this time and hencforward Disowne and Empty myselfe my heires Executors and Administrators of all my right title and Interest which formerly I had vnto the abouesaid land granting and giueing vnto the abouesayd

PART I, FOL. 106.

Arthur Hughes all my right and titell therein with warranty from all persons whatsoever, and moreover I Doe by these presents Declare at the signeing and sealeing hereof the sayd land is properly my owne Estate and is free from all sales and Mortgadges whatsoever and shall from this time Disowne any propriety therein giueing & granting my sole and proper right which formerly I Did enjoy vnto the abousayd Arthur Hughes his heires Executors Administrators and Assignes for evermore as Wittness my hand and seale this twenty fourth Day of May Anno Dom 1694

Signed Sealed and Delivered   the marke of
   in the presence of vs   John ⟨ Bonighton (Seale)
Elihu Gunnison
Samuell Winkley

John Bonighton came and acknowledged this Instrument to be his act and Deed vnto Arthur hughes this 24th Day of May 1694// Before me Francis Hooke, of ye Councill

the aboue written is a true Coppie of the originall Deed of John Bonighton to Arthur Hughes here Entred on record this 20th Day of June 1694
                 p me John Wincoll Cleric:

To all Christian People to whom this Deed of Sale or Instrument in writeing shall come to be seene read or heard Know ye that I Robert Elliot Mercht in the towne of Portsmouth in the province of New hampsheire in New England for and in Consideration of the sum of ten pounds receiued by me Robert Elliot at and before the Ensealeing and Delivery hereof of and from Nathaniell Kene now Inhabitant in Spruce Creeke in the province of Maine in New England Carpenter Have Giuen Granted Bargained sold Aliened Assigned and set over, and by these presents Doe for my-

Part I, Fol. 107.

selfe my heires Executors Giue Grant Bargaine sell Alien Assigne and set over vnto the said Nathaniell Kene his heires Executors Administrators and Assignes, All that right, title, Interest Claime and proerty which I haue or ever had, In, of or vnto a certaine lot or tract of land containeing ten acres: scittuate lyeing and being on the Westward side of Spruce Creek in the Tounship of Kettery in the province of Maine in said New England betweene the land of Mr John Shapleigh and John Shepard begining at the water side and so runing back vntill ten acres be accomplished, which ten acres of land was Giuen by the town of Kittery to Ephraim Crocket and laid out by the select men of the said town the third Day of June in the yeare of our lord one thousand six hundred seventy and two, And which lot or ten acres of land was afterwards sold by Ephraim Crockett to Charles OGrado of portsmouth yeoman 'Dwelling in the river of piscataqua in said New England and afterward was sold by said Charles Ogrado to me the said Robert Elliot as by 'the originall deed or bill of sale may and Doth appeare By assignment on the the backe side thereof, And which originall Deed of Sale to sd Charles Ogrado by the said Ephraim Crocket beares Date the sixteenth Day of September in the yeare of our lord one thousand six hundred seventy and two and in the twenty fourth yeare of the Reigne of our soveraigne lord King Charles the Second &c: To Haue and to Hould the said ten acres of land according to the tenour of the aboue Mentioned [107] Writeing or deed of sale togather with all the priviledges or appurtenances thereof vnto him the said Nathaniell Kene his heires Executors Administrators and Assignes free of all former Gifts Grants Dowryes and titles of Dowries and all other Incombrances whatsoever, And I the said Robert Elliot for myselfe my heires Executors and Administrators and for every of them do Couenant and Grant to

Part I, Fol. 107.

and with the said Nathaniell Kene his heires Executors Administrators and Assignes and to and with every one of them to defend the title thereof (as it was Granted to me as by writeing and Assignment aboue exprest) vnto Him the said Nathaniell Kene his heires Executors Administrators and Assignes against any Person Claimeing any right title or Interest to it, In Witness whereof I the said Robert Elliot do herevnto sett my hand and seale without fraud this third Day of July in the yeare of our lord one thousand six hundred Eighty and seaven and the third yeare of the reigne of our sovereigne Lord King James the Second

Signed Sealed and deliverd   Robert Elliot ($_\text{Seale}^\text{a}$)
   in presence of   Nicholas Heskins & Joseph Read made
   Robert Jordan   oath this 17th Day of January 1690
   Nicholas Heskins   that they Did see Mr Robert Elliot
   Joseph Read   signe seale & deliver the aboue writ-
   ———   ten deed to Nathaniell Kene before
                     me   Nathaniell Fryer Jus : peac :

The aboue written is a tru Coppy of the originall Deed o : M Robert Elliot to Nathaniell Kene Compared and here Entred on Record June 25th 1694

                      p me John Wincoll Cleric :

To all Christian people to whom these presents shall Come Greeteg Know ye that I James Emery Senr of Kittery in the County of yorke in the province of the Massathusets bay in New England for Many Good Causes and Considerations me moueing herevnto Especially for the Naturall loue and affection that I beare vnto my two sones Daniell Emery and Job Emery haue freely and absolutely Giuen and Doe by these presents for myselfe my heires Executors and Administrators freely and Absolutely Giue Grant Alien Infeoffe pass

Part I, Fol. 108.

over and Confirme vnto my foresaid two sones Daniell Emery and Job Emery a Certaine parcell of land scittuate and lieing in the towne of Kittery aforesaid containing a hundred forty and three acres more or less as it is bounded on the East with the land of John Thompson and a pond called yorke pond, and on the north bounded with the land of Peter Grant and on the west bounded with the land of Edward Hayes and Jabez Jenkins and bounded on the South with the land of Edward Waymouth and is partly vpland, partly swamp, partly Meadow and partly Heathy land and was partly giuen to me by my late father Anthony Emery and the rest was granted to me by the towne of Kittery and now by me the aforesaid James Emery Senr freely Giuen to my aforesaid two sones Daniell Emery and Job Emery in Equall halues so to be divided when they see cause To Haue and To hold the aforesaid tract of land together with all and singular the appurtenances priviledges and Commodities of woods timber trees vnderwoods waters water Courses &c : to them the said Daniell Emery and Job Emery their heires and Assignes for ever without lett Interuption or molestation of me the said James Emery Senr or any other person or persons by from or vnder me my heires or Assignes, onely whereas Major Charles Frost James Emery Junr and Noah Emery lately built a sawmill on a brooke in the foresaid land I doe reserue a liberty for the said Major Charles Frost and James Emery Junr to Improue their parts in the said sawmill according to what Agreement was made betweene them and said Noah Emery, I also giue vnto the aforesaid Daniell Emery and Job Emery my whole right in that part of the said Sawmill that lately belonged vnto the foresaid Noah Emery, they paying to me or [**108**] to my order tenn pounds, and for confirmation of the premises I the said James Emery Senr herevnto sett my hand and seale this seaventh Day of May Anno Dom̃ one thousand six hundred ninety foure an

PART I, FOL. 108.

in the sixth yeare of their majestyes reigne of England Scotland Françe and Ireland Defenders of the faith &c:
Signed Sealed & delivered James Emery Sen' (Seale)
 in the presence of vs Kittery in the County of yorke
 Daniell Stone   June 23 1694 James Emery Sen'
 Silvanus Nocke   acknowledged the aboue written
 John Wincoll   Instrument to be his act and Deed
     Before me Charles Frost Just of peace
 James Emery Sen' acknowledged to haue received full Satisfaction of his two sones daniell & Job for the tenn pounds aboue mentioned this 23. of June 1694
     Before Me Charles Frost Just peace
 A true coppy of the originall Deed here Entred on Record this 30th Day of June 1694

Province To all to whom these p'sents shall Come I
of Mayne Peter Ware of Cape Nedock and Mary Ware
   Ihabitors in the aforesd Province send Greetting &c.
Know ye that I the sd Peter Ware and Mary my wife for and in Consideration of the sum of twelue pounds in money vnto vs in hand paid by our sone Daniell Ware of Cape Nedock in the aforesd province before the Ensealing & Delivery hereof (the receipt whereof I the sd Peter Ware Mary my wife doe hereby acknowledge) and ourselues therewith to be fully satisfied, Haue for ourselues Giuen Granted Bargaind sold delivered and Confirmed and by these presents doe fully freely and Absolutely Giue Grant Bargaine sell deliver and Confirme vnto our sone Daniell Ware his heires Executors Administrators and Assignes, a certaine parcell of land Containing sixty acres more or Less Formerly bought of M' John Gooch for a certaine sum of

Part I, Fol. 108.

about fourteene pounds which land is Knowne by the name of Gooches Neck lyeing and being Neare Cape Nedock in the aforesaid province, the bounds begining at the seaside one the north Eeast side of a small pond which the stormes wash over Into there being a small heape of stones : and from thence North West forty and seven rods vnto a forked Walnut tree marked and from thence it runneth North and by East Eighty rode vnto a black birch Marked, and from thence it runeth Northeast vnto a small brooke which said brooke is the bounds betweene the lands of Thomas Avery and the land aboue mentioned and sold with all and singular the Timber, Timber trees, woods vnderwoods priviledges and appurtenances whatsoever to the said land now belonging or in any wayes Appertaining : To Haue and to Hold the sd land and premises hereby bargaind and sold vnto our said sone Daniell Ware his heires Executors Administrat[rs] and Assignes as his and theire owne proper Goods and Estate for ever and to his and theire owne proper vse & behoofe for evermore, and I the said Peter Ware and Mary my wife for our selues our heires Execut[rs] Administ[rs] & assigns and every of them Doe Covenant promise and Grant to & wth our said sone Daniell Ware his heires Exeqt[rs] Admist[rs] and assigns by these presents that I the said Peter Ware and Mary my wife are the Day of the Date hereof and at the time of the Ensealing & delivery hereof haue in ourselues full power Good right & lawfull Authority to giue Grant bargaine sell dd[r] and Confirme the said land and premises hereby bargained & sold vnto our sd sone Daniell Ware his heires Executors Administ[rs] and Assignes for evermore in Mañer and forme aforesd And also that he our sd sone Daniell Ware his heires Exeqt[rs] Admist[rs] and Assigns or any of them shall & may lawfully frome time to time and at all times hereafter peaceably & quietly haue, hold vse and Injoy ye sd land & premises hereby bargained

PART I, FOL. 109.

and sold w{th}out any manner of lett suite trouble Evicēn Ejecēn Molestation disturbance Challenge Claime Deniall or demand whatsoever of or by me the sd Peter Ware & Mary my wife our heires Exeqt{rs} Admist{rs} and Assigns or any of y{m} or of or by any other person or persons whatsoever lawfully Claimeing or to Claime frome by or vnder vs oure act or title, our sd sone Daniell Ware his heires Execqt{rs} Admist{rs} and Assigns paying all such acknowledgment or acknowledgments as the proprietor shall require from time to time and at all times and to make and Maintaine a sufficient fence betweene my land & his land so bounded as aboue mentioned for the space of fifteene yeares from the Day of the Date hereof In Witness whereof wee haue herevnto Put our hand & seal this 28{th} Day Anno R R{s} Jacobi Secundi tertio Annoq, Dom̄ 1687//

Signed sealed & Delivered in y{e}   Peter Weare Seale (Seale)
   presen of vs   her
   John Penwill   Mary ᴜ Ware (Seale)
   John H Herman : Henry Godard   marke
    his marke

[109] M{r} John Penwill cam and made oath that he saw m{e} Peter Weare & Mary his wife signe seale and Deliver this Instrument as their act & Deed vnto Daniell Weare,
   Taken this third March 169¾   Just
        Before Me Francis Hooke, pea//

John Herman cam & made oath that he saw M{r} Peter Weare and Mary his wif signe seale & Deliver this Instrument as their act & Deed vnto Daniell Weare vnto which he put his hand as a witnes   Taken 23 June 1694
       Before Me Francis Hooke : Just pea :

M{rs} Mary Weare owneth this Instrument to be her act & Deed vnto Daniell Wyer this 26 of June 1694 :
       before Me Francis Hooke Just. pea :

PART I, FOL. 109.

This aboue written with the Deed of Sale on the other side Is a true coppy of the originall Deed of Sale from Mr Peter Ware & Mary his wife to their sone Daniell Ware here Entred on record this 7th Day of July 1694

      p me John Wincoll Cleric:

Know all men by these presents that Whereas I Joshua Crocket sone to Thomas Crocket some times of Kittery Deceased haue sometime since the Death of my said father Laid Claime to some part of a neck of land at the mouth of Spruce Creeke Comonly called Crockets Necke and was so accounted, and was in the possessione of of his said Father Thomas Crocket when he Dyed and and now is in the posession of my Elder brother Ephraim Crockett, and for as much as. I haue some right vnto the said neck of land abouesd not only by Inheritance but also by a promise of my father abouesaid Deceased yet notwithstanding to the Intent that there may arise no controversye betweene my said Elder brother Ephraim Crocket and my selfe nor his heires nor mine for ever I Doe by this and other valuable Considerations me Moueing therevnto but More Especially for and in Consideration of twenty pounds to me secured before the Delivery hereof, I doe Disowne and Disclaime any right title or Interest to or in the said Necke of land abouesaid and Doe by these presents own and acknowledge my selfe to be fully satisfied and contented for all and every part or percell thereof that Doe now or may hereafter belong to me my heires Executors or Administrators for evermore, And moreover I Doe by these presents oblidge myselfe my heires Executors and Administrators from henceforth never to trouble Demand Chalenge or molest my said brother Ephraim Crocket his heires Executors Administrators or Assignes in the peaceable and Quiet posession of the abouesaid Necke of land and that without the least Mollestation from me my heires Executors Administ[rs] or assignes for evermore as Witness my hand and seale this tenth Day of July 1688

Signed Sealed & Deliverd　　　　The marke of
　in the presence of vs　　　Joshua 🇨 Crocket (Seale)
　Francis Hooke　　　Joshua Crocket cam & acknowledged
　Mary Hooke　　　　this Instrument to be his act &
　　　　　　　　　　　Deed this 10th July 1688
　　　　　　　　Before me Francis Hooke Just pea :

A true coppy of the originall Deed here Entred on record this 15th Day of Augst 1694/

　　　　　　　　p me John Wincoll Cleric:

This Indenture made this twenty fifth Day of March in the thirty seventh yeare of the reign of our Sovereigne Lord Charles the Second by the Grace of god of England Scotland France and Ireland King Defender of the faith Between Robert Nickolson of Casco bay and formerly of Scarborough in the province of Maine in New England yeoman of the one part And Robert Elliot of the towne of Portsmouth in the province of New Hampsheir New England Merchant of the other part Witnesseth That the said Robert Nickolson for and In Consideration of the sum of thirty eight pounds of good and lawfull Money of and In New England to him in hand paid by the said Robert Elliot at or before the Ensealeing and delivery of these presents the receipt whereof he Doth hereby acknowledge and himselfe therewith satisfied contented and paid : Hath granted bargained sold and Aliened And by these presents Doth Clearely and absolutely grant bargaine sell and Aliene vnto the said Robert Elliot his heires Executors Administrators or assignes for ever, All

Part I, Fol. 110.

that parcell of vpland Medow land and Marsh scittuate lyeing and being in the Village of Dunster in the town of Scarbrow in the Easter parts of New England aforesaid: or howsoever Conteyning in all two hundred and Thirty acres by Estimation be it more or less, And which vpland Medow land and Marsh the said Robert Nickolson bought and purchased formerly of Henry Watts as appeares by Deed vppon record Dated the twentieth Day of May In the yeare of our lord one thousand six hundred and seventy, And which Medow and Marsh ground and vpland were formerly in the posession of George Barlow Edward Shaw John Wakefeild or whomsoever: and containes all the lott of George Barlowes and two thirds of a lott of Edward Shawes and is bounded on the North north east or there about with a Creek comonly called Arthur Augers Creek then Westward [110] by the side of the river vntill it come to Westward of sd Barlowes land and so vp into the Country To Haue and to Hold all and singular Every part and parcell of the said vpland and Medow land Marsh and Marshes swamps, pastures, woods trees, bushes, fences waters free boards, wayes, Easements, propertyes and Emoluments whatsoever therevnto properly appertaining vnto him the said Robert Elliot his heires Executors Administrators and assignes for ever And by him or them to be peaceably had occupied posesed and Injoyed without lett, law, trouble Eviction or Molestation from any person whatsoever: And the said Robert Nickolson for himselfe his heires Executors and Administrators Doth by these presents Warrant and Defend vnto the said Robert Elliot his heires Executors Administrators and Assignes for ever the sale of all and every part of the aboue recited premises against all other person or persons Claimeing or to Claime right or title therein or to any part thereof In Witness whereof the said Robert Nickolson hath herevnto put his hand and seale without fraud Dated this

Part I, Fol. 110.

25th Twenty fifte Day of March in the yeare of our Lord One thousand six hundred Eighty and fiue

Signed Sealed and   Robert Nickals (Seale)
  Delivered in presens of   Robert Nickolls cam and ac-
  Phillip Foxwell   knowledged this Instrument
  Jeames Wiggens   to be his act and Deed vnto
                            Mr Robert Elliot this twen-
                            ty fift Day of March 1685
                   Before me Francis Hooke Just pe

A true Coppy of the originall Deed here Entred on record this 15th Day of August 1694

                         p me John Wincoll Cleric:

and on the back side of the aboue Deed is as followeth

Memorandum full and peaceable livery and seisin and possession was Giuen by the within mentioned Robert Nickolson by turfe and twigg to Robert Elliot of all the premises according to the true Intent and Meaning of this Indenture in presence of vs

Phillip Foxwell
The Marke of
John I Jackson

Robert Nickolls cam and Acknowledged that he did this Day Deliver vnto Mr Robert Elliot the land within specified by twigg and turff as is aboue Mentioned as also the Marsh within specified this 25 Day of March 1685/

             Before me Francis Hooke Just. pea :

This Livery & seisin here Entred on record August 15 : 1694

          p me John Wincoll Cleric:

To all Christian People to whom this present writeing shall Come Greeting Know ye that I Francis Champernoon of Kittery in the province of Maine in New England Esqr

Part I, Fol. 110.

for and in Consideration of the Naturall loue and affection that I beare to Elizabeth Elliot the Daughter of Mary my beloued wife, and in Consideration of a marriage already had & solemnized betweene Humphrey Elliot of Great Island in y[e] province of New Hampsheire in New England Marin[r] & the said Elizabeth, and for Divers other good Causes & Considerations haue by and with the Consent & approbation of my said beloued wife Giuen and Granted and hereby Doe freely & absolutely Giue Grant bargaine sell Infeoffe and Confirme to the said Humphrey & Elizabeth Elliot their heires and assignes from & after my Decease the Moiety or half part of all that parcell of land and Marsh lieing and being in Kittery aforesaid called or knowne by the name of Champernoons Island and now in My possession together with all and singular y[e] Comodities priveledges & appurtenances to the same in any wise belonging or apertaining and the reversion & reversions remainder and remainders and all the Estate right title possession Interest Claime & Demand whatsoever in and to the said Moiety or halfe part of the said parcell of land Marsh & premises and every part thereof To Haue & to hold y[e] sd Moiety or halfe part of the sd land Marsh and premises from and after My Decease to y[e] sd Humphrey & Elizabeth Elliot their heires & assigns to the only vse & behoofe of them their heires and assignes for ever, And I the said Francis Champernoon for me my heires Executors & Administrators Do hereby Couenant with the said Humphrey & Elizabeth Elliot their heirs and ass[ns] That they the said Humphrey & Elizabeth Elliot their heires and assignes from and after my Decease shall and may from time to time and at all times thereafter peaceably and Quietly haue hold possess & injoy y[e] said hereby granted p[r]mises & every part thereof free & Cleare and freely & clearely Discharged and kept harmeless from all former & other Gifts grants bargaines sales feoffments

vses Dowers thirds Jointures Judgm^{ts} Execuc̄ons Extents titles troubles Claimes Demands & incumbrances w'soever And the same premises to the sd Humphry & Elizabeth Elliot their heires & assignes against all persons w'soeuer I shall & will warrant & for ever hereby Defend. In Witness whereof I haue hereto set my hand & seale the thirteenth Day of July in ye first yeare of the reign of our Sover^n lord James ye Second King of England &c Anoq̄ Dom̄ 1685
Signed Sealed & Deliverd
  in presens of vs
  Sarah Elliot   ffran : Champernoun
  Nicholas Heskins   Mary Champernown
                                    (Seale)

A true coppy of the originall Deed in parchm^t is here Entred on record August 16th 1694
                   p me John Wincoll Cleric:

[111] To all Christian people to whom these presents may come — Know ye that Thomas Spencer of Kittery in the County of Yorkesheire & in the Massathusets Collony in New England plantor and Patience his Wife for many good Causes and Considerations them Moueing therevnto especially for that Naturall loue and affection that they beare vnto Humphrey Spencer their sone and Grace his wife and for their better liuelichood hath passed over Giuen Granted Aliened Infeoffeed and Confirmed and Doe by these presents for themselues their heires Executors and Administrators pass over, Giue Grant Alienate Infeoffee and Confirme vnto the aforesaid Humphry Spencer and Grace his wife Dureing the whole terme of their naturall liues or the longest liuer of either of them and after the Decease of the said Hum-

phrey Spencer and Grace his wife vnto ther heires of the said Humphrey Spencer one Messuage or tenement scittuate and being in the towne of Kittery aforesd Containeing one Dwelling house and about thirty acres of land adjoyning to it more or lesse as it is bounded on the south west with the house lot of Daniell Goodin in part and the land of John Wincoll in part and the land of the aforesd Thomas Spencer in part and on the southeast with a small brooke running out of a swampe called parkers Marsh into a meadow of Daniell Goodins called Sluts corner and on the northeast bounded with the land of Daniell Gooddin in a litle part and the rest of that Northeast side bounded with the land of Mr William Hutchinson and bounded on the north west with the high way that leadeth towards yorke which parcell of land is part of a lott of two hundred acres of land formerly Granted by the towne of Kittery vnto the said Thomas Spencer and now by the said Thomas Spencer and patience his wife passed over and Giuen as aforesaid vnto the said Humphrey Spencer and Grace his wife To Haue and to Hold all the aboue Granted premises with all the appurtenances and previledges thereto belonging or in any wise appertaining to him the said Humphrey Spencer and Grace his wife Dureing the whole terme of their naturall liues or the longest liuer of Either of them and from after the Decease of both of them to the lawfull heires of the said Humphrey Spencer & Grace for ever without any lett sute or molestation of the said Thomas Spencer or Patience his wife or any other person or persons whatsoever by from or vnder them the said Thomas Spencer or patience his wife or any of their heires: The foresd Thomas Spencer alwayes reserueing vnto himselfe and to Patience his wife free liberty of felling Cutting and Carrying away timber and firewood from the said tract of land or aboue Granted premises Dureing the whole terme of their Naturall liues or the longest liuer of

PART I, FOL. 111.

Either of them it being for the Nessesary vse of their famely; and for confirmation of the truth hereof the foresd Thomas Spencer and Patience his wife haue setto their hands and seales this fiue and twentieth Day of July in the yeare of our lord one thousand six hundred seventy and six

Signed Sealed and Delivrd Thomas Spencer (a Seale)
  in the presence of vs   his ⌒ marke
  John ✝ Terrie   Patience Spencer (her Seale)
    his marke
  William Spencer   The aboue written deed of gift was acknowledged by the aboue named Thomas Spencer and Patience his wife to be their act and Deed this 25^t Day of July 1676:
    Before me John Wincoll Assotiate

These presents Declare and Witness that I humphrey Spencer mentioned in this Deed of Gift or Instrument in writeing hereby Do Make Over Surrender and Deliver vnto Mr Robert Elliot Merch^t in portsmouth in New Hamshiere in New England this Deed or writing togather with all the perticulars therein Mentioned and all my Interest and Concernes I haue or might haue therein from me and mine to him and his Witness my hand this Eleaventh Day September in the yeare of our Lord One thousand six hundred Eighty three

  September 11th 1683   Marke of
Then came before me Edwd Humphry H S Spencer
  Cranfeild Esqr Gouern^r the
  aboue named Humphry
  Spencer and acknowledged
  the aboue written to be his
  act and Deed
      Edw: Cranfeild

Part I, Fol. 112.

These afore written are true Coppyes of the originall Deed and the surrender of it to Mʳ Robert Elliot here Entred Septᵐᵇʳ 13ᵗʰ 1694

p me John Wincoll Cleric͠:

[112] To all Christian people to whom these presents may Come to be seene read or heard Know ye that I humphrey Spencer of the great Island in the township of Portsmouth in New Hamsheir in New England Carpenter for and In Consideration of the sum of ten pounds to me in hand paid by Mʳ Robert Elliot merchᵗ the receipt whereof I doe hereby acknowledge and myselfe therewith fully satisfied contented and paid at and before the Ensealeing and delivery of these presents Haue Bargained and sold and by these presents Doe fully Clearely and Absolutely bargaine and sell vnto the sd Robert Elliot Merchant and Inhabitant in the towne of portsmouth in New hamsheir in New England aforesaid One Certain tract of land containing fifty acres being a town grant and ten acres of swampe bounded with the land of George Gray on the west Nicholas Gillison on the East and Thomas Spencer and Richard Nasons Marsh; and bounded on the South with the brook that runs out of wilcocks pond and his owne addition, and bounded on the north with the Com̄ons next the river, all which demised premises are scituate lieing and being in Newichawanick in the province of Maine in New England aforesd To Haue and to hold the said fifty acres of land and ten acres of swamp bounded as aboue and laid out and measured by John Wincoll and Roger Plaisted surveyers and as the said premises are recorded or howsoever vnto the said Robert Elliot his heires Executors Administrators and assignes to his and theire proper vse and behoofe for ever and I the said Humphrey Spencer my heires Executors and Adminis-

Part I, Fol. 112.

trators and Every of vs the said fifty acres of land and ten acres of swampe aboue specified: vnto the said Robert his heires Executors Administrators and Assignes shall and will warrant, and for Ever Defend, hereby revoakeing makeing void and Disanulling all and all manner of promises Contracts writeings or agreements formerly made or Don to any other person or persons in New England In of or concerning the premises demised as abouesaid or any part thereof and the said Humphrey Spencer Doth and by the vertue of these premises Hath, aliene sell Infeof and grant vnto the abouesaid Robert Elliot his heires Executors Administrators and assigns two fifth parts of the Marsh comonly called the farther Marsh and lyeing and Adjoining to Richard Nasons and the land abouesaid and which Marsh was formerly belonging to Thomas Spencer Deceased the father of said Humphrey Spencer and the said Humphrey Spencer, all the first and last Demised land swampe and Marsh for myselfe my heires Executors and Administrators together with all the priviledges accomodations thereof shall and will warrant and for ever defend by these presents Witness my hand and seale without fraud this second Day of Aprill in the yeare of our lord one thousand six hundred Eighty and six — 1686/

Signed Sealed and Delivered
  in presence of vs   mark of
  Nicho: Heskins   Humphrey $H\!S$ Spencer (Seal)
  William Broad   Grace $R\!L$ Spencer (Seal)

Nicholas Heskins Came before me Nathanill Fryer and made oath that Humphrey Spencer and Grace Spencer in his sight Did signe seale and Deliver this Deed in his sight and that he saw William broad write his name and was witness with himselfe to the same September 12 : 1694

                         Nathan[ll] Fryer Jus. pes

A true coppy of the originall Deed here Entred on Record this 13th Day of Septemb[r] 1694

                      p me John Wincoll Cleric:

Part I, Fol. 113.

To all Christian People to whom this present Deed of Sale or Instrument in writeing shall Come Know ye that John Griffin formerly of blue point in the township of Scarborough in the province of Mayne in New England Cooper and planter for and in Consideration of the sum of ten pounds to me in hand paid at and before the Ensealling and delivery of these presents by Robert Elliot Merchant and Inhabitant in the Town ship of portsmouth in the province of New hamsheire in said New England and with which sum of ten pounds I said John Griffin Doe acknowledge myselfe fully satisfied contented and paide, Haue for my selfe my heires Executors and Administrators Granted, sould giuen Aliened and by these presents doe Grant sell Giue Aliene Infeofe and confirme vnto the said Robert Elliot his heires Executors Administrators & Assignes for ever one certaine tract or parcell of vpland meadow and Marsh land scittuate lyeing and being at blue point aforesaid be it one hundred acres more or less: being bounded on the one side with the land of the abouesaid Robert Elliot and on the other side with the land of Giles Barge And which tract or parcell of vpland meadow and Marsh was formerly possesed by and imployed and in the teneur of my father Phillip Griffin Deceased To Haue and To Hould all that said tract or parcell of land together with all the priveledges Commonages Easements and accomodations thereof and therevnto belonging vnto him the said Robert Elliot his heires [113] Executors Administrators & Assignes for ever hereby revoaking makeing void and Disanulling all former promises contracts Mortgadges or writeings in or about the said Demised premises, And I the said John Griffin my heires Executors and Administrators vnto the said Robert Elliot his heires Executors Administrators or assignes Shall and will warrant and Defend for ever against all persons whatso ever all the said tract of land and marsh Togather with all the appurtenances aboue recited In Witness whereof I the sayde John Griffin haue setto my hand and seale this seaventeenth Day of March in the yeare of our lord one thousand six hundred ninety and two 169¾ and in the fifth yeare of the reigne of William and Mary King and Queene of England &c :

Signed Sealed and Delivered   John Greiffon (Seal)

  In presence of vs
  after Interlineing   Nicholas Heskins before me Nathan[ll]
  Peter Coffin   Fryer and made oath that the
  Tho. Davis   abouesaid John Griffin Signed
  Nicho Heskins   sealled and Delivered the aboue writeing in his sight and that he saw the two witnesses M[r] Coffin and Thomas Davis set their hands as witnesses Sep : 12 1694

                                  Nathan[ll] Fryer Jus peis

A true Coppy of the originall Deed of Sale from John Griffin to M[r] Robert Elliot here Entred this 14th Day Septemb[r] 1694

                         p me John Wincoll Cleric :

I John Griffin mentioned in this Deed of Sale Do Engage myselfe to Deliver the land Mentioned therein to M[r] Robert Elliot or his assignes by turfe and twig and to Giue him perfect Livery and Seizin according as the law requires on demand Witnes My hand 17th March 169¾

  Witness   John Greiffen
  Nathaniell Martyn

A true coppy of a writing on the back side of the abouesd Deed of Sale here Entred Septem[br] 14th 1694

                         p me John Wincoll Cleric :

Know all men by these presents that I Christian Remich of Kittery in the County of yorke in the province of the Massa-

PART I, FOL. 113.

thusets bay in New England plantor with the consent of Hannah my wife haue demised Granted and to farme letten vnto my loueing sone Joshua Remich my home stall of Dwelling house barne orchard Garden planting land pasture and Meadow lieing on the neck of land by the boyleing rock in Kittery together with ten acres of land in the woods lieing at the head of Peter Dixons land, and fifteene acres of Land more lyeing in the place called Simons his Marsh on the South side of Stephen paulds land, To Haue hold and faithfully to Improue as a tennant (vppon the termes following) Dureing the whole terme of My Naturall life and the life of the said Hannah my wife and after my Decease and the Decease of my said wife his mother To Haue and to Hold the said Home stall of Dwelling house barne orchard Garden planting land pasture and Meadow together with the ten acres of land and the fifteene acres of land before Mentioned with all the appurtenances and priviledges thereto belonging, to him the said Joshua Remich and his heires for ever, and also I haue lett vnto my said sone Two oxen of seven yeares old, fiue cowes and a bull of three yeares old: two steres of two yeares old and two heifers of two yeares old and twenty Ewes for the terme of the Naturall liues of mee and my wife aforesaid And for and In Consideration of the premises the foresaid Joshua Remich shall allow and pay vnto me his said father yearely and vnto his mother If she outliue me the one halfe of the Increase and proffits of all the foresd lands as English or Indian corne, orchard and Garden fruites and also the one halfe of the Increase of the Neate Catle to be devided once in three yeares and the butter and Cheese with the lambs and wooll to be devided in Equall halues one every yeare, and to allow to me and to his said mother the vse of the one halfe of the foresaid Dwelling house Dureing the whole terme of our Naturall liues And for the true performance thereof and every part of it the foresaid Joshua Remich Doth hereby bind himselfe his heires Executors and

PART I, FOL. 114.

Administrators to his said father and mother and his or her assignes: he said Joshua to deliver the aforesaid stock of neat Catle & sheepe within six monthes after the Decease of his [114] said father and mother to whomsoever they or the longest liver of them shall haue Disposed them vnto in their liues time and for Confirmation of all the aboue written premises both partyes to these presents haue herevnto sett their hands and seales this Eighteenth Day of October Anno Dom͞: one thousand six hundred ninety and three

Signed sealed & delivered   Christian Remich (seal)
   in the presence of vs   the marke of
   Jacob Remich
   Isaac Remich   Hanah ✕ Remich (seal)
   John Tomson   the word after Interlined between the Eight and ninth lines & the word: hay: blotted out in the Eighteenth line before the signe- ing & sealeing hereof

Christian Remich and Hanah his wife Came and acknowledged this Instrument to be their act and Deed vnto their sone Joshua Remich this thirteenth Day of Septemb'r 1694/
    Before me Francis Hooke of the Councill & Just. pea
    A true Coppy of the originall Deed of Christian Remich & Hanah his wife to their sone Joshua Remich here Entred Sep't 15th 1694/   p me John Wincoll Cleric:

To all Christian People to whom these presents shall come greeting Know ye that I Richard Nason of Kittery in the County of yorke & in the province of the Massathusets bay in New England yeoman with the consent of Abigail my wife For and in consideration of that Naturall loue and affection that wee beare vnto our two sones Benjamin Nason and Baker Nason and Especially for and in Consideration of their helpe to vs in our old age by paying rent and other helps for our comfortable Maintenance Dureing our naturall liues to which they are Ingadged as is hereafter perticularly Expressed, the performance will be our full content and satisfaction Haue Giuen Granted bargained sold Infeoffed and confirmed And Doe by these presents for our selues our heires Executors and Administrators Absolutely Giue Grant barguine sell Infeoffee and Confirme vnto the aforesd Benjamin Nason and Baker Nason all my houseing out houseing barnes and lands being my home stall of two hundred acres besides the pastures bounded on the North with the lands that were late Thomas Spencers deceased, and on the west with the tide river and on the south with the land of the Widdow Lord and bounded on the East with the town Comons, Together with all other outlands and Meadowes which belong or Appertaine vnto me the said Richard Nason and being all of them in this towne of Kittery together with six Cowes and six Calues, foure young oxen, twenty seven sheepe and all my horses and horse kind either at home or in the wods as also two sowes and seven pigs with all oxe tackling and all other tackling belonging to the farme either of Iron or wood To Haue and To Hold all and singular the aboue mentioned houses lands Meadowes out lands with all and singular their appurtenances and previledges therevnto belonging or in any wise appertaining together with all the cowes sheepe oxen calues horses swine ox tackling and other the vtencills for husbandry to them the said Benjamin and Baker theire heires Executors Administrators and Assignes for ever in as ample manner to all Intents whatsoever as I the said Richard Nason can or may Estate them, and I the said Richard Nason for myselfe my heires Executors and Administrators Doe Covenant and promise to and with the said Benjamin Nason and Baker Nason that they their heires Executors Administrators or Assignes shall from henceforth and forever Quietly and peaceably haue

PART I, FOL. 115.

hold vse and Injoy all the aboue granted premises with all and singular the appurtenances thereof as I the said Richard Nason haue formerly Done: The aforesaid Benjamin Nason and Baker Nason they or either of them or either of y^r heires Executors Administrators or Assignes shall performe [115] vnto their said father and mother the articles following vizt first that they build or cause to be built a good and warme house of twenty six or twenty eight foote long and Eighteene foote wide with a good chimney every way fitted for their said father and mother to liue in as long as either sd father or mother shall liue and sd Benjamin and Baker shall Doe it at their owne charge as soone as it may be Done after sd father Demands it Secondly the said Benjamin Nason and Baker Nason shall pay sixteene pounds p annem rent in Currant Mony of New England the whole terme of their said father and Mothers liues & to pay it Quarterly and If their said father shall Dye before sd mother then they are to pay to her twelue pounds p annem Dureing her life in Money as aforesaid and then they said Benjamin and Baker to be free from all the other Articles: and in the Meanetime as long as their said father liues sd Benjamin and Baker are to provide and maintaine at their own charge a sufficient Maid for their said father and Mothers helpe and vse as long as they shall both liue and to allow them the milke of a cow yearely such as their sd father shall Choose and two Ewe lambs which he shall choose and to maintaine them for sd fathers vse and to allow them the fruite of his two aple trees and such garden fruite and tobacco as they may haue occasion for and to provide them sufficient fire-wood and make the fires for them constantly and to cause all such graine or mault, as they shall haue occasion to vse to be ground and to be borne to their house and to make them a celler vnder the aforesd house fitt & sufficiently Done and to allow them what wooll they shall haue occasion for at twelue pence per pound, and all the

Part I, Fol. 115.

aboue bargained premises of houses lands and cattell &c to stand bound vnto the said Richard Nason and Abigaille his wife (their sd father and Mother) for the true performance of all the articles to which the said Benjamin Nason and Baker Nason are bound, And for true performance of all the premises both parties to these presents haue herevnto set their hands and seales this twentieth Day of September 1694 in the 6ᵗ yeare of their Majestyes Reigne

Signed Sealed and Richard Nason (seal) Benjamin Nason (seal)
Delivered in pres- his ◯ marke Baker Nason (seal)
ence of vs
John ffoste John Wincoll Abigaile 𝒜 Nason (seal)
John Coopper her marke

     Richard Nason and Abigaile his wife and Benjamin Nason and Baker Nason acknowledged the aboue written Instrument to be their act and Deed this 20ᵗʰ Day of Septᵇʳ 1694
     before me Charles Frost Just : peace

A true coppy of the originall Deed is here Entred on record this 5ᵗ Day of october 1694
     p me John Wincoll Clericː

The within named Richard Nason and Abigaile his wife delivered possession by turf & twigg of the within Mentioned lands and houses &c vnto the within named Benjamin Nason and Baker Nason this twentieth Day of September 1694

in the pʳsence of vs John ffoste
John Coopper : John Wincoll/

This also Entred on record this 5ᵗ Day of october 1694 being on the back side of the originall Deed
     p me John Wincoll Clericː

Part I, Fol. 115.

Know all men by these prents that I James Emery Sen[r] of Barwick in the County of York, of the Prouince of the Massachusets in N : England for diuers good causes and considerations me hereunto mouing, but Especially for the loue I doe bear unto my Son in law Siluanus Knock of the Town and Prouince abouesaid haue granted giuen Alienated and confirmed and doe by these presents giue grant Alienate and confirm unto my aboue named Son, a certain parcell of land lying and being in Town and County aboue said containing Eighteen Acres more or less as appeareth by Sundry marked trees bounded Southerly on the land of Nathan Lord westerly on the land of John Playsted and on the land of Zechariah Emery till you come to a Small white oak Northerly which said white oak is marked with I: E on the North Side of the tree and S N on the South Side and soe to run on the North Side by seuerall marked trees of the same marks to an ash tree, and then to run South East by seuerall marked trees till you come to the Rockie hill to a white oak marked and then to run from that said white oak on a Southeast line twenty Rods, and soe to run to a marked tree which is Nathan Lords bound mark, all which parcell of land together with all its appurtenances of woods waters &c shall be to my son Sylvanus Nock his heires Execut[rs] Administrat[rs] and Assignes for euer. To haue and to hold the same as a quiet and peaceable possession free from all Molestation from me the aboue said James Emery my heires Execut[rs] Administrat[rs] and Assignes or any other pson or psons laying any Leagall Claime thereunto/ In confirmation of the aboue written I the said James Emery haue set to my hand and Seal this March y[e] Second one thousand Six hundred

Part I, Fol. 116.

Ninety and four fiue In the sixth yeare of William and Mary by the grace of God King and Queen of England &c Signed Sealed and deliuered in the presents of us.

James Emery Senr ◯

Job Emery ⎫
Lemuel Smith ⎬ James Emery Senr acknowledged th
Edward Tompson ⎭ aboue written Instrum^t to be his act & deed this 18° of March : 169⅜

before me – Charles ffrost Just peace

A true Copie of ye origenall deed Transcribed & compared this 20° day of March : 169⅜ : p me Jos Hamond Regist^r

[116] To all Christian people to whom this present Deed of gift shall come, John Purrington sometimes of York in the Prouince of Mayn in New England Sendeth Greeting/ Now Know ye that I the said John Purrington for and in consideration of the kindness rec^d of my Louing Cousin Joseph Weare of York aforesaid in ye Province aforesaid in New England aforesaid and alsoe for the loue and affection that I the said John Purrington doe bear unto the aforesaid Weare, haue giuen and granted and by these presents doe giue and grant unto the said Joseph Weare, all the Interest right title or benefit that I the said John Purrington now haue or hereafter may haue in Revertion as I am an heir to my father George Purrington his lands or Estate in York Viz^t I giue and grant to the said Weare all that Tract or pcell of land which was formerly possessed by my father afores^d which land the said Weare hath a dwelling house upon, and the said land hath in part fenced, John Penwill of York hauing alsoe a dwelling house on part of said land he the said Penwill setting the said house there by my leaue and Allowance and onely to Enjoy one halfe Acre of said land where his house now standeth, which said halfe Acre was to him ffrom ye town high way to ye Eastward of said Penwills

house down to the Creek in York called the Meeting house Creek/ the said land being bounded as followeth/ Imprimis — to ye Southeast, or nere it, by a little gut before the s^d Penwills house, which gut cometh out of the afores^d Meeting house Creek, to the Eastward by the town high way aforesaid, and to the Northward by a piece of Marish Now in the possession of Joan Young Widow & by the Meeting house Creek aforesaid the s^d tract of land wholy and solely to ye use and behoofe of the said Weare, I giue and grant all my Interest and title I haue therein now at this prs^t or after the Decease of my Mother/ To haue and to hold to him his heires Execut^{rs} Administrat^{rs} and Assignes for euer, all and euery part and pcell thereof Except what before is Excepted Viz^t, one halfe acre before Expressed allowed to John Penwill afores^d, together with all the priuiledges and appurtenances thereunto belonging or appertaying to him the said Wear his heirs Execut^{rs} Administrat^{rs} and Assigns for euer/ ffurther promising for my selfe my heires and Assigns unto ye said Weare his heirs and Assigns that the said tract of land with all its priuiledges or benefits is free & clear and freely and clearly acquitted from all and former Deeds Sales conveiances gifts grants promises engagements Judgements Executions Joyntures Dowryes Wills Testaments or any other hinderance or Incombrance whatsoeuer done or made from by or under me or my procurement/ And alsoe that I haue good right to conuey and giue the said premises as aforesaid, and alsoe that the said Wear shall and may him his heirs and Assignes Enjoy hold use ocupie and possess the premises aforesaid euen all the Interest I haue therein at present or in Revertion, against the suit let or deniall of any psons whatsoeuer from by or under me, and doe alsoe Engage for my selfe my heires and Assignes unto the said Weare his heires and Assignes to doe any further act or [117] acts that may be needfull in the law for further confirmation.

PART I, FOL. 117.

In witness whereof I hereunto set my hand and affix my seal this twenty fourth day of ffebruary one thousand six hundred Eighty Nine Ninety : 168 $\frac{9}{90}$

Signed Sealed and   John Purrington (his seal)
   deliuered in presents of us
   John Parsons
   Timothy Yealles } the 24° ffebruary 168 $\frac{9}{90}$

John Purrington came before me and acknowledged this Instrument to be his act and Deed/ John Daues Dep : Presid^t

A true Copie of the origenall Deed is here Entred upon Record : and therewith compared : this 12° day of Aprill : 1695   p Jos Hamond Regist^r

Know all men by these presents that I Richard Green of the Town of Kittery in the Prouince of Mayn doe for diuers good Considerations me mouing thereunto, but more Especially the ffatherly affection and tender care and loue that I bear unto my beloued Son John Green, doe by these presents ffreely grant and giue unto him my beloued Son aforesaid and to his lawfull heires for euer, a certain tract & parcell of land be it more or less, Scituate and lying in ye afores^d Town & Prouince of Mayn Joyning to ye land of James Tobey on ye North side, and on y^t side beginning at ye Coue on ye uper side of ffranks fforte butting to ye home lot of the foresaid Richard Green, & from James Tobeys land runing on a square to a hemlock tree and on ye same line till it comes to ye Middle of the afores^d lot of land of ye afores^d Richard Green And then to run up through ye Middle of ye lot to ye head sad Richard Greens land, the other halfe of sad Greens land remains on ye South side, the aforesad land thus butted and bounded on ye North side with James Tobeys land and on ye South side with ye remaining halfe of sad Greens land, the aforesad land contains

PART I, FOL. 118.

halfe halfe sad Greens land running back into y[e] woods to y[e] head of sad Greens land To haue & to hold y[e] aboue said land to him & his heires for euer as aboue said with all y[e] priuiledges and apportances thereunto belonging, without any let or hinderance or Molestation by me or any under me/ unto which daly gift I doe hereby ffreely and Voluntaryly giue and grant as aboue said unto my Son John Green as aboue said for euer unto which Deed of gift I doe hereunto ffreely set my hand and seale, this nineteenth day of June An: Dom 1687.

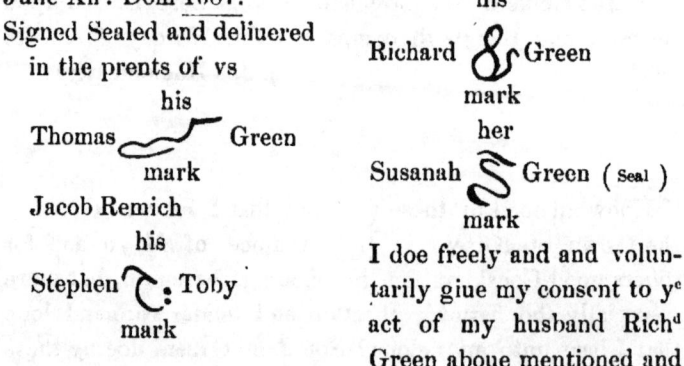

Signed Sealed and deliuered in the prents of vs

Thomas (his mark) Green

Jacob Remich

Stephen (his mark) Toby

Richard (his mark) Green

Susanah (her mark) Green (Seal)

I doe freely and and voluntarily giue my consent to y[e] act of my husband Rich[d] Green aboue mentioned and doe hereby promise and ingage neuer to disturb or Molest y[e] said John Green on y[e] said land nor hinder him or any of his from quietly possessing of y[e] aboue said land In witness whereof I Susanah Green wife of sad Richard Green doe freely set my hand and seale this nineteenth of June: 1687

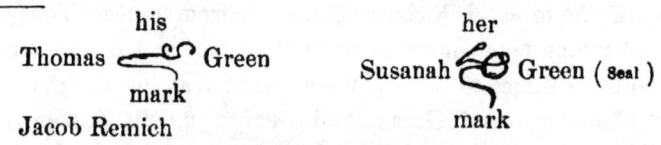

Thomas (his mark) Green

Jacob Remich

Susanah (her mark) Green (Seal)

acknowledgem[t] on y[e] other side

[118] Richard Green and Susanah Green his wife appeared before me this 24. August 1687 — and acknowledged y[e] aboue Instrum[t] to be their acts and Deeds before me

John Hinckes of y[e] Councill

Part I, Fol. 118.

A true Copie of y⁰ origenall Deed transcribed & compared this 22⁰ of June 1695   p Jos Hamond Regist'

For as much as the Law of the Prouince Cause how persons claiming interests in house or Lands either to sue out such claim or claims or enter their claim before the term of the Law be expired — These are therefore to Inform and giue notice y' I Joshua Downing of Kittery in the Prouince of Main do by these presents lay and shall in time Conuenient make out Just & right interest to one hundred and sixty acrees of Land giuen & granted unto him the said Downing by y⁰ Town of Kittery as p y⁰ grant will more at Large appear which Land is good part of it detained from me the said Downing by Maj' Hutchinson of Boston and others by his order without Just right

Dated 27⁰ of Septemb' 1695

p Me Joshua Downing

A true Coppy of the Originall is here entred upon Record and therewith Compared this 28⁰ of Sept' 1695

p John Newmarch Clericᵐ

This is to giue notice to all persons to whom this writing shall come that Sarah Morrill of Boston in the Colony of the Massachusetts hauing lately had Administration granted to y⁰ Estate of John Ugroue sometime of Kittery in the Prouince of Main wᶜʰ said Estate Consists in Land and is lying and being between Watts fort and ffranks fort in afore said Kittery These are therefore to signify to all persons concerned that I John Pickerin of Portsmouth in y⁰ Prouince of Newhampshire attorney to y⁰ said Sarah Morrell do in her behalf lay Just claim to all that tract of Land

Part I, Fol. 119.

aforesaid and forbid all persons of medling or improuing any part thereof without Leaue from y⁶ said Morrill This to preserue her right till oppertunity giues Leaue for triall of her title

Dated 27° Sept^r : 1695   John Pickerin Attorney as afores^d

A true Coppy of the Originall is here entred upon Record & therewith Compared this 28° Septr 1695

p J^no Newmarch Regist^r

[119] To all Christian People to whom this present writing or deed of Gift shall come Know ye that Michael Endle and his wife Wilmot Endle now inhabitants in the Township of Kittery in the Prouince of main in New England (in Spruce Creek) of their own uoluntary wills and mutuall Consents and for diuers good reasons them thereunto mouing haue giuen granted surrendered And by these presents do for themselues their Heirs Executors & Administrators give graunt surrender and giue quiet possession of all that house and Land Tenement Hereditament Purchase and Estate wch they now have and do Enjoy in Spruce Creek in the Prouince of Main aforesaid unto John Mogridg Bricklayer and Sarah his Wife Inhabitants in said Spruce Creek, To him and her & their Heyres Executors Administrators and Assignes for euer, To haue and to Hold the said demised premises together with all the priuiledges Conueniences Profitts Emoluments thing and things thereunto belonging Unto the said John Mogridg and his wife and their Heirs Executors Administrators and Assignes for euer prouided always and it is y⁶ true intent and meaning of this present Deed of Gift that the said John Mogridge and Sarah Mogrige their Heirs Execut^rs Administrators & Assigns Do & Shall from time to Time and all times during y⁶ Naturall Life of y⁶ said Michaell Endle and Wilmot Endle, find Pro-

Part I, Fol. 120.

uide Yeild; Supply and giue and grant to them either and both them Sufficient meat drink apparrell Lodging roome fire and Candle & all things necessary and Conuenient for aged persons as aforesaid at the sole and proper Charge of · ye said John Mogridge and Sarah Mogridge both and either of them their heirs Executors Administrat^{rs} and Assigns, During their naturall Life as aboue said, In Wittness and for Confirmation whereof we ye said Michaell Endle and Wilmot Endle to this aboue mentioned Deed haue set our hands and seals this fifteenth day of December, in ye Year of Lord One thousand Six hundred Ninety one.

Signed Sealed and Deliuered
   In Presence of us   Michaell [mark] Endle (seal)
   Robt Elliot
   Nicho Heskins
   Thomas Wise   Wilmot [mark] Endle (seal)

Michaell Endle and Wilmot Endle his wife came and acknowledged this Instrument to be their act and deed unto John Mogridg and Sarah his wife this Second day of August 1693

                 Before me Francis Hooke Just pe

A true Coppy of the originall Deed is here Entred upon Record: and therewith Compared this 20° Day of Nouemb^r 1695

                p Jno Newmarch Regist^r

[120] Know all men by these presents that I John Alcot Shipwright of ye Town of Kittery in the Prouince of Maine with ye consent of my Mother Abigail Rowsley of the Town of Portsm^o in ye Prouince of New-Hampshiere for and in consideration of a valluable sum of money already in hand payd with which sum I doe acknowledge myselfe fully sat-

isfied/ Haue bargained and sold and doe by these presents bargain sell alien enfeoff and make ouer a parcle of land containning fifteen acres, unto Peter Dickson of ye Town of Kittery afores^d Shipwright his heires Execut^{rs} Administrat^{rs} & Assignes which said parcle of land lies in ye town of Kittery afores^d nere ye boyling Rock hauing ye Riuer of Piscataqua on ye Southwest side thereof and is bounded on ye South East with ye land of Thomas Spinney and on the Northwest with ye land of Christian Remax and on ye north East with ye land of the aforesaid Peter Dickson. To Haue & to Hold to him ye said Peter Dickson his heires Execut^{rs} Administrat^{rs} and Assignes, all ye abouesaid fifteen acres of land soe butted and bounded as aforesaid with all the priuiledges and appurtenances thereunto belonging for Euer, And I ye said John Alcot doe hereby Engage to Warrant and Defend all ye aboue mentioned premises unto ye said Dickson his heires &c. from all manner of pson or psons whatsoeuer that shall lay any claim thereunto from by or under me/ In witness whereof I haue hereunto set my hand and seal ye 10º day of Aug^o 1681 — and in the three & thirtieth year of ye Reign of our Souereign Lord Charles ye Second by ye grace of God, of England Scotland ffrance & Ireland King Defend^r of ye ffaith.

Signed Sealed and Deliuered   John Alcocke (seal)
  in ye presents of
  John ffletcher   John Alcot came & acknowledged the
  Edward Melcher aboue Instrum^t to be his free act &
                              deed & his Mother Abigail Rowsley
came & acknowledged that she did approue of ye aboue Sale of the s^d land and doth freely rend^r up all her Interest in ye aboue mentioned premises to ye s^d Peter Dickson &c. Portsm^o Aug^o 10º 1681 before me Richd Martyn of ye Council

  A true Copie of ye origenall here Entred on Record Jan: 13 : 169½

                          p Jos Hamond Regist^r

PART I, FOL. 120.

In the Name of God Amen/ the xxvth of June in ye year of our Lord one thousand Six hundred fforty Seuen, I George Puddington the unprofitable Seruant of God, weake in body but Strong in mind, doe willingly and with a free heart render and giue again into ye hands of my Lord God and Creat^r my Spirit which he of his ffatherly goodness gaue unto me when he first fashioned me in my Mothers Wombe, making me a liuing and a reasonable Creature, Nothing Doubting but that for his infinite Mercye, Set forth in ye precious blood of his Dearly beloued Son Jesus Christ our onely Saui^r & Redeem^r he will receiue my Soul into his Blessed Saints.

And as concerning my body Euen with a good will & free heart I giue ouer, recomending it to ye earth whereof it came nothing doubting but according to ye Article of my faith at ye great day of generall Resurrection when we shall appear before the Judgement Seat of Christ, I shall receiue ye Same again by ye mighty power of God whereas he is able to Subdue all things to himselfe, Not a corruptable, Mortall weak and vile body as it is now but an incorruptable, immortall, Strong and perfect body in all points.

ffirst as concerning my wife with whome I Coupled my Selfe in ye fear of God refusing all other women I linked my Selfe unto her, liuing with her in ye Blessed State of Honourable Wedlock, by whom alsoe by the Blessing of God I haue now two Sons and three daughters, John & Elias Mary ffrances and Rebecca. And albeit I doubt not but that God after my departure according to his promise will be unto her a husband yea a father and a Patron and Defender, and will not Suffer her to lack if She trust fear and Serue him dilligently calling upon his holy name, yet for as much as God hath Blessed me with Worldly Substance and She is my own flesh, and whosoe prouideth not for his, denieth the ffaith and is worse than an Infidell/ I therefore giue & bequeath unto John my Eldest Son, and Elias my youngest Son all my land

and houses and out houses which are now in my Possession where I now dwell in Gorgeana in New-England and alsoe all my Marsh ground, or land, in Gorgeana aforesaid with all ye appurtenances thereunto belonging to them and to their heires for euer Equally to be Deuided, but if any of my Sons doe die without heires of his body lawfully begotten that then the land and Marishes aforesaid remain to y^o longest liuer and to his heires ffor Euer. [121] But if it shall please God that both my Sons doe die wthout heires of their bodyes lawfully begotten, that then I giue and bequeath the aforesaid lands and Marish groud unto my three daughters Mary Rebecca & ffrances, and and to their heires for Euer/ And if any of them shall die without Issue of their bodies lawfully begotten then to the longest liuer and their heires for euer/ but if all my Children doe die without heires that then I giue and bequeath my aforesaid land and Marish ground unto my brother Robert Puddington and his heires for Euer Prouided alwayes that Mary my wife haue ye Said land and Marsh ground during this her Mortall life for ye bringing up and Maintainance of my said Children — moreouer I giue and bequeath unto Mary my Eldest daughter one cow called or known by ye name of Ladd and fiue pounds Starling when She Shall come unto the age of Sixteen yeares/ I doe giue and bequeath unto my Second Daughter ffrances one Cow called or known by the name of young finch, and fiue pounds of money, and the which to be payd unto her at ye age of Sixteen yeares ffurther I doe giue and bequeath unto my youngest daughter Rebecca one heifer called or known by the name of young Ladd, and fiue pounds of money and the said 5^{lb} to be payd unto her at ye age of Sixteen yeares And all ye aforesaid Cattle to remain in Mary my wiues Custody untill they or Either of them Shall come unto ye age of Sixteen years without any fraud or Couin And my meaning is that my three daught^{rs} Shall haue the thirds of ye Increase of the afores^d Cattle in the mean to their use/ My Will is further that I doe giue unto John my Eldest Son, my best feather bed with all things Else thereunto belonging, and one long Table and a Brewing ffurnis, but Mary my wife to haue ye use of them untill he come unto ye age of one and twenty years but if he Shall die in the meantime that then my Will is that ye ffether bed with that thereunto belonging, and the Table and the Brewing ffurnis I giue unto Elias my youngest Son and to his heires for Euer/ My Will is further that I doe giue unto Mary my Eldest daughter, one fflock bed and Bolster with all things Else belonging, also my Will is that Mary my Wife I doe make and ordaine to be full and wholly Executrix of this my last Will and Testament/ Alsoe my desire is that my Brother Robert Puddington and Mr Edward Johnson Mr Abraham Preble & Mr John Alcock to be Supervisors of this my Will/ And in token of my loue unto them, I bequeath unto these my Supervisers ten Shillings.

Witnesse hereof I haue hereunto Set my hand and Seal in the presents of/

John Alcock George Puddington

The mark of B Bartholomew Barnet (Seal)

The mark of A Arthur Bragdon

A true Copie of ye origenall here Entred on Record this 18º of January : 169⅔ p Jos Hamond Regist^r

SECOND PART.

[1*] Province   1689
of Maine

At a meeting of the Deputy p^{r}sident and Justices of this pvince viz. Major John Davese Deputy p^{r}sident, Major Charles Frost Capt Francis Hooke : Samuell Wheelewright and John Wincoll Esq^{rs} By authority of their Maties King William and Queene and by order of the Honble president of this province : the sd Justices being first sworne before the sd Deputy p^{r}sident this twentieth Day of December at york. in sd province and the said Deputy p^{r}sident sworne be . . . . said Justices the publick officers Chosen are as foll . . . . .

John Wincoll Chosen Clarke of the Courts and recorder of ye pvince and sworne before the Deputy president
Arthur Bragdon Chosen Marshall of the province
Thomas Harris Chosen prison keeper

A Court of sessions of the peace appointed to be held at wells the fir . . tuesday of March Next and a Court of pleas to be held at the same place the next Day following .

William Card bound to the Good behaviour in the sum of twenty pounds to our sov^{rain} lord the king till the next sessions of the peace and to appeare and Answere there

A Court of sessions of the peace held at Wells the fourth Day of Mar . . 16$\frac{89}{90}$ before Maj^r John Davese Esqr Deputy

Part II, Fol. 2.

p'sident Capt Francis Hooke Mr Samuell Wheelewright and John Winc . . . Justices of the peace

The Grand	Jonathan Hamonds. John Preble . . . Hill
Jury were	William Plaisted M . . . .
	Ens: Thom . . . . .
	Thomas . . . . .

Nathaniell . . . .
the oath th . . . .
Silvester . . . .

Maj^r Davese . . . .

Leiut Joseph . . . .

Christopher . . . .
is licenced . . . .

Richard . . . .
on both J . . . .
of them . . . .

[2]

Administration of the Estate of Samuell L . . . . Barwic. Deceased is Granted vnto his Brother Abraham Lord who together with William Plaisted Did acknowledg themselues bound to our Soveraine lord the King in the sum of one hundred pounds sterling that the sd Abraham Lord shall on sd Estate according to law

William Card by proClamation Cleard from his bond for Good behauior : fees pd

Mr Francis Litlefeild being approued of by the select men of wells is licenced to keepe a house of publick Entertainment according to law

PART II, FOL. 2.

Letters of Administration granted to Mary Barrett of Cape porpus of the Estate of her husband John Barrett deceased and sd Mary Barret and Capt John Litlefeild Doe acknowledg themselues bound vnto o^r soveraign lord the King in the sum of fiue hundred pound that the sd Mary Barret shall Administer on sd Estate acording to law

Letters of Administration granted to Anthony Bracket of falmouth of the Estate of his father Anthony Bracket Deceased and the said Anthony Brackett of falmouth and John Reding of wells Doe ackowledg themselues bound vnto o^r soveraign Lord the King in the sum of two hundred and fourteen pounds that the sd Anthony Bracket shall Administer on sd Estate according to law

Thomas Rice being bound by recognisance to Answere at this Court and being Called appeared not, his bond is declared forfeit

James Warren Junr being bound to this Court to answere Elizabeth Gattensby for being the father of a Child which shee then was great withall and being now delivered & not Capeable of appearance at this Court the sd James Warren appeared and his bond is continewed till the next Court of sessions of the peace and is by proclamition Cleared from his bond for the good behaviour

Daniell God . . . . . n^r his Licence to keepe a house of publick Entertai . . . .   ewed

.   ♦   .   .   .   nce granted to sell Drinke by
.   .   .   .   .   tinewed

PART II, FOL. 3.

. . . . . . Molton haue both
. . . . . . ses of publicke
. . . . . . rmination to
. . . . . . hall be licenced
. . . . . . Court

. . . . . l the estate

. . . . . is left in the
. . . . . f her selfe
[3]

Mr Samuell Daniell of yorke his Licence for keeping a house of publick Entertainment is renewed and Continewed for the yeare Ensueing and the said Samuell Daniell Doth acknowledg himselfe bound vnto our soveraigne Lord the King in the sum of twenty pounds sterling that in keepeing sd house of publick Entertainment to obser . . the Stat--utes and lawes in that Case provided

Robert Steuart came before this Court and Ingadged to pay vnto Jonathan Hamond twenty shillings in mony for the vse of Mrs Bray within a fortnights time

James Warren Junr appearing to answere his bond the young woman his accuser being newly Delivrd of a Child was prevented appearance & his bond for appearance Continewed to another sessions the 25. Instant at Major Frosts house & is Cleared of his bond of good behaviour

The Grand Jurys presen tments were as followeth vizt

witness: wee p^rsent George Norton of yorke for re-
Thomas: taileing of rum Cyder and beare in his house
Harris:
witnes   Wee p^rsent William More of yorke for re-
Thomas   taileing of strong Drinke in his house this winter
Harris

Part II, Fol. 3.

Thomas Bradgdon
Phillip Frost

Wee present Timothy yeales William Hilton and John Longmead for not frequenting the publick worship of god vppon the lords Day

John preble

Wee present the wife of Samson Anger for not frequenting the publick worship of god vppon the lords Day

Wee present Jeremiah Shiers for not frequenting the publick worship of god vpon the lords Day

A Court of Pleas held at Wells the 5ᵗ Day of March 16⅞⅞ befor Majʳ John Davese Esqʳ Deputy pʳsident Capt Francis Hooke Mʳ Samuell Wheelewright and John Wincoll Justices of the peace

No actions appeareing the Jury is Dismissed

Grand Jurymen to be speedily Chosen in every town vizᵗ Kittery : 5 : yorke 3 — wells. 2. Sacoc. 2 : Scarburoug and Falmouth. 2 :

The returnes of the Juryes of Inquest vppon the vntimely Death of Samuell Lord of Barwick Robert Houston of Dover and Thomas Litlefeild of Wells the said Juryes are are allowed one shilling p man, to say twelue shillings each Jury, fiue shillings each Coroner and two shillings each Constable to be paid out of the respectiue Estates of the deceased

Lycence is Granted to Capt Edward Sargent of Sacoe to keepe a house of publick Entertainment for the yeare Ensueing

PART II, FOL. 4.

June 18th 1690
p 2 Justices
& ye Clarke

Letters of Administration is granted vnto Sarah Whinicke of Scarborough on the Estate of her husband Joseph Whinicke late of Scarburough deceased and shee is to bring in a true Inventor. and giue bond according to law at the next Court of sessions

[4]

Province of Maine July 15 : 1690

In their Maties names A Court of sessions of the peace held at yorke before Maj^r John Davese Deputy p^{r}sident Capt Francis Hooke Maj^r Charles Frost and John Wincoll Justices of the peace

The Grand Jury : vizt Mr Nathaniell Raines foreman
Nicholas Weekes   Ichabod Plaisted   Jesper Pulman
Jabez Jenkins   John Harman   Dominicus Jordan
John Heard   Arthur Kane   John Bray
Thomas Rice   Samuell Bragdon   Thomas Adams

George Norton sumond to answere his p^{r}sentment for selling rum Cyder and beere by retaile is Cleared

George Norton bound by recognisance to answere for retailing strong Drinke without licence is fined to our soveraign lord the King the sum of fiue pounds & Court fees, George Norton desired apeale which could not be granted because ye law is positiue in that case

William More sumoned to answere his p^{r}sentment pleading his licence to sell Drinke is Cleared paying fees

Letters of Administration Granted to Richard Endle of Kittery on the Estate of his brother John Endle Deceased

Part II, Fol. 3.

amounting to the Vallue of nineteen pound sixteen shillings and nine pence and phillip Addams acknowledged himselfe Indebted by way of recognisance vnto our soveraigne lord & lady William & Mary King and Queen of England & in the sum of forty pounds mony On condition that Richard Endle shall truely Administer acording to law & sd Richard Endle tooke oath to the Inventory any more Estate appeare to add it

Timothy yeales sumoned to answere his pʳsentment for not frequenting the publick worship of god on the lords Dayes vppon his promise of reformation is Cleared paying Court fees

William Hilton Called to Answere his pʳsentmᵗ for not frequenting the publick worship of god on the lords Dayes vpon his promise of reformation is Cleared paying Court fees·

Sarah the wife of Samson Anger presented for not frequenting the publick worship of god on the lords Day vppon her acknowledgment & pmise of amendmᵗ is passed by shee paying fees

Nathaniel Kene not appeareing to answere his recognisance of twentie pounds Currant Mony Dated June 19ᵗʰ 1690: his sd recognizance is Declared forfeit but vpon his petition his recognizance is respited and Continewed to the next Court

Joshua Dowing his recognizance respited till the next Court of sessions

Jeffery Currier for abuseing one of their Maᵗⁱᵉˢ Justices of the peace Mʳ Andrew Deumant in open Court and for say-

PART II, FOL. 5.

ing the said Deamant was a lyer is fined to our soveraine Lord & Lady the king & Queene the sum of fiue pounds and to be bound to the good behauiour with sure . . . in the sum of fifty pounds vntill the next sessions of the . . ace & to stand Comitted till it be performed

[5]

The Grand Jury Exhibited a p'sentm' against Samuell Mathews and Abraham Kelly for abusing their Maties Constable of the northern Isles of Shoules both strikeing of sd Constable & sd Kelly taking away his staff The said Mathewes is fined forty shillings and the sd Kelly is fined fifty shillings to their Maties and to pay Court fees and to stand Comitted till payment be made   paid for Kelly By Alex : Maxwell

Thomas Mawaring Chosen and sworne Grand Jury man for ye northen Isles of Shoules

Jeffery Currier being brought by warrant before this Court for speakeing Mutanous words in publick tending to the breach of their Maties peace is to be admonished and to pay costs and fees of Court

Samuell Cater and Hugh Allard being Comitted to yorke Goale by vertue of a Mittimus from Mr Roger Kelly appeared at this Court and no pson appeareing to prosecute against them haveing paid officers fees

Joseph Banks Complained of for strikeing Nathaniell Adams while he was on their Maties service gaurding of a prisoner, is fined to y^r Maties ten shillings in Mony

Thomas Harris fined to y^r Majesties three shillings and fourpence for sweareing

Part II, Fol. 5.

Whereas there is Great Complaint made of severall abbuses taken notice of in ordinaryes by excessiue Drinking of rum, flipp &c: the Il consequence whereof is pubickly seene in the misbehaviour of severall persons in ye presence of authority and otherwise, for the prevention of the like for the future it is therefore ordered

That from henceforth there shall not be any rum or other strong liquor or flip be sold vnto any Inhabytant of the town by any ordinary keeper therein Directly or Indirectly, Except in Case of great nesessity as in Case of sickness &c: nor shall any ordinary keeper sell vnto any stranger more then one gill for a person at one time, and all Ciuell officers, Especially select men and constables in the respectiue townes in this province are required to take Espcciall Care by Inspecting any suspitious house or houses where any such abuses or profanenesse may be acted, and in Case any ordinary keeper shall presume to transgress this order he shall Imediately forfeit his licence

   The Gran Jurys presentments vizt
Inprimo: Jeffery Currier for swearing:
   Abraham Parker for theft:
   William More for retailing liq^r:
   Abraham Preble for marrieing Contrary to law:
   William Hilton for not Comeing to Mitting:
   Joseph Doniell for not Comeing to Mitting:
   Adrian Fry & famely for not Coming to Mitting
   William Munsay for not Comeing to mitting
   John Longmaid for not Comeing to Mitting
   Thomas Langly for not Comeing to Mitting
   John Billin for not Coming to Mitting
   Richard White for not Coming to Mitting
   John Linscott for fornication

Province [6]
of maine In their Maties names

A Court of pleas held at yorke the 16th Day of July 1690 Before Major John Davese Dep^ty p^rsident Capt Francis Hooke Maj^r Charles Frost and John Wincoll Justices of the peace

The Jury of tryalls vizt John penwill Foreman
John Harman	Thomas Rice	Jesper Pulman
Nicholas Weekes	Ichabod Plaisted	Dominicus Jordan
Jabez Jenkings	Arthur Kane	John Bray
John Heard	Sam^ll Bragdon	Thomas Adams

Mr Peter Weare is plaintiff in an action of the Case for a Debt Due by bill to the vallue of Nine pound currant mony &c Contra Elizabeth Stover Executrix and relict of Silvester Stover Defendent/ The Jury finds for the defendent Costs of Court

Maj^r John Davese is plaintiff in an action of the Case for non payment of fiue pounds six shillings and twopence in Mony or there abouts Contra Charles Brisson defendent The Jury finds for the plaintiff fiue pounds six shillings and two pence in mony or as mony or goods Equivalent and Costs of Court

A day of solemn fasting and prayer appointed to be kept throughout this province on the 24th Day of this Instant July

William Bray apointed keeper of the Goale at yorke and is to be paid foure pounds p Annem as mony

George Norton Complaind of for vain sweareing and proued by 3 witnesses is fined ten shillings and for his abusiue words against the Court and Minister of yorke is to giue bond of ten pound for his good behauiour till the next Court and stands Comitted till it be Effected

Joseph Johnson being brought before this Court vppon suspision of killing Samson Aingers horse vppon Examination Ingeniously Confessed that he went to Capt Alcocks Garrison and fetched a speare and kild sd Aingers horse being himselfe alone and no other pson Confederate with him

Province [7]
of Maine In their Maties names

A Court of sessions of the peace held at yorke the 24th Day of february 1690: before Maj^r John Davese Dep^ty p^rsident Capt Francis Hooke & John Wincoll Justices of the peace

The Grand Jury vizt John Penwill Foreman : Jeremia Stover

John Harman	Arthur Beale	Samuell Bragdon
Jabez Jenkins	Silvanus Nock	Jesper pulman
John Heard	John Wheelewright	Dominicus Jordan
Thomas Rice	Arthur Kane	William More
James Sayword	Joseph Weare	Jacob Remich

John Longmaid p^rsented for not Coming to meetting vppon his his acknowledgment is Cleared paying fees 2^s

Letters of Administration is granted to m^rs Elinor Foxwell of the Estate of her Husband phillip Foxwell late of Kittery deceased the Inventory Deliverd in vppon her oath and surety taken

Nicholas Frost Indicted for theft is by the Grand Jury found guilty and puts himself vppon tryall by god & the King : he is fined forty shillings or whipt fifteene lashes and

Part II, Fol. 7.

to pay Costs and giue bond for the good behauiour In the sum of fifty pound

Administration is granted to M{r} Samuell Penhallow of the estate of Christopher Grant late of Barwick deceased and Cap{t} Franc . . Hooke stand bound with sd Sam{ll} Penhallow that he shall bring Inventory of y{t} Estate & administer according to law, a the sd Penhallow paid seven shillings and six pence for the same by order of the Deputy president

Nathaniell Kene for abuse of the Constable in the Execution of his office is fined ten shillings and to pay Costs & stand Comitted till it be Done, the Costs allowed are ten shillings

Whereas the Justices of this province haue no publick allowance for their time and Charges at Courts &c : wee Doe therfor according to pattent previledge and grant of the proprietor take seven shillings and six pence for probats of Wills, grants of Administration, Licences for ordinarys & six shillings p action for the Jurys of tryalls besides Entry mony & this by order of the Councill/

Richard Ellett Constable of Kittery owned in Court that Nicholas Frost never offered any abuse when he had him by by warrant in his Custody

The grand Jurys presentments viz{t}   Sarah Anger for not frequenting the publick worship of god
Joseph Carline & Elizabeth his wife for not coming to y{e} publick worship of god
John Linscott for being fudled
George Norton & Hannah Grant for not Coming to y{e} publick worship of god
Margaret Buckland for fornication
Nicholas Frost for theft

Part II, Fol. 8.

Province [8]
of maine   February 25 16$\frac{8}{9}$?   In their Ma[ties] names

A Court of Comon pleas held at yorke Maj[r] John Davese Dep[ty] p[r]sident Maj[r] Charles Frost Capt Francis Hooke M[r] Samuell Wheelewright and John Wincoll, theire Ma[ties] Justices of y[e] peace

The Jury of tryalls :   M[r] John Penwill foreman
John Harman	Daniell Stone	Thomas Baston
William Young	Andrew Neale	Richard Cutt
Joseph Molton	Humphrey Axell	James Sawyer
Silvanus Nock	Steven Toby	

James Litlefeild and Mary Litlefeild are plaintiff in an action of trespass vpon the case for withholding of ten thousand foote of merchantable pine boards Contra William Sayer defendant   The Jury finds for the plaintiff ten thousand foote of Merchantable pine to be delivered according to Covenant or the vallue of the boards, and Costs of Court, two pound fourteen shillings mony

George Norton Appelant Contra Samuell Daniell from a Judgment obtaind against him before Maj[r] John Davese of twenty two shillngs and the pence, the Court finds for y[e] Appellant the revercion of the former Judgment & Costs of Court

Nathaniell Raines appellant versus William More from a Judgment obtained before Maj[r] John Davese of thirty six shillings Damage and seven shillings ten pence Costs the Jury finds for the appellant the reversion of the former Judgment and costs of Court twenty Eight shillings Mony

Henry Goddard by vertue of a letter of atturney from Elizabeth Stover Did in her name & behalfe appeare before this Court and acknowledge a Judgment of six pounds in mony to Peter Weare and Costs of Court allowed seven shillings nine pence

Maj^r John Davese is plaintiff in an Action of trespass on the Case Contra Samuell Hill defendent for damage Done to his said Sloope to the vallue of thirty pound mony: The Jury finds for the plaintiff six pounds eight shillings and fiue pence Damage Mony and Costs of Court twenty four shillings and six pence: The Defendent appeales to the next Court of appeales

Administration is granted to Israell Harden on the Estate of William Frost Senr Late of wells Deceased and sd Harden & William Frost Junr stand bound to o^r soveraigne Lord & lady the King & Queene in the sum of eighty pounds y^t the said Israell Harden shall administer on sd estate according to law

Administration is Granted to John Wooddin & Katherne his wife of the Estate of James Litlefeild late of wells Deceased and said Wooddin and Joseph Stover stand bound vnto our soveraigne lord and lady the King and Queen in the sum of two hundred and seventy pounds that the said John Wooddin and his sd wife shall Administer on sd Estate according to law

[9]

Robert Stewart not prosecuting his appeale against John Reding is according to law fined forty shillings

A Court of sessions of the peace appointed to be holden at yorke on the first Tuesday of June next and a Court of Comon pleas the next Day following in the same place

A Day of publick humiliation appointed to be kept the third Wednesday in March next & all servile labour is forbidden on that Day

PART II, FOL. 9.

Administration is granted vnto Nathaniell Kene of the Estate of John Wilson Late of Kittery Deceased

Whereas Nathaniell Kene hath taken away a certain Jersey boy named Joseph Eastknop (by warrant from Maj^r Davese) from John Alcock who had receiued him by Execution and being put into the Constables hands and thereby occasioned great Charges to the said Alcock and to the Constable Joseph Curtis, vpon heareing of the case the Court finds for John Alcock ten shillings costs and for Joseph Curtis the Constable one pound eighteene shilling six pence Costs

John Linscot bein p^{r}sented by ye Grand Jury for fornication referring his triall to god & the King is fined twenty shillings or to receiue ten stripes at the post and to pay fees of Court: fiue shillings

Administration is granted to m^{rs} Mary Hull of the Estate of her deceased father Mr Edward Rishworth and the sd Mary hull & John Wheelwright stand bound to our soveraigne Lord and Lady the King and Queen in the sum of seventy eight pounds that the sd Mary hull shall Administer on sd Estate according to law

Licence is granted to Lieut: Joseph Storer of wells to keepe a house of publick Entertainment for retailing of strong liquor wine beere and Cyder &c. for the yeare Ensueing he keepeing good order according to law and no other to be granted in wells for the time being

Capt Francis Hooke and Mr Samuell Wheelewright are Chosen and Impowred a Comittee to setle the Estate of Lewes Beane (late of 'yorke Deceased) amongst his Children

PART II, FOL. 10.

Province [10]
of Maine   In their Maties names June 2^d 1691
 A Court of sessions of the peace held at yorke before y^r Maties Deputy p^rsident & Justices of the peace

The names of the Grand Jury vizt
James Sawyer   Andrew Neale   Alexander Maxwell
Joseph Molton   Steven Tobie   Richard Ellett
William Young   Humphry Axtell   Richard Cutt
Daniell Stone   William Peprill

 This Court Grants Administration to Daniell Maning of Ipswich of the Estate of Samuell Saward late of yorke Deceased and the sd Daniell Maning James Sayward & Joseph Molton stand bound to our soveraine Lord and Lady the King & Queen in the sum of thirty four pound that the sd Daniell Maning shall Administer on sd Estate according to Law

 Ordered that James Emery late Constable of Barwick shall with a fortnight make vp his accounts with the select men and pay what he is behind in gathering vp the rates Comitted to his hands or be liable to pay it out of his owne Estate

 Joshua Downing is Cleared from his bond of the good behauior hee paying Court fees

 Ordered that the select men of Kittery shall forthwith veiue and Lay out such highwayes in the town of Kittery as are in any wise Interupted or hindred by fences or otherwise and Especially in the lower part of the towne that they may be made conveniently passable for horse and foote because of the present Complaint mad to this Court

PART II, FOL. 11.

It appearing to this Court that the garrison formerly in the possession of m^r Thomas Holmes at Quamphegon is and will be of great vse for the security of those parts against the Comon Enemy it being now in the Custody of m^r William Patridge he haueing men there & promiseing to keepe the same for the vse aforesd so long as he can or vntill this Court or the authority of this pvince shall see cause otherwise to Dispose of the same for the vse aforesd & Whereas sd Court is Informed that sd Holmses widdow with some other abettors haue threatened the destruction thereof it is further ordered that Maj^r Charles Frost is appointed and Impowred to send for sd widdow Holmes & her abettors letting her and them know this Court order & If he find the Information to be true to punish as the matter of fact may require or bind the party or partys offending against this order over to the next Court held in sd province there to answere the same

This Court is adjorned vntill the last tuesday of this Instant June as also the Court of pleas adjorned to the next Day following which will be the first Day of July next where all persons shall haue liberty to bring new Comenced actions as well as those already Depending & all Jurors & others already sumoned for both Courts are to attend sd Courts at the time appointed

Province [11]
of Maine   In their Maties names July 1st 1691

A Court of pleas held at yorke before the deputy p^rsident and two Justices of the peace

A Court of sessions of the peace is appointed to be holden at yorke on the first tuesday of october next and a Court

PART II, FOL. 11.

of Comon pleas is appointed to be held at yorke aforesd the next Day following and this present Court is adjorned to the same Day and all recognizances presentments and actions depending to stand good for trieall at sd Courts where all persons shall haue liberty to bring New Comenced actions and all Jurors in p'sent are to appeare and serve at sd Courts

Ordered y[t] the Comittees of Militia of yorke and wells are Impowred to Impress and take any fatt Cattell (for the suply of Country soldiers) from any person whatsoever Especially from such persons as Desert the province the giueing a true account of what cattell they shall so take

Province In their Ma[ties] names, October 6[t] 1691
of maine
        At a court of sessions of the peace held at yorke before their Ma[ties] Justices of the peace: Capt Francis Hook Deputy p[r]sident, Major Charles Frost and M[r] Samuell Wheelewright

Letters of Administration granted vnto Mary Daves of the Estate of her husband Maj[r] John Daves late of yorke Deceased and sd Mary Daves tooke oath to the Inventory of three hundred forty foure pound nineteene shillings and If any More Estate shall appear shee will ad 'it to sd Inventory And the said Mary Daves John Herman & Thomas Trafton bind themselues Jointly and severally to Our soveraine Lord and Lady the King and Queen in the sum of six hundred Eighty nine pound Eighteene shillings that the sd Mary Daves Administratrix to the sd Estate of her deceased husband Major John Daves shall resond all Just Debts Due from the said Estate

Part II, Fol. 12.

Lett[rs] of Administration granted vnto Rachell Preble of the Estate of her deceased husband Stephen Preble the Estate being vallued one hundred seventy one p[d] 12s : & Natt[ll] Preble and Sam[ll] Bragdon security to the vallue of three hundred forty three pound four shillings that the sd Rachell Preble respond all Just Debts

Administration Granted vnto Sarah Preble of the Estate of her Deceased husband Joseph Preble the Estate being vallued at ninty nine pound ninteene shillings Abraham Preble & John Reding security

Administration granted vnto Hannah Milbery of the Estate of her Deceased husband william Milbery the Estate being vallued thirty nine pound ten shillings Abraham Preble & Natt[ll] Preble securyty

| Grand Jurys p[r]sentm[ts] | George Norton for not attending the publick worship of god William Hilton for the same Crime | The town of Kittery for not maintaining & allowing the kings highway according to law |

[12]

Charles Brissum Complaines against Jos Carline

It is ordered that the Constable shall deliver vnto Elizabeth Carline one Coate, and Manty Coate, one gold ring, two silke Hoods, one siluer bodkin, which was formerly her Mothers and the rest of the goods into the hands of Charles Brissume

Whereas Sarah Trickie widdow Complaines against George Lidden trespassing vpon her land in pulling Downe her fence and hindring her from planting these severall yeares. for the prevention thereof this Court Doth order

Part II, Fol. 12.

John Wincoll Lieut William Fernald & Mr William Screven to veiw their bounds and Make returne theirof to the next Court of sessions held in yorke in the province of Maine

It is ordered by this Court that the select men of ye town of yorke Doe forthwith meet together and make a rate for ye payment of Mr Shubaell Dumers sallary being for the yeare past

It is ordered that there be a Day of publick thanksgiueing kept on the fift Day of November next & all servile worke on that Day is hereby prohibited

Whereas Elizabeth Carline was Justly Convicted of her great abuses Done to their Maties Constable of yorke and was ordered to be gagged, Mrs Mary Weare became bound for her Good behaviour promising that If the sd Elizabeth shall in any ways act Contrary to their Maties lawes with her tongue in abusing any person : she will suffer in her owne person for sd Elizabeth·

Province   In their Maties names October 7th 1691/
of maine

A Court of pleas held in yorke before their Maties Justices of ye peace Capt Francis Hooke Deputy p^rsident Maj^r Charles Frost and Mr Samuell Wheelewright

It is ordered that the first fines that shall come into the treasury of this pvince shall be to satisfie the expences of the Grand Jury at the house of Joseph Molton in yorke

It is ordered that there shall be a Court of sessions on the last tuesday of December next held at yorke

Part II, Fol. 13.

It is Declared in Court that William Hillton hath forfeited his bond of ten pounds

It is ordered that there be a speedy warrant Issued out for delinquents

Licence is granted to Joseph Molton of yorke for retaileing of wine beere and Liquor and is bound to our soveraign lord the king in the sum of ten pound that he shall keepe good order according to law ·

Province [13]
of maine In their Maties names December 29 : 1691
    A Court of sessions of the peace holden at yorke before their Maties Deputy p^rsident & Justices of the peace of this pvince

The names of the Grand Jury viz : Mr John Penwill foreman
Daniell Stone   Thomas Rice   Henry Simson
Andrew Neale   Jonathan Hamond   John Harman
Stephen Tobie   Nicholas Cole   Thomas Wise ·
Thomas Hunscome   Josiah Litlefeild   Pendleton Flecther
Richard Cutt

George Norton and William hilton being Sumoned & called to answere their presentments appeared not, therefore a especiall warrant to be Issued out against them to the next Court

William Hilton being bound in ten pounds to answere the Complaint of Thomas Wise at this Court & not appeareing his bond is Declared forfeit

Part II, Fol. 13.

Thomas Wise appeareing to prosecute is Cleared of his bond and is now bound in the sum of ten pounds to o^r sov^{rne} Lord the King to prosecute his Complaint against sd Hilton at the next Court

Jonathan Hamond and Josiah Litlefeild for non appearance on the Grand Jury are fined Each of them thirteen shillings & foure pence

George Snell is plaintiff in an action of Scire Facias to the vallue of seven pound fifteen shillings Money Contra Stephen Hardison defend^t the Court finds for the plaintiff seven pound fifteen shilling Damage in Money and Costs of Court eighteene shillings

A Court of sesssions of the peace appointed to be held at yorke on the first Tuesday in June Next and a Court of Comon pleas to be held the next Day following in the same place

Thursday the fourteenth Day of January next is appointed to be kept a Day of sollemn fasting and prayer throughout this province

Licence is Granted to Francis Litlefeild of Wells to sell strong beere victualls by retaile in his house

Nathaniell Kene ownd himsefe bound vnto our soveraign Lord & Lady the King and Queen in the sum of twenty pounds that he will personally appeare at the next Court of sessions of the peace in this pvince and in the meane time to be of good to their Maties and all their leidg subjects

In answere to a petition of Mr Richard Cutt of Kittery this Court Doth Impower the select men of Kittery with

PART II, FOL. 14.

the towns surveigher to bound his land according to the former agreement of M{r} Robert Cutt with the sd towne

The grand : Jurys pre : sentments : viz :
Wee present the lower part of Kittery for want of a ferry at sd point
Wee present phillip babs and Liddia Bragden for fornication
Wee p'sent George Norton & William Hilton for not frequenting the publick worship of God

Stephen Tobie
presents John Cater and Mary Wittam for fornication
Wee present Thomas Adams for theft

Jn⁰ Penwill
presents John Bracy for a comon lyer

[14]
At a court of sessions of peace held at yorke before Capt Francis Hooke, Maj{r} Charles Frost M{r} Sam{ll} Wheelewright & M{r} Abraham Preble, their Ma{ties} Justices of the peace in this County of yorkshiere the first Day of Novem{br} 1692/

Viz{t} :
John Wincoll Chosen Clarke

The names of the Grand Jury viz{t}
John Harman foreman
Thomas Rice James Plaisted Nicholas Cole John Nason
John Alcock Thomas Trafton Jeremy Storer Thomas Spiney
John Banks Samuell Hath Daniell Goodin Alexander Denett

The new Highway lately cutt by order of Major Hutchinson betweene yorke & pascataque river from Thomas Traftons to John Woodmans is approued of and a ferry to be kept from Withers point to Strawbery banke and to be al-

Part II, Fol. 14.

lowed fifteen pence for a man & horse & fiue pence for a man when he goes alone The sd ferry being setled vpon John Woodman & his heires, he and they keeping and attending it with sufficient boate or Gundelo for horse and man

The Constables of yorke & well Complaining to this Court that they prosecuting hue & cry after Thomas Healy, a soldier vnder Capt Converse and John Boden a soldier vnder Capt Rogers, they both stood vpon their gaurd and would not be taken, it is therefore ordered that their respectiue Captains shall be desired to secure them that they may be forth comeing for their answere

A ferry appointed to be kept at Thomas Traftons over york river & to be allowed six pence for horse & man & two pence for a single person

Margaret Buckland p'sented for fornication is sentenced to receiue eleven stripes on the bare skin or to pay a fine of forty shillings to their Maties forthwith & Mr Sam^ll Wheelewright to see ye Execution Done

This Cour orders Jno Wincoll y^r Clarke to take the records of this County into his Custody (that are with Mr Hutchinson in Boston) and to pervse them as occasion may require

Administration is Granted to Hannah Preble on the Estate of her husband John Preble late of yorke deceased and the said Hannah Preble and Leiut Abraham Preble stand bound to our soveraigne Lord & lady the King & Queene in the sum of a hundred & fifty pounds that the sd Hannah Preble shall Administer on sd Estate according to law

Part II, Fol. 15.

Thomas Adams ownes himselfe equally bound with Sarah Masterson & Arthur Bragden in the late Administration Granted to said Sarah Masterson March 8th 169½

[15]
The widdow Elizabeth Addams is Joined with her sone Thomas Adams in the Administration on her deceased husbands Estate

The Estate of Nathaniell Addams being 60£ 18ˢ is to be delivered to the widdow Elizabeth Addams fo the vse of Nath Adams Child

Administration is granted vnto Leiut Abraham preble of yorke on the Estate of Henry Simson late of yorke deceased and said Leiut Abraham Preble and Lewes Beane stand bound vnto yr Maties in ye sum of foure hundred and thirty pounds that the sd Abraham Preble shall Administer on sd estate according to law

Administration is granted to Benjamin Preble on the Estate of Cooper, & sd Benjamin Preble and Job Curtis stand bound to oʳ souᵐ Lord & Lady the King & Queene in the sum of seventy six pound that the said Benjamin Preble shall Administer on sd Estate according to law

John Woodman freed from his bond for the peace

Administration granted to Mʳˢ Mary Were on the Estate of her deceased Husband Peter Were late of yorke an sd Mary Were as principle and John Harman as surety stand bound vnto oʳ sovernigne Lord & Lady the King & Queen in the sum of foure hundred sixty & two pounds that sd Mary were shall Administer on sd Estate according to law

A court of sessions of yᵉ peace appointed to held at yorke on the last tuesday of March next

Part II, Fol. 16.

Administration is Granted vnto Abraham Preble Jun[r] and John Harman on the Estate of Nathaniell Preble deceased and sd Abraham Preble Jun[r] & John Harman stand bound vnto our soveraigne Lord & Lady the King & Queen in the sum of two hundred pounds that they the sd Abraham Preble Jun[r] and John Harman shall Administer on sd Estate According to law

Administration is granted to Elizabeth Parsons on the Estate of John Parsons her husband Deceased and sd Elizabeth parsons as principle and William Hilton and Thomas Trafton as suretyes stand bound to our soveraigne Lord and Lady the King and Queen in the sum of a hundred and twenty pounds that the sd Elizabeth Parsons shall Administer on sd Estate according to law

Matthew Austin of yorke hath Lycence to keepe a house of publicke Entertainement giueing twenty pound security and sd Austin ownes himselfe bound vnto o[r] soveraigne Lord & Lady the King & Queen in the sum of twenty pounds to obserue the lawes provided in that Case for the regulating of ordinaryes

[16]
Phillip Bab and Liddia his wife presented for fornication are sentenced to receiue seven stripes a peece on the bare skin or to pay forty shillings and M[r] Preble to see Execution Done

Thomas Addams p[r]sented for suspision of theft is Cleared paying 5[s]

Ordered that what Damage shall be done to Nicholas Weeks by the New highway goeing through his land he shall be satisfied according to law:

Part II, Fol. 17.

Ordered that the twenty acres of land between bass coue and the Mill in yorke that was John perses be forth with laid Laid out by the select men of york according to yᵉ grants

The grand Juryes pʳsentmᵗˢ

Wee present James Warrin & Mary his wife of barwick for fornication

Wee also pʳsent William Fost & Margery his wife of Barwick for fornication

Wee pʳsent Mathew austin of yorke for selling strong drinke by retale

Wee present Jeremiah Molton of yorke for selling strong drink by retale

Wee pʳsent Hannah Frethy widdow of yorke for selling strong drink by retayle

Wee pʳsent Rachell Credefur yᵉ wife of Joseph Credefur for fornication

of wels   Wee present Jane Litlefeild for selling strong Drinke by retaile

of wells   Wee pʳsent John Clais & Nathaniell Clais for selling strong drink by retaile

[17]

County of yorkshiere   A Court of sessions of the peace held at yorke Aprill 4 1693 before Capᵗ Francis Hooke Majʳ Charles Frost Mʳ Samˡˡ Wheelewright and Leiuᵗ Abraham Preble Esquʳ their Maᵗⁱᵉˢ Justices of this County

The names of yᵉ grand Jury vizᵗ   Thomas Donell John Alcock Thomas Abbet Senʳ John Banks Jonathan Hamond Richard Bryer Daniell Goodin Junʳ Samˡˡ Hatch John Claise Thomas Spiney James Plaisted Mʳ Jnᵒ Wheelewright Alexander Denet Thomas Trafton John Heard

Part II, Fol. 17.

Capt Francis hooke chosen Treasurer of the County of yorke

M[r] John Woodman freed by proclamation from his bond to y[e] peace paying fees

Francis Avant freed by proclamation from his bond to y[e] peace paying fees

Hannah Frethy being presented by the Grand Jury for selling strong Drinke by retaile vppon her acknowledgment is Cleared paying fees 3[s] and hath liberty to sell beare sider & victualls

Lycence Granted to M[r] John Wheelewright to sell strong beere cyder and victualls in the town of Wells for y[e] yeare Ensueing pd 5[s]

John Clayse & Nathaniell Clayse being presented for selling strong Drinke by retaile are Cleared paying Cour fees: 6[s] pd

Mathew Austin being presented for selling strong Drinke by retaile is Cleared paying Court fees, 3[s]

Joseph Storer of wells is licenced to sell strong beere cyder and victualls in the town of wells for the yeare ensueing

Jeremy Molton presented for selling strong Drinke vppon his submission to the Court is Cleared paying fees 3[s] 6[d]

The Constable of yorke ordered to Deliver the Goods taken out of the hands of Nathaniell Blackledg in to the hands of Henry Milbery for his security

PART II, FOL. 18.

Mr William Screven & Richard Cutt for non apearance on the Jury are fined 13ˢ 4ᵈ a peece — passed by

County of yorke   A Court of Common pleas held at yorke before Capt Job Alcock Capt Francis Hooke Maj^r Charles Frost and Mr Samuell Wheelewright y^r Maties Justices of peace aprill 5 1693

no business appearing the court is Dissolued

Arthur Beale being apprehended on suspision of stealeing a Jett or boat buckett & a peece of a roade from Capt Hooke and being found in his boate saith he knowes not how they came there is sentenced to pay thirty shillings to Capt Hooke and to pay a fine of twenty shillings to y^r Maties or to receiue ten stripes and to pay Costs 5 shillings

Arthur beale stands bound in fiue pounds to appeare at the next Quarter sessions to answer John Reding in behalfe of Roger Kelly for a Coate of his found in sd beals boate

[18]

John Reding in behalfe of Roger Kelly stands bound in fiue pounds to prosecute Arthur beale at the next Quarter sessions

Vppon complaint of Dorathy Moore of yorke, the select men of yorke to lay out a highway to the land that was formerly James Wiggens land

Administration is granted to James Emery Junr on the Estate of Phineas Hull late of yorke Deceased and sd James & his father James Emery Senr stand bound in the sum of

Part II, Fol. 18.

thirty pounds that the said James Emery Jn^r shall bring in a true Inventory of sd Estate to the next Quarter sessions and Administer on sd Estate according to law

A Court of oyer and Terminer held by especiall Comission for tryall of Murther &c before Capt Francis Hooke Maj^r Charles Frost & Mr Samuell Wheelewright at yorke: Aprill 5^t 1693/

The Grand Jury:

Jonathan Hamond:	William Sayer	James Litlefeild
Nicholas Cole	Jeremy Molton	John Banks
John Claise	Lewes Beane	Thomas Spiney
John Wheelewright	Thomas Donell	Alexander Denett
		Thomas Trafton

The Grand Jury passing vpon the Indictme againt Baker Nason brought in their verdict and found that Baker Nason Did Kill his brother Jonathan Nason

The names of the Jury of life and Death
Joseph Hamond foreman

Mr John Shapleigh	John Morrell	John Harman
Nicholas Weeks	Nathaniell Raines	Richard Bryer
Peter Dixon	Lt Joseph Storer	John Alcock
Richard King	Arthur Cane	

The Juryes Verdict vizt

Whereas Baker Nason was Indicted to this Court for wilfully murthering of his brother Jonathan Nason

The Jury finds him not Guilty

Jos Hamond foreman

The Court accepts y^e verdict
& allows for costs 14$^£$: 15^s : 06^d

PART II, FOL. 19.

County [19]
of yorke   A court of sessions of the peace held at yorke
July 4th this 4th Day of July 1693 before Capt Francis
1693   Hooke Maj^r Charles Frost Esq^{rs} and others their
Maties Justices of y^e peace of this County of
yorke

The Constable of Wells Joseph Taylor being called & not Makeing returne of his warrant to sumon in the Grand Jury is fined 13^s 4^d

    The names of the Grand Jury
Mr William Screven foreman
Leiut William Fernald   Benoni Hodsden   Arthur Kane
  Mr John Shapleigh   James Emery Junr Nathaniell Raines
    Richard King   Thomas Manaring   Lewes Beane
  Jonathan Hamond Samuell Bragden   Richard Cutt

Lycence is Granted to James Stagpole of barwick to sell by retaile beere Cyder rum provision and lodging he giueing ten pounds bond to their Maties to obserue the laws in that case provided

As an adition to Mr John Wheelewrights licence Aprill 4th he hath liberty to sell wine Rhum

    The Grand Jury for the next yeare
Mr William Sceven Benoni Hodsden James Emery Junr Robert Cutt John Leighton Richard Rogers Richard Endle Samuell Bragdon Senr Arthur Bragdon Senr Richard Bray Ezekiell Knights Daniell Litlefeild Jonathan Litlefeild
Iles of Shoules to Choose a man & Mr Kelly to giue him his oath

Part II, Fol. 20.

Rachell Credefur p'sented for fornication appeared not but her husband appeareing in her behalfe referd it to the Court and is fined twenty shillings or the woman to receiue seven stripes on the bare skin at the post and Mr Wheelewright to see the Execution speedily Done

Mr William Screven & Mr Richard Cutt being fined 13ˢ 4ᵈ a peece for non appearance on the Jury giuoing satisfieing answere were Cleared payin fees 2ˢ

Jane Litlefeild being presented for selling strong Drinke witho .. Lycence by retaile in two presentments refers it to the Court is fined twenty shillings & costs of Court fiue shillin .. eight shillings is remitted and the rest paid

Arthur Beale appeareing to answere his bond giuen of 5 p ..... at the last Quarter sessions to answer John Reding in beha .. of Roger Kelly for a Coate of sd Kellys found in sd beales boate beale is fined ten shillings to their Maties & to pay 15ˢ to Mr Roger Kelly and fees 5ˢ

Richard Beale answering to his presentment is to . . . . . . monished and to pay fees fiue shillings: which . . . . .

[20]

Alice Mathrell being Called to answere her presentment appeared not she not appeareing is to answere before three Justices

James Smith answereing in behalfe of his wife who was p'sented for fornication refers it to ye Court & is fined twenty shillings & fees 5ˢ

Hannah Freathy hath Liberty granted to sell beere cyder and victualls she keeping good order in her house

Part II, Fol. 20.

Mr Roger Kelly hath lycence granted to sell rhum wine beere cyder for the yeare Ensueing & victualls

Lycence is Granted to John Woodman to keepe a publick Entertainment for men and horses to sell Rhum wine Cyder beere & victualls giueing bond to obserue the lawes

The widdow Elizabeth Parsons Complaining against William Hilton for taking a cow from her sd Hilton is ordered to returne the cow to her or another as Good in her roome

At a quarter sessions this 4th of July 1693/
presentments made to sd Court by the grand Jury

Wee present the Constable of Barwick for breach of his oath in not Makeing a returne of a somons according to law wherein he was required to sumon in to this Court severall Delinquents as in page 60

Wee present Capt John Litlefeild of Wells for selling Drinke by retale without lycence

Wee present Jane Litlefeild of wells for selling Drinke without lycence in page 26

Wee present Mr John Wheelewright and Joseph Storer of wells Inkeepers for keeping keeles and boules at their houses Contrary to law page 27.

Wee present the Constable of the northerne parts of the Isles of Shoules for breach of oath in not makeing a true returne of a warrant wherein he was required to warne a town meetting and to sumon in the Jury men according to law page 60:

Signed by me William Screven foreman
& by consent & order of ye Grand Juror

County [21]
of york   October 3ᵈ 1693

At a Court of sessions of the peace held at wells befor yᵉ majesties Justices of the peace vizᵗ Majʳ Francis Hooke Mʳ Samuell Wheelewright Mʳ Roger Kelly & Mʳ Abraham Preble Esquⁿ this 3ᵈ Day of October 1693

The names of the Grand Jury Vizᵗ Mʳ William Screven foreman

Mʳ Richard Cutt	Benoni Hodsden	Arthur Bragden
Richard Endell	James Emery Junʳ	Jonathan Litlefeild
Richard Rogers	Samuel Bragden	Daniell Litlefeild
John Leighton	Richard Bray	Ezekiell Knights

Thomas Manary of the Isles of Shoules sumoned to serue of the Grand Jury & not appeareing Is fined thirteen shillings & 4 pence

Nathan Lord Constable of Barwick in answere to his presentment for not makeing returne of his warrant to sumon delinquents is Cleared paying fees

Lieuᵗ John Wheelewright pʳsented for keeping Keeles neare his ordinary is Cleared

Leiuᵗ Joseph Storer is also Cleared of the like pʳsentment

George Perkins of the Isles of Shoules Constable pʳsented for breach of oath in not Makeing returne of a warrant &c Mʳ Roger Kelly is Impoured to heare & Determine it

James Warren and Mary his wife and William Fost & his wife being presented for fornication & doe withdraw & will not be found by the Constable it is ordered that the Clarke shall giue Especiall warrant to seize them and take tenn

Part II, Fol. 22.

pounds bond of each for their appeareance at the next sessions or keepe in safe Custody for their appeareance there

Arthur Beale appeareing to answere his bond & the Complaint of Mr Nathaniell Raines for stealeing a bay mare & colt & sd Raines not being in Capasity to make out the Charge at present but saith he can & will Doe it their bonds are continewed vntill the next sessions in January next

Matthew Austin of yorke his lycence for keepeing of the ordinary is Renewed for the yeare Ensueing

The Jury for the next yeare

Leiut Storer	Thomas Adams	Nicholas Tucker
Jonathan Hamonds	Job Young	Thomas Dering
Samuell Hatch	Thomas Abbett Senr	John Morrell
Daniell Levingstone	William Spencer	Samuell Spiney
	William Lakeman	

Jeremiah Molton being brought before this Court for threatening the Constable of yorke to shoot him when he was in the Execution of his office & sd Molton haueing a gun in his hand Did also threaten to shoot a Justice of ye peace vizt Leiut Preble that was present with the Constable, is fined to y^r Majesties the sum of ten pounds and to giue fifty pounds bond to y^r Maties for his good behaviour and appearan .. at the next Quarter sessions and to pay Costs: vizt

[22]

	£	s	d
To the Constable of yorke	00	03	00
To Phillip welch a witness	00	03	00
To Andrew Shaw a witness	00	01	00
To the recognisance	00	02	06
To the Sherriff	00	08	06
To fees of court	00	04	00
	01	02	00

vppon his humble acknowledgm^t and request the Court remits three pounds of the said fine of ten pounds, the other seven pounds to be forthwith payd.

Part II, Fol. 22.

Jeremiah Moulton appeareing before this Court Did acknowledg himselfe to stand bound to our soveraigne Lord and Lady King William and Queen Mary in the sum of fifty pounds that he will be of good behaviour toward their Maties and all their leidge subjects and to make his personall appeareance before their Maties Justices at the next Quarter sessions to be held at wells on the first tuesday of January next and for security binds over his houses and lands in yorke whereon he now Dwells

Ordered that the hay in controversy between Leiut Abraham Preble and Jeremiah Molton be by the Constable of yorke delivered to said Abraham Preble haueing giuen forty shillings bond to answere sd Molton at the next Quarter sessions in what Claime he may make to the said hay

Vppon Complaint of Dyvers persons for want of the records It is ordered that the Clarke of the court shall goe to Boston for the records that are with Mr Hutchinson and with Captin Scottow takeing the aprobation of his Exelency and Councill

At a Court of Quarter sessions held by their Maties Justices of ye peace at Wells October ye 3. 1693/

Wee the Grand Jury hereafter Mentioned

of Kittery

Wee present John Gowen alias Smith and Mercy Hamon that was for fornication presentable p the law fo : 16

Wee present William Saunders and Sary his wife for vnnessesary travaileing on the lords Day — page : 28 : 29

Wells presented for want of a paire of stockes
p the appointment & in the behalfe of ye Grand Jury
     Signed by me William Screven foreman

Wee present Kittery : Barwick yorke & Wells for not takeing due Care to provide them Ministers according to law   Signed p me William Screven foreman

[23]

County of yorke   January 2ᵈ 169¾
A Court of sessions of the peace held at Wells before Majʳ Francis Hooke Majʳ Charles Frost & Mʳ Samuell Wheelewright Esquⁿ their Maᵗⁱᵉˢ Justices of yᵉ peace in yᵉ County of yorke

The names of the Grand Jury vizᵗ
Jonathan Hamond foreman

Leiut Joseph Storer	Job young	Samuell Spiney
Samuell Hatch	Nicholas Tucker	Isack Remich
Thomas Adams	Thomas Dering	Jabez Jenkins
Daniell Levingstone	John Morrell	Rowland young

William Spencer fined 13s 4d for non appeareance on the Grand Jury

William Sanders & his wife presented the last quarter sessions for vnnessesary travelling on the lords Day the heareing of it is referd to the next Quarter sessions at yorke

Arthur Beale bound by recognisance in ten pound to this Court appeared

Complaint being Entred the last sessions by mʳ Nathaniell Raines against Arthur Beale for stealeing a bay mare and Colt and their bonds Continewed till this Court for tryall Arthur Desires a Jury which is Granted for the tryall of yᵉ Case and the Jury of tryalls are as followeth vizᵗ

Jonathan Hamond foreman,	Job young	Samuell Spiney
Samuell Hatch	Nicholas Tucker	Isack Remich
Thomas Adams	Thomas Dering	Jabez Jenkins
Daniell Levingstone	John Morrell	Rowland young

Part II, Fol. 24.

M{r} Nathaniell Raines plaintiff against Arthur Beale defendent the Jury finds for the defendent Costs of Court one pound seventeene shillings and three pence and twelue shillings to the Constable of yorke

The Grand Jury for the next yeare   Richard Tozer Joshua Downing Rouland young John Morrell John Cooper M{r} John Wheelewright M{r} William Peprill Joseph Wilson Jeremy Storer Nicholas Tucker Jabez Jenkins Nathaniell Clayes Thomas Dering

Joshua Remich being bound to this Court with suretyes his bonds are Continewed till the next sessions

M{r} Preble & Jeremiah Moltons Case about the hay is continewed till the next sessions

James Warren Jun{r} Voluntarily appeareing for his owne and his wifes presentment for fornication is fined twenty shillings & to pay 5{s} fees which he paid Down

Mercy Gowen Alias Smith being presented for fornication vpon her Humble petition to Excuse her absence is fined thirty shillings & to pay fiue shillings fees which was paid

[24]
Arthur Beale bound by recognisance to apeare at this Court to answere for Discorageing a soldier who was hired to goe to Sacoe to reliue Daniell Merrey and Convaying said soldier away is fined fifteene shillings and to pay Costs viz{t} the recognisance 2{s} Cour fees 5{s} the bill of costs 8{s} in all 15{s}

Jeremiah Molton being bound over vnto this Court vppon the Good behaviour & being vppon his delivery from his bonds there came in New Evidence against him by Maj{r}

PART II, FOL. 24.

Hooke for threatening sd Maj^r Hooke in the high way: at the first sd Molton denied that he met sd Maj^r Hooke alone but soone after said that If he did threaten him the sd Maj^r Hooke provoaked him to it: the Court vppon the sd Moltons request for respiting the case till the next Quarter sessions at yorke, Did grant it, and his bonds are continewed vntill sd Court.

Robert Hilton presented by ye grand Jury for Exessiue Drinkeing & it appeareing to be at least the second time is fined fiue shilings to the pore of the towne of wells and to stand bound to the good behaviour with suretyes in the sum of ten pounds till the next Quarter sessions & sd Robert Hilton to pay ye Clarks fees 2^s pd

Robert Hilton as principle & m^r John Wheelewright and Jonathan Hamond as suretyes acknowledg themselues bound vnto our soveraigne lord & Lady the King & Queene in the sum of ten pounds that the said Robert Hilton shall be of good behaviour till the next Quarter sessions and sd Robert Hilton acknowledgeth his land & meadowes in wells to stand Engaded to sd Wheelewright & sd Hamond for their security

Whereas there is great Complaint for want of the records this Court with the advice of the grand Jury Doe order that the records of this County which are at Boston shall be speedily sent for and brought to Leuit william Fernalds House vppon his Island and Kept there till further order and ye Clarke of this Court to fetch them as soone as may be and the sheriff to Deliver him thirty shillings to pay for the bookes in Capt Scottows hand which are a part of the County records

Presentments made by the Grand Jury at a Court of sessions held at wells this second Day of January 1693/

Wee present Samuell Miller and Mary Neale the wife of the sd Samuell Miller for fornication

Wee present Robert Hilton for Excessiue Drinking

Jona^t Hamond foreman

[25]

At a court of sessions of the peace held at yorke the 3^d Day of Aprill 1694 before Maj^r Francis Hooke Maj^r Charles Frost & Mr Abraham Preble Esqu^{rs} theire Maties Justice of this County of yorke

The Grand Jury were M William Peprill foreman

Mr Josua Downing	Nathaniell Clayes	John Morrell
Mr John Wheelewright	Rowland Young	Joseph Wilson
Jeremy Storer	Nicholas Tucker	Richard Tozer
Nathaniell Raines	Thomas Dercing	John Cooper

Josuua Remick appeareing to answere his bond for apearance at this Court the woman that was the occasion of his bonds by Charging him sd Remich of being the father of the Child she was great withall and being not yet delivered sd Remich his bonds are continewed to the nex Quarter sessions

Samuell Miller appeareing to answere his presentment for fornication ownes the fact and is fined thirtie shillings and court fees or ten stripes and fees and his wife to be sumoned to answere at the next sessions

Robert Hilton Cleared from his bond of the good behauiour by proclamation

Thomas Rice fined for sweareing ten shillings to the pore of the towne of Kittery & fees

PART II, FOL. 26.

John Woodman fined ten shillings to the poore of the towne of Kittery for sweareing & fees

John Wooman Thomas Rice Jabez Jenkins and John Wormwood are fined fiue shillings a peece for Quarrelling and fees of Court and John Woodman to stand bound to their Ma[ties] in fiue pound to the Good behaviour till the next sessions

Lycence is Granted vnto Sarah Nason to keepe a house of publicke Entertainment to sell wine, Rhum Cyder beere &c for the yeare Ensuing and stand bound vnto y[r] Ma[ties] and Jabez Jenkins stands bound with her that shee shall obserue the law in that Case provided

Lycence is granted to Leiut Joseph Storer to keepe a house of publicke Entertainment to sell wine rhum cyder beere &c: for the yeare Ensueing and ownes himself bound to their Ma[ties] in the sum of tenn pounds to obserue the laws provided in that Case

[26]

Lycence is Granted to M[r] John Wheelewright to keepe a house of publicke Entertainment to sell wine, Ruhm, Cyder, beere &c for y[e] yeare Ensueing and ownes himselfe to stand bound vnto their Ma[ties] in the sum of ten pounds to obserue the lawes provided in that Case

Lycence is Granted to M[r] William Peprill to sell wine, ruhm, Cyder, and beere &c: by retale out of Dores for the yeare Ensueing

Presentments made by the Grand Inquest for the body of this County of yorke at a Court of Quarter sessions held at yorke the 3[d] day of Aprill 1694

PART II, FOL. 26.

<small>witnes
Christian
Remick</small>
Wee present James Stagpole for selling strong drinke by retale

<small>Witnes
Major ffrost</small>
Wee p^rsent Edward Baile & Elizabeth Baile for Co͞mitting fornication

We p^rsent John Lisen & Mary his wife for Committing fornication

Wee present John Furbush for breach of the sabbath

Wm Peprell foreman

At an Inferiour Court of Comon pleas held at yorke Aprill 4th 1694

Phillip Atwell acknowledged a Judgement of ten pounds in fish at price Currant to Mr Francis Tucker of New Castle in the province of New Hamsheire Merc^t

John Tiney Senr acknowledged a Judgment of foure pounds : vizt fifty shillings thereof to be paid in fish at price Currant and the other thirty shillings in Mony to Mr Francis Tucker of the towne of New castle in the province of New hamshiere Merch^t

The Grand Jury for the Court Ensueing are
John Harman foreman

Thomas Goodin	James Plaisted	William Lakeman
Abraham Lord	Nathaniell Raines :	William Sayer
Enoch Hutchins	Peter Dixon	John Eldredg
Joseph Weekes	Richard Gowell	Thomas Cole
Leiut Joseph Storer	Jonathan Litlefeild	

[27]

William and Mary by the Grace of god of England Scotland France and Ireland King and Queen defenders of the faith &ᶜ To our trustey & welbeloued William Stoughton, John Richards, Nathanael Saltonstall, Wait Winthrop, John Phillips, James Russell, Samuell Sewall, Samuell Appellton, Bartholomew Gedney, John Hathorn, Elisha Hutchinson, Robert Pike Jonathan Corwin John Joyliffe, Adam Winthrop, Richard Midlecutt, John Foster, Peter Sergeant, Joseph Lynde, Samuell Hayman, William Bradford, John Walley, Barnabas Lathrop, Job Alcock, Samuell Donnel, Silvanus Davis, Isaac Addington, Francis Hooke, Charles Frost, Samuell Wheelewright, Abraham Preeble, Roger Kelly, and William Lakeman Esquires Greeting, Know ye that wee haue Assigned you and Every one of you Jointly and severally our Justices to keepe our peace in our County of yorke within our province of the Massachusetts bay in New England, and to keepe and Cause to be kept all lawes & ordinances made for the Good of the peace and for the Conservation of the same and for the quiet rule and government of our people in all and every the articles thereof in the County aforesaid according to the force forme and Effect of the same, And to Chastise and punish all persons offending against the fforme of these said lawes and ordinances or any of them in the County aforesd as according to the fforme of these lawes and ordinances shall be fit to be done, And to Cause to Come before you, or any of you all those persons who shall threaten any of our people in their person or in burning their houses, to find Sufficient security for the peace or for the good behauiour towards vs and our people and If they shall refuse to find such securitie then to Cause them to be kept safe in Prison vntill they find such security We haue also assigned you and every three or more of you (wherof any of you the sd

PART II, FOL. 28.

Job Alcock Samuell Donnell Francis Hooke Charles Frost & Samuell Wheelewright shall be one) our Justices to Enquire by the oath of good and lawfull men of the County aforesaid by whom the truth may be the better knowne, of all and all manner of petty larcenys, thefts trespasses fforestallings Regratings Ingrossings and Extortions whatsoever and of all and singular other Misdeeds and offences of which Justices of the peace May or ought lawfully to Enquire, [28] by whomsoever or howsoever Done or perpretated or which hereafter shall happen howsoever to be Done or attempted in the County aforesaid, And of all those who in the county aforesaid haue either gone or Ridden or that hereafter presume to goe or ride in Companyes with armed force against the peace to the Disturbance of our people; and also of all those who in like manner haue lien in waite, or hereafter shall præsume to lie in waite to maim or kill our people, And also of Innholders and of all and singular other persons who haue offended or attempted or hereafter shall presume to offend or Attempt in the abuse of waights or Measures or in the sale of victualls against the formes of the lawes and ordinances or any of them in that behalfe made for the common good of this province and the people thereof in the County aforesd; And also of all sherriffs, bayliffs, Constables goalers and other officers whatsoever who in the Execution of their offices about the premises or any of them haue vnlawfully demeaned themselues, or hereafter shall presume vnlawfully to demeane themselues, or hereafter shalbe Careless remiss or Negligent in the County aforesaid and of all and singular articles and Circumstances, And all other things whatsoever by whomsoever and howsoever Done or perpetrated in the County aforesaid or which shall hereafter happen howsoever to be done or attempted in any wise more fully concerning the truth of the premises or any of them And to Inspect all Indictm[ts] whatsoever so before you or any of you taken or to be taken or made or taken before others late Justices of the peace in the County aforesaid and not as yet determined and to make and continew the process therevpon against all and singular persons so Indicted before you vntill they be apprehended. render themselues, or be outlawed; And to heare and determin all and singular ye petty larcenys, thefts trespasses, forestallings Regrateings, Ingrossings, Extortions, vnlawfull assemblyes, Indictments aforesaid, And all and singular other the p^{r}mises according to law And therefore We Command you and Every of you that you dilligently attend the keeping of the peace lawes and ordinances and all and singular other the p^{r}mises, And at certaine Dayes and places, which you, or any such three, or more of you as is aforesd shall in that behalfe appoint, or by law shall be appointed to make Inquiry vppon the premises, And heare and determin all and singular the p^{r}mises and performe and fullfill [**29**] the same in forme aforesaid Doeing therein that which to Justice apperteineth according to the Laws and ordinances aforesaid And we Command by vertue of these presents the Sherriffe of the said County of yorke that at certaine Dayes and places which you or any such three or more of you as aforesaid shall make known vnto him, or that shall be by law appointed as aforesd he cause to come before you or such three or more of you as aforesaid, such and so many good and lawfull men of his Bailiwick by whom the truth in the premises may be the better known and Enquired of In Testimonie whereof wee haue Caused the publick seal of our province of the Massachusetts bay in New England to be herevnto affixed: Witness Sr William Phips K^{nt} our Captain Generall and Governour in Cheife in and over our said province of the Massachusets bay at Boston the thirtieth Day of May in the fourth yeare of our Reign Annoq$_3$ Dmi 1692   William Phips

By order of his Ex^{cy} the
  Gouerno^r and Councill
   Jsa: Addington Sec$\tilde{r}$y

PART II, FOL. 30.

[30]

County of yorke   At their Majestyes Court of Quarter sessions of the peace holden at yorke the 3ᵈ Day of July 1694 before their Maᵗⁱᵉˢ Justices : viz Majʳ Francis Hooke, Majʳ Charles Frost and Mʳ Abraham Preble Esquʳˢ

The names of the Grand Jury vizᵗ : Mʳ John Harman foreman
Leiut Joseph Storer   James Plaisted   Thomas Goodin
Abraham Lord   Peter Dixon   William Sayer
Enoch Huchins   Richard Gowell   John Eldredge
Joseph Weekes   Jonathan Litlefeild :   Thomas Cole

John Furbush being pʳsented for breach of sabbath is sentenced to be Admonished & is Cleared payin officers fees : 5ˢ

James Stagpole for selling strong drinke by retale nothing appeareing and haueing lycence is Cleared

Edward Baile and Elizabeth Baile pʳsented for fornication : are fined to their Maᵗⁱᵉˢ twenty shillings a peece or to receiue fiue stripes a peece & pay fiue shillings fees : yᵉ fine & fees payd

John Lisson and mary wife presented for Comitting fornication are fined to yʳ Maᵗⁱᵉˢ 25ˢ a peece or to receiue fiue stripes a peece and fees 5ˢ : paid

Nicholas Morrell bound to this Court : his bond is Continewed to the next sessions

The verdict of the Jury of Inquest on the vntimely Death of Richard Pope is allowed in Court

The verdict of the Jury of inquest on the vntimely Death of Thomas Milfort is allowed in Court

Part II, Fol. 31.

Peter Dixon hath Lycence Granted to him to sell beer Ale Cyder perry & Cakes at a litle house Distant from the publick meetting neare Christian Remichs for the yeare Ensueing and to giue ten pounds bond according to law

James Emery Sen[r] bound by recognisance to this Court is fined to their Ma[ties] twenty shillings for his abuse of Major hooke and stopping the highway and to giue ten pounds bond for the Good behaviour till the next sessions for his abuseiue carriage before the Court this Day and to stand Comitted till payd

Daniell Emery bound by recognisance to this Court is fined 3s 4d and 5s fees & to stand Comitted till payd : & is all paid

Job Emery bound by recognisance to this Court is fines to y[t] majisties 25[s] and fees 5[s] .& to stand Comitted till paid is

Lycence Granted to John Morgridg to sell beer, cyder bread and victualls for y[e] yeare Ensueing & to giue bond according to law

[31]

Lycence granted to James Stagpole to sell by retale beer Cyder victualls horsmeate & lodgeing for y[e] yeare Ensueing and to giue bond according to law

John Woodman Cleared of his bond by proclamation & fees paid

Isaac Remich his offence forgiuen vppon his pettition : & fees paid

Part II, Fol. 31.

Mr Jeremy Molton cleard of bond by pclamation vppon his humble pettition, & fees paid

Joshua Remich bound by recognisance continewed to this Court for being the reputed father of a bastard Child by Sarah Lisson being legally proued is sentenced to pay two shillings six pence p weeke from ye birth of the Child towards the Maintenance of it for seven yeares Ensueing and to Giue sufficient bond to pay it Quarterly in mony to said Sarah Lisson at her fathers house and to giue bond with sufficient surety for his good behauiour till the next Quarter sessions and to pay Costs & to stand Comitted till it be performed as aboue, : the Costs allowed said Lisson is twenty shillings : which was paid to sd Lisson in Court

Sarah Lisson being convicted of fornication in haueing a bastard Child is fined to their Majesties to pay 30^s or to receiue 9 lashes on the bare skin at the post, the fine being paid she is Cleared

John Tomson bound by recognisance to this Court for his vncivell Carriage with Sarah Lisson, Lieing on the bed with her is fined to their Maties to pay ten shillings & costs 3^s is payed & Cleared

Ordered that the Sheriff shall pay ten shillings to James Warren Constable of Kittery out of the fines for his labour and Charges about James Emery Senr and his sones

Christian Remich and Peter Dixon stand bound with Joshua Remich in ten pounds to their Majestyes that said Joshua Remich shall be of good behaviour towards their Majestyes and all their leidg subjects till the next Quarter sessions

Part II, Fol. 32.

Joshua Remich as principle and Christian Remich and Isaac Remich as sureties acknowledge themselues Jointly and severally to stand bound vnto their Majesties in the sum of fifty pounds that the said Joshua Remich shall pay two shillings and six pence p weeke in money to Sarah Lisson or to her order at her fathers house in Kittery for seven yeares from the birth of her Child according to the sentence of this Court this 4th Day of July 1694/

The presentments of the Grand Jury : vizt
Wee present Sarah Lesson for fornication
Wee present Mary Theyfts for fornication
         John Harman foreman

County [32]
of York   At their Majesties Inferi^r Court of Comon pleas holden at York July ye 4° 1694 — before Maj^r ffrancis Hook Major Charles ffrost and Cap^{tn} Job Alcock Esq^{rs} their Majesties Justices of this County of York

	1 James Plaisted fforeman/	7 Thomas Trafton
Jury	2 Benjamin Nason	8 Benjamin Preble
of tryall	3 William Gooden	9 John Green
	4 Joseph Tayler	10 Rowland Williams
	5 Moses Littlefield	11 John Spinney
	6 Jeremiah Molton	12 Jonathan Littlefield

John Shepard is Plaintiff in an action of ye case for unjustly and forcebly detayning land as p attachment, versus Nathaniell Keen Defendant. The Jury ffinds for the Plaintiff the land in Controuersy and Costs of Court

PART II, FOL. 33.

The Court acceps the verdict and ye Costs allowed, 2^£ : 10^s : 10^d / The Execution serued Septemb^r the 5° : & returned Octob^r 2^d

John Pickerin is Plaintiff in an action of ye case versus m^rs Mary Champernoun Defendant for detayning a pcell of Marsh or money as p attachm^t
The Plaintiff withdraws his action/

James Emery Senr & Joshua Downing in behalfe of the town of Kittery are Plaintiffs versus John Leighton Defendant for not fulfilling an agreement with ye Selectmen of Kittery &c as p attachment
Cast out of Court
                        Bill of Costs allowed : 11s

[33]
Abraham Lord is Plaintiff in an action of the Case, versus Ensigne Thomas Abbet and Sarah Nason Defendants for entring upon and holding in possession a Certain Legasie in Land giuen by Abraham Conley as p attachment, The Jury finds for ye Plaintiff the Marsh and land in Controuersie and Cost of Court — The Defendant appeales to the next Superi^r Court

Thomas Abbet & Sarah Nason Principles and John Morrell & Jabes Jinkins Sureties own themselues bound to their Majesties in 200^li to prosecute ye appeale to Efect at ye s^d Super^r Court

Cap^tn Joseph Hamond is Plaintiff in an action of Slander, Contra: Joshua Downing Defend^t for saying he was a great lyer &c. The Jury ffinds for ye plaintiff ten shillings & cost of Court 1^li : 12^s : 8^d — which ye Defendant payd in Court : 2^li : 12^s : 8^d

PART II, FOL. 34.

2ᵈ Jury of tryall	1 Mʳ Wᵐ ffernald fforeman	1	Jeremiah Molton
	2 Mʳ John Shapleigh	2	Thomas Trafton
	3 Benjamin Nason	3	Benjamin Preble
	4 William Gooden	4	John Geer
	5 Joseph Tayler	5	Rowland Williams
	6 Moses Littlefield	6	John Spinney
		7	Jonathan Littlefield

The Case of appeale of John Ball Plaintiff Contra Elizabeth Berry Entred yᵉ last Court Aprell: 4°: 1694 and referred to this Court, is referred to the next Court of pleas at Wells

[34]

County of York

October: 2°: 1694 At their Majesties Court of Session of yᵉ peace held at Wells before Majʳ ffrancis Hooke Major Charls ffrost Mʳ Samuell Wheelright Mʳ Samuell Donnell and Lieuᵗ Abraham Preble Esqʳˢ, their Majesties Justices of yᵉ peace

The names of yᵉ Grand Jury

1 Jonathan Hamond fforeman
2 Jeremiah Molton   8 William Goodin
3 Rowland Williams   9 Jonathan Littlefield
4 Thomas Trafton   10 Joseph Tayler
5 Benjamin Nason   11 Moses Littlefield
6 Lewis Bean   12 Benjamin Preble
7 John Spinney   13 Humphrey Spencer

John Geer not appearing on the Grand Jury is fined to their Majesties : 13ˢ : 4ᵈ

Nicholas Brown not appearing on the Grand Jury is fined to their Majesties 13ˢ : 4ᵈ

PART II, FOL. 35.

Nicholas Morrell bound to y⁰ last Sessions by recognisauince and continued to this Court is continued to y⁰ next Sessions

Mary Theyfts presented by y⁰ Grand Jury for ffornication is fined to their Majesties thirty shillings or to receiue seuen stripes at y⁰ post and pay fiue shillings ffees/ the Sentance to be Executed before Maj^r Hook within Eight dayes

John Gowen Alias Smith presented by y⁰ Grand Jury for ffornication being Sumoned & called and not appearing a speciall warrant to be Isued out for his contempt of Authority and for his appearance at y⁰ next Sessions

[35]

Lysence is granted to Mrs Joan Amerideth to sell bere sider and victualls by retayle and to giue ten pound bond to keep good order according to law in that case prouided

Joshua Remich is by proclamation cleared from his bond of the good behauiour

Mary Miller being presented & sumond to answer for ffornication & resining herselfe to the pleasure of the Court is fined to their Majesties thirty shillings or to receiue seuen stripes and pay 5⁰ ffees and Sentance to be Executed within Eight dayes before Maj^r Hooke

Lycence is granted to Matthew Austin to keep a house of publique Entertaynment according to law in the house he now liues in for y⁰ year Ensuing upon y⁰ bond that he formerly gaue, Octob^r 1692

William ffost and Margery his wife presented for ffornication and submitting themselues to this Court, are ffined to

PART II, FOL. 36.

their Majesties 20ˢ a piece and Costs of Court 5ˢ or to receiue seuen stripes a piece at yᵉ post & 5ˢ ffees

ordered that: fforty shillings p anñ be payd to a Prison keper at York

James Emery Senʳ being called and not appearing to answer his bond for yᵉ good behauiour his bond is continued till the next Sessions

[36]
Octobʳ 2º 1694

At an Inferiour Court of Comõn pleas held at Wells the 2ᵈ· day of Octobʳ 1694

John Ball is Plaintiff in an action of appeale Contra: Elizabeth Berry Defendant from a Judgement giuen by Majʳ Hook in an action of Trespass the   day of   169
The Jury finds for yᵉ Defendant a confirmation of the former Judgement & costs of Court: 6ˢ

The Grand Jury for yᵉ next Sessions
Jonathan Hamõnd fforeman

Jeremiah Molton   Moses Littlefield
Rowland Williams   John Spinney
Thomas Trafton   William Goodin
Benjamin Nason   Jonathan Littlefield
Lewis Bean   Joseph Tayler
                     Benjamin Preble

[Pages 37, 38 and 39 are blank]

William and Mary by the grace of God of England Scotland ffrance and Ireland **King** and **Queen** Defenders of the ffaith &c. **To all** to whom this shall come Greeting, **Know ye** that we haue assigned and doe hereby Constitute and appoint You Samuel Wheelwright Job Alcott Charles ffrost and William Peperill Esq[rs] our Justices of our Inferiour Court of Comon pleas within our County of York, And you or any three of you to hear Try and Determine all causes and Matters Ciuill by by law Cognizeable in said Court, And to award Execution thereupon accordingly, with authority to use and exercise all powers and Jurisdictions belonging to y[e] said Court, pursuant to an Act of our great and Generall Court or Assembly of our Prouince of the Massachusets Bay in New England Entituled an Act for y[e] Establishing of Judicatories and Courts of Justice within y[e] same/ And to doe that which to Justice doth appertain according to law. In Testimony whereof we haue Caused the Seal of our said Prouince to be hereunto affixed. **Witness** William Stoughton Esq[r] our Lieu[t] Gouern[r] and Comander in Chiefe in and ouer our said Prouince of y[e] Massachusets Bay with y[e] aduise and consent of y[e] Councill at Boston the Sixth day of March 169¾ In y[e] seuenth year of our Reign W[m] Stoughton

By order of the Lieuten[t]
  Gouernour and Council
  Is[a] Addington Secr̃y

  A true Copie of y[e] origenall Comission Transcribed and compared   p Jos Hamond Regist[r]

[The following five pages are blank and without page numbers]

PART II, FOL. 47, 48.

[47]

Anno
1694-5

County of York

At their Majesties Court of Quarter Sessions held the 1st day of January 169¾ at Wells before

Justices

ffrancis Hook Charles ffrost Samuel Wheelwright & Samuel Donnell Esqrs Justices of their Majesties peace for this County

Proclamation being made, the Grand Jurors sumoned to appear, to inquire between our Soueraign Lord & Lady the King and Queens Majesties and ye body of this County were as ffolloweth.

Jurors

Jurors

1	Jonathan Hamond foreman		
2	Jeremiah Molton	Moses Littlefield	8
3	Rowland Williams	Benjamin Preble	9
4	Thomas Trafton	Edmund Gatch	10
5	Lewis Bean	James Warren	11
6	Jonath: Littlefield	Joseph Weare	12
7	Joseph Taylor	Nicholas Cole	13

John Spinney being warned and not appearing upon the Grand Jury is fined to their Majesties : 13s 4d

[48]

Anno
1694-5

Nich Morrell

Nicholas Morrell being bound to this Court by recognesance & not appearing in time his bonds are Continued till the next Quarter Sessions

John Braun and Annah Langley

John Braun being bound to this Court by Recognisance for comitting ye act of ffornication with Annah Langley appeared in Court & owned the ffact and is sentenced to receiue seuen stripes upon the Naked back : or to pay thirty shillings to their Majesties & ffees 4s

PART II, FOL. 49.

the ffees being payd, he is acquitted
and the said Annah to be sumoned to y° next Quarter Sessions

Richd Rogers of Spruce Creek — Richard Rogers being bound to this Court by Recognisance for abusive carriage toward m^r Joseph Curtes is fined fiue shillings to their Majesties & fees : 4^s

fine & ffees being payd hee is acquitted

Richd Briar — Richd Bryar being bound to this Court by the Complaint of Nathanil Keen and appearing in Court was Cleared by proclamation — ffees payd

[49]

Anno 169 4-5 Nathaniel Keen — Nathaniell Keen bound to this Court by Recognisance by the Complaint of Richd Briar appeared in Court and cleared by proclamation. ffees payd

Benja: Nason for Swearing &c — Benjamin Nason being bound to this Court by Recognesance for Swearing Cursing and taking the name of God in vaine ffrequently and being Leagally Convicted he is Adjudged to pay ten shillings to y° Select men of Kittery for y° use of y° pore thereof, and to be Admonished — ffees payd

Bridge at Spruce crek — It is ordered at this Court that Lieu^t Jeremiah Storer Mr James Plaisted and Peter Dixon shall view the bridge built by Mr Joseph Curtes ouer Spruce Creek and Judge of the Cost thereof according to the best of their understanding and make return thereof to y° next Quarter Sessions

Presentmts of ye grand Inquest

Presentments brought into this Court by the Grand Jury is as follows

We pres^t Nathaniell Keen for suspicion of Murdering a Negro woman as appears by seuerall Euidences

[50]

Anno 1694-5

Wee present Mr William Godsoe for not ffrequenting the publique worship of God upon the Lords day

presentmts

We present Sarah Sanders the wife of William Sanders for not ffrequenting the publique worship of God upon the Lords day

We present Constant Rainking and his wife for not ffrequenting ye publique worship of God upon ye Lords day.

We present John More for selling Rhum without Lycence by retayle

Jonathan Hamond
ffloreman.

[51]

Anno 1695
Justices

At their Majesties Court of Sessions held at York at York Aprill 2° : 1695 : before Charles ffrost Samuel Wheelwright Samuel Donnell Abraham Preble & Roger Kelly : Esq^{rs} Justices of their Majesties peace for this County of York

Proclamation made the Grand Jury sumoned to appear are as ffolloweth

	Mr John Wheelwright	1	ffloreman	
	Lieu^t Jeremiah Storer	2	Christian Remich	8
Jurors	Nicholas Cole	3	Peter Dixon	9
	Mr Nathaniel Rayns	4	Joseph Couch	10
	John Parker	5	Peter Lewis	11
	Joseph Banks	6	John Heard	12
	Arthur Bragdon	7	Thomas Gooden	13

Part II, Fol. 51ᵃ.

Nicholas Morrell

Nicholas Morrell being bound to this Court by the continuance of his Recognisance for being the reputed ffather of a Bastard Child by Sarah ffry, made his appearance and noe Euidence appearing against him he is acquitted, — paying ffees : 16ˢ 6ᵈ

Sarah Sanders

Sarah Sanders being presented for not ffrequenting yᵉ publique worship of God upon the Lords day, appeared in Court and upon promise of reformation she is acquitted, paying ffees : 2ˢ and to be admonished

Admonition giuen & ffees payd in Court

[51ᵇ]

Anno 1695
Constant Rainking and his wife

Constant Rainking and his wife being presented for not ffrequenting the publique worship of God upon yᵉ Lords day the said Rainking apearing in Court to answer for himself and his wife, promising reformation are acquitted paying ffees : 4ˢ and to be Admonished/ which was done in Court

Will Godsoe

Mʳ William Godsoe being presented by the Grand Jury for not frequenting the publique worship of God upon yᵉ Lords day appeared in Court and being Admonished & paying ffees he is acquitted

Jno More

John More being presented for selling Rhum without Lycence, appeared in Court, and is acquitted paying ffees : 3ˢ

John Nelson & his wife

John Nelson & Elizabeth Hayly yᵉ now wife of John Nelson being presented by the grand Jury for Comitting ffornication, he appearing in Court and being Leagally Convicted are ffined to their Majesties fiue & twenty shillings a piece, or to be whipt fiue stripes

Part II, Fol. 51ᵇ.

a peece upon their naked backs/ ffine & ffees 5ˢ payd in Court

Presentments

Presentments made by the Grand Jury are as ffolloweth

We present William Staey of Barwick for not ffrequenting yᵉ publique worship of God upon yᵉ Lords day

[51ᵇ]

Anno 1695

Wee present the Town of Kittery for not haueing a pound

We present Alice Methrill of Kittery for not ffrequenting the publique worship of God upon the Lords day

We present Richᵈ Kearle of Kittery for not ffrequenting the publique worship of God upon yᵉ Lords day

Presentmts

We present John Granger of Kittery ffor not ffrequenting the publique worship of God upon the Lords Day

We present Richᵈ Carter of York for not ffrequenting yᵉ publick worship of God upon yᵉ Lords dayes

We present Phillip Atwell of Kittery for not ffrequenting yᵉ publique worship of God upon the Lords day

We presᵗ Annah Braun of York for ffornication

We present William Thomas of Kittery for not ffrequenting the publique worship of God upon the Lords day

We present Robert Clark of Kittery for a Comon Drunkard and an Idle pson

We present Arthur Bale of York for fencing in the Kings high way

We presᵗ Mʳ Wᵐ Pepprell of Kittery for hauing Tan pits uncouered & unfenct in or Joyning to yᵉ Kings high way wᶜʰ is very dangerous both for man & beast

[52]

Anno 1695
Abraham Preble & Mary his wife

We present Abraham Preble, of York Junr, & Mary Bragdon his now wife for comitting ffornication. Abraham Preble and Mary his wife appeared at this Court and owned the ffact and are ffined to their Majesties fifty shillings and to pay ffees 5^s, or to receiue fiue stripes upon their naked backs & pay ffees 5^s and to stand Comitted till it be done The ffine and ffees payd in Court & they Acquitted

These presentments Agreed upon & consented to by ye Grand Jury, and brought into Court by John Wheelwright fforemã

Lieu^t Jeremiah Storer m^r James Plaisted and Peter Dixon for obseruing ye Court order in viewing ye bridge at Spruce Creek and makeing their return to this Court:

Spruce Creek Bridge

are allowed : 10^s that is 6^s to Lieu^t Storer and 2^s a piece to each of ye other.

Aprell 1st 1695/ we underwritten being ordered by the Court to set a Valluation of the worth of the Bridge at Spruce Creek built by Mr Curtes haue vallued it at ten pounds in mony.

       Jeremiah Storer
       James Plaisted
       Peter Dixon

It is ordered & agreed by ye Justices in Quarter Sessions that the Judges of the next Superi^r Court at Kittery are to be requested to determine whether the County of York in generall or town of Kittery shall be at ye Charge of ye Bridge aboue mentioned

PART II, FOL. 53, 54.

[53]

Anno 1695 Lycence is granted to Thomas More to keep a fferry ouer York Riuer nere his dwelling house he keeping a sufficient boat or vessell to transport horse & man and to giue good attendance, for which he giues bond of ten pounds to their Majesties.

Lycences
Lycence granted to Lieu^t Joseph Storer to keep a publique house of Entertainment and to retayle all sorts of Strong drink: giuing bond of ten pounds to their Majesties to obserue the law in such cases provided.

Lycences
Lycence granted to m^r John Wheelwright to keep a publique house of Entertaynment and to retayle all sorts of strong drink at his now dwelling house in Wells, giuing bond of ten pounds to their Majesties to obserue the law in such Cases prouided.

Lycence granted to Sarah Nason to keep a publique house of Entertaynment at her now dwelling house in Barwick and to retayle all sorts of strong drink she Entring into recognisance of ten pounds to their Majesties to obserue the law provided in such cases.

Lycence granted to Matthew Austine to keep a publique house of Entertaynment at his now dwelling house at York and to retayle all sorts of strong drink, giuing bond of ten pounds to their Majesties to observe the law provided in such Cases.

[54]

Anno 1695
Lycence
Lycence granted to Mr William Peprell to retayle all sorts of strong drink at his now dwelling house at Kittery giuing bond of ten pounds to their Majesties to obserue the law provided in such Cases.

PART II, FOL. 55.

County of York

At their Majesties Inferi^r Court of Comon pleas held at York. the 2º day of Ap^{ll} 1695 before Samuel Wheelwright Job Alcock Charles ffrost and William Peprill Esq^{rs} their Majesties Justices of this County.

Justices

Proclamation made
The Jury of tryalls are as ffollows

Jurors sworn

1 Mr John Wheelwright fforeman
2 Lieu^t Jeremiah Storer   7 Arthur Bragdon
3 Nicholas Cole   8 Joseph Couch
4 Nathaniel Rayns   9 Peter Lewis
5 John Parker   Jury   10 John Heard
6 Joseph Banks   Sworn   11 Christian Remich
                                12 Peter Dixon

Captn Pickerin Mrs Champrnoun

Cap^{tn} John Pickerin is Plaintiff in an action of Debt versus Mrs Mary Champernoun Defendant for wthholding twenty pounds payd by ye Plaintiff for Cap^{tn} ffran: Champernoun Deceased as p attachment

verdict

The Jury finds for ye Plaintiff twenty pounds in money sued for twenty one pounds Interest money and Cost of Court/ The Court accepts ye verdict
Bill of cost: 1^l: 17^s: 3^d: allowed in Court.

[55]

Anno: 1695

County of York

At his Majesties Court of Sessions held at York July 2, 1695 before Charles ffrost, Samuel Wheelwright, Job Alcock Samuel Donnell Willm Pepprell and Abraham Prebble Esq^{rs} Justices of his Majesties peace for the County of York

Justices

PART II, FOL. 56.

The names of the Grand Jury sumoned to appear are as followeth.

1 M^r Jn° Wheelwright	8 Christian Remich
2 Jeremiah Storer	9 Peter Dixon
Jurors 3 Nicholas Cole	10 Joseph Couch
4 Nath: Raines	11 John Heard
5 Jn° Parker	12 Ensign Abbet
6 Joseph Banks	13 Nicholas.Brown
7 Arthur Bragdon.	

Peter Lewis   Peter Lewis not appearing upon the Jury: is fined to his Majestie thirteen shillings and four pence

William Stacy being presented for not frequenting the publick Worship of God upon ye Lords Day appeared in Court and promising reformation is acquitted paying fees 5^s

Willm Stacy

John Grangiar being presented for not frequenting ye Publick Worship of God upon the Lords day: he making application to Maj^r ffrost one of his Maj^{ties} Justices & submitting himself & promises reformation is acquitted paying fees 5^s.

John Grangiar

[56]

Ri........   Richd Karle being presented for not frequenting the Worship of God &c and making application to this Court by his humble petition is sentenced to be admonished before the next Justice of Peace & to pay fees 5^s.

Part II, Fol. 57.

Walter Burks Walter Burks being bound to this Court by Recognisance for abusing Mr Sam^{ll} Donnell one of his Maj^{ues} Justices by lifting up his hand against him and giuing him threatning speeches is sentenced to be Whipt, fiue strip . . upon the naked back & pay fees 8^s or to pay fifty shillings fine to his Majestie and pay fees : 8^s

Upon his humble petition the Court has remitted 25^s of his fine and clear'd of his bonds paying fees

Arthur Beale Arthur Beale being presented by the Grand Jury for fencing in the Kings high way This Court orders that the Select men of York & survey^{rs} forthwith lay out a convenient high way from the Lower ferry at York . . Capt Rains his Braue boat harbour and w^t other ways are needfull : And to make return of their doings theirin to the next Quarter Sessio . . and especially to make report referring to the way for which s^d Beale is presented.

Wm Godsoe In answer to the petition of Mr William Godsoe the Court orders that Capt W^m ffernald Mr Elihu Gunnison and Mr Richd Cutt Select men of Kittery shall forthwith Lay out the land mentioned in s^d petition according to Grant

There being seuerall persons summoned to appear at this Court, which haue made default, it is ordered by this Court that a Speciall Warrant shall be [57] forthwith granted to the Sheriff to seize the s^d persons and secure them so that they appear at the next Quarter Sessions to answer their Contempt

PART II, FOL. 58.

Presentment

Presentment made by the Grand Jury is as followeth

We present Andrew Shaw for a common Drunk-
<small>wittness
Hugh Crocket</small> ard and for a common Lyar

This presentment 'greed upon and Consented to by the Grand Jury and brought into Court by John Wheelwright, foreman

Licence is granted to James Stagpole to keep a publick house of Entertainm^t he giuing bond wth security as the Law directs : Ensign Abbet & Wm Stacy suretys

Licences

Licence is granted to John Shepard to retayle bear syder perry & Victualls giuing bond with security as the Law directs

Licence granted to John Morgrage to retayle bear ale sider perry and victualls he giuing bond of ten pounds payable to his Maj^{tie} to obserue the Law provided in such Cases

Licence is granted to Peter Dixon to keep a publick house of entertainm^t & to retayle all sorts of strong drink at his now dwelling house, and also to keep a ferry over the Riuer Piscataqua from Kittery to Portsm^o side near his s^d dwelling house he giving bond with

<small>Anno
1695</small>

[58] Sureties according to Law to obserue and perform the law in such cases made and provided

Licence granted to Joan Dearing Widdow to keep a publique house of entertainment giuing bond according to Law.

Licence granted to the widow Hannah ffreathy to retayle bear sider ale perry and Victualls giuing bond according to law

Licence granted to Katherine Paul to sell bear &c

Part II, Fol. 59.

County of York

At his Majesties Inferior Court of Common Pleas held at York July 2ᵈ 1695, before Samuel Wheelwright Job Alcock Charles ffrost & William Peprell Esqʳˢ his Majesties Justices for this County of York

Justices

Proclamation made
The Jury of Tryalls are as followeth

Jurors

1. Mʳ John Wheelwright foreman
2. Jeremiah Storer
3. Nicholas Cole
4. Nathˡˡ Raines
5. Jnᵒ Parker
6. Joseph Banks
7. Arthur Bragdon
8. Christian Remich
9. Peter Dixon
10. Joseph Couch
11. Jnᵒ Heard
12. Thoˢ Abbitt

[59]

Anno 1695.
Philip White & Eliz: Gowen

Mʳ Philip White Plaintiff in an action of the Case versus Eliz: Gowen Defendant for detaining & wᵗʰholding from the Plaintiff one half part of all yᵉ Estate both reall and psonall belonging to Trustrum Harris or Harriden Deceased

Verdict

The Jury finds for the Plaintiff the premises sued for and Costs of Court

Jnᵒ Wheelwright foreman.

The Court accepts the Verdict

The Defendant appeales to the next Superiʳ Court holden for this County of York according to Law Eliz: Gowen as Principle & Leiuᵗ Jnᵒ Shapleigh & John Heard as Sureties own themselues bound to his Majᵗⁱᵉ King Willᵐ his successors in 80ˡᵇ bond to prosecute the said appeal to Effect at the sᵈ Superiʳ Court.

PART II, FOL. 60.

Elihu Gunnison *versus* Richd Endle

Elihu Gunnison Plaintiff in an action of the Case versus Rich⁴ Endle Defendant for Entring upon a pcell of Land in Spruce Creek as p Attachm⁺ Richard Endle appeared in Court and owned a Judgment for the Land sued for

[60]

Anno 1695

County of York

Justices

At his Maj^ties Court of Quarter Sessions held at Wells Octob^r 1st 1695 before Charles ffrost Sam^ll Wheelwright Job Alcock, Sam^ll Donnell Willm Peprill Abraham Preble & Roger Kelly Esq^rs Justices of his Maj^ties peace for the County of York

Roger Kelly Esqr non appearance

Jno Newmarch

John Newmarch chosen to be Clerk of ye Courts for this County and sworn to the true Discharge of y^t office in Court.

Proclamation made

The names of the Grand Jury summoned to appear are as followeth.

Jurors

1 John Wheelwright foreman
2 Jeremiah Storer   8 Thomas Abbit
3 Nicholas Cole   9 John Heard
4 Nath^ll Rains   10 Peter Dixon
5 Jno Parker   11 Peter Lewis
6 Joseph Banks   12 Joseph Couch
7 Arthur Bragdon   13 Richd Gowell

Peter Lewis

Whereas Peter Lewis not appearing in time at the last Quarter Sessions of the peace upon the Grand Jury was fined to his Maj^tie 13^s 4^d it is ordered by this Court that the said Lewis hath his fine Remitted.

Part II, Fol. 61.

Andrew Shaw Anna Brawn & Richd Carter being summoned psonally to appear in Court to answer their presentments Exhibited against them by the Grand Jury they not

Andrew Shaw Anna Brawn Richd Carter & Sarah ffry

appearing it is ordered by this Court that Charles Frost Sam^ll Donnell & Willm Pepprill Esq^rs shall cause the said Shaw Brawn and Carter also Sarah ffry now the wife of Nicholas Morrell who was presented for fornication to appear before them when and where they shall think fitt and determine their Contempt of authority and presentm^ts

Elisha Engerson Anno 1696

Elisha Engerson being bound to this Court by Recognizance [61] on suspicion of Adultery it not being proued against him is discharged paying fees 11^s 6^d fees paid

Alice Metherill

Alice Metherill of Kittery made Oath in Court that Jno Thomson of Kittery is the father of that respectiue bastard Child which she hath lately brought forth and no other man

Alice Metherill

Alice Metherill being brought before this Court for hauing a Bastard child and it being aggrauated by seuerall Circumstances It is ordered by this Court y^t she be whipped 10 stripes upon the naked back & pay fees 15^s or to pay five pounds to his Maj^tie & fees and to stand Committed untill the Judgm^t be answered

John Thomson

John Thomson being brought before this Court by Recognizance for being the reputed father of a bastard child which Alice Metherill charges him with it is ordered by this Court y^t ye said Thomson shall pay towards the maintainance of the Child to Alice Metherill 2^s 6^d p week to be paid monthly in money from the time of the childs birth being brought forth ye 21st of

Part II, Fol. 62.

August, During the Courts pleasure and to pay fees 11ˢ 6ᵈ and to stand Committed till he bring sufficient suretys for his true performance thereof.

<small>Mary Remich</small>   Mary Remich being brought before this Court by Recognizance for scolding and fighting it is ordered by yᵉ Court yᵗ she receiue publick admonition & pay fees 6ˢ 10ᵈ publick admonition giuen in Court & fees paid

Willᵐ Thomas & Philip Atwell being brought before this Court by a speciall warrant for their Contempt of authority in not answering to presenᵗ Exhibited against [62] then by

<small>Anno 1695
Wm Thos & Philip Attwell</small>   the Grand jury for not frequenting the publick worship of God upon the Lords day as p summons warned it is ordered by this Court that they Receiueing publick admonition and promising future reformation & paying fees 6ˢ a peice are discharged & to stand Committed untill the Judgmᵗ be answered, fees payd.

There being seuerall persons at this and yᵉ Last Court of Quarter Sessions wᶜʰ haue made default it is ordered by this Court yᵗ a speciall Warrant shall be granted to the Sheriff to seize yᵉ said psons and them secure so that they may appear before any two of the Justices of yᵉ peace of this County when and where they shall be appointed to answer for their contempt & presentments. Also yᵗ a Warrant be giuen to the Sheriff or his deputy psonally to summons Sarah ffry now yᵉ wife of Nichˢ Morrell to answer to a presentmᵗ Exhibited against her by yᵉ Grand Jury for fornication, before any two or more of yᵉ Justices of this County when and where said Justices shall appoint.

It being hazardous trauelling wᵗʰ prisoners to the Comon goale by reason of yᵉ Indian Enemy also yᵉ Goal being

PART II, FOL. 63, 64.

much out of Repair it is ordered by this Court y^t ye Sheriff shall Constitute any house which he thinks most conuenient for a common County Goale for the present.

Licence Licence is granted to Joan Crafts to keep a publick house of Entertainm^t at the house w^r she now liues She giuing in bond wth security as ye Law directs at the next meeting of three of ye Justices of ye peace of this County at Mr Pepprills.

Presentmts Presentments made by ye grand Jury at ye Court are as followeth

We present Sarah Gullishaw of Kittery for Committing fornication

[63]

Anno 1695 We present ye Town of Kittery, The Town of York & the Town of Wells for not Choosing a county Treasurer John Wheelwright foreman

[64]
County of York

At his Majesties Inferior Court of Common pleas held at Wells Octob^r 1st 1695 before Samuell Wheelwright Job Alcock Charles Frost and Willm Pepprill Esq^{rs} his Maj^{ties} Justices for this County of York

Proclamation made

No actions entred the Jury are discharged

PART II, FOL. 65.

County of York

The Reasons of Appeal of Eliz* Gowen alias Smith Adminestratrix to y⁰ Estate of her late husband William Gowen alias Smith of Kittery dec⁴ Appell' against Phillip White Defendant from the Judgm' of y⁰ Inferior Court of Comōn pleas held at York for the County of York on the first tuesday of July last To y⁰ Superior Court of Judicature to be held at Boston for the s⁴ County of York on the last tuesday of Octob' Anno Doin 1695.

Eliza Gowens reasons of appeall uersus White

1 That y⁰ Judgment rendred at y⁰ s⁴ Inferiour Court of Pleas for y⁰ now Defend' against y⁰ p'sent appellant is erroneous and contrary to Law and ought to be reversed for y' an action of Detinue cannot by Law be maintained ag' an Administ' of an Administ' for withholding goods Chattells &c.

2 That if y⁰ Appellant was liable to such action as y⁰ Defend' comēnced against her there is no evidence to make her lyable to respond the defend' demaund for y⁰ proof against her is a Judgm' of a Generall Court wch is still in force for any that appears to y⁰ Contrary to y⁰ Court and the Defendant must either bring a Scire facias or comēnce a new action upon y⁰ Judgm' but cannot bring y' originall action and make y' Judgment his evidence and ground of action

3 That y' is such incertainty in the writt for the things in Demaund as no Judgment can be rendred for or any Execution [65] granted upon such Judgm' the Law requires certainty in all actions and the things sued for must be certainly set forth & expressed in the writt so y' y⁰ same may be plain and intelligible to y⁰ Court and Jury and y⁰ writt claims only one half part of y⁰ reall and personall Estate of one Trustrum Harridon, wch is as great an incertainty w' it is as may be for There is no certainty of w' y⁰ reall Es-

tate sued for is how many number of acres, or wheather they are upland or meadow, what houses mills or buildings or in what County Town province or territory they lye in or how butted and bounded all which ought to haue been particularly specifyed & set forth in yᵉ attachment otherwise yᵉ reall Estate sued for is as incertaī as yᵉ Land in the moon.

<small>Eliza Gowens Reasons of Appeall</small>

That the personall Estate is as incertainly specified in yᵉ writt as yᵉ Reall there being no mention made therein of any particular nor of any vallue not so much as yᵉ name of beds Chairs pewter brass or any manner of houshold stuff wᶜʰ ought to haue been set forth in yᵉ writt otherwise right can not be administered to either party

That yᵉ Defendᵗ Doth not shew forth any title to yᵉ Reall Estate for he deriues his Right from an Administration granted him by yᵉ prerogatiue Court of yᵉ Archbishop of Canterbury which can giue him no interest in yᵉ Reall Estate.

That yᵉ Action commenced is both for a reall and Personall Estate wᶜʰ cannot be connexed in one processe all which being duly weighed and Considered by yᵉ Honourable Court and Jury the Appellant hopes they will see good Reason to reuerse yᵉ former Judgmᵗ and allow her Reasonable Costs.

Thoˢ Newton Attorney
for yᵉ Appellant.

A true Coppy of the originall transcribed & therewith Compared here Entred upon Record this 14º day of October 1695 p Jnº Newmarch Clericum

[66]

County of York

By vertue of an order of the Last quartʳ sessions which was held at wells on the first tuesday of octobʳ 1695 Charles

Part II, Fol. 67.

ffrost Samuel Wheelwright and William Peprill Esq^{rs} Justices of his majesties peace for this County, met this 29º of Octob^r 1695, In Kettery to hear and determine seuerall defaults wch should haue been answered at ye sd Court:

Anna Brawn being brought before us by uertue of a speciall warrant for her contempt of authority in not appearing at his majesties Court of Quarter Sessions held at York on the first tuesday of July Last past to answer to a presentm^t Exhibited against her for fornication, it is ordered that she pay ten shillings for her contempt of authority, or be whipt three stripes upon her naked back and pay fees, and to pay thirty shillings for committing of fornication or be whipt seuen stripes upon her naked back & pay fees thirteen shillings and to stand committed till ye Judgm^t be answered ·

Anna Brawn

John Brawn and Anna his wife humbly petitioning to us for a remission of part of her fine upon consideration of their Condition we haue seen Cause to remitt her ten shillings.

Andrew Shaw being brought before us by uertue of a speciall warrant for his contempt of authority in not answering to a Presentment Exhibited against him by ye Grand Jury for being a common drunkard and a common Lyar when he was summoned, it is ordered that he pay ten shillings for his contempt and fees and stand committed till it be done and that he pay fifteen shillings [67] for his Presentm^t for ye use of the poor of ye Town and pay fees or to sit in the stocks three hous and pay fees 13^s & 3^d and to stand committed 'till ye Judgm^t be answered

Andrew Shaw

Richard Carter being brought before us by uertue of a

Part II, Fol. 68.

Richd Carter

speciall warrant for his contempt of authority in not answering to a presentm^t Exhibited against him by ye Grandjury for not frequenting ye Publick Worship of God on the Lords day it is ordered that the sd Carter receiue publick admonition and promising Reformation for ye future and paying fees 8^s 6^d is discharged & to stand committed untill ye Judm^t be answered, admonition giuen:

Thos Trafton

Thomas Trafton addressing to us for liberty to keep a publick house of entertainm^t, it is granted to him till the next Quarter Sessions prouided he make his address to the Court for a licence and that till then he obserue ye Law made and prouided in such cases

At a meeting of Charles ffrost Sam^{ll} Wheelwright & William Pepprell Esq^{rs} three of his Majesties Justices for the County of York

These are to order yee' Select men for the Town of Kittery that yee forthwith take y^t Care of and make y^t Prouision for Alice Metherill and her Children wch the Law requires of you they being persons destitute of any habitation.

[68]

169 5-6 Anne

Justices

County of Yorke

At his Majesties Court of Quarter Sessions holden at Wells January 7° 169$\frac{5}{6}$ Before Charles ffrost Samuel Wheelwright Job Alcock Sam^{ll} Donnell and William Peprell and Abraham Preble Esq^{rs} Justices of his Majesties peace for this County of Yorke

PART II, FOL. 69.

Proclamation made
The Grand Jury Sumoned to appear are as follows

  1 John Wheelwright fforeman

Jurors
2 Nicholas Cole   7 Thomas Abbet Senr
3 Jeremiah Storer   8 John Heard
4 James Plaisted   9 Peter Lewis
5 William Sayer   10 Joseph Couch
6 John Parker   11 Arthur Bragdon Senr
       12 Richd Gowell

Grand Jurrs

Ju^rn Sworn : in Cour.   13 Isaac Remich

Nath’ll Rayns and Joseph Banks not appearing on ye Jury according to Sumons are fined to his Matie 13s 4d each

Wm Goodens prsentmt

William Goodden being presented to this Court by the Grand Jury for Retailing Rhum & sider is sentenced to pay forty shillings to ye Selectmen of Kittery for ye use of ye pore of s^d Town. and to pay ffees : 4^s. ffees payd in Court

Mr Curtis prsentmt

Mr Joseph Curtes being presented to this Court by the Grand Jury for Retayling of Rhum & sid^r is sentenced to pay forty shillings to ye Select men of Kittery for ye use of ye pore of said Town and to pay fees : 4^s — ffees payd in Court

Joshua Remichs petition

This Court taking into serrious consideration ye humble Petition of Joshua Remich praying liberty to take into his charge & care or to put out to some [69] other pson the child that was laid to his charge by Sarah Lisson — This Court orders that the said Sarah Lisson shall be sumoned to appear at ye next Quarter Sessions to giue her Reason why ye s^d Remich may not dispose of s^d Child as aforesd.

Part II, Fol. 69.

Point Meeting house

There being complaint made to this Court that the Meeting house at Kittery point is very much out of repair soe y^t it is very uncomfortable to meet in — Therefore this Court orders that ye Select men of that part of Kittery forthwith cause ye same to be repayred, and to rayse money upon ye Inhabitants belonging to that p^t of ye Town by way of rate for ye doing of it.

Cape Porpus Records

Whereas the Records or Town Books of Cape Porpus are not to be found in this County, for want whereof seuerall of the propriet^{rs} of land there are very like to come to Damage, And this Court being aduised that said Records were comitted to the care & custody of John Puddington late of Cape Porpus by Sr Edm^d Andros, doth order that ye Clerk shall with all conuenient speed send to James Puddington, son of s^d John Puddington, in whose custody they are supposed to be that he forthwith send them safely to ye Clerk of this Court — and he to keep them till further order.

high way from ye pt to Sirgeon Creek

This Court orders that ye Select men of ye lower part of Kittery shall with all couenient speed lay out a conuenient high way from Kittery point to Stirgeon Creek and other conuenient high ways into ye woods to ye seuerall out lots in that part of the Town — And that Mr William Peprell shall & is hereby ordered to be with ye s^d Select men at ye doing of it. And to make return of their doing therein to ye next Quarter Sessions/ Mr Peprill to appoint ye time when to doe it, and to giue notice to the Select men.

Part II, Fol. 70.

[70]

^{high way from York to Cape Nuddeck &c}
It is ordered by this Court that yᵉ Select men of York shall lay out a conuenient high way or Country Rode from York Town through yᵉ woods to yᵉ head of Cape Nuddeck Riuer by yᵉ Mill and from thence to yᵉ back side of Auerells pond or where they shall find it most conuenient to come to yᵉ old Road.

^{Cul'er of leathr}
Itt is ordered by this Court that yᵉ Select men of yᵉ lower part of Kittery shall appoint some meet pson in that part of the Town for a Sealer of Leather it being neglected in yᵉ season of it and complaint being made to this Court for want of that officer it is ordered as aforesᵈ

^{Euerits complaint again.. Woodman}
Whereas Complaint is made to this Court by Capᵗⁿ John Eueret & Sargeant Daniel Black against John Woodman of Kittery for not giuing due attendance at yᵉ fferry from Kittery to Portsmᵒ — Itt is ordered by this Court that yᵉ said Woodman shall be sum̄oned to answer at yᵉ next Quarter Sessions to be holden at York.

^{Lycenses}
Lycence is granted to Mʳ Joseph Curtes to retayle all sorts of drink & victualls &ᶜ, he giuing bond wᵗʰ sureties according to law well & truly to oscrue the law in such cases made & prouided.

Lycence is Granted to John Woodman to Retayle all sorts of strong drink victualls &ᶜ giuing security to obserue yᵉ law in such Cases made and prouided

Lycence is Granted to John Leighton to retayle all sorts strong drink victualls &ᶜ giuing bond wᵗʰ sureties to obserue yᵉ law in such cases made and prouided

Part II, Fol. 71, 72.

[71]

Lycence Granted to Thomas Trafton to retayle all sorts of drink victualls &c Giuing bond wth sureties duly to obserue ye law in such Cases made & prouided

Allowed ye Constables for sumoning ye Select men to answer the presentm^ts of ye seuerall Towns in this County for not Chusing a County Tresu^r

      vizt To John Cooper.................... : : 03:
        To Richd Endle.................... : : 03:
        To Sephn Tobey.................... : : 01:
        To Moses Littlefield................ : : 01:

Witness
Josiah Clark Presentm^ts giuen by the Grand Jury to this Court
Wm Sanders We present William Goodden of Barwick for
Jno Thorne
Ephrm Joy selling by retayle Rhum & Sid^r / this presentm^t
Benjm Louell answ^rd

Witness   We present Jeremiah Molton of york for sell-
Richd Comer ing Rhum by Retayle
Thos ffauor

    We present Mr Joseph Curtes of Kittery for selling by retayle strong drink/ answered in Court

    We present John Nelson of Kittery for a comon
presentmts Drunkard and for Cursing Swearing & Quarrelling in his drink

We present Richd Green & his wife of Kittery for not ffrequenting ye publique worship of God

We present Alice Hanscum & Mary Miller of Kittery for not ffrequenting ye publique worship of God.

[72]

Witness
Wm Gooden We present James Stagpole of Barwick for
Eph: Joy suffering seuerall psons to sit drinking in his
Walter Abet House at unseasonable times to Excess & many of them Inhabitants and on ye Sabbath day.

We present Alexander Maxell of Yorke for selling sider by Retayle.

PART II, FOL. 73.

We present Robert Junkins of York for selling sider by Retayle

John Wheelwright fforeman.

[73]

1695-6 Anno

Justices of Inferr Court

County of York

At his Majesties Inferiour Court of Common pleas holden at Wells: before Samuell Wheelwright Job Alcock Charles ffrost & William Pepprill Esq^{rs} his Majesties Justices for this County, January 7° 169⅚

Proclamation Made

The names of the Jury of Tryalls sumoned to appear are as followeth, vizt:

Jurrs

1 John Wheelwright fforeman
2 Jeremiah Storer
3 Nicholas Cole
4 James Plaisted
5 Wm Sayer
6 John Parker
7 Thomas Abbet Senr
8 John Heard
9 Peter Lewis
10 Joseph Couch
11 Joseph Hill
12 Lewis Bean

Jur^{rs} Sworn in Court

Nicholas Gowen alias Smith is plaintiff in an action of Trespass for cutting and carrying away about fiue or 6 load of hay from ye Widow Mary Twisdens Marsh at York as p attachment versus Sarah Chadbourn Defendant

The Jury finds for ye Defend^t Costs of sute

the Court accepts y^e verdict/ Costs Alowed 1[£] : 19^s/ : 6^d

John Thomson Plaintiff in an action of y^e case for Defam-

PART II, FOL. 74.

ing and Injuring him in his name & Estate as p attachm^t, versus Alice Medrell Defendant

The Jury finds for y^e Defend^t Costs of sute
Costs Allowed 00$^£$:16^s : 06^d.

1696 Anno
Justices

[74]
County of York

At his Majesties Court of Quarter Sessions held at york, April y^e 7° 1696 before Charles ffrost Samuel Wheelwright Job Alcock Samuel Donnell Willi Pepperill & Abraham Preble Esq^{rs} Justices of y^e peace for this County.

The names of y^e Grand Jury are as follows

Jurrs

1 Jonathan Hamond fforeman
2 Daniel Littlefield   8 Jacob Remich
3 Jonath Littlefield   9 Thomas Hunscom
4 Thomas Donnell   10 Daniel Goodwin
5 Arthur Cane   11 Nicholas Gowen
6 Richd Hunniwill   12 Richard Briar
7 Abraham Preble   13 Richard Endle

Roger Dearing not appearing to serue on ye Jury according to sumons : is fined to his Majesty : 13^s : 4^d

Wm Peperll Esqr Tresur

Mr William Pepperill is Chosen Tresu^r for this County of York.

John Nelson to answr

John Nelson of Kittery not appearing according to sumons to answer his presentm^t : It is ordered by this Court that a Speciall warrant be giuen out to seize ye s^d Nelson and secure him soe that he appear at ye next Quarter Sessions to be holden for this County to answer for his contempt, as also for his presentm^t

PART II, FOL. 75.

Richd Green & his wife to be Admonished and pay ffees

Richd Green & his wife being presented for not ffrequenting the public worship of God, And making their humble supplication to Maj^r ffrost one of his Maties Justices and promising reformation are sentenced to be admonished before ye next Justice, & to pay fees : 8^s.

[75]

Mary Miller being presented for not ffrequenting the public worship of God and not appearing according to sumons the Court orders that a special warrant be Issued forth to seize & secure ye s^d Mary Miller soe that she appear before his Maties Justices at ye next Quarter Sessions to be holden for this County to answer her contempt as alsoe for her presentm^t

James Stacpole being presented to this Court for suffering bad orders in his house &^{c} as p ye presentment, is for his ofence sentenced to pay twenty shillings for ye use of his Matie and to be Admonished : & pay fees 5^s

Admonition rec^d & ffees payd in Court

Alexander Maxel being presented for selling sider by retaile without lycence, is sentenced to pay forty shillings to ye Select men of York for use of pore thereof And to pay ffees : 5^s : fees payd in Court.

Ensign Nathaniel Rayns being bound to this Court by Recognizance by ye complaint of Arthur Beal, appeared in Court to answer and at ye hearing thereof is Adjudged to pay to his Majestie : 15^s and to pay ffees : 5^s : 9^d :
ffees payd in Court — and he is cleared of his Bonds.

Arthur Beal being bound to this Court by recognezance by complaint of Ensign Raynes, appeared in Court and at ye hearing thereof is sentenced to pay to his Majestie

Part II, Fol. 76.

twenty shillings, and to pay ffees : 5ˢ : 9ᵈ/ ffees payd and he is cleared of his bonds.

[76]

John Woodman being bound to this Court by recognezance, by complaint of Isaac Remich & John Staple for swearing, appeared in Court and at yᵉ hearing thereof is sentenced to pay 8ˢ to yᵉ Select men of Kittery for yᵉ use of yᵉ pore thereof, and to pay ffees : 5ˢ ffees payd in Court, and he is cleared of his bonds

Isaac Remich & John Staple being bound to this Court by recognezance, by complaint of John Woodman for abusing him sᵈ Woodman & drawing blood of him, appeared in Court and upon Leagall conuiction are sentenced to pay to his Majestie 20ˢ a piece and to pay ffees 5ˢ each, And to stand bound to his Majestie his successⁿ in yᵉ sum of ten pounds for their good behauiʳ till yᵉ next Quarter Sessions.

Capᵗⁿ John Pickerin is surety for Isaac Remich and Jacob Remich is suretie for John Staple.

Jeremiah Molton being presented by yᵉ Grand Jury for selling Rhum by retayle, is sentenced to pay ffourty shillings to yᵉ Select men of York for yᵉ use of yᵉ pore thereof, and to pay ffees 5ˢ

ffees payd in Court.

Lycence is granted unto Lieuᵗ Joseph Storer to keep a public House of Entertainment & to retayle all sorts of strong drink he giuing bond according to law/

Mʳ John Wheelright has Lycence granted him to sell all sorts of strong drink by retayle & to keep a public house of Entertainment.

Part II, Fol. 77.

Lycence is granted to M{r} James Playsted to retayle bear syder and victualls at his now dwelling house

[77]

Lycence is granted to Matthew Austine to keep a public house of Entertainment & to retayle all sorts of strong drink at his now Dwelling house

<small>Prison to be re- payred</small>

It is ordered by this Court that M{r} Samuel Donnell Lie{t} Preble & m{r} James Playsted shall forthwith view the Prison at york & see whats amiss in it, and cause it to be repayred and to be payd by y{e} Sheriff out of that ten pounds which was giuen to y{e} County by y{e} Generall Court.

It is ordered that y{e} Sheriff forthwith prouide a payr of Iron Bilbows for y{e} Prison & to be payd out of y{e} afores{d} ten pound

It is ordered that twenty pounds be forthwith raysed upon this County of York, by warr{t} from y{e} County Tresur{r}, Whereof Kittery is to pay ten pounds: york: 5£ and Wells fiue pounds for y{e} Defraying of y{e} public Charge of y{e} County.

County of York   At his Majesties Inferio{r} Court of pleas held at York Apr{ll} 7º 1696 before Samuel Wheelwright Job Alcock Charles ffrost & W{m} Pepperill Esq{rs} his Majesties Justices for this County of York

PART II, FOL. 78.

The names of y⁰ Jury of tryalls are as followeth viz⁰
1 Jonathan Hamond foreman
2 Daniel Littlefield   8 Jacob Remich
3 Jonath Littlefield   9 Thomas Hunscomb
4 Thomas Donnell   10 Daniell Goodwin
5 Arthur Cane   11 Nich° Gowen
6 Rich⁴ Huniwill   12 Rich⁴ Briar
7 Abraham Preble

[78]
William Parsons is Plaintiff in an action of the Case for withholding a horse as p attachm⁰, versus Baker Nason Defend⁰

The Jury for y⁰ Plaintiff y⁰ horse sued for and Costs of sute/ Costs allowed 2£ : 13ˢ : 00ᵈ

Cap¹ⁿ John Pickerin is Plaintiff in an action of the case for a Debt of 3£ : 11ˢ : 3ᵈ due by bill from the Estate of John Deament Deceased, versus John Woodman & Nathaniel Raynes Defend¹ˢ The Jury finds for y⁰ Plaintiff his Debt sued for and Costs of sute/ Costs allowed 1£ : 14ˢ : 00ᵈ

John Woodman & Nath¹¹ Rayns appeal to y⁰ next Supʳ Court to be holden for this County of York & sd Woodman & Rayns as principles and Thomas Rice as surety own themselues bound to his Maᵗᵗᵉ King William his Succesʳˢ in 7£ bond to prosecute their appeal to Effect

Mʳ Samuell Cutt Suruiuing heir of John Cutt Esqʳ Decᵈ is plaintiff in an action of y⁰ Case for a debt due by Book to y⁰ vallue of six pounds fourteen shillings and nine pence, versus Thomas Rice Defendant. The Jury finds for y⁰ Defendant Costs of Court/ Cost allowed 0£ 9ˢ 6ᵈ

PART II, FOL. 79.

Maj^r William Vaughan is plaintiff in an action of Debt of twenty six pounds as p attachm^t versus John Buckland Defend^t

John Buckland came into Court & owned a Judgement of thirty one pounds fourteen shillings due to Maj^r vaughan from s^d Buckland in money which is in full of all acco^{ts} & concerns between said Vaughan & Buckland relating to y^e Estate of Cap^{tn} Richd Cutt Deceased.

John Woodman Appeal^t from a Judgm^t obtayned against him of thirty seuen shillings & nine pence at a hearing of y^e case March 16 : 169$\frac{4}{5}$ before Wm Pepprell Esqr versus Thomas Trafton Defend^t.

The Jury finds for y^e Appeal^t a Reuersion of y^e former Judgm^t and costs of Court. Costs allowed 2$^£$: 0^s : 6^d

[79]

Thomas Rice came into Court and owned a Judgment of nine pounds & 2^d due to Maj^r William Vaughan from s^d Rice in money.

Presentments made by y^e Grand Jury at y^e Quart^r Sessions held at York : Apr^{ll} 7° : 1696

We present Thomas Walters for doing Seruile Lab^r that is to say lading his sloop upon ye day of Humiliation which was upon ye second day of this Ins^t

presentmts We pres^t Thomas More of York for selling strong drink without Lycence

We present Nicholas Smith and Hannah Hodsden, now the wife of s^d Smith for comitting ffornication.

Nicholas Smith and Hannah his wife appeared in Court and submitting themselues are sentenced to pay to ye use of his Majestie twenty shillings a piece & to pay fees 5^s : or to receiue fiue stripes a piece upon ye Naked back : & pay fees : The fine and ffees both payd down in Court

Part II, Fol. 80.

We present Richd Bray for not ffrequenting ye public worship of God upon ye Lords day

We present Abraham Parker of York for not ffrequenting ye public worship of God upon ye Lords day

We present Edmund Gage of Kittery for profane swearing & for being Drunk.

We present Thomas Hooper for not ffrequenting the public worship of God upon ye Lords day

We present John Braun Junr for not ffreqenting ye public worship of God upon ye Lords day.

[80]

We present John Thompson & Elizabeth Paul now ye wife of s^d Thompson for comitting ffornication.

We present Katherine Paul for selling Rhum and wine by Retayle without Lycence.

We present Christopher Banfield and Grace Banfield his wife for not ffrequenting ye public worship of God upon ye Lords day.

Presentmts   We present Edward Waymouth & Hester his wife for not ffrequenting ye public worship of God upon ye Lords day.

We pres^t ye Widow Taylor for not ffrequenting ye public worship of God upon ye Lords day.

We present Wm Godsoe and wife for not ffrequenting ye public worship of God upon ye Lords day.

We present Mary ye wife of Walter Allen for not ffrequenting ye public worship of God upon the Lords day

We pres^t Nich Turbet & Eliz : his wife for not ffrequenting ye publick worship of God upon ye Lords day.

We present Peter Wittum Senr & Peter Wittum Junr for not ffrequenting ye public worship worship of God upon ye Lords day   Jonath : Hamond fforeman

PART II, FOL. 82, 83.

Anno 1696

[82]
County of York

At his Majesties Court of Quarter Sessions held at York July y⁰ 7⁰ 1696, Before Charles ffrost Sam¹¹ Wheelwright Job Alcock Samuel Doñel Wᵐ Peprill Abraham Preble and Roger Kelly Esqʳˢ Justices of the peace for this County

Justices

Proclamation made
The Jury sumoned to appear are as follows
1 Jonathan Hamond fforeman
2 Daniel Littlefield   8 Jacob Remich
3 Jonathan Littlefield   9 Thomas Hunscom
4 Thomas Donnell   10 Daniel Goodwin
5 Arthur Cane   11 Nicholas Gowen
6 Richᵈ Hunniwill   12 Roger Dearing
7 Abraham Preble   13 Joseph Couch

Jurrs

Richᵈ Bryar being sumoned and not appearing on yᵉ Jury is fined to his Maᵗⁱᵉ 13ˢ 4ᵈ

Thomas Walters being presented for doing seruile labour upon yᵉ day of Humiliation presenting his resons of Nessessity of his soe doing, is acquitted, paying fees: 5ˢ

Isaac Remich & John Staple being bound to yᵉ good behauiour, appeared in Court and nothing appearing against them; are Cleared of their bonds.

[83]
John Nelson being brought to this Court by special Warrant for his contempt in not appearing at yᵉ last Quarter Sessions according to Summons to answer a presentment of the Grand Jury Exhibited against him for being a common Drunkard and for cursing swearing and quarreling, is for

his ofences fined fiue and twenty shillings, to be payd to ye Selectmen of Kittery for ye use of the pore thereof and to pay ffees of Court: 10^s: And to stand comitted till done/ And to giue bond of ten[£] to be of good behaui^r till ye next Quarter Sessions. ffine & ffees payd in Court.

John Nelson Principle and Edmund Gage and Thomas Hooper Sureties doe own themselues firmly bound and obliged to our Soueraigne Lord King W^m his Success^{rs} in the sum of ten pounds sterling, Joyntly & seuerally that the said John Nelson shall be of good behaui^r till the Next Quarter Sessions.

Nelsons bond

Mary the wife of Samuel Miller being brought to this Court by Special Warrant for her contempt in not appearing at the last Quarter Sessions according to Sumons, to answer a presentm^t of the Grand Jury for not ffrequenting the public Worship of God upon ye Lords day, is for her ofence to be admonished and to sit one hour in ye Stocks at Kittery point on Monday ye 20th of this Instant and to pay ffees: 5^s.

ffees payd in Court.

[84]

John Thomson and Elizabeth his wife presented for Comitting ffornication, s^d Thomson appeared for himselfe and in behalfe of his wife, owned ye ffact and referr^d it to the Court, Are sentenced to receiue fiue stripes a piece upon their Naked backs. & pay fees 10^s or to pay fiue & twenty shillings a piece to his Majestie and to pay ffees of Court: 10^s and to stand comitted till done.

William Godsoe and his wife presented for not ffrequenting ye public worship of God upon the Lords day: the s^d Godsoe appeared, and being Legally couicted is for his ofence to pay 5^s for ye use of the pore of Kittery: And to pay ffees 5^s

Presentmts answered

PART II, FOL. 85.

his wife bringing Euidence that she often frequ[ts] y[e] public Worship of God : is acquitted.

Rich[d] Bray not being sumoned to answer his present[t] at this Court is to be sumoned to answer at y[e] next Quarter Sessions to be holden at wells.

Christoph[r] Banfield and his wife presented for not ffrequenting y[e] public worship of God upon the Lords day they making application to Maj[r] ffrost one of his Ma[ties] Justices, are acquitted paying fees of Court 4[s] a piece.

Edward Waymouth & his wife presented for not frequenting y[e] public worship of God, producing Euidence that they haue been sometimes at Douer Meeting are acquited, paying ffees of Court : 4[s] a piece

[85]

The widow Martha Tayler presented for not ffrequenting y[e] public worship of God upon y[e] Lords day she presenting her humble petition & promising reformation is acquitted paying ffees 4[s]

Mary y[e] wife of Walter Allen, & Nicholas Turbet & his wife presented for not ffrequenting y[e] public worship of God upon y[e] Lords day : presenting their Humble petitions to this Court, are acquitted paying ffees : 4[s] each

Peter Wittum Sen[r] and Peter Wittum Jun[r] not appearing to answer their presentm[ts] according to Sumons It is ordered that a special warr[t] be forthwith granted to y[e] Sheriff or Constable, to answer their contempt at y[e] next Sessions

Rich[d] Milberry and Mary his wife formerly Mary Winchester, being presented to this Court for comitting ffornication s^d Milberry appeared in Court for himselfe and in behalfe of his wife to answer the s^d presentment, And owning the ffact they are sentenced to receiue fiue stripes a piece upon their Naked backs and to pay ffees of Court 5ˢ a piece. or to pay fiue & twenty shillings a piece. and pay ffees : 5ˢ a piece and to stand comitted till done.

ffine & ffees payd in Court.

<small>Jurrs to be payd by the Towns where they dwell</small> It is ordered at this Court that ye Grand Jur^n shall be payd by the seuerall Towns to which they doe belong, considering there is at pres^t noe money in ye Tresu^rs hand, And this to continue till ffurther order/

Constant Raynking & his wife being presented to this Court for not frequenting ye public worship of God upon ye Lords day, he apeared in Court to answer for himselfe [86] and his wife, are for their ofence fined fiue shillings a piece, to be payd to the Select men of York for ye use of ye pore thereof, and to pay ffees of Court : 2ˢ

ffees payd in Court

Abraham Parker being brought to this Court by speciall order to answer his contempt in not appearing to answer his presentment according to sumons, is for his ofence sentenced to sit in ye Stocks one hour : & to pay fees 5ˢ and to be Admonished for his not Attending ye public worship of God upon ye Lords day : for which which he was presented.

Alexand^r Maxell and Agnes his wife presented to this Court for not ffrequenting ye public worship of God he apeared in Court and being Admonished, promised reformation, is acquitted paying fees of Court : 2ˢ which was payd in Court

Part II, Fol. 87.

Daniell ffurbish presented to this Court for endeavouring to catch ffish upon ye Lords day appeared in Court, and is for his ofence to pay : 5^s for ye use of pore of ye Town of Kittery and to pay fees : 1^s

Lycence granted to Katherine Paul to keep a public house of Entertainment, and to retayle all sorts of strong drink victualls &^{c} She giuing bond with suretys as ye law directs.

[87]

Lycence granted to Mr Wm Pepril to retayle Rhum wine sider &^{c}, he giuing bond with sureties to obserue the laws made & prouided for ye Regulation of such houses

Lycence granted to James Stackpole to keep a public house of Entertainment at his now dwelling house, and to retayle all sorts of strong drink & victualls he giuing bond with sureties to observe ye law made and provided in such Cases.

Lycences

Lycence granted to John Shepard to retayle bere Cyder and cakes and ale he keeping & obseruing ye law made and prouided in such Cases

Lycence granted to Joanna Dearing, widow, to keep a public house of Entertainment And to retayle Rhum wine Cyder bere &^{c} giuing bond with sureties to obserue and keep ye law made & provided in such Cases.

Lycence granted to ye Widow ffrethy to keep a public house of Entertainm^t And to retayle Rhum wine bere Cyder &^{c} giuing bond with sureties to obserue & keep ye law made for ye Regulation of such houses.

Lycence Granted to Thomas More to keep a ferry ouer

PART II, FOL. 88.

York Riue^r as formerly he giuing due attendance as ye Law Directs in such Cases.

Presentments made by the Grand Jury to this Court are as ffolloweth —

York   We present Richd Milberry & Mary   answered
Winchester, now the wife [88] of s^d Milberry for comitting ffornication

We present George Norton & Shedrach Norton his son for doing seruile labour upon ye Lords day by breaking ground Rowing and Sayling out of York Harbour this was done on the Lords day.

Answered   We present Alexander Maxel & Agnes his wife for not ffrequenting ye public worship of God upon ye Lords day

Answered   We pres^t Constant Reignking & Hannah his wife for not ffrequenting ye public worship of God upon ye Lords day

answered   We present Abraham Parker and Sarah his wife for not ffrequenting ye public worship of God upon the Lords day.

Kittery   We present ye Lower part of Kittery for not keeping a ffery ouer ye Riu^r to ye Great Island according to law.

Presentamts   We present ye Lower part of Kittery for not hauing a pound according to law.

We present m^r Joseph Curtis for Incombring ye Kings High way namely ye bridge near his house by setting a Gate and Piling of wood upon s^d Bridge to ye great Hinderance of Trauailers.

We present ye Middle part of Kittery for not keeping the Kings high way Clear & ffeazable between m^r Joshua Downings & Thomas Hunscoms.

PART II, FOL. 89.

We present yᵉ Town of Kittery for not keeping a sufficient bridge ouer Stirgeon Creek.

Answered We present Daniel ffurbish for Indeauouring to cath fish on the Lords day/ We present Joseph Abbet for breaking yᵉ Kings peace by throwing a man down and striking him seuerall blows/ We present Katherine Neal for doing seruile work, to say making a shirt upon yᵉ last day of thanksgiving

Answered We present Mʳ Peprils two Tanners Namely John Robinson and James Tryworgye for doing seruile work vpon yᵉ last day of thanksgiving by scraping of hides vpon yᵗ day and doing other work in the Tanyard.

These presentmᵗˢ agreed on by yᵉ Grand Jury/

Jonathan Hamond foreman

[89]

Anno 1696
County of York

Court of Pleas
At his Majesties Inferiour Court of Comon pleas held at York July yᵉ 7º 1696 Before Samuel Wheelwright Job Alcock Charles ffrost & William Pepril Esqʳˢ his Majesties Justices for this County of York.

Justices

Proclamation made
The names of the Jury of tryalls are as follows

Jurrs
1 Jonathan Hamond fforeman
2 Daniel Littlefield   7 Abraham Preble
3 Jonath: Littlefeild   8 Jacob Remich
4 Thomas Donnel   9 Thomas Hunscom
5 Arthur Cane   10 Daniel Goodwin
6 Richᵈ Hunniwell   11 Nicholas Gowen
   12 Roger Dearing

PART II, FOL. 90.

Samuel Cutt is Plaintiff in an Action of the case for a Debt Due by Book to ẙ vallue of ffifty fiue pounds versus Joseph Wear : Defendᵗ
The Plaintiff withdraws his Action
Costs allowed y͏ᵉ Defendᵗ 00ᴸ : 14ˢ : 06ᵈ

The Quarter Sessions is Adjourned till the 20° of this Instᵗ at Kittery point at y͏ᵉ house of M͏ʳ W͏ᵐ Peprill

[**90**]

Anno 1696
Adjournment of ye Sessions

At an Adjournment of the Quarter Sessions from York July 7° : 1696, held at Kittery : July : 20° 1696 before Maj͏ʳ Charles ffrost Samuel Wheelwright Job Alcock Samuel Donnel and William Peprel Esq͏ʳˢ Justices of his Majesties peace for this County

Peter Wittum Jun͏ʳ appeared in Court to answ͏ʳ his contempt &c, is for his ofence to sit in the Stocks one hour and is to pay ffees : 5ˢ : and to stand comitted till done

John Robertson and James Treworgie being presented for doing seruill labour on a day of thanksgiuing, appeared in Court and pleading Nessessity are acquitted paying ffees 5ˢ a piece and to stand comitted till done.

John Robertson & his wife appeared in Court to answer for their not ffrequenting the public worship of God upon y͏ᵉ Lords day, Are for their ofence to be Admonished, And to pay ffees : 2ˢ.

Sarah Gullishaw appeared in Court to answer her presentment Exhibited against her for comitting ffornication, is for her ofence to receiue fiue stripes upon her Naked back, at y⁰ post, And to pay ffees fiue shillings, or to pay fiue & twenty shillings to his Majestie, and ffees 5ˢ, And to stand comitted till done/ the fine & ffees payd in Court

Stephen Hardison & his wife appeared in Court to answer for their not ffrequenting the public Worship of God upon y⁰ Lords day are for their ofence to be Admonished, And to pay ffees : 4ˢ

Admonition receiued and ffees payd in Court.

[91]

Anno 1696

Elisha Clark and his wife appeared in Court to answer for their not ffrequenting the public worship of God upon the Lords day, Are for their ofence to be Admonished, and pay fees three shillings.

Admonition receiued in Court

Thomas Dearing appeared in Court to answer for his not ffrequenting y⁰ public worship of God upon y⁰ Lords day, Is for his ofence to be Admonished and to pay ffees : 2ˢ : 6ᵈ.

Adjournmt of ye Sessions

Admonition receiued and ffees paid in Court.

Mary Miller the wife of Samˡˡ Miller, for her Contempt of Authority in not appearing according to Sumons to answer her presentment, and further Agreuations therein, Is for her ofence to receiue fiue stripes at y⁰ post upon her Naked back and to pay ffees 2ˢ, or to pay twenty shillings and ffees : 2ˢ / 12ˢ payd in Court and fees, and she is acquitted.

PART II, FOL. 92.

[92]

Anno 1696

County of York

Justices

At his Majesties Court of Quarter Sessions held at Wells Octob^r The 6th 1696, before Charles ffrost Samuel Wheelwright Job Alcock Sam^{ll} Donnel William Peprel and Abraham Preble Esq^{rs}

Proclamation made
The names of the Grand Jury are as followeth

Jurors

1 Jonathan Hamond fforeman
2 Daniel Littlefield   9 Thomas Hanscome
3 Jonath Littlefield   10 Roger Dearing *
4 Arthur Kane *   11 Richard Briar
5 Thomas Donnell   12 Andrew Neal
6 Daniel Goodwin   13 Benjamin Preble
7 Nicholas Gowen   14 Job Young
8 Jacob Remich   15 James Spinney

Jos: Abbett presentmt Answered

Joseph Abbet being presented for breach of the Kings peace, by throwing down a man and striking of him seuerall blows, Is for his ofence fined to his Majestie six shillings, and to pay ffees: 4^s: 6^d, and to stand committed till it be payd.

Katherine Neals prsentment answered

Katherine Neal being presented for doing of seruile labour on ye day of thanksgiuing, her husband appearing in her behalfe, and pleading Ignorance, she is acquitted, paying ffees: 4^s 6^d ffees payd in Court

Richd Briar Acquitted

Richard Briar being Delinquent in not appearing on ye Jury ye Last Sessions: and amerced to pay to our Soueraign Lord ye King: 13^s: 4^d. Upon his Application to this Court is acquitted, paying ffees: 2^s 6^d/ ffees payd in Court.

1696 annoq   John Nelson is Cleared of his bonds of good behau* by proclamation

[93]

Humphrey Scamon being brought to this Court by the Sheriff as a prison* for some Misdemeni*/ And the said Scamon as principle and M* Rich* Cutt as surety do own themselues bound and firmly obliged Joyntly & Seuerally to our Souereign Lord King William his Successors in the sum of ten pounds that y* said Scamon shall psonally appear at y* next Quarter Sessions holden for this County, and there to answer to what shall be aleged against him by William Pepril Esqu* on y* Kings behalfe and to abide the order of Court therein and not to depart w*th*out Lycence, and to be of the good behau* till then.

The Town of Kittery being presented for not keeping a sufficient Bridge ouer Stirgen Creek, &*/ M* Josh: Downing to answer in behalfe of s* Town.

It is ordered by this Court that y* s* Bridge shall built within six weeks from y* date hereof, upon the fforfiture of fiue pounds to be payd to the Tres* of this County, for y* use of the s* County, and to pay ffees: 4*: 6*.

Job Young appearing in Court and owning himselfe Guilty of breach of y* Kings peace by Striking of a man Is for his ofence fined to his Majestie: 6* and to pay fees: 1* and to stand Comitted till done.

Presentments
[94]
Presentments made by the Grand Jury this Court

York   We present Constant Rainking and Hannah his wife for not ffrequenting the public worship of God upon the Lords day.

PART II, FOL. 95.

We present Abraham Parker & Sarah his wife for not attending the public worship of God on ye Lords day

We present m^{rs} Mary Plaisted wife of m^r James Plaisted for not attending ye public worship of God upon ye Lords day.

Presentmts — We present Rowland Young Senr for Swearing seuerall sinfull oaths.

Kittery — We present John Staple and Mary his now wife for committing fornication.

We present Peter Staple & Mary his wife for fornication

We present Peter Staple for swearing & cursing.

We present John Staple for swearing and cursing

We present Samuel Pray for Cursing.

We present William Graunt & Martha his now wife, for comitting ffornication.

Jonathan Hamond fforeman

[95]

Anno 1696-7

County of York

At a Court of Quarter Sessions held at wells January the 5°: 169$\frac{6}{7}$ before the Honour^d Charles ffrost Samuel Wheelwright Samuel Donnel Wm Pepril and Abraham Preble Esq^{rs}, Justices of his Majesties Peace in this Countie of York.

Proclamation made/ the Comission for holding s^d Court Read

The names of the Jury of Inquest to Enquire betwixt

our Soueraign Lord the King and the body of this County are as followeth vidz'

Grand Jurrs

1 Jonathan Hamond fforeman
2 Daniel Littlefield
3 Jonathan Littlefield
4 Thomas Donnel
5 Daniel Goodwin
6 Nicholas Gowen
7 Jacob Remich
8 Thomas Hunscom
9 Abraham Preble
10 Abraham Lord
11 Arthur Bragdon
12 Benjamin Preble
13 Jeremiah Storer

Mr Roger Dearing and Arthur Came not appearing to serue on the Jury according to Summons are fined to his Majestie: 13^s: 4^d a piece.

Humphrey Scamon appearing at this Court to answer his bonds of good behauiour, and nothing appearing against him he is acquitted from his s^d bonds paying the ffees of Court. ffees payd in Court.

Abel Molton of york being brought to this Court to answ^r for some Misdemenio^rs as p Euidence giuen in against him desires to be tryed by a Jury, the Court grants it/ The Jury are the psons aboue named except Arthur Bragdon onely

The Jury finds Abel Molton Guilty of speaking abusiue words against authority, for which abusiue speeches the s^d Molton is sentenced by this Court to pay three pounds to the use of his Majestie and to pay ffees: 12^s and to stand Comitted till it be payd/ ffine & ffees payd in Court.

he presenting his humble petition, the Court remits 30^s of his fine

Baker Nason being brought to this Court by Recognesance nothing appearing against him he is discharged of his said Recognezance by Proclamation/ fees of Court payd.

Part II, Fol. 97.

Rowland Young Sen[r] appearing at this Court to answer a presentment Exhibited against him by y[e] Grand Jury for Swearing seuerall Sinfull oaths, is for his ofence to pay to the Select men of York: six shillings for the use of the pore of said Town, and to pay ffees: 4[s]: 6[d]

ffine and ffees payd in Court.

Abraham Parker and Sarah his wife being presented for not ffrequenting the public worship of God upon y[e] Lords day they applying themselues to one of his Majesties Justices of this County and promising reformation are acquitted paying ffees 4[s]/ ffees payd in Court.

Seuerall of the Town of Barwick presenting their humble Petion to this Court relating to the Irrigular and Illeagall proceeding of the Select men thereof by giuing warrant for the raysing of money upon the Inhabitants to satisfie for y[e] building of a house for the Ministry without Consulting the s[d] Inhabitants the Court Thinks Meet upon Mature Consideration to order that there shall be a public Meeting of the Inhabitants, and that the gathering of the rate comitted to the Constable shall be suspended till y[e] s[d] Inhabitants haue had a Meeting for their better satisfaction and in Case of none agreement between said Select men and Town, they shall chuse two Indifferent men which are unconcerned, who shall view y[e] s[d] house and Compute the Cost as near as may be and alsoe Examine the Select mens Accounts and giue their Determination thereof under their hands which shall be Complyed with, and a Rate Imediately made to reimburse y[e] s[d] Select men what is adjudged their due to be payd in Money or otherwise as shall be ordered.

[97]

Samuel Spinney presenting his humble Petition to this Court to haue a conuenient high way from his homesteed to

PART II, FOL. 98.

his out Lot This Court taking it into Consideration doe order a high way to be Layd out according to his Petition if there be Land there to be found.

William Grant of Barwick and Martha his now wife being presented by the Grand Jury for comitting ffornication s^d Grant appearing to answer for himselfe and wife, giuing satisfying reasons for his s^d wiues not appearing, and he owning the ffact, they are sentenced to pay to the use of Majestie fiue and twenty shillings a piece and ffees: 10^s, or to receiue fiue stripes a piece upon their Naked backs at the Post, and to pay ffees afores^d, and to stand Comitted till the fine be payd or Execution done/ ffine and ffees payd

Lycence Granted to John Woodman to keep a public house of Entertainment and to retaile all sorts of strong drink he obseruing the laws and orders made and prouided for the regulation of such houses.

Lycences

Lycence is granted to John Leighton to keep a public house of Entertainment and to retayle all sorts of strong drink &^{c} he obseruing the Law made and prouided for ye regulation of such houses.

Mr Joseph Curtis has Lycence granted him to keep a public house of Entertainment and to retaile all sorts of strong drink he obseruing the Law made and prouided for y^e Regulation of such houses.

[98]

Presentments made by the Grand Jury to this Court of Sessions at wells upon the 5º day of January: 169$\frac{4}{5}$

Wells

We present William Parsons and Hannah Wheelwright the now wife of s^d Parsons for Comitting ffornication/

Part II, Fol. 99.

We present Joseph Credifor and Rachel his wife for not ffrequenting the pubic worship of God upon the Lords day.

We present Elizabeth Denmark the wife of James Denmark for not ffrequenting ye public worship of God upon the Lords day/ We present Rebeckah Mackanney the wife of Robt Mackanney for not ffrequenting the public worship of God upon the Lords day/ We present William Sawyer and Joseph Sawyer for doing seruile Labour upon ye Lords day, by trauailing from Kittery to Wells with burdens.

Presentmts

We present Matthew Young and Elin^r Hayns his now wife for comitting ffornication.

York

We present Peter Nowel for selling deliuering and receuing pay for a horse upon ye Lords day.

We present Martha Taylor for not ffrequenting ye public worship of God upon ye Lords day/ We present Mary Allen the wife of Walter Allen for not ffrequenting ye public worship of God upon ye Lords day/ We present Elizabeth the wife of Nicholas Turbet for not ffrequenting the public worship of God upon ye Lords day.

Kittery

We present the widow Sarah Chadborn for not ffrequenting the public worship of God upon the Lords day/

We present Moses Woster for striking and abusing his wife upon the Lords day seuerall times/

We present Elizabeth Bracket for not ffrequenting the public worship of God upon the Lord day.

Jonathan Hamond fforeman

William Parsons appearing at this Court to answer a presentm^t Exhibited against himselfe and wife, by the Grand Jury as apears aboue for Comitting ffornication, s^d parsons owning the ffact are [99] ffor said ofence sentenced to pay to the use of his Majestie fiue and twenty shillings a piece and to pay fees: 2^s: 6^d/ his s^d wife for resons shewed to ye Courts satisfaction Excused for her not appearing/ fine and ffees payd in Court.

Part II, Fol. 99.

Joseph Credifor and his wife and Elizabeth Denmark appeared to answer their presentm⁺ for not frequenting the public worship of God upon yᵉ Lords day, are for their ofence, admonished by the Court, and to pay fees: 1ˢ 6ᵈ a piece/ fees payd

Peter Staple Junʳ and Mary his wife, and John Staple and Mary his wife being presented by the Grand Jury for Comitting fornication, and sᵈ Peter and John Staple for swearing and Cursing, the said Peter Staple and his wife being sumoned to appear at this Court to answer for their ofence, And for theyr not appearing according to Sumons It is ordered that a speciall warrant be granted by the Clerk of sᵈ Court to seize yᵉ sᵈ psons and bring them before his Majesties Justices at yᵉ Next Quartʳ Sessions to be holden at york to answer for their Contempt and alsoe for their sᵈ presentment. And alsoe a speciall warrᵗ to be granted for Constant Rainking & Hannah his wife for their not appearing according to Sumons to answer their presentmᵗ at this Court. And Sumons granted for Jnᵒ Staple & his wife to answer.

Anno 1696-7

Inferir Court of pleas

County of York
An Inferiour Court of Comon pleas held at Wells on the 5ᵒ day of January: 169¾ Before Samuel Wheelwright Charles ffrost Samuel Donnel & Wᵐ Peppril Esqʳˢ/

Proclamation made, and Comission Read for holding sᵈ Court/ Noe business appearing the Court is Desoluᵈ/

PART II, FOL. 100.

[100]

William the third by the grace of God, of England Scotland ffrance and Ireland King Defend[r] of the ffaith &c/ To our trusty and beloued Samuel Wheelwright Charles ffrost W[m] Peppril and Samuel Donnel Esq[rs] Greeting/ Whereas the Great and generall Court or Assembly of our Prouince of the Massachusets Bay in New England in America haue lately reviued the Act ffor establishing of Judicatories and Courts of Justice within our s[d] Prouince Except such paragraphs, articles clauses and sentences thereof as haue been heretofore repealed altered or otherwise prouided for by the Generall Assembly and with such further alterations and amendments as we have signified our Royall plesure to be necessary, upon our disallowance of the s[d] act to cōtinue and abide in full force untill the end of the first Sessions of the Generall Assembly of our said Prouince to be begun and held upon the last Wednesday in May next anno 1697 and noe longer, We have Assigned and Doe hereby Constitute and appoint you o[r] Justices of our Inferiour Court of Comon Pleas within our County of Yorke during the continuance of the s[d] act and you or any three of you to here try and Determine all causes and Matters ciuil by Law cognizeable in s[d] Court With authoritie to use & exercise all powers and Jurisdictions belonging to the same, and to award Execution and to doe that w[ch] to Justice doth appertain according to Law In Testimony whereof We have caused the publick Seal of our Prouince of the Massachusets Bay afores[d] to be hereunto affixed Witness William Stoughton Esq[r] our Lieu[t] Gouern[r] and Comand[r] in Chief in and over our s[d] Prouince at Boston the Sixteenth day of octob[r] 1696, In the Eighth year of our Reign.   W[m] Stoughton
By order of the Lieu[t] Gouern[r]
  and Council
    Is[a] Addington Secr̃y

PART II, FOL. 101.

A true Copie of the origenall Comission Transcribed and Compared this third day of ffebruary : 169¾
p Jos: Hamond Regist^r

[101]

Anno 1697   County of York

At his Majesties Court of Quarter Sessions held at York Apr^{ll} 6th 1697 Before Charles ffrost Sam^{ll} Wheelwright Sam^{ll} Donnell William Peprill and Abraham Preble Esq^{rs} Justices of his Majesties peace for s^d County

Proclamation made & Comission read for hold s^d Court

The names of Grand Jury are as follows
1 John Leighton fforeman
2 Wm Sayer   8 Sam^{ll} ffernald
3 Josiah Littlefield 9 Richard Rogers
4 Sam^{ll} Hatch   10 James Goodwin
5 Jeremiah Molton   11 Arthur Bragdon
6 Lewis Bean   12 Abraham Lord
7 Robert Cutt   13 Arthur Came

Mr William Pepril Chosen County Tresur^r for this year

Roger Thomas being bound ouer to this Court by Recognesance upon suspicion of Stealing a parcel of Money from Mary Dixon, Nothing appearing against him he is Cleared of his bonds.

Alexander Thompson Cleared of his bons for appearing at this Court by Proclamation.

William Sawyer being presented for doing serule Labour

upon ye Lords day, being Legally Conuicted is for his said ofence to pay fiue shillings fine to ye Select men of Wells for ye use of ye pore thereof, and to pay fees: 4ˢ 6ᵈ

ffine and ffees payd in Court

[102]

Moses woster appearing to answer his presentment for striking his wife upon ye Lords day, he being Leagally Conuicted thereof is sentenced to pay twenty shillings fine for ye use of his Majestie for breach of the peace in striking his wife, and to pay fiue shillings for breach of ye Sabbath, and ffees: 4ˢ: 6ᵈ, and to stand Comitted till done/ payd in Court.

Sarah Chadborn appearing to answer presentment for not ffrequenting ye public worship of God upon ye Lords day is for her ofence to be admonished and to pay ffees of Court fiue shillings 6ᵈ and to stand Comitted till done.

Admonition giuen and fees payd in Court.

Peter Nowell appearing to answer his presentment for breach of Sabbath as appears p sᵈ presentmᵗ on Record, he Submitting himselfe to ye Court is for his ofence fined fiue shillings for ye use of ye pore of York and to pay fees of Court: four shillings 6ᵈ and to stand Comitted till done, payd in Court

Matthews Young and Ellinʳ his wife appearing to answer their presentments for Comitting ffornication, they owning the ffact are Sentenced to receiue nine stripes a piece upon their Naked backs at ye post, or to pay fiue & twenty shillings a piece for ye use of his Majestie, and to pay fees nine shillings, and to stand Comitted till it be done.

Upon their humble petition ten shillings of their fine is remitted, the rest payd in Court.

PART II, FOL. 103.

Elias Weare & Magdalen his wife being presented to this Court for Comitting ffornication they owning ye fact are sentenced to Receiue nine stripes a piece upon ye Naked back or to pay fiue & twenty shillings a piece and ffees : 9^s : 3^d and to stand Comitted till done/ ffees payd in Court

[103]

Thomas Trafton being presented to this Court for Retaileing of Strong drink without Lycence, he pleading of ye time of renewing his Lycence is sentenced to pay ten shillings to ye use of ye pore of York, and to pay ffees : 2^s : 6^d. ffees payd in Court.

Elizabeth Trafton being brought to this Court by Complaint of Sargeant Daniel Black, for her and her sons abusiue Carriage toward him s^d Black in the Execution of his office she being Leagally Conuicted is sentenced to be admonished and to pay ffees of Court : 5^s 6^d — payd in Court

Mr James Plaisted appearing to answer in behalfe of his wife to answer her presentm^t for not ffrequenting ye public worship of God upon ye Lords day, she being under some bodily Infirmity hindering her own appearance, Is for her ofence to pay ffees : 4^s 6^d and to be admonished : ffees payd in Court.

Lycence is granted to Lieut Joseph Storer of Wells to keep a public house of Entertainment and to retale all sorts of strong drink and Victualls he giuing bond to obserue ye law made and prouided in such Cases.

Mr John Wheelwright has Lycence granted to keep a public house of Entertainment and to retale all sorts of strong drink and victualls he giuing bond to obserue ye law made and prouided in such Cases

[104]

Lycence is Granted to M{r} James Plaisted of York to retail all sorts of strong drink and Victualls, he giuing bond to obserue y{e} Law made and prouided in such Cases

Lycences

Matthew Austine has Lycence granted him to keep a public house of Entertainment and to retale all sorts of strong drink and victualls he giuing bond to obserue y{e} law in such Cases made & prouided

Lycence is granted to Joan Crofts to keep a public house of Entertainment and to retaile all sorts of strong drink and victualls she giuing bond to obserue y{e} law in such Cases made and prouided

Lycence is granted to John Morgrage to retail Victualls beer and Cyder he giuing bond to obserue y{e} law in such Cases mad and prouided

Thomas Trafton has Lycence granted him to retaile all sorts of strong drink and victuall and to keep a public house of Entertainment he giuing bond to obserue the Law made and prouided in such Cases

presentments

Presentments made by the Grand Jury to y{e} Court of Quarter Sessions held at York Apr{ll} y{e} 6{th} 1697.

We present Elias Weare & Magdaleen Adams his now wife for Comitting ffornication.

We present George Spencer & Brawn his now wife for Comitting ffornication

We present Thomas Trafton for retayling strong drink without Lycence.

We present The Towns of York and Kittery for the Defect of Braue boat Harb{r} Bridge.

Part II, Fol. 105, 106.

[105]

We present the Town of Kittery for not repairing the High way from York bounds to Spruce Creek

York Apr^{ll} 6. 1697   John Leighton forem̃

At his Majesties Inferiour Court of Com̃on pleas held at York April ye 6th 1697, before Samuel Wheelwright Charles ffrost Samuel Doñell and William Pepril Esq^{rs} his Majesties Justices appointed to hold s^d Court.

The Names of ye Jury of Tryalls are as ffolloweth —

1	John Leighton fforeman	7	Sam^{ll} ffernald
2	Wm Sawyer	8	Robert Cutt
3	Josiah Littlefield	9	Richd Rogers
4	Sam^{ll} Hatch	10	James Goodwyn
5	Jeremiah Molton	11	Arthur Bragdon
6	Lewis Bean	12	Abraham Lord

James ffoul is Plaintiff in an Action of ye Case for Detaining three pounds in money as p Attachm^t Versus Nathaniel Johnson Defendant

The Jury finds for y^e Plaintiff three pounds sued for and Cost of sute. John Leighton fforeman

Bill of Costs brought in and allowed: two pounds ffifteen shillings & 6^d p Sam^{ll} Wheelwright

[106]
County of York

At his Maties Court of Sessions held at York Jan^{ry} 4th 169$\frac{7}{8}$

PART II, FOL. 107.

Before Sam^ll Wheelwright Sam^ll Donnell William Pepprill and Abraham Preble Esq^rs his Maties Justices of y^e peace for s^d County.

Proclamation made
The names of the Grand Jury are as followeth
1 John Leighton fforeman
2 William Sayer
3 Josiah Littlefield
4 Samuel Hatch
5 Lewis Bean
6 Jeremiah Molton
7 Arthur Bragdon
8 Baker Nason
9 John Heard
10 Richard Rogers
11 Robert Cutt
12 Samuel ffernald
13 Nicholas Gowen

John Staple appearing to answer a presentment of the Grand Jury Exhibited against himself & his now wife for comitting ye act of ffornication, the s^d Staple owning the ffact are sentenced to receiue seuen stripes a piece on ye Naked back at ye post or to pay unto his Majestie 25^s a piece, and to pay ffees : 9^s and to stand Comitted till done/
ffine & ffees both payd in Court & they are Acquitted

John Staple appearing to answer a presentm^t brought against him by the Grand Jury for cursing & swearing and being Leagally Conuicted is for his offence to pay 5^s fine for ye use of ye pore of Kittery and to be admonished or to sit one houre in the Stocks, and to pay ffees : 4^s 6^d and to stand Comitted till done/ Admonition receiued, and ffees paid

[107]
George Spencer and his now wife appearing to answer a presentm^t of ye grand Jury brought in against them for comitting the act of ffornication, they owning the ffact are sentenced to be whipt seuen stripes a piece upon ye Naked back or to pay a fine of fiue & twenty shillings a piece to his Maj-

Part II, Fol. 108.

estie and to pay fees nine shillings. ffine and ffees payd in Court, and they are Cleared.

The Towns of York & Kittery being presented to this Court for y{e} defect of Braue-boat Harb{r} bridge, Matthew Austine appearing to answer for y{e} Town of York and Lieu{t} John Shapleigh for y{e} town of Kittery, The Court orders that s{d} Bridge be repaired by the last of Apr{ll} next on y{e} forfiture of fiue pound a piece for each town, for his Ma{ties} use, and to pay ffees 4{s} 6{d} each town

Lieu{t} John Shapleigh appearing at this Court to answer a presentm{t} of the grand Jury Exhibited against y{e} town of Kittery for not repairing the highway between Kittery bounds & Spruce Creek this Court ordereth that s{d} high way be repaired by the last of June next upon y{e} forfiture of fiue pounds to be payd by s{d} town for the use of his Majestie, and to pay ffees : 4{s} : 6{d}

Samuel ffernald presenting his humble Petition to this Court for a conuenient high way from his Land lying in y{e} great Coue as p his Petition the Court taking it into Consideration doe order that y{e} Select men for y{e} Town of Kittery or y{e} Maj{r} part of them, shall lay out from s{d} ffernalds Land to y{e} water side a conuenient way prouided that if it be any considerable damage to any other man it shall be made up to him in some other place/ And this to be done by the first of Aprill next. And to make return thereof under their hands to y{e} town Clerk

[108]

Richard Rogers presenting his humble Petition to this Court to haue his Land in the long Reach layd out, that is to say his the line to be run on that side next Peter Staples according to grant the Court taking it into consideration doe order that the Sureir of Kittery shall run sd line by the first of Aprill next. And that according to grant/ And make return thereof under his hand to ye Town Clerk.

Lycence is granted to Arthur Beal of York to Keep a fferry ouer york Riuer for one year, where Thomas More formerly kept it he keeping a sufficient Boat to transport horse and man and to giue good attendance/ And to be allowed 6d for a man & horse that is 2d a man & 4d an horse, for wch he stands bound to our Soueraign Ld the King in ye sum of ten pounds.

Jeremiah Moulton being complained of to this Court for retailing strong drink without Lycence, he appearing in Court and owning the ffact, the Court taking it into consideration and duly weighing all circumstances doe acquit him from any fine that might by law be Imposd he giuing bond as ffolloweth & to pay ffees : 3s : 6d

Jeremiah Molton owns himselfe bound & firmly obliged to our Souern Ld King William his Successrs in the sum of ten pounds that for time to come he will neither directly nor Indirectly sell any strong drink without Lycence.

Samuel Bragdon Senr being complained of to this Court for retailing of strong drink without Lycence he appearing in Court and being Legally Conuicted is adjudged to pay 40s to ye use of the pore of York, and to pay ffees : 2s 6d and to stand comitted till payd/

Upon his humble Petition the one half of ye fine is remitted

[109]

Samuel Bragdon Junr being Complained to this Court for his abusiue carriage toward Abraham Preble Esqr one of his Majesties Justices, appearing in Court and being Legally

Part II, Fol. 109.

Conuicted is fined to his Majestie 30ˢ and to pay ffees : 8ˢ 10ᵈ and to stand Committed till it be payd/ And stands bound & firmly obliged to oʳ Soueraign Lord yᵉ King in yᵉ sum of ten pound to be of yᵉ good behauioʳ till the Next Sessions of yᵉ Peace

Thomas Rice and his two Sons Thomas and Richard brought to this Court as Prisoners upon of ffelloniously taking away and conceasealing of goods from seuerall psons. And upon Examination in Court the sᵈ Thomas Rice Junʳ owned & confessed in Court that he had stolen a shallops foresaile fishing lines bread and pork out of James Blagdons shallop and a parces of ffish from Clarks Island belonging to Richᵈ oliuer & William Tucker the sᵈ goods being found in the Custodie of Thomas Rice Senʳ giues Just cause of Judging him Guilty of being priuie to yᵉ fact — the sᵈ foresaile fishing lines bread & pork taken from Blagdons boat vallued at 4ᶠ and yᵉ fish taken from Clarks Island valᵈ at 1ᶠ 2ˢ The sᵈ psons submitting themselues to yᵉ Court are sentenced as ffolloweth vidzᵗ the sᵈ Thomas Rice Senʳ for concealing sᵈ goods is to receiue ffifteen stripes upon yᵉ Naked back or to pay 4ᶠ fine to his Majestie and to pay to Mʳ James Blagdon twelue pounds and to Richᵈ olliuʳ & Will Tucker 3ᶠ : 6ˢ : And Thomas Rice Junʳ is sentenced to pay ffiftie shillings to his Maᵗⁱᵉ or to receiue twelue stripes at yᵉ post upon his Naked back, And Richᵈ Rice to be admonished and soe acquitted/ And yᵉ sᵈ Thomˢ Rice Senʳ to pay ffees & other Charges as ffolloweth.

That is to say

	s	d
To Wm Pepprill Esqr....................£01	07	00
To ye Coustable Weeks & ye Sheriff............. 02	11	06
To Mr James Blagdons charges................. 01	14	09
To the Kings Atturney, Capt Pickerin............ 00	10	00
To the Clerk of ye Court....................... 00	07	00
	6 10	3

and to stand Comitted till done.

Part II, Fol. 110.

[110]

Lycence is granted to Mrs Mary ffrost to keep a publick house of entertainment she giuing bond to obserue the laws made and prouided in such Cases.

Lycence is granted to John Leighton, he obseruing the laws made & prouided in such cases.

Lycence granted to Mr Saml¹ Donnell he obseruing the laws made & prouided such cases

Lycence granted to Mr William Pepperill he obseruing the laws made & prouided in such cases.

Lycence granted to Mr Joseph Curtis he obseruing the laws made and prouided in such cases.

Lycence granted to Joanna Dearing she obseruing the laws made and prouided in such Cases.

All these aforenamed haue liberty to sell all sorts of strong drink.

It is ordered by this Court that thirty pounds shall be raysed by rate upoh ye Inhabitants of this Countie for defraying of the charge thereof/ And that there shall be a Comissionr Chosen in each Town who are to meet at York ye last Tuesday of March next to compute ye Towns Estate, in order to raysing sd sum of Money

PART II, FOL. 111, 112.

[111]

County York

Presentments agreed upon and brought in by the grand Jury Jan'y 4th 169¾, to y'e Court of Sessions at York.

Wells   We pres't Sarah King for comitting ffornication.

York   We present Sam'll Bragdon Sen'r for retailing strong strong drink without Lycence — answered in Court.

We present Alexander Maxell for drinking to Excess

We present John Bracie for cursing

We present Thomas ffeauo'r & Ruth Donnel his now wife for comitting ffornication.

Kittery   We present Thomas Starboard for not frequenting the public Worship of God upon y'e Lords day.

We present y'e Town of Kittery for not laying out high ways according to Law in s'd Town.

We present John Hoight for swearing.

We present ffrancis Herloe for swearing he would cut his wiues throat.

We present y'e Widdow Taylor, Walter Allens wife, Nicholas Turbet & his wife Sam'll Brackett & his wife & John ffosts wife, for not ffrequenting the public worship of God upon the Lords day.

                        John Leighton fforeman

[112]

County York

Anno 169 7-8   At an Inferiour Court of Comon pleas held at York Jan'rn 4th 169⅞ Before Samuel Wheelwright William Pepperill & Samuel Donnell Esq'rs his Majesties Justices for s'd County —

Part II, Fol. 113.

Proclamation made.

The Comission for holding s^d Court Read.
and the Jury Impenneled.
The names of ye Jury of trialls are as ffolloweth —
John Leighton fforeman

William Sayer	Arthur Bragdon
Josiah Littlefield	Baker Nason
Samuel Hatch	John Heard
Lewis Bean	Robert Cutt
Jeremiah Molton	Sam^ll ffernald
	Nicholas Gowen

John Woodman is Plaintiff in an Action of the Case for none paym^t of four pounds as p ye attachment
  Versus Richard King Defendant
The Jury ffinds for ye Defendant Costs of suit.
Costs allowed : 1^£ : 4^s : 0^d

Capt ffrancis Raynes is Plaintiff in an Action of Debt due upon Acco^t to ye vallue of 11^£ : 18^s : as p attachment
  Versus Richard Carter Defendant
The Jury ffinds for ye Defendant Costs of suit
Costs allowed : 16^s : 9^d :

[113]

Christian Remich is Plaintiff in an action of Trespass to ye vallue of twenty fiue pounds money for cutting down trees upon his Land to ye Numb^r of about Sixtie, as p Attachm^t versus Sam^ll Spinney Defend^t
The Jury finds for ye Defendant Costs of suite
The Plaintiff Appeals to ye next Superi^r Court to be holden for the County of York — And ye s^d Remich Apellant as principle & Jacob Remich of Kittery & Jaruis Ring of Salisbury as Sureties own themselues bound to our Sou-

eraign Lord King William his Success[rs] in the sum of ffiftie pounds that y[e] s[d] Christian Remich shall prosecute his Appeal to Effect at s[d] Superi[r] Court

Nathaniel Keen is Plaintiff in a suite to compell y[e] making and acknowledging a Deed of Sale for a hundred Acres of Land as p Attachm[t] versus Lieu[t] John Shapleigh Defend[t]
The writ abates by reson there is noe Action Mentioned Costs allowed y[e] Defend[t] twentie shillings   £1 : 0 : 0

Nathaniel Keen is Plaintiff in an Action of y[e] case for y[e] fforfiture of a bond of Eighty pounds, versus Lieu[t] John Shapleigh Defend[t]
The writ abates by reason it is not mentioned what y[e] forfiture is for.
Costs allowed y[e] Defend[t] 19[s] 0[d]

[114]

Christian Remichs Reasons of Appeal from the Judgment of the Inferi[r] Court of Pleas holden at York the first Tuesday in January: 1697 unto the next Superi[r] Court to be holden for The County of Yorke In a case wherein he was Plaintiff against Sam[ll] Spinney, Which are as followeth

first. My first and generall reson is because I fairly and fully proued my case and yet y[e] Verdict was giuen against me.

2[ly]/ That it was soe we make it thus appear/ our Action was an Action of Trespass for falling of seuerall trees, to the number about Sixty, upon the Land of the Plaintiff/ Now that such trees were fell, and fell upon y[t] very land doe appear by the Testimony of Jacob Remich Joshua Remich Daniel Green & Thomas Spinney Sen[r]/ All these Testifie to the cutting of the trees and that they were Cut upon the Plaintiffs Land, wherein the Case or action is fully proued/ the Jury are to goe by law and Euidence, and by y̆ᵉ law, by the mouth of two or three witnesses euery word shall be Established but here are four substantiall knowing Euidences to the whole soe that what is more is more then is Needfull

3ᵈˡʸ But we haue alsoe produced the seuerall grants of said land to sᵈ Remich and layd out all in one day and bounded and that the sᵈ and that yᵉ sᵈ bounds were run and owned by him and yᵉ Defendᵗ, and seuerall years according to law renewed between them.

4ˡʸ We haue a generˡˡ order of Legall Town Meeting in Kittery Dated June yᵉ 24ᵗʰ 1687 wherein they being sensable of some Inconueniency that might come by the naming of the numbʳ of Acres or breadth of bounds in mens Lands did pass this ordʳ for preuention thereof that those antient bounds set between one mans land and an other through yᵉ whole Town either by yᵉ Select men or Surueiʳˢ for yᵉ laying out of land, shall stand as the true and lawfull bounds between euery mans Land And what can more be said in yᵉ case if firm foundations be remoued what can yᵉ Righteous doe or when can [115] any man be safe or quiet, troubling Courts with many woes is not to Clear but darken truth which to auoyd we humbly add that all their Allegations on yᵉ dispute are too friuelous to abuse the eares of the Honoured Court and Jury with any further taking Notice of them by way of Answer/ humbly hopeing that yᵉ case will soe appear to yʳ Honʳˢ as to reuerse the former Judgement All which I leaue with yʳ honʳˢ Subscribeing myselfe, yʳ Honʳˢ humble Seruant

         Christian Remich

A true Copie of yᵉ origenall Reasons Transcribed and Compared this 11ᵗʰ day of Aprill, 1698

         p Jos Hamond Clerᵏ

PART II, FOL. 116, 117.

[116]

County York

At a Court of Sessions held at Wells July y° 5th 1698 Before Samuel Wheelwright Samuel Donnell William Pepperrell & Abraham Preble Esqr, his Majesties Justices of peace in s^d County.

Proclamation made
The names of the Grand-Jury are as follows
Imp^r Joshua Downing, fforeman

2	Thomas Spinney	8	Andrew Brown
3	Christopher Mitchell	9	Joseph Pray
4	Thomas Thompson	10	John Clayce
5	James Emery	11	Dauid Littlefield
6	Lewis Bean	12	Nicholas Gowen
7	Joseph Banks	13	John Eldridge

The Jury swrne in Court

Joseph Wilson Philip Hubbord & Eliab Littlefield being sumoned to appear on ye Jury and they being defectiue are fined for their Delinquency to s^d County : 20^s a piece.

Alexand^r Maxell being presented to this Court for drinking to Excess, he making application to Mr Samuell Donnell, one of his Maties Justices for s^d County and promising reformation, he is acquitted paying fiue shillings fine for ye use of ye pore of ye Town of York and to pay ffees : 5^s

[117]

John Bracy being sumoned to appear at this Court to answer a presentment of ye Grand Jury Exhibited against him for Cursing/ And this Court being made senceable that he was not Capable to appear is sentenced to sit in ye Stocks at York not exceeding three houres/ Mr Donnell & L^t

PART II, FOL. 118.

Preble to see ye Execution done within one Moneth of ye Day hereof and he is to pay ffees of Court, 5s

Sarah King appearing at this Court to answer a presentmt Exhibited against her for comitting ye act of ffornication/ She owning the ffact is sentenced to receiue seuen stripes at ye Post upon ye Naked back, and to pay ffees of Court 5s, or to pay fiue & twenty shillings fine to his Majesty & pay ffees as aforesd and to stand Comitted till done
 ffine and ffees payd in Court.

Thomas ffcauaugh and his wife being sumoned to apear at this Court to answer a presentmt of the Grand Jury Exhibited against them for comitting ffornication and they not apearing, its ordered by the Court that a speciall warrant be granted by the Clerk for their appearance at ye Next Sessions at York to answer Contempt as alsoe their presentmt

John Hoit appearing to answer a presentmt against him for swearing, and being Legally Conuicted is fined fiue shillings for ye use of ye pore of Kittery and to pay fees of Court : 5s and to stand comitted till done
 ffine and ffees payd in Court

[118]
The Widow Martha Taylor, Walter Allens wife, Nicholas Turbet & his wife Samll Bracket & his wife & John ffosts wife not apearing at this Court to answer their presentmts Exhibited against them by ye Grand Jury for not ffrequenting ye public worship of God upon ye Lords day/ Its ordered by the Court that a speciall Warrant be granted by the Clerk for their appearance at ye Next Sessions to be held at York to answer for their Contempt as alsoe to answer their sd presentment

PART II, FOL. 119.

The Town of Kittery being presented to this Court, for not laying out high wayes in s^d Town according to Law/ Mr William Pepperrell appearing in Court to answer in s^d Towns behalf this Court orders that the Select men of Kittery shall some time between this and ye next Sessions lay out such high ways in said Town as are nessessary & conuenient on penalty of paying fiue pounds to ye County Tresu^r for ye use of ye County of York, and to pay ffees of Court 5^s

ffees payd in Court.

The Town of Wells being presented for not making a nigh way from John Littlefield Junr to Sam^{ll} Hatchs, Mr John Wheelwright appearing to answer in s^d Towns behalf/ The Court orders that a conuenient high way be made there between & y^e next Sessions upon penalty of fiue pounds to be payd to y^e County Tresu^r for y^e use of s^d County and to pay fees: 2^s 6^d/ ffees payd.

[119]

Mr Jeremiah Molton Cleared of bonds of: 10$^£$

Edmund Gatch brought to this Court by recognezence for stealing a siluer spoon, he owning y^e ffact is sentenced to receiue fiue stripes at y^e post upon the Naked back, and to pay ffees of Court 4^s or to pay 15^s fine to his Majesty & fees afores^d, and to stand Comitted till done.

Thomas Spinney Senr presenting his humble Petition to haue a Survigh upon his old Lott in the great Coue behind Sam^{ll} Spinneys house And the Addition at the head thereof and on ye North side next Christian Remichs land where there is a present controuersie between his son Sam^{ll} and s^d Remich/ In answer whereunto after Mature Consideration. This Court has appointed Mr William Pepperrell Maj^r

Part II, Fol. 120.

Joseph Hamond M{r} Richard Cutt Ensign John Leighton and M{r} William Godsoe Surueigh{rs} to meet upon y{e} place and to run y{e} line between y{e} Petition{r} and s{d} Remichs lands according to y{e} antient grants & returns/ And to make true return of their doing therein to y{o} next Sessions to be holden for or w{th}in this County.

Lycence Granted to Matthew Austine of York to keep a public house of Entertainment and to retayle all sorts of strong drink, he giuing bond to obserue in that behalf made and Prouided

[120]
Lycence granted to Thomas Trafton to keep a house of public Entertainment and to Retaile all sorts of strong drink, he giuing 10$^£$ bond to obserue the Law made and provided in such Cases.

Lycence granted to James Plaisted to kepe a house of Entertainment he giving 10$^£$ bond to observe and keep the Law, in such cases made and Provided

Lycence Granted unto Katharine Paul of Kittery to Keep a house of public she giving bond of 10$^£$ to observe and keep the Law in such cases made and provided.

Lycence granted to James Stackpole to keep a house of public Entertainm{t} he giving bond of 10$^£$ to observe and keep the Law in such Cases made and provided

Lycence granted to L{t} Joseph Storer of Wells to keep a house of public Entertainm{t} he giueing bond of 10$^£$ to observe and keep y{e} Law in such Cases made and provided.

PART II, FOL. 121.

Mr John Wheelwright has Lycence granted to keep a house of public Entertainm.^t and to retaile all sorts of strong drink/ he giuing bond to observe and keep the Law In such cases made & Provided

Lycence granted to John Morgrage to retaile all sorts of strong drink, he giuin 10.[£] bond to obserue the Law In such cases made and Provided

[121]
Presentments brought in by the Grand Jury

Wells — We pres.^t ye Town of Wells for not making a convenient high way betwixt the house of John Littlefield Junr & Samuel Hatches/ Answered

York — We Present Susana Young, daughter of Rowland young for Comitting ffornication.

We present Arthur Beal for selling strong drink by retale without Lycence.

We Present Elizabeth Parsons for selling strong drink by retayle without Lycence.

We Present Sarg.^t Daniel Black for selling strong drink by retale without Lycence.

We Present Thomas Hains for falling trees athwart the Kings high way & for Cumbring ye same

We present Hannah ffrethy for selling strong drink by retale without Lycence.

Kittery — We present Hugh Tucker & his now wife for comitting the act of ffornication

We present Hugh Crocket & his now wife Committing the act of ffornication.

p me Joshua Downing fforeman

PART II, FOL. 122.

Anno 1698

[122]
County of York

At his Majesties Court of Quarter Sessions held at York January y° 3ᵈ 169⅝/ Before Samuel Wheelwright, Samˡˡ Donnell William Pepperrell & Abraham Preble Esqʳˢ Justices of the Peace for sᵈ County of York.

Proclamation made
The names of the Grand Jury are as ffolloweth vizᵗ
1ˢᵗ Joshua Downing fforeman
2 Tho: Spinney   8 Joseph Banks
3 Joseph Wilson   9 Joseph Pray
4 Christophʳ Mitchell   10 John Clayce
5 Phillip Hubbord   11 David Littlefield
6 Thomas Thomson   12 Eliab Littlefield
7 Andrew Brown   13 Richard King

Susana Young appearing at this Court to answer a presentment Exhibited against her by the grand Jury for comitting the act of ffornication/ She owning the ffact and humbly submitting herselfe, is sentenced to receive fiue stripes upon the naked back at yᵉ Post and to pay fees 5ˢ/ or to pay 25ˢ fine to his Majᵗⁱᵉ and fees as aforesᵈ/

The sᵈ Young presenting her humble Petition and seuerall Circumstances moveing yᵉ Court thereto, have Metigated her fine to 12ˢ, She standing Comitted till done/ ffees payd in Court.

Arthur Beale appearing in Court to answer his presentmᵗ Exhibited against him by yᵉ Grand Jury for selling strong drink by retale without Lycence he making it appear that he had liberty from one of his Maᵗⁱˢ Justices of yᵉ Peace to sell drink for yᵉ reliefe of Trauailers till yᵉ Sessions, he is acquitted paying ffees: 5ˢ/ ffees paid in Court.

Part II, Fol. 123.

[123]

Elizabeth Parsons appearing to answer her presentm^t for selling strong drink by retale without Lycence and being Legally convicted/ She is Adjudged to pay: 40^s fine to ye Select men of York for ye use of ye pore y^{r}of and to pay ffees : 5^s, and to stand Comitted while done/ fees payd

Daniel Black appearing in Court to answer his presentm^t for seling strong drink by retale without Lycence and being Legally convicted is Adjudged to pay 40^s to ye Select men of York for ye use of ye pore thereof and to pay ffees : 5^s and to stand Comitted till done/ ffees paid

Thomas Haines appearing in Court to answer his presentm^t for felling trees athwart ye Kings high way, it not Legally appearing against him, he is acquitted, paying ffees : 3^s : 6^d/ paid in Court

Hannah ffrethy appearing in Court to answer her presentm^t for selling strong drink by retale without Lycence, is sentenced to pay 40^s to ye Select men of York for ye use of ye pore thereof, and to pay fees 5^s. ffees paid in Court.

Hugh Crocket appearing in Court to answer a presentm^t Exhibited against himselfe & his wife by ye grand jury, for comitting ye act of ffornication/ he owning ye ffact they are sentenced to receiue fiue stripes a piece upon ye Naked back at ye post, & to pay ffees 5^s each, or to pay 25^s a piece to his Majestie & fees as afores^d, and to stand Comitted till it be performed. He presenting his humble Petition the Court thinks Meet to remit 20^s of the fine ffees paid in Court.

William Gooden appearing in Court to answer his presentm^t for selling stron drink by retaile without Lycence is Adjudged to pay : 40^s to ye Select men of Kittery for ye use of ye pore thereof, and to pay ffees fiue shillings and to stand Comitted till done.

William Gooden for refusing to giue bond for his good behavr when requid thereto by one of his Majtis Justices of ye Peace, was comitted to Prison & from thence brought to this Court to answer ffor ye same, is sentenced to pay all charges arising through his disorder, which is 15s 4d and to stand Comitted till it be satisfied.

[124]

ffrancis Herlow appearing to answer his presentment for swearing he would cut his wiues throat, being legally conuicted is sentenced to sit in ye Stocks one houre, and to pay ffees fiue shillings and to stand comitted till Executed/

Thomas ffevaugh & Ruth his wife appearing in Court to answer their presentment Exhibited against them by the Grand jury for comitting ye act of ffornication, they owning the ffact are sentenced to receiue fiue stripes a piece upon ye Naked back at ye Post & to pay ffees 5s each, or to pay fiue & twenty shillings a piece & fees as aforesd, and to stand Comitted till done. They presenting their humble Petition the Court remits 20s of their fine

John ffost appearing to answer in behalfe of his wife for her contempt in not appearing to answer her presentment at ye last Court, as alsoe to answer sd presentment in not attending the Public worship of God upon ye Lords day, is Adjudged (all circumstances duely weighed) to pay ffees, 7s and to stand committed till done.

Nicholas Turbut and his wife being brought to this Court for their contempt in not appearing at ye last Court of Sessions held at Wells July : 1698, to answer their presentment for not frequenting the Public worship of God upon ye Lords day, as alsoe to answer s^d presentment s^d Turbet is sentenced to sit in ye Stocks one houre, and his wife to be Admonished. And they to pay ffees: 20^s and to stand comitted till done.

Samuel Bracket appearing to answer in behalfe of his wife for her not ffrequenting ye public worship of God upon ye Lords day, is sentenced to pay fees 5^s & she to be Admonished.

Joseph Wilson Eliab Littlefield & Philip Hubbord appearing to answer their Delinquencie for not attending his Maj^{ties} service on ye Grand jury & Jury of tryalls at the last Sessions and Court of Pleas holden at Wells, they giuing reasons to satisfaction are Acquitted.

[125]

Philip ffollet bound by recognesance to this Court to answer for his uncivill carriage wth Grace Lewis by attempting to take up her coats & lying upon her, is for his offence, sentenced to receiue fiue stripes upon ye Naked back at ye Post, or to pay 20^s for ye use of his Majestie, and to pay ffees & other Charges arising thereby. ffees paid.

Mary Hutchins bound by recognezance to this Court to be of ye good behav^r in ye sum of fiue pounds for abusing & striking some of her Neighb^{rs}/ She appearing to answer for her Misdemen^r & being legally convicted is sentenced to pay ten shillings to his Maj^{tie} and her bonds to be continued till ye next Sessions and to pay ffees: 5^s 6^d/ paid in Court.

Henry Barnes being bound to this Court by recognezance for his wiues good behav^r, and nothing appearing against her, he is acquitted of his bonds.

Part II, Fol. 126.

It is ordered by this Court that twenty pounds be forthwith raised by way of Rate upon y° Inhabitants of this County for paying y° Grand jury & other charges of y° County and to be deliuered to y° County Tresu^r for ye use afores^d

ordered that y° Clerk of this Court shall make up all accounts with y° Sheriff for what he has rec^d & paid in reference to his ofice since he has bin in y° place & ofice of Sheriff.

Lycence granted to John Woodman to keep a public house of Entertainment and retale all sorts of strong drink giuing bond according to Law

Lycence granted to Charles Kelley to retaile all sorts of strong drink out of Dores, not under a pint he giuing bond according to law

Lycence granted Arthur Beal to retale all sorts of strong drink he giuing bond according to law.

Lycence granted to John Leighton to keep a public house of Entertainment and to retale all sorts of strong drink giuing bond &c

Lycence granted to Mr William Pepperrell to retale strong drink giuing bond &c

[126]

Lycence granted to Mr Joseph Curtis to retaile strong drink he giuing bond &c

Lycence granted to Joanna Dearing to retale strong drink, giuing bond &c

Part II, Fol. 126.

Lycence granted to Mr Samll Donnell to keep a public house & to retale strong dring, giuing bond as ye Law Directs.

Presentmts made by ye Grand Jury

Kittery

We present Henry Barns & his wife, & Elisha Crocket, & Jane Hamons all of Kittery, for not frequenting ye public worship of God on ye Lords day

We present Joanna Crafts, Widow for retaling of strong Liqrs without Lycence

We present Mary Lisson for retaling of strong liqr without Lycence

York

We present in York ye high way between broad boat harbr & Thomas Mores

Wells

We present in Wells John Cyas & Ann Pitman wch is now his wife for for comitting ffornication.

Joshua Downing fforeman

County }
York } At his Mattes Inferir Court of Comon Pleas held at York Janry 3d 169$\frac{8}{9}$, before his Matts Justices of sd County appointed for holding sd Court.

The names of ye Jury of Tryalls are as followeth vizt
1 Thomas Spinney   7 Daniel Black
2 Joseph Wilson   8 Joseph Banks
3 Christophr Mitchell   9 Joseph Pray
4 Philip Hubbord   10 John Claise
5 Thomas Tomson   11 David Littlefield
6 Andrew Brown   12 Eliab Littlefield

Peter Wear Plaintiff in an Action of ye Case for a Debt due from ye Estate of Gabriel Tetherly as p Attachmt, versus: Richd King Defendt/ The Jury finds for ye Defendt

Part II, Fol. 127.

Costs of suit/ The Plaintiff by his Atturney vizt Cap^{tn} John Pickerin, appeales to ye next Superi^r Court to be holden within this s^d County of York, And ye s^d John Pickerin Woodman & Samuel Spinney own themselues bound & obliged to our Soveraign Ld King William his Success^{rs} in ye sum of twenty pounds that ye s^d Weare shall prosecute his Appeal with Effect.

Sam^{ll} Spinney is Plaintiff in an Action of the Case for laying Claim to a pcle of land and timb^r as p Attachm^t, versus Christian Remich Defend^t/ The Jury finds for ye Plaintiff ye land sued for, ten pound : 10^s : 6^d Damage & Costs of suite The Defend^t appeals to ye next Superi^r Court to holden within or for this County of york/ And ye s^d Remich Appell^t as Principle and Jarvis Ring of Salisbury and Joshua Downing of Kittery as Sureties own themselues bound & obliged to our Soveraign Ld King William his Success^{rs} in ye sum of fffiftie pounds that ye s^d Remich shall Prosecute his Appeal to Effect

[127]
Christian Remich his Reasons of Appeal/
ffrom ye Judgement of ye Inferi^r Court of Pleas holden at York ye first Tuesday in January 1698, unto the next Superio^r Court to be holden for ye County of York in a case where he was Defend^t against Samuel Spinney the Judgement was for ye Plaintiff the Land sued for ten pounds & ten shillings and six pence Damage and Cost of Court which Judgment is wrong and eronious & ought to be reversed, for reasons following.

1st Reason because there was noe cause of Action/ we were sued in an Action of ye Cause for claiming Right unto & Propriety in a certain pcell of land and timb^r belonging to the Plaintiff/ which had we soe done it was not suable.

PART II, FOL. 128.

2dly The Land and timb^r which I claim Right in is my own wch has fully appeared by record and Evidence and confirmed by the Judgement of two Superio^r Courts held for ye County of York in my Possession And I humbly conceive the Inferio^r Court had not power to reverse ye Judgment of the Superi^r Court for ye ten pounds ten shillings & six pence Which Spinney hath recovered a Judgement for, from which we appealed, was that same Money which I recevered at ye Superiour Court and to be recovered back again at an Inferi^r Court is contrary to Law & Reason the Premises considered we make noe Doubt but the Honoured Court will see cause to reverse the former Judgement and find for ye Appell^t his Just Costs   Christian Remich

A true Copie of ye origenall Reasons of Appeal Transcribed and Compared this 10th day of Aprill 1699
                 Jos Hamond Cler

[128]

Know all men by these presents that I Robert Bronsdon of Boston In New England Merch^t for Diuers good Causes and considerations me hereunto moueing Haue Assigned ordained and made, and in my stead & place by these presents put & constituted my trusty ffriend Mr John Watson of Boston afores^d, to be my true sufficient and Lawfull Atturney Giuing and hereby granting unto my s^d Atturney full power Authority and speciall Comission for me and in my name & to my use and behoofe, to Ask Demand Sue for Leuie require recouer receiue and take out of the hands Custodie and possession of Nathaniel ffryer sometime of ye County of York in New Eng^d Gent and of all and euery pson & psons whomsoeuer it doth shall or may concern, All and singular such Lands. Island Tenem^{ts} houses Hereditam^{ts} their rights memb^{rs} and appurtenances, scituate lying and being in ye County of York and Prouince of ye Massachusets Bay in N. E. Goods Chattells rents arrears of rent, Effects of things and other Estate whatsoeuer which is, are, or hereafter shall be due owing belonging or appertaining unto me by any manner of wayes or means whatsoeuer And upon recouery and receipts thereof to giue due Acquittances and discharges And if need be to appear and ye pson of me constituant to repres^t before any Gouern^r Judges Justices or Minist^rs of ye Law in any Court or Courts of Judicature and there in my behalf to answer defend and reply to all actions matters and things relating to the premises And to sue arrest attach Cite Plaint prosecute Implead Imprison & condemn and out of prison again when need shall be to Deliu^r, As alsoe to contest in Law in most ample manner until Definitiue sentence, with full power to make and substitute one or Atturneys under him my s^d Atturney and the same again at pleasure to reuoke and generally in touching & concerning the premises and ye Dependencies thereof to doe say transact execute Determine & finish all and whatsoeuer the constituant myself might or could do personally pres^t Ratifying allowing & holding firm & valled all & whatsoeuer my s^d Atturney shall Lawfully doe or cause to be done in and about ye premises by vertue of these presents/ In Witness whereof I haue hereunto set my hand and seal this Seuenteenth day of June Anno Dom one thousand six hundred Ninety & eight, In the tenth year of the Reign of our Soueraign Ld William ye third ouer Engl^d &^ct

Robert Bronsdon (Seal)

[129]

Signed Sealed & Deliuerd
  in presents of us
  Antho: Stoddard
  Elias Purinton
  Suffolk ss Boston Prim^o August 1698

Part II, Fol. 129.

the within named Robert Bronsdon psonally appearing Acknowledged the within written Instrument or letter of Atturney to be his Act & Deed, Cor : Is⁴ Addington
Jus : peace
A true Copie of the origenall Transcribed & compared this 19ᵗʰ day of Augst 16⁷8,   p Jos Hamond Cler̄

INDEX OF

Date.	Grantor.	Grantee.	Instrument.
1689, Mar. 4	ADAMS, Margaret	William Fernald	Deed
1681, Aug. 10	ALCOCKE [Alcot], John and Abigail Rowsley	Peter Dickson	Deed
1690, Jan. 19	ALDEN, John et ux.	Simeon Stoddard	Mortgage
1691, Feb. 13	ALLEN, Robert	Adrian Fry	Deed
1693, Jan. 20	ANGER, Samson, estate of, by Arthur Hughes and Sarah Hughes, adm'rs	John Partridge	Deed
	BALL, John, see William Godsoe		
1694, May 24	BONIGTON, John	Arthur Hughes	Deed
1678, May 25	BRAGDON, Arthur, sen.	Thomas Bragdon	Conditional Deed
1698, June 17	BRONSDON, Robert	John Watson	Power atty
1693, May 15	BUTLAND [Buckland], John	Daniel Littlefield	Deed
1693, May 3	CARELL, Richard	Samuel Spinney	Deed
1691, Dec. 22	CARTER, Joan	John Diamond	Deed
1685, July 13	CHAMPERNOUN, Francis et ux.	Humphrey Elliot et ux.	Deed

GRANTORS.

Folio.	Description.
97	30 acres at the head of Spruce Creek, in *Kittery*.
120	15 acres on Piscataqua river, opposite Boiling Rock, in. *Kittery*.
68	One-eighth in common of the tract between Kennebunk river and Saco river, from the seashore to the Salmon Falls, in the latter river; also 1000 acres on west side of Kennebunk river; also one-fourth part of a saw-mill and appurtenances at Saco river falls.
74	6 acres, part of town grant at Cold Harbor, in *Kittery*; also one acre more adjoining same.
95	Messuage of the deceased on the main river, between Edward Rishworth and John Penwill in *York*.
106	A neck of land on the Eastern side of Saco river, between Page's Creek, the Flying Hill and the Great Swamp.
26	His whole estate [in *York*], conditioned for support of himself and wife.
II, 128	General power of attorney.
92	2 acres adjoining Wheelwright's Neck and the sea wall in *Wells*.
103	6 acres, part of a town grant, at Great Cove, in *Kittery*.
67	10 acres at Crooked Lane; also town grant of 8 acres adjoining; also 10 acres, by gift from John Dymand sr., all in *Kittery*.
110	One-half of Champernoun's island, in *Kittery*, reserving a life estate therein.

INDEX OF GRANTORS.

Date.	Grantor.	Grantee.	Instrument.
1687, Mar. 18	CHILD, Henry et ux	Samuel Lord	Deed
1648, June 24	CONLEY, Abraham	Thomas Jones	Deed
1693, Sept. 15	COXHALL Proprietors	Jacob Perkins Nathaniel Fuller	Vote
1693, Sept. 15	COXHALL Proprietors	Christopher Pottle	Vote
1693, Oct. 13	COXHALL Proprietors	Joseph Gerrish	Vote
1686, Apr. 27	CROCKET, Ephraim et ux	Richard White	Deed
1688, July 10	CROCKET, Joshua	Ephraim Crocket	Deed
1693, Dec. 16	CUTT, Richard	Richard Bryer	Deed
1693, Sept. 19	DOWNING, Joshua and John Leighton	Each other	Deed
1687, July 3	ELLIOT, Robert	Nathaniel Kene	Deed
1694, May 7	EMERY, James, sen.	Daniel Emery Job Emery	Deed
1695, Mar. 2	EMERY, James, sen.	Sylvanus Nock	Deed
1694, Mar. 20	EMERY, James, jun. et ux	John Searle	Deed
1691, Dec. 15	ENDLE, Michael et ux	John Mogridg	Deed
1689, Mar. 4	FERNALD, Thomas et ux	William Fernald	Deed
1671, Aug. 26	FOXWELL, George	James Robinson	Deed

Index of Grantors.

Folio.	Description.
60	40 acres at Post Wigwam, on Newichawannock river, in *Berwick*, with a dwelling-house, but excepting Mr. Leader's grant of pine trees.
102	Field and house in *Kittery*, next to William Everett's.
86	Admitting them to shares (200 acres each) in the lands in *Lyman*.
86	Admitting him to a share (200 acres) in the lands in *Lyman*.
86	Admitting him to a share (200 acres) in the lands in *Lyman*.
76	90 acres at Broad-[Brave-]boat Harbor Creek and adjoining York line in *Kittery*, and all the marsh between the above and the creek below the bridge, and a strip of marsh above the bridge.
109	Quit-claiming all right &c. to Crocket's Neck, at the mouth of Spruce Creek in *Kittery*.
100	A mill privilege on Long Creek, at the mouth of Broad Cove in *Kittery*, with rights of flowage, and to scour its tributaries.
83	Fixing the dividing line between their house lots, near the [Piscataqua] river, in *Kittery*.
106	10 acres on the west side of Spruce Creek, in *Kittery*, between lands of John Shapleigh and John Shepard.
107	143 acres on York pond, in *Kittery*.
115	18 acres at Rocky Hill, in *Berwick*.
98	42 acres upland and 8 acres marsh adjoining at Long Reach, in *Kittery*.
119	Messuage at Spruce Creek, in *Kittery*.
119	30 acres at the head of Spruce Creek, in *Kittery*.
64	One-half of the plantation at Black Point, in *Scarborough*, bought of Richard Foxwell.

Index of Grantors.

Date.	Grantor.	Grantee.	Instrument.
1688, Oct. 26	FRYER, Nathaniel	Robert Bronsdon	Mortgage
1690, July 17	GIBBONS, James and Thomas Gibbons	Elizabeth Sharp	Deed
	GIBBONS, Thomas, see James Gibbons		
1692, Oct. 6	GODSOE, William and John Ball	Each other	Deed
1687, June 29	GOODIN, Sarah and Nicholas Turbet et ux.	Harlakenden Symonds	Deed
1644, Mar. 20	GORGES, Sir Ferdinando, by Richard Vines, Steward General	Thomas Withers	Grant
1687, June 19	GREEN, Richard et ux.	John Green	Deed
1693, Mar. 17	GRIFFIN, John	Robert Elliot	Deed
1690, Aug. 12	HOLE, John	Elizabeth Hole	Power atty
1694, June 15	HUGHES, Arthur et ux.	Arthur Hughes	Deed
1691, Apr. 3	JENKENES, Stephen	Jonathan Nason	Deed
1686, Nov. 30	JONES, Thomas	John Leighton	Deed
1679, Mar. 29	KITTERY, Town of	Peter Staple	Grant
1693, Sept. 6	KITTERY, Town of	Peter Staple	Survey
1679, Dec. 24	KITTERY, Town of	Peter Staple	Grant
1693, Sept. 7	KITTERY, Town of	Peter Staple	Survey

INDEX OF GRANTORS.

Folio.	Description.
48	Champernoun's island, in *Kittery*, except 80 acres conveyed to John Hinks, with certain live stock.
45	100 acres on Saco river, with marsh adjoining; also marsh on Fresh Water Creek, all in *Saco*.
76	Fixing the dividing line between their lands at Spruce Creek, in *Kittery*.
86	One-third in common of the tract called Coxhall, now *Lyman*
58	600 acres between two creeks, at the head of Spruce Creek, in *Kittery*.
117	A tract at the cove on the upper side of Frank's Fort, in *Kittery*.
112	100 acres at Blue Point [in *Scarborough*], between lands of Grantee and Giles Barge.
99	To manage his estates in *Kittery*, or elsewhere in New England.
105	A neck of land east of Saco river, between it and Page's Creek, the Great Swamp and the Flying Hill.
73	2 acres of marsh in two pieces, at Sturgeon Creek, in *Berwick*.
102	6 acres between two other lots of Grantee's, on Piscataqua river; also all meadow at Heathy Marsh; also 40 acres by town grant, adjoining said marsh, all in *Kittery*.
87	10 acres adjoining his house lot at the Long Reach, in his own right, and 5 acres in right of his wife.
87	Of the above 15 acres.
87	30 acres adjoining Christopher Biddle's and Richard Rogers' lands.
87	Of the above 30 acres.

Index of Grantors.

Date.	Grantor.	Grantee.	Instrument.
	LEIGHTON, John, see Joshua Downing		
1692, Apr. 18	LIDDEN, (Letten) Katherine and Sarah Trickey	Each other	Deed
1683, Mar. 28	LITTLEFIELD, Francis, sen.	Daniel Littlefield	Deed
1683, Mar. 29	LITTLEFIELD, Francis, sen.	Dependence Littlefield	Deed
1682, Mar. 20	LITTLEFIELD, James, sen.	Francis Littlefield, sen.	Deed
1687, Apr. 14	LITTLEFIELD, James, et ux.	John Buckland	Deed
1678, Apr. 27	MORE, Agnes	John Se[a]ward	Deed
1674, June 13	MORE, John	John Se[a]ward	Deed
1686, Aug. 11	NACODUMIAH, *alias* Dony, *alias* Robert, and Robert, his son	Harlakinden Symonds	Deed
1694, Sept. 20	NASON, Richard, et ux.	Benjamin Nason Baker Nason	Conditional Deed
1675, July 24	NEWBERRY, Thomas	Thomas Homes	Bond
1675, July 24	NEWBERRY, Thomas	Thomas Homes	Mortgage
1685, Mar. 25	NICKALS [Nicholson], Robert	Robert Elliot	Deed
1692, June 10	PARKER, Abraham	Francis Hooke	Deed

INDEX OF GRANTORS. 9

Folio.	Description.
75	Fixing the dividing line between their house lots at Crooked lane in *Kittery*.
90	150 acres on the north side of Ogunquet river, with 10 acres of meadow; also 150 acres northeast of said river adjoining Joseph Cross, with 2 acres of salt marsh; also 4 acres of marsh; also 10 acres of marsh at the island in Webhannet river, all in *Wells*. Reserving the use of 5 acres of marsh till Daniel comes of age.
91	All his homestead in *Wells*, except what had been conveyed to James Littlefield and Daniel Littlefield, reserving life estate to himself and wife, with reversion to said James and Daniel.
89	Land in *Wells* by the same description as the second above (except the ten acres of marsh).
92	House and 174 acres on the sea next the river with an island and several parcels of marsh; also 100 acres of upland at Merryland, with 10 acres of marsh, all in *Wells*.
97	Quitclaim to the next below.
97	Of land [probably in *Kittery*] endorsed on a previous deed.
86	Land about Coxhorne pond, in Coxhall, now *Lyman*.
114	Homestead of 200 acres, and pastures between tide-water and town commons in *Kittery*.
60	Conditioned to pay £8 in eleven months.
59	House and town grant of 50 acres, of and in *Kittery* as further security for the above debt.
110	230 acres upland and meadow between the river and Arthur Auger's Creek, at Dunster, in *Scarborough*.
81	House and 50 acres, extending from west side of river to Kittery line, in *York*.

Index of Grantors.

Date.	Grantor.	Grantee.	Instrument.
1687, July 13	PENNYWEL, Walter	Edward Sergeant	Deed
1693, July 6	PLAISTED, Elisha, estate of, by Elizabeth Plaisted, Exe'x	John Plaisted	Deed
1690, Feb. 24	PURRINGTON, John	Joseph Weare	Deed
1686, Oct. 16	REMICH [Remick] Christian	Isaac Remick	Deed
1693, Oct. 18	REMICH [Remick] Christian, et ux.	Joshua Remick	Conditional deed
1686, Oct. 16	REMICH [Remick] Jacob	Isaac Remick	Deed
1690, Jan. 4	RICE, Thomas, et ux.	Samuel Spinney	Deed
	ROBERT, Indian, see Nacodumiah		
	ROWSLEY, Abigail, see John Alcocke		
1690, Mar. 29	SCOTTOW, Joshua, et ux.	Samuel Sewall	Deed
1688, Sept. 11	SPENCER, Humphrey	Robert Elliot	Deed
1686, Apr. 2	SPENCER, Humphrey, et ux.	Robert Elliot	Deed
1674, Dec. 18	SPENCER, Moses	Daniel Goodden [Goodwin]	Deed
1676, July 25	SPENCER, Thomas, et ux.	Humphrey Spencer, et ux.	Deed
1694, Mar. 22	SPINNEY, Thomas, et ux.	James Spinney	Deed

INDEX OF GRANTORS. 11

Folio.	Description.
49	50 acres at Scadlock's or Little river, and 7 acres of marsh near said river, on the sea-wall in *Saco*.
87	80 acres at Birch Point Cove, on the Great river and the new meadow near York line, in *Kittery* [*Berwick*].
116	About half an acre under and around grantee's house, at Meeting-house Creek, in *York*.
71	House and 30 acres, at the Great Cove, behind Thomas Spinney's, in *Kittery*.
113	Homestead on the neck, opposite Boiling Rock, and 10 acres in the woods, and 15 acres marsh in *Kittery*, reserving life estates to himself and wife.
71	Quitclaim to the land at Great cove, in *Kittery*.
103	20 acres near Spruce Creek, between Shapleigh's, Withers' Shepherd's and Thos. Spinney's lands, in *Kittery*.
64	500 acres, between Little or Crooked Lane river and Sandy point, on Merriconeag neck, now *Harpswell*, granted to Grantor by the General Court.
111	House and 30 acres on the brook running from Parker's marsh swamp to the marsh called Slut's Corner, in *Kittery* [*Berwick*].
112	50 acres and 10 acres of swamp, on the brook running from Wilcocks' pond and the commons next the river, at Newichewannock [in *Berwick*].
98	25 acres on Newichawannock Little river [in *Berwick*].
111	House and 30 acres, on the brook running from Parker's marsh swamp to the marsh called Slut's Corner, in *Kittery* [*Berwick*].
104	Part of his homestead, on Piscataqua river, in *Kittery*, with reversion to John Spinney.

INDEX OF GRANTORS.

Date.	Grantor.	Grantee.	Instrument.
1694, Mar. 23	SPINNEY, Thomas	John Spinney	Deed
1688, June 12	SYMONDS, Harlakinden	Roger Haskens Edward Bishop William Baker Geo. Herrick Thos. Edwards Sam'l Ingalls jun. John Low jun. William Dixey Thos. Shepherd Wm. Goodhew Samuel Gittins Barnett Thorne Michael Farlo Meshech Farlo Moses Bradstreet Matthew Perkins John Gitting sen Paul Thorndick Isaac Fellows Richard Walker John Browne Nathan'l Browne Zachary Herrick Thomas Higginson John Stanford Thomas Low sen Sam'l Ingalls sen. Robert Lord jun. Robert Bradford Nicholas Woodbury Mark Haskell William Haskell William Cleeves John Harris John Burnam Nathaniel Rust sen. Andrew Elliot jun.	Deed
1693, Apr. 11	SYMONDS, Harlakinden	Thomas Baker	Deed

Folio.	Description.
104	The remainder of his homestead at Great Cove, on Piscataqua river, in *Kittery*, reserving life estates to himself and wife.
84	Part of the tract of land called Coxhall, now *Lyman*, six miles by four miles in extent. *Mem.* It appears by the votes of these Coxhall proprietors, fol. 86, that these substitutions were made: Jacob Perkins, in place of Samuel Giddins; Nathaniel Fuller, in place of John Giddins; Christopher Pottle, in place of Nathaniel Rust sen.; Joseph Gerrish, in place of Thomas Low sen.
93	1500 acres in Coxhall, now *Lyman*, next north of the above tract, 135 rods broad and six miles in length, between Saco river and Mousam river.

Index of Grantors.

Date.	Grantor.	Grantee.	Instrument.
1693, Apr. 11	Symonds, Harlakinden	Timothy Dorman	Deed
	Trickey, Sarah, see Katherine Lidden		
1690, Jan. 6	Trustrum, David	Edward Sergent	Deed
	Turbet, Nicholas, et ux., see Sarah Goodin		
1638, Jan. 1	Ugroufe, John	Abraham Conley	Deed
1687, —— 28	Weare, Peter, et ux.	Daniel Weare	Deed
1688, May 24	White, Richard	Ephraim Crocket	Deed
1689, Jan. 4	White, Richard	John Moore	Deed
1692, Sept. 28	White, Richard	Henry De[e]ring	Deed
1692, Sept. 27	White, Richard	Henry De[e]ring	Deed
1692, Sept. 27	White, Richard	Henry De[e]ring	Deed
1692, Sept. 27	White, Richard	Francis Hooke Samuel Kease	Power atty
1675, July 22	Withers, Thomas	Thomas Rice et ux.	Deed
1689, Apr. 19	Woodbridge, Benjamin	William Pepperrell	Deed
1689, Apr. 19	Woodbridge, Benjamin	William Pepperrell	Bond

Folio.	Description.
94	500 acres in Coxhall, now *Lyman*, next north of the above tract, of the same length, but 45 rods broad, between the same bounds.
95	30 acres at Winter Harbor in *Saco*, adjoining to Grantee's land and a brook on the southwest.
102	House and 6 acres in *Kittery*.
108	60 acres called Gooch's Neck, near Cape Neddick, in *York*.
76	By quit-claim, revoking the deed from Grantee to Grantor in folio 76.
54	All Grantor's marsh on the northeast side of Broad-[Brave-]boat Harbor creek, from land of Capt. Raines, to the head of the creek, in *Kittery*.
77	Quit-claiming all right, &c., in the above.
77	90 acres at Broad-[Brave-]boat Harbor creek and adjoining York line, in *Kittery*, and all the marsh between the above and the creek below the bridge, and a strip of marsh above the bridge.
78	60 acres of upland between the above parcel and York line in *Kittery*.
78	To enter upon and deliver possession of the above parcels of land to Henry Deering.
43	A tract at Eagle point, on Piscataqua river, in *Kittery*.
62	12½ acres between Crocket's creek and Piscataqua harbor mouth, in *Kittery*.
	In a penalty of £24, to observe the covenants in the above deed.

INDEX OF

Date.	Grantee.	Grantor.	Instrument.
1693, Apr. 11	THOMAS BAKER	Symonds, Harlakinden	Deed
	BAKER, William, see Roger Haskens		
	BISHOP, Edward, see Roger Haskens		
	BRADFORD, Robert, see Roger Haskens		
	BRADSTREET, Moses, see Roger Haskens		
1678, May 25	BRAGDON, Thomas	Arthur Bragdon, sen.	Conditional Deed
1688, Oct. 26	BRONSDON, Robert	Nathaniel Fryer	Mortgage
	BROWN, John, see Roger Haskens		
	BROWN, Nathaniel, see Roger Haskens		
1693, Dec. 16	BRYER, Richard	Richard Cutt	Deed
1687, Apr. 14	BUCKLAND, John	James Littlefield, et ux.	Deed
	BURNAM, John, see Roger Haskens		
	CLEEVES, William, see Roger Haskens		

GRANTEES.

Folio.	Description.
93	1500 acres in Coxhall, now *Lyman*, next north of the above tract, 135 rods broad and six miles in length, between Saco river and Mousam river.
26	His whole estate [in *York*], conditioned for support of himself and wife.
48	Champernoun's island, in *Kittery*, except 80 acres conveyed to John Hinks, with certain live stock.
100	A mill privilege on Long Creek, at the mouth of Broad Cove in *Kittery*, with rights of flowage, and to scour its tributaries.
92	House and 174 acres on the sea next the river with an island and several parcels of marsh; also 100 acres of upland at Merryland, with 10 acres of marsh, all in *Wells*.

INDEX OF GRANTEES.

Date.	Grantee.	Grantor.	Instrument.
1638, Jan. 1	CONLEY, Abraham	John Ugroufe	Deed
1688, May 24	CROCKET, Ephraim	Richard White	Deed
1688, July 10	CROCKET, Ephraim	Joshua Crocket	Deed
1692, Sept. 28	DE[E]RING Henry	Richard White	Deed
1692, Sept. 27	DE[E]RING Henry	Richard White	Deed
1692, Sept. 27	DE[E]RING, Henry	Richard White	Deed
1691, Dec. 22	DIAMOND, John	Joan Carter	Deed
1681, Aug. 10	DICKSON, Peter	John Alcocke [Alcot], and Abigail Rowsley	Deed
	DIXEY, William, see Roger Haskens		
1693, Apr. 11	DORMAN, Timothy	Harlakinden Symonds	Deed
	EDWARDS, Thomas, see Roger Haskens		
	ELLIOT, Andrew, jun. see Roger Haskens		
1685, July 13	ELLIOT, Humphrey, et ux.	Francis Champernoun, et ux.	Deed
1683, Sept. 11	ELIOT, Robert	Humphrey Spencer	Deed

Folio.	Description.
102	House and 6 acres in *Kittery*.
76	By quit-claim, revoking the deed from Grantee to Grantor in folio 76.
109	Quit-claiming all right &c. to Crocket's Neck, at the mouth of Spruce Creek in *Kittery*.
77	Quit-claiming all rights, &c., in the deed Richard White to John More, fol. 54.
77	90 acres at Broad-[Brave-]boat Harbor creek and adjoining York line, in *Kittery*, and all the marsh between the above and the creek below the bridge, and a strip of marsh above the bridge.
78	60 acres of upland between the above parcel and York line in *Kittery*.
67	10 acres at Crooked Lane; also town grant of 8 acres adjoining; also 10 acres, by gift from John Dymand sr., all in *Kittery*.
120	15 acres on Piscataqua river, opposite Boiling Rock, in *Kittery*.
94	500 acres in Coxhall, now *Lyman*, next north of the Baker tract, fol. 93, of the same length, but 45 rods broad, between the same bounds.
110	One-half of Champernoun's island, in *Kittery*, reserving a life estate therein.
111	House and 30 acres on the brook running from Parker's marsh swamp to the marsh called Slut's Corner, in *Kittery* [*Berwick*].

Index of Grantees.

Date.	Grantee.	Grantor.	Instrument.
1685, Mar. 25	Elliot, Robert	Robert Nickals [Nicholson]	Deed
1686, Apr. 2	Elliot, Robert,	Humphrey Spencer, et ux.	Deed
1693, Mar. 17	Elliot, Robert	John Griffin	Deed
1694, May 7	Emery, Daniel, and Job Emery	James Emery, sen.	Deed
	Emery, Job, see Daniel Emery		
	Farlo, Meshech, see Roger Haskens		
	Farlo, Michael, see Roger Haskens		
	Fellows, Isaac, see Roger Haskens		
1689, Mar. 4	Fernald, William	Margaret Adams	Deed
1689, Mar. 4	Fernald, William	Thomas Fernald, et ux.	Deed
1691, Feb. 13	Fry, Adrian	Robert Allen	Deed
	Fuller, Nathaniel, see Jacob Perkins		
1693, Oct. 13	Gerrish, Joseph	Coxhall Proprietors	Vote
	Gittings, John, senior see Roger Haskens		
	Gittings, Samuel, see Roger Haskens		
	Goodhew, William, see Roger Haskens		

Folio.	Description.
110	230 acres upland and meadow between the river and Arthur Auger's Creek, at Dunster, in *Scarborough*.
112	50 acres and 10 acres of swamp, on the brook running from Wilcocks' pond and the commons next the river, at Newichewannock [in *Berwick*].
112	100 acres at Blue Point [in *Scarborough*], between lands of Grantee and Giles Barge.
107	143 acres on York pond, in *Kittery*.
97	30 acres at the head of Spruce Creek, in *Kittery*.
119	30 acres at the head of Spruce Creek, in *Kittery*.
74	6 acres, part of town grant at Cold Harbor, in *Kittery;* also one acre more adjoining same.
86	Admitting him to a share (200 acres) in the lands in *Lyman*.

Date.	Grantee.	Grantor.	Instrument.
1674, Dec. 18	GOODDEN [Goodwin], Daniel	Moses Spencer	Deed
1687, June 19	GREEN, John	Richard Green, et ux.	Deed
	HARRIS, John, see Roger Haskens		
	HASKELL, Mark, see Roger Haskens		
	HASKELL, William, see Roger Haskens		
1688, June 12	HASKENS, Roger	Harlakinden Symonds	Deed
	HERRICK, George, see Roger Haskens		
	HERRICK, Zachary, see Roger Haskens		
	HIGGINSON, Thomas, see Roger Haskens		
1690, Aug. 12	HOLE, Elizabeth	John Hole	Power atty
1675, July 24	HOMES, Thomas	Thomas Newberry	Bond
1675, July 24	HOMES, Thomas	Thomas Newberry	Mortgage
1692, June 10	HOOKE, Francis,	Abraham Parker	Deed
1692, Sept. 27	HOOKE, Francis, and Samuel Kease	Richard White	Power atty
1694, May 24	HUGHES, Arthur	John Bonigton	Deed
1694, June 15	HUGHES, Arthur	Arthur Hughes, et ux.	Deed

Index of Grantees. 23

Folio.	Description.
98	25 acres on Newichawannock Little river [in *Berwick*].
117	A tract at the cove on the upper side of Frank's Fort, in *Kittery*.
84	Part of the tract of land called Coxhall, now *Lyman*, six miles by four miles in extent.
99	To manage his estates in *Kittery*, or elsewhere in New England.
60	Conditioned to pay £8 in eleven months.
59	House and town grant of 50 acres, of and in *Kittery* as further security for the above debt.
81	House and 50 acres, extending from west side of river to Kittery line, in *York*, fols. 77 and 78.
78	To enter upon and deliver possession of the lands to Henry Deering.
106	A neck of land on the Eastern side of Saco river, between Page's Creek, the Flying Hill and the Great Swamp.
105	A neck of land east of Saco river, between it and Page's Creek, the Great Swamp and the Flying Hill.

Index of Grantees.

Date.	Grantee.	Grantor.	Instrument.
	INGALLS, Samuel, sen., see Roger Haskens		
	INGALLS, Samuel, jr., see Roger Haskens		
1648, June 24	JONES, Thomas,	Abram Conley	Deed
	KEASE, Samuel, see Francis Hooke		
1687, July 3	KENE, Nathaniel	Robert Elliot	Deed
1686, Nov. 30	LEIGHTON, John	Thomas Jones	Deed
1683, Mar. 28	LITTLEFIELD, Daniel	Francis Littlefield sen.	Deed
1693, May 15	LITTLEFIELD, Daniel	John Butland [Buckland]	Deed
1683, Mar. 29	LITTLEFIELD, Dependence	Francis Littlefield, sen.	Deed
1682, Mar. 20	LITTLEFIELD, Francis, sen.	James Littlefield sen.	Deed
	LORD, Robert, jun., see Roger Haskens		
1687, Mar. 18	LORD, Samuel	Henry Child, et ux.	Deed
	Low, John, jun., see Roger Haskens		
	Low, Thomas, sen., see Roger Haskens		

Folio.	Description.
102	Field and house in *Kittery*, next to William Everett's.
106	10 acres on the west side of Spruce Creek, in *Kittery*, between lands of John Shapleigh and John Shepard.
102	6 acres between two other lots of Grantee's, on Piscataqua river; also all meadow at Heathy Marsh; also 40 acres by town grant, adjoining said marsh, all in *Kittery*.
90	150 acres on the north side of Ogunquet river, with 10 acres of meadow; also 150 acres northeast of said river adjoining Joseph Cross, with 2 acres of salt marsh; also 4 acres of marsh; also 10 acres of marsh at the island in Webhannet river, all in *Wells*. Reserving the use of 5 acres of marsh till Daniel comes of age.
92	2 acres adjoining Wheelwright's Neck and the sea wall in *Wells*.
91	All his homestead in *Wells*, except what had been conveyed to James Littlefield and Daniel Littlefield, reserving life estate to himself and wife, with reversion to said James and Daniel.
89	Land in *Wells* by the same description as the third above (except the ten acres of marsh).
60	40 acres at Post Wigwam, on Newichawannock river, in *Berwick*, with a dwelling-house, but excepting Mr. Leader's grant of pine trees.

Index of Grantees.

Date.	Grantee.	Grantor.	Instrument.
1691, Dec. 15	Mogridg, John	Michael Endle et ux.	Deed
1689, Jan. 4	Moore, John	Richard White	Deed
	Nason, Barker, see Benjamin Nason		
1694, Sept. 20	Nason, Benjamin and Baker Nason	Richard Nason et ux.	Conditional Deed
1691, Apr. 3	Nason, Jonathan	Stephen Jenkenes	Deed
1695, Mar. 2	Nock, Sylvanus	James Emery, sen.	Deed
1693, Jan. 20	Partridge, John	Samson Anger, estate of, by Arthur Hughes and Sarah Hughes, adm'rs	Deed
1689, Apr. 19	Pepperrell, William	Benjamin Woodbridge	Deed
1689, Apr. 19	Pepperrell, William	Benjamin Woodbridge	Bond
1693, Sept. 15	Perkins, Jacob and Nathaniel Fuller	Coxhall Proprietors	Vote
	Perkins, Matthew, see Roger Haskens		
1693, July 6	Plaisted, John	Elisha Plaisted, estate of, by Elizabeth Plaisted, Exe'x	Deed
1693, Sept. 15	Pottle, Christopher	Coxhall Proprietors	Vote
1686, Oct. 16	Remick, Isaac	Christian Remich [Remick]	Deed

INDEX OF GRANTEES.

Folio.	Description.
119	Messuage at Spruce Creek, in *Kittery*.
54	All Grantor's marsh on the northeast side of Broad [Brave] boat Harbor Creek, from land of Capt. Raines, to the head of the creek, in *Kittery*.
114	Homestead of 200 acres, and pastures between tide-water and town commons in *Kittery*.
73	2 acres of marsh in two pieces, at Sturgeon Creek, in *Berwick*.
115	18 acres at Rocky Hill, in *Berwick*.
95	Messuage of the deceased on the main river, between Edward Rishworth and John Penwill in *York*.
62	12½ acres between Crocket's Creek and Piscataqua harbor mouth, in *Kittery*.
63	In a penalty of £24, to observe the covenants in the above deed.
68	Admitting them to shares (200 acres each) in the lands in *Lyman*.
87	80 acres at Birch Point Cove, on the Great river and the new meadow near York line, in *Kittery* [*Berwick*].
86	Admitting him to a share (200 acres) in the lands in *Lyman*.
71	House and 30 acres, at the Great Cove, behind Thomas Spinney's, in *Kittery*.

Index of Grantees.

Date.	Grantee.	Grantor.	Instrument.
1686, Oct. 16	REMICK, Isaac	Jacob Remich [Remick]	Deed
1693, Oct. 18	REMICK, Joshua	Christian Remich [Remick] et ux.	Conditional deed
1675, July 22	RICE, Thomas, et ux.	Thomas Withers	Deed
1671, Aug. 26	ROBINSON, James	George Foxwell	Deed
	RUST, Nathaniel, see Roger Haskens		
1694, Mar. 20	SEARLE, John	James Emery, jun., et ux.	Deed
1678, Apr. 27	SE[A]WARD, John	Agnes More	Deed
1674, June 13	SE[A]WARD, John	John More	Deed
1687, July 13	SERGEANT, Edward	Walter Pennywel	Deed
1690, Jan. 6	SERGEANT, Edward	David Trustrum	Deed
1690, Mar. 29	SEWALL, Samuel	Joshua Scottow et ux.	Deed
1690, July 17	SHARP, Elizabeth	James Gibbons Thos. Gibbons	Deed
	SHEPHERD Thomas, see Roger Haskens		
1676, July 25	SPENCER, Humphrey, et ux.	Thomas Spencer, et ux.	Deed
1694, Mar. 22	SPINNEY, James	Thomas Spinney, et ux.	Deed
1694, Mar. 23	SPINNEY, John	Thomas Spinney	Deed

Index of Grantees.

Folio.	Description.
71	Quitclaim to the land at Great cove, in *Kittery*.
113	Homestead on the neck, opposite Boiling Rock, and 10 acres in the woods, and 15 acres marsh in *Kittery*, reserving life estates to himself and wife.
43	A tract at Eagle point, on Piscataqua river, in *Kittery*.
64	One-half of the plantation at Black Point, in *Scarborough* bought of Richard Foxwell.
98	42 acres upland and 8 acres marsh adjoining at Long Reach, in *Kittery*.
97	Quitclaim to the next below.
97	Of land [probably in *Kittery*] endorsed on a previous deed.
49	50 acres at Scadlock's or Little river, and 7 acres of marsh near said river, on the sea-wall in *Saco*.
95	30 acres at Winter Harbor in *Saco*, adjoining to Grantee's land and a brook on the southwest.
64	500 acres, between Little or Crooked Lane river and Sandy point, on Merriconeag neck, now *Harpswell*, granted to Grantor by the General Court.
45	100 acres on Saco river, with marsh adjoining; also marsh on Fresh Water Creek, all in *Saco*.
111	House and 30 acres, on the brook running from Parker's marsh swamp to the marsh called Slut's Corner, in *Kittery* [*Berwick*].
104	Part of his homestead, on Piscataqua river, in *Kittery*, with reversion to John Spinney.
104	The remainder of his homestead at Great Cove, on Piscataqua river, in *Kittery*, reserving life estates to himself and wife.

INDEX OF GRANTEES.

Date.	Grantee.	Grantor.	Instrument.
1690, Jan. 4	SPINNEY, Samuel	Thomas Rice et ux.	Deed
1693, May 3	SPINNEY, Samuel	Richard Carell	Deed
	STANFORD, John, see Roger Haskens		
1679, Mar. 29	STAPLE, Peter	Town of Kittery	Grant
1693, Sept. 6	STAPLE, Peter	Town of Kittery	Survey
1679, Dec. 24	STAPLE, Peter	Town of Kittery	Grant
1693, Sept. 7	STAPLE, Peter	Town of Kittery	Survey
1690, Jan. 19	STODDARD, Simeon	John Alden et ux.	Mortgage
1686, Aug. 11	SYMONDS, Harlakinden	Nacodumiah, alias Dony, alias Robert, and Robert, his son	Deed
1687, June 29	SYMONDS, Harlakinden	Sarah Goodwin and Nicholas Turbet et ux.	Deed
	THORNDICK, Paul, see Roger Haskens		
	THORNE, Barnett, see Roger Haskens		
	WALKER, Richard, see Roger Haskens		
1698, June 17	WATSON, John	Robert Bronsdon	Power atty
1687, —— 28	WEARE, Daniel	Peter Weare et ux.	Deed

Index of Grantees. 31

Folio.	Description.
103	20 acres near Spruce Creek, between Shapleigh's, Withers' Shepherd's and Thos. Spinney's lands, in *Kittery*.
103	6 acres, part of a town grant, at Great Cove, in *Kittery*.
87	10 acres adjoining his house lot at the Long Reach, in his own right, and 5 acres in right of his wife.
87	Of the above 15 acres.
87	30 acres adjoining Christopher Biddle's and Richard Rogers' lands.
87	Of the above 30 acres.
68	One-eighth in common of the tract between Kennebunk river and Saco river, from the seashore to the Salmon Falls, in the latter river; also 1000 acres on west side of Kennebunk river; also one-fourth part of a saw-mill and appurtenances at Saco river falls.
86	Land about Coxhorne pond, in Coxhall, now *Lyman*.
86	One-third in common of the tract called Coxhall, now *Lyman*.
II, 128	General power of attorney.
108	60 acres called Gooch's Neck, near Cape Neddick, in *York*.

Index of Grantees.

Date.	Grantee.	Grantor.	Instrument.
1690, Feb. 24	WEARE, Joseph	John Purrington	Deed
1686, Apr. 27	WHITE, Richard	Ephraim Crocket et ux.	Deed
1644, Mar. 20	WITHERS, Thomas	Sir Ferdinando Gorges, by Richard Vines, Steward General	Grant
	WOODBURY, Nicholas, see Roger Haskens		

Folio.	Description.
116	About half an acre under and around Grantee's house, at Meeting-house Creek, in *York*.
76	90 acres at Broad-[Brave-]boat Harbor Creek and adjoining York line in *Kittery*, and all the marsh between the above and the creek below the bridge, and a strip of marsh above the bridge.
58	600 acres between two creeks, at the head of Spruce Creek, in *Kittery*.

INDEX OF OTHER PERSONS.

N. B. For Administrations, Depositions, Inventories and Wills, see the General Index.

Abbett, Abbot,
  Ensign, II. 55, 57.
  John, I. 49.
  Joseph, I. 73, II. 88, 92.
  Thomas, I. 25, 55, II. 17, 21, 33, 58, 60, 68, 73.
Addams,
  Elizabeth, II. 15.
  Magdalen, II. 104.
  Margaret, I. 96.
  Nathaniel, II, 5, 15.
  Philip, I. 18, 42, II. 4.
  Thomas, I. 81, II. 4, 6, 13. 14, 15, 16, 21, 23.
Addington, Isaac, I. 65, II. 27, 29, 40, 100, 129.
Aignew, Agnew, Niven, I. 27, 55.
Alden, John, I. 68.
Allard, Hugh, II. 5.
Allen, Allin,
  Edward, I. 73.
  James, I. 88.
  Mary, II. 80, 85, 98, 111, 118.
  Robert, I. 74.
  Walter, I. 59, 71, II. 80, 85, 98, 111, 118.
Allexander, Richard, I. 10, 20.
Allcocke, Alcott,
  Abigail, I. 61.
  Captain, II. 6.
  Elizabeth, I. (26), 96.
  Joan, I. 61.
  Job, I. 3, 4, 30, 33, 36, 44, 73, 81, 82, II. 17, 27, 32, 40, 54, 55, 58, 60, 64, 68, 73, 74, 77, 82, 89, 90, 92.
  John, I. 61, 62, 76, 96, 121, II. 9, 14, 17, 18.
  Mary, I. 61.
  Widow, I. 26.
Allison, Ann, I. 2, 3.
Amerideth,
  Joan, I. 61, 62, II. 35.
  John, I. 61, 62.

Andrews, Edmund, I. 45.
  John, I. 47.
Andros, Sir Edmund, II. 69.
Anger,
  Samson, I. 4, II. 4, 6.
  Sarah, I. 57, II. 4, 7.
Appleton, Samuel, II. 27.
Ashley, William, I. 91.
Atherton. See Etherington.
Atwell,
  John, I. 37.
  Philip, II. 26, 51[b], 61.
Auger, Arthur, I. 109.
Austen, Austine,
  Joseph, I. 102.
  Matthew, I. 56, 75, 88, II. 15, 16, 17, 35, 53, 77, 104, 107, 119.
  Samuel, I. 24, 29.
Avant, Francis, II. 17.
Avery, Thomas, I. 108.
Axell, Axtell, Humphrey, II. 8, 10.

Babb,
  Lydia, II. 16.
  Philip, I. 73, II. 13, 16.
Backhouse, Backus,
  Elizabeth, I. 28.
  Francis, I. 11, 89, 90.
Baile,
  Edward, II. 26, 30.
  Elizabeth, II. 26, 30.
Baker,
  Lieutenant, I. 94.
  Thomas, I. 94.
Ball, John, II. 33, 36.
Bane, Bean,
  Lewis, I. 83, II. 9, 15, 18, 19, 34, 36, 47, 73, 101, 105, 106, 112, 116.
Banefield,
  Christopher, I. 24, 74, II. 80, 84.
  Grace, II. 80, 84.
Banks,
  John, II. 14, 17, 18.

Index of Other Persons. 35

Joseph, I. 79, II. 5, 51, 54, 55, 60, 68, 116, 122, 126.
Richard, I. 3, 6, 18, 21, 30, 65.
Samuel, I. 66.
Barge, Giles, I. 112.
Barlow, George, I. 109.
Barnard,
  Benjamin, I. 43[b].
  George, I. 37.
Barnes, Henry, II. 125 ['s wife 125, 126,] 126.
Barnet, Bartholomew, I. 121.
Barrett,
  John, I. 29, 36, 61.
  Mary, I. 25, II. 2.
Barsham, John, I. 88.
Bass, Peter, I. 2.
Baston, Thomas, II. 8.
Batson, Elizabeth, I. 36.
Beal,
  Arthur, II. 7, 17, 18, 19, 21, 23, 24, 51[b], 56, 75, 108, 121, 122, 125.
  Richard, II. 19.
Bedford,
  Ann, I. 6.
  (son of Nathan,) I. 6.
  William, I. 96.
Belcher, John, I. 98.
Bennett,
  Edward, I. 5.
  Nicholas, I. 97.
Berry, Elizabeth, II. 33, 36.
Bidle, Christopher, I. 87.
Billing, John, I. 76, 77, II. 5.
Black, Daniel, II. 70, 103, 121, 123, 126.
Blackledg, Nathaniel, II. 17.
Blagdon, James, II. 109.
Bly, John, I. 47.
Boden, John, II. 14.
Bolls,
  Beckey, I. 34.
  Joseph, I. 24, 25, 34.
  Mary, I. 23, 34.
  Mercy, I. 34.
  Samuel, I. 84.
  Thomas, I. 33.
Bonighton, John, I. 8, 22, 45.
Botts, Isaac, I. 98.

Bouden, Ambrose, II. 64.
Brackett,
  Anthony, I. 37, II. 2.
  Elizabeth, II. 98, 111, 118, 124.
  Lieutenant, I. 1.
  Samuel, II. 112, 118, 124.
  Thomas, I. 37.
Bracy, John, II. 13, 111, 117.
Bradford, William, II. 27.
Bragden, Bragdon,
  Arthur, I. 24, 38, 51, 52, 71, 121, II. 1, 14, 19, 21, 51, 54, 55, 58, 60, 68, 95, 101, 105, 106, 111, 112.
  Lydia, II. 13.
  Mary, II. 52.
  Samuel, I. 31, 82, II. 4, 6, 7, 11, 19, 21, 108.
  Samuel, junior, II. 109.
  Thomas, I. 21, II. 3.
Braun, Brawn,
  Annah, II. 51[b], 60, 66.
  John, II. 48, 66, 79.
  ———, II. 104.
Bray,
  Joan, I. 9, 46, 47.
  John, I. 9, 46, 47, 62, 63, II. 4, 6.
  Mary, I. 46, 47.
  Mrs., II. 3.
  Richard, I. 18, II. 19, 21, 79, 84.
  William, II. 6.
Bready,
  John, I. 24.
  Sarah, I. 13.
Breeden, William, I. 28, 29.
Brian, Richard, I. 56.
Brisson, Brissan, Charles, II. 6, 12.
Broad, William, I. 112.
Brondon, Joseph, I. 48.
Broughton,
  George, I. 22, 40, 61, 99.
  Peru, I. 61.
Brown,
  Andrew, I. 22, II. 116, 122, 126.
  Joshua, I. 84.
  Nicholas, II. 34, 55.
Bryard, Elisha, I. 102.
Bryer, Briar, Richard, II. 17, 18, 48, 49, 74, 77, 82, 92.

Bryce, Patrick, I. 26.
Buckland,
  John, II. 78.
  Margaret, II. 7. 14.
Burks, Walter, II. 56.
Burrine, William, I. 22.
Bush, John, I. 5, 86, 93, 94.
Buss, Mr., I. 11.

Cahan, Katherine, I. 55.
Came, Caime, Cane,
  Arthur, I. 26, 51, 52, 53, 57, II. 18, 74, 77, 82, 89, 95, 101. See Kane.
Card,
  Annas, I. 82.
  Elizabeth, I. 82.
  John, I. 18, 82.
  Mary, I. 82.
  Thomas, I. 82.
  William, I. 82, II. 1, 2.
Carline,
  Elizabeth, II. 7, 12.
  Joseph, II. 7, 12.
Carter, Richard, I. 4, 19, II. 51[b], 60, 67, 112.
Cater,
  John, II. 13.
  Samuel, II. 5.
Chadborn,
  Elizabeth, I. 40.
  Humphrey, I. 82, 99.
  James, I. 20, 24.
  Sarah, II. 73, 98, 102.
  ——, I. 82.
Champernown.
  Captain, I. 18.
  Francis, I. 18, 48, II. 54.
  Mary, II. 32, 54.
  Miss or Mrs, I. 18, 40.
Chick, Thomas, I. 24.
Child, Sarah, I. 70.
Churchwell, John, I. 50.
Clark,
  Elisha, II. 91.
  ('s wife II. 91).
  Josiah, II. 71.
  Major, I. 32.
  Robert, II. 51[b].
  Thomas, II. 41, 72.

Cleamons, Job, I. 13.
Clemens, Richard, I. 62.
Cloyce, Clais, Clays,
  Hannah, I. 25.
  John, II. 16, 17, 18, 116, 122, 126.
  Nathaniel, I. 11, 23, II. 16, 17, 23, 25.
  Peter, I. 25.
Coffin, Peter, II. 113.
Cole,
  Nicholas, II. 13, 14, 18, 47, 51, 54, 55, 58, 60, 68, 73.
  Thomas, II. 26, 30.
Comer, Richard, II. 71.
Conley, Abraham, I. 30, 102, II. 33.
Converse, Captain, II. 14.
Cook, Edmund, I. 82.
Cooper,
  John, I. 26, 115, II. 23, 25, 71.
  ——, II. 15.
Corben, Robert, I. 37.
Corwin, Curwine,
  Jonathan, I. 82, II. 27.
  Mr., I. 1.
Couch, Joseph, II. 51, 54, 55, 58, 60, 68, 73, 82.
Crafts, Joan, II .62, 104, 126.
Cranfield, Edward, I. 111.
Credefur, Credifor,
  Joseph, II. 98, 99.
  Rachel, II. 16, 19, 98, 99.
Crocket,
  Ann, I. 40.
  Ephraim, I. 32, 39, 40, 77, 106.
  Elihu, I. 45.
  Elisha, II. 126.
  Hugh, II. 121, 123.
  Joseph, I. 45.
  Thomas, I. 109.
  ——, I. 76, 77, II. 121, 123.
Cross,
  John, I. 11.
  Joseph, I. 5, 11, 89, 90.
  Mary, I. 29.
Crown, Henry, I. 96, 105.
Crusey, Elizabeth, I. 81.
Currier, Jeffery, I. 8, II. 4, 5.
Curtis,
  Job, II. 15.

Joseph, I. 56, II. 9, 48, 49, 68, 70, 71, 88, 97, 110, 126.
Mr., II. 52.
Cutt, Cutts,
 Eleanor, I. 30.
 John, I. 30, 60, II. 78.
 Mr., I. 40.
 Richard, II. 8, 10, 13, 17, 19, 21, 56, 78, 93, 119.
 Robert, II. 13, 19, 101, 105, 106, 112.
 Samuel, II. 78, 89.
Cyas,
 Ann, II. 126.
 John, II. 126.

Daniell,
 Samuel, II. 3, 8.
 Thomas, I. 81.
Davess, Davis,
 Captain, I. 19.
 John, I. 4, 17, 21, 26, 33, 38, 48, 53, 76, 77, 82, 117, II. 1, 3, 4, 6, 7, 8, 11.
 Major, I. 48, II. 9.
 Mary, I. 66, II. 11.
 Sylvanus, I. 41, 64, II. 27.
 Thomas, I. 113.
Davison, Daniel, jun., I. 84.
Dearing, Dereing, Deering,
 Henry, I. 78.
 Joan, I. 46, 47, II. 58, 87, 110, 126.
 Mr., I. 5.
 Roger, I. 32, 39, 43°, 47, II. 74, 82, 89, 92, 95.
 Thomas, II. 21, 23, 25, 91.
Denmark,
 Elizabeth, II. 98.
 James, II. 98.
Dennett, Alexander, I. 18, 83, II. 14, 17, 18.
Diamond, Deament, Diament, Dyament,
 Andrew, I. 67, II. 4.
 Goodman, I. 50.
 Joan, I. 40.
 John, I. 39, 43, 67, II. 78.
 William, I. 67.
Dixon,

Mary, II. 101.
Peter, I. 25, 62, 104, 113, II. 18, 26, 30, 31, 49, 51, 52, 54, 55, 57, 58, 60.
Donel, Donnell, Dunnell,
 Captain, I. 30,
 Henry, I. 4.
 Joseph, II. 5.
 Mr., II. 117.
 Ruth, II. 111.
 Samuel, I. 3, 30, 33, 36, 66, II. 27, 34, 47, 51, 55, 56, 60, 68, 77, 82, 90, 92, 95, 99, 100, 101, 105, 106, 110, 112, 116, 122, 126.
 Thomas, I. 81, II. 17, 18, 74, 77, 82, 89, 92, 95.
Dorman,
 Ephraim, I. 94.
 Timothy, I. 94.
Downing, Joshua, I. 67, 118, II. 4, 10, 23, 25, 32, 33, 88, 93, 116, 121, 122, 126.
Downs, Richard, I. 7.
Dudley, Joseph, I. 5, 21.
Dummer,
 Mr., I. 33, 96.
 Shubael, I. 19, II. 12.

Eastknop, Joseph, II. 9.
Edgscome,
 Robert, I. 8.
 Wilmot, I. 8.
Edwards, Thomas, I. 85.
Elldridg, Eldreg, John, I. 6, II. 26, 30, 116.
Ellet, Richard, II. 7, 10.
Ellingham, William, 15.
Elliott,
 Robert, I. 6, 38, 100, 119.
 Sarah, I. 110.
Ellkins, Henry, I. 17.
Emery,
 Anthony, I. 107.
 Daniel, II. 30.
 James, I. 24, 37, 40, 74, 87, II. 10, 18, 30, 31, 32, 85, 116.
 James, junior, I. 107, II. 18, 19, 21.
 James, senior, I. 98.

INDEX OF OTHER PERRONS.

Job, I. 115, II. 30.
Noah, I. 107.
Zachariah, I. 115.
Endle,
  John, II. 4.
  Richard, II. 4, 19, 21, 59, 71, 74.
Engerson, Elisha, II. 60.
Etherington, Etherton, Euerington,
  Mary, I. 12.
  Patience, I. 12.
  Thomas, I. 12.
Evans, Jonathan, I. 48.
Everell, James, I. 27.
Everet, John, II. 70.

Favor, Feavaugh,
  Ruth, II. 111, 117, 124.
  Thomas, II. 71, 111, 117, 124.
Fayerfield, Walter, I. 84.
Fellows, John, I. 86.
Felt, Aaron, I. 37.
Fernald, Furnald, Furnell,
  John, I. 71, 103, 104.
  Samuel, I. 104, II. 101, 105, 106, 107, 112.
  Thomas, I. 97.
  William, I. 7, 15, 26, 30, 47, 99, II. 12, 19, 24, 33, 56.
Fletcher,
  John, I. 120.
  Katherine, I. 37.
  Mr., I. 5.
  Pendleton, I. 5, 35, II. 13.
Fluellin, Indian, I. 68, 86, 93, 94.
Follet, Philip, II. 125.
Forgisson, Mary, I. 30.
Fost,
  John, I. 71, 115, II. 111, 118, 124.
  Margaret, II. 16, 21, 35.
  Mary, I. 71, II. 111, 118, 124.
  William, II. 16, 21, 35.
Foster, John, II. 27.
Foxwell,
  Eleanor, I. 56, II. 7.
  Philip, I. 110, II. 7.
  Richard, I. 64.
Foul, Fowl, James, II. 105.
Freathy,
  Hannah, II. 16, 17, 20, 58, 121, 123.

  John, I. 30, 31.
  Mary, I. 52.
  Samuel, I. 4.
  Widow, II. 87.
Frost,
  Captain, I. 21, 30, 73.
  Charles, I. 2, 5, 13, 14, 17, 39, 81, 83, 98, 107, 108, 115, II. 1, 4, 6, 8, 10, 11, 12, 14, 17, 18, 19, 23, 25, 27, 30, 32, 34, 40, 47, 51, 54, 55, 58, 60, 64, 66, 67, 68, 73, 74, 77, 82, 89, 90, 92, 95, 99, 100, 101, 105.
  Charles, junior, I. 98.
  Major, I. 55, II. 3, 55.
  Mary, II. 110.
  Nicholas, I. 30, 39, II. 7.
  Philip, II. 3.
  William, senior, II. 8.
  William, junior, II. 8.
  ——, I. 34.
Fry,
  Adrian, I. 74, II. 5.
  Mr., I. 11.
  Sarah, II. 51, 60, 62.
Fryer, Nathaniel, I. 2, 30, 107, 112, 113, II. 128.
Furbush,
  Daniel, II. 86, 88.
  John, II. 26, 30.

Gage, Edmund, II. 79, 83.
Gatch, Edmund, II. 47, 119.
Gattinsby,
  Elizabeth, II. 2.
  John, I. 12.
  Susanna, I. 12.
Gedney, Bartholomew, II. 27.
Geer, John, II. 33, 34.
Gibbenes,
  James, I. 22.
  Judith, I. 8.
Giddins,
  John, I. 85.
  Samuel, I. 85.
Gillison, Nicholas, I. 112,
Gilman,
  Elizabeth, I. 62.
  John, I. 62.
Goddard, Henry, I. 108, II. 8.

Godfrey, Mr., I. 42.
Godsoe,
　William, I. 62, 104, 105, II. 50, 51ᵃ, 56, 80, 84, 119.
　's wife, II. 80, 84.
Gooch,
　James, I. 93.
　John, I. 108.
Goodin, Goodwin,
　Daniel, I. 12, 59, 111, II. 2, 14, 74, 77, 82, 89, 92, 95.
　Daniel, junior, II. 17.
　James, II. 101, 105.
　Thomas, I. 88, II. 26, 30, 51.
　William, II. 32, 33, 34, 36, 68, 71, 123.
Gorges,
　Ferdinando, Esq., I. 68.
　Sir Ferdinando, I. 68.
　Thomas, I. 58.
Gowell, Richard, II. 26, 30, 60, 68,
Gowen, Nicholas, I. 54, II. 73, 74, 77, 82, 89, 92, 95, 106, 112, 116.
Gowine *alias* Smyth,
　Elizabeth, I. 39, II. 59, 64.
　John, II. 22, 34.
　Mercy, II. 23.
　William, I. 21, 37, II. 64.
Granger, John, II. 51ᵇ, 55.
Grant,
　Christopher, II. 7.
　Elizabeth, I. 27, 28.
　Hannah, II. 7.
　James, I. 1.
　James, junior, I. 27.
　Joan, I. 27.
　Martha, II. 94, 97.
　Peter, I. 26, 27, 30, 72, 107.
　Peter, junior, I. 27.
　William, II. 94, 97.
Graves, John, I. 1, 18.
Gray, George, I. 26, 27, 112.
Green,
　Daniel, II. 114.
　Gemmer, I. 35.
　John, I. 98, II. 32.
　John, junior, I. 103.
　Nicholas, I. 42.
　Percival, I. 29.
　Richard, I. 30, 35, 117, II. 71, 74.

　's wife, II. 71, 74.
　Thomas, I. 117.
Griffin, Philip, I. 112.
Gullishaw, Sarah, II. 62, 90.
Gullison, see Gunnison.
Gunnison,
　Elihu, I. 7, 46, 75, 106, II. 56, 59.
　Mary, I. 18.
Gyndall, Walter, 17.

Haines, see Heines.
Haley, Elizabeth, II. 51ᵃ.
Hamon, Mercy, II. 22.
Hammond, Hamonds,
　Jane, II. 126.
　Jonathan, I. 11, 92, 93, II. 1, 3, 13, 17, 18, 19, 21, 23, 24, 34, 47, 74, 77, 80, 82, 89, 92, 95.
　Joseph, I. 3, 10, 17, 20, II. 33, 36, 100, 115, 119, 127, 129.
　Mr., I. 5.
Hanscum, see Hunscum.
Harden, Harding, Israel, I. 6, II. 8.
Hardison,
　Stephen, I. 55, II. 13, 90.
　's wife, II. 90.
Harman, Harmon, Herman,
　John, I. 2, 6, 66, 67, 73, 79, 80, 81, 82, 108, II. 4, 6, 7, 8, 11, 13, 14, 15, 18, 26, 30, 31.
Harriden *alias* Harris, see Harris.
Harris, Nathaniel, I. 86.
　Thomas, II. 1, 3, 5.
　Trustrum, II. 59, 65.
Harvy, Thomas, I. 30.
Hatch, Samuel, II. 14, 17, 21, 23, 101, 105, 106, 112, 118.
Hathorn, John, II. 27.
Hayes, Ann, I. 10.
　Edward, I. 107.
　Elizabeth, I. 10.
　Joseph, I. 10.
　Philadelphia, I. 10.
　William, I. 10.
Hayman, Samuel, II. 27.
Healey, Thomas, II. 14.
Heard, Abigail, I. 19, 40.
　Ann, I. 19.
　Elizabeth, I. 19, 20.
　Isabel, I. 20.
　James, I. 19.

Index of Other Persons.

John, I. 20, 30, 40, II. 4, 6, 7, 17, 51, 54, 55, 58, 59, 60, 68, 73, 106, 112.
Katherine, I. 19.
Mary, I. 19, 20.
Susanna, I. 20.
Hearle, John, I. 30.
Heines, Hains, Haynes,
Elinor, II. 98.
Robert, I. 8.
Thomas, II. 121, 123.
William, I. 36, 51.
Herlow, Francis, II. 111, 124.
Herrick, George, I. 85.
Heskins, Nicholas, I. 107, 110, 112, 113, 119.
Hill, John, I. 28, 29, 49.
Joseph, I. 28, 29, II. 73.
Samuel, I. 28, 29, II. 8.
———, I. 1.
Hilton, Robert, I. 89, 90, 91, II. 24, 25.
William, II. 3, 4, 5, 11, 12, 13, 15, 20.
Hinckes, Hinks, John, I. 17, 48, 71, 102, 118.
Hodsden,
Benoni, I. 54, II. 19, 21.
Hannah, II. 79.
John, I. 71.
Nicholas, I. 87.
Hoight, Hoit, John, II. 111, 117.
Holmes,
Joanna, I. 59, II. 10.
Thomas, I. 13, 21, II. 10.
Hooke,
Captain, I. 36, 46.
Francis, I. 2, 5, 6, 9, 13, 14, 15, 18, 31, 35, 36, 39, 40, 43, 44, 45, 46, 47, 51, 53, 54, 63, 67, 71, 72, 76, 77, 82, 96, 100, 103, 104, 105, 106, 109, 110, 114, 119, II. 1, 3, 4, 6, 7, 8, 9, 11, 12, 14, 17, 18, 19, 21, 23, 25, 27, 30, 32, 34, 36, 47.
Major, II. 24, 30, 34, 35.
Mary, I. 54, 109.
Mr., I. 32.
William, I. 42, 44, 46, 54, 63, 76, 77.
Hookely, William, I. 30.

Hole, Hoole, John, I. 15, 35, 50.
Hooper, Thomas, II. 79, 83.
Horell, Mr., I. 59.
Houston, Robert, II. 3.
Hovie, John, I. 51, 52, 53.
Hubbord, Philip, II. 116, 122, 124, 126.
Hughes, Hews,
Arthur, I. 37, 95, 96.
Sarah, I. 95, 96.
Hull,
Mary, I. 56, II. 9.
Phineas, I. 22, 35, 60, 70, II. 18.
Hunniwell, Richard, II. 74, 77, 82, 89.
Hunscom, Hanscom,
Alice, II. 71.
Thomas, II. 13, 74, 77, 82, 88, 89, 92, 95.
Hutchins, Huchin, Houtchin,
Enoch, I. 2, 76, II. 26, 80.
Mary, II. 125.
Hutchinson,
Elisha, I. 69, II. 27.
Major, I. 118, II. 14.
Mr., II. 14, 22.
William, I. 111.

Ingersall, Ingersoll,
George, I. 37.
Lieutenant, I. 22.

Jackson,
Elizabeth, I. 19.
James, I. 19.
John, I. 7, 110.
Jefferys, John, I. 32.
Jenkin, Jinkens,
Jabez, I. 10, 107, II. 4, 6, 7, 23, 25, 33.
Robert, I. 19, II. 72.
———, I. 30, 73.
Jocelyn, Henry, I. 58, 64.
Johnson,
Benjamin, I. 9.
Edward, I. 58, 121.
James, I. 17.
Joseph, II. 6.
Nathaniel, II. 105.
Samuel, I. 2.

INDEX OF OTHER PERSONS. 41

Jones,
  Alexander, I. 58.
  George, I. 41.
Jones, *alias* Pearce, *alias* Mattown, I. Sarah, 3.
Jordan,
  Dominicus, I. 41, 64, II. 4, 6, 7.
  Hannah, I. 81.
  John, I. 3, 6. 7.
  Robert, I. 6, 7, 107.
Joy, Ephraim, I. 24, 71, II. 71.
Joyliff, John, II. 27.
Junkines, see Jenkin.

Kane, Arthur, II. 4, 6, 7, 19, 92. (See Came).
Kearle, Karle, Richard, II. 51[b], 56.
Kelly,
  Abraham, II. 5.
  Charles, II. 125.
  Mr., II. 19.
  Roger, I. 8, 105, II. 5, 17, 18, 19, 20, 21, 27, 51, 60, 82.
Kemble, Thomas, I. 48.
Kene, Keen, Nathaniel, II. 4, 7, 9, 13, 48, 49, 113.
Key,
  Goodman, I. 27.
  John, I. 28.
King,
  Richard, I. 25, 61, 71, II. 18, 19, 112, 122, 126.
  Sarah, II. 111, 117.
Knight,
  Ezekiel, I. 92, II. 19, 21.
  Samuel, I. 43, 103.
Knollys, Hansard, I. 102.
Lakeman, William, II. 21, 26, 27.
Langley, Langleigh,
  Hannah, I. 9, II. 48.
  Thomas, II. 5.
Lathrop, Barnabas, II. 27.
Lawd, see Lord.
Leader, Mr., I. 60.
Leads,
  John, I. 32.
  's wife, I. 32, 33.
Leighton,
  Elizabeth, I. 20.
  John, I. 17, II. 19, 21, 32, 70,

97, 101, 105, 106, 110, 112, 119, 125.
Letten, Litten, Litton, Lidden, see Lisen,
  George, I. 26, 44, II. 12.
  Sarah, I. 44.
Levingstone, Daniel, II. 21, 23.
Levitt, James, I. 96.
Lewis, Lewes,
  Grace, II. 125.
  Peter, I. 50, II. 51, 54, 55, 60, 68, 73.
  Thomas, I. 45.
  ———, I. 50.
Libby
  Daniel, I. 22.
  Matthew, I. 22.
  ———, wife of John, I. 22.
Lidden, see Letten.
Linn, Mrs, I. 58.
Linscott, John, I. 73, 98, II. 5, 7, 9.
Litchfield, Thomas, I. 56.
Littlefield,
  Daniel, I. 91, II. 19, 21, 74, 77, 82, 89, 92, 95.
  David, II. 116, 122, 126.
  Eliab, II. 116, 122, 124, 126.
  Francis, I. 1, 11, 24, 92, II. 2, 13.
  James, senior, I. 90, 91, II. 8, 18.
  Jane, II. 16, 19, 20.
  John, I. 3, 25, II. 2, 20.
  John, junior, II. 118, 121.
  Jonathan, II. 19, 21, 26, 30, 32, 33, 34, 36, 47, 74, 77, 82, 89, 92, 95.
  Joseph, I. 92.
  Josiah, II. 13, 101, 105, 106, 112.
  Mary, II. 8.
  Meribah, I. 25.
  Moses, II. 32, 33, 34, 36, 47, 71.
  Rebecca, I. 91.
  Thomas, I. 24, 25, 92, II. 3.
Lisen, Lisson, see also Letten.
  John, II. 26, 30.
  Mary, II. 26, 30, 126.
  Sarah, II. 31, 69.
Locke, ———, I. 34.
Longmead, Longmaid, John, II. 3, 5, 7.
Lord, Lawd,

INDEX OF OTHER PERSONS.

Abraham, I. 43[b], 74, II. 2, 26, 33, 95, 101, 105.
Nathan, I. 25, 30, 40, 74, 115, II. 21.
Nathan, junior, I. 74.
Samuel, II. 2, 3.
Widow, I. 114.
Love, William, I. 1.
Lovell, Benjamin, II. 71.
Low, Thomas, senior, I. 85.
Lynde, Joseph, II. 27.

Mackanney,
   Rebecca, II. 98.
   Robert, II. 98.
Mackeyntire, Micum [Malcom], I. 19.
Manary, Thomas, II. 21.
Maning, Daniel, II. 10.
Ma[n]waring, Thomas, II. 5. 19.
Mare, Mayre, Walter, I. 4, 32.
Martin, Martyne,
   Nathaniel, I. 113.
   Richard, I. 5, 14, 88, 95, 96, 97, 120.
Mason, Robert, I. 64.
Massey, Jeffrey, I. 92.
Masterson, Sarah, II. 14.
Mathews, Samuel, II. 5.
Mattoon, Mattown, *alias* Pearce, *alias* Jones,
   Sarah, I. 3.
   Hubertus, I. 45.
Maxell, Maxwell,
   Agnes, II. 86, 88.
   Alexander, I. 42, II. 5, 10, 72, 75, 86, 88, 111, 116.
Mayne, Mane, John, I. 18, 37.
Maysterson, Nathaniel, I. 26.
Mears, Samuel, I. 65.
Melcher, Edward, I. 120.
Mendum,
   David, I. 14.
   Goodman, I. 35.
   Jonathan, I. 14.
   Mary, I. 15.
   Robert 14, 43.
Merry, Daniel, II. 24.
Metherell, Mathrell, Alice, II. 20, 51[b], 61, 67, 73.

Michamore, Robert, I. 14.
Midlecutt, Richard, II. 27.
Milberry,
   Hannah, II. 11.
   Henry, I. 72, II. 17.
   Mary, II. 85, 87.
   Richard, II. 85, 87, 88.
   William, II. 11.
Milborne, William, I. 49.
Milfort, Thomas, II. 30.
Miller,
   Mary, II. 24, 35, 71, 75, 83, 91.
   Samuel, II. 24, 25, 83, 91.
Mitchell,
   Christopher, II. 116, 122, 126.
   Robert, I. 63, 81.
Moghiggin, Indian, I. 68.
Moody,
   Ann, I. 5.
   Eleazer, I. 65, 69.
   Joshua, I. 5, 14.
More, Moore,
   Ann, I. 57.
   Dorothy, I. 57. II. 18.
   Eleanor, I. 57.
   Jeremiah, II. 108.
   John, 57, 71, 78, II. 50, 51[a].
   John, junior, I. 97.
   Mary, I. 57.
   Robert, I. 57.
   Thomas, I. 57, II. 53. II. 79, 87, 108.
   William, I. 57. II. 3, 4, 5, 7.
Morgradg, Mogridg, John, I. 44, II. 30, 57, 100, 104, 120.
Morrall, Morrill,
   John, I. 30, 96, 97, II. 18, 21, 23, 25, 33.
   Nicholas, II. 30, 34, 48, 51, 60, 62.
   Sarah, I. 118, II. 60, 62.
Morris, John, I. 36.
Moulton, Mowlton,
   Abel, II. 95.
   Jeremiah, I. 21, 26, 31, 38, II. 16, 17, 18, 21, 22, 23, 24, 31, 32, 33, 34, 36, 47, 71, 76, 101, 105, 106, 112, 119.
   Joseph, II. 8, 10, 12.
Muggridg, John, I. 100.

Munsay, William, II. 5.

Nason,
  Baker, II. 18, 78, 96, 106, 112.
  Benjamin, I. 73, II. 32, 33, 34, 36, 49.
  John, II. 14.
  Jonathan, I. 25, 71, II. 18.
  Richard, I. 12, 13, 24, 26, 55, 70, 112.
  Sarah, I. 72, II. 25, 33, 53.
Neale,
  Andrew, I. 54, II. 8, 10, 13, 92.
  James, I. 54.
  John, I. 54.
  Katherine, II. 88, 92.
Nelson,
  Elizabeth, II. 51[a].
  John, II. 51[a], 71, 74, 83, 92.
Newmarch, John, I. 118, 119, II. 60, 65.
Newton, Thomas, II. 65.
Nocke, Sylvanus, I. 108, II. 7, 8.
Norton,
  George, II. 3, 4, 6, 7, 8, 11, 13, 88.
  Shadrach, II. 88.
Nowel, Peter, II. 98, 102.
Nutter, Elder, I. 87.

Oakeman, Mary, I. 1, 5.
O'Grado, Charles, I. 106.
Oliver, Richard, II. 109.
Otis, Richard, I. 17, 40.

Page, George, I. 8.
Paine,
  Richard, I. 102.
  William, I. 65.
Palmer,
  John, I. 17.
  Richard, I. 5, 11.
  wife of Richard, I. 5.
Parker,
  Abraham, II. 5, 79, 86, 88, 94, 96.
  Basil, I. 102.
  John, I. 80, II. 51, 54, 55, 58, 60, 68, 73.
  Sarah, II. 88, 94, 96.
  Thomas, I. 96.
Parsons,
  Elizabeth, I. 78, 81, II. 20, 121, 123.
  Hannah, II. 98.
  John, I. 117, II. 15.
  William, II. 78, 98.
Partridge, William, junior, I. 105.
Patee, John, I. 100.
Paul,
  Elizabeth, II. 80.
  Katherine, II. 58, 80, 86, 120.
  Stephen, I. 98, 113.
Pearce,
  Eleanor, I. 31.
  John, II. 16.
  Joseph, I. 8, 9.
  Mary, I. 3, 8, 9, 31.
    alias Jones, *alias* Mattown, Sarah, I. 3, 8, 9. 31.
Peard, Richard, I. 37.
Pearson, George, I. 12, 89, 90, 91.
Pendleton,
  Bryan, I. 5, 32, 41.
  Captain, I. 6.
  Eleanor, I. 5.
  Hannah, I. 5.
  James, I. 5.
  James, junior, I. 5.
  Major, I. 1.
  Mary, I. 5.
  ———, I. 5.
Penhallow, Samuel, II. 7.
Penwell, Penwill, Pennywel,
  John, I. 39, 95, 108, 116, II. 7, 8, 13.
  Mary, I. 22.
  Walter, I. 18, 49.
Pepperrell,
  Andrew, I. 46.
  Margery, I. 46.
  Mr., II. 62, 88.
  William, I. 100, II. 10, 23, 25, 26, 40, 51[b], 54, 55, 58, 60, 64, 66, 67, 68, 69, 73, 74, 77, 78, 82, 87, 89, 90, 92, 93, 95, 99, 100, 101, 105, 106, 109, 110, 112, 116, 118, 119, 122, 125.
Perkins, George, II. 21.
Phillips,
  John, II. 27.

Major, I. 32.
William, I. 5, 49, 68, 69, 84.
Phips, William, II. 29.
Pickerin,
   Captain, II. 109.
   John, I. 17, 118, II. 82, 54, 76, 78, 126.
Pike, Robert, II. 27.
Pitman,
   Ann, II. 126.
   William, I. 64.
Plaisted,
   Elisha, I. 100.
   Elizabeth, I. 87, 88.
   Ichabod, II. 4, 6.
   James, I. 75, II. 14, 17, 26, 30, 32, 52, 68, 73, 76, 77, 94, 103, 104, 120.
   John, I. 115.
   Mary, II. 94, 103.
   Roger, I. 112.
   William, II. 1, 2.
Pope, Richard, II. 30.
Powle (Powell?) Mr., I. 33.
Præsbury, William, I. 35.
Pray,
   Joseph, II. 116, 122, 126.
   Samuel, II. 94.
Preble,
   Abraham, I. 6, 18, 20, 21, 38, 53, 56, 65, 66, 79, 80, 82, 83, 88, 121, II. 5, 11, 14, 15, 17, 21, 22, 25, 27, 30, 34, 51, 55, 60, 68, 74, 77, 82, 89, 92, 95, 101, 106, 109, 116, 122.
   Abraham, junior, I. 80, II. 15, 52.
   Benjamin, I, 79, II. 15, 32, 33, 34, 36, 47, 92, 95.
   Hannah, I. 79, II. 14.
   John, II. 1, 3, 14.
   Joseph, II. 11.
   Lieutenant, I. 83, II. 21, 77, 117.
   Mary, II. 52.
   Mr., II. 16, 23.
   Nathaniel, I. 26, II. 11, 15.
   Rachel, II. 11.
   Sarah, II. 11.
   Stephen, II. 11.
Price, (Bryce,) Patrick, I. 27.
Puddington,
   Elias, I. 120, 121.
   Frances, I. 120, 121.
   James, II. 69.
   John, I. 120, 121, II. 69.
   Mary, I. 120, 121.
   Rebecca, I. 120, 121.
   Robert, I. 121.
Pullman,
   Goody, I. 36.
   Jasper, I. 4, 57, II. 4, 6, 7.
   John, I. 4.
   Mary, I. 4.
Pumrey, Pomrey,
   Thomas, I. 3, 8.
Purinton, Purrington,
   Elias, II. 129.
   George, I. 116.
   John, I. 36.

Raines, Raynes,
   Captain, I. 54, II. 56.
   Francis, II. 112.
   Nathaniell II. 4, 8, 18, 19, 21, 23, 25, 26, 51, 54, 55, 58, 60, 68, 75, 78.
Ramach, Ramich, Remich,
   Christian, I. 14, 15, 30, 35, 98, 120, II. 30, 31, 51, 54, 55, 58, 113, 114, 115, 119, 126, 127.
   Isaac, I. 114, II. 23, 31, 68, 76, 82.
   Jacob, I. 30, 114, 117, II. 7, 74, 76, 77, 82, 89, 92, 95, 113, 114.
   Joshua, II. 23, 25, 31, 35, 68, 69, 114.
   Mary, II. 61.
Randell,
   Edward, I. 95.
   Richard, I. 95.
Randolph, Edward, I. 48.
Raynkine, Rainking,
   Constant, II. 50, 51*, 85, 88, 94, 99.
   Hannnah, II. 85, 88, 94, 99.
   Matthew, (Martha?) I. 24.
Read, Joseph, I. 107.
Redding,
   Elias, I. 37.
   John, II. 2, 11, 17, 18, 19.
Remick, see Ramach.

INDEX OF OTHER PERSONS. 45

Rice, Ryce,
  Mary, I. 35, 36, 50.
  Richard, II. 109.
  Thomas, I. 15, II. 2, 4, 6, 7, 13, 14, 25, 78, 79, 109.
  Thomas, junior, II. 109.
Richards, John, II. 27.
Ring, Jarvis, II. 113, 126.
Rishworth,
  Edward, I. 2, 3, 4, 9, 10, 11, 17, 18, 20, 22, 23, 27, 29, 30, 32, 37, 38, 39, 95, II. 9.
  Edward, recorder, I. 51
  Mr., I. 19, 42.
Roads, Thomas, I. 40.
Roberts, Thomas, I. 13.
Robinson, Robertson,
  John, II. 88, 90.
  's wife, 90.
Rockwell, Ebenezer, I. 94.
Roe, Anthony, I. 17, 22.
Rogers,
  Captain, II. 14.
  Goody, I. 35.
  Richard, I. 87, II. 19, 21, 48, 101, 105, 106, 108.
  William, I. 37.
Ross, John, I. 19, 20.
Rously, Robert, I. 100.
Russell, James, II. 27.
Rust, Nathaniel, senior, I. 85.

Saltonstall, Nathaniel, II. 27.
Sanders, Saunders,
  John, I. 86, 93.
  Lieutenant, I. 94.
  Sarah, II. 22, 23, 50, 51.
  William, II. 22, 23, 50, 71.
Sargent, Sergeant,
  Benjamin, I. 95.
  Edward, II. 3.
  John, I. 2, 4, 32, 41, 95.
  Peter, II. 27.
Sawyer, Sayer,
  James, II. 8, 10.
  Joseph, II. 98.
  William, II. 8, 13, 26, 30, 68, 73, 98, 101, 105, 106, 112.
Sayword,
  Henry, I. 82.

James, II. 7, 10.
  Mary, I. 1, 8, 32, 33, 88.
  Samuel, I. 31, 32, II. 10.
Scadlock, Samuel, I. 50.
Scammon, Humphrey, I. 1, 8, II. 93, 95.
Scottow,
  Captain, II. 22, 24.
  Joshua, I. 1, 3, 5, 8, 22.
  Thomas, I. 43ª.
  Thomas, clerk, 43ª.
Screven, Scrivine, William, I. 18, 40, 43ª, 75, II. 12, 17, 19, 20, 22.
Searle, Andrew, I. 59, 60, 74.
Sewall, Samuel, I, 77, 78, II. 27.
Seward, Richard, I. 97.
Shapleigh, Alexander, I. 35, 50, 62.
  Alice, I. 17, 35, 50, 83.
  John, I. 10, 20, 35, 50, 61, 103, 106, II. 18, 19, 33, 59, 107, 113.
  Nicholas, I. 3, 20, 62.
Sharpe, John, I. 22.
Shaw,
  Andrew, II. 22, 57, 60, 66.
  Edward, I. 109.
  Peter, I. 3.
Shears,
  Goody, I. 19.
  Jeremiah, II. 3.
Shephard, John, I. 44, 103, 106, II. 32, 57.
Simson, Symson, Henry, I. 3, 20, 21, 30, 88, II. 13, 15.
Skilline, Thomas, I. 37.
Smale, Small,
  Francis, I. 20, 74.
  Samuel, I. 83.
Smith, Smyth,
  Hannah, II. 79.
  Henry, I. 37.
  James, I. 40, II. 20.
  John, I. 18, 19.
  Lemuel, I. 115.
  Mr., I. 19.
  Nicholas, II. 79.
  alias Gowen, Gowine, Elizabeth, I. 39.

William, I. 21.
Snell,
  George, I. 19, 72, II. 13.
  John, I. 96.
  Samuel, I. 96.
Sosowen, Indian, I. 86, 93, 94.
Souden, Robert, I. 57.
Spencer,
  Elizabeth, I. 12.
  George, II. 104, 107.
  Humphrey, I. 1, 12, 24, II. 34.
  Moses, I. 13, 24.
  Patience, I. 12.
  Susanna, I. 12.
  Thomas, I. 112, 114.
  William, I. 12, 20, 21, 24, 27, 59, 71, 111, II. 21, 23.
Spiller, Abraham, I. 96.
Spinney,
  James, I. 104, II. 92.
  John I. 103, 105, II. 32, 33, 34, 36, 47.
  Margery, I. 104.
  Samuel, II. 21, 23, 97, 113, 114, 119, 126, 127.
  Thomas, I. 71, 103, 120, II. 14, 17, 18, 114, 116, 119, 122, 126.
Sprague, Samuel, I. 69.
Stacie, William, I. 74, II. 51[a], 55, 57.
Stagpole, Stackpole, James, I. 14, II. 19, 26, 30, 31, 57, 72, 75, 87, 120.
Staple,
  John, II. 76, 82, 94, 99, 106.
  Mary, II. 94, 99.
  Peter, II. 94, 108.
  Peter, junior, II. 99.
Starboard, Thomas, II. 111.
Stoddard, Anthony, II. 129.
Stone, Daniel, I. 24, 108, II. 8, 10, 13.
Storer, Jeremiah, II. 14, 23, 25, 49, 51, 52, 54, 55, 58, 60, 68, 73, 76, 95.
  Joseph, I. 1, 23, 29, 34, II. 9, 17, 18, 20, 21, 23, 25, 26, 30, 53, 103, 120.
  Lieutenant, II. 21.
Stoughton, William, II. 27, 40, 100.

Stover, Elizabeth, II. 6, 8.
  Jeremiah, II. 7.
  Joseph, II. 8.
  Sylvester, I. 18, 42, II. 6.
Stuart, Robert, II. 3, 9.
Styleman,
  Elias, I. 13, 61, 97.
  Richard, I. 30.
Symonds,
  William, I, 25, 34.
  William, junior, I. 34.

Taylor,
  Abigail, I. 55.
  Deliverance, I. 55.
  John, I. 26, 27.
  Joseph, II. 19, 32, 33, 34, 36, 47.
  Martha, I. 55, II. 85, 98, 111, 118.
  Mary, I. 55.
  Sarah, I. 55.
  Widow, II. 80, 85, 111.
Terrie, John, I. 111.
Tetherly,
  Gabriel, II. 126.
  William, I. 62, 87, 98.
Theyfts, Mary, II. 31, 34.
Thomas,
  Roger, II. 101.
  William, II. 51[b], 61.
Thorne, John, II. 71.
Tilton, Abraham, I. 89, 90.
Tiney, John, II. 26.
Tobey,
  James, I. 117.
  Stephen, I. 117, II. 8, 10, 13, 71.
Thompson, Tomson,
  Alexander, II. 101.
  Edward, I. 115.
  Elizabeth, II. 80, 84.
  John, I. 25, 107, 114, II. 31, 61, 73, 80, 84.
  Thomas, II. 116, 122, 126.
Torner, Deliverance, I. 69.
Tozier, Richard, I. 22, II. 23, 25.
Trafton,
  Elizabeth, I. 57, II. 103.
  Thomas, II. 11, 14, 15, 17, 18, 32, 33, 34, 36, 47, 67, 71, 78, 103, 104, 120.

Tricky,
  John, I. 7.
  Sarah, I. 7, 39, II. 12.
Trustrum, Ralph, I. 41, 95.
Treworgie, Tryworgye, James, II 88, 90.
Tucker,
  Francis, I. 57, II. 26.
  Hugh, II. 121.
  Nicholas, II. 21, 23, 25.
  William, II. 109.
  ——, II. 121.
Turbett,
  Elizabeth, II. 80, 85, 98, 111, 118, 124.
  Nicholas, I. 71, II. 80, 85, 98, 111, 118, 124.
  Peter, I. 86, 93. 94.
Turner,
  John, I. 55.
  Thomas, I. 35.
Tuttle, John, I. 72.
Twisden,
  John, I. 6, 18, 19, 21, 52, 66, 67.
  Mary, II. 73.
  Samuel, I. 20.
Tyng, Ting, Edward, I. 64.
Tynny, John, I. 5.

Ugroufe,
  John, I. 118.
  Mary, I. 102.
Usher, John, I. 84.

Vahan, Vaughan, William, I. 80, 100, II. 78, 79.
Vines,
  Mr., I. 42.
  Richard, I. 58.

Wade, Thomas, I. 94.
Waddock,
  Henry, I. 1.
  Jane, I. 4.
Waite, Thomas, I. 94.
Wakefield,
  Elizabeth, I. 25.
  John, I. 109.
  Katherine, I. 25.
Walden, Waldron,

  Richard, I. 16.
  Richard, junior, I. 17.
  William, I. 58.
Walford, Jeremy, I. 67.
Walker, Richard, I. 85.
Walley, John, II. 27.
Walters, Thomas, II. 79, 82.
Warren, Warrine,
  Gilbert, I. 12, 59.
  James, I. 26, II. 16, 21, 31, 47.
  James, junior, I. 26, II. 2, 3, 23.
  Mary, II. 16, 21.
Watts, Henry, I. 109.
Waye, William, I. 96.
Waymouth,
  Edward, I. 107, II. 80, 84.
  Hester, II. 80, 84.
Weare,
  Elias, II. 102, 104.
  Joseph, II. 7, 47, 89.
  Magdalen, II. 102, 104.
  Mary, I. 80, II. 12, 15.
  Peter, II. 6, 8, 15, 126.
Webber, Samuel, I. 3, 30.
Weeks,
  Constable, II. 109.
  Joseph, I. 53, II. 26, 30.
  Nicholas, I. 44, 53, 71, II. 4, 6, 16, 18.
Welch, Philip, II. 22.
Welcom, Sarah, I. 57.
Wells,
  John, I. 11.
  Lucy, I. 62.
Wentworth,
  John, I. 30, 77, 78.
  Samuel, I. 77, 78.
West,
  John, I. 5.
  Mr., 5.
Wheelwright,
  Hannah, II. 98.
  John, I. 29, II. 7, 9, 17, 18, 19, 20, 21, 23, 24, 26, 52, 53, 54, 55, 57, 58, 59, 60, 63, 68, 72, 73, 76, 103, 118, 120.
  Mr., I. 25, II. 19, 25, 51.
  Samuel, I. 11, 12, 20, 29, 34, 85, 86, 89, 90, 91, 92, II. 1, 3, 8, 9, 11, 12, 14, 17, 18, 21, 23,

Index of Other Persons.

27, 34, 40, 47, 51, 54, 55, 58, 60, 64, 66, 67, 68, 73, 74, 77, 82, 89, 90, 92, 95, 99, 100, 101, 105, 106, 112, 116, 122.
  Samuel, junior, I. 86.
Whinick,
  Joseph, II. 3.
  Sarah, I. 45, II. 3.
White,
  John, I. 74.
  Philip, II, 59, 64.
  Richard, I. 71, II. 5.
  Samson, I. 16.
Whitefoot, John, I. 87.
Wiggens, James, I. 7, 37, 76, 77, 78, 110, II. 18.
Williams,
  Gregory, I. 97.
  Rowland, II. 32, 33, 34, 36, 47.
Wills, Thomas, I. 40.
Willson,
  Gowine, I. 2.
  John, II. 9.
  Joseph, II. 23, 25, 116, 122, 124, 126.
Winchester, Mary, II. 85.
Wincoll,
  Captain, I. 24, 39.
  John, I. 5, 10, 12, 13, 14, 22, 24, 27, 28, 35, 39, 43[b], 44, 45, 46, 47, 55, 60, 61, 71, 72, 74, 75, 76, 78, 79, 80, 81, 82, 83, 86, 87, 88, 99, 103, 108, 111, 112, 115, II. 1, 3, 4, 6, 7, 8, 12, 14.
  John, junior, I. 12, 27.
  Mary, I. 12.
Winkley, Samuel, I. 106.
Winthrop,
  Adam, II. 27.
  Wait, II. 27.
Wise, Thomas, I. 119, II. 13.
Withers,
  Elizabeth, I. 35, 43, 50, 70.

Jane, I. 35, 43, 50.
  Mr., I. 103.
  Thomas, I. 58, 70.
Wittam, Wittum,
  Mary, II. 13.
  Peter, I. 83, II. 80, 85.
  Peter, junior, II. 80, 85, 90.
  William, I. 54.
Wollcocke, Edward, I. 4, 33.
Wollcott, Mr., I. 19.
Woodbridge, Benjamin, I. 47.
Wooddin,
  John, II. 8.
  Katherine, II. 8.
Woodman, John, II. 14, 15, 17, 20, 25, 31, 70, 76, 78, 97, 112, 125, 126.
Wormwood,
  John, II. 25.
  William, I. 39.
Woster,
  Moses, II. 98, 102.
  wife of, II. 102.

Yeales, Timothy, I. 31, 32, 38, 117, II. 3, 4.
Young,
  Elinor, II. 98, 102.
  Joan, I. 37, 38, 116.
  Job, II. 21, 23, 92, 93.
  Matthew, II. 98, 102.
  Robert, I. 1.
  Rowland, II. 23, 25, 94, 96, 121,
  Susanna, II. 121, 122.
  William, I. 82, II. 8, 10.

Surnames not given,
  John (Freathy?) I. 39.
  Capt. Joshua (Scottow?) I. 1.
  Lewis (Bean?) I. 35, 50.
  Meribah (Littlefield?) I. 24.

INDEX OF PLACES.

Barbadoes, island of, I. 99.
Batson's river, I. 68.
Berwick. I. 13, 26, 27, 28, 39, 43ᵇ, 54, 55, 60, 70, 73, 86, 115. II. 2, 3, 7, 10, 16, 19, 20, 21, 22, 51ª, 53, 71, 72, 96, 97.
  garrison at, I. 54. II. 10.
  Newgewanake, Newichewanock. I. 10, 12, 59, 60, 87, 112.
  commons, I. 60.
  Post Wigwam, I. 60.
  Little river, I. 98.
  river, I. 60.
  Parker's marsh, I. 12, 111.
  Quamphegon, II. 10.
  Rocky hills, I. 55, 72, 115.
  Slut's corner, I. 111.
  Sturgeon creek, I. 39, 72, 73.
  Third hill, I. 39.
  Wilcock's pond, I. 13, 24, 112.
  York line, 39.
Black Point, see under Scarborough.
Blue Point, see under Scarborough.
Boston. I. 1, 27, 41, 48, 64, 65, 68, 69, 77, 78, 84, 118. II. 14, 22, 24, 29, 40, 100, 128, 129.
Boxford, Mass. I. 94.

Cape Elizabeth. I. 7.
Cape Porpoise. I. 5, 84, 86. II. 2, 69.
  islands at, I. 5, 6.
  Prince's Rock, I. 5.
Cape Porpoise, alias Mousam river. I. 3, 86, 93, 94.
Casco. I. 1, 3, 30.
Casco Bay. I. 37, 64, 109.
  New Damariscove sound, I. 64.
  Pulpit island, I. 64.
Coxhall, now Lyman. I. 11, 84, 85, 86, 93, 94.
  called Swansfield, I. 93, 94.
  by description, I. 86.
  Coxhorne pond, I. 86.

Dartmouth, England. I. 61.
Dover, N. H., I. 59, 60, 73. II. 3, 84.
  Oyster river, I. 73.
Duxbury, Mass. I. 68.

Eastward, at the. I. 56.
England, I. 46, 59, 61. See Dartmouth, Jersey, Plymouth.
Essex county, Mass. I. 84, 93, 94.

Falmouth. I. 37. II. 2, 3.
  Ammongungon river, I. 37.
  Bastine's or Bustian island, I. 87.
  Capisic, called Tewissicke, I. 37.
  House island, I. 37.
  Long creek, I. 37.
  Pischataqua, i. e., Piscataquis, I. 37.
  Tewissicke, i. e., Capisic, I. 37.

Gorgeana. I. 120.
Great island, N. H. I. 5, 6, 67, 97, 112. II. 88.

Harpswell, see Mericaneeg.

Ipswich, Mass. I. 84, 85, 86, 93, 94 II. 10.
Isles of Shoals. I. 7, 44. II. 5, 19, 21.
  the northern, II. 5, 20.
  Smutty Nose island, I. 44.

Jersey, island of. II. 9.

Kennebeck river. Recorder's error for Kennebunk river. I. 68.
Kennebunk, islands in. I. 68.
  river, I. 68.

Index of Places.

Kittery. I. 1, 3, 7, 10, 12, 13, 14, 15, 17, 19, 20, 22, 25, 26, 27, 30, 40, 43, 44, 45, 46, 47, 54, 59, 60, 61, 62, 63, 67, 71, 74, 75, 76, 77, 78, 83, 87, 96, 97, 98, 99, 100, 102, 103, 104, 106, 107, 108, 109, 110, 111, 113, 114, 117, 118, 119, 120. II. 3, 4, 7, 9, 10, 11, 13, 22, 25, 31, 32, 49, 51[b], 52, 54, 56, 57, 61, 62, 63, 64, 66, 67, 68, 69, 70, 71, 74, 76, 77, 79, 83, 84, 88, 89, 90, 93, 98, 104, 105, 106, 107, 108, 111, 114, 118, 120, 123, 126. See Piscataqua.
Ballyhock, I. 22.
Birch point cove, I. 87.
Boiling rock, I. 113, 120.
Brave-[or Broad]-boat harbor. I. 46, 47, 77, 78, II. 104, 107.
  creek, I. 54, 76.
Broad cove, I. 61, 100.
Champernoon's island, I. 48, 110.
Clark's island, II. 109.
  commons, I. 78.
Cool harbor, I. 74.
Crooked lane, I. 40, 67, 75.
Crocket's creek, I. 62.
  neck, I. 109.
Eagle point, I. 43, 50, 58.
Frank's fort, I. 117, 118.
Great cove, I. 103, 104. II. 119.
  islands in, I. 40, 70.
Long creek, I. 100.
Long reach, II. 108.
mills, grist mill, I. 15.
  saw mill, I. 15.
Nine noches, I. 27.
Oak point, I. 50.
Pine point, I. 58.
Piscataqua harbor mouth, I. 62.
  point, I. 17. II. 69, 83, 89.
Simmons' marsh, I. 98, 113.
Spruce Creek, I. 14, 40, 43[a], 46, 47, 58, 75, 96, 97, 103, 106, 109, 119. II. 49, 52, 105, 107.
Sturgeon Creek, I. 15, 20, 25, 30, 40, 74. II. 69, 88, 93.
Tomson's point, I. 19, 20.
Watts' fort, I. 118.
Withers' point, II. 14.

York pond, I. 107.

Massachusetts. See Boston, Boxford, Duxbury, Essex county, Ipswich, Middleborough, Plymouth, Plymouth county, Salem, Salisbury, Suffolk county, Topsfield, Wenham.
Mericaneeg neck, now Harpswell. I. 64.
Little or Crooked Lane river, I. 64.
  Sandy point, I. 64.
Middleborough, Mass. 1. 68.
  Decayed neck, I. 68.
  Pechague, I. 68.
  Rooty brook, I. 68.
Mousam. I. 3, 30.
  river, I. 86.
  alias Cape Porpoise river, I. 86, 93, 94.
  falls, I. 85.

Newcastle, N. H. II. 26.
New Hampshire. I. 13, 73, 87, 95, 118. See Dover, Great island, Newcastle, Portsmouth, Portsmouth county, Strawberry bank.
North Yarmouth. I. 64.

Piscataqua. I. 6, 58, 81, 99. See Kittery.
Piscataqua river. I. 5, 10, 20, 43, 48, 78, 102, 104, 106, 114, 120. II. 14, 57, 88.
  called Great river, I. 87.
Plymouth, England. I. 46.
Plymouth, Massachusetts. I. 68.
Plymouth county, Mass. I. 69.
Portsmouth, N. H. I. 5, 87, 95, 97, 100, 105, 106, 109, 111, 112, 118, 120. II. 57, 70.
Portsmouth, N. H. county of. I. 44.

Richman's island. I. 6.

Saco. I. 2, 5, 8, 37, 45, 49, 95, 105, 106. II. 3, 24.
  Flying hill, I. 105, 106.
  Fresh Water creek, I. 45.

Index of Places. 51

Great swamp, I. 105, 106.
Little river, I. 5, 11, 22, 49.
Page's Creek, I. 105, 106.
Timber island, Little river, I. 5.
West's brook, I. 5.
Winter harbor, I. 5, 6, 17, 22, 41, 49, 95.
Saco river, I. 1, 4, 5, 45, 49, 86, 93, 94, 105, 106.
  falls in, I. 5, 6, 68.
Scadlock's river, I. 49.
Salem, Mass. I. 1, 82.
Salisbury, Mass. II. 113, 126.
Scarborough. I. 45, 64, 109, 112. II. 3.
  Arthur Augers creek, I. 109.
  Black Point. 1. 3, 5, 17, 64.
  garrison at, I. 3.
  Blue Point. I. 7, 112.
  Dunster, I. 109.
  Spurwink, I. 7.
  Spurwink river, I. 7.
Strawberry bank, Portsmouth, N. H. I. 1, 70, II. 14.
Suffolk county, Mass. I. 65, 68. II. 129.
Swansfield, a former name of Lyman. I. 93, 94.

Tardodous. (?) I. 17.
Topsfield, Mass. I. 93.

Wells. I. 1, 3, 5, 6, 10, 11, 19, 23, 27, 28, 30, 68, 84, 86, 89, 90, 91, 92, 94. II. 1, 2, 3, 8, 9, 11, 13, 14, 16, 17, 19, 20, 21, 22, 23, 24, 34, 36, 47, 53, 60, 63, 64, 66, 68, 73, 77, 92, 95, 98, 99, 103, 116, 118, 120, 121, 124, 126.

Drake's island, I. 10, 28, 29.
Epiford, I. 11. 28.
islands in, I. 92.
Merryland, I. 92.
mills, grain, I. 25.
Ogunquet, I. 10.
  river, I. 89, 90.
Webhannet river. I. 90.
the Great river, I. 92.
the ridge, I. 92.
Wenham, Mass. I. 85.

York. I. 1, 3, 7, 17, 18, 19, 26, 31, 36, 38, 42, 51, 52, 53, 57, 66, 72, 78, 79, 81, 82, 87, 95, 96, 111, 116. II. 3, 4, 5, 6, 7, 8, 9, 10, 11, 12, 13, 14, 15, 16, 17, 18, 19, 21, 22, 23, 24, 25, 26, 30, 32, 51, 51^b, 52, 53, 54, 55, 56, 58, 63, 64, 70, 71, 72, 73, 74, 75, 76, 77, 79, 82, 86, 89, 95, 96, 101, 102, 103, 104, 105, 106, 107, 108, 110, 111, 112, 114, 116, 117, 119, 122, 123, 126, 127.
Agamenticus hills, I. 87.
Alcock's garrison, II. 6.
Averell's pond, II. 70.
Bass cove, I. 66, II. 16.
Brave-boat harbor, II. 56, 104, 107, 126.
Brave-boat Harbor creek, I. 54.
called Gorgeana, I. 120.
Cape Neddick, I. 79, 108.
Gooch's neck, I. 108.
harbor, II. 88.
line, I. 77.
lower ferry, II. 56.
Meeting-house Creek, I. 116.
New Mill Creek, I. 31.
Old Mill Creek, I. 42, 82.
Preble's garrison, I. 83.
river, I. 42. II. 42, 70.
Scituate highway, I. 42.
York river, I. 31, 42, 66, 67, 78, 81, 95. II. 14, 53, 87, 108.

GENERAL INDEX.

Accounts stated and rendered, I. 19, 30.
Administration, on the estate of,
  Adams, ——II. 15.
  Barrett, John, II. 2.
  Bedford, Nathan, I. 6.
  Biss, Samuel, I. 6.
  Brackett, Anthony, II. 2.
  Cooper, ——, II. 15.
  Davis, John, II. 11.
  Endle, John, II. 4.
  Fox(w)ell, John, I. 2.
  Fox(w)ell, Philip, II. 7.
  Frost, William, II. 8.
  Grant, Christopher, II. 7.
  Hull, Phineas, II. 18.
  Littlefield, James, II. 8.
  Lord, Samuel, II. 2.
  Milberry, William, II. 11.
  Milton, Nathaniel, I. 1.
  Oakeman, Samuel, I. 1.
  Oliver, Joseph, I. 2.
  Parsons, John, II. 15.
  Pearce, Joseph, I. 3.
  Preble, John, II. 14.
    Joseph, II. 11.
    Nathaniel, II. 15.
    Stephen, II. 11.
  Pullman, John, I. 4.
  Raynkine, Andrew, I. 24.
  Rishworth, Edward, II. 9.
  Robbines, William, I. 3.
  Sayword, Henry, I. 1.
    Samuel, II. 10.
  Simson, Henry, II. 15.
  Weare, Peter, II. 15.
  Whinick, Joseph, II. 3.
  Wilson, John, II. 9.
Administrators' accounts, I. 4, 19, 30, 35.
Annuity, I. 26, 34, 67, 113, 114. (see Support and maintenance.)
Appeals, II. 33, 36, 64, 78, 127.
Apprentices,

Irish boys, I. 16.
Arms, accoutrements and ammunition, I. 62, 72.
  ammunition, I. 3, 13, 72.
  armor, I. 62.
  back-sword, I. 39.
  bandoleers, I. 6, 27, 29, 52.
  belts, I. 36.
  blunderbuss, I. 16, 44.
  bullets, see under shot.
  carbines, I. 13. 65.
    double-barrelled, I. 65.
  cutlasses, I. 21, 26, 33, 51, 52, 66, 67, 80.
  dagger-knives, I. 16, 17.
  flints, I. 33.
  fowling-pieces, I. 4, 8, 9, 15, 16, 33, 38, 40.
  guns, I. 1, 6, 13, 23, 27, 29, 31, 32, 36, 39, 41, 51, 52, 53, 57, 59, 66, 67, 71, 79, 80, 82, 88.
    barrels, I. 81.
    great, I. 16.
  gun carriages, I. 16.
  holsters, I. 23, 41.
  muskets, I. 2, 4, 6, 8, 13, 16, 28, 33, 34, 55, 65.
    fire-lock, I. 15, 27, 33.
  pistols, I. 23, 31, 41.
  powder, I. 16, 17, 29, 33, 34, 38, 41, 44, 51, 52, 53.
    horns, I. 33, 36, 38, 44.
  rapiers, I. 6, 32, 41, 80.
  swords, I. 3, 11, 27, 28, 29, 30, 32, 52, 53, 82.
    belts, I. 6, 11, 21, 26, 27, 28, 44.
  shot and bullets, I. 29, 31, 33, 34, 41, 44, 52.
    moulds, I. 34, 41.
    pouch, I. 44.
  watch-bill, I. 79.
Assistants, members of the Governor's council in Massachusetts,

Isaac Addington, I. 65.
Joseph Dudley, I. 21.
Elisha Hutchinson, I. 69.
Associates, Yorkshire magistrates,
Edward Rishworth, I. 9, 10, 11, 20.
Samuel Wheelwright, I. 11, 12, 20, 32.
John Wincoll, I. 10, 27, 60, 99, 111.
Attorneys, I. 118, II. 8, 109, 126.
Authority, i.e. those in, I. 2, 6, 7, 22, 24.
Courts of, I. 19.

Berwick, see Index of Places.
selectmen, I. 1, II. 96.
grants recorded, see Index of Grantors under the names following:
Child, Henry, et ux., I. 60.
Emery, James, sen., I. 107, 115.
Jenkenes, Stephen, I. 73.
Plaisted, Elisha's estate, I. 87.
Spencer, Humphrey, I. 111, 112.
Moses, I. 98.
Thomas et ux., I. 104, 111.
grants referred to:
town (Kittery) to [Richard] Leader, I. 60.
Nyven Agnew to John Taylor, I. 55.
John Gattinsby to Thomas Etherington, I. 12.
Thomas Spencer to John Gattinsby, I. 12.
Thomas Spencer to Thomas Etherington, I. 12.
Bilboes, shackles for the feet, to be provided in the prison, II. 77.
Bill of sale, I. 29.
Bills, debts, etc., I. 25, 30, 33, 35, 37, 40, 54.
Board for soldiers, I. 11.
per week, I. 11.
Books, I. 3, 7, 11, 23, 28, 29, 30, 33, 34, 37, 40, 41, 54, 65, 72, 75, 79, 80.

Bibles, I. 3, 9, 11, 17, 24, 28, 30, 33, 36, 39, 41, 57, 80.
Key of the Bible, I. 80.
Practice of Piety, I. 9.
sea, I. 33.
Divinity, I. 39.
new book of records for the Province, I. 6.
Bridges, II., 52, 104, 107.
Buildings and their appurtenances and divisions.
barns, I. 11, 13, 23, 26, 29, 31, 39, 43,[b] 46, 52, 55, 57, 65, 66, 67, 71, 73, 75, 79, 82.
brew-house, I. 16.
canopy rooms, I. 16.
chamber, I. 47.
cow-house, I. 81, 88.
dairy, I. 16.
garret, I. 16.
garrisons, I. 3, 54, 83, II. 10.
hall, I. 47.
hall-chambers, I. 16.
houses, houseing and dwellings, I. 2, 3, 4, 5, 7, 9, 10, 11, 12, 18, 14, 17, 18, 20, 21, 22, 24, 25, 26, 27, 29, 31, 43,[a] 43,[b] 46, 52, 55, 57, 62, 65, 66, 67, 71, 72, 73, 75, 79, 81, 82, 88.
hovel, I. 31.
kitchen, I. 16, 47.
lean-to, I. 16, 47.
lodgings, I. 2.
rooms, I. 16.
mansion, I. 31.
mill-buildings, I. 3, 30, 31.
on leased land, I. 18, 19.
out houses, I. 12, 13, 14, 29, 55, 65.
parlor chamber, I. 16.
porch, I. 47.
sheep-house, I. 31.
shop, I. 31, 54.
ware-house, I. 4, 65.
wharf, I. 65.
Burying place reserved, I. 28.

Cattine, i.e. kitchen, I. 31.
Cattle, names given to, I. 35, 50, 121.

54 GENERAL INDEX.

Cautions, i.e. caveats, I. 6, 118.
Chitchine, kitchen, I. 16.
Church of England, I. 20.
Clerks of the Province (See Recorders).
  Newmarch, John, II. 60.
  Scottow, Thomas, I. 43.[a]
  Wincoll, John, I. 43.[b]
  Wincoll John, II. 1.
Clerk of the writs, I. 6.
Cloths and fabrics, I. 3, 6, 24, 28, 38, 39, 66.
  blanket cloth, I. 72.
  brins, I. 72.
  broadcloth, I. 4, 14, 17, 33, 34.
  calico, I. 38, 41.
  canting, kenting, cantoon, a fustian, I. 6, 43,[a] 72.
  canvas, I. 11, 16, 65.
  cotton, I. 6, 16, 19, 24, 32, 34, 39, 65, 67, 72.
    wool, I. 21, 23, 54, 80.
    yarn, I. 72.
  diaper, I. 65, 72.
  dimity, I. 41.
  Dowlas, a coarse linen, I. 24, 34, 65, 72.
  drusline, I. 8.
  flax, I. 72.
    yarn, I. 72.
  fustian, I. 44.
  galloon-trimming, I. 34.
  hair-cloth, I. 7.
  Hollands, I. 8, 17, 41, 65.
  homespun, I. 14, 17, 52.
  kersey, I. 4, 7, 13, 16, 23, 34.
  lace, I. 33.
  leanells, I. 7.
  linen, I. 7, 16, 17, 19, 23, 24, 25, 27, 29, 31, 32, 33, 34, 38, 44, 56, 67, 70, 80.
  locerum, I. 15, 17.
  nowells, I. 7.
  Osenbridg, Osnaburg, a coarse linen, I. 6.
  paragon, I. 7.
  pennystone, a coarse woolen, I, 15, 21, 24, 29.
  ribbons, I. 33.
  Scotch, I. 15, 17.
  searge, I. 7, 11, 14, 17, 21, 33, 34, 38, 41, 67, 70.
  sheared, homespun, I. 4.
  silk, I. 6, 21, 23, 33, 41.
  thread, I. 7, 23, 33.
  ticking, I. 3, 31, 34.
  twine, I. 7, 88, 39.
  wool, I. 7, 17, 24, 39, 67, 79, 80.
  woolen, I. 23, 25, 27, 34, 44, 88.
  yarn, I. 6, 21, 23, 37, 39, 54, 67, 72, 79, 82, 88.
Commissions to the Justices, II. 27, 40, 100.
Commissioners, inferior magistrates of Yorkshire.
  Walter Gyndall, I. 17.
  Francis Hooke, I. 4.
  Edward Johnson, I. 53.
  Roger Kelley, I. 8.
  in New Hampshire.
  Richard Martin, I. 97.
  Elias Styleman, I. 97.
Commissioners on intestates estate I. 17, II. 9.
Commissioners on County Jail, II 77.
Common Law, I. 6.
Constables, II. 22, 23, 71, 85, 109.
Council of the Province, I. 1, 7, 17, 36.
Councillors of Massachusett, I. 82, 103, 106, 114.
Councillors of New England, I. 84.
Councillors of New Hampshire, I. 71, 102, 118, 120.
Cousin,
  for nephew, I. 28, 61, 116.
  for niece, I. 4, 28.
Courts of Common Pleas, I. 1, 6, 21, 22, 25, II. 10.
  held at Wells, I. 1, 3, II. 3, 36, 60, 64, 73, 99.
  held at York, I. 58, 96, II. 1, 6, 8, 9, 11, 12, 17, 26, 32, 54, 58, 77, 89, 105, 112, 114, 126.
Court of Oyer and Terminer, special, II. 18.
Courts of Quarter Sessions, I. 1, 2, 4, II. 1, 10.
  held at Kittery. I. 1, 3, II. 90.

GENERAL INDEX. 55

held at Wells, I. 6, 19, 27, II. 1, 21, 22, 23, 24, 34, 47, 66, 67, 68, 92, 95, 116.
held at York, I. 87, II. 1, 4, 7, 9, 10, 11, 12, 13, 14, 15, 17, 19, 20, 25, 26, 30, 51, 55, 74, 79, 82, 89, 101, 106, 122.
of New Hampshire, I. 13.
Superior, see Superior Courts.
Court, expenses at, I. 30.
Computation of the church of England, i.e. Old Style, I. 20.

Defendants.
  Abbet, Thomas, et al., Abraham Lord vs. II. 33.
  Atwell, Philip, Francis Tucker vs. II. 25.
  Beal, Arthur, Nathaniel Raines vs. II. 23.
  Berry, Elizabeth, John Ball apl't. vs. II. 33, 36.
  Brisson, Charles, John Davis vs. II. 6.
  Buckland, John, Wm. Vaughan vs. II. 78.
  Carter, Richard, Francis Raines vs. II. 112.
  Chadbourn, Sarah, Nicholas Gowen *alias* Smith vs. II. 73.
  Champernoon, Mary, John Pickerin vs. II. 33, 54.
  Daniell, Samuel, George Norton, apl't vs. II. 8.
  Downing, Joshua, Joseph Hammond vs. II. 33.
  Endle, Richard, Elihu Gunnison vs. II. 59.
  Gowen, Elizabeth, Philip White vs. II. 59, 65.
  Hardison, Stephen, George Snell vs. II. 13.
  Hill, Samuel, John Davis vs. II. 8.
  Hilton, William, Elizabeth Parsons vs. II. 20.
  Johnson, Nathaniel, James Foul vs. II. 105.
  Keen, Nathaniel, John Shepard vs. II. 32.
  King, Richard, John Woodman vs. II. 112.
  Leighton, John, Town of Kittery vs. II. 32.
  Lidden, George, Sarah Trickey vs. II. 12.
  Metherell, Alice, John Thomson vs. II. 73.
  More, William, Nathaniel Raines apl't vs. II. 8.
  Moulton, Jeremiah, Abraham Preble vs. II. 22, 33.
  Nason, Baker, William Parsons vs. II. 78.
  Nason, Sarah, et al., Abraham Lord vs. II. 33.
  Raines, Nathaniel et al., John Pickerin vs. II. 78.
  Reding, John, Robert Stewart apl't, vs. II. 9.
  Remich, Christian, Samuel Spinney vs. II. 126, 127.
  Rice, Thomas, John Cutt's estate vs. II. 78.
  Sayer, William, James Littlefield et al. vs. II. 8.
  Shapleigh, John, Nathaniel Keen vs. II. 113.
  Spinney, Samuel, Christian Remich vs. II. 113, 114.
  Stover, Sylvester's estate, Peter Weare vs. II. 6.
  Tetherly, Gabriel's estate, Peter Weare vs. II. 126.
  Tiney, John, Francis Tucker vs. II. 25.
  Trafton, Thomas, John Woodman vs. II. 78.
  Weare, Joseph, John Cutt's estate vs. II. 89.
  Woodman, John et al., John Pickerin vs. II. 78.
Deer-skins, I. 3.
Deputy President.
  John Davis, I. 33, 38, 117, II. 1, 3, 4, 6, 7, 8.
  Francis Hooke, I. 72, II. 11, 12.
  Bryan Pendleton, I. 1.
Diet, I. 11, 30.
Doctor's bill, I. 8.

GENERAL INDEX.

Depositions.
Aignew, Nivine, I. 27.
Alexander, Richard, I. 20.
Allcocke, Job, I. 4, 96.
Anger, Sarah, I. 57.
Bonighton, John, I. 8.
Bools, Joseph, I. 25.
Bouden, Ambrose, I. 64.
Brookin, Henry, I. 70.
  Sarah, I. 70.
Bragdon, Samuel, I. 82.
Bray, Joan, I. 9.
Bryard, Elisha, I. 102.
Carter, Richard, I. 4.
Combes, Anthony, I. 85.
Deament, John, I. 43.
Dennett, Alexander, I. 18.
Donnell, Henry, I. 4.
Donnell Samuel, I. 82.
Evans, Jonathan, I. 48.
Freathy, Samuel, I. 4.
Fry, Adrian, I. 74.
  Sarah, I. 74.
Gibbines, Judith, I. 8.
Graves, John, I. 18.
Gray, George, I. 27.
Hardison, Stephen, I. 55.
Heines, William, I. 51, 70.
Herman, John, I. 109.
Heskins, Nicholas, I. 107, 112, 113.
Hill, John, I. 85.
Hooke, Francis, I. 9, 47, 51.
Jocelyn, Henry, I. 58.
Johnson, Edward, I. 58.
Jones, Alexander, I. 58.
King, Richard, I. 61, 82.
Knight, Samuel, I. 43.
Moody, Joshua, I. 5, 14.
Morgradge, John, I. 44.
Moulton, Jeremiah, I. 38.
Paine, Richard, I. 102.
Patee, John, I. 100.
Pears, John, I. 75.
Penwill, John, I. 109.
Pitman, William, I. 64.
Price, Patrick, I. 27.
Raines, Nathaniel, I. 82.
Ramach, Christian, I. 14.
Randell, Edward, I. 95.
Read, Joseph, I. 107.
Rousley, Robert, I. 100.
Sargent, Benjamin, I. 95.
Shepard, John, I. 44.
Small, Francis, I. 20.
Souden, Robert, I. 57.
Symonds, William, I. 25.
Taylor, John, I. 27, 55.
Tetherly, William, I. 61.
Tucker, Francis, I. 57.
Wheelwright, John, I. 29.
  Samuel, I. 29.
Wincoll, John, I. 27.
Woodbridge, Benjamin, I. 47.
Yealls, Timothy, I. 38.
Young, William, I. 82.
Domestic animals:
  barrows, I. 23, 27.
  bulls, I. 11, 14, 21, 28, 29, 56, 59, 72, 79, 81, 83.
  calves, I. 2, 4, 7, 11, 14, 18, 21, 22, 23, 24, 26, 27, 29, 30, 34, 36, 38, 39, 41, 43,[b] 44, 51, 52, 53, 54, 55, 56, 59, 65, 66, 67, 70, 73, 75, 79, 83, 88.
  cattle, I. 5, 6, 8, 14, 18, 19, 40, 48, 51, 55, 59, 62, 82, 83.
  colts, I. 2, 11, 21, 36, 53, 65, 66, 67, 71, 79, 88.
  cows, I. 2, 3, 4, 5, 7, 9, 10, 11, 13, 14, 18, 20, 21, 22, 23, 24, 26, 27, 28, 29, 30, 33, 34, 35, 36, 38, 39, 41, 43,[a] 43,[b] 45, 47, 48, 50, 51, 52, 53, 54, 55, 56, 57, 59, 65, 66, 67, 70, 71, 72, 73, 75, 79, 80, 81, 82, 83, 88.
  ewes, I. 44, 47, 55, 71.
  fowls, I. 37.
  heifers, I. 2, 4, 5, 9, 10, 14, 17, 18, 21, 22, 26, 27, 28, 34, 35, 38, 39, 40, 43,[b] 44, 45, 47, 52, 53, 65, 66, 67, 71, 79, 80, 82.
  hogs, I. 11, 14, 18, 39, 47, 48, 57, 65.
  horses, I. 2, 5, 10, 11, 13, 15, 18, 21, 22, 24, 26, 27, 29, 34, 38, 39, 44, 47, 52, 53, 56, 57, 59, 70, 72, 81, 82.
  lambs, I. 15, 44, 55, 65.
  mares, I. 2, 6, 11, 13, 21, 23, 27,

GENERAL INDEX. 57

31, 36, 39, 40, 43,* 47, 48, 53, 57, 66, 67, 71, 72, 79, 80, 81, 88.
nags, I. 2.
oxen, I. 7, 11, 14, 15, 24, 27, 29, 34, 36, 43,[b] 48, 50, 52, 54, 56, 57, 59, 65, 66, 67, 70, 72, 82, 88.
pigs, I. 7, 11, 17, 21, 23, 38, 44, 53, 65, 66, 72.
sheep, I. 2, 4, 11, 13, 15, 19, 21, 22, 36, 38, 40, 48, 51, 52, 55, 57, 65, 66, 67, 72, 75, 79, 80, 81, 82, 88.
shoats, I. 14, 21.
sows, I. 7, 17, 21, 23, 39, 53, 59, 83.
stears, I. 5, 7, 9, 11, 13, 14, 18, 20, 21, 23, 24, 27, 28, 33, 38, 47, 52, 65, 66, 70, 71, 79, 80, 83.
swine, I. 11, 13, 15, 18, 20, 21, 22, 24, 26, 27, 28, 29, 30, 34, 38, 39, 40, 43,* 52, 53, 55, 56, 62, 66, 67, 70, 71, 72, 73, 79, 80, 81, 82, 83, 88.
yearlings, I. 7, 9, 10, 11, 13, 14, 15, 18, 20, 21, 22, 24, 26, 27, 28, 30, 39, 40, 41, 43,* 57, 59, 66, 71, 72, 79, 80, 88.
Execution, I. 30.

Fast day appointed, II. 9. II. 79.
Fees,
 appraisers, I. 35, 39.
 commissioners, II. 52.
 constables, II. 71.
 coroners jury, II. 3.
 court, I. 30, II. 109.
 entry fees, II. 7.
 ferriage, I. 1, II. 108.
 for administration, I. 4, 19, II. 7.
 for licences, II. 7.
 for probating wills, II. 7.
 for recording accounts, I. 19, 30.
 for recording inventory, I. 4, 19.
 jury trials, II. 7.
 of grand jurors to be paid by the towns, II. 85.

Feofees in trust, see Trustees.
Ferries, II. 1, 13, 14, 53, 70, 87, 88, 108.
Fish, fishing and appurtenances. see also under Vessels.
 barrels, I. 33, 38, 41.
 boats, I. 29.
 breams, a fresh water fish, I. 7, 17, 43.*
 casks, I. 6, 17.
 cod, I. 32, 33, 38.
 cod, dried, I. 4.
 cod-lines, I. 32.
 flake-room, I. 38.
 fish, I. 6, 7, 22, 41.
 gutters, I. 33.
 hake, I. 33.
 hooks, I. 16, 32, 33, 38, 41.
 leads, I. 4, 33, 38.
 lines, I. 4, 7, 33, 38, 41.
 mackerel, I. 41.
 nets, I. 4, 6, 22, 33, 41.
 oil, I. 6, 7, 33, 41.
  -cask, I. 30.
 refuge, i.e. refuse, I. 4, 7, 38.
 splitters, I. 33.
 stock, I. 32.
 salt I. 6, 17, 41.
 scale-fish, I. 18.
 squid lines, I. 32, 41.
 stages, stage-room, I. 38, 41, 57.
 summer, I. 43.*
Funeral charges, I. 4, 8, 13, 30, 35, 66.

Garrison, at Black Point, I. 3.
 York, I. 83.
 Quamphegon in Berwick, II. 10.
General Assembly, of the Province, I. 17.
 held at York, I. 17.
General Court of Massachusetts, I. 64.
Gentle, cows so named, I. 25, 35, 50.
Goal, County, II. 6, 62.
Governor of Massachusetts, William Phips, II. 29.
Governor of New Hampshire, Edward Cranfield, I. 111.

Grants referred to.
  Grantors:
    Agnew, Nyven, I. 55.
    Alcock, Job, I. 81.
    Alden, John, sen., I. 68.
    Ameredith, John, et ux., I. 62.
    Andrews, John, I. 47.
    Berwick, or Kittery, town of, I. 60.
    Bush, John, I. 5, 93, 94.
    Champernown, Francis, I. 48.
    Crockett, Ephraim, I. 106.
    Cross, Joseph, I. 29.
    Diamond, John, I. 67.
    Downing, Joshua, I. 67.
    Emery, Anthony, I. 107.
      James, I. 74.
      James, sen., I. 98.
    Fletcher, Mr., I. 5.
    Fluellin, Indian, I. 68, 86.
    Foxwell, Richard, I. 64.
    Gattinsby, John, I. 12.
    Gilman, John, et ux., I. 62.
    Gorges, Ferdinando, jun., I. 68.
      Thomas, I. 58.
    Gooch, John, I. 108.
    Hammond, ——, I. 5.
    Hooke, William, I. 42.
    Kittery, town of, I. 40, 59, 60, 67, 74, 87, 103, 106, 111, 118.
    Littlefield, Francis, I. 89, 90.
    Massachusetts General Court, I. 64.
    Moghegin, I. 68.
    O'Grado, Charles, I. 106.
    Pendleton, Bryan, I. 5.
    Phillips, William, I. 5, 49, 68, 69.
    Sanders, John, I. 93, 94.
    Shapleigh, Alice, I. 83.
    Sosowen, Indian, I. 86, 94.
    Spencer, Thomas, I. 12.
    Turbet, Peter, I. 93, 94.
    Vines, Richard, I. 42.
    Watts, Henry, I. 109.
    Wells, Lucy, I. 62.
    West, ——, I. 5.
    Withers, Thomas, I. 70.
    York, town of, I. 42.

  Grantees:
    Alden, Elizabeth, I. 68.
      John, I. 68, 69.
    Allen, Robert, I. 74.
    Austin, Samuel, I. 29.
    Bray, John, I. 47.
    Bush, John, I. 86, 94.
    Carell, Richard, I. 103.
    Carter, Joan, I. 67.
    Conley, Abraham, I. 74.
    Crocket, Ephraim, I. 106.
    Diamond, William, I. 40, 47.
    Downing, Joshua, I. 83, 118.
    Elliot, Robert, I. 106.
    Emery, James, jun., I. 98.
      James, sen., I. 107.
    Etherington, Thomas, I. 12.
    Fletcher, Pendleton, I. 5.
    Foxwell, George, I. 64.
    Fryer, Nathaniel, I. 48.
    Gattinsby, John, I. 12.
    Littlefield, James, sen., I. 89, 90.
    Nickolson, Robert, I. 109.
    Norton, Henry, I. 42.
    O'Grado, Charles, I. 106.
    Parker, Abraham, I. 81.
    Pendleton, Bryan, I. 5.
    Pennywell, Walter, I. 49.
    Phillips, William, I. 68.
    Rice, Thomas, I. 103.
    Sanders, John, I. 86, 94.
    Scottow, Joshua, I. 64.
    Spencer, Thomas, I. 111.
    Symonds, Harlakinden, I. 86, 93, 94.
    Taylor, John, I. 55.
    Turbett, Peter, I. 86, 94.
    Weare, Peter, I. 108.
    Wincoll, John, I. 87.
    Withers, Elizabeth, I. 70.
      Thomas, I. 58.
    Woodridge, Benjamin, I. 62.
Grave-digging, I. 19.
Guardian, I. 54.
Gunter's scale, I. 33.

Hardware, see also under tools, I. 23.
  brass rings, I. 16.

chains, I. 6, 7, 9, 11, 24, 27, 29, 34, 57, 83.
fetters, I. 81.
hook and ring, I. 9.
iron, I. 2, 6, 11, 16, 56, 79, 83.
lead, I. 17, 33, 41, 51, 53.
lock, I. 54.
nails, I. 11, 16, 31, 33, 34, 41, 81.
padlocks, I. 17.
shoe nails, I. 51.
spikes, I. 7, 41.
Spanish iron, I. 17.
staples, I. 35.
Harpswell, see Index of Places under Mericoneeg, grant recorded; see Index of Grantors under the name following:
Scottow, Joshua et ux., I. 64.
Hides, I. 11, 14, 24, 65.
  bear, I. 39.
  beaver, I. 15.
  deer, I. 3.
  moose, I. 15, 16.
  otter, I. 15.
Highways, I. 12, 27, 46, II. 10, 14, 16, 18, 69, 70, 88, 97, 105, 107, 118, 121, 123, 126.
House-frame, I. 33.
Hue and cry, II. 14.
Household goods, furnishings and wares.
  andirons, I. 2, 5, 7, 8, 9, 16, 23, 28, 41, 56, 65.
    called cob-irons, I. 56.
  bags, I. 24, 29, 31, 33, 34, 57.
  barrels, I. 16, 23, 27, 29, 34, 39, 52, 53, 57, 81, 82.
  baskets, I. 8, 9, 24, 31, 40.
  basons, I. 6, 8, 9, 13, 23, 24, 27, 40, 41, 43ª, 55, 66, 72.
  beakers, I. 15, 43ª.
  beds, I. 2, 3, 5, 7, 8, 10, 11, 13, 14, 16, 16, 17, 23, 24, 25, 28, 32, 34, 39, 40, 41, 46, 54, 56, 65, 66, 71, 80, 88.
    down, I. 40.
    feather, I. 2, 6, 7, 13, 16, 22, 27, 29, 31, 34, 36, 39, 40, 41, 43ª, 51, 55, 59, 65, 66, 70, 72, 73, 82.
    flock, I. 34, 72.
    standing, I. 16.
    trundle, I. 3, 10, 16, 39, 53.
  bed-sack, I. 38, 53.
  bed-steads, I. 8, 9, 16, 23, 28, 29, 31, 37, 39, 40, 51, 53, 55, 65, 72, 80.
    covering, I. 10.
    curtains, I. 16, 39, 40, 51.
  bedding, I. 2, 4, 5, 11, 13, 14, 16, 18, 23, 25, 29, 30, 34, 37, 38, 39, 52, 54, 56, 57, 62, 66, 72.
  beer barrels, I. 15.
  beer bowls, I. 8.
  bellows, I. 14, 15, 22, 29, 34, 51.
  blankets, I. 2, 3, 6, 7, 10, 13, 16, 17, 21, 22, 23, 25, 27, 28, 31, 32, 33, 39, 40, 41, 51, 52, 53, 57, 59, 70, 72, 82.
  board-cloth, I. 8, 65.
  bolsters, I, 2, 3, 6, 7, 10, 13, 15, 16, 17, 22, 23, 24, 25, 27, 28, 29, 31, 32, 33, 34, 39, 40, 41, 51, 52, 53, 55, 57, 59, 70, 72, 73, 80, 82, 88.
    drawers, I. 40.
  bottles, I. 8, 9, 15, 29, 31, 33, 34, 38, 39, 52, 54, 56, 57, 72.
    cases of, I. 8, 9, 31, 39, 56.
  bowls, I. 8, 16, 25, 31, 32, 34, 51.
    silver, I. 8.
  boxes, I. 8, 9, 10, 14, 17, 23, 30, 31, 35, 36, 56, 65, 70, 71, 81.
  brass-ware, I. 7, 23, 28, 30, 34, 47, 62, 82.
  brewing-vessels, I. 16.
    copper, I. 16.
  brushes, I, 31.
  buckets, I. 2, 3, 9, 30, 45, 55.
  butter-dish, I. 10.
    firkin, I. 15.
    pot, I. 23, 38, 51, 57.
    tub, I. 52.
  calibashes, I. 31.
  candle-sticks, I. 6, 8, 9, 10, 16, 24, 32, 35, 40, 43ª, 56, 59, 65, 80.
  candle case, I. 16.

General Index.

cans, I. 8, 16, 23, 31, 33.
cards for wool, I. 3, 10, 11, 14, 17, 39, 40, 72, 80, 81.
carpets, I. 11, 13, 16, 29, 33, 34, 40, 65, 72.
case, iron-bound, I. 16.
casks, I. 39, 51, 54, 65, 72.
caudle-cup, I. 23.
chafing dishes, I. 9, 29, 56, 65.
chairs, I. 2, 6, 7, 8, 9, 10, 11, 13, 14, 15, 16, 22, 23, 28, 30, 31, 32, 34, 39, 40, 43*, 52, 56, 62, 65, 72, 81.
chamber pots, I. 9, 16, 23, 24, 31, 39, 41, 52, 54, 66.
chargers, I. 9.
cheese press, I. 16, 39.
    vats, I. 9, 29.
chest bed, I. 10.
chests, I. 2, 3, 4, 7, 8, 9, 13, 14, 17, 21, 22, 23, 25, 29, 31, 33, 34, 35, 37, 38, 39, 40, 41, 43*, 46, 51, 52, 53, 54, 55, 56, 57, 59, 62, 65, 70, 71, 72, 73, 80, 81, 82.
    chests of drawers, I. 16.
    Spanish, I. 16.
churns, I. 11, 15, 16, 29, 34, 38, 39, 57, 79.
collenders, I. 6.
comb case, I. 6, 38.
court cupboard, I. 16, 46.
coverlets, coverlids, coversides, I. 2, 8, 13, 15, 29, 31, 32, 33, 35, 51, 53, 70, 72, 83.
cradle, I. 39, 52.
crooks, I. 5, 40, 41, 45.
cupboards, I. 9, 16, 28, 40, 43*, 56, 65, 72.
    cloths, I. 9, 16, 31, 56, 72.
cups, I. 9, 10, 23, 40, 80.
    silver, I. 6, 8, 13, 28, 29, 31, 80.
curtains, I. 10, 13, 16, 28, 31, 34, 40, 72, 79, 80.
curtain rods, I. 9, 82.
cushions, I. 6, 9, 31, 66, 72, 80.
desks, I. 8, 9.
dishes, I. 7, 22, 23, 32, 41, 70, 72, 79, 80.
    Lisbon, I. 9, 23.

    Spanish, I. 31.
dogs, fire, I. 16.
dram cups, I. 9, 23, 43*.
dripping pans, I. 6, 8, 9, 16, 24, 29, 31, 65.
earthen ware, I. 8, 9, 10, 13, 14, 23, 28, 30, 34, 39, 40, 51, 65, 72.
ewers, I. 13.
feathers, I. 31.
fire-pans, I. 13, 17.
flagons, I. 6, 41, 65.
flask, I. 57.
flesh-hooks, or forks, I, 15, 16, 59.
forms, or benches, I. 13, 16, 34, 65.
frying-pans, I. 2, 7, 10, 14, 16, 17, 21, 22, 24, 29, 32, 34, 35, 36, 38, 39, 40, 41, 43*, 51, 52, 53, 54, 56, 57, 59, 71, 72, 75, 79.
funnels, I. 9, 22, 33.
furniture, I. 8, 36, 40, 47, 62, 71.
gallipots, I. 39, 57.
glasses, I. 8, 31, 41.
goose-wings, I. 33.
graters, I. 6, 17, 33.
grid-irons, I. 8, 9, 10, 29, 40, 51, 56.
hackle, I. 72.
hammocks. I. 7, 15, 23, 39, 57.
hangers, I. 6, 8, 9, 11, 41.
hat-case, I. 16.
heaters, I. 9.
hogsheads I. 24, 27, 34, 57, 81, 82.
hour-glass, I. 29, 39.
household stuff, I. 11, 18, 22, 29, 36, 41, 46, 47, 55, 59, 88.
ink-horns, I. 6, 7, 38.
iron ware, I. 62.
jacks, I. 16.
jackenapes-plate, I. 31.
jar, I. 54, 81.
joint-stools, I. 9, 10, 28, 31, 62, 72.
jugs, I. 10, 59.
keelers, I. 2, 52, 55, 59, 81.
kettles, see under pots.
kitchen-ware, I. 22, 33.
knitting-needles, I. 17.

General Index.

Household Goods, continued.
  knives, I. 6, 9, 14, 32.
  knot bowls, I. 8.
    dishes, I. 8, 9.
  ladles, I. 21, 45.
  lamps, I. 9.
  lanterns, I. 6, 65.
  latten-ware, I. 39, 72.
  linen-wheel, I. 72.
  lock and key, I. 31, 38.
  looking-glasses, I. 9, 16, 29, 32, 72.
  lumber, I. 16, 39.
  malt-mill, I. 66.
  meal-bags, I. 37.
  meal-sieves, I. 8, 51, 52, 53.
  meal-troughs, I. 3, 15, 54, 57.
  milk-pails, I. 57.
  milk-pans, I. 16, 38, 57, 70.
  milk-tubs, I. 6, 16.
  milk-vessels, I. 34.
  minute-glass, I. 31.
  mortars, I. 8, 9, 24, 29, 34, 38, 39, 56, 57.
    and pestles, I. 15, 31, 56, 79.
  napkins, I. 2, 3, 6, 7, 10, 14, 15, 16, 23, 29, 31, 34, 39, 40, 41, 57, 65, 72, 73, 79.
  pails, I. 11, 14, 15, 16, 22, 29, 38, 39, 40, 51, 52, 54, 59, 70, 72, 80.
  pans, I. 5, 6, 39.
  pewter and pewter dishes, I. 2, 5, 6, 8, 9, 10, 13, 15, 21, 22, 23, 24, 25, 26, 27, 28, 29, 30, 31, 34, 38, 39, 40, 41, 43ª, 47, 51, 55, 56, 57, 59, 62, 66, 71, 72, 79, 80, 82, 83.
  pictures, I. 9, 31.
  pillows, I. 4, 6, 7, 8, 9, 10, 14, 16, 21, 22, 23, 31, 32, 33, 34, 38, 39, 40, 53, 55, 57, 70, 72, 82.
  pillow-bears, I. 7, 8, 9, 10, 14, 16, 21, 31, 34, 35, 38, 41, 65, 72, 73.
  pillow-cases, I. 51.
  pillow drawers, I. 16, 32, 34, 40, 79, 82.
  pillow-napkins, I. 16.
  pins, I. 17, 23.

Household Goods, continued.
  pin-cushions, I. 31.
  pint-cups, I. 65.
  pint-pots, I. 6, 7, 8, 35.
  pipkins, I. 34.
  pitchers, I. 25.
  plate of displeasure, I. 31.
  plates, I. 43ª, 72.
  plate, silver, I. 31, 47, 62, 65.
  platters, I. 7, 8, 9, 10, 23, 35, 41, 43ª, 65, 66, 72, 88.
  porringers, I. 7, 8, 9, 10, 23, 28, 32, 35, 39, 41, 43ª, 52, 55, 57, 72.
  posnets, I. 8, 9.
  pots and kettles, I. 2, 3, 4, 7, 9, 10, 13, 15, 20, 21, 24, 25, 26, 28, 29, 30, 31, 32, 36, 39, 40, 41, 45, 51, 52, 53, 54, 55, 56, 57, 59, 70, 72, 75, 79, 80, 81, 82.
    brass, I. 2. 8, 9, 15, 16, 27, 29, 31, 32, 33, 39, 40, 41, 55, 56, 59, 65, 79.
    copper, I. 6, 8, 9, 13, 16.
    iron, I. 2, 5, 6, 7, 9, 10, 16, 17, 22, 23, 27, 28, 29, 30, 32, 33, 34, 38, 40, 41, 43ª, 47, 55, 56, 65, 66, 70, 72, 75, 79, 82, 88.
    pewter, I. 32.
  pot-hooks, I. 2, 10, 13, 15, 16, 17, 20, 21, 22, 23, 34, 39, 40, 45, 51, 57, 59, 65, 66, 79, 82.
  powdering-tubs, I. 24, 25.
  pressing-iron, I. 10, 15.
  prospect-glass, I. 9.
  pudding-pan, I. 9.
  quart-pot, I. 27, 52, 55, 65.
  quilts, I. 8, 32.
  racks, I. 16.
  rugs, I. 3, 4, 6, 7, 10, 13, 16, 17, 23, 24, 25, 27, 34, 38, 39, 41, 52, 55, 57, 59, 65, 70, 73, 75, 82.
  runlets, small tubs, I. 9, 33.
  sacks, I. 39, 40.
  salt-cellars, I. 8, 9, 23.
  salve, I. 39.
  sash, I. 83.

General Index.

Household Goods, continued.
saucers, I. 6, 9, 57.
scales, I. 9. 15, 16, 17, 31, 43ª, 51, 56, 72, 79.
scissors, I. 9, 14, 16, 17, 38.
settles, I. 39, 71.
shears, I. 10.
sheets, I. 2, 4, 6, 7, 9, 10, 13, 14, 15, 16, 21, 22, 23, 24, 25, 27, 28, 31, 32, 34, 39, 40, 41, 53, 55, 65, 70, 72, 73, 79, 82, 88.
shovels, I. 6, 28, 29, 35, 41, 51, 59, 65.
sieves, I. 9, 10, 15, 17, 22, 29, 32, 34, 39, 51, 57, 59, 72.
skillets, I. 2, 4, 6, 8, 9, 10, 11, 13, 15, 16, 21, 23, 24, 26, 28, 31, 32, 34, 39, 40, 41, 51, 55, 56, 57, 65, 71, 79.
skimmers, I. 6, 13, 15, 16, 21, 24.
sleightstone, slickstone, I. 8, 72.
smoothing-irons, I. 6, 9, 10, 16, 21, 34, 39.
spinning-wheels, I. 3, 14, 16, 28, 37, 39, 40, 52, 53, 54, 57, 59, 72, 80, 81.
spits, I. 2, 6, 7, 8, 11, 15, 16, 28, 29, 32, 36, 40, 51, 56, 57, 65, 79, 81.
spoons, I. 8, 10, 13, 14, 15, 17, 22, 23, 32, 39, 43ª, 51, 55, 57, 72, 80.
steel-box, I. 35.
stew-pan, I. 34.
still, I. 16.
stilyards, I. 3, 7, 9, 16, 17, 23, 25, 29, 31, 39, 56, 65, 80, 81.
stools, I. 14, 54.
syllabub-pot, I. 16.
tables, I. 10, 13, 16, 22, 23, 28, 29, 30, 34, 40, 51, 52, 62, 65, 80.
table-boards, I. 3, 8, 9, 31, 43ª, 65.
table-chair, I. 15, 23.
table-cloths, I. 6, 7, 9, 10, 11, 14, 15, 16, 21, 23, 29, 31, 32, 34, 39, 40, 41, 57, 65, 72, 79, 82.
linen, I. 62, 72.

Household Goods, continued.
tankard, silver, I. 43ª, 72.
tapistry, I. 23.
thimbles, I. 6, 9, 31.
ticking, I. 3, 4, 22, 32, 34.
tin-ware, I. 7, 10, 13, 28.
tongs, I. 6, 7, 9, 11, 15, 16, 17, 22, 23, 24, 28, 29, 30, 35, 36, 39, 40, 51, 57, 59, 65, 72.
towels, I. 6, 16, 28, 31, 32, 41, 65, 72.
trammels, I. 2, 7, 13, 15, 16, 17, 20, 21, 22, 23, 24, 27, 28, 30, 32, 34, 35, 36, 39, 40, 51, 52, 53, 55, 56, 57, 65, 66, 72, 79, 80, 81.
trays, I. 8, 9, 10, 11, 13, 14, 15, 30, 31, 39, 52, 57.
trenchers, I. 8, 9, 13, 14, 17, 22, 31, 32, 35, 72.
trunks, I. 16, 17, 23, 29, 36, 59, 62, 72, 80.
tubs, I. 2, 9, 15, 16, 29, 38, 53, 57, 65, 72, 80, 81, 82.
Turkey carpet, I. 16.
chairs, I. 16.
urine-pot, I. 20.
valances, I. 10, 31, 39, 51, 72, 83.
wainscot-chest, I. 10.
warming-pans, I. 6, 8, 9, 13, 15, 24, 29, 31, 34, 38, 39, 43ª, 56, 57, 59, 65, 72, 80, 82.
weights, for scales, I. 15, 17, 72.
wine-cups, I. 15, 32, 72.
wooden dishes, I. 2, 10, 13, 16, 17, 22, 25, 35, 45, 54, 55, 57.
ware, I. 6, 28, 30, 37, 39, 40, 43ª, 51, 52, 53, 71, 81,
yarn-pot, I. 21.
Husbandry, Implements and Appurtenances; see also Provisions.
axel-trees, I. 70.
bags, I. 11.
barley, I. 28, 53, 55.
barrels, I. 13.
bridles, I. 13, 37, 41, 56, 59, 66, 72.
carts, I. 10, 16, 29, 34, 39, 72, 81.
cart-wheels, I. 65.

Husbandry, continued.
  cart-wheel hoops, I. 13.
  casks, I. 11.
  cattle, see under Domestic Animals.
  cider, I. 23.—press, I. 72.
  clevis, I. 10, 13, 24, 27, 36, 40, 57, 72.
  cops, I. 2, 13, 15.
  cops-pin, I. 9.
  cops-yoke, I. 22, 41.
  cord-wood, I. 55, 71.
  corn, I. 4, 11, 15, 18, 19, 21, 23, 24, 25, 27, 28, 37, 39, 53, 55, 72.
  coulters, I. 5, 10, 15, 34, 51.
  crupper, I. 32.
  draught-chain, I. 24, 55, 70.
  farms, I. 5, 20, 46.
  fences, fencing, I. 19, 25, 30, 102.
  fire-wood, I. 55.
  fodder, I. 13.
  forks, I. 10, 57.
  grain,
    English, I. 13.
    Indian, I. 13.
  halter, I. 11.
  harnesses, I. 11. 52, 88.
  harrow-teeth, I. 11, 13.
  hay, I. 13, 18, 19, 22, 23, 27, 34, 53.
  hay-knife, I. 55.
  hoes, I. 3. 11, 15, 17, 21, 22, 24, 26, 27, 51, 52, 55, 57, 72, 81.
  hooks and staples, I. 10, 22, 23, 25, 36, 39, 52, 55.
  hoops, I. 70.
  horse-collar, I. 11.
  horse tackling, I. 39.
  mattocks, I. 15.
  pales, fences, I. 102.
  pease, I. 11, 28, 39, 54.
  pillions, I. 11, 23, 29, 71.
  pillion cloths, I. 23, 29.
  pins, I. 70.
  pitchforks, I. 15, 21, 29, 34, 39, 51, 52, 55, 72, 81.
  plantations, I. 5.
  plows, I. 10, 21, 22, 27, 34, 65, 66, 72.

Husbandry, continued.
  plow-chains, I. 15, 23, 65, 66, 71.
  plow-irons, I. 13, 21, 36, 39, 65, 70, 81.
  plow-shares, I. 5, 10, 15.
  racks, I. 34.
  rails, I. 54.
  reaping-hook, I. 24, 57.
  rings, I. 36, 41, 52, 57.
  ropes, I. 10.
  rye, I. 11. 23.
  saddles, I. 6, 13, 20, 25, 28, 29, 37, 39, 51, 56, 59, 65, 66, 67, 71, 72, 81.
  saddle-cloths, I. 72.
  scythes, I. 11, 15, 16, 30, 38, 39, 44, 52, 57, 66, 72.
  scythe-nibs, I. 3, 15, 52.
  scythe-rings, I. 23, 52, 66.
  sickles, I. 39, 52.
  sleds, I. 11. 29, 34, 39, 40, 65, 72, 81.
  sleighs, I. 11, 52, 88.
  spades, I. 15, 16, 21, 27, 51, 56.
  staples, I. 13, 30, 41, 57.
  utensils for, I. 5, 6, 11.
  wheat, I. 3, 11, 15, 23, 24, 25, 28, 53.
    smutty, I. 21.
  wheels, 11, 22, 29, 34, 39, 70, 72.
  winnowing-sheet, I. 39.
  wintering, fodder, I. 22.
  wool, I. 11, 52, 53, 57, 80, 82, 88.
  yokes, I. 10, 11, 13, 15, 23, 27, 29, 34, 39, 40, 52, 57, 71, 72.
  yoke chains, I. 34, 40.
Indian enemy, II. 62.
  war, I. 3.
Interest, rate of, I. 59.
Inventory, of the estate of:
  Adams, Philip, I. 73.
  Allcocke, Joseph, I. 25.
  Amerideth, John, I. 62.
  Batson, John, I. 36.
  Bean, Lewis, I. 21.
  Bedford, Nathan, I. 6.
  Billing, John, I. 53.
  Biss, Samuel, I. 6, 7.
  Bonighton, Gabrigall, I. 22.

Inventory, continued.
 Bools, Joseph, I. 23, 34.
 Bragdon,
  Arthur, I. 26, 52.
  Daniel, I. 52.
  Thomas, I. 51.
 Bray, John, I. 47.
 Bready, John, I. 13.
 Card, John, I. 82.
 Cawley, Tobias, I. 37.
 Chadborne, James, I. 40.
 Child, Henry, I. 70.
 Cirmihill, John, I. 21.
 Cleverly, Thomas, et ux., I. 17.
 Cocks, Edmund, I. 18.
 Conley, Abraham, I. 25.
 Cooper,
  Alexander, I. 27.
  Philip, I. 79.
 Crocket, Thomas, I. 40.
 Cross,
  John, I. 10.
  John, jun., I. 11.
  Joseph, I. 29.
 Davis, John, I. 65, 66.
 Diamond, William, I. 40.
 Donnell,
  Benjamin, I. 33.
  Margaret, I. 36.
 Dummer, Shubael, I. 72.
 Edgecome, Nicholas, I. 8.
 Endell, John, I. 44.
 Farrow, George, I. 11.
 Fletcher, Jonathan, I. 36.
 Fox(w)ell,
  John, I. 2.
  Philip, I. 56.
 Frethy,
  James, I. 52.
  Samuel, I. 38, 39.
 Gouch,
  James, I. 11.
  Ruth, I. 11.
 Gowen, *alias* Smith, William, I. 39.
 Grant, James, I. 28.
 Harris, Tristram, I. 21, 24.
 Hayes, Edward, I. 10.
 Hill, John, I. 18, 40.
 Hodsden, Joseph, I. 71.

Inventory, continued.
 Holmes, Thomas, I. 59.
 Jackson, James, I. 18, 19.
 Leads, John, I. 33.
 Libby, John, I. 22.
 Littlefield, Annas, I. 24.
 Lord, Samuel, I. 43[b].
 Martyne, Charles, I. 31.
 Masterson, Jonathan, I. 73.
 Mendum, Robert, I. 14.
 Milberry, William, I. 66.
 Moor, John, I. 43[a].
 More, William, I. 57.
 Moulton, Joseph, I. 83.
 Munjoy, George, I. 37.
 Nason, Jonathan, I. 72.
 Norton, Henry, I. 42.
 Oakeman, Samuel, I. 5.
 Oliver, Joseph, I. 3.
 Palmer, John, I. 21.
 Parker, George, jun., I. 21.
 Parsons, John, I. 81.
 Pearce,
  Eleanor, I. 9.
  John, I. 9.
  Joseph, I. 31.
 Pendleton, Bryan, I. 6.
 Penwell,
  Joseph, I. 17, 18.
  Walter, I. 22.
 Phillips, John, I. 2.
 Præsbury, John, I. 32, 35.
 Preble,
  John, I. 79.
  Joseph, I. 67.
  Nathaniel, I. 80.
  Stephen, I. 66.
 Pullman, John, I. 4.
 Raynkine, I. 24.
 Rishworth, Edward, I. 56.
 Roanes, William, I. 20.
 Robbines, William, I. 8.
 Sayword,
  Henry, I. 2, 30, 31.
  Jonathan, I. 88.
  Samuel, I. 71.
 Searle, Andrew, I. 54.
 Shapleigh, Nicholas, I. 15, 16, 17.
 Simson, Henry, I. 79.

GENERAL INDEX. 65

Inventory, continued.
  Smith, *alias* Gowen, William,
    I. 39.
  Spencer,
    Patience, I. 23, 24.
    Thomas, I. 13.
  Taylor, John, I. 55.
  Tompson, John, I. 30.
  Tozier, Judith, I. 22.
  Tricky,
    Francis, I. 7.
    John, I. 39.
    Sarah, I. 39.
  Trustrum,
    Benjamin, I. 41.
    Nathaniel, I. 41.
    Ralph, I. 41.
  Waddocke, Henry, I. 4.
  Weare, Peter, I. 79.
  Whinick, Joseph, I. 45.
  Wormwood, William, I. 53.
  Young, Rowland, I. 38.
Irish boys, apprentices, I. 16.

Joint tenancy, I. 5, 14, 19, 46, 61, 74, 96, 107.
Joyrn, iron, I. 79.
Judgment, *pro confesso*, I. 3.
Justices of the Inferior Courts.
  Job Alcock, II. 32, 60, 64, 68, 73, 74, 77, 82, 89, 92.
  John Davis. I. 4, II. 1, 3, 7, 8.
  Samuel Donnell, II. 34, 47, 51, 60, 68, 74, 82, 90, 92, 95, 101, 105, 106, 112, 122.
  Charles Frost, I. 2, 39, 55, II. 1, 8, 11, 14, 17, 18, 25, 30, 32, 34, 47, 51, 60, 64, 66, 67, 68, 73, 74, 77, 82, 89, 90, 92, 95, 101, 105.
  Francis Hooke, 1. 2, II. 1, 3, 7, 8, 11, 14, 17, 18, 21, 25, 30, 32, 34, 47.
  Roger Kelley, II, 21, 51, 60, 82.
  Bryan Pendleton, I. 1.
  William Pepperrell, II. 60, 64, 65, 67, 68, 73, 74, 77, 82, 89, 90, 92, 95, 101, 105, 106, 112, 122.

Justices of the Inferior Courts, continued.
  Abraham Preble, II. 14, 17, 21, 25, 30, 34, 51, 60, 68, 74, 82, 92, 95, 101, 106, 122.
  Samuel Wheelwright, II. 1, 3, 11, 14, 17, 18, 21, 34, 47, 51, 60, 64, 66, 67, 68, 73, 74, 77, 89, 90, 92, 95, 101, 105, 106, 112, 122.
  John Wincoll, I. 39, 55, II. 1, 3, 7, 8.
Justices of the Peace.
  John Davis, I. 4, 88.
  Andrew Diamond, II. 4.
  Charles Frost, I. 5, 6, 13, 14, 55, 81, 98, 108, 115.
  Francis Hooke, I. 5, 6, 13, 14, 15, 18, 35, 36, 39, 43, 44, 45, 46, 47, 51, 54, 63, 70, 71, 77, 82, 96, 100, 103, 104, 105, 109, 110, 114, 119.
  Henry Jocelyn, I. 58.
  Roger Kelley, I. 105.
  Dedimus Justice, II. 19.
  Abraham Preble, II. 22.
  Edward Rishworth, I. 3, 4, 18, 22, 27, 29, 33, 37, 39.
  Joshua Scottow, I. 3, 5, 8.
  Samuel Wheelwright, I. 29, 85, 89, 90, 91, 92.
  John Wincoll, I. 5, 6, 13, 14, 27, 44, 45, 47, 57, 59, 61, 71, 72, 74, 65, 82, 88.
Justices of the Peace.
  of Massachusetts.
  Isaac Addington, II. 129.
  Jonathan Corwin, I. 82.
  Thomas Wade, I. 94.
  Samuel Sewall, I. 77, 78.
Justices of the Peace.
  of New Hampshire.
  Nathaniel Fryer, I. 107, 112, 113.
  Richard Martin. I. 88, 95, 96, 97.
  Robert Mason, I. 64.
  Thomas Parker, I. 96.
  William Vaughan, I. 100.

Kittery, see Index of Places,
  selectmen, I. 1, II. 32, 67, 68, 69, 70, 71, 76, 107, 114, 118, 123.

Kittery, continued.
  town book, I. 87.
  town meeting, II. 114.
  town grants, I. 87.
  other grants recorded; see Index of Grantors under the names following:
  Adams, Margaret, I. 97.
  Alcocke, John, I. 120.
  Allen, Robert, I. 74.
  Carell, Richard, I. 103.
  Carter, Joan, I. 67.
  Champernoun, Francis, et ux., I. 110.
  Conley, Abraham, I. 102.
  Crockett, Ephraim, et ux., I. 76.
    Joshua, I. 109.
  Cutt, Richard, I. 100.
  Downing, Joshua, I. 83.
  Elliot, Robert, I. 106.
  Emery, James, sen., I. 107.
    James, jun., et ux., I. 98.
  Endle, Michael, et ux., I. 119.
  Fernald, Thomas, et ux., I. 119.
  Fryer, Nathaniel, I. 48.
  Godsoe, William, I. 76.
  Gorges, Sir Ferdinando, I. 58.
  Green, Richard, et ux., I. 117.
  Jones, Thomas, I. 102.
  Lidden, Katherine, I. 75.
  More,
    Agnes, I. 97.
    John, I. 97.
  Nason, Richard, et ux., I. 114.
  Newberry, Thomas, I. 59.
  Plaisted, Elisha's estate, I. 87.
  Remich, Christian, I. 71, 113.
    Jacob, I. 71.
  Rice, Thomas, et ux., I. 103.
  Spinney, Thomas, et ux., I. 104.
  Ugroufe, John, I. 102.
  White, Richard, I. 54, 76, 77, 78.
  Withers, Thomas, I. 43.
  Woodbridge, Benjamin, I. 52.
  grants referred to:
    town to Robert Allen, I. 74.
    to Richard Carell, I. 103.
    to Ephraim Crocket, I. 106.
    to William Diamond, I. 40, 67.

Kittery, continued.
    to Joshua Downing, I. 118.
    to Thomas Newberry, I. 59.
    to Thomas Rice, I. 103.
    to Thomas Spencer, I. 111.
    to John Wincoll, I. 87.
  John Ameredeth, et ux., to Benj. Woodbridge, I. 62.
  John Andrews to John Bray, I. 47.
  Francis Champernown to Nathaniel Fryer, I. 48.
  Ephraim Crockett to Charles O'Grado, I. 106.
  John Diamond to William Diamond, I. 67.
  Joshua Downing to Joan Carter, I. 67.
  Anthony Emery to James Emery, sen., I. 107.
  James Emery to Abraham Conley. I. 74.
  James Emery, sen., to James Emery, jun., I. 98.
  John Gilman, et ux., to Benj. Woodbridge, I. 62.
  Thomas Gorges to Thomas Withers, I. 58.
  Charles O'Grado to Robert Elliot, I. 106.
  Alice Shapleigh to Joshua Downing, I. 83.
  Lucy Wells to Benj. Woodbridge, I. 62.
  Thomas Withers to Elizabeth Withers, I. 70.

Lad, name of a cow, I. 121.
Leaseholds, I. 18, 19, 46, 74.
Licenses granted:
  for ferries, I. 1, II. 14, 53, 87, 108.
  for public houses, I. 1, 2, II. 3, 9, 12, 13, 14, 15, 17, 19, 20, 25, 26, 30, 31, 35, 53, 57, 62, 70, 71, 76, 77, 86, 87, 98, 103, 104, 110, 119, 120, 125, 126.
Lieutenant Governor of Massachusetts,
  William Stoughton, II. 40, 100.

General Index.

Life estate, I. 5, 14, 20, 35, 37, 46, 61, 96.
   reserved, I. 12, 19, 20, 28, 57, 91, 113.
Lime, I. 81.
Logging, see under Mills.
Lumbering, see under Mills.
Lyman, see Index of Places.
   grants recorded; see Index of Grantors under the names following:
      Coxhall Proprietors, I. 86.
      Goodin, Sarah, et als., I. 86.
      Nacodumiah, I. 86.
      Symonds, Harlakinden, I. 73, 84, 93.
   grants referred to :
      John Bush to Harlakinden Symonds, I. 93, 94.
      Fluellin to Harlakinden Symonds, I. 86.
      John Sanders to Harlakinden Symonds, I. 93, 94.
      Sosowen to Harlakinden Symonds, I. 86.
      Sosowen to John Bush, John Sanders, and Peter Turbet, I. 86, 94.
      Peter Turbet to Harlakinden, Symonds, I. 93, 94.

Maine,
   book of records for, I. 6, 69.
   commissions to the Justices, II. 27, 40, 100.
   Council of the Province, I. 1, 7, 17, 36.
   Courts of Common Pleas, I. 1, 6, 21, 22, 25, II. 10.
   Courts of Common Pleas held at Wells, I. 1, 3, II. 3, 36, 60, 64, 73, 99.
   Courts of Common Pleas held at York, I. 58, 96, II. 1, 6, 8, 9, 11, 12, 17, 26, 32, 54, 58, 77, 89, 105, 112, 114, 126.
   Court of Oyer and Terminer, special, II. 18.
   Courts of Quarter Sessions, I. 1, 2, 4, II. 1, 10.

Maine, continued
   Courts of Quarter Sessions held at Kittery, I. 1, 3, II. 90.
   Courts of Quarter Sessions held at Wells, I. 6, 19, 27, II. 1, 21, 22, 23, 24, 34, 47, 66, 67, 68, 92, 95, 116.
   Courts of Quarter Sessions held at York, I. 87, II. 1, 4, 7, 9, 10, 11, 12, 13, 14, 15, 17, 19, 20, 25, 26, 30, 51, 55, 74, 79, 82, 89, 101, 106, 122.
   Courts, Superior, II. 52, 54, 113, 114, 127.
   Courts, Superior, to be held at Boston, II. 64.
   Courts, Superior, to be held at Kittery, II. 62.
   General Assembly of the Province, I. 17.
   General Assembly of the Province held at York, I. 17.
   Goal, county, II. 6, 62.
   Magistrates, see President, Deputy President, Assistants, Associates, Commissioners, Justices of the Inferior Courts, Justices of the Peace, Clerks of the Province, Marshal of the Province, Recorders, Register, Sheriff, Steward General, Treasurer, Valuation Commissioners.
   Patent of the Province, I. 68.
   Submission to Massachusetts, I. 86.
   Valuation Commissioners, II. 110.
      John Davis, deputy president of, I. 33, 38, 117, II. 1, 3, 4, 6, 7, 8.
      Francis Hooke, deputy president of, I. 72, II. 11, 12.
      Francis Hooke, treasurer, I. 17.
      Bryan Pendleton, deputy president, I. 1.
      William Pepperrell, treasurer, I. 101.
      Richard Vines, steward general, I. 58.

68   GENERAL INDEX.

Majority, attainment of, I. 14, 26, 28.
Marked trees, I. 75 and elsewhere.
Marriage portion, I. 43, 110.
Marshal of the Province,
　Arthur Bragdon, II. 1.
Massachusetts:
　assistants, see under, for members of the governor's council.
　commissioners of, see under, for Yorkshire Inferior Magistrates
　councillors, I. 82, 103, 106, 114.
　General Court of, I. 64.
　governor of, William Phips, II. 29.
　Justices of the Peace of, other than those in Maine, I. 77, 78, 82, 94, II. 129.
　lieutenant governor of,
　　William Stoughton, II. 40, 100.
　Plymouth County, recorder of, Samuel Sprague, I. 69.
　Secretary of, Isaac Addington, II. 29, 40, 100.
　Suffolk County, clerk of, Isaac Addington, I. 65.
　Superior Court to be held at Boston for Yorkshire, II. 64.
Meeting-houses:
　at Berwick, II. 96.
　at Kittery Point, II. 69.
　contribution toward seating of, I. 14.
Meeting at Dover, II. 84.
Militia, Committee of, II. 11.
Mills and their appurtenances:
　bark-mill, I. 13.
　barrel staves, I. 39.
　boards, I. 15, 18.
　board-logs, I. 39.
　corn, I. 3, 15, 24, 25, 30, 31, 82, 100, II. 16.
　dams, I. 31.
　draught chains, I. 16.
　fulling, I. 100.
　log-chains, I. 70.
　logging wheels, I. 16, 40.
　mast-chains, I. 16.
　mast wheels, I. 16.

Mills, continued.
　pine slabs, I. 18.
　pipe-staves, I. 21.
　saw, I. 3, 15, 30, 31, 36, 100, 107.
　staves, I. 72.
　timber of, I. 15, 44.
　timber chains, I. 16.
　turning-mill tools, I. 2.
　utensils, I. 31.
Ministers' salary, II. 12.
Money, I. 4, 12, 14, 15, 19, 24, 29, 30, 33, 35, 54, 57, 59, 66, 67, 82.
　five shilling piece, I. 31.
　gold, I. 9, 31.
　silver, I. 6, 8, 56, 82.
　equivalent to, or as money, I. 12, 25, 26.
Negroes,
　men, I. 7.
　women, II. 49.
New Hampshire,
　Commissioners of, I. 97.
　Councillors of, I. 71, 102, 118, 120.
　Court of Quarter Sessions of, I. 13.
　Governor of, Edward Cranfield, I. 111.
　Justices of the Peace of, I. 64, 82, 88, 95, 96, 97, 100, 107, 112, 113.
　Recorder of, I. 13.
Note, I. 72.
Notice of administration to be posted, I. 1.
Nuncupative wills,
　of Alexander Cooper, I. 26.
　of John Libby, I. 22.
Nursing, I. 19.

Occupations,
　accountant, I. 30.
　bricklayer, I. 119.
　carpenter, I. 106, 112.
　cooper, I. 61, 64, 82, 112.
　cordwainer, I. 60.
　farmer, I. 84.
　ferryman, I. 1.
　fisherman, I. 44, 57.
　husbandman, I. 32.

GENERAL INDEX. 69

Occupations, continued.
  inn-keeper, I. 1, 2, II. 2, 3, 12, 15, 17, 19, 21, 25, 26, 30, 31, 35, 53, 54, 58, 62, 70, 71, 76, 77, 86, 87, 97, 104, 110, 119, 120, 125, 126.
  mariner, I. 62, 63, 68.
  merchant, I. 6, 30, 48, 64, 87, 106, 109, 111, 112, II. 128.
  millwright, I. 3.
  minister, I. 62, 63, 85, II. 12, 22.
  notary public, I. 96.
  planter, I. 49, 52, 53, 60, 95, 99, 111, 113.
  school-master, I. 51.
  scrivener, I. 65, 105.
  servant-man, I. 43ª.
  shipwright, I. 96, 97, 99, 120.
  shoemaker, I. 24.
  shopkeeper, I. 68.
  soldier, II. 14, 24.
  surveyor, I. 62, 74, 87, 103, 112, II. 108, 114, 119.
  tailor, I. 51.
  tanner, II. 88.
  vintner, I. 95.
  weaver, I. 24, 38, 49.
  yeoman, I. 19, 28, 89, 91, 92, 100, 103, 104, 109, 114.
Old style, I. 20.
Orders of Court,
  about Henry Sayword's estate, I. 1.
  about John Lead's estate, I. 33.
  about Nicholas Shapleigh's estate, I. 17.
  appointing fast-days, II. 9, 79.
  appointing thanksgiving days, II. 12, 90.
  regulating sales of liquor, II. 5.
Oyeren, iron, I. 72.

Patent of the Province, I. 68.
Pay, see under money.
  as silver, I. 25.
  current of New England, I. 10, 48, 49, 60, 62, 63, 89.
  current specie, I. 30.
  good, I. 57.
  lawfull money, I. 59, 87.

Pay, continued
  other pay, I. 25, 57.
  soldiers, I. 3.
Pine trees, standing, grant of, I. 60.
Plaintiffs:
  Ball, John, apl't, vs. Elizabeth Berry, II. 33, 36.
  Cutt, estate of John, vs. Thomas Rice, II. 78.
  Cutt, estate of John, vs. Joseph Weare, II. 89.
  Davis, John, vs. Charles Brisson, II. 6.
  Davis, John, vs. Samuel Hill, II. 8.
  Foul, James, vs. Nathaniel Johnson, II. 105.
  Gowen, *alias* Smith, Nicholas, vs. Sarah Chadbourn, II. 73.
  Gunnison, Elihu, vs. Richard Endle, II. 59.
  Hammond, Joseph, vs. Joshua Downing, II. 33.
  Keen, Nathaniel, vs. John Shapleigh, II. 113.
  Kittery, Town of, vs. John Leighton, II. 32.
  Littlefield, James, et al. vs. William Sayer, II. 8.
  Lord, Abraham, vs. Thomas Abbet and Sarah Nason, II. 33.
  Norton, George, apl't, vs. Samuel Daniel, II. 8.
  Parsons, Elizabeth, vs. William Hilton, II. 20.
  Parsons, William, vs. Baker Nason, II. 78.
  Pickerin, John, vs. Mary Champernoon, II. 33, 54.
  Pickerin, John, vs. John Woodman and Nathaniel Raines, II. 78.
  Preble, Abraham, vs. Jeremiah Moulton, II. 22, 33.
  Raines, Francis, vs. Richard Carter, II. 112.
  Raines, Nathaniel, apl't, vs. William More, II. 8.
  Raines, Nathaniel, vs. Arthur Beal, II. 23.

70   GENERAL INDEX.

Plaintiffs, continued.
  Remick, Christian, vs. Samuel Spinney, II. 113, 114.
  Shepard, John, vs. Nathaniel Keen, II. 32.
  Snell, George, vs. Stephen Hardison, II. 13.
  Spinney, Samuel, vs. Christian Remick, II. 126, 127.
  Stewart, Robert, apl't, vs. John Reding, II. 9.
  Thomson, John, vs. Alice Metherell, II. 73.
  Trickey, Sarah, vs. George Lidden, II. 12.
  Tucker, Francis, vs. Philip Atwell, II. 25.
  Tucker, Francis, vs. John Tiney, II. 25.
  Vaughan, William, vs. John Buckland, II. 78.
  Weare, Peter, vs. Estate Sylvester Stover, II. 6.
  Weare, Peter, vs. Estate of Gabriel Tetherly, II. 126.
  White, Philip, vs. Elizabeth Gowen, II. 59, 65.
  Woodman, John, vs. Thomas Trafton, II. 78.
  Woodman, John, vs. Richard King, II. 112.
Plate, silver, I. 15.
Plymouth County,
  Recorder of, Samuel Sprague, I. 69.
Poor, the, I. 5, II. 24, 67, 76, 84, 86, 123.
Posting notice of Administratorship, I. 2.
Pound, town, II. 51^b, 88.
Poyse, i.e., avordupois, or weight.
Preference to elder children, I. 19.
  to males over females, I. 19.
President of the Province, I. 1.
Prices. See under the various Inventories for second-hand articles.
  barrel-staves, I. 39.
  beaver, I. 15.
  beef, per barrel, I. 15, 72, 81.
  board, per week, I. 11.

Prices, continued.
  board, per year, I. 30.
  boards, per thousand, I. 15, 18, 31.
  bodys, corsets, I. 19.
  bread, per hundred weight, I. 41.
  bulls, I. 11, 14, 21, 28, 29.
  calves, I. 2, 4, 8, 21, 22, 23, 24, 26, 29, 30, 32.
  cod, per quintal, I. 38.
  cod-lines, I. 7.
  colts, I. 2, 11, 23.
  corn, per bushel, I. 11, 15, 18, 21.
  cotton cloth, I. 6, 19.
  cows, I. 2, 3, 4, 5, 8, 10, 11, 14, 15, 18, 20, 21, 23, 24, 26, 29, 30, 32, 39.
  days labor, I. 19, 39.
  drawers, I. 30.
  feathers, I. 31.
  fish, per quintal, I. 6, 18, 22, 33, 38.
  flour, per barrel, I. 6.
  funeral charges, I. 30.
  hake, per quintal, I. 33.
  hay, per cock, I. 18.
  hay, per load, I. 23.
  heifers, I. 2, 4, 5, 7, 9, 10, 14, 17, 18, 21, 22, 24, 26, 32.
  hides, I. 14.
  hogs, I. 11, 14, 21.
  horses, I. 2, 5, 10, 15, 18, 21, 22, 24, 26, 29.
  lambs, I. 15.
  land, per acre, I. 2, 5, 6, 10, 13, 14, 15, 21, 22, 24, 31.
  land, inland, I. 5.
  lime, per hogshead, I. 31.
  linen, per yard, I. 19.
  mackerel, per barrel, I. 41.
  making a suit of clothes, I. 19.
  malt, per bushel, I. 6.
  mares, I. 2, 7, 11, 21, 31, 40.
  marsh, per acre, I. 5, 6, 8, 13, 15, 23, 25.
  meadow, per acre, I. 4, 13, 22.
  mills, I. 3.
  molasses, per barrel, I. 21, 29.
  molasses, per hogshead, I. 7.
  moose skins, I. 15.
  nags, I. 2.

GENERAL INDEX. 71

Prices, continued.
 neck cloth, I. 30.
 negroes, I. 7, 15.
 oars, per foot, I. 21, 39.
 oil, per barrel, I. 6.
 otter skins, I. 15.
 oxen, I. 7, 11, 14, 15, 24, 29.
 pease, per bushel, I. 11.
 pine boards, I. 40.
 pine slabs, per hundred, I. 19.
 pipe staves, white oak, I. 21.
 pork, per barrel, I. 6, 15, 41, 72.
 pork, per pound, I. 19.
 powder, per barrel, I. 17.
 rum, per gallon, 1. 21, 33.
 salt, per bushel, I. 19.
 salt, per hogshead, I. 6.
 scale fish, per quintal, I. 18.
 servant, per year, I. 43.
 sheep, I. 2, 11, 15, 18, 22, 23.
 shoats, I. 14.
 silver plate per oz., I. 15, 62.
 spikes, per pound, I. 7.
 stears, I. 5, 7, 11, 14, 18, 20, 21, 22, 23, 24.
 stockings, I. 30.
 swine, I. 7, 11, 13, 18, 20, 22, 24, 26, 29, 30.
 upland, per acre, I. 3, 4, 6, 8, 26.
 wheat, per bushel, I. 11, 15.
 wheat in the straw, I. 11.
 winding sheet, I. 30.
 woodland, I. 21.
 yearlings, I. 7, 10, 11, 14, 15, 20, 21, 22, 23, 24, 26, 29, 30.
Prison, see Goale.
Prison-keeper, II. 1, 6.
Provisions (for cereals see under Husbandry), I. 18, 54, 72.
 beef, I. 10, 15, 21, 34, 37, 39, 54, 55, 72, 81.
 bread, I. 4, 41.
 butter, I. 18, 23, 29, 34.
 cheeses, I. 10, 18, 23, 29, 33, 34, 39.
 cocoa nuts, I. 9.
 corn, I. 10, 11, 21, 29, 34, 40, 41.
 flesh, I. 27.
 flour, I. 6.
 garden stuff, I. 34.
 lard, I. 39.

Provisions, continued.
 meal, I. 14, 29, 41, 53.
 meat, I. 14, 21, 75.
 molasses, I. 7, 13, 14, 21, 29, 34, 41.
 pease, I. 11.
 pork, I. 4, 6, 15, 27, 28, 34, 39, 41, 55, 72.
 suet, I. 34.
 wine, I. 41.
Rates, see Taxes.
Records, new book of for the Province, I. 69.
 of the Province in Boston, II. 14, 24.
Records of Town of Cape Porpoise, II, 69.
Recorders of the Province,
 Joseph Hammond, I. 117-120, II. 40-129.
 John Newmarch, I. 118, 119, II. 60.
 Edward Rishworth, I. 2 — 43.
 John Wincoll, I. 35, 43, II. 1, 14.
Recorder of New Hampshire,
 Elias Styleman, 1. 13.
Register,
 Joseph Hammond, I. 47.
Rent, I. 114, 115.
Requisition for the Country's use of a cow, I. 11.
Residuary Legatees, I. 25, 27, and elsewhere.
Reversions, I. 19, 46, 47.
Revocation of a clause in a will, 1. 29.
Realty and appurtenances, see also the various deeds in the Index of Grantors.
 corn land, I. 12, 13.
 farms, I. 5, 20, 25, 46.
 fields, I. 15.
 gardens, I. 12, 35, 47, 55.
 home-stall, homestead, I. 13, 15, 21, 27, 28, 31, 37, 70.
 house lots, I. 8, 27, 34, 82.
 islands, I. 4, 6, 11, 24, 37.
 land, I. 2, 5, 6, 7, 8, 10, 11, 13, 14, 15, 17, 18, 19, 21, 22, 24, 25, 26, 28, 29, 30, 31, 32, 33,

General Index.

Realty, continued.
34, 35, 37, 38, 39, 40, 42, 43ª, 43ᵇ, 46, 47, 53, 62, 66, 72, 73, 82.
  marsh, I. 2, 4, 5, 6, 7, 8, 10, 13, 15, 18, 20, 25, 26, 30, 34, 38, 42, 46, 47, 53, 66, 72, 79, 82.
  meadow, I. 4, 5, 11, 12, 13, 20, 22, 24, 27, 28, 29, 32, 34, 35, 42, 73.
  mills and privileges see under mills.
  orchards, I. 12, 13, 15, 20, 27, 28, 31, 39, 43, 55, 81.
  out lands, I. 15, 27.
  pasture, I. 12, 15, 42, 79.
  swamp, I. 25, 28, 31, 73.
  tan yard, I. 13.
  upland, I. 3, 4, 5, 6, 8, 10, 11, 18, 26, 28, 34, 42, 46.
  woodland, I. 13, 66, 82.
Reddle, red-chalk, I. 51.
Riding horse and caparison, I. 15.
Rosin, I. 81.
Rum, I. 21, 33.

Saco, see Index of Places.
  grants recorded, see Index of Grantors under the names following:
    Alden, John, I. 68.
    Bonighton, John, I. 106.
    Gibbons, James, I. 45.
    Hughes, Arthur et ux., I. 105.
    Pennywell, Walter, I. 49.
    Trustrum, David, I. 95.
  grants referred to:
    John Bush to Bryan Pendleton, I. 5.
    Mr. Fletcher to Bryan Pendleton, I. 5.
    —— Hammond to Byran Pendleton, I. 5.
    Byran Pendleton to Pendleton Fletcher, I. 5.
    William Phillips to Byran Pendleton, I. 5.
    William Phillips to Walter Pennywell, I. 49.

Saco, continued.
    William Phillips to John Alden et ux., I. 69.
    John West to Byran Pendleton, I. 5.
Saco River, Ferry over, I. 1.
Schooling, I. 19.
Sealer of Leather, II. 70.
Secretary of Massachusetts,
  Isaac Addington, II. 29, 40, 100.
Sedule, schedule, i.e., codicil 5.
Selectmen,
  of Berwick, I. 1, II. 96.
  of Kittery, I. 1, II. 32, 67, 68, 69, 70, 71, 76, 107, 114, 118, 123.
  of Wells, II. 2, 71.
  of York, I. 18, II. 12, 16, 18, 56, 70, 71, 75, 76, 86, 96, 123.
Scarborough, see Index of Places.
  grants recorded, see Index of Grantors under the names following:
    Foxwell, George, I. 64.
    Griffin, John, I. 112.
    Nickals, Robert, I. 110.
  grants referred to:
    Richard Foxwell to George Foxwell, I. 64.
    Henry Watts to Robert Nicholson, I. 109.
Sheriff,
  II. 62, 77, 85, 109, 125.
Skins, various, see under Hides.
Star, a cow so named, I. 35, 50.
Steward-General of the Province,
  Richard Vines, I. 58.
Stocks, II. 83, 90, 117, 124.
Submission to Massachusetts, I. 86.
Suffolk County, Clerk of,
  Isaac Addington, I. 65.
Superior Court, II. 52, 64, 113, 114, 127.
Superior Court to be held at Boston, II. 64.
Superior Court to be held at Kittery, II. 52.
Support and maintenance, see Annuity, I. 26, 113, 114, 119.
Survivorship, Inheritance by, I. 14, 20.

Tan
vats, I. 14.
yard, I. 14.
Taxes,
rates, I. 30.
country rates, I. 19, II. 77, 110, 125.
town rates, I. 19, II. 77, 96, 110.
Thanksgiving day, II. 12, 90.
Threshing corn, I. 11.
Titles,
Captain, I. 1, 2, 4, 6, 18, 19, 21, 24, 30, 35, 36, 39, 46, 47, 48, 51, 53, 54, 64, 69, 73, 78, 81, 85, 87, 96, 103, II. 1, 2, 3, 4, 6, 7, 8, 9, 11, 12, 14, 17, 18, 19, 20, 24, 32, 33, 54, 56, 70, 76, 78, 113, 126.
Ensign, II. 1, 33, 57, 75, 119.
Esquire, I. 13, 14, 64, 110, II. 1, 47, 51, 54, 55, 58, 60, 64, 66, 67, 68, 73, 74, 77, 78, 82, 89, 90, 92, 93, 95, 99, 100, 101, 105, 106, 109, 112, 116, 122.
Gammer, I. 35.
Gentleman, I. 33, 34, 48, 68, 84, 93, 94, II. 128.
Goodman, I. 27, 35, 39, 50.
Goody, I. 35, 36.
Lieutenant, I. 1, 2, 10, 53, 83, 93, 94, 100, II. 1, 9, 14, 15, 17, 21, 22, 23, 24, 29, 34, 49, 52, 53, 54, 103, 107, 113, 117, 120.
Major, I. 1, 3, 4, 5, 6, 15, 17, 20, 32, 41, 49, 55, 62, 65, 66, 82, 84, 107, 118, II. 1, 3, 4, 6, 7, 8, 10, 11, 12, 14, 17, 18, 19, 21, 23, 24, 25, 29, 30, 32, 34, 35, 36, 55, 78, 79, 84, 90, 119.
Mis, Mrs., I. 7, 11, 17, 18, 32, 34, 39, 40, 47, 56, 58, 59, 62, 66, 80, 83, 88, 109, II. 3, 12, 15, 35, 54, 110.
Mr. I. 1, 3, 5, 6, 7, 9, 10, 14, 16, 17, 19, 22, 23, 25, 29, 30, 31, 32, 33, 34, 36, 37, 38, 42, 45, 47, 51, 54, 56, 58, 60, 62, 63, 64, 70, 72, 78, 83, 85, 89, 90, 91, 92, 94, 95, 96, 100, 102, 103, 104, 105, 106, 107, 108,

Titles, continued.
109, 110, 111, 112, 113, 121, II. 1, 2, 3, 5, 6, 7, 8, 9, 11, 12, 13, 14, 16, 17, 18, 19, 20, 21, 23, 25, 26, 29, 30, 31, 33, 34, 48, 49, 50, 51, 51ª, 51ᵇ, 52, 53, 54, 55, 56, 58, 59, 62, 68, 69, 70, 71, 74, 76, 77, 78, 88, 89, 93, 96, 101, 103, 104, 109, 110, 118, 119, 120, 125, 126, 128.
Sergeant, II. 70, 103.
Tobacco, I. 33, 34, 37.
tongs, I. 33.
Tools and Implements, I. 2, 11, 15, 23, 29, 30, 40, 62, 67, 79, 80.
(See also under Hardware and Husbandry.)
adzes, I. 2, 3, 11, 15, 27, 55, 72.
augurs, I. 2, 3, 11, 15, 27, 32, 39, 52, 53, 55, 79, 81.
axes, I. 3, 10, 13, 15, 16, 17, 22, 26, 27, 29, 34, 36, 38, 39, 40, 43ª, 44, 52, 53, 54, 55, 56, 57, 59, 65, 66, 67, 70, 72, 75, 79, 80.
broad, I. 15, 21, 23, 24, 26, 32, 33, 39, 52.
felling, I. 3.
mortising, I. 32.
square, I. 27.
barking knife, I. 81.
beetles, I. 13, 23, 24, 26, 38, 57, 72.
rings, I. 10, 11, 13, 21, 26, 29, 30, 33, 34, 38, 39, 40, 43ª, 52, 72.
bench-hook, I. 3.
briar-bill, I. 2.
carpenters' tools, I. 16, 28.
chalk-line, I. 3.
chisels, I. 2, 3, 11 25, 38, 39, 52, 53, 55, 59.
cold-chisel, I. 35.
compasses, I. 3, 27, 39.
cross-cut saws, I. 2, 6, 15, 25, 57, 70.
crows, I. 15, 57.
curing-knife, I. 81.
dogs, I. 9.

Tools and Implements, continued.
　edges, I. 26.
　files, I. 2, 21, 41.
　frows, used to split staves I. 32, 39, 57.
　gimlets, I. 3.
　gouges, I. 2, 3, 11, 53.
　grind-stones, I. 2, 6, 15, 17, 29, 32, 34, 39, 40, 43ᵇ, 53, 65, 83.
　hammers, I. 2, 3, 9, 11, 22, 39, 40, 81.
　hand-saws, I. 2, 15, 27.
　hand-screws, I. 16.
　hatchets, I. 2, 25, 32, 33, 54, 55.
　hold-fast, I. 2.
　　ring, I. 3.
　jack-plane, I. 2.
　jointer, I. 2.
　joint-plane, I. 24.
　last-knife, I. 81.
　looms, I. 11, 52, 54, 72, 88.
　　gears, I. 72.
　　reeds, I. 54.
　marking-iron, I. 34.
　nippers, I. 81.
　pick-axes, I. 2.
　pincers, I. 25, 81.
　planes, I. 3, 26.
　　irons, I. 3, 15, 53.
　　stocks, I. 15.
　punches, I. 2.
　reaming-iron, I. 2.
　rub-stone, I. 14.
　rules, I. 39, 53.
　saws, I. 21, 29, 34, 38, 39, 40, 41, 51, 52, 53, 57.
　　tenon, I. 15, 40.
　shaves, or knives, I. 2.
　　bark, I. 81.
　　draw, I. 2, 3, 15, 16, 22, 26, 39, 53, 57.
　　hook, I. 2.
　　lock, I. 26.
　　spoke, I. 2.
　sledges, I. 39.
　small tools, I. 36.
　smiths' bellows, I. 16.
　spades, I. 10, 11.
　squares, I. 2, 39.
　tailor's goose, I. 51.

Tools and Implements, continued.
　turning hooks, I. 2.
　turning mill tools, I. 2.
　　tools, I. 16.
　two-bill, I. 2.
　vises, I. 32.
　warping pins, I. 54.
　wedges, I. 9, 10, 13, 23, 24, 26, 27, 29, 30, 32, 33, 34, 36, 39, 40, 41, 43ᵃ, 55, 57, 72, 82.
　whip-saw, I. 15.
　wimble-bitt, I. 2.
　　breast, I. 2.
Town book of Kittery, I. 87.
Town lands of Wells, I. 28.
Treasurer of the Province, I. 1, 2, 3, 24, II. 17, 63, 77, 85, 93, 101, 118, 125.
　Francis Hooke, I. 17.
　William Pepperrell, I. 101.
Trustees, I. 26, 36.
Turf and twig, delivery by, I. 50, 54, 70, and elsewhere.
Twilt, *i.e.*, quilt, I. 32.

Valuation Commissioners, II. 110.
Vessels, and appurtenances,
　anchors, I. 6, 7, 33, 41.
　blocks, I. 38, 41.
　boats, I. 4, 6, 22, 33, 38, 41.
　buckets, I. 38.
　cables, I. 33.
　calks, I. 40.
　canoes, 3, 7, 11, 15, 20, 29, 30, 33, 40, 43ᵃ, 52, 57, 71.
　canvas, I. 41.
　coasting canoe, I. 16.
　compass, I. 30, 33, 38, 41.
　cordage, I. 41.
　foresail, I. 38, 41.
　furniture, I. 16, 41, 43ᵃ, 57.
　glass, I. 33.
　grappers, grapnels, I. 6, 41.
　gundelo, I. 43ᵃ, 57.
　hammocks, I. 33.
　hay-canoe, I. 16.
　junk, I. 6.
　ketch I. 43ᵃ.
　lighter, I. 16.
　main sail, I. 38, 41.

General Index. 75

Vessels, continued.
  moorings, I. 7.
  oars, I. 21, 39.
  quadrant, I. 43ª.
  rigging, I. 16, 41.
  roads, cables, I. 38, 41.
  sails, I. 32.
  sail-needles, I. 38.
  shallops, I. 16, 41.
  skiffs, I. 7, 82.
  sloop, I. 66.
  standing rigging, I. 6.
  tackling, I. 38.
  tar, I. 4, 33, 41.
  yards, I. 38.
Votes of Town Proprietors, I. 85.
Vre, ewer, I. 13.

Wages, *i.e.*, pay, a soldiers, I. 3.
Wearing Apparel and Personal Appliances. I. 2, 4, 5, 6, 7, 8, 11, 13, 15, 17, 19, 21, 22, 23, 25, 27, 28, 29, 38, 39, 40, 43ª, 43ᵇ, 51, 52, 53, 54, 55, 56, 57, 59, 65, 66, 67, 70, 72, 73, 80, 82, 88.
  aprons, I. 17, 23, 24, 32, 35.
  bands, I. 72.
  bodys, pair of, corsets, I. 9, 17, 19.
  boots, see under shoes.
  breeches, I. 2, 3, 7, 8, 10, 14, 20, 24, 26, 31, 32, 33, 37, 41, 44, 51, 52, 71, 79.
  brushes, I. 9.
  buttons, I. 3, 21, 32, 33, 38, 41.
  caps, I. 7, 8, 9, 21, 35, 72.
  castors, hats, I. 31.
  children's clothes, I. 32, 35.
  clasps, I. 9, 36.
  cloaks, I. 14, 16.
  clouts, I. 35.
  coats, I. 3, 6, 7, 8, 10, 14, 20, 21, 23, 24, 26, 31, 32, 33, 36, 37, 38, 41, 44, 52, 53, 71, 79, 80.
  coifs, I. 9, 35.
  combs, I. 33, 37.
  doublets, I. 24, 31.
  drawers, I. 2, 3, 6, 7, 8, 14, 15, 30, 31, 33, 36, 37, 41, 44, 57.
  dressing-case, I. 15.

Wearing Apparel, continued.
  garters, I. 31.
  gloves, I. 3, 6, 19, 23, 32, 33, 35, 36, 37, 72.
  gold pin, I. 31.
  gowns, I. 32, 34.
  half-sleeves, I. 72.
  handkerchiefs, I. 6, 7, 9, 33, 37, 41, 52, 72.
  hats, I. 3, 6, 7, 8, 9, 15, 16, 17, 21, 24, 26, 31, 32, 33, 35, 36, 38, 41, 44, 51, 52, 57, 66.
  bands, I. 37, 38.
  head-bands, I. 9.
  head-wear, I. 17, 23.
  hoods, I. 9, 17, 32, 35.
  jackets, I. 2, 3, 36, 44.
  knife, I. 33.
  lace, I. 9.
  mantua, I. 72, 83.
  mittens, I. 14, 37.
  muff, I. 9.
  neck-cloths, I. 6, 7, 8, 9, 17, 21, 30, 33, 36, 37, 38, 41, 44, 52, 72, 79.
  neck-kerchief, I. 9.
  oil-skins, I. 17.
  old clothes, I. 18, 37.
  petticoats, I. 9, 17, 24, 32, 35, 72, 83.
  pins, I. 17, 23.
  purses, I. 9, 31.
  razors, I. 9, 32, 33, 38, 41.
  rings, gold, I. 8, 9, 17, 21, 31, 33.
  sashes, I. 15, 17.
  saymarr, semare, simar, a long robe, I. 32, 35.
  scarfs, I. 41.
  shifts, I. 8, 17, 19, 32, 41.
  shirts, I. 6, 7, 15, 30, 33, 37, 38, 39, 41, 44, 51, 52, 57, 71, 72.
  shoes and boots, I. 2, 3, 4, 6, 8, 9, 16, 17, 21, 29, 32, 33, 35, 37, 38, 41, 44, 52, 57, 71.
  shoe buckles, I. 33.
  skirts, I. 41.
  sleeves, I. 17, 32, 35.
  socks, I. 17.
  stockings, I. 3, 6, 7, 8, 9, 14, 17, 19, 21, 30, 31, 33, 35, 37, 38, 44, 52, 71.

Wearing Apparel, continued.
  suits, I. 17, 19, 26, 27, 33, 36.
  swaths, I. 8, 9, 31, 35.
  trowsers, I. 33, 37, 38.
  vest, I. 3.
  waistcoats, I. 7, 8, 9, 14, 17, 23, 24, 26, 31, 32, 33, 35, 37, 41, 44, 79.
  walking-staff, I. 33.
  whisk, a tippet, I. 9, 32.
  winding-sheet, I. 30.
Wells, see Index of Places.
  selectmen, II. 2, 71.
  town lands, I. 28.
  grants recorded, see Index of Grantors under the names following:
    Butland, John, I. 92.
    Littlefield, Francis sen., I. 90, 91.
    Littlefield, James, sen., I. 89, 92.
  grants referred to.
    Joseph Cross to Samuel Austin, I. 29.
    Francis Littlefield to James Littlefield sen., I. 89, 90.
Whipping-post, II. 91, 122, 124.
Wills:
  Alcock, Elizabeth, the lost will of, I. 96.
  Amerideth, John, I. 61.
  Boaden, Walter, I. 44.
  Boolls, Joseph, I. 33.
  Bray, John, I. 46.
  Bready, John, I. 13.
  Card John, I. 82.
  Conley, Abraham, I. 74.
  Cooper, Alexander, I. 26.
  Cross, Joseph, I. 28.
  Grant, James, I. 27.

Wills, continued.
  Hayes, Edward, I. 10.
  Heard, John, I. 19.
  Hill, John, I. 18.
  Leads, John, I. 32.
  Libby, John, I. 22.
  Littlefield, Annis, I. 25.
  Mendum, Robert, I. 14.
  More, William, I. 57.
  Pearce Eleanor, I. 8.
  Pendleton, Bryan, I. 5.
  Puddington, George, I. 120.
  Spencer, Thomas, I. 12.
  Taylor, John, I. 55.
  Withers, Thomas, I. 35, re-recorded I. 50.
  Young, Rowland, I. 37.
York. See Index of Places.
  selectmen, I. 18, II. 12, 16, 18, 56, 70, 71, 75, 76, 86, 96, 123.
  grants recorded; see Index of Grantors under the names following:
    Anger, Samson's estate, I. 95.
    Bragdon, Arthur, sen., I. 26.
    Parker, Abraham, II. 81.
    Purrington, John, I. 116.
    Weare, Peter, et ux., I. 108.
  grants referred to,
    town to Henry Norton, I. 42.
    Alcock, Job, to Abraham Parker, I. 81.
    Gooch, John, to Peter Weare, I. 108.
    Hooke, William, to Henry Norton, I. 42.
    Vines, Richard, to Henry Norton, I. 42.
Young Finch, name of a cow, I. 121.
Young Lad, name of a heifer, I 121.

7

CPSIA information can be obtained
at www.ICGtesting.com
Printed in the USA
LVHW081948070521
686793LV00002B/77